ALLIED MILITARY LOCOMOTIVES
OF THE
SECOND WORLD WAR

R. TOURRET

© R. Tourret 1976, 1977 and 1995.
First published in 1976 and 1977. Revised and augmented for republication in 1995.

All rights reserved. No part of this book may be reproduced or transmitted
in any form or by any means, electronic or mechanical, including photocopying,
recording or by any information and retrieval system, without prior
written permission from the Publisher.

ISBN 0–905878–06–X

Published by Tourret Publishing, 5 Byron Close, Abingdon, Oxon OX14 5PA, GB.
Typeset and Printed by Shearprint, Homesteads Road, Basingstoke, Hants. RG22 5RP

CONTENTS

Page

Introduction

Section 1 Campaign Notes

Chapter 1	Britain & WD General Notes	1
Chapter 2	USA/TC General Notes	3
Chapter 3	Middle East	5
Chapter 4	Persia (Iran)	9
Chapter 5	North Africa	11
Chapter 6	Sicily	13
Chapter 7	Italy	13
Chapter 8	Northern France, Belgium & Holland	15
Chapter 9	Southern France	20
Chapter 10	Europe	20
Chapter 11	India & Burma	22
Chapter 12	New Caledonia & Philippine Islands	25
Chapter 13	Japan	26
Chapter 14	Korea	26

Section 2 War Department

Chapter 15	WD Locomotive Stock List	28
Chapter 16	LMS Diesels, WD 3–7, 16–27, 49–64, 213–8/24/5/33/60–73	36
Chapter 17	LMS Standard Class 3F 0–6–0Ts, WD 8–15	43
Chapter 18	Standard WD 150hp 0–4–0Ds, WD 29–48, 2220–31/5–9	44
Chapter 19	Ex-LNE Class J69 0–6–0s, WD 78–91	47
Chapter 20	Ex-GWR "Dean Goods" 0–6–0s, WD 93–200	48
Chapter 21	Stanier LMS Class 8F 2–8–0s, WD 300–449, 500–24/40–623	56
Chapter 22	Locomotives of the Italian North African Colonies, WD 70624–44	69
Chapter 23	Robinson LNE (GCR) Class O4 2–8–0s, WD 700–91	75
Chapter 24	Standard WD 2–8–0s, WD 800–79, 7000–7509, 8510–8718, 9177–9312	79
Chapter 25	Whitcomb 650hp Diesel Locomotives Used in Middle East and Italy, WD 1200–51, 1537–96, MRS 1200–8/32–71	97
Chapter 26	Standard WD 0–6–0STs, WD 1437–56/62–1536, 5000–5199, 5250–5331	103
Chapter 27	Hudswell Clarke 2–8–2T, WD 2200	112
Chapter 28	Ex-LBSCR Atlantic Tanks, WD 2400/1	113
Chapter 29	Federated Malay States Railway Class C2c 4–6–4Ts, WD 2600–5	115
Chapter 30	Sudan Type 4–6–2s, WD 2800–54	117
Chapter 31	Standard WD 2–10–0s, WD 3650–3799	120
Chapter 32	60cm gauge 2–8–2s, WD 4000–4	129
Chapter 33	2ft 6in gauge 2–8–0s, WD 4005–10	131
Chapter 34	Light Beyer-Garratt Locomotives, WD 4200–43	132
Chapter 35	Heavy Beyer-Garratt Locomotives, WD 4400–24	136
Chapter 36	LNE Armoured 2–4–2Ts, WD A–M (& spares)	138
Chapter 37	Indian Class YD (Modified) Metre-gauge 2–8–2s, WD (India) 1 & 2	140
Chapter 38	Locomotives from China	142
Chapter 39	The Longmoor Military Railway	144
Chapter 40	The Melbourne Military Railway	154
Chapter 41	WD Tramway, Shoeburyness	155
Chapter 42	Shropshire & Montgomeryshire Railway	157
Chapter 43	Martin Mill Military Railway	158
Chapter 44	The Kowloon-Canton Railway	160

Section 3 United States Army Transportation Corps

Chapter 45	USA/TC Locomotive Stock List	162
Chapter 46	The Camp Claiborne Locomotives, USA/TC 1–7, 10/11 & 20/2	187
Chapter 47	Standard USA/TC "MacArthur" Narrow-gauge 2–8–2s, USA/TC 3000–29, 130–249, 257–890 & 4281–4312	190

Chapter 48	Standard USA/TC Standard-gauge 2–8–2s, WD & USA/TC 1000–1199	200
Chapter 49	Standard USA/TC 0–6–0Ts, USA/TC 1252–1316/87–1436, 1927–2001, 4313–41/72–4401, 5000–60, 6000–23/80–6103/60–83	207
Chapter 50	Standard USA/TC Standard-gauge 2–8–0s, USA/TC 1600–1926, 2032–2382, 2400–59, 2500–2989, 3200–3749, 4402–83, 5155–99, 5700–5859 & 6024–78	223
Chapter 51	Metre-gauge 0–4–0P Locomotives, USA/TC 2383–99, 2990–7 & 8288–95	255
Chapter 52	Porter Steam Locomotives for Russia, USA/TC 3030–75	256
Chapter 53	USA/TC 2–10–0s for Russia, USA/TC 3925–95, 4143–4280, 4500–4999, 5200–5699, 5860–5999, 6104–54, 6240–6739, 10000–99 & 10500–619	257
Chapter 54	Standard USA/TC 0–6–0s Used in the United States, USA/TC 4000–79	260
Chapter 55	Finnish State Railways 0–6–0STs, USA/TC 6740–63	262
Chapter 56	The Lima 2–8–0s, USA/TC 6994–9	264
Chapter 57	General Electric 75 ton Diesel Locomotives, USA/TC 7228–37	265
Chapter 58	Evans Autorailers 235hp 0–6–0Ds, USA/TC 7731–8	266
Chapter 59	General Electric 25 ton Diesel Locomotives, USA/TC 7770–9	267
Chapter 60	General Electric 45 ton Diesel Locomotives, USA/TC 7800–29, 7924–9, 8390, 8499–8528 & 8532–9/60–73	269
Chapter 61	Whitcomb 65 ton Diesel Locomotives, USA/TC 7961–90, 8120–47, 8400–98, 8800–11 & MRS 1300–67	274
Chapter 62	Alco-GE 127 ton Diesel Locomotives, USA/TC 8000–56 & 8600–99	280
Chapter 63	Japanese Mikai Class 2–8–2s, USA/TC 9400–32	284
Chapter 64	Broad-gauge 2–8–2s for Indian Railways	285
Chapter 65	The MRS Numbering Scheme Used in Italy	292
Chapter 66	The White Pass & Yukon Route	299
Chapter 67	Alaska Railroad	302
Index		303

INTRODUCTION

The origin of this book lies in the Railway Correspondence and Travel Society who initially sponsored my research into the activities of the British and American military locomotives of World War Two. Some of the information so gained was published in a series of articles in the Railway Observer from 1949 to 1958, now long out of print. Based on further research carried out for nearly forty years, two books were published, "War Department Locomotives" in 1976 and "United States Army Transportation Corps Locomotives" in 1977. The majority of the data given had not been published before, and the two books gave the most detailed history of WD and USA/TC locomotives ever assembled up to that date.

Since these two books were published, further research has been carried out, more photographs obtained, some drawings specially prepared, better maps obtained and, most importantly, much more data has been accumulated. "War Department Locomotives" was the first book published by Tourret Publishing, and inevitably some financial trepidation was felt, so the work was published in two volumes. In some ways, placing all the information between one pair of covers has advantages, so the two books are now being republished under a new title "Allied Military Locomotives of the Second World War". There is so much new information that the new title is considered justified.

The histories of the locomotives are best reviewed class by class. However, it is difficult in these class histories to give an idea of the general progress of the campaigns. Accordingly, this work begins in the first Section with descriptions of the campaigns in the different theatres of war from the railway point of view, followed in the second and third Sections by the class histories of the British and American locomotives. The last two Sections each start with a numerical list of the locomotives which gives the key to the numbering structure. The bulk of the Chapters then deal with separate classes of locomotives, but these are followed by one or two Chapters dealing with odd topics such as various military railways. The layout of the Chapters can be seen from the Contents list.

In many countries, several different spellings of place names were used. In this book, the spelling most frequently used by the military forces is employed but this may not, of course, be correct, then or now.

Locomotive dimensions are generally given in British units for British designs and in American units for American designs, since these data are intended for an international readership. Locomotives are renumbered in sequence unless stated otherwise. Post-war allocations and withdrawals of the engines in British Railways service have been omitted because they are readily available elsewhere. Some attempt has been made to list those locomotives which are preserved, but it must be remembered that preserved locomotives often change location and/or ownership, so details may not be up-to-date.

I would like to thank the RCTS again for sponsoring my work for several years. I also thank the many individuals who have corresponded with me, in some cases over a period of many years. I would particularly like to thank the following for help in providing and correlating information: D. W. Allen, B. W. Anwell, G. Balfour, J. Benson, J. D. Blythe, H. D. Bowtell, K. R. M. Cameron, K. W. Clingan, Paul Cotterell, E. A. S. Cotton, H. R. Cox, H. M. Dannatt, G. H. Daventry, L. Desrosiers, C. K. Dunkley, R. G. Farr, H. L. Goldsmith, R. S. Grimsley, R. N. Higgins, H. C. Hughes, P. M. Kalla-Bishop, A. J. Knight, A. P. Lambert, M. A. Lane, G. Lanham, R. Leitch, W. S. Love, R. K. McKenny, M. T. McHatton, E. R. Mountford, W. Nicholls, J. Quanjer, D. R. Pollock, P. Proud, B. Reed, R. C. Riley, A. Rough, R. A. Savill, Paul Spencer, A. G. Wells and D. E. White.

Some informants from Eastern Europe prefer to remain anonymous, but are thanked nevertheless. The officers of the then Birmingham Locomotive Club and the Industrial Locomotive Society also gave much help. Thanks are also due to the Office of the Chief of Transportation Department of the U.S. Army, the SNCF, Mr R. F. Corley of the Canadian General Electric Co., Mr C. S. Alexander, Superintendant of the BB&SR; the Commandant of the Transportation Centre, Royal Engineers, Longmoor; Mr G. A. Benedict, Motive Power Superintendant of the Alaska Railroad and to Mr C. J. Rogers, President of the White Pass and Yukon Route. Mr Ben Ashworth is thanked for certain photographic work.

Finally, while every care has been taken to ensure accuracy, it will be appreciated that official records for this wartime period are somewhat scarce and not necessarily accurate. If anyone should notice any mistakes or be able to supply additional information, I should be pleased if he would contact me.

R. Tourret

SECTION 1   CAMPAIGN NOTES

Chapter 1

BRITAIN AND WD GENERAL NOTES

British locomotives played their part in support of the fighting fronts. Locomotives were withdrawn from service for use in France at the beginning of the war, and these were lost after Dunkirk. Heavy freight locomotives were later withdrawn and sent to the Middle East for use in Egypt, Syria, Persia and Palestine. As the threat of German invasion diminished, Britain became the centre of military build-up for the counter attack on mainland Europe. To help British railways, many WD 2–8–0s, WD 2–10–0s and USA/TC 2–8–0s were placed on loan until they were needed abroad.

In 1940, some new connections were made between the different railways around London (see Map 1), so as to improve flexibility of operations, to serve various military dumps, and to provide alternative routes in case of London bomb damage blocking lines. In 1941/42, one or two more connections were put in, with the aim of improving routes to the south coast.

With the fall of France on 18 June 1940, Southampton became too dangerous as a loading point for convoys. Furthermore, the bombing of other ports such as Liverpool, the general diversion of shipping from the east coast ports to the west coast ports, and the expectation of receiving extra traffic from the USA, meant that there was a need for increased military port capacity, preferably in the north-west as far as possible out of harm's way, and with adequate road and rail facilities. During the period August to November 1940, plans were made to proceed with two new deep-water ports, at Faslane on the east side of Gare Loch and at Cairn Point on Loch Ryan.

Priority was given to Military Port No 1 at Faslane and by February 1941 some 1000 men were at work and a connection to the LNER had been laid in. In May 1941, further air raids on Liverpool and Clydeside gave increased impetus to the work, but it was not until April 1942 that a Port Operating Superintendent was appointed. The Port was officially opened in August 1942, with six berths taking vessels up to 33ft draught, with 30 cranes plus a 150 ton floating crane. There was a shed near the foreshore, a three-roof steel-framed structure mainly clad with corrugated iron sheeting. One of its main uses was to accept incoming ships with aircraft as deck cargo, but by May 1944 it was also used for outgoing troopships.

The first locomotives used at Faslane were Dean Goods WD 94, "Cossack" 0–6–0ST P 723/98 and 0–6–0ST MW 1425/98 (both on loan from contractors Sir Lindsay Parkinson) by April 1941. Around May 1942, J69 0–6–0Ts WD 79, 80/3/6/7 & 90 were sent to Faslane, followed by J68 WD 85. LNE J50 1058 WD 220 came to Faslane briefly in early 1942, but then moved to Cairnryan by May 1942. These 0–6–0Ts were adequate for yard shunting but were rather underpowered and underbraked for the gradient up and down to Faslane Bay, and so the WD borrowed SR Z Class 0–8–0Ts 951/5/6 (WD 213-5) in January, May and April 1942 respectively, as well as WD 2000/1 2–6–0STs by the end of September 1942. By March 1943, six engines were said to be allocated to Faslane, although it is not entirely clear which they were. WD 2–8–0s 7223 & 7369 went to Faslane on being built in October 1943, and on their arrival the SR Z Class 0–8–0Ts were returned to the SR. WD 7168 came to Faslane from Longmoor, releasing WD 7223 which was sent to Cairnryan. A number of other WD 2–8–0s 7226/7/34 also worked at Faslane before going on loan to the LNE in October 1943.

In March 1945, the War Office decided that Military Port No 1 (Faslane) would not be needed after the war with Germany ended, and that Military Port No 2 (Cairnryan) would be able to cope with future requirements. Military Port No 1 closed for port operations on 31 March 1946. Since when it had been set up, it had been promised that it would not become a commercial port, so the ship-breaking firm of Metal Industries Ltd took over the port from 31 July and formally on 15 August 1946. The LNE took over responsibility for operating the branch down to the port area, and subsequently singled the track, although it continued to be MoD property. In July 1946, WD 70086/7 were still in use on military tasks "de-storing" Admiralty ships. The last large engine, WD 2–8–0 77369, went on loan to the LNE in May 1946 and was subsequently sold to the LNE. WD 70078/9/83/5-7/90 were subsequently sold to MIL.

Regarding Military Port No 2 at Cairnryan, which developed into the Cairnryan Military Railway, this large military port also with six deep-water berths, was built between January 1941 and the middle of 1943 on the east shore of Loch Ryan, about seven miles north of Stranraer. A rail connection was made to the LMS about 1½ miles east of Stranraer, with extensive sidings and a signal box at Cairnryan Junction. The railway swung north, crossed the A75 road and then ran parallel to the A77 road. An engine shed was sited at the Leffnol, four miles from the Junction. As at Faslane, this was a three-road steel-framed structure mainly clad with corrugated iron sheeting.

The first locomotives were Dean Goods WD 93 in November 1941, followed by WD 94/5 and 177/8. Around May 1942, they were joined by J69 0–6–0Ts WD 78, 81/2/8/9 & 91 and probably LNE J50 0–6–0Ts WD 216-8/20. As will be discussed in later Chapters, various other locomotives were later allocated here, such as LMS 8F 2–8–0s and WD 0–6–0STs. After the war, the Port was used to load ships with unwanted munitions being taken out to sea for disposal. The WD left in 1959.

Throughout the war, the UK was a major centre of operations for military locomotives, which were used at many depots. Some were new, some were based on existing industrial facilities. The major ones were Bicester Central Ordnance Depot, Cairnryan (military port), Corsham underground ammunition depot, Donnington Ordnance Depot, Kineton (ammunition), Long Marston (RE stores), Longtown (ammunition), Marchwood (military port), Newbury (RE hutting depot), Steventon (motor transport) and West Moors (petroleum).

Liphook Central Ordnance Depot and Marchwood Port Operating Depot, both in Hampshire, were both supplied with locomotives by the Longmoor Military Railway. The WD Depots at Donnington, Harlech and Wem were maintained from the Depot on the Shropshire & Montgomeryshire Railway. Allocations of these subsidiary Depots were frequently exchanged with those of the main Depot.

Various military dumps were established as follows. At Islip, between Oxford and Bicester, a petrol depot was reopened. There was another petrol depot at Husband Crawley, on the Midland line

Coulomiers, Vitry le Francois, Paris, Brussels, Furth and Frankfurt.

As can be seen, the first ROB to be organised was No 711. Its first task was to rehabilitate the 4½ mile railway serving Fort Belvoir in Virginia. Sleepers were replaced, several bridges rebuilt, culverts installed and fresh ballast laid, all in 48 days. Its second task was to construct a new railway for training purposes, running 47½ miles between Camps Claiborne and Polk in Louisiana. It followed the terrain closely to minimise earthworks and used second-hand rail. The golden spike was driven in on 11 July 1942. Further details, including the locomotives, are given in Chapter 46.

In August 1942, the USA/TC ordered 400 2–8–0s and 15 0–6–0Ts for use in the UK, and later the orders were expanded. Because British railways were sufficiently organised, there was no call for the USA/TC to participate in UK operations, but the USA/TC did take over the responsibility for shunting operations at their own depots (often British depots passed over to the US Army) and by April 1943 the USA/TC was responsible for shunting at eight USA/TC depots, using 18 locomotives. Later, these operations were expanded.

Apart from locomotives, the USA/TC ordered many wagons, the main types being bogie petroleum tank wagons, bogie & 4w box wagons and bogie flat wagons (for carrying heavy items such as armour). There were also some bogie refrigerator cars, 4w 20 ton and bogie 40 ton open wagons and 4w caboose wagons (guards vans). These were made chiefly for use in the European Theatre of War, and so were made to British loading gauge. As mentioned in Chapter 1, some were put to use on British railways prior to the invasion of Europe. At 8 May 1944, there were also stored in England 375 petroleum tank wagons, 3327 box cars, 64 flat wagons, 151 refrigerator cars, 730 open wagons and 325 cabooses, a total of 4972 wagons in store. All told, some 22,000 wagons were ordered, but many of these were sent in from North Africa or Italy, while later ones were assembled on the Continent.

USA/TC hospital trains were obtained in the UK, probably because British coaches would fit any European loading gauge whereas American coaches would not necessarily do so. Coaches were converted for ambulance use at Swindon under USA/TC control. By 1 September 1943, there were 15 trains available and by D-Day 27. At the end of 1944, 25 of these trains were on the Continent, while some were still in the UK for use in the UK (casualties from USAF flying operations).

By June 1945, the Americans had built and exported for use world-wide by the US or Allied forces no less than 5578 locomotives, 106 railway cranes and 83,875 items of rolling stock. In addition, some diesel locomotives had been purchased from American railroads for use in Iran, and some narrow-gauge equipment for the White Pass and Yukon Route railway. About 43,500 men and women employees of the American railroads served in the various units of the Military Railway Service.

While the box cars and refrigerator wagons were rather flimsy and did not survive long after the war, the petroleum tank wagons, flat wagons and railway cranes proved to be very durable and some may still be seen today in odd corners of Europe.

Towards the end of the war, thought was given to supplying new locomotives to various countries to assist in the post-war rehabilitation. It was considered that large numbers of locomotives would be required, and that production would be greater if a standard design was produced, which led to the concept of an all-purpose "Liberation" 2–8–0. The UK manufacturer Vulcan Foundry was chosen to design one such version of this locomotive, and in the USA a similar type was designed.

As war turned to peace, the UNRRA (United Nations Relief and Rehabilitation Administration) was set up to provide emergency relief. UNRRA became involved with these locomotives. Countries such as China, Czechoslovakia, Greece, Poland and Yugoslavia did not have the money to pay for new locomotives, while Belgium, France & Luxembourg were reckoned to be able to pay.

Of course, it did not work out entirely as planned. France, the largest customer and one who was paying, did not want 2–8–0s considering them to be too small (having experience of the USA/TC and WD 2–8–0s), but wanted a 2–8–2, which became the R141 class. The first of these were ordered by the USA/TC, as shown below:

USA/TC Nos	Maker & Works Nos	SNCF Nos
8867–9046	Lima 8867–9046/45	141 R1–180
10250–509	Alco 74054–313/45	141 R181–440
10760–11019	Baldwin 72254–513	141 R441–700
–	–	141 R701–1340

Shortly after the war ended, large numbers of USA/TC 2–8–0s, often virtually unused, became available, and it was pointless building new engines, so S160s were supplied instead (as described in Chapter 50) and the UNRRA orders were cancelled. However, for some reason, Belgium was left as the only customer for the USA "Liberation" 2–8–0. Accordingly, the SNCB had some say in its design which became its Class 29. Details are as follows:

SNCB Nos	Makers & Works Nos
29.001–60	Montreal 74498–557/45
29.061–160	Montreal 74558–657/46
29.161–220	Canadian 2288–347/46
29.221–300	Alco 74706–85/46

These engines had side buffers and screw couplings for European use, plus small smoke deflectors. They were used on passenger and freight workings. SNCB 29.013 worked the last regular steam train in Belgium, just before Christmas 1966, and was subsequently preserved.

Later, it became clear that more locomotives would be needed for China, and so some UNRRA orders for the USA "Liberation" 2–8–0 were reinstated. These became Class KD7. Details were as follows:

UNRRA Nos	Makers & Works No
1001–35	Alco (S) 74388–422/46
1036–115	Baldwin 73247–326/46
1116–60	Lima 9212–56/47

They were built with Chinese type knuckle couplers. In China, they were distributed amongst the various Chinese railways, and subsequently they became China Railways Class KD7 501–660. The chimney and combined dome/sandbox covers were increased in height. The original curved running plate at the front was replaced by straight ladders. "Bay" windows were fitted to the cabs to facilitate shunting operations. Tender sides were build up to carry more coal.

FC Mexicano, a private railway later absorbed into the national system, also needed locomotives at this time and ten units were supplied as a follow-on order, as follows:

FCM Nos	Maker & Works Nos
211–20	Baldwin 73237–46/46

These had knuckle couplers, and ran freight trains for about 20 years.

Chapter 3

MIDDLE EAST

Apart from the UK, during the first part of World War Two, the main centres of military locomotive operations were in the Middle East and the Near East. The railways in the Middle East, in particular the Western Desert Extension Railway, were used to supply the British forces during the fluctuating war in the desert. Before World War Two, the Egyptian Western Desert Railway was a single-track standard-gauge line along the coast, extended to Mersa Matruh on strategic grounds in April 1936. Thus, Mersa Matruh was connected to Alexandria some 200 miles away by this line. The war naturally brought considerable traffic to this line, and the WD were responsible for an extension which was called the Western Desert Extension Railway.

a counter-offensive. El Agheila fell on 24 March, and the German forces crossed the 150 miles to Benghazi in a few days. The British evacuated Benghazi on 3 April and by 13 April, the Germans had reached Bardia near the Egyptian frontier, leaving Tobruk as an isolated British garrison. As an aside, on 6 April 1941, Greece and Yugoslavia were invaded, and by 28 April the British and Commonwealth forces had left Greece. The British reinforced Tobruk by sea with some Australian units, and the Germans failed to take it. During May and June, there were attacks and counter-attacks in the Sollum and Fort Capuzzo areas, but no large scale offensive was launched against Egypt.

The Allies in the Middle East had other distractions at this time. The Abyssinian

Egypt under WD jurisdiction (see Chapter 21). Some of these engines were used by the Railway Operating Companies on the Western Desert Extension Railway and, for a while, also on the Daba to Mersa Matruh section of the Egyptian State Railway Western Desert line. It was realised that if the Western Desert branch was to be extended, to Tobruk or even further, diesel locomotives would be required, as the use of steam locomotives would necessitate major developments. Accordingly, orders were placed with the Whitcomb Locomotive Co for fifty-two 0–4–4–0 diesel-electric locomotives (see Chapter 25).

On 18 November 1941, the Eighth Army took the offensive and after much fighting of mixed fortunes eventually relieved Tobruk on 10 December. By early January, the German forces had withdrawn once more to El Agheila. However, German reinforcements arrived, while Allied forces were diverted or withdrawn to strengthen the Far East following the shock of Pearl Harbour. On 21 January, the Germans launched a counter-attack and on 29 January recaptured Benghazi. The Allies withdrew and for four months, the front was just east of Derna.

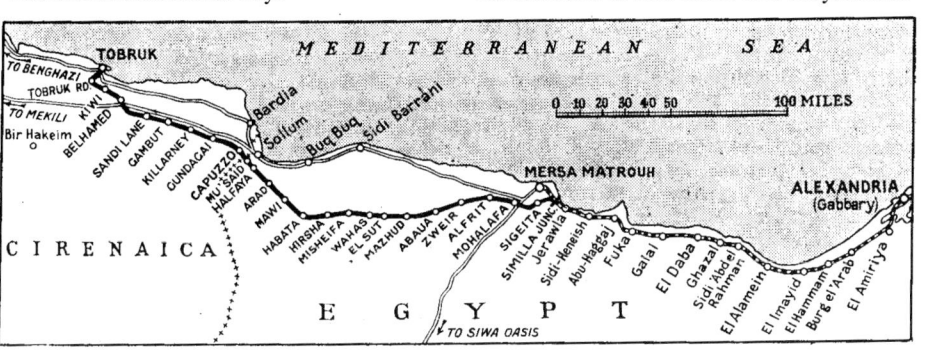

Map 2   Sketch map of the Western Desert Extension Railway from Similla Junction (near Mersa Matruh) to Tobruk (Courtesy Railway Magazine)

The Italians entered the war on 10 June 1940, and invaded Egyptian territory, proceeding to a point east of Sidi Barrani, but west of Mersa Matruh. In October 1940, the New Zealand 16 & 17 Rly Op Coys Royal Engineers began an extension ready for a military offensive. To climb the escarpment behind Mersa Matruh, it was decided to begin the extension at a point roughly midway between Jerawla and Mersa Matruh, which became known as Similla Junction. The first British advance began on 9 December 1940, and Benghazi was occupied on 7 February 1941. In view of this advance, work stopped on the extension in January 1941. The British advance reached El Agheila and thus covered virtually the whole of Cirenaica.

At this time, Churchill directed that major effort should be directed towards Greece and the Balkans. The best military units and equipment were stripped from the desert front. However, on 12 February 1941, Rommel arrived in Africa! At the end of March, the German forces launched

campaign did not end until mid-May. On 20 May, the Germans invaded Crete and by 31 May, the British forces were driven out. The Royal Navy had lost so many surface ships in the Mediterranean Sea that convoys could no longer safely pass from Gibraltar to Egypt.

With the position in the western desert more or less stabilised, it was decided in June 1941 to carry on with the extension to the WDR for some 108 miles to a railhead immediately behind the British lines. By September, the railhead had reached Mohalafa ("Alliance") and by December 1941 the New Zealanders had reached Misheifa which lay south of Sidi Barrani. This was also the head of the Western Desert water pipeline. At Misheifa, a large circular depot was laid out (similar in principle to Bicester or Bramley) to minimise enemy attack, and a dummy railhead was built further west which took most of the bombing!

At the end of 1941, forty-two ex-LMS Class Stanier 2–8–0s were put to work in

The British authorities had decided, as soon as the way to Tobruk was clear, that the Western Desert Extension Railway should be further extended to that point. By March 1942, the line had been extended to Capuzzo, being operated by steam locomotives. Construction continued and by 12 June 1942, the railhead was opened at Bel Hamed, only 15 miles from Tobruk. The British were getting ready to attack.

However, the Germans moved first and on 26 May a heavy attack was launched. Unfortunately, the British had 10,000 tons of stores at Tobruk and 26,000 tons at Bel Hamed ready for their own attack, and the need to protect these dumps hampered the Eight Army's freedom of manoeuvre. The Eighth Army counter-attacked unsuccessfully on 5 June, and by 11 June Rommel was up in the Ed Adem area, and by 13 June the Eighth Army was forced to withdraw to the Egyptian frontier. Thus, the Capuzzo to Bel Hamed section of the WDER did not come into full use because five days later the Eighth Army withdrew. Tobruk was attacked on 20 June and surrendered on 21 June. Three days later, the Germans reached a point beyond Sidi

Barrani; on 27 June they reached Mersa Matruh and on 30 June El Daba. The British positions at El Alamein were then established. Rommel attempted to attack on 1 July but failed.

It was not possible in the limited time available for the track to be demolished effectively, but no locomotives were allowed to fall into enemy hands, except one ESR 2–6–0 590 which had failed at El Daba and was immobilised by charges in the frames, but some wagons were left behind. The railhead for the British forces became Burg El'Arab. The Germans repaired the part of the railway that they held. German and Italian diesel locomotives were shipped to Africa and by October the Germans were regularly working the 280 miles between Bel Hamed and El Daba with captured British wagons. In addition, the line was extended by the Germans from Bel Hamed to Tobruk.

The British forces had to consider anti-aircraft defences. Some LMS 2–8–0s were fitted with either armour plate or concrete slabs to protect the cabs and boilers. Some trains had box wagons at each end with twin machine guns, or barrage balloons attached by steel cables! Some Whitcomb diesels were also fitted with armour plate and/or disguised as box vans and marshalled in the middle of the trains!

Rommel attacked again between 31 August and 3 September 1942, but failed again. Rommel had come to a dead end. American supplies were beginning to arrive in the Middle East, Malta had survived and was being reinforced and could therefore intercept supplies going to Rommel.

The next Allied offensive, the famous Battle of Alamein, started with massed artillery fire on 23 October 1942. After hard fighting, by 4 November the German forces started to retreat. By 5 November, the Allies were in the Fuka area. On 6 November, it rained heavily turning the desert into a quagmire but the Allies reached Sidi Heneish. The chase was on! About this time, the Allies were landing in North Africa (see Chapter 5), convoys were getting through to Malta, and the Royal Navy was active again.

For this offensive, the Whitcomb diesel locomotives took over the operation of the Western Desert line from the Stanier 2–8–0s, which were then mostly loaned to the ESR, with the exception of two which remained to operate passenger trains. In the early stages of the advance, it was essential that the railway should be repaired and operated as rapidly as possible and that the railhead be advanced as quickly as the tactical situation allowed. Construction trains were operated on a shuttle service from Gabbary, the marshalling yard at Alexandria. The railhead was advanced to El Imayid by 27 October and then to El Alamein by 5 November, progress being limited by the rate at which the permanent way could be repaired, the provision of water for the locomotives and by the need for adequate signal communications.

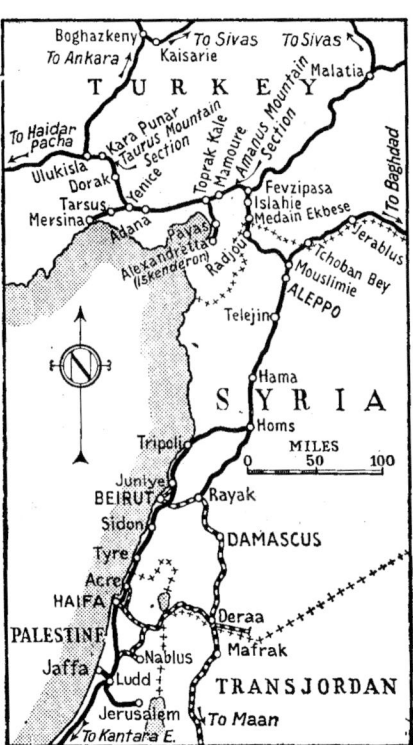

Map 3 Sketch map of the railways of Syria and adjoining countries. Full lines represent standard gauge track and dotted lines narrow gauge (Courtesy Railway Magazine)

Heavy work was required to open the section through the battle area westwards to El Daba by 9 November 1942 owing to the damage caused by enemy demolitions as well as by our own shelling and bombing. The enemy had also constructed many dugouts in the railway embankments. Less work was required west of El Daba, although track demolitions had occurred and points, crossings and lengths of track had been removed. Teller mines had been laid in the track, every yard of which had to be examined before the line was opened as far as Mersa Matruh on 14 November and Tobruk on 18 November. By 20 November, the railhead was at Capuzzo and on 22 November a construction train reached Bel Hamed. By 28 November, about a month after the offensive started, the line was open to Tobruk Road, situated on top of the escarpment about seven miles from the harbour, and by 1 December was in operation to that point. No less than 355 miles of railway had been cleared and repaired in a month. ESR 590 was recaptured at El Daba, remaining exactly as it had been left!

The heavy traffic on the Western Desert Extension Railway caused by the advance of our forces was foreseen and a mobile shop train was constructed containing machine tools and maintenance gear to ensure that locomotives were repaired as rapidly as possible.

As the railhead advanced, it was followed by the water pipeline. The custom was for steam power to be used up to and sometimes on the section immediately after the pipe head and for diesel power to be used further west. To begin with, water was available at Hamman, which was carried forward to El Daba by rail tank wagons. Later, water was similarly carried from El Daba to Similla Junction, the diesel locomotives being moved forward to operate the line further west. On 25 November, the water pipe was extended to Similla, whence it was carried by rail to Misheifa while the pipe was being extended that far. Steam locomotives then operated to Misheifa and the diesel locomotives were moved westward to Capuzzo. On 7 December, the water pipe reached Misheifa and the steam locomotives then worked to Capuzzo and the diesels from Capuzzo to Tobruk Road, the railhead.

Originally, the railway was operated throughout by a New Zealand Railway Operating Company but when the line was opened to Mersa Matruh this naturally was too big a job for one Company so that shortly afterwards the 6th Railway Operating Group consisting of the 193 (British) and 115 (Indian) Railway Operating Companies took over the Alexandria to Mersa Matruh section, leaving the original NZ Company free to concentrate on the line west of Mersa Matruh. Eventually the service through to Tobruk Road averaged six 450-ton trains a day, with a maximum of eight trains on peak days, so that Tobruk Road was operating at 2700 tons a day.

As the advance continued, Benghazi was occupied and the 0.95 metre gauge Benghazi Barce and Soluch Railway came under British control (see Chapter 22). The German forces had started to extend the Barce line to Tobruk but had built only the track foundations without laying any track. The British authorities considered carrying on with this work, and also extending the line westwards to connect with the Tripolitanian Railway, but neither project was ever started.

Supplies had to come to Benghazi either by the single road hundreds of miles back to the Egyptian bases, or by rail to Tobruk and then mostly by sea to Benghazi port. Plans called for about 2380 tons per day by road and 2200 tons per day by rail and sea. On 3/4 January 1943, there was a bad gale and the mole of Benghazi

Harbour, already weakened, was cracked. Ships were damaged or even sunk, and berths and warehouses damaged. For a time, getting supplies forward took priority over advancing. Fortunately, the German forces had their own supply problems. For example, only 30 tanks survived Alamein and by 6 November only four of these were intact!

Finally, as the advance continued further westwards, the 0.95 metre gauge Tripolitanian Railway (see Chapter 22) was captured. Besides serving several areas close to Tripoli, there was a 70 mile line to Zuara to the west. The British authorities decided to restore the local lines, before the Zuara branch, in order to facilitate clearing the port for operation. Two locomotives and twelve wagons were shipped from the BB&SR to augment the captured Tripolitanian Railway stock.

Some German and Italian military diesel locomotives were captured in the advance. The German engines were referred to by a numbering system best explained by an example; WR 200 B 14 in which "WR" was "Wehrmacht Reichsbahn", 200 was the horsepower, the letter represented the wheel arrangement (B 0–4–0, C 0–6–0, etc) and the number was the axleload. A WR200B14 was captured at Tunis and became WD 235, while four others became WD 246–9. Seven Italian Badoni/Fiat 0–4–0Ds, works numbers 4172/90/2/4/7, 4207/9, were captured, of which 4172/90 and 4209 became WD 250–2. The others were derelict and did not receive WD or MEF numbers. WD 246/8/9 were later used at Beirut, 250–2 at Fanara and 247 at an American base at Darb el Hag.

The Western Desert operations provided an interesting comparison of steam and diesel power. Naturally, the water economy of the diesel locomotive showed to advantage. The Whitcomb diesels required 70 gallons for 24 hours operation and could be refilled in 10 minutes. On the other hand, the Stanier steam 2–8–0s, which carried 250 gallons in the boiler and 4000 gallons in the tender, required some 60 to 80 gallons per mile under desert conditions. The maintenance of the diesel locomotives was found to be as simple as that of the steam engines, but when breakdowns occurred they were sometimes serious and expert knowledge was required. The diesels provided a more flexible power unit for general operations because while two diesels were required to equal a steam engine for hauling heavy freight trains, these two could be split up and operated as single units for shunting duties if so required. Sufficient spare parts were not available for either the Stanier 2–8–0s or the Whitcomb diesels and badly damaged locomotives had to be stripped of parts in order to repair less badly damaged locomotives.

After the war, the BB&SR and the Tripolitanian Railway continued to operate under WD supervision but the amount of military traffic dropped and gradually the lines were handed back to civilian control. The need for the Western Desert Extension Railway largely lapsed when the war ended and the Tobruk-Capuzzo section was closed on 20 December 1946.

Considering the eastern end of the Mediterranean, in April 1941, the German forces invaded Greece and a drive to dominate Iraq looked probable. British forces were sent to Iraq to develop the port of Basra and to develop the railways from Baghdad to the Syrian and Turkish borders, and to Mosul.

"British Troops Iraq", later known as Paiforce ("Persia and Iraq Force"), landed in May 1941 to find that the metre-gauge line between Basra and Baghdad had been cut by rebels, while the line to Syria and Turkey from Baghdad was standard-gauge, rendering through running between Basra and Syria and Turkey impossible. Three miles up the river from Basra was Maqil, the terminus of the IqSR and a small port. Gradually the line was repaired and by 16 June 1941 it was reopened to Baghdad. The troops then pressed on 200 miles to Mosul, along the standard-gauge railway, and eventually took Tel Kotchek on the Turkish border.

From 1941 onwards, Iraq became involved in the war effort as one of the supply routes for aid to Russia. One route was from Basra to Khaniqin, and then by road through Iran. In December 1942, a metre-gauge line was opened from Kut-El-Amara to Baquba (see Map 5). Freight was carried from Basra to Kut by river barges up the River Tigris. A new port was built at Um Qasr, with rail connection to the metre-gauge railway. The standard-gauge line was extended in May 1942 to Hindiyah on the metre gauge, avoiding Baghdad. Use was made of the metre-gauge branch to Maqil, close to Basra, in December 1943 by building the Hull Bridge across the Shatt-al-Arab waterway, leading to exchange sidings at Tanuma on the east bank from which a standard-gauge line was built to the Iraqi border and on to the Iranian railway system. A notable feature of the Hull Bridge was that it had a *sinking* span 90 ft long so that ships could pass *over* it when lowered!

After the war, the lines were closed of course. Kut to Baquba shut in June 1945, the Tanuma branch in July 1945 and the Um Qasr line was lifted in April 1946.

With the Mediterranean route becoming difficult for British shipping, and the risk of Suez being heavily attacked from the air, it was decided to improve the alternative route via the Cape. Accordingly, a railway line was built from Qena on the ESR, about 320 miles south of Cairo, 116 miles to Sofaga on the Red Sea coast, where an alternative port was created. Surveys were carried out in July 1941 and work started in August 1941. Whatever materials were available were used, mostly from India, and this led to the line being built metre gauge. However, the line was actually built by the ESR but at WD expense. The line was completed in May 1942, the last section to Sofaga using the existing Egyptian Phosphate Company's line, but was not in operation until July 1942 due to lack of water tank wagons necessary for the arid terrain.

Rolling stock, as well as permanent way, was imported from the metre-gauge lines of India (see Chapter 15), as well as the FMSR 4–6–4Ts WD 2600–5 (see Chapter 29). Fortunately, there was never any need for the line to carry much traffic, and by the beginning of 1944, the potential need for it had disappeared. The ESR did not want the line, so it was closed in February 1944 and lifted later that year.

When the war started, there was a standard-gauge railway between Kantara East (on the east bank of the Suez Canal) and Haifa, operated by the Palestine Railways,

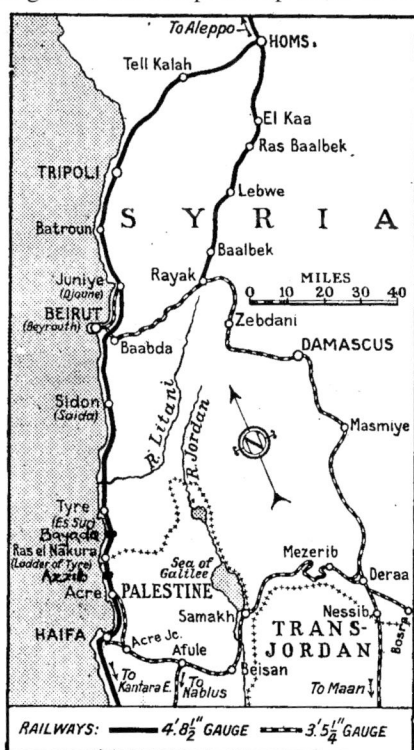

Map 4 Approximate course of the new standard-gauge railway built by the Allied military forces between Haifa and Tripoli, known as the Haifa-Beirut-Tripoli Railway (Courtesy Railway Magazine)

the Kantara East to Rafa (on the border between Egypt and Palestine) being known as the Sinai Military Railway. There was a daily passenger service, with dining and sleeping cars, between Kantara and Haifa, connection being made with the ESR Cairo to Port Said trains at Kantara West by ferry across the Suez Canal. In June 1941, the Australian Royal Engineers started to build a standard-gauge line along the eastern side of the Suez Canal some 71 miles from Kantara south to El Shatt opposite Suez. This was to guard against the Suez Canal being blocked by enemy military action. This new railway was completed in July 1942 and turned over to the ESR for operation. To connect the line to the ESR, a new swing bridge was built across the Canal at Firdan. This was opened for traffic in August 1942. A new through passenger service was started from Cairo to Haifa via the bridge, operated jointly by ESR and PR, each administration providing one set of coaches.

When the Vichy government was ousted from Syria in July 1941, and faced with the possibility that the German forces might strike south through Turkey, it was decided to build a standard-gauge link between Haifa and the Syrian railways, so that equipment could be moved quickly, without transhipment problems, from Egypt and Palestine to Iraq and right through to the Turkish border.

Following surveys, it was decided to build the line along the coast, connecting Haifa with Beirut and Tripoli. This involved some difficult work negotiating steep cliffs where headlands met the sea, but was considered preferable to the alternative of Haifa to Rayak. Initial construction of the 90 mile section between Haifa and Beirut was carried out by the South African Railway Construction Engineers, with later work by the New Zealand Royal Engineers, while the 50 mile section from Beirut to Tripoli was built by the Australian Royal Engineers, with help from South African miners.

The Haifa to Beirut section included the problems presented by the two big headlands on the Palestine/Syrian frontier, Ras Nakura and Ras Bayada, where high cliffs drop down straight into the sea. At Ras Nakura, it was decided that the line could be taken round the headlands by two short tunnels 360 and 250 feet long and the construction of a sea wall. At Ras Bayada, it was decided to cut a ledge in the cliff face about 20 feet above sea level. The sea walls were a problem, at some places having to be built in water over 8 feet deep. Concrete blocks, varying from 15 to 100 tons, were cast on the rock ledges and tipped into the sea, sometimes 100 feet

Map 5   Map of the railways in Iraq (Courtesy Railway Magazine)

below. The interstices between the blocks were filled up with bags of concrete. The Haifa-Beirut section was opened in August 1942.

For the Beirut to Tripoli section, two tunnels, one almost a mile long, had to be built near Cheka. Since this was beyond the capacity and equipment of an ordinary railway construction group, a special tunnelling group of South African miners was recruited which worked under the control of the Australian Royal Engineers. The 14 mile section from Tripoli to Cheka was opened in July 1942, and the whole line from Beirut to Tripoli in December 1942.

This completed a rail link from Suez and Cairo to the Bosphorus. Seven major bridges had been built, as well as eight smaller ones and 98 culverts. Marshalling yards were built at Azzib and Beirut, and crossing stations every 10 to 12 miles. A central control office was opened at Beirut and train crews were based at Haifa, Azzib and Beirut. As locomotives and rolling stock were obtained, up to 32 trains a day were operated.

Fortunately, Germany did not strike through Turkey, and, despite hopes by the Allies, Turkey maintained its neutrality. This limited the need to pass military stores north of Aleppo. However, locomotives were transferred to and from Iraq by the Haifa-Beirut-Tripoli Railway as it became known, and ex-MEF engines were delivered to Turkey.

In the wartime period, there were two Railway Workshop Squadrons in the MEF, No 169 with headquarters at Suez and No 199 first at Haifa and then at Jaffa from October 1942. No 199 had a carriage and wagon detachment (31 Det) at Azzib, North Palestine, on the HBT. No 199 was later responsible for maintaining the locomotives at depots at Wadi Sarar (Ammunition), Rafah (Ordnance) and El Jiya (Fuel). No 169 was similarly responsible for Fort Agrud, Adabiya, Romana and Fayid. The Western Desert line motive power was looked after by the No 3 Mobile Workshops, which were at Similla, near Mersa Matruh. Formerly they were at Azzib when the Whitcomb diesels were operating the HBT line.

The HBT was operated by No 193 Operating Squadron with headquarters at Beirut, a detachment at Azzib and individuals up and down the line. When the British came out of the Lebanon, No 193 went to Suez, later to Lydda and finally formed their headquarters at Azzib, with detachments working at El Jiya, Rafah, Wadi Sarar (which had previously been operated by the No 155 Indian Operating Squadron), and also at the Palestine Railway depots at Haifa and Lydda.

There were five Transportation Stores Depots, which were renumbered in 1944. These were 400 (ex 6) at Suez, 401 (ex 8) at Azzib, 402 (ex 16) at Ein Shams near Cairo, 403 (ex 15) at Alexandria and 404 (ex 4) at Helwan. TSD 402 carried locomotive spares. These were the numbers of the depots. The Squadron running all of them was latterly No 198 Transportation Stores Squadron, and previously a different Squadron, but the depots had the same numbers all the time. No 400 TSD was adjacent to No 169 Railway Workshop Squadron and supplied them, except for locomotive spares. No 401 TSD supplied No 199 Rly Wksp Sqn although some 94 miles away, No 31 Detachment who were in the same camp and No 193 Optg Sqn when on the HBT. No 402 TSD, until they closed, supplied only locomotive spares to all units, not direct but through No 401 TSD for No 199 Rly Wksps and through No 400 TSD for No 169 Rly Wksps. When No 402 TSD closed, their stock went mostly to No 400 TSD although some 8F 2–8–0 parts went straight to No 401 TSD for No 199 Rly Wksps. The Palestine Railway also used to obtain parts for their 8F 2–8–0s from No 401 TSD.

Locomotives in store at Suez were almost all in No 400 TSD yard, so were the Sudan type 4–6–2 parts (see Chapter 30) and the FMSR 4–6–4Ts ex Qena-Sofaga Railway (see Chapter 29). Locomotives in store at Azzib were generally in the running sheds on PR ground. The PR maintained the HBT track to the frontier at Ras en Nagura, just north of Azzib. The Sudan type 4–6–2s here, however, were again on stores ground, in No 401 TSD.

The American 760 RSB Diesel, which was activated for training at Camp Claiborne in June 1942, arrived at Suez in November 1942 to maintain the diesel-electric locomotives which were then in use in Egypt, Libya, Palestine and Syria.

There were, of course, many WD depots with railway connections which required shunting locomotives. In Egypt there were Abu Sultan, Agrud, Amiriya, Ataqa, Barrage, Fanara, Gilbana, Gineifa, Qasfareet and Suez Junction; and in Palestine there were Azzib, El Jiya, Rafah and Wadi Sarar.

Chapter 4

PERSIA (IRAN)

Starting in 1927, a 866-mile long railway was built from Bandar Shahpur on the Persian Gulf to Bandar Shah on the Caspian Sea, via Teheran, the capital. One of the railway engineering feats of the world, the railway crossed 150 miles of desert after leaving Bandar Shahpur, then wound up and across the mountains for 100 miles boring through 130 tunnels to reach a height of 7270ft at Arak. In the next 250 miles, it fell some 3000ft to Teheran. The next 300 miles included crossing the Elburz Mountains on gradients of up to 1 in 36 with more bridges and tunnels. In all, there were 231 tunnels and 4102 bridges.

Subsequently, several branches were built, including one from the port of Khorramshahr 77 miles to Ahwaz, and one from Teheran 272 miles to Mianeh. The country was mountainous and largely desert.

At the end of 1941, the Iranian State Railway was operating two trains a day from Ahwaz to Andimeshk and one train to Bandar Shahpur, with a passenger and mail train to Teheran three times a week. The locomotive stock at Ahwaz was generally in bad condition except for two German Ferrostaal 2–10–0s which were used for the mail trains between Ahwaz and Do-Rood. The remaining engines were seven Ferrostaal 2–8–0s, two Beyer Peacock 2–8–0s, two Baldwin 2–6–0s, a Krupp 2–6–0 and a Decauville 0–4–0T, and two ex-Austrian 0–10–0 two-cylinder compounds in store. There were 52 passenger coaches, about 900 covered 4w wagons, about 420 open wagons, some bogie wagons, tank wagons, ballast hopper wagons and some flat wagons. There were also some 50 American bogie wagons in poor condition and with centre buck-eye couplers. The existing staff was sufficient for only one shift, train control was by telephone and hardly necessary since no trains were booked to cross each other between Bandar Shahpur and Andimeshk. Night working was discouraged. All water used by the locomotives at Bandar Shahpur was hauled from Ahwaz in tank wagons. The water at Gor-Gor was saline and unsuitable.

This was the state of the IrSR at the time that it was proposed to start sending heavy traffic through to Russia. British interest in the Southern Division began in September 1941, while the Russians took over responsibility for the Northern Division, that is, north of Teheran, in January 1942. The British No 190 Rly Op Co arrived in December 1941. The first tasks were to clear 30,000 tons of goods which lay at the port of Bandar Shahpur, to lay new yards at Bandar Shahpur, Ahwaz and Andimeshk, to prepare a junction at Ahwaz with the new railway then being surveyed to Khorramshahr, to supply track to Abadan where arriving engines were to be put ashore for transhipment into barges, and to erect a derrick at Ahwaz jetty to lift the engines from barge to rail.

The port at Bandar Shahpur at that time possessed a short jetty which could berth two medium-sized ships and which had three rail tracks but no dock cranes. For jetty shunting, axle-loads were limited, and the work was carried out by two Nohab 0–6–0s with 4w tenders, and a Baldwin 2–6–0. The yard was small and inconvenient and there was little room for expansion owing to the land being reclaimed from estuary mud. There was no road access.

The first WD Stanier 8F 2–8–0s arrived in December 1941, WD 337 IrSR 41.100 being the first steamed on 10 December. Engines were thenceforth turned out to traffic at a rate of one every 36 hours and they were immediately sent to increase the service between Bandar Shahpur and Andimeshk. Shortly afterwards, it was possible to release some of the German engines to go to the Northern Division. Wagon parts also began to arrive in December 1941, some 840 WD 20-ton high-sided wagons being sent to the IrSR. Also, 24 diesel shunters ordered by the IrSR before the WD arrived were delivered in 1942.

The main problem of the Southern Division and the bottleneck of the whole railway was the 208 km section between Andimeshk and Do-Rood in which the line rose from 146 to 1454 metres above sea level with a ruling gradient of 1:67. At the beginning, there were six Ferrostaal '51' class 2–10–0s at Andimeshk which were in fair order and could handle 450 tons gross. To supplement these, some Ferrostaal 2–8–0s of the '41' class were transferred from Ahwaz, being replaced by coal-burning Stanier 2–8–0s. These could handle around 300 tons in theory. However, their injectors would not deliver water to the boiler when the temperature of the tender water was around 40°C. So tenders were sometimes painted white to try to bring the water temperature down and cure the trouble. Water was so hard that the boiler suffered from considerable deposits.

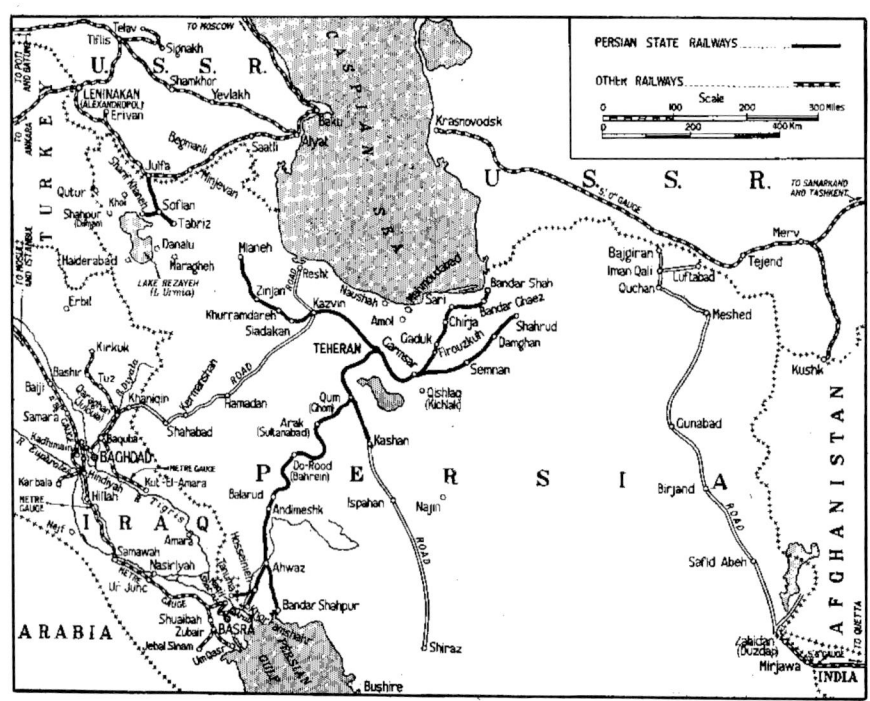

Map 6 Map of the railways of Persia (now Iran) and adjacent territories, showing also the principal road links used in sending supplies to Russia (Courtesy Railway Magazine)

Sandboxes proved inadequate for the mountain sections. American 2–8–2s from the WD/USA/TC 1000–1199 series arrived but needed some changes before being put into service. Buck-eye couplings had to be replaced by screw type, running gear was converted from oil to grease lubrication. Electric headlamps had to be fitted for the tunnels.

Crews of steam trains were almost asphyxiated by the fumes from their engines, despite stocking up, opening the regulator, wrapping a wet cloth round their faces and climbing down on to the footsteps. If the locomotives started slipping, they were in real trouble! Thus, coal-firing was quite inadequate for regular work on this line and hence no WD engine could be used until February 1942 when oil-burning Stanier 2–8–0s began to arrive at Andimeshk. The 2–10–0s were then gradually released for service in the Northern Division. A Beyer Peacock 2–8–0 was stationed at Do-rood for shunting. The Andimeshk detachment was withdrawn on the arrival of No 192 Rly Op Co in June 1942.

Another job was the development of increased port facilities at Khorramshahr, since Bandar Shahpur could not be developed sufficiently, and linking these facilities by rail with Ahwaz (120 km). Survey was begun in November 1941, earthwork in December 1941 and ballasting in January 1942. The laying of rail was completed in April 1942, although ballasting was only half completed. Traffic started at the end of May 1942.

Various wagons were put into service at Ahwaz. In addition to the WD high-sided wagons already mentioned, these included eight SR brake vans (used for sanding), 50 WD "Warflats", 51 French cross-Channel ferry covered vans, 166 covered vans from India converted to 4ft 8½in gauge, some Indian coal wagons, 24 bogie oil tanks and ten pairs of pipe-carrying single-bolster wagons from the Iraqi State Railway. During the last three months of 1942, a large number of new wagons were received from the United States including covered vans, flat wagons and oil tank wagons.

English wagons were not fitted with continuous brakes and even the American wagons were inadequately braked and their couplings were too weak for the 1 in 36 sections. Shunters and pointsmen were illiterate, so sorting had to be done by colour coding the sidings and wagons.

On the civil engineering side, 40 new passing loops were blasted out of the rock. Many new sidings were installed at Teheran, Andimeshk, Ahwaz, Khorramshahr and Tanuma.

In late 1942, it was agreed that the USA/TC should take over from the British, and in December 1942, No 711 ROB landed at Khorramshahr and, as the first part of No 702 RGD, began taking over from the WD in January 1943. No 703 ROB arrived in February, 754 RSB Steam and 762 RSB Diesel in March. The whole formed the 3rd MRS. It was considered that diesel-electric locomotives were the type of motive power most suited to the conditions on the IrSR, and it was felt that the standard 1000hp locomotive was the best type to send (see Chapter 62). Some 57 of these locomotives had just been delivered to American railroads or were being built, and these were all sent to Iran. In addition, 91 USA/TC steam 2–8–2s were brought in (see Chapter 48) and nearly 3000 freight wagons. The first diesel-powered train went from Ahwaz to Andimeshk on 10 March 1943. Even the diesels operated with the engine access doors removed because the heat was so intense, despite the greater risk of damage due to sand. In March 1943, an extension was opened from Zinjan to Mianeh on the line towards Russia.

It was found that two ROBs were insufficient to handle the mileage and accordingly No 791 ROB was activated in Iran by transfers from other units. By May 1943, the position was that 711 ROB had its HQ at Ahwaz and was responsible for lines south of Andimeshk through Ahwaz to the ports of Bandar Shahpur, Khorramshahr and Tanuma; No 791 ROB had its HQ at Arak and operated between Andimeshk and Arak; and No 730 ROB with its HQ at Teheran operated from Arak to Teheran.

The three ROBs began to deliver trains to Teheran yards faster than the Russians could handle them. Also, many wagons were floated across the Caspian Sea and not returned. By 1943, the turn-around time for loaded tank cars leaving the Gulf and returning from Russian depots was 30 days instead of the 15 days considered an ample allotment. By August 1943, virtually the entire fleet of about 5000 serviceable freight wagons was at the north end of the line waiting to be unloaded! In desperation, the MRS clamped a six-day embargo on shipments to Russia, during which time no freight was loaded at the ports and nothing sent to Teheran. The situation soon improved! Towards the end of 1943, a branch was opened from Hosseinieh to Tanuma into Iraq to facilitate supplies coming from Iraq. In February 1944, eight GE 45 ton diesels USA/TC 8532–9 arrived for shunting operations (see Chapter 60).

Traffic increased up until January 1945 but the new units and locomotives were able to cope with all the traffic. In January 1945, a new route to Russia opened through the Bosphorus and the Dardanelles, and traffic then diminished until May 1945 when the war ended in Europe. On 25 June, the MRS relinquished control to the British authorities who shortly afterwards returned control to the IrSR. No 791 ROB and 762 RSB Diesel left in May 1945, 730 ROB in June 1945, 711 ROB in July 1945, while 754 RSB Steam was inactivated in Iran in July. The northern lines were handed back by the Russians in May 1946.

Chapter 5

NORTH AFRICA

The railways of North Africa in 1942 totalled 5082 miles, consisting of 2741 miles standard and metre gauge Chemin de Fer Algeriens, 1001 miles standard and metre gauge Chemins de Fer Tunisiens, 867 miles standard gauge Chemins de Fer du Maroc, 276 miles metre gauge Chemin de Fer de Sfax à Gafsa and 197 miles standard gauge Chemin de Fer de Tanger à Fez. Most of the CFT was metre gauge but the main line from Souk Ahras through to Bizerta and Tunis was standard gauge.

In November 1942, the Allies landed in force at various ports in North Africa, with the intention of moving east to push Rommel and the retreating Germans out. In the event, the Allied advance was stopped temporarily short of Tunis by the influx of fresh German troops facing west. The main Allied supply route was a single-track standard-gauge railway line stretching 1410 miles from Casablanca via Fez, Oujda, Oran, Algiers and Constantine to Tunis. The branches were mainly metre gauge.

The USA/TC used 703 RGD in the North African invasion, landing at Casablanca in November 1942. Shunting at Oran was taken over immediately by 761 RTC (Railway Transportation Company). By the end of 1942, 727 ROB was operating the metre-gauge line running between Ouled Rhamoun through to Tébessa. The CFA shops at Sidi Mabrouk in Constantine were taken over by 753 RSB. The British First Railway Operating Group disembarked at Algiers in November 1942 and took over operations on the CFA between Algiers and Constantine.

In February 1943, 713 ROB arrived, at which time the American II Corps forces were concentrated in the Kasserine Pass area and on a front from Gafsa to Fondouk. The British First Army forces were in north Tunisia from La Calle to near Bou Arada, connected by a small French force to the American II Corps at Kairouan. Early in March 1943, 703 RGD moved to Constantine and, using 727 ROB and the newly-arrived 713 ROB, was operating the CFA from Beni Mancour through Kroubs to Souk Ahras, from Philippeville to Kroubs, from Ouled Rhamoun to Tébessa and from Ouled Kebérit to Tébessa, with HQ at Constantine. No 154 Rly Op Coy operated the line from Bône to La Calle. No 189 Rly Op Coy operated the metre-gauge line from Ouled Rhamoun to Tébessa until relieved by 727 ROB. No 163 Rly Wksp Coy operated in the shops at Algiers. No 2 Rly Wksp Mob was at Guelma and No 5 Rly Wksp Mob was at Ghardimaou, with HQ at Algiers.

The final German offensive, at Kasserine Pass, was in February 1943. No 727 ROB was operating the line from Ouled Rhamoum through Tébessa and into south-east Tunisia on the Sfax-Gafsa Railway, a few men having moved to Gafsa. On 3 February, there were rumours of a German advance (discounted at headquarters, of course!). There were six dead engines in the sheds at Sened, and an engine in steam was moved over from Gafsa to remove what could be taken. A train left Sened with four dead engines and various wagon loads, bound for Gafsa. On 14 February, HQ at Tébessa sent five train crews down to Gafsa by road trucks, MRS operations now being in front of the Allied lines! On 14 & 15 February, the yards at Gafsa were cleared by five fully-loaded trains, the last leaving at 3 am on 15 February. Unfortunately, a problem occurred when the US Army engineers, not realising that the trains were coming, blew up the large bridge at Sidi Bou Daker! Five spans out of a total of 40 were out! The first train had already safely passed but the other four were cut off! One train loaded with ammunition was hidden in a tunnel, safe from the Luftwaffe. The Americans hid eight locomotives in tunnels in phosphate mines, stripped them of their side rods and valve motion, loaded these parts on to their trucks and returned to Allied lines. The lost ground was recovered by the American forces on 21/22 February. A few days later, the ammunition train was brought back to the wrecked bridge and the ammunition transferred to trucks. The hidden locomotives were also recovered.

The Spring offensive started in March 1943 when the British Eighth Army reached Sousse. The British First Army was just east of Natour, Djedeida and Pont du Fahs. As more MRS troops arrived, the British Rly Op troops were gradually concentrated behind the British First Army, and at the end of March were responsible only for the main line east of Souk Ahras, the Bône to La Calle line and the Algiers base and dock area.

The final phase began on 1 May 1943. The battle line was shortened from the south when the British Eighth Army moved to a line between Bou Arada and Enfidaville. The American II Corps transferred to a line from the Mediterranean down to Tebourba. Then came the British First Army and the French units. The offensive was successful, and Bizerta and Tunis were occupied on 7 May. Hostilities ceased on 12 May 1943. The first Allied train entered Tunis on 13 May and Bizerta on 20 May.

Railway equipment was still being received from the USA in preparation for the invasion of Sicily and mainland Italy, and a base supply depot was established at Oran, followed by others elsewhere. In May 1943, No 701 RGD HQ only, and 704 RGD arrived at Oran, together with Nos 715, 719 and 759 ROBs. At the end of May, the railway troops held the fol-

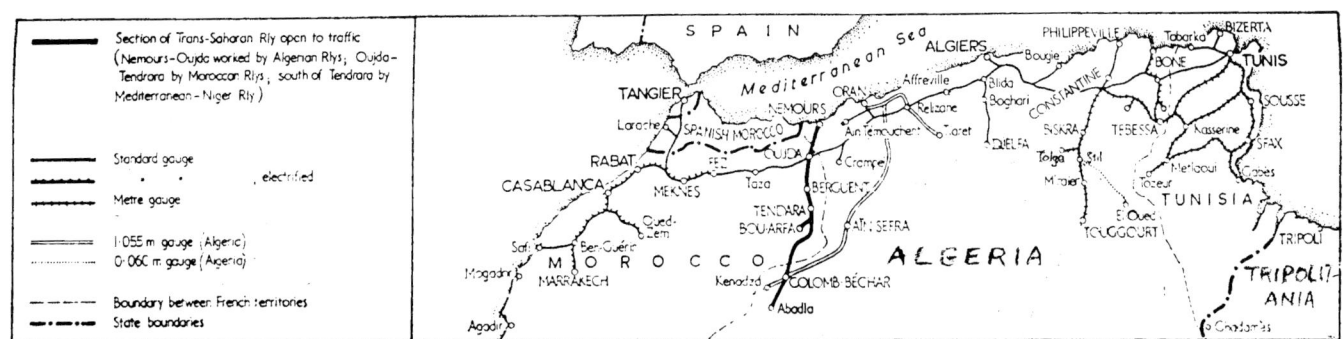

Map 7　Railway route used by the Allies from the ports of Casablanca in Morocco and Oran and Algiers in Algeria, through to Tunisia.

lowing responsibilities, and did so until departure for Sicily and Italy. No 701 RGD HQ, without any units, directed the CFM west of Oujda. No 703 RGD at Constantine headed the following units. No 713 ROB ran the line from Sousse to Tébessa, 715 ROB operated the line between Krouba and Duvivier, and Bône to Oued Keberit, 727 ROB continued to operate the metre-gauge between Ouled Rhamoum and Tébessa, and 753 RSB was still in the CFA shops at Sidi Mabrouk.

No 704 RGD was at Maison Carrée in Algeria heading the following units. No 719 ROB operated from Sétif through Constantine to Philippeville, 759 ROB from Orléansville to Algiers, then to Sétif, plus the line from Beni Mancour to Bougie, and 761 RTC continued with the yard operations at Oran.

The British No 1 Rly Op Group based in Souk Ahras had No 154 Rly Op Coy operating the metre-gauge line from Bône to La Calle, No 189 Rly Op Coy was half in the Algiers area and the other half behind the British First Army, No 163 Rly Wksp Coy was in the railway shops in Algiers, No 2 Rly Mobile Wksp was at Guelma and No 5 Rly Mobile Wksp at Ghardimaou.

In December 1942, military traffic was handled at a rate of nine million ton-miles per month over 1300 miles of track. By March 1943, the traffic was 19 million ton-miles per month over 1750 miles of track, and in June 1943, 33 million ton-miles per month over 2000 miles. This last figure was about the peak traffic and represented deployment of stores for the invasion of Sicily and Italy. Troop, hospital and POW trains are not included in the above figures.

USA/TC standard-gauge 2–8–0s (see Chapter 50) and metre-gauge 2–8–2s (see Chapter 47) were used in North Africa. The original plans called for 250 standard-gauge 2–8–0s and 175 metre-gauge 2–8–2s, but these requirements were later reduced to 105 sg 2–8–0s and 60 ng 2–8–2s. They began arriving in early 1943, the first two ng 2–8–2s arriving in March 1943, and all are believed to have been landed at Oran. The 2–8–0s were received already assembled but the freight wagons and metre-gauge 2–8–2s were received in CKD state (completely knocked down). The metre-gauge locomotive and freight wagons in crates were moved on flat cars from Oran to Sidi Mabrouk in Constantine, assembled there by 753 RSB, and then placed on special well wagons and sent the short distance to Ouled Rhamoun where they were railed on to metre-gauge track. By April 1943, the MRS at Oran had placed 38 sg 2–8–0s in service. By July 1943, 1000 American freight wagons were in service. Sixty metre-gauge freight wagons and 25 2–8–2 locomotives were erected, followed by seven more 2–8–2s in October, making 32 in all.

There is some uncertainty about the USA/TC 2–8–0s. Major General Carl R. Gray, who was Director General of the MRS 1942-5, says in his book "Railroading in Eighteen Countries" that in North Africa, "there had been 149 2–8–0 locomotives received, 135 assembled and 126 in service with nine stored". The official USA/TC history states that approximately 16 locomotives were "lost to the enemy", without giving any details as to the type(s) or when or how this happened. No MacArthur metre-gauge 2–8–2s appeared to have been lost in the Kasserine Pass offensive, and as discussed in Chapter 50, some North African standard-gauge 2–8–0s are unaccounted for, so it seems probable that the locomotives "lost to the enemy" were these 2–8–0s. For a period, the German Luftwaffe had aerial superiority in North Africa, so possibly some 2–8–0s were destroyed, or sufficiently damaged as to render them not worth repairing when there was an adequate supply of them, in some German raid?

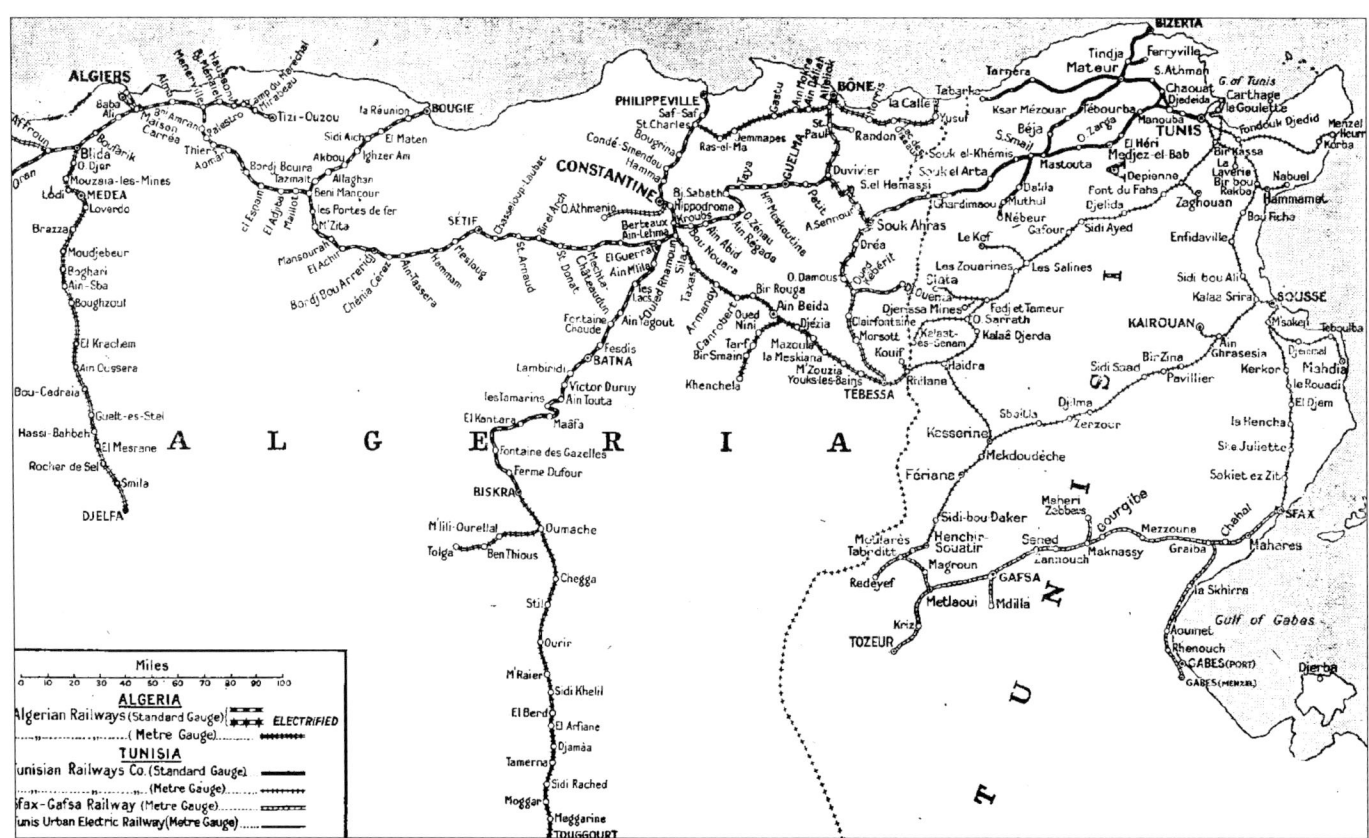

Map 8 Tunisian Railways (CFT), Sfax-Gafsa Railway and part of the Algerian Railways (CFA) (Courtesy Railway Magazine)

Chapter 6

SICILY

On 9/10 July 1943, the invasion of Sicily began. The British Eighth Army landed just south of Syracuse and the American Seventh Army at Licata. The Eighth Army went north along the coast until meeting resistance at Mount Etna. The Seventh Army went north-west through Caltanissetta and Marsala to capture Palermo on 25 July, and then went east. The German and Italian forces were driven into the north-east corner of the island.

Sicily had about 1500 miles of standard and narrow gauge railway, all steam operated. Starting at Palermo, the standard-gauge line went east to Messina, south to Ragusa, west to Licata and Agrigento and back to Palermo, thus circling the island. The American No 727 ROB was used and the British First Rly Op Group.

Only two days after the invasion, an advance party from 727 ROB landed at Licata, fired up a locomotive and ran 15 miles north to the front at Campobello. They made some repairs to the track and started a supply service the same day, moving 400 tons to the front. On 13 July, 600 tons were carried, on 14 July 800 tons until by 30 August about 170,000 tons of military freight had been handled.

The first British railhead was opened on 22 July inland at Scordia and the line was progressively lengthened to St Bicocca, Motta and finally Catania, 106 miles away. By early August, seven 1500-ton trains were operated daily. By September, 90 captured locomotives and 900 freight wagons were in use. There was virtually an unlimited supply of captured locomotives and wagons in good condition, and no Allied locomotives were landed in Sicily. Telegraph and telephone lines were very scarce, however, and radio was largely used for controlling the trains.

The narrow-gauge railway from Licata to Margonia was opened and a few trains operated but after 20 July there was no further need and operations were stopped. By 12 August, the railway was open from Palermo to San Stefano in the north and Licata to Etna in the south. By 30 August, No 727 ROB opened the line from Catania to Gerbini in the British sector. In all, No 727 ROB operated about 1375 miles of Sicilian railway, used 300 captured locomotives and 3500 freight wagons.

Sicily was completely captured in just 38 days and it then became a staging area for the forthcoming Italian campaign. The Sicilian railways were returned to civilian control in March 1944.

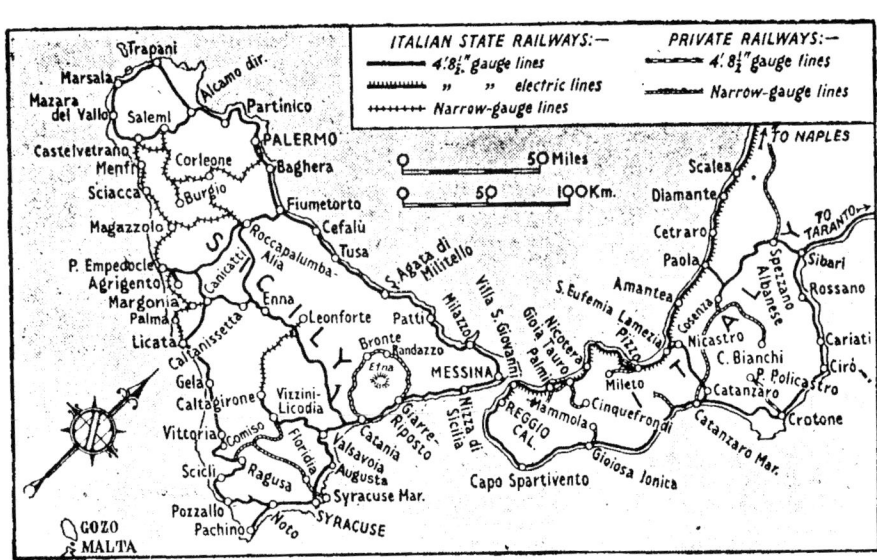

Map 9   Railways of Sicily and the toe of Italy (Courtesy Railway Gazette)

Chapter 7

ITALY

The invasion of Italy started on 3 September 1943, when two divisions of the British Eighth Army went across the straits of Messina from Sicily to Reggio di Calabria in Italy, and started towards Brindisi and Bari. The Armistice with Italy was signed the same day and on 8 September the surrender of Italy was announced. On 9 September, the American Fifth Army landed at Salerno near Naples. The Germans resisted the landing but Naples was captured on 1 October. In the meanwhile, the Eighth Army had advanced through the Liri Valley and captured the Foggia airfields. By 1 October, the battle line went from the west coast just north of Naples to the Adriatic coast just north of Foggia.

It was agreed around this time that the American MRS would support the US Fifth Army looking after the west coast lines and ports, including the cross line from Salerno through Potenza to Taranto; while the British units, which came into the MRS structure, would support the British Eighth Army looking after the east coast to the Calabrian lines and ports. This division of responsibility held throughout practically all the Italian campaign.

The first MRS troops to support the US Fifth Army were 703 RGD, the advance party from HQ 703 RGD landing at Naples on 4 October. No 713 ROB landed in Naples of 7 October, four days after it had been captured. The US railway troops started repairing the yards and dock lines at Naples and the main line from Naples to Aversa. The first train ran on 10 October and by 23 October nine locomotives were in service. Naples became the main supply port for the US Fifth Army. On 22 October, MRS HQ in North Africa was closed and reopened in Naples, which became the centre of MRS activities in Italy. By 29 October, military trains were being operated from the port to a dump near Aversa. By the first week in November, trains were being operated to Caserta. By December, 15,000 tons per day were being handled from Naples.

The British used railway troops from Sicily, North Africa and the MEF in support of the British Eighth Army. No 1 Rly Op Group moved from Tunis to Bari,

0–4–0Ds loaded on adapted tank-transporter vehicles. At Normandy, the wagons came ashore via floating bridgework designed to allow for the tides. Tracks were laid across the beach direct to the SNCF! The first USA/TC locomotives were USA/TC 150hp diesels unloaded directly on to the beach at Utah Beach on 10 July 1944, and hauled to the railway at Chef-Dupont. These beach connections were the only source of railway wagons and other supplies for several weeks in the early stages of the invasion, before the capture and return to service of the ports of Cherbourg and Le Havre.

In readiness for the invasion of Europe, and since it was anticipated that captured European ports would not have train-ferry type tidal connecting ramps in working order, it was considered necessary to be able to cope with the task of landing locomotives and rolling stock without such ramps. Accordingly, the former SR train ferry ships "Hampton Ferry" and "Twickenham Ferry" were fitted with special lifting gear at the stern capable of lifting up to 60 tons and thus enabling the engines to be unloaded direct to the quayside. This lifting gear added 260 tons to the ships' weight, and jutted out by 35ft. These ships could take 16 locomotives and about 20 wagons at a time. SR railway staff prepared the locomotives at the port of embarkation by emptying the boilers and tenders of water, but filling the tenders with coal, and providing kindling wood and military fire-iron tools. The cab roof was removed and stored on the locomotive, so that the lifting gear could be used. These ships carried both USA/TC and WD locomotives, and both steam and diesel types.

In general, ships coming to Cherbourg were loaded at Southampton; later on when Dieppe was also used, the ships were loaded at Dover. Some engines were also later carried on ordinary ships from Cardiff.

The first military operations were the advance from the beaches, the drive to Saint-Lô and around the northwest side of the peninsular to Cherbourg and a drive south to Caen. Carentan was captured on 12 June, Cherbourg on 26 June, Caen on 9 July and Saint-Lô on 18 July. Within five weeks after the capture of Cherbourg, the port and rail facilities were sufficiently repaired for heavy locomotives to be unloaded directly from ships. The first train ran from Cherbourg to Carentan on 11 July 1944 and by 31 July, 48 diesel and steam locomotives had arrived.

Once the Allies landed, the SNCF personnel cooperated in getting trains running again. Bridges were temporarily rebuilt with the assistance of army engineers. For instance, the line from Cherbourg to Caen was repaired by the USA/TC. In July 1944, HQ 707 RGD arrived, together with 720 and 729 ROBs and 757 RSB. In August, HQ 706 RGD and HQ 708 RGD arrived, together with 712, 718 and 740 ROBs and 755 and 764 RSBs.

The British 181 ROC established its HQ at Bayeux on 18 June 1944. By July, 181 ROC had moved to Caen, and started to restore the main lines. The train ferries started working from Southampton to Cherbourg on 4 August, enabling the supply of large military locomotives to begin in larger numbers, as well as a 45-ton Ransome & Rapier crane to help clear the line from Bayeux to Caen. Three SNCF Pacifics and two 2–8–2Ts were put back into service. By August, the lines from Caen west to Bayeux and east to

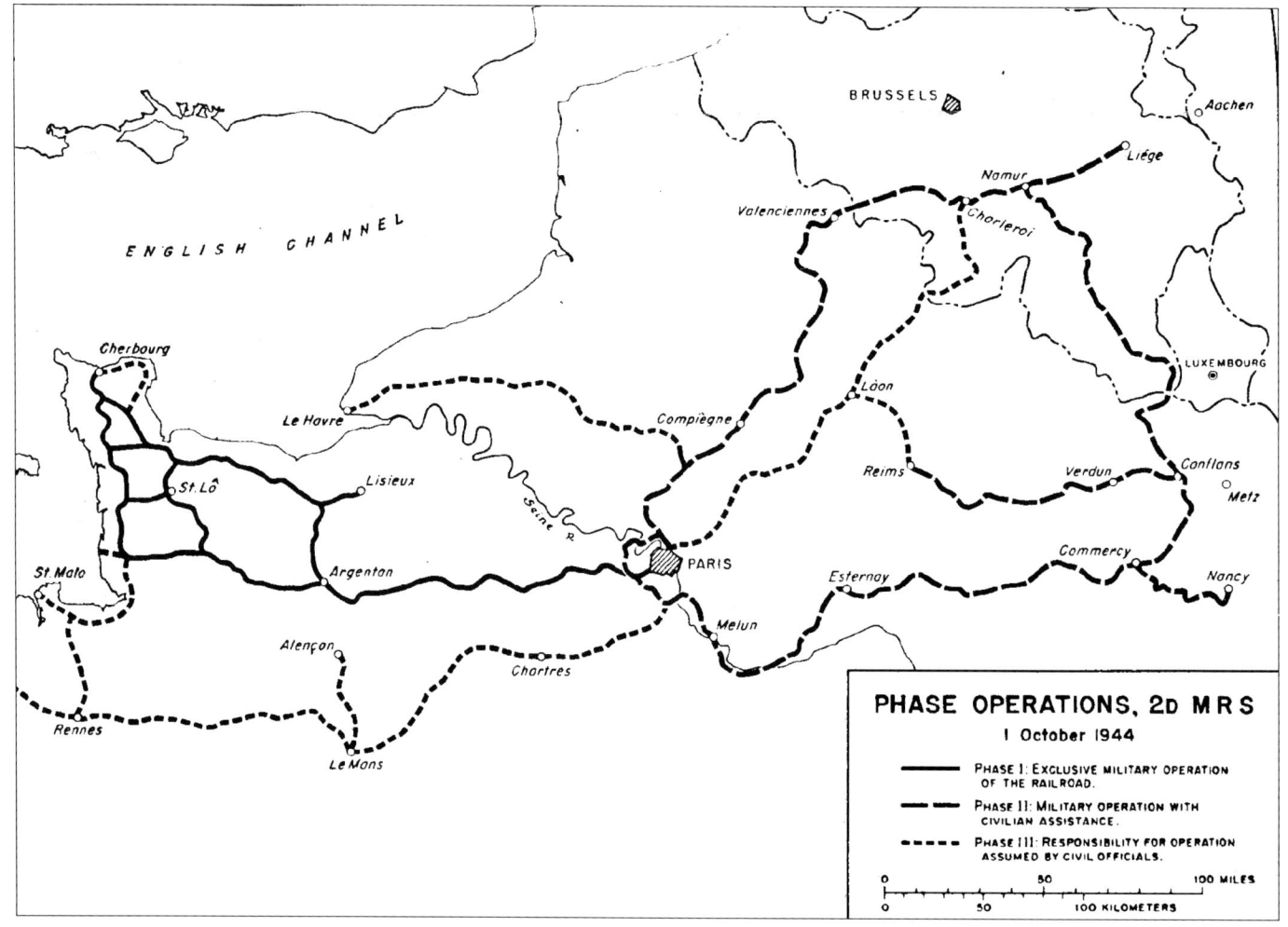

Map 10 Military rail routes in France and Belgium as at 1 October 1944 (C. F. Cornelius, Courtesy US Army)

Mezidon were made operational, so at this stage the military stores service was using the coastal line from Ouistreham to Courseulles and to Port en Bessin and Bayeux, and the main line from Bayeux to Caen. An ambulance train section was set up at Bayeux, and from 1 September, two 14-coach ambulance trains ran through to Mezidon. The docks at Caen were opened at the end of August, but with the capture of Dieppe and Ostend, this rather small port was not used much except for coal imports.

Between 17 and 24 June 1944, the first American railway troops arrived at Omaha Beach. Entering Cherbourg after its capture, they observed that the line between Lison and Cherbourg was not badly damaged and discovered to their surprise the existence among the SNCF locomotives at Cherbourg some dozen of the First World War locomotives from the US Army still in service. One was SNCF 140.A.575 Alco 57851/18, which was checked over and put back into service. Another SNCF locomotive at Cherbourg was 030.C.828 of 1882, used to pull USA/TC diesel locomotives off the ferry ships. The first troop train ran on 22 July 1944, and the first ambulance train with wounded soldiers from Saint-Lô on 4 August.

On 25 July 1944, the battle line went east from a point on the Cherbourg Peninsular west of Saint Lô to Caen and then north to the Channel. On this day, there was a breakthrough at Saint Lô. No 740 ROB arrived at Mayenne on 14/15 August and rehabilitated the rail facilities there. The yards at Le Mans were almost totally destroyed but 712 and 740 ROBs arrived on 20 August to commence its reconstruction, and on 1 September, 764 RSB moved into the workshops there. In mid-August to enable the US Third Army under General Patton to strike out for Paris, 31 trains of ammunition, rations and gasoline were worked in six days from Cherbourg through Saint Lô, Flers, Mayenne to a dump at Le Mans. Paris was captured on 25 August. Four days after the Allied troops entered Paris, the first military train, a diesel autorail, entered St Nazaire Station. The first MRS locomotive, Whitcomb USA/TC 8125, reached Paris on 30 August. The route was from Cherbourg via Mezidon, Alencon, Le Mans, Chartres, Dreux and Maintenon!

By mid-September 1944, Allied troops had pushed the German forces out of France, and were clearing Belgium and parts of Holland. Antwerp was captured on 4 September and Brest on 17 September. At this stage, supply lines stretched back to the ports in France, and military traffic was heavy and operating over long distances. Railwaymen were busy trying to sort out and repair the damage. In September 1944, the line from Brittany via Rennes, Le Mans and Chartres to Paris was given back to the French, releasing MRS personnel for other jobs. By 1 October 1944, it was possible to travel from Paris to Lyon and Marseilles, and lines to the east and north of Paris had been reopened. In Holland, only 204 locomotives were fit for work, and another 198 founded damaged. Some 464 locomotives had just disappeared! By mid-October 1944, 1300 locomotives and 20,000 loaded wagons had been delivered to the shores of France by the MRS and WD. In October, 798 freight trains arrived in Paris from Normandy and Brittany, and 999 freight trains departed for northern and eastern destinations (trucks brought the rest to Paris). On 21 October 1944, Aachen was captured. During the rest of 1944 and early 1945, most of the remaining French main lines were re-established.

During August, two more British ROCs and a Canadian ROC arrived. During September, the supply route was extended to Le Foret de Londe. On 22 September, through working started to Serqueux, and the British gave facilities for the USA/TC to work over the line Lison-Mezidon-Argentan. The line from Argentan to Le Mans had already opened on 31 August. Through US services were worked by US crews to Caen, British to Lisieux, and then Canadian onwards. With the opening of the line west of Bayeux to Cherbourg, some British WD locomotives were landed at Cherbourg and worked through to Caen. The British supply services from Cherbourg were then worked to Caen and on to Lisieux where they were also handed over to the Canadians.

Dieppe was captured on 2 September and reopened for ships on 8 September. The SR train ferries started working on 29 September from Southampton to Dieppe, bringing in WD 2-8-0s amongst other railway equipment. An LNER train ferry also started on 29 September bringing in WD 2-8-0s. Le Havre was captured on 12 September and handed over to the US forces for shipping purposes. Ostend was captured on 9 September and reopened for ships by 28 September. Boulogne was captured on 22 September and Calais on 30 September. The train ferry terminal at Calais was rebuilt by 15 November and the first vessel arrived on 21 November. With Dieppe, Ostend, Boulogne and le Havre all brought into use, direct working over the original invasion beaches and Mulberry harbours were no longer required and ceased early in September. The import of military stores through Dieppe ceased on 28 December.

From 23 October to 1 November, control of the sector east of Bayeux was transferred from British to the USA/TC. The British moved on to Brussels and Antwerp, arriving at Antwerp on 3 November. Operation of the section from Serqueux to Lille and to the Belgium border was given back to the SNCF. Although Antwerp had been captured in September, it could not yet be used as a port because the north bank of the Scheldt was still occupied by German forces. The first task for the British was to clear the Antwerp-Roosendaal line which was blocked by a bombed ammunition train.

The 21st Army Group Transportation Services concentrated on the repair and bringing into operation a railway line from the vicinity of Caen into Belgium and Holland. This involved the repair or rebuilding of over 100 bridges over the rivers Orne, Seine, Somme, Maas, Rhine and Ems, as well as the Albert Canal. In September 1944, the Royal Canadian Engineers (RCE) No 1 Rly Op Coy took responsibility for the line from Lisieux to Elbeuf (south of Rouen), and RCE No 2 Rly Op Coy took over the line from Elbeuf to Serqueaux. In October 1944, they worked 699 trains, mostly via Paris. The main trouble was getting crews and engines back from Paris! Two missing engines that had gone to Paris were eventually found near Dijon close to the Swiss border, having been appropriated by the American forces!

A site at Le Manoir near Pont de l'Arche was selected for the Seine crossing by No 197 Rly Construction Coy. It required the removal of 90,000 cubic yards of earth for the approach tracks, and Lt Col Everall's Unit Construction Railway Bridging material (the less-known railway equivalent to the Bailey Bridge for road crossings) was used to make a 520ft six-span long bridge. After 14 days work, the bridge was opened to traffic on 22 September 1944. For two months, until the Channel ports north of the Seine were opened for traffic, this bridge was the main line of supply for the British forces. There were several anxious periods in November 1944 and again in February 1945, when the Seine suffered its worse floods for 40 years, and several times the water level came up almost to the rails, but the bridge held and trains continued. At one time, coal wagons were loaded on to the bridge to weigh it down, and at another time trains of wagons were coupled together and pushed across

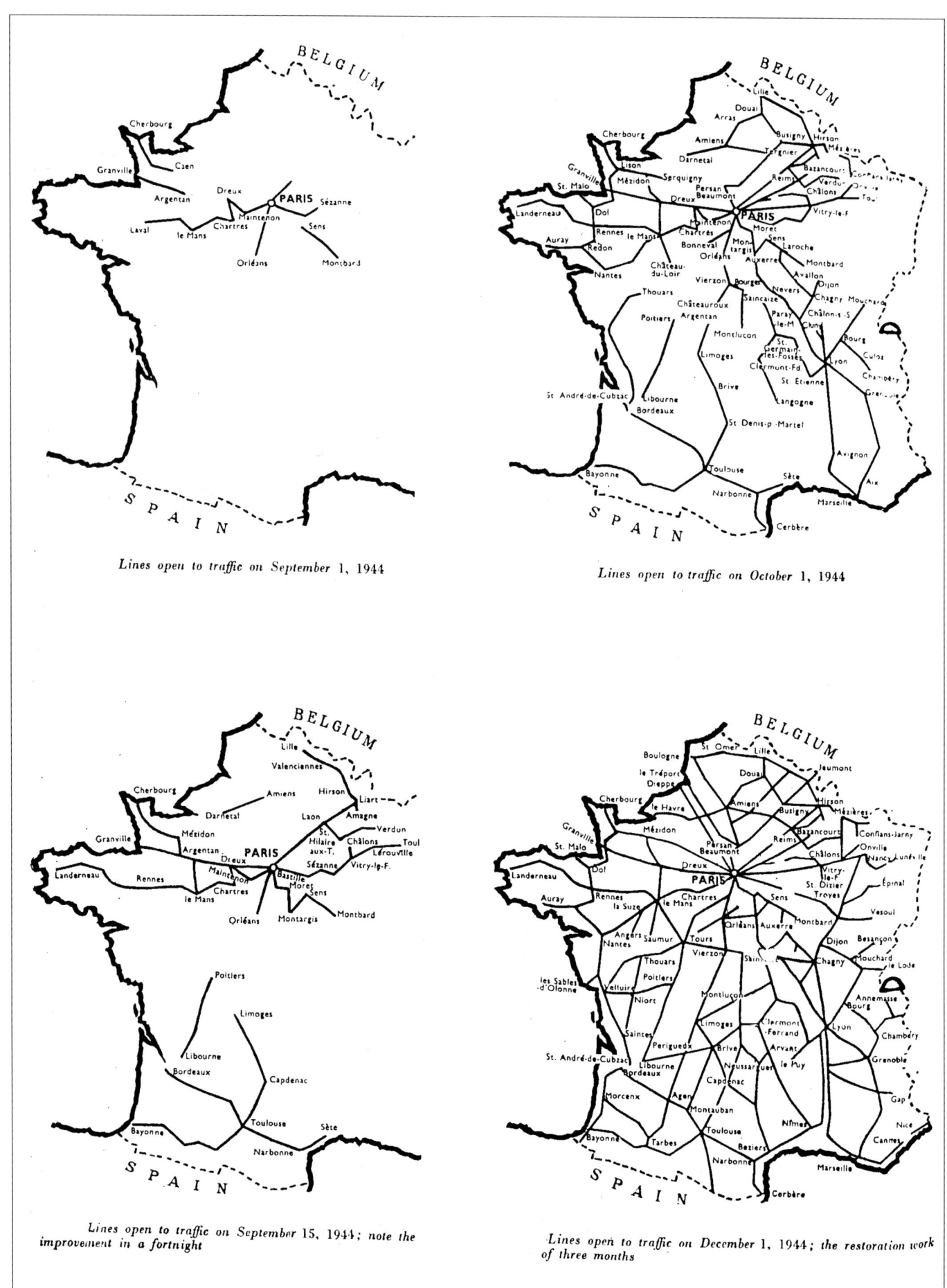

Map 11 Series of sketch maps showing the restoration of rail services in France in 1944 (Courtesy Railway Gazette)

without locomotives passing on to the bridge, with the wagons receiving other engines on the far side!

By the end of September, Brussels had been liberated, and ambulance trains were being run from Brussels to Hasselt, Eindhoven and Amiens. With the building of the bridge over the Seine at Le Manoir, the ambulance trains were worked through to the base hospital now set up at Bayeux.

No 707 RGD directed operations over the lines in the Cherbourg port area to Vire. No 708 RGD directed the activities on the lines from Brest to Le Mans, Pontaboult via Fougères to Mayenne and from Granville via Vire and Flers and Mayenne to the line between Brest and Le Mans. No 706 RGD took control of the line from Vire through Surdon, Dreux and Paris, from Surdon to Le Mans, and from Le Mans to Paris. No 729 ROB, the first MRS unit to land in France, operated the lines from Cherbourg south through Sottevast, Valognes, Montebourg and Carentan to Lison. No 720 ROB operated from Lison east through Bayeux, Caen, Mézidon and Lisieux. Both battalions became units of 707 RGD. No 757 RSB set up in the repair shops at Cherbourg, and 755 RSB went to Rennes. Temporary MRS stores were first established near Omaha Beach, but later on SNCF stores in Paris were taken over. Another depot was established at Liége, as soon as Antwerp was captured and by January 1945, 75% of rail supplies on the Continent were at Liége.

More MRS units arrived in France, including 709 RGD, 710/6/22-4/8/32-5/41/3/4/6/50/2 ROBs and 763/5 RSBs. On 1 October 1944, No 706 RGD operated Valenton Yard in Paris to Nancy via Sommesous and Commercy, and railheads off this line except within Belgium and Luxembourg; from Pantin Yard in Paris to the Belgium and Luxembourg border via Meaux, Reims, Verdun, Conflans, and to army railheads in France and Germany off this line. Its units were 712 ROB at Coulommiers, 718 ROB at Sézanne and 733 ROB at Toul.

No 707 RGD operated from Cherbourg to Vire via Lison, Sottevast to Folligny, Carteret to Carentan, Saint-Lô to Coutances, Granville to Vire, and Lison to Lisieux via Caen. Its units were 728/9 ROBs at Cherbourg, 720 ROB at Lison, 735 ROB at Coutances and 757 RSB at Cherbourg.

By November 1944, No 708 RGD was in Belgium operating from Erquelinnes and Quiévrain on the French/Belgium border to Liége via Charleroi, Gembloux and Landen, Gambloux to Namur to Liége, Athus to Namur and Liége, and Liége to railheads of the US First and Ninth Armies in Belgium, Netherlands, Luxembourg and Germany. Its units were 740/1 ROBs at Liége and 755 RSB at Namur.

No 709 RGD operated from Versailles-Matelots to the Belgian frontier via Creil, Tergnier, Busigny, Cambrai, Denain and Valenciennes, from Le Havre to Creil, from Batignolles Yard in Paris to the Belgian frontier via Soissons and Laon, and from Laon to Reims. Its units were 722 ROB at Valenciennes, 724 ROB at Compiègne and 743 ROB at Beauvais.

No 710 RGD operated from Vire to Valenton Yard in Paris, Argentan to Mezidon, and Valenton Yard to Batignolles Yard. Its units were 716 ROB at Versailles, 723 ROB at Dreux, 732 ROB at Argentan, 744 ROB at Vire and 764 RSB at Paris.

From July to November 1944, the port of Cherbourg despatched about 28,000 wagons per month. More than 400,000 men passed through this port between July 1944 and June 1945.

In September 1944, the British railway services were largely north of Brussels and the USA/TC south of Brussels. The port of Antwerp was reopened gradually between 20 and 28 November 1944. This made Boulogne redundant and it was closed for the import of military stores on 13 January 1945. Antwerp became USA/TC 709 RGD territory and 743 ROB shunted the port. The British and the USA/TC (729 ROB) took the trains out of the port, both using the same route to Louvain. Hasselt then became the border between the British and the US, so both WD 2–8–0s and USA/TC 2–8–0s could be seen at Hasselt. By December 1944, 740 ROB was operating as far forward as Malmedy in Belgium and 734 ROB was operating to Herzogenrath and Geilenkirchen in Germany.

In mid-December 1944, the Germans made a counter-offensive in the Ardennes, known at the time as the "Battle of the Bulge", against the Third Army. At one time, 732 ROB was delivering artillery ammunition by rail direct to the guns without any need of trucking it up from the railheads. During this period, 718 ROB moved four divisions of the Third Army across the front and into the south flank in 48 hours. A double-track railroad was operated in one direction (both tracks) for sixteen hours, then reversed for eight hours. Trains were operated in blocks of six trains at a time on each track, holding to ten minutes minimum headway. During this time, there was a heavy snowfall and no proper snow equipment was available. This counter-offensive closely threatened the big depot at Liége, and at one stage, about half the stores were loaded ready for transfer to a safer location. By mid-January, the Germans had been driven back.

By January 1945, some 1523 military locomotivs had been placed in service. The railway was reopened for British traffic to the south of the Netherlands via Roosendaal, rail depots being established at Borstel-mill, Breda, Roosendaal and Tilburg; and through Belgium via Aarschot to Hasselt, Neerpelt to Eindhoven and Helmond. The SNCB through to Lille and Namur was in service for the USA/TC. Initially, military services came from the coastal ports west of Brussels, and then east for WD and south for USA/TC. With the recovery of the western area of the Netherlands, from January 1945, Antwerp became the chief port, the route from Antwerp to Louvain being used by both USA/TC and WD trains, the USA/TC then working south to Liége and Namur, and the WD working east to Hasselt, Eindhoven and Maastricht.

Forty hospital trains served the US forces on the Continent, 25 of British origin, 14 of French material and one American (experimental). British ambulance trains went to Dieppe and Ostend. From September 1944, these trains had worked from Hasselt via Brussels to Amiens. When the Seine bridge opened in September, they then worked through to Bayeux. Two ambulance trains were stabled at Merelbeek for service from Brussels to Ostend. By January 1945, British ambulance trains, generally made up of 10 to 12 Gresley LNER coaches, worked daily from the forward areas to Ostend.

On 22 January 1945, the USA/TC inaugurated the "Toot Sweet Express" to carry high-priority freight on a fast schedule from Cherbourg to Paris, where it was split into two 20-car freight trains, one to Namur (and later to Liége) in Belgium, and the other to Verdun in France. Specially marked railway equipment was used. The time taken from Cherbourg to either terminal was 36 hours. This train followed the US Armies into Germany until the end of the war. In March 1945, a similar special train, the "Meat Ball Express", began hauling perishable food, mainly meat, from Namur to the US First and Ninth Armies.

Chapter 9

SOUTHERN FRANCE

Southern France was invaded near Marseille on 15 August 1944, and Marseille was captured on 28 August. The Sixth Army Group, consisting of the US Seventh Army and the French First Army, drove up the Rhône River valley to meet the US Third Army just west of Dijon on 11 September 1944. The First MRS supported the Sixth Army Group, and 703 RGD HQ, and 713 & 727 ROBs, arrived in France in August from Italy. The first trains were run eight days after the invasion. No 759 ROB arrived in Marseille in September 1944, and in the same month First MRS was established. The Grenoble route to Lyon was used first because it had suffered less damage, then the railway on the east bank of the Rhône River was opened on 20 September 1944. Rail traffic to Lyon opened on 25 September 1944. The railway on the west bank was opened on 27 September, and this enabled use of the difficult Grenoble line to be abandoned. In November 1944, 798 trains ran over the two Rhône River lines carrying 415,404 tons.

No 703 RGD was first assigned all lines in southern France. No 713 ROB operated Marseille Terminal, Marseille-Valence, San Raphael-Toulon, Marseille-La Barque, Aix-en-Provance to Grenoble, Valence-Moirans, Port-de-Bouc-Avignon via Miramas and Chevel Blanc-Pertuis. Nos 727 & 759 ROBs operated Lyon Terminal, Valence to Lyon, Lyon to Dijon, Lyon-Chagny-Grenoble, Grenoble-Bougr, Bougr-Railhead and Dijon-Railhead. No 750 ROB arrived in November and was assigned the main line east of Dijon. No 756 RSB arrived from England in November and went to work at Marseille. No 704 RGD arrived from Italy in December 1944, together with 761 RTC which was placed at Sarrebourg. No 766 RSB arrived in April 1945 and was established in Marseille.

The first four 65 ton Whitcomb diesel-electric locomotives were received on 25 October and were soon followed by six USA/TC 2–8–0s. By the end of 1944, 812 SNCF locomotives and about 15,000 freight wagons were in service. Some 102 USA/TC locomotives were brought in from North Africa and USA, of which 87 were in service and 15 were being assembled and repaired, and some 250 special wagons. The MRS had to overhaul all the USA/TC locomotives from North Africa owing to neglected maintenance after the MRS had departed.

The first priority for rail rehabilitation around October to December 1944 was Epinal-Blainville-Luneville-Sarrebourg-Strasbourg for the Seventh Army, second priority Vesoul-Lure-Belfort-Mulhouse for the French First Army, and third priority Epinal-St Die-Strasbourg for the Seventh Army. In January 1945, battle conditions changed and first priority was allocated to Lure-Belfort, Bruyères-St Die-Saales-Molsheim and Sarrebourg-Berthelnung-Sarralbe, second priority to Belfort-Mulhouse, the connection from St Die to St Marie and the vicinity of Sélestat. Marseille remained the main port for supplies for the Sixth Army Group and most spares were also stocked there. Peak traffic out of Marseille was on 26 October 1944, when 24 trains were moved. Peak tonnage delivered to the Seventh Army railheads was on 14 January 1945, and for the French First Army on 21 December 1944. The largest number of military trains operated in any one day was on 23 November 1944, when 233 were run northbound and 166 southbound.

On 29 May 1945, No 756 RSB erected its 10,000th wagon at Marseille. The last wagon erected was on 29 August 1945 and this was the 28,801st. No 764 RSB was set up at Marseille Docks for the purpose of unloading USA/TC 2–8–0s and making them fit for service.

Chapter 10

EUROPE

Around the beginning of 1945, the Allied forces in northern France and Belgium were linked up with those in southern France. In February 1945, a joint MRS HQ was therefore established in Paris. Units of the MRS were reorganised. A boundary was established between First and Second MRS as being a line extending from Paris along the divisional line between the Nord and Est Regions of the SNCF, to Hirson, and then along the Belgium and German boundaries, and thence north-east. Territory north and west of this line was under Second MRS, with its HQ transferred from Paris to Brussels, and south and east was under First MRS with HQ still at Lyon.

The British Twenty-First Army Group was on the extreme left flank. The US Ninth Army was on its right flank, then the US First Army and the US Third Army, these three armies comprising the Twelfth Army Group. The Sixth Army Group had the line south of Kaiserlautern with the US Seventh Army on the left flank and the French First Army on the right flank.

The final assault on Germany began on 8 February 1945 by the British Twenty-First Army Group driving north-east. On 23 February, the Twelfth Army Group began to advance east, and on 13 March the US Third and Seventh Armies attacked.

To support the advance, the MRS units were extremely active. For example, in February 1945, No 704 RGD handled over 175 million gross ton miles. Also in February, No 712 ROB, based on Verdun, moved 649,280 net tons in serving 12 active railheads.

The process, begun in North Africa and Italy, of converting USA/TC 2–8–0s from coal to oil burning continued, with instructional classes for the European drivers on how to handle these oil-fired locomotives! No 765 RSB set up in the Basse Yutz shops outside Thionville specialising in diesel locomotives.

In February and March 1945, the RCE No 2 Rly Op Coy moved to Nijmegen to prepare for railway operations on the other side of the Rhine. The Rhine was crossed on 23 March 1945, and in April RCE No 2 Rly Op Coy moved to Rheine on the River Ems to operate the line from Emmerich to Rheine. Soon afterwards, RCE No 1 Rly Op Coy took over the line from Rheine to Kirchweye There was then no bridge across the Rhine in the area worked by the British Transport Service, so that heavy breakdown and repair equipment, and rolling stock, had to be

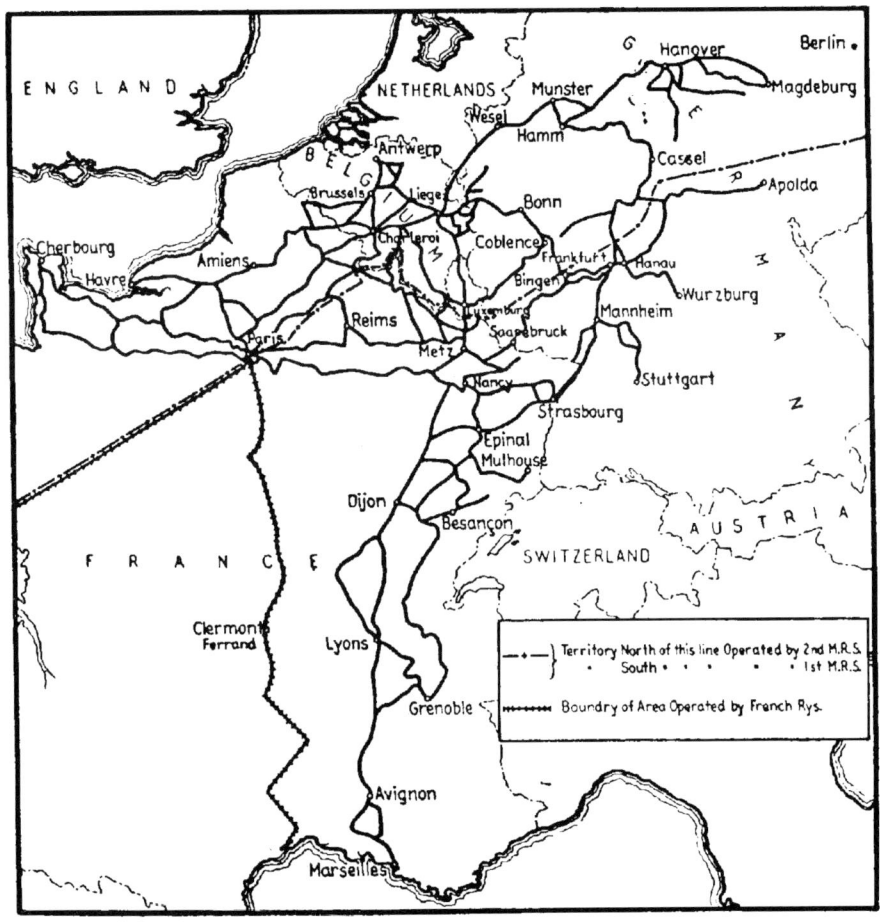

Map 12 The European railways which were being operated by the Military Railway Service when the war ended (Courtesy US Army)

worked from Nijmegen, through the American sector on a roundabout route to Rheine. By mid-April 1945, enough stock had been collected around Osnabruck to operate 18 return trains per day between Rheine and Kirchwere. The German condenser engines were much appreciated because of fewer delays taking on coal or water.

British units were used at Calais, where some American locomotives were unloaded. The British units later moved into Belgium and Holland. One unit moved to Eindhoven and then to s'Hertogenbosch. At this time, there were several German air attacks on the Allied trains. As mentioned above, the line was opened to Nijmegen and British units worked the line from Nijmegen 26 miles to Cleves. Austerity 2-8-0s were used but disliked because of rough riding and lack of cab lighting and dropping/rocking grates. Later on, the British units ran the leave trains from Gott to Krefeld and Tilburg.

On 10 February 1945, No 732 ROB of 706 RGD operated the first train into Germany from Thionville to the Moselle Valley town of Perl. By 22 February, the railway line was opened to Mulhouse. By 1 March, the various MRS units were assigned as follows. First MRS had 703 RGD at Marseille and 704 RGD at Nancy, while Second MRS had 706 RGD at Luxembourg, 707 RGD at Wesel, 706 RGD at Liége, 709 RGD at Brussels and 710 RGD at Paris. On 5 March 1945, No 706 RGD was transferred from Second to First MRS, without change of its own responsibilities. On 15 March, No 741 ROB ran its first train into Germany, destination Krefeld. On 30 March, No 718 ROB, operating in Luxembourg and north thereof, ran its first train into Germany from Luxembourg City to Bleialf.

The battle line in March 1945 extended from Arnheim near the German-Netherlands border down the west bank of the Rhine to Switzerland, and included most of the Saar Region but not the Ruhr on the east side of the Rhine River.

In pushing towards the Rhine, the First Army captured the Ludendorff rail bridge at Remagen, south of Cologne, on 7 March 1945, but unfortunately ten days later it collapsed due to battle damage! On 22 March, the Third Army crossed the Rhine south of Mainz and the British Second Army crossed north of Wesel on 24 March. The first rail link, a 1752ft single-track line, across the Rhine was opened on 8 April 1945 at Wesel, and was called the Major Robert A Gouldin Bridge. By VE-Day, it had carried 273,141 tons eastbound, chiefly POL (petrol, oil & lubricants), rations and ammunition; 403,656 tons westbound and 309,000 displaced persons! Six diesel-electric shunters were used in the yards at Wesel. On 14 April, the President Roosevelt Bridge was built at Mainz with 732 ROB operating the first (work) train over it, while the first service train was 34 wagons of rations hauled by two USA/TC diesels operated by 718 ROB. This bridge carried 10,000 net tons per day. On 23 April, another bridge was built at Ludwigshafen, on 29 April one at Karlsruhr, and on 8 May one at Duisberg known as the Victory Bridge. This carried peak traffic on 26 June of 32 trains carrying 14,702 net tons. Finally, another bridge was built at Strasbourg on 7 July.

On 8 May 1945, VE-Day, Germany surrendered. At this time, the MRS disposition was as follows. First MRS at Strasbourg had 703 RGD at Furth, with 712 ROB at Hanau, 728 ROB at Nürnberg, 750 ROB at Würzburg and 761 RTC at Augsburg; 704 RGD at Nancy with 713 ROB at Ludwigshafen, 727 ROB at Heilbronn and 733 ROB at Neustaft; 706 RGD at Frankfurt with 716 ROB at Metz, 718 ROB also at Metz, 732 ROB at Saarbrücken and 759 ROB at Hanau, while reporting directly to First MRS were 756 RSB at Marseille, 765 RSB at Thionville and 766 RSB at Bischheim. Second MRS at Brussels had 707 RGD at Wesel with 720 ROB also at Wesel, 723 ROB at München-Gladbach, 729 ROB at Hanover and 735 ROB at Hamm; 708 RGD at Warburg had 722 ROB at Warburg, 740 ROB at Bonn, 746 ROB at Warburg and 757 RSB at Kassel; 709 RGD at Brussels had 734 ROB at Maastricht, 741 ROB at Liège, 743 ROB at Antwerp, 744 ROB at Charleroi, 752 ROB at Namur, 755 RSB at Namur and 763 RSB at Louvain; and 710 RGD at Paris had 724 ROB at Compiègne and 764 RSB in Paris, On 9 May, 704 RGD moved to Esslingen and during the month of May operated 106,399,107 gross ton miles.

Much effort, by both MRS troops and German railway workers, was immediately put into repairing the railway facilities. Operation of the railways was rapidly turned back to the German authorities, at first under MRS supervision, the first being some lines at Kassel which were returned on 10 May 1945. No 722 ROB was assigned to Bremerhaven and Bremen, and ran the first train into Bremen, a coal train, on 18 May 1945.

While direct military traffic lessened, there were many trains needed for prisoners of war and displaced persons, as well as for food for the civilians. In May 1945, 729 ROB handled 977 trains carrying 772,391 net tons, 153,240 displaced persons and 88,800 prisoners of war; 735 ROB handled 1222 trains carrying 1,588,600 tons; 741 ROB handled 2905 trains covering 56,507 train miles of military traffic.

No 757 RSB at Kassel took over the Henschel plant there. Kits for condenser 2–10–0 "Kriegslok" locomotives were found there, and these were assembled. The first one assembled under MRS jurisdiction, L52 1960, was given a "pilot" (or cow-catcher in English), the only one so fitted! Another interesting locomotive was a streamlined 2–8–2 No 19.1001, fitted with twin V-type steam drives mounted on both sides!

HQ Second MRS moved from Brussels to Frankfurt. No 707 RGD went to Haltern-Herne and then to Fürth in July 1945. In June 1945, 709 RGD moved to Marseille and then in August 1945 to Calais departing for Manila. However, VJ-Day intervened and the unit in fact went to Boston in the USA, and then Fort Eustis in January 1946, being disbanded in 1950. No 710 RGD moved to Brussels in June 1945 and then to Marseille in July 1945. It was the intention to send 710 RGD to the Pacific but in the event this did not occur. The other units were inactivated in Europe. The last units (first in, first out) were 734, 735, 741, 746, 750 and 752 ROBs and 766 RSB which were inactivated in February 1946, and 716 ROB which left for the USA in the same month. MRS operations closed in October 1945.

In the British area, German railway staff were ready to resume railway operation at the end of May 1945. RCE No 1 Rly Op Coy ceased to function as a unit in June 1945 and RCE No 2 Rly Op Coy in July 1945. However, because, not surprisingly, the Belgian and German railway staffs did not cooperate very well, RCE No 1 Rly Op Coy was recalled in late July to take over seven miles of track across the Belgian frontier into Aachen, which they continued to operate until October 1945, when they were disbanded.

Chapter 11

INDIA AND BURMA

In 1940, the Mediterranean supply route to Britain was cut and the railways of India were used to support the Middle East. Rails were lifted from certain sections of Indian railways and sent to the Middle East. Locomotives, rolling stock and personnel followed. Twenty-one Bombay, Baroda and Central India Railway Class G2 4–6–0s and two Class F1 0–6–0s were sent to the Qena-Sofaga Railway as MEF 100-20 and 160/1 in 1942. Most returned to the BBCI in 1944.

However, in 1941 and early 1942, the Japanese over-ran South-East Asia and approached the Indian frontiers. They were in Arakan threatening an attack on Chittagong and on the Indo-Burma border threatening to attach the Brahmaputra Valley. Instead of military traffic to the west, the need was now to the east. Supplies were required for Allied forces and also for the Chinese who were fighting the Japanese. Air attack was expected, although in fact surprisingly few air-raids took place.

The railway service was meagre. From Calcutta, the main Allied supply base, the broad-gauge Bengal Assam Railway main line went 300 miles north to Silguri. From Parbatipur on this line, a metre-gauge single track went across eastern Bengal and north Assam to the bank of the Brahmaputra at Amingaon where a ferry connected to Pandu. From Pandu, a metre-gauge single track went through the Brahmaputra Valley to Tinsukia and Ledo in the north-east corner of Assam. Roughly half-way along this last line was Dimapur (also known as Manipur Road), the beginning of the Manipur Road, the only road into Burma. Calcutta to Dimapur was 612 miles, and to Ledo 809 miles. From here on, supplies were sent to China by air or by lorry over the Ledo and Burma Roads.

Calcutta was connected to the rest of India to the west by the Willingdon Bridge near Dum Dum, and the Jubilee Bridge near Naihati, five and twenty-four miles respectively from Calcutta, both of which bridges spanned the Hooghli and brought East Indian Railway traffic to the BAR. Another link with the rest of India was via Barbatipur, from whence a metre-gauge BAR branch went to Katihar and linked up with the Oudh and Tirhut system, which in turn connected with other systems reaching the west of India. This provided an all metre-gauge route and avoided the need for transhipment. Another route not using Calcutta was from Chittagong across the plains to Badarpur and then over the "Hill" section to Lumding and thence to Dimapur.

In 1942, the BAR was in a poor state of repair. Locomotives and rolling stock were in short supply and in bad condition, and the traffic was leisurely. Initially, engines and rolling stock were brought in from other Indian railways, then a flood of American and Canadian equipment arrived such as 171 "MacArthur" metre-gauge 2–8–2s and the broad-gauge CWD class. Indian railway troops arrived, together with one British Rly Op Coy, and two Rly Construction Coys. However, the Indian effort was the greater since there were no less than 34 Indian Rly Op Coys, 22 Rly Construction Coys, and many other units.

At the beginning, the broad-gauge main line was double track for only 135 miles at Abdulpur. To pass the maximum amount of traffic, only up traffic used the line for a period, then only down traffic for the next period. Eventually, double track was extended to Santahar, together with some sections between Santahar and Parbatipur.

As already mentioned, only one British Railway Operating Company of about 400 troops was available, who had been trained at Longmoor and Melbourne. The main work done by this Rly Op Coy was to handle the motor vehicle traffic on the BAR, trucks being needed in the Brahmaputra Valley but they had to go by rail because there were no main roads there from Calcutta. The railway troops took over the twice-daily trains at Ishurdi, 124 miles from Calcutta, and ran them 108 miles to Parpatipur and 193 miles to Siliguri, using the broad-gauge CWD class locomotives. These trains were worked by the British troops until February 1945.

At Christmas 1942, the Japanese made light air raids on Calcutta, and in particular on the Kidderpore Docks, and many people left the area. Since Calcutta docks were then of the utmost importance to the war effort, the main force of British railway troops was moved there, providing crews for five locomotives, to staff five signal boxes and to provide shunters to work the two large yards and the coal berth lines at Kidderpore Docks. All equipment was in a very bad state of maintenance, and operating methods were very lax, but the British troops managed to get things moving. The British Rly Op Coy also assisted at Chittagong Docks.

In January 1944, the American No 705 RGD started to take over the operation of the 804 mile metre-gauge line from Katihar to Ledo. Operation of the BAR by the MRS began officially on 1 March 1944. The following units arrived. No 721 ROB had its HQ at Parbatipur and operated the railway from Khatihar, where the BAR joined the Oudh and Tirhut Railway, east through Parbatipur to Lalmanirhat, some 120 miles. No 725 ROB HQ was at Lalmanirhat and they operated from there 175 miles to Amingaon on the Brahmaputra. No 726 ROB has its HQ at Pandu on the other side of the Brahmaputra and operated 160 miles from there to Lumding, as well as the ferry operations across the river. No 745 ROB with its HQ at Lumding was responsible for 108 miles to Mariani. No 748 ROB had its HQ at Mariani and operated 100 miles to Tinsukia, Ledo and Dibrumukh. No 758 RSB set up operations in the BAR shops at Dibrumukh.

In March 1944, there were 154 metre-gauge USA/TC locomotives on the BAR under Lease-Lend. By March 1945, there were 262. The 48 mile bottleneck track between Lumding and Dimapur was double tracked by the British during 1944. The MRS used their own "MacArthur" or MAWD locomotives almost exclusively and tended to ignore BAR engines. Trains were standardised with either 50 or 100 wagons, and either one or two MAWD engines respectively were used. The trains of 100 wagons were operated double-headed eastbound, while westbound trains of 50 wagons took to the sidings, which could just accommodate 50 wagons when the trains met. This permitted the general flow of traffic to be considerably increased. This was merely an interim solution, however, and 67 passing loops were lengthened east of the Brahmaputra to handle 100 wagons, and 26 west of the river were lengthened to take 150 wagons. A point of interest is that when diesel or steam power was not available, shunting was often carried out by elephants. For instance, No 748 ROB used the elephant "Moonbeam" frequently near Bogpani.

The greatest single obstacle was, of course, the Brahmaputra River, forming a tremendous water barrier between the Calcutta base and the front line. Even at its upper reaches, it was seldom less than two miles wide, and in some places, six miles. In 1942, it was completely bridgeless. The principal crossing was between

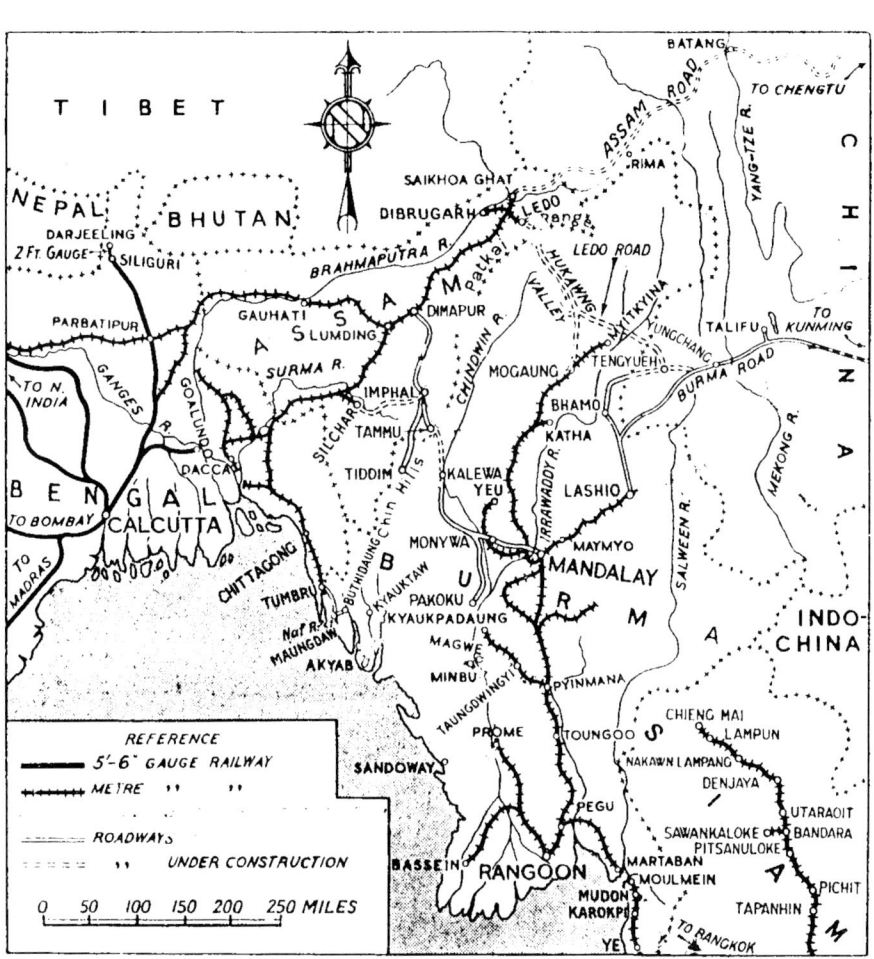

Map 13 The transport links between India, Burma and China (Courtesy Railway Gazette)

Amingaon and Pandu, where solid shore masses brought the width of the river down to 1¼ miles, and provided shore bases for ferry stations. In early 1942, there was heavy refugee traffic from Burma moving west. The existing wagon ferry could handle 90 wagons per day, say 16,000 tons per month. The military wanted to work 200,000 tons per month!

The wagon ferry was a barge with nine tracks laid crosswise on its deck, each track taking two metre-gauge vans. A floating landing stage provided the link between the shore and the ferry. The empty barge was brought up to the landing stage by tug and secured in position so that the last (down-stream) track was in alignment with the ramp line. Meanwhile, a locomotive picked up a pair of wagons on the end of a string of runners, and propelled them down to the ferry. When the wagons were on the barge, the runners were on the landing stage and bridge, while the locomotive was still on firm ground! While the locomotive withdrew to bring in two more wagons, the mooring ropes of the ferry were eased off and the barge allowed to drift downstream until the second track was in alignment with the approach line. By this time, the next two wagons would be arriving! The process was repeated until the barge was fully loaded. At Pandu, the barges were unloaded in a similar fashion.

In May 1942, a new ferry was opened about a mile downstream from the original ferry. Some troop trains were diverted to Dhubri, and a fleet of steamers ferried the troops up river to Pandu, an 18-hour voyage. It was at one time decided to build a bridge across the Brahmaputra River above Amingaon, but later thoughts were that the burden of bringing up constructional materials would interfere too much with the war traffic, and the railway and the Indians operating the ferries promised to work everything that the military brought up. A third ferry came into operation in September 1944. While a fourth ferry was planned, in the event it was never required. The capacity of the wagon barges was also increased. On the biggest, 17 tracks were laid enabling 34 wagons to be ferried at a time. At the peak period, 442,000 tons per month were ferried across, well above the original requirement.

In the Spring of 1944, the Japanese penetrated to within 4½ miles of the line at Mariani and were only beaten back by

British and American troops rushed to the spot by train. Raiding was quite common at one time and rail motorcars with machine guns were operated ahead of the trains to watch for damage to the track.

The maximum traffic of 34,000 wagons per month was handled in March to May 1945. In the event of a derailment, little or no attempt was made to recover the wagons. The most urgent need was considered to be clearing the line, and damaged vehicles were usually pushed off the line and left. Traffic then declined and in September and October 1945, the railway was returned to civilian BAR operation and the last MRS unit left India for the United States in October.

Reverting to the "Hill" section, this was in the middle of the line linking Chittagong with the Brahmaputra Valley. It presented difficulties since it included eleven miles of 1 in 37 up to Jatinga and had 33 tunnels and numerous viaducts, which cut down the maximum practical capacity of the line to eight trains per day.

The "Hill" section began at Badapur, a railway settlement on the plains about 17 miles from the foot of the Cachar hills. The climb into the hills began at Chandranathpur and rose to Harangajao. Here began the eleven miles of 1 in 37 to Jatinga. The track then went down to Lower Haflong and up to the summit at Mahur, from where the line fell at 1 in 60 to Lumding.

The engines doing the bulk of the work were 20 of the old Assam-Bengal Railway "K" class 4–8–0s, plus five ex–A–B "T" class 2–6–2+2–6–2 Garratts. The "K" class could take 16 wagons over the "Hill" and the "T" class 22. Every train made up for the "Hill" was put on an inspection pit and checked, a process taking at least two hours. All trains were vacuum braked and only 25% piped wagons were allowed, no two of which could run together. So when a long train arrived from the plains, say 70 wagons with 35 of them piped, much thought and work were necessary before trains could be remarshalled and passed fit for the "Hill". Indeed, often such a train would have to be split into three separate trains. Badapur had to supply three engines to do the work of one engine over the plains, plus bankers for the 1 in 37 section. The shops to which Badapur engines normally went to for major repairs had been closed, and so locomotives had to be sent to Dibrugarh or across the Brahmaputra to Saidpur.

At first, extra war traffic was not too heavy, but during the 1942 monsoon the Beki Bridge fell and incapacitated the main line on the north side of the Brahmaputra and threw a heavy burden on the "Hill" section. Everything that could run was pressed into service, such as a "K" class double-headed with an ex–A–B "H" class 4–6–0, with a little "F" class 0–6–0 attached at the rear in case of brake failure!

A peculiar feature of the "Hill" section was that motive power was available only at the Badarpur end, since no "Hill" engines were allocated to Lumding. In peacetime, the engine workings usually balanced, but in wartime loads sometimes accumulated at Lumding, requiring locomotives to work light 115 miles from Badarpur, for example a Garratt with two brake vans.

To increase the capacity of the line, extra stations with crossing facilities were built, using Indian railway construction troops. British RE troops also assisted. The locomotive position was eased by the arrival in early 1944 of twelve 2–8–2+2–8–2 MWGH WD Light Garratts (see Chapter 34), which could take 30 wagons over the "Hill". In late 1945, these were replaced by sixteen 4–8–2+2–8–4 MWGX WD Light Garratts, the largest engines ever then used. By VJ-Day, three were in service and others were on their way. As they arrived, the MWGH Garratts were withdrawn and sent to the then just liberated Burma Railways. The introduction of these heavy locomotives meant that the permanent way had to be improved. In six weeks in 1944, the 50 lb rails in the "Hill" section were replaced by 60lb rails and the number of sleepers increased, by Indian railway construction troops.

The "Hill" bankers were housed in a small locomotive shed at Harangajao. The bulk of the work was carried out by "C" class 2–6–2Ts, but they had limited water and coal capacities. "T" class Garratts were also used. Several MAWD 2–8–2s arrived and were adapted for the "Hill" and put into service, first as bankers and later on main line duties passed for 18 wagons. Bankers were also attached to all down passenger trains, and goods trains if available, to give increased braking power. Bankers were always placed on the train with the normal train engine leading.

As to activities in Burma, these began on 12 May 1944 when Allied bombers attacked the airfield at Myitkyina, the terminal of the railway running north from Rangoon through Mandalay. Thus began the struggle for Myitkyina station which ended in a fight between the Allied forces in four freight vans and the Japanese in the next four vans in the same train! The MRS flew into the captured airfield at Myitkyina in August 1944 and started reactivating the railway 38 miles from Myitkyina to Mogaung. Freight carried in August 1944 amounted to 1883 tons.

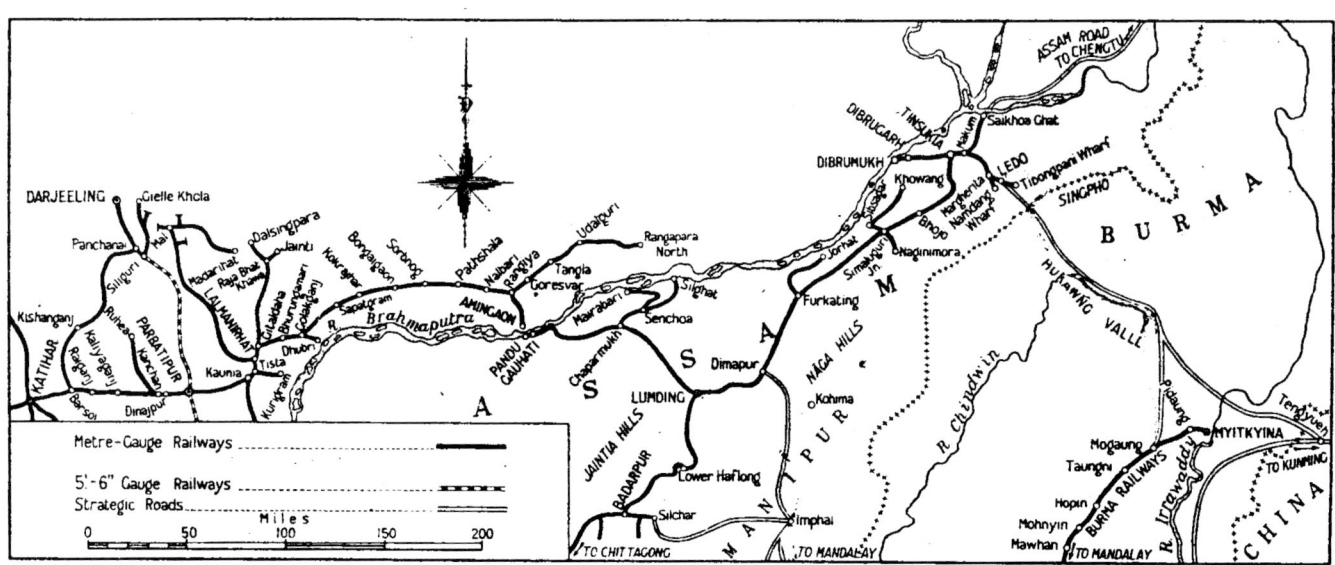

Map 14   The Bengal and Assam Railway approach lines to the supply routes to China and to the Burma front (Courtesy Railway Gazette)

By October 1944, the Allied forces were proceeding down the railway from Mogaung to Naba Junction, near Katha on the Irrawaddy River. American troops fitted flanged wheels to a pair of army jeeps and put them at each end of a train of six wagons or so to form a "push-pull" train! Not to be out-done, REME troops countered by producing "Windsor Castle" and "Lancaster Castle" made from salvaged Burmese railway wagons, some British motor engines and some Japanese gearboxes! Performance was about the same as that of the rail jeeps!

By the end of January 1945, the railway extended 128 miles to Mawlu. In February, the line was operational to Katha and Indaw, with seven steam locomotives and two diesels. The peak traffic was January 1945 with 73,312 tons of freight moved, after which the need for traffic at this northern end of the line rapidly declined.

Around April 1945, when Mandalay was liberated but not Rangoon, three USA/TC MacArthur 2–8–2s made a 300 mile journey by road from the BAR to the re-captured part of the Burma Railway, as discussed in Chapter 47. Road trailers were used and a mobile crane travelled with the convoy to lift the ends of the engines round bends in the road! These three locomotives were erected in the engine shed at Myingyan, about 50 miles south-west of Mandalay, and were initially used between Myingyan-Thazi-Tatkou. Six USA/TC 0–4–0P locomotives were flown into Myingyan in April 1945, as discussed in Chapter 51.

By May 1945, Rangoon had been captured, and thoughts turned to the postwar rehabilitation.

Chapter 12

NEW CALEDONIA AND PHILIPPINE ISLANDS

The Chemin de Fer Colonial in New Caledonia ceased operation in January 1940, the Vichy government being overthrown with Australian help. On 7 December 1941, Japanese bombers attacked Manila in the Philippine Islands for the first time and on 22 December 1941, the Japanese landed in the Philippines. On 5 May 1942, the fortress of Corregidor fell and the Philippines were conquered.

Also in 1942, the USA/TC arrived in New Caledonia and in April 1942, the Chemin de Fer Colonial, the Noumea to Paita Railway, was reopened by No 790 ROC, using French and Javanese employees. It was used for hauling freight from the port at Noumea 20 miles to the end of the line at Paita, from where it was sent by lorries to Tontouta Airfield 29km further west, and to various supply dumps. The USA/TC brought with them two GE and two Brookville diesel locomotives. In February 1944, the tide of war had moved on and the USA/TC closed its operation.

The American forces returned to the Philippines in October 1944 and the first MRS troops arrived in January 1945, being No 790 ROC (Railway Operating Company) from New Caledonia, which became part of No 775 RGD which arrived in February 1945. They began rehabilitating the railway from Dagupan south towards Manila. The Manila Railway Company had 712 miles of 42 inch gauge track on the island of Luzon but the MRS were responsible for only 234 miles known by them as the Luzon Military Railway. No 790 ROC operated their first train from Dagupan 30 miles to

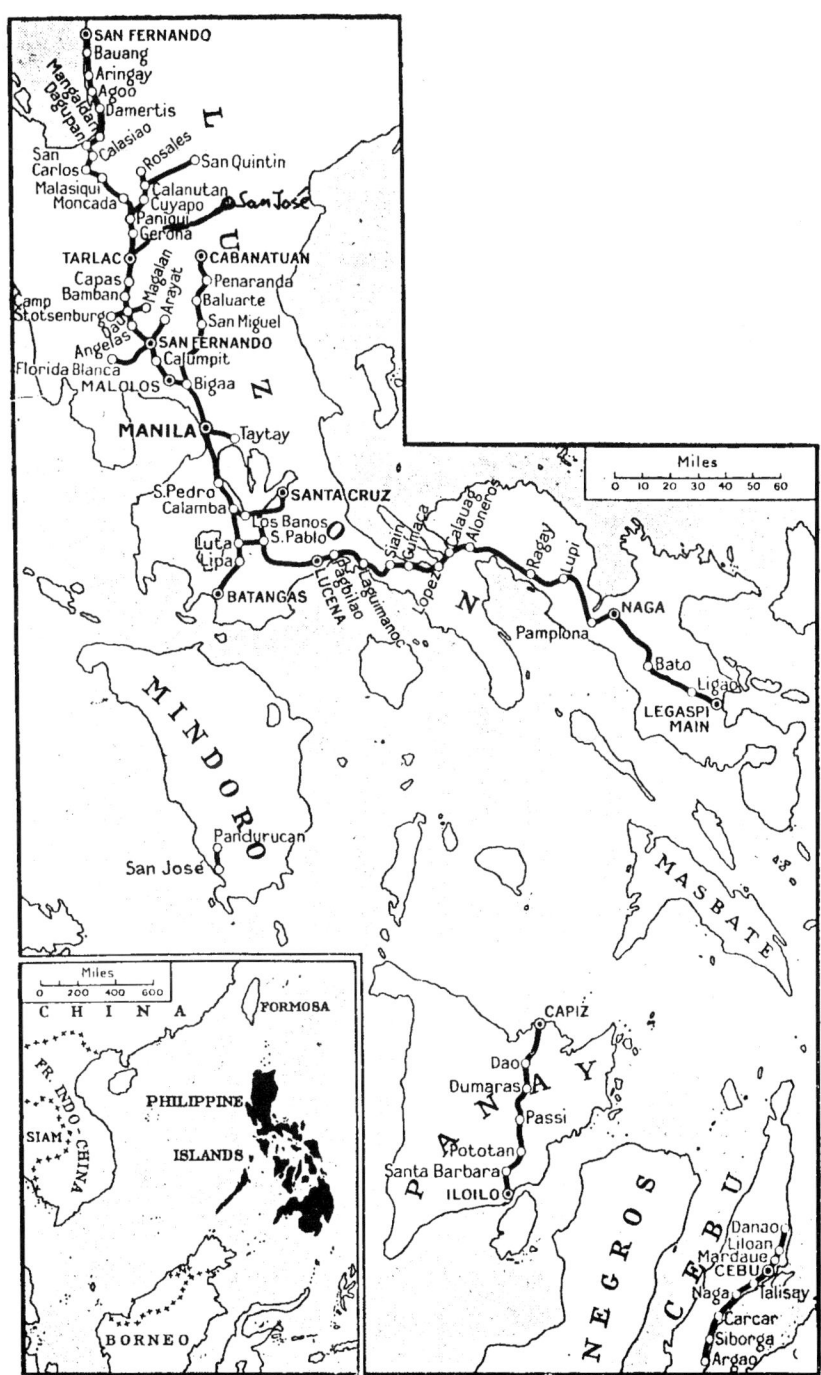

Map 15   The railways of the Philippine Islands, with insert showing the strategic relationship of these islands to other countries (Courtesy Railway Gazette)

Bayambang on 19 January 1945. By 24 January, the line was open 70 miles to Capas, and by 15 March 150 miles right through to Manila.

In April 1945, 737 and 749 ROBs arrived and the responsibilities became as follows. No 790 ROC operated the San José branch line. No 737 ROB operated 127 miles from San Fernando (Pampanga) north to San Fernando (La Union). No 749 ROB operated from San Fernando (Pampanga) south through Manila to Calamba, a distance of 70 miles. No 753 RSB arrived from Italy in September 1945, and was located in Caloocan workshops.

The first USA/TC railway supplies arrived in February 1945 and eventually 53 locomotives and 990 wagons were put into service. The 53 locomotives included 45 "MacArthur" 2–8–2s (see Chapter 47) and five GE B-BDEs USA/TC 8584–8. Possibly the three unaccounted for would be from GE B-BDEs USA/TC 8588–93 landed temporarily en route to Japan? Peak traffic was 152,628 tons in July 1945. The Japanese accepted peace terms on 14 August 1945, VJ-Day. On 15 August, Nos 737 ROB and 790 ROC were relieved and sent to Japan and Korea. On 1 January 1946, the USA/TC returned the railway to civilian control and 775 RGD was considerably reduced in size, and was inactivated in May 1946. No 749 ROB left for Korea in February 1946, while No 753 RSB was inactivated in April 1946.

Chapter 13

JAPAN

American forces landed on Honshu Island on 28 August 1945 and MRS forces were used to supply these units. The MRS took over for a short while the Japanese National Railway line from Sapparo on Hokkaido Island in the north, across the train ferry between Hakodate on Hokkaido to Aomori on Honshu, through Yokohama and Tokyo to Shimonoseki on the southern tip of Honshu, and then by underwater tunnel to Moji on Kyushu Island.

These lines were rapidly handed back to civilian control.

Chapter 14

KOREA

When the surrender terms were signed by the Japanese in 1945, Korea was taken from Japan, the north part above the 38th parallel going to Russian control and the south part below the 38th parallel to American control. In 1950, the United Nations led by America and the North Koreans directed by Russia began fighting. Accordingly, MRS operations were first as suppliers to the Army of Occupation following World War 2, and then in support of the United Nations fighting the Communist armies of North Korea in 1950.

In 1945, there were 4000 miles of railway in Korea, all steam-operated, of which 1700 miles were south of the 38th parallel. Practically all the railway track was 4ft 8½in gauge. Workshops were situated at Seoul and Pusan.

The MRS moved into Korea in September 1945, and found 474 locomotives of which some 166 were serviceable. Accordingly, the MRS requisitioned USA/TC 2–8–0 locomotives from Europe which were no longer needed there. The first arrived in March 1947, and eventually 101 arrived. Fifteen locomotives were brought in from Japan, and most of the Korean engines repaired.

The first unit to arrive was No 790 ROC from the Philippine Islands in September 1945, and they took over duties at Seoul. No 737 ROB arrived from the Philippines in November 1945 and operated in the Seoul region, the Taiden terminals and lines in the southwest. No 770 ROB also arrived from the Philippines in November and operated the Pusan region and the main line up to Taiden. No 749 ROB arrived in March 1946 but was inactivated on arrival. By July 1947, Nos 737 and 770 ROBs were inactivated. No 790 ROB left Korea in December 1948 for Japan were it was inactivated in January 1949.

The first trains were operated on 15 September 1945 from Seoul to Pusan, and traffic was built up until by November 1947 twelve or fourteen freight trains were handled daily between Pusan, Taiden and Seoul, in addition to passenger trains.

On 25 June 1950, the North Koreans invaded South Korea. In July 1950, some MRS troops arrived. In August 1950, Nos 714 ROB and 765 RSB arrived. These units were under strength and when strengthened only 20% of the troops were experienced railwaymen. HQ was set up at Pusan and in September 1950, 272 miles were under MRS direction. On 1 October, this mileage was increased to 359 by taking over responsibility for the railway to Riri in the south-west and Waegwan in the north. Some 153 locomotives, 340 passenger coaches and 3600 wagons were available. Equipment was shipped in, such as diesel locomotives from the United States and steam locomotives from Japan.

In October, the enemy was retreating and the mileage increased to 1074. Demolitions were experienced. HQ was established at Seoul. No 712 ROB arrived in December 1950, when the enemy began a counter-offensive south. The MRS were in retreat. On 10 December, the yards at Sinmak were destroyed, and later facilities at Susack and in the Hamhung-Hungnam area. On 14 December, HQ was moved back from Seoul to Taikyu. On 26 December, facilities north of Uijongbu were destroyed. On 1 February 1951, the enemy advance was finally halted on a line east and west across the peninsular south of Suwon and Wonju, which cut the railways out of Taiden and Taikyu.

The United Nations turned to the attack and by 1 March the port of Inchon was recaptured and the Han River reached. On the east coast the line was just north of Samchok. By 1 April, the United Nations forces had pushed north of the 38th parallel just south of Haeju and recaptured Yangyang on the east coast. There the battle line remained except for minor changes until hostilities ceased on 27 July 1953.

No 724 ROB arrived in June 1951, but slow progress was made with rehabilitating the railways owing to the extensive demolition and bombing by both sides. Guerrilla action was frequent and there were over 50 engagements between MRS units and the enemy. Wagons filled with sandbags and manned by fighting troops with machine guns were placed at the front and rear of each train.

During June and July 1951, the fighting gradually became stationary. In August 1951, No 714 ROB returned to the United States. No 765 RSB was inactivated in Korea in December 1954, and No 712 ROB in January 1955. No 724 ROB remained for a further period.

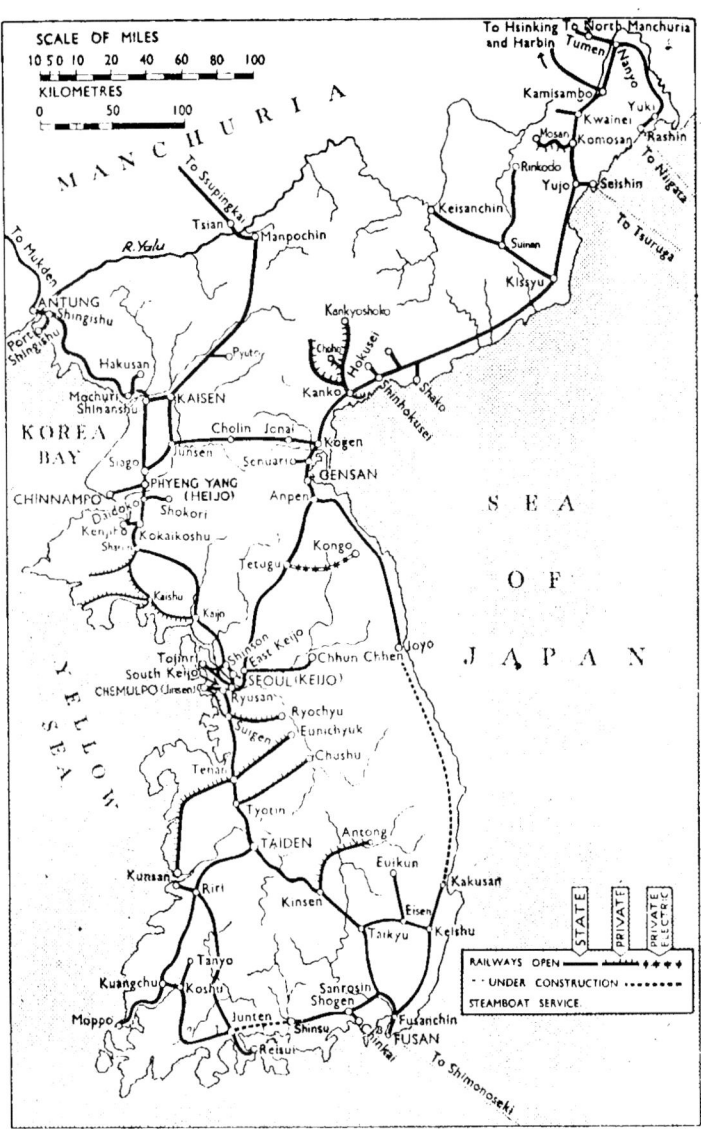

Map 16   The railways of Korea as around 1942 (Courtesy Railway Gazette)

SECTION 2

Chapter 15

WD LOCOMOTIVE STOCK LIST

Practically all the War Department locomotives were numbered in one WD series. A separate MEF list was used in the Middle East during the first part of the war. Apart from certain miscellaneous engines, the MEF numbers were obtained be adding 6000, 8000 or 9000 to the WD number. This was done to avoid confusion with Egyptian State Railway engines. A separate list was also used in India.

In the late summer of 1944, when the invasion of Europe was being contemplated, it was considered desirable to give all military engines numbers which would not clash with the numbers of existing locomotives on any line over which they might be called upon to operate. Thus, the 7XXXX scheme was devised, in which all existing WD numbers were given a "7" prefix.

The main WD list is given following these introductory notes. When the classes are dealt with in detail, reference is made to the appropriate Chapter, otherwise brief details of the locomotives are given. Afterwards, the WD (India) and the MEF series are listed.

The 7XXXX prefix used in the latter part of the war is frequently omitted in this book to avoid unnecessary repetition. Several locomotives were never renumbered into the 7XXXX series, while others, in particular those numbered in the MEF series and those built in the later years of the war, were never without the "7" prefix. Some further information on this point is given in the Chapters dealing with individual classes. The numbers given in brackets in the main WD list were never actually used but are given here to complete the list and thereby demonstrate the structure of the WD numbering scheme.

When works numbers are shown as WD running numbers, it is possible that these were not official WD Nos but merely convenient reference numbers for administrative purposes. In many cases, these numbers were not shown on the locomotive, other than on the works plates.

The first WD of all in this list, WD 1, was a Hunslet diesel locomotive fitted with a 200bhp Gardner engine. It was built to a low loading gauge for surface and underground use at the War Office depot at Corsham. The drive was taken via a Hunslet friction clutch, flexible coupling and three-speed gearbox. Westinghouse straight air brakes were fitted, air being provided by a belt-driven Broom & Wade compressor. The weight was 22 tons and a maximum speed 18mph.

MEF 1–7 were the survivors of sixteen used on the Haifa Harbour Works Department construction work, the others having been sent back to the UK. They were given their MEF numbers by No 199 Rly Wksp Sqn in January 1941 and served at various Palestine depots. MEF 2 was withdrawn in July 1941 and its boiler used on MEF 4. MEF 1/3/4 were withdrawn in May 1944 and so did not receive WD numbers in the 7XXXX series. MEF 6 "Doreen" went to Ataqa in Egypt in February 1944 and then to No 169 Rly Wksp Sqn. MEF 7 was rebuilt by No 199 Rly Wksp Sqn and became works shunter at Jaffa Workshops.

MEF 31–7 were existing pre-war Middle East locomotives. MEF 31 "Sahel" was at Qasfareet but transferred to Palestine in January 1943. By 1952 it was dumped at Haifa. MEF 32 "Karour" was at Ataqa and Suez and finally became No 169 Rly Wksp Sqn works shunter. MEF 33–5 continued to work at their original locations, but were withdrawn before 1944 and so did not receive WD numbers in the 7XXXX series. MEF 36 "Haren" was employed as works shunter at No 169 Rly Wksp Sqn. MEF 37 "Mechelen" was at Ataqa but transferred to Palestine in November 1942 and worked at Wadi Sarar and Jaffa. By 1952 it was dumped at Haifa.

MEF 100–20/40–5/60/1 were all metre-gauge locomotives brought in for

WAR DEPARTMENT LOCOMOTIVE STOCK LIST

WD Nos	Maker, Works No & Date	Type	Notes
1	HE 1846/37	0–6–0D	
2	JF 22500/38	0–4–0D	Rn WD 810 1952
3–7	Ex LMS	0–6–0D	See Chapter 16
8–15	Ex LMS	0–6–0T	See Chapter 17
16–27	Ex LMS	0–6–0D	See Chapter 16
28	JF 22889/39	0–4–0D	Rn WD 852 1952
29–48	WD	0–4–0D	See Chapter 18
49–64	Ex LMS	0–6–0D	See Chapter 16
65	HE 2412/41	0–6–0ST	
66	HE 2414/41	0–6–0ST	
67	HE 2416/41	0–6–0ST	
68	HC 1529/24	0–6–0ST	
69	HC 1513/24	0–6–0ST	Named "Staines"
70	HC 1719/43	0–6–0T	
71	HC 1720/43	0–6–0T	
72	? 1212/?	0–6–0D	
73	WGB 2643/41	0–6–0PT	
74	AE 1572/10	0–6–0ST	Rn WD 010 1952, Longmoor museum engine
75	VF 4564/36	0–6–0D	Temporarily WD 4564, named "Vulcan"
76	? ?	? D	Junkers engine
77	AB 1769/21	0–6–0ST	MEF 32, named "Karour"
78–91	Ex LNE	0–6–0T	See Chapter 19
92	MW 654/77	0–6–0ST	Originally WD 654
93–200	Ex GWR	0–6–0	See Chapter 20
201	HE 304/83	0–4–0ST	Rn WD 1689
202	AE 1407/99	0–4–0ST	Named "Tartar"
203–8	LMR stock	–	See Chapter 39
209	MW 1334/97	0–6–0ST	
210	P 1691/25	0–6–0ST	
211	HC 1102/15	0–6–0ST	Ex PLA 46
212	STR –/89	0–6–0	Ex LNE J15 7835
213–5	BTN –/29	0–8–0T	Ex SR Z 951/5/6

WD Nos	Maker, Works No & Date	Type	Notes
216	DON 1414/13	0-6-0T	Ex LNE J50 3157
217	DON 1500/19	0-6-0T	Ex LNE J50 3219
218	DON 1418/14	0-6-0T	Ex LNE J50 3160
213-8	Ex LMS	0-6-0D	See Chapter 16
219	STR –/01	0-6-0T	Ex LNE J67 7169
219	MEF	–	See MEF 9805
220	DON 1659/26	0-6-0T	Ex LNE J50 1058
220	MEF	–	See MEF 9801
221	STR –/88	0-6-0	Ex LNE J15 7541
222	AB 859/00	0-4-0ST	Named "Sapper"
223	MW 863/83	0-4-0ST	Named "Wyn"
224	Ex LMS	0-6-0D	Ex WD 25, see Chapter 16
225	Ex LMS	0-6-0D	Ex WD 26, see Chapter 16
226	HE 1858/37	0-4-0D	Rn WD 811 1952
227	Pl 2016/?	0-4-0D	Rn WD 812 1952
228	P 1204/10	0-6-0ST	Named "Daisy"
229	?	0-6-0T	
230	JF 22905	0-4-0D	
231	RH 187075/38	0-4-0D	Rn WD 800 1952
232	RH 221648/44	0-4-0D	Rn WD 801 1952
233	Ex LMS	0-6-0D	See Chapter 16
234	D&S ?/80	0-4-0ST	Named "Victory", built by Dick & Stevenson
235	M ?/41	0-4-0D	German type WR200B14, built by Mannheim
236	HC 845/?	0-6-0T	
237	WGB 2652/41	0-4-0ST	Rn WD 013 1952
238	JF 22976/42	0-4-0D	Rn WD 853 1952
239	RH 221645/44	0-4-0D	Rn WD 802 1952
240	HE 1649/31	0-6-0ST	MEF 6, named "Doreen"
241	HE 1657/31	0-6-0ST	MEF 5
242	HE 1658/31	0-6-0ST	MEF 7
243	AB 1898/27	0-4-0ST	MEF 31, named "Sahel"
244	B 43120/16	0-4-0ST	MEF 36, named "Haren"
245	B 45337/17	0-4-0ST	MEF 37, named "Mechelen"
246	Henschel ?/?	0-8-0DH	German type WR550D14, No 11118
247	? ?	0-4-0D	German type WR200B14, No 3610
248	Henschel ?/?	0-6-0DH	German type WR360C14, No 11465
249	Henschel ?/?	0-6-0DH	German type WR360C14, No 11464
250	B/F 4172/?	0-4-0D	Italian, built by Badoni/Fiat
251	B/F 4190/?	0-4-0D	Italian, built by Badoni/Fiat
252	B/F 4209/?	0-4-0D	Italian, built by Badoni/Fiat
260-73	LMS type	0-6-0D	See Chapter 16
(274-99)	(LMS type)	(0-6-0D)	Cancelled order
300-449	Ex LMS	2-8-0	See Chapter 21
500-24	Ex LMS	2-8-0	See Chapter 21
540-623	Ex LMS	2-8-0	See Chapter 21
624-44	Italian	–	See Chapter 22
654	–	–	See WD 92
700-91	Ex LNE	2-8-0	See Chapter 23
800-79	WD	2-8-0	See Chapter 24
1000-1199	American	2-8-2	See Chapter 48
1200-51	Whitcomb	0-4-4-0D	See Chapter 25
1252-1316	American	0-6-0T	See Chapter 49
(1317-86)	(American)	(2-8-2)	Cancelled WD order
1302-6	USA/TC	0-6-0T	See Chapter 49
1387-1436	American	0-6-0T	See Chapter 49
1437-1536	WD	0-6-0ST	See Chapter 26
1537-96	Whitcomb	0-4-4-0D	See Chapter 25
(1597-1636)	(Whitcomb)	(0-4-4-0D)	Cancelled order
1659	HE 1643/30	0-6-0ST	Named "Bramley No 4", ex Haifa HWD 3
1660	HE 1644/30	0-6-0ST	Named "Bramley No 6", ex Haifa HWD 4
1677	HC 1510/23	0-6-0ST	Rn WD 011 1952
1678	AB 1297/15	0-6-0ST	
1681	HE 2065/40	0-4-0D	Rn WD 847 1952
1682	HE 2066/40	0-4-0D	Rn WD 848 1952
1687	JF 22890/39	0-4-0D	Rn WD 854 1952
1689	–	–	See WD 201
1769	AE 1769/17	0-4-0ST	Named "Betty", RN WD 4199

use on the Qena-Sofaga line. MEF 160/1 left the BBCI in October 1941 and were put into service by December 1941. MEF 100-14 left the BBCI between January and March 1942. Three were put into service in April 1942 and the other twelve in June 1942. MEF 115-20 left the BBCI in January and February 1943, but were not put into service until June 1943. Originally another nine BBCI 4-6-0s were due to be sent to the Qena-Sofaga line, but the movement of these was cancelled. The MEF numbers were alloted early in 1943. MEF 101-9/11-3 were returned to the BBCI in India between December 1943 and April 1944. MEF 110/6/8 and one other went to Tanganyika in 1947.

Several locomotives were sent from one railway to another to assist in meeting the needs of wartime traffic. Although these loans/transfers were arranged by the WD, the engines were not given WD numbers. It is convenient to summarise these movements here.

Sixteen South African Railway 4-6-0s of Class 6, built by Dubs & Co in the 1890s and by Neilson Reid & Co in 1898, were acquired by the WD and shipped to the Sudan in February 1942. They became Sudan Railways 700-15 and were later purchased by the SR. Details were as follows (see page 33).

At least four were used for shunting at Wadi Halfa in 1945/6. By March 1948, many tenders had been changed, as can be seen from the Table. Also by March 1948, 703/11 were in Atbara Works, 702/7/9/13/4 at Atbara shed, 701/4/5/8/15 at Port Sudan, 706/10 at Khartoum and 700/12 at Wadi Halfa.

Ten standard-gauge Class G8 0-8-0s from the Chemin de Fer Damas, Hamah et Prolonguements (Syria) were loaned to the IqSR in 1941, becoming IqSR 1001-10. These were returned in 1942.

A total of 179 metre-gauge locomotives of various types acquired from various Indian railways was shipped in to Iraq, four more being lost en route, in 1941/2. These were mostly 4-6-0s, but there were some 4-8-0s, 0-6-0s and a few 0-6-2s. They were given local military numbers 601-779, and then hired to the IqSR. Twelve were returned in May 1943, 18 in February 1944, 68 were purchased by the IqSR and became IqSR 154-94, 201-14/21-33, and the remaining 81 were sold or scrapped. Full details are given in "Middle East Railways" by Hugh Hughes, published by the Continental Railway Circle in 1981.

As an interesting "might have been", it may be mentioned that around March 1941 there was a proposal by Mr R. L. D.

WD Nos	Maker, Works No & Date	Type	Notes
1872	AE 1872/20	0–6–0ST	Named "Ashford"
2000	RSH 7017/42	2–6–0ST	KCR S15 October 1946, Rn 1
2001	RSH 7018/42	2–6–0ST	KCR S16 October 1946, Rn 2
2200	HC 1678/37	2–8–2T	See Chapter 27
2210	RH 224341/44	0–4–0D	Rn WD 803 1952
2211	RH 224342/44	0–4–0D	Rn WD 804 1952
2212	RH 224343/44	0–4–0D	Rn WD 805 1952
2213	RH 224344/44	0–4–0D	Rn WD 806 1952
2214	RH 224345/45	0–4–0D	Named "Caen", Rn WD 807 1952
2215	RH 224347/45	0–4–0D	Rn WD 808 1952
2216	RH 224348/45	0–4–0D	
2217	RH 224349/45	0–4–0D	Rn WD 809 1952
2218	RH 235513/45	0–4–0D	
2220–31	WD	0–4–0D	See Chapter 18
2235–9	WD	0–4–0D	See Chapter 18
2400/1	Ex LBSCR	4–4–2T	See Chapter 28
2600–5	FMSR	4–6–4T	See Chapter 29
2800–54	Sudan	4–6–2	See Chapter 30
(3000–3500)	(American)	(2–8–2)	WD order taken over by USA/TC, see Chapter 47
3031–60	USA/TC	2–8–2	See Chapter 47
3600–5	Krupp	2–10–2	See Chapter 38
3606–9	Ex China	–	See Chapter 38
3650–3799	WD	2–10–0	See Chapter 31
3800	BP 7045/42	2–6–2+2–6–2	SLR 57 (2ft 6in gauge)
3801	BP 7046/42	2–6–2+2–6–2	SLR 58 (2ft 6in gauge)
3802	BP 7047/42	2–6–2+2–6–2	SLR 59 (2ft 6in gauge)
3803	BP 7048/42	2–6–2+2–6–2	SLR 60 (2ft 6in gauge)
3804	BP 7049/42	2–6–2+2–6–2	SLR 61 (2ft 6in gauge)
3805	BP 7050/42	2–6–2+2–6–2	SLR 62 (2ft 6in gauge)
4000–4	Vici-Congo	2–8–2T	See Chapter 32
4005–10	Ex SIR	2–8–0	See Chapter 33
4114	AE 1742/16	0–6–0ST	Named "Avonside", Rn WD 4114 1944
4199	–	–	See WD 1769
4200–43	Light Garratt	–	See Chapter 34
4400–24	Heavy Garratt	–	See Chapter 35
4553	AE 1807/18	0–6–0ST	Named "Bramley No 1", Rn WD 012 1952
4554	AE 1808/18	0–6–0ST	Named "Bramley No 2"
4559	HL 3347/18	0–6–0ST	Named "Bramley No 3"
4564	–	–	See WD 75
4584	P 820/00	0–4–0ST	Named "Douglas"
5000–5199	WD	0–6–0ST	See Chapter 26
(5200–49)	–	–	Originally intended for USA/TC 0–6–0T
5215/7	USA/TC	0–6–0T	See Chapter 49
5250–5331	WD	0–6–0ST	See Chapter 26
5519	HE 2067/40	0–4–0D	Named "Don 1", Rn WD 849 1952
5520	HE 2068/40	0–4–0D	Named "Don 2", Rn WD 850 1952
5521	HE 2078/40	0–4–0D	Named "Don 3", Rn WD 851 1952
6909	Sent 6909/27	0–4–0VB	Named "Molly"
7000–7509	WD	2–8–0	See Chapter 24
(7510–8509)	–	–	Originally intended for USA/TC 2–8–0
7979	HE 2407/41	0–4–0ST	
8108	Crewe 1869/74	0–6–0	Ex LMS 8108, Rn SMR 2 May 1939
8182	Crewe 2333/80	0–6–0	Ex LMS 8182, SMR
8236	Crewe 2459/81	0–6–0	Ex LMS 8236, SMR
8510–8718	WD	2–8–0	See Chapter 24
(8719–9176)	–	–	Originally intended for USA/TC 2–8–0
9177–9312	WD	2–8–0	See Chapter 24
A–M	Armoured	2–4–2T	See Chapter 36
E1 1	EE 533/22	0–4–0BE	
E1 2–5	EE ?/22	0–4–0BE	

Maunsell of the Sudan Railways that some Irish narrow-gauge locomotives could be purchased, refurbished and converted to work on the 950mm Eritrean Railways. Possibilities listed at the time were LMS(NCC) 101/2/4/10/1/3/4, CDR 1–20, L&LSR 1–8/10/2–6, GSR (West Clare) 1,3,7,10/1 and GSR (Tralee & Dingle) 1–6/8. It is not known how seriously this proposal was taken by the UK military authorities, but it is perhaps fortunate that it was not taken up.

By 1952, the WD had disposed of most of the large war-time fleets of locomotives, leaving a residual number which they then considered necessary for peacetime operations. Accordingly, at the beginning of 1952, the WD renumbered virtually all the military locomotives remaining in service at that time. The existing numbers, which remained from the large war-time numbering scheme, were cumbersome and scattered. The aim of the new system was to use smaller numbers in a more compact arrangement.

It subsequently became clear that the allocation of batches of numbers was on the following basis:

010–039	Miscellaneous tank engines
040–079	Miscellaneous tender engines
100–299	WD 0–6–0STs
300–399	USA/TC 0–6–0Ts
400–499	WD 2–8–0s
500–599	LMS 8F 2–8–0s
600–699	WD 2–10–0s
700–799	USA/TC 2–8–0s
800–819	Diesel-mechanical up to 60hp
820–869	Diesel-mechanical 100 to 195hp
870–889	Diesel electric 350hp
890–899	Diesel electric 650hp
900–999	Railcars

The War Office issued an official list but remarked that "certain gaps or discrepancies may be noticed" and "no explanation can be offered as to the reasons for these". The renumbering list which follows is based on the official list but has been augmented from other sources and is now believed to be essentially complete. At the time, all the old WD numbers were in the 7XXXX series but the "7" prefix is omitted in the table to save space. One engine, 508, retained its old number in the renumbering.

From 1961, locomotives from many of the smaller Royal Ordnance Factories, which had never been listed in the WD series, were taken over by the WD and renumbered into the 1952 WD series. Since they served during wartime, they are included here. In April 1964, the War

WAR DEPARTMENT (INDIA) LOCOMOTIVE STOCK LIST

WD(I) Nos	Maker, Works No & Date	Type	Notes
1	WGB 2625/42	2–8–2	See Chapter 37
2	WGB 2626/42	2–8–2	See Chapter 37
3–112	USA/TC	2–8–2	See Chapter 47
400–23	Light Garratt	–	See Chapter 34

MIDDLE EAST FORCE LOCOMOTIVE STOCK LIST

MEF Nos	Maker, Works No & Date	Type	Notes
1	HE 1683/31	0–6–0ST	Ex Haifa HWD 16
2	HE 1586/29	0–6–0ST	Ex Haifa HWD 2
3	HE 1646/30	0–6–0ST	Ex Haifa HWD 6
4	HE 1585/29	0–6–0ST	Ex Haifa HWD 1
5	HE 1657/30	0–6–0ST	See WD 241, Ex Haifa HWD 9
6	HE 1649/30	0–6–0ST	See WD 240, Ex Haifa HWD 7
7	HE 1658/30	0–6–0ST	See WD 242, Ex Haifa HWD 10
11–8	–	–	See WD 49–54/6/7
19–22	–	–	See WD 19–22
23	? ?	0–4–0T	
26	RMM 721/26	0–4–0WT	90cm gauge, Fanara
27	RMM 714/26	0–4–0WT	90cm gauge, Fanara
28	RMM 713/26	0–4–0WT	90cm gauge, Fanara
29	RMM 719/26	0–4–0WT	90cm gauge, Fanara
31	AB 1898/27	0–4–0ST	See WD 243
32	AB 1769/21	0–6–0ST	See WD 77
33	? ?	0–4–0T	
34	HL 3247/17	0–4–0ST	Originally ROD 4211, Named "Napoleon"
35	? ?	0–4–0T	
36	B 43120/16	0–4–0ST	See WD 244
37	B 45337/17	0–4–0ST	See WD 245
38	? ?	?	90cm gauge, Fanara
39	? ?	?	90cm gauge, Fanara
40/1/3–5	–	–	See WD 34-8
70	–	–	See WD 250
71	–	–	See WD 251
72	–	–	See WD 252
100	Ajmer ?/26	4–6–0	Ex BBCI 33
101	Ajmer ?/26	4–6–0	Ex BBCI 34
102	Ajmer ?/26	4–6–0	Ex BBCI 40
103	Ajmer ?/24	4–6–0	Ex BBCI 100
104	Ajmer ?/25	4–6–0	Ex BBCI 127
105	Ajmer ?/24	4–6–0	Ex BBCI 161
106	Ajmer ?/24	4–6–0	Ex BBCI 202
107	Ajmer ?/24	4–6–0	Ex BBCI 208
108	Ajmer ?/25	4–6–0	Ex BBCI 210
109	Ajmer ?/25	4–6–0	Ex BBCI 214
110	Ajmer ?/25	4–6–0	Ex BBCI 219
111	Ajmer ?/25	4–6–0	Ex BBCI 239
112	Ajmer ?/25	4–6–0	Ex BBCI 248
113	Ajmer ?/27	4–6–0	Ex BBCI 249
114	Ajmer ?/25	4–6–0	Ex BBCI 506
115	Ajmer ?/25	4–6–0	Ex BBCI 209
116	Ajmer ?/24	4–6–0	Ex BBCI 247
117	Ajmer ?/25	4–6–0	Ex BBCI 216
118	Ajmer ?/26	4–6–0	Ex BBCI 233
119	Ajmer ?/25	4–6–0	Ex BBCI 251
120	Ajmer ?/26	4–6–0	Ex BBCI 95
140–5	–	–	See WD 2600–5
160	Dubs 2908/92	0–6–0	Ex BBCI 709
161	Ajmer ?/03	0–6–0	Ex BBCI 759
6200–51	–	–	See WD 1200–51
6537–96	–	–	See WD 1537–96
9000–9199	–	–	See WD/USA 1000–1199
93XX & 94XX	–	–	See WD 300–449, 500–24/40–623
97XX	–	–	See WD 700–91
9801–7	–	–	See Chapter 38

Department became the Army Department, and in 1968 there was another systematic renumbering into a new series. However, by this time, only a few war-time locomotives still existed, so this can be considered to fall outside the scope of this book. Details can be obtained from "Locomotives of the Ministry of Defence" published by the Industrial Railway Society in 1992.

Plate 1　　Port of London Authority 0–6–0ST 79 (ex WD 70066) at Custom House shed in November 1946. This engine was a prototype of the WD Standard 0–6–0ST class (Photo: A. G. Wells)

Plate 2　　WD 73 0–6–0PT at Normanton (Derby) in May 1948 (Photo: H. C. Casserley)

Plate 3　　WD 70228 "Daisy" at Longmoor after the war (Photo: E. C. Griffiths)

SR No	SAR No	Maker	Works No	SAR Class	Cab	Tenders as supplied SAR No	Tenders as supplied SAR Class	Wheels	Tenders March 1948 SAR No	Tenders March 1948 SAR Class	Type
700	402	Dubs	3050/93	6	Small	414	6	6w	–	–	Bogie high flush sides
701	403	Dubs	3051/93	6	Small	524	6B	Bogie	–	–	Small bogie original
702	406	Dubs	3054/93	6	Small	454	6A	6w	1238	8F	Small bogie original
703	417	Dubs	3070/93	6	Large	1168	8C	Bogie	–	–	Ex Khor Class No 82
704	421	Dubs	3060/93	6	Small	428	6	6w	–	–	Small bogie original
705	423	Dubs	3088/93	6	Small	537	6B	Bogie	–	–	Small bogie
706	436	Dubs	3067/93	6	Small	631	6H	Bogie	631	6H	Small bogie original
707	465	Dubs	3447/96	6A	Small	1235	8F	Bogie	1065	7C	Small bogie original
708	472	Dubs	3467/97	6A	Small	582	6D	Bogie	–	–	Small bogie
709	475	Dubs	3463/97	6A	Small	1197	8D	Bogie	428	A	6w weather board
710	479	Dubs	3475/97	6A	Small	1238	8F	Bogie	–	–	SR Port C1 or Atlantic
711	534	NR	5319/98	6B	Small	617	6H	Bogie	582	6D	Small bogie original
712	538	NR	5323/98	6B	Large	571	6D	Bogie	–	–	6w weather board
713	548	Dubs	3343/96	6C	Small	1065	7C	Bogie	–	–	SR Port C1 or Atlantic
714	572	NR	5250/98	6D	Small	408	6	6w	537	6B	Small bogie flush sides
715	587	NR	5269/98	6D	Small	770	10C	Bogie	–	–	Small bogie

Details of the WD 1952 renumbering scheme are as follows:

WD	0	1	2	3	4	5	6	7	8	9
01X	74	1677	4553	237	2200	(a)	–	–	–	–
04X	(b)	(b)	(b)	(b)	(b)	–	–	–	–	–
10X	5028	5031	5035	5036	5037	5039	5040	5041	5042	5044
11X	5072	5075	5076	5078	5079	5096	1437	1487	1505	1527
12X	1528	5045	5047	5048	5049	5063	5099	5100	5102	5103
13X	5107	5111	5113	5114	5118	5121	5122	5126	5133	5141
14X	5142	5144	5151	5152	5158	5162	5165	5171	5180	5181
15X	5186	5187	5189	5191	5192	5193	1438	1443	1444	1445
16X	1446	1448	1449	1450	1477	1529	1530	1531	5019	5176
17X	5179	5250	5251	5252	5253	5254	5274	5275	5277	5278
18X	5280	5282	5283	5284	5285	5286	5290	5292	5294	5295
19X	(c)	(c)	(c)	(c)	(c)	(c)	(c)	(c)	(c)	(c)
20X	(c)	(c)	(c)	(c)	–	–	–	–	–	–
30X	4382(d)	1267(d)	1271(d)	1275(d)	1276(d)	1290(d)	1294(d)	1295(d)	1297(d)	1302(d)
31X	1303(d)	1304(d)	–	–	–	–	–	–	–	–
40X	7337	9250	–	–	–	–	–	–	–	–
50X	307	320	607	387	392	393	395	501	508	516
51X	574	575	583	593	373	613	–	–	–	–
60X	3651	3797	–	–	–	–	–	–	–	–
70X	3257(e)	–	–	–	–	–	–	–	–	–
80X	231	232	239	2210	2211	2212	2213	2214	2215	2217
81X	2	226	227	(f)	(g)	(h)	–	–	–	–
82X	30	31	32	42	43	44	46	47	48	2220
83X	2221	2222	2223	2224	2225	2226	2227	2228	2229	2230
84X	2231	2235	2236	2237	2238	2239	224	1681	1682	5519
85X	5520	5521	28	238	1687	(i)	(i)	(i)	(j)	(j)
86X	(j)	(j)	(j)	(j)	(j)	(j)	(j)	(j)	(j)	(j)
87X	49	50	51	53	56	57	270	271	272	273
88X	20	22	215	216	(k)	–	–	–	–	–
89X	1232(l)	1233(l)	–	–	–	–	–	–	–	–

(a) German 0–4–0WT OC "Jasper" at RE Adabiya, Suez
(b) LNE O4 2–8–0s taken into WD service in 1952, see Chapter 23
(c) The fourteen new standard WD 0–6–0STs which were built in 1952/3 became WD 190–203
(d) USA/TC 0–6–0Ts, see Chapter 49
(e) USA/TC S160 2–8–0
(f) 4wDE EE 687/35
(g) 4wDM RH 218046/42
(h) 0–4–0DM JF 22503/38
(i) Hunslet 204hp 0–6–0DM cut down for tunnel work at Corsham, HE 1846/36, HE 2063/40 and HE 2064/40
(j) Standard 150 hp 0–4–0DM ex ROF, AB 346/41, 347?/41, DC 2172/42, AB 331/38, DC 2168/42, DC 2169/42, DC2170/42, DC 2171/42, AB 337/40, AB 342/40, AB 338/39 and AB 344/41. See Chapter 18 for description of similar, but later, locomotives built for WD.
(k) Ex WD 813 in 1952 series
(l) Whitcomb BoBoDE

Plate 4 WD 011 0–6–0ST at Shoeburyness in May 1953. This engine was previously WD 1677 (Photo: A. G. Wells)

Plate 5 WD 72214 at Longmoor in 1947 (Photo: R. Tourret)

Plate 6 Works shunter at Jaffa Workshops, 0–6–0ST MEF 7 (later WD 242), Hunslet built and originally used before the war by the contractors who built Haifa Harbour. Rebuilt by No 199 Rly Wkshp Co, RE (Photo: K. R. M. Cameron)

Plate 7   WD 70245 awaiting shops at Jaffa, Palestine Railways, in June 1945. Baldwin-built 0–4–0ST rebuilt by No 199 Rly Wkshp Co and fitted with top-feed (Photo: H. D. Bowtell)

Plate 8   Captured German diesel locomotives at Beirut on the HBT. The nearest one is WD 70246 (Photo: F. Saville)

Plate 9   WD ex LMS 0–6–0 8236 at Kinnerley on the Shropshire & Montgomeryshire Railway in February 1946 (Photo: R. Tourret)

Chapter 16

LMS DIESELS, WD 3–7, 16–27, 49–64, 213–8/24/5/33/60–73

Many LMS diesel locomotives were used by, or built for, the WD and they served in several theatres of war. They will be considered in order of construction by the LMS (or WD), since this enables the technical development of the designs to be studied. Indeed, around this time, probably the WD experience of diesel shunting locomotives was as great, if not greater, than that of the LMS.

In 1932, the LMS ordered nine diesel shunters from five different manufacturers. Delivery took place during 1933/4, but some were not put into running stock until 1935. They were allocated Nos 7400–8 but were soon renumbered 7050–8. LMS 7050 was built under Lot 106, 7051–4 under Lot 107, 7055/6 under Lot 108, 7057 under Lot 109 and 7058 under Lot 110. The first five of these locomotives, LMS 7053/2/0/4/1, were taken over in 1940 and became WD 23–7. All were 0–6–0Ds built by Hunslet, except WD 25 which was an 0–4–0D built by Drewry. Later LMS 7057 became WD 233. They were used at WD depots in Britain throughout the war.

WD 23 (LMS 7053) had a 150hp Brotherhood-Ricardo six-cylinder sleeve-valve diesel engine fitted with a Vulcan-Sinclair hydraulic coupling and two-speed epicyclic gearbox designed by David Brown, with integral manual reverse. Final drive was by jackshaft and side rods. Starting was by an air starter motor, with air for the compressed air reservoir being supplied either by an air compressor driven off the main engine or by an auxiliary petrol-driven compressor. It entered LMS stock in November 1934. The epicyclic gearbox was not satisfactory in service and was replaced about 1936 by a Cotal four-speed gearbox with separate manual reverse gearbox. This was not too satisfactory either! In late 1939, it was loaned to the WD and noted at Hamworthy Quay and Poole Harbour in April and June 1940 respectively. It was at Bournemouth SR shed in July and August 1940, and by January 1941 it was on loan to the SR for use at Eastleigh Works. In May 1941, it was loaned to the Admiralty until December 1942, when it was nominally returned to the LMS but in fact withdrawn and sold back to Hunslet, with a view to rebuilding and resale, and it may even have been rebuilt but it was never sold and it was finally scrapped in March 1954 at Hunslet.

WD 24 (LMS 7052) had a 150hp McLaren-Benz eight-cylinder diesel engine with friction clutch and a two-speed preselector gearbox. Final drive was by jackshaft and side rods. For starting, it had a twin-cylinder Scott petrol engine. It was purchased by the LMS in January 1934. It was on loan to the WD (Air Ministry at Stafford) in 1940, returned to the LMS in February 1942. It was then withdrawn and sold to the Admiralty in 1943. It was modified to flashproof standard by Hunslet and then used at the Royal Navy Armament Depot at Broughton Moor in Cumberland until November 1966. It was sold to Birds Commercial Motors Ltd at Long Marston who used it until they scrapped it in 1969.

WD 25 (LMS 7050) was the only 0–4–0D. It was designed by Drewry but actually built at the English Electric Co works at Preston. It originally had a prototype 180hp W. H. Allen 8-cylinder engine fitted with Vulcan-Sinclair fluid coupling and four-speed Wilson epicyclic gearbox. It was arranged for electric starting, the only one to be so fitted. The reverse and final drive unit was by Bostock & Bramley incorporating a layshaft reverse and worm-gear final reduction. LMS 7050 worked initially at Agecroft and then at Salford goods depot. The original cab was fully enclosed after the first few months of service. It was loaned to the WD (Air Ministry) in August 1940, returned to the LMS in August 1941 and used at Stanlow until withdrawn in 1942 due to connecting-rod failure. The Allen engine was replaced by a Gardner 6L3 153hp engine of the type then in use on the standard WD 0–4–0Ds (see Chapter 18). As the Allen engine had been of anti-clockwise rotation, it was not possible to retain the original gearbox, so this was replaced by a Wilson SE-type unit again as fitted to the standard WD 0–4–0Ds. The original reverse unit was retained however. The unit had been purchased by the WD in March 1943, and the conversion was carried out by Vulcan Foundry Ltd in 1944. The engine was renumbered WD 70224 and started work at the Feltham Central Ordnance Depot in February 1945. In 1952, it was renumbered WD 846 in the postwar series. This locomotive worked at West Hallam from October 1953, at Stirling from August 1956 to May 1957, stayed six weeks at Bicester Workshops, and then worked at Hilsea from June 1957 to 1961. From April 1961 she was at Bicester awaiting repair, and in November 1961 she moved to Elstow and then in April 1964 to West Moors Supply Depot where she was still working, as Army 240, in 1973. She remained in service with the Ministry of Defence until going to the National Railway Museum in November 1979, and the Museum of Army Transport at Beverley in June 1987. It was latterly named "Rorke's Drift", the famous Zulu battle in Natal in 1879, at which Victoria Crosses were awarded to soldiers serving with the Royal Engineers and what became the RASC, the two principal army corps involved in military railway operations.

WD 26 (LMS 7054) had a 180hp Davey Paxman six-cylinder diesel engine, again with a Vulcan-Sinclair fluid coupling but with a David Brown three-speed preselector gearbox with integral manual reverse. Final drive was by jackshaft and side rods. Starting was by air starter motor with air for the compressed air reservoir

Plate 10   LMS 7061 on heavy gun train at Catterick in December 1940. This engine later became WD 70214. The gun is "HMG Boche Buster" and it has its attendant armoured ammunition wagon, which went to the Elham Valley Military Railway as described in Chapter 43. (Photo: R. Tourret Collection)

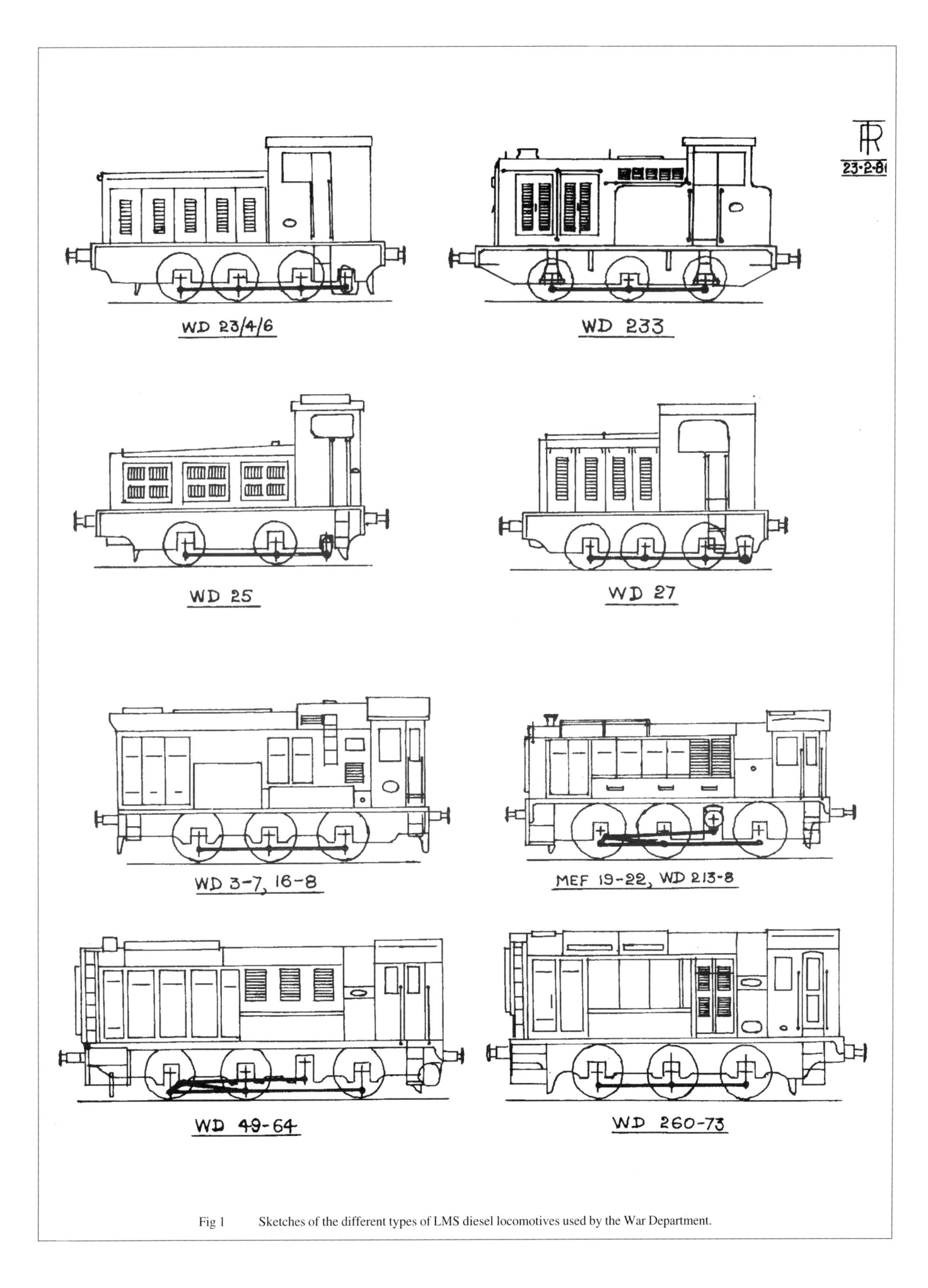

Fig 1   Sketches of the different types of LMS diesel locomotives used by the War Department.

Plate 11   MEF 17 (ex WD 51) English Electric 0–6–0D shunting in the Suez Canal area on the Egyptian State Railway (Photo: F. Saville)

being supplied either by an air compressor driven off the main engine or by an auxiliary compressor driven by a Scott twin-cylinder petrol engine. It entered LMS stock in November 1934. It was loaned to the WD in June 1940 for use at Longmoor and Melbourne. It carried its LMS number until March 1941 when it was renumbered WD 26. It returned to the LMS in July 1941, reloaned to the WD in March 1942 and returned to the LMS in July 1942. In November 1942 it reverted to LMS 7054. The LMS withdrew it in May 1943 and sold it to the WD, who renumbered it WD 225 and later 70225. It went to Highbridge WD Depot in 1943 and Bicester Central Ordnance Depot in 1947, but was then sold back to Hunslet in 1947, where it was refurbished. In 1954, it was hired to Brodsworth Colliery, near Doncaster, and later it was purchased by the NCB. It had brief spells on loan to Hickleton Main, Bullcroft, Goldthorpe and Frickley Collieries. and then in December 1972 it moved to Hickleton Main from where it was sold to T. W. Ward of Sheffield for scrap in October 1974.

WD 27 (LMS 7051) was the Hunslet prototype unit of February 1932, purchased by the LMS in May 1933. It had a German MAN diesel engine producing 150hp, with Hunslet clutch and a preselector gearbox. Final drive was by jackshaft and side rods. For starting, it was fitted with a 1100cc twin-cylinder JAP petrol engine. It was loaned to the WD (Ministry of Works and Buildings at Capenhurst, near Chester) in August 1940, but returned to the LMS in June 1941. In August 1944 it was loaned to the WD again, becoming WD 70027, but returned to the LMS in June 1945. It was withdrawn in December 1945 and sold back to Hunslet who stored it for a while and then overhauled it in 1949 and fitted it with a 132hp McLaren engine. It was used as a hire locomotive and works shunter until it went to the Middleton Railway, at first on loan from June to August 1960 and then after return to Hunslet, sold to the Middleton Railway in September 1960, who named it "John Alcock", a name it retained until 1982. In January 1979, it went on loan to the National Railway Museum. It was stored for some years but restored to working order in 1989.

WD 233 (LMS 7057) was an 0–6–0D built by Harland and Wolff of Belfast under Order 2503 in 1934, which was added to LMS stock in 1936. It had a Burmeister & Wain design engine, built by Harland & Wolff under licence. This was a 175hp four-cylinder two-stroke diesel engine, fitted with a Vulcan-Sinclair hydraulic coupling and a SLM two-speed gearbox with integral manual reverse. Drive was by cardan shaft to a Bostock & Bramley worm-gear unit on the front axle, all wheels being coupled. It had direct air starting, with air for the reservoir being supplied either by an air compressor driven off the main engine or by an auxiliary compressor driven by a petrol/paraffin engine. In 1935, a new SLM two-speed gearbox with separate manual reverse was fitted. During the war, it was loaned to the WD and became WD 233. It was used at Sinfin Lane WD Depot. It was withdrawn from the LMS in January 1944 and in January 1945 sold back to Harland and Wolff, who rebuilt it to 5ft 3in gauge, gave it a 225hp diesel engine and raised the engine hood to full cab height. It was loaned to the Northern Counties Committee who renumbered it 22. It was bought by the NCC in October 1949. It was withdrawn in April 1965 and scrapped later that year.

In the light of experience gained with the experimental locomotives LMS 7050–8, the LMS decided to use more powerful engines and to use electrical transmission. Two batches of ten locomotives were ordered. The first batch were ten 0–6–0DEs LMS 7059–68 built by Armstrong Whitworth under Lot 134, works numbers D54–63, and delivered between May 1935 and November 1936.

They each had a 350hp Armstrong Sulzer diesel engine directly coupled to a Crompton Parkinson generator, with a Crompton Parkinson single forced-ventilation traction motor with double-reduction gear drive. Final drive was by jackshaft and side rods. The jackshaft was placed within the wheelbase, which resulted in an unequal spacing of the wheels (5ft 3in and 9ft 3in) and a larger wheelbase, which made some of the connecting rods heavy to handle.

Six of these locomotives, LMS 7059/61–4/7, were loaned to the WD in 1940 for use on the MMMR and Elham Valley Military Railway where they became the permanent locomotives, at first helping in construction work and then hauling the rail-mounted guns stationed on these lines. LMS 7062 moved from the Martin Mill Military Railway to the Melbourne Military Railway in March 1941, and stayed until 1944. They were not renumbered into the WD series until 1944, when they were finally officially withdrawn from the LMS and sold to the WD, becoming WD 70213–8 in order. WD 213/4/6/7 were named "Old Joe", "Pluto", "Flying Scotsman" and "Royal Engineer" while on the MMMR, in block lettering on the radiators.

With the tide of war turning, the long-range guns were no longer required and WD 213/4/7/8 were sent to France in February 1945. WD 213 was stored at Ghent Merelbeke in September 1945 and later at Antwerp South. WD 214 was at Malines Works in March 1945 and then stored at Merelbeke in May 1945. WD 217 was at Ostend in June 1945 and Utrecht in September 1945. WD 218 was at Vilwoorde in February 1945, Halle in March 1945 and stored at Antwerp South later that year. WD 214/7 spent a short period on trial with the Nederlandsche Spoorwegen as 521/2 at the end of 1945, but subsequently all four locomotives, WD 213/4/6/7, became SNCB property in April 1946. They carried their WD numbers for a long time but were renumbered SNCB 230.01–4 in January 1952 and then 230.001–4 in April 1954. SNCB 230.001 was withdrawn in March 1958, while the other three were renumbered SNCB 231.101–3 in October 1960. They were withdrawn in February 1965, May 1961 and January 1966 respectively.

WD 215/6 stayed in the UK working at various depots. WD 215 arrived at Bicester COD in 1945 for repair, was at Burton Dassett WD Depot in October 1945, and then moved to Honeybourne WD Depot in November 1945, Long Marston in May 1947 and Bicester Central Ordnance Depot in 1950. WD 216 went to Longmoor in May 1946 and to Stranraer in December 1948. WD 215/6 were renumbered WD 882/3 in 1952. WD 215 (882) went to Germany in 1957 and was sold there about 1959. It was last heard of at Dortmund in May 1974. WD 216 (883) was at Cairnryan in 1952 and Bicester Central Ordnance Depot in October 1955. It was named "Royal Engineer" in 1959. WD 216 (883) was sold in 1963 to R. Fenwick & Co of Brackley, where it was overhauled and then hired to the CEGB Hams Hall Power Station. By the middle of 1967 it was stored out of use, and it was scrapped in November 1967.

The other four locomotives of this batch, LMS 7060/5/6/8, also went to the WD, being taken over in February 1941 and being renumbered WD 19–22. They were sent to the Middle East where their existing WD numbers 19–22 fitted conveniently into the MEF numbering system. They were withdrawn officially from the LMS in December 1942, it having become obvious that they were unlikely to return! They were delivered to the Middle East in May 1941 and entered service in June 1941. They were normally employed at British Army or Air Force Depots and also at the forward circular (or "Balloon") depots. In January 1942, MEF 19 & 20 were at Fanara, 21 at Gineifa and 22 at Abu Sultan. All four remained in the Canal Zone. MEF 20 was at Ataka and 22 at Fort Agrud in 1951. MEF 19 was can-nibalised for spares and MEF 19 and 21 were scrapped around 1951/2. WD 70020/2, as the remaining two had become, were renumbered WD 880/1 in the post-war renumbering, but they were sold to the ESR around 1952/3 and became ESR 4022/1 respectively around 1954. They were withdrawn by 1974.

The second batch of ten locomotives were ten 0–6–0DEs LMS 7069–78 built by Hawthorn Leslie works under Lot 135, works numbers HL 3841–50, and delivered in 1936. English Electric supplied the diesel engines and transmissions and Hawthorn Leslie supplied the mechanical parts. The design was based on that of the private-venture prototype which later became LMS 7079. These were the first English Electric shunters built for the LMS. They were, of course, built for comparison with the Armstrong Whitworth units just discussed.

They each had a 350hp English Electric Type 6K diesel engine direct coupled to an English Electric generator, with two self-ventilated axle-hung traction motors with single reduction gear on the outer two axles. Outside frames were used. All wheels were coupled by side rods. Starting was by electric batteries.

The intention had been to use LMS 7069–78 on trip freight trains as well as shunting, and the higher speed requirement led to single-reduction gearing rather than double-reduction gearing to give a higher speed. In fact, these locomotives were almost entirely used for shunting and it was found that the self-ventilated motors tended to overheat. In 1938, LMS 7074 was modified with force-ventilated motors, and in 1940 with double-reduction gearing, bringing the maximum speed down to 20mph.

Eight of these locomotives, LMS 7069–73/5/7/8, were taken over by the WD, LMS 7070/3/5/7/8 becoming WD 3–7 in December 1939 and January 1940, and LMS 7071/2/69 becoming WD 16–8 in March and April 1940 They were officially withdrawn from the LMS in December 1940. These locomotives went to France early in 1940. It is believed that WD 3, 4 & 7 were destroyed at Dunkirk in June 1940 and WD 6, 16/7 were lost in Brittany in June 1940 and probably destroyed, since nothing further has been heard about any of them. WD 5 (7075) was captured at Dunkirk and used by the German army until 1944. After the war, it was acquired by a machinery merchant in Paris, who sold the locomotive to a waterworks at Chartres, where the diesel engine and generator were removed to serve as a standby generating set. WD 18 (7069) was abandoned near Nantes in Brittany, where the Germans captured it and put it into use, until in turn they abandoned it in mid-1944 during their retreat following the D-Day landings in Normandy. WD 18 was found by the Allied forces north of Le Mans. The French army used it in that area at a General Reserve Munitions Depot, probably until 1957 when it became the property of a minor French railway, Chemin de Fer de Mamers à Saint Calais No 7, near Le Mans until 1973. In 1975, it was in the premises of the locomotive dealer Louis Patry in Paris, but in December 1987, it returned to the UK and went to the Swanage Railway for restoration!

Experience with the two batches of ten 350hp locomotives being generally favourable, a new design was drawn up taking what was then considered the best features from the two previous designs. Production was brought "in-house" and in 1939, Derby started manufacturing 0–6–0DEs. Forty new locomotives, LMS 7080–7119, were built, approximately ten each year 1939–42. LMS 7080–99 were built under Lot 141, LMS 7080–4 under order number 458 in 1939, and LMS 7085–99 under order number 486 in 1939/40. LMS 7100–19 were built under Lot 156, LMS 7100–9 under order number 1333 in 1941 and LMS 7110–9 under order number 1334 in 1942. However, LMS 7100–9 appeared in late 1941 as WD 49–58; WD 49/50 in October, WD 51–4 in November and WD 55–8 in December, while LMS 7110–5 appeared in early 1942 as WD 59–64; WD 59/60 in January, WD 61–3 in February and WD 64 in March.

They each had an English Electric Type 6K 350hp diesel engine direct coupled to an English Electric generator, with one large force-ventilated traction motor set above a double-reduction geared jackshaft drive with side rods similar to the Armstrong Whitworth design. Starting was by electric batteries. The mechanical portion built at Derby was based wholly

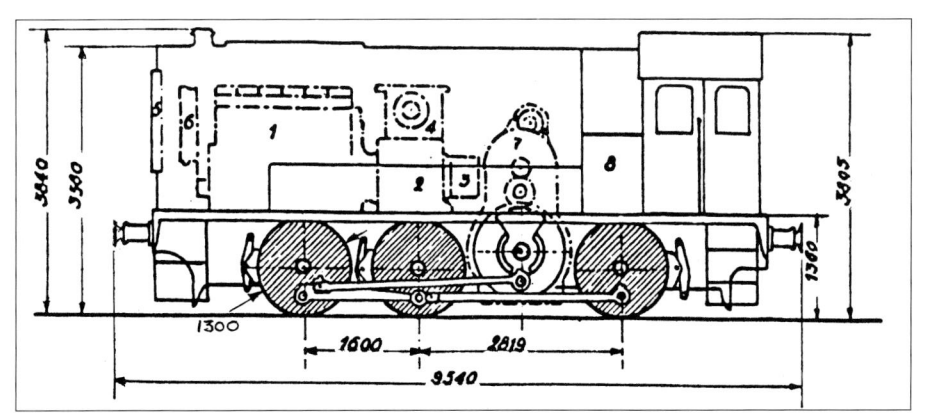

Fig 2 Diagram of Armstrong Whitworth WD 0–6–0DE as used by the SNCB, showing the layout of the main components; 1 diesel engine, 2 main generator, 3 auxiliary generator, 4 automatic rheostat, 5 radiator, 6 fan, 7 traction motor, and 8 fuel tank (Courtesy SNCB).

on that of the Armstrong Whitworth type, Armstrong Whitworth having by this time gone out of the diesel traction market. LMS 7106–9 WD 55–8 were fitted with neat little cowcatchers front and rear.

WD 49 and 58 worked at Toton in March 1942, and WD 51/4 were also used by the LMS in early 1942. Also in 1942, WD 60/1 were working at Willesden, to be replaced at the end of 1942 by WD 55/8.

WD 49/50/2/3/7/6/1/4 went to the Middle East and became MEF 11–18 in that order. They entered service during April to October 1942. By June 1942, MEF 14/5 were on the Western Desert Extension Railway at Capuzzo and Misheifa respectively, disguised as box wagons because of the risk of air attack! By November 1942, MEF 11/3/8 were also on the WDER. By March 1943, by which time the German forces had been driven back, MEF 13/4/8 were at Alexandria Docks, two were at Abu Sultan and single units at Gineifa, Suez, Agrud and Gilbana. Three were under repair at No 169 Rly Wksp Sqn. This makes a total of 12, and thus covers MEF 11–22. This remained the general pattern but by the end of 1943, some were on hire to the ESR. WD 55/8 went to North Africa in February 1943, worked on the CFT June 1943 and went to Italy in March 1944, where they were joined by WD 52/4 from MEF in April 1945. At this time, April 1945, WD 49/50/3/6/7 were on hire to ESR and the remainder were under WD control in the MEF.

In 1952, WD 70049–51/3/6/7 were renumbered WD 870–5 in the postwar system, but soon afterwards they were sold to the ESR and became ESR 4018/20/19/16/17/23 respectively. WD 52/4/5/8 were sold to the FS in Italy in 1946 and became FS Ne 700.001–4 in order. The first two were still in service in 1978, while the other two still existed but were not in service. They were finally all withdrawn in 1984. Ne 700.001 was sold to a scrap dealer in Arquata Scrivia, who reconditioned it and resold it to permanent way constructor Cariboni di Colico. It was at Vercelli in February 1995. In 1991, Ne 700.003 was sold to FSAS (Ferrovie Sinalunga-Arezza-Stia) and was noted at Arezzo Pesciaolo depot in November 1994. The other two locomotives apparently still exist and were last noted at Arquata Scrivia.

WD 59–64 stayed only two or three months under WD control and when it became apparent that there was no immediate military need for them, they passed back to the LMS, WD 59–61 in March 1942 and WD 62–4 in May 1942. They reverted to their LMS numbers in November 1942.

When the WD LMS diesels needed works attention, they were sent to Derby and it was normal for the LMS to loan the WD a substitute meanwhile, so as to keep the military railways such as MMMR and LMR fully functional. In fact, some of these locomotives stayed with the WD for appreciable periods. While these locomotives did not acquire WD numbers, their WD service merits listing. Those known are as follows:

7058	Longmoor 1941–3
7059	Longmoor
7074	MMMR
7076	MMMR 1939–41
7092	EVMR
7095	EVMR, MMMR 1941
7098	Replaced 7058 at Longmoor, June 1943 to Nov 1944

LMS 7080–7119 gave good service, both with the LMS and under arduous conditions in the Middle East, but some disadvantages became apparent. The presence of the jackshaft within the wheelbase made the fixed wheelbase rather long for shunting on sharply-curved track, and led to undue stressing of the frames. The tooth loading on the final drive gearing was rather high. By 1942, WD immediate needs had been met, and wartime restrictions on the use of steel and non-ferrous metals prevented further construction for the LMS. However, by 1943 preparations for the invasion of Europe were being made and the WD wanted some more diesel shunters. This enabled Derby to restart production and the opportunity was taken to improve the design.

This time, two traction motors were used as in the Hawthorn Leslie batch, but with double-reduction gearing. This eliminated the jackshaft drive, enabling the wheelbase and weight to be reduced. The smaller wheel diameter was used. This made a shorter and better balanced locomotive. Thus was developed the basic

Plate 12   SNCB 0–6–0D 230.22 (ex WD 70214) at Brussels North in October 1952 (Photo: R. C. Riley)

Plate 13   WD 70270 at Detmold Military Railway, Germany, in May 1949 (Photo: J. Firth)

Plate 14   WD 878 (ex 70272) "Basra" at Longmoor in 1963 (Photo: R. Tourret Collection)

0–6–0DE shunter used on the LMS and then British Railways.

The LMS locomotives each had a 350hp English Electric Type 6KT diesel engine direct coupled to an English Electric generator, with two force-ventilated axle-hung traction motors with double-reduction gearing on the two outer axles. Starting was by electric batteries.

WD 260–9 were produced in 1944 and WD 270–3 in 1945, all under Lot 173, WD 260–4 under order number 3239 and WD 265–73 under part of order number 3240. No LMS numbers were allocated against these locomotives. WD 70263–73 were prefixed with the "7" prefix when first built. Further production was planned as WD 70274–9 but these, the remainder of order number 3240, were not required by the WD and were taken over by the LMS as 7120–5 and never ran as WD locomotives.

When first built, WD 260–3 went to Longmoor for a while, then WD 262/3 went to France in November 1944, followed by WD 260/1 in December 1944. WD 264–8 went direct to France in January and February 1945, followed by WD 269 in April and WD 270 in May 1945. WD 271–3 went to Longmoor in June, July and August 1945 respectively.

After the war, WD 214/7 were on loan to the NS for comparative trials with WD 269 before NS decided which type they wished to purchase. Having decided on the latter type, WD 260–9 were purchased, WD 214/7 being exchanged with WD 262/3. WD 260/1/4–9 were renumbered NS 501–8 in March 1946, and WD 262/3 renumbered NS 510/09 in April 1946 (although 265 retained its WD number until at least August 1948).

The NS were satisfied with the performance of these locomotives and ordered more of the same type, eventually no less than 115 of them. They were built between 1949 and 1957 by the Dick Kerr works of English Electric, and are very similar to the BR classes 08 and 09, being numbered NS 511–45 (without train brakes), 601–65 (with train brakes) and 701–15. The ex-WD locomotives NS 501–10 were withdrawn around 1973, but NS 508 (ex-WD 70269) survives in the Utrecht Railway Museum.

WD 270 went to the Detmold Military Railway in 1946, was renumbered WD 876 in 1952 and returned to Longmoor in 1956. It was the second 0–6–0DE to be named "Bari", but was withdrawn in 1968 and scrapped in May 1969. WD 271/2 remained at Longmoor, were renumbered WD 877/8 in 1952 and named "Bari" and "Basra". WD 271 was scrapped in 1956 following the Palmers Ball collision. WD 272 was renumbered WD 601 in 1968 and outlived Longmoor, being transferred to Shoeburyness in April 1970. It went to Bicester in 1977 and was sold to the Lakeside & Haverthwaite Railway in July 1980. WD 273 went to the NS after the war, becoming NS 511 in 1949, but later returned to WD service in the UK in September 1949 and was renumbered WD 879 in 1952. It went to Germany where it was used in the Ruhr for some years. In 1957, it was noticed lying out of use at Hamm by some Danes, and as a result it was purchased by the Danske Statsbaner in December 1957. Early in 1958, it was classified ML and given DSB No 6. For some years it was used for shunting at Copenhagen, particularly at the Carlsberg breweries, and so it was nicknamed the "Hof-tractor", "Hof" being a special beer from Carlsberg. In the early 1970s, it had several changes of allocation, but following a failure in 1973, it was stored at Copenhagen and scrapped in 1974.

In preservation, there are WD 18 (LMS 7069) on the Swanage Railway, WD 25 (LMS 7050) at the Museum of Army Transport at Beverley and WD 27 (LMS 7051) at the National Railway Museum, while WD 52/5 are in engineering service in Italy. WD 70269 (NS 508) is in the Dutch Railway Museum at Utrecht.

Dimensions of LMS Diesel Locomotives Used by the WD

WD No	23	24	25	26	27	233	MEF 19–22 WD 213–8	3–7, 16–8	49–64	260–73
LMS No	7053	7052	7050	7054	7051	7057	7059–68	7069 etc	7080–7119	–
Maker, Works No & date	HE 1723/24	HE 1721/34	DC 2047/34 EE 847/34	HE 1724/34	HE 1697/32	See Text	See Text	See Text	See Text	See Text
Length over buffers	25ft 0in	24ft 8½in	23ft 10½in	24ft 8½in	23ft 2in	25ft 4½in	31ft 4½in	30ft 6¾in	32ft 5½in	29ft 1½in
Length over buffer beams	21ft 8¼in	21ft 8¼in	20ft 10in	21ft 8¼in	19ft 8in	22ft 6in	28ft 0¼in	28ft 0¼in		
Height	12ft 1in	12ft 1in	12ft 8in	12ft 5in	11ft 4¾in	12ft 0in	12ft 6in	12ft 9¾in	12ft 7in	12ft 6in
Width	8ft 3in	8ft 3in	8ft 5in	8ft 8in	8ft 2in	8ft 6in	8ft 7in	8ft 11½in	8ft 7in	8ft 7in
Wheelbase	9ft 0in	9ft 0in	7ft 0in	9ft 0in	8ft 0in	12ft 0in	14ft 6in	11ft 6in	15ft 3in	11ft 6in
Wheel diameter	3ft 4in	3ft 4in	3ft 0in	3ft 4in	3ft 0in	3ft 2in	4ft 3in	4ft 0½in	4ft 3in	4ft 0½in
Tractive Effort, max, lb	15950*	12800*	11200	15780*	10520	17500*	34000	30000	35000	35000
Weight in WO	26t 6c	26t 8c	25t 8c	30t 10c	21t 8c	27t 10c	52t 0c	51t 0c	55t 5c	47t 5c
Rated engine hp	150	150	160	180	150	175	350	350	350	350
Maximum speed, mph	14	8	12	15	30	10	20	30	20	20

Notes: Dimensions are given to the nearest ¼ inch. For some locomotives, more than one figure has been given for tractive effort, doubtless due to different assumptions as to rated or maximum engine power, use or not of 85 percent, etc. These figures are marked with an asterisk.

Chapter 17

LMS STANDARD CLASS 3F 0–6–Ts, WD 8–15

Early in 1940, eight LMS 0–6–0Ts, 7613/11/07/60/59/63, 7589 and 7617, were withdrawn and prepared for service with the WD as WD 8–15. These locomotives passed to WD control in March 1940 and were shipped to France in the same month, where they were overrun by the German forces in the retreat to Dunkirk. They were officially withdrawn by the LMS in December 1940.

LMS 7587 was originally prepared as WD 8 but was later exchanged for 7613. LMS 7638/31/43/29/20/24 were also prepared for WD service as WD 19–24 in order but were retained at the last moment owing to the collapse of France, and remained in LMS service. In addition, LMS 7591 and 7609 were earmarked for WD service but were not actually prepared.

It is believed that WD 8, 13 and 15 were destroyed by the British in the evacuation, and some say that they were then pitched off the quayside into the sea at some Channel port in order to impede future use by the German forces. Certainly the rest were captured by the German Army and handed over to the SNCF who used them on their former Etat system and renumbered them into SNCF stock as 030T042–4 and 030T026/7 in order. They were later renumbered in the style 030TW0XX, although not all the locomotives received numbers of the second type. As can be seen from Chapter 20, they were numbered in the same SNCF series as the ex-GWR "Dean Goods" 0–6–0s, but had a "T" included to denote tank locomotive.

While little is known of their war-time service, three of the class, SNCF 030T042–4, were allocated to Savenay and two, SNCF 030T026/7, to Brest. By 1947 they were out of use and they disappeared from SNCF lists in 1947, presum-

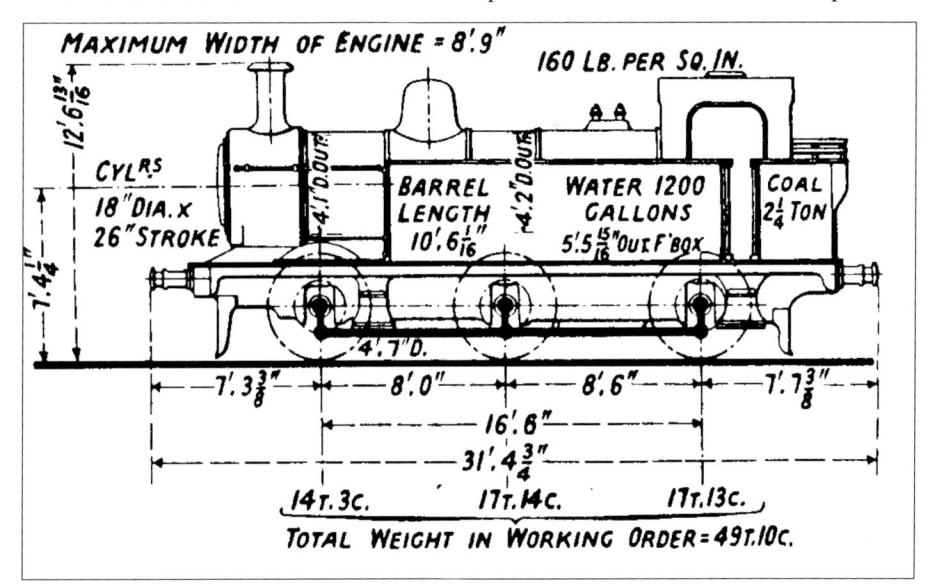

Fig 3   LMS Standard Class 3F 0–6–0T (Courtesy Railway Gazette)

Plate 15   SNCF 030TW044 (ex WD 11 and LMS 7660) at Cricklewood in August 1948, after return from France and on the way to Derby Works for re-conditioning (Photo: British Rail)

ably because they had been claimed back by the British authorities.

These five remaining locomotives, which had surprisingly survived the war, were returned to the UK via the Dunkirk-Dover train ferry in August and September 1948. They passed through Derby Works and came back into service on the LMS, now the London Midland Region of British Railways, between October and December 1948, using their original LMS numbers plus 40,000. They were finally withdrawn between 1961 and 1966.

WD No	LMS No	SNCF No	Return UK	Return BR	Notes
8	7613	–	–	–	
9	7611	030T042	8/48	11/48	
10	7607	030T043	9/48	12/48	
11	7660	030T044	8/48	10/48	
12	7659	030T026	9/48	12/48	(a)
13	7663	–	–	–	
14	7589	030T027	9/48	11/48	(b)
15	7617	–	–	–	

(a) Named "Corsair" in France
(b) When returned, fitted with chimney from GWR Dean Goods 0-6-0

Chapter 18

STANDARD WD 150hp 0-4-0D, WD 29-48 & 2220-31/5-9

These small diesel locomotives were designed by A. Barclay & Sons of Kilmarnock, and were built by them and the Drewry Car Co, to Ministry of Supply order. Drewry subcontracted part of the work on some of the later locomotives to the Vulcan Foundry. The locomotives were fitted with a Gardner 6L3 engine with a hydraulic coupling. Their dimensions were:

Horse-power	153
Cylinders	5½in x 7¾in
Tractive effort, 1st gear	10,540 lb
Tractive effort, 4th gear	2,580 lb
Max. speed, 1st gear	4.2mph
Max. speed, 2nd gear	7.4mph
Max. speed, 3rd gear	11.6mph
Max. speed, 4th gear	17.2mph
Total weight in working order	21tons 6cwt
Height (above rails)	11ft 4⅜in
Minimum curve	60ft radius
Wheel diameter	3ft 3in
Wheelbase	6ft 3in
Overall length	23ft 8⅞in
Fuel capacity	100gl

Of the first batch of twenty locomotives, WD 29-38 were built DC 2156-65 in 1941, WD 39-44 by AB 354-9 in 1941 and WD 45-8 by AB 360-3 in 1942. They were immediately put to use at various military depots in the UK, WD 29 going to Longmoor.

In 1941, five (WD 34-8) were sent to the Middle East, where they received MEF numbers 40/1/3/4/5 respectively. They arrived in rather a poor state due to lack of protection on board ship, and seem to have been too small a power unit to be of much use. These five reverted to their WD numbers when they received the "7" prefix in late 1944, but 34 became 35 and vice versa. One was used at Qasfareet from 1942 onwards; in 1945 this was 70035. The other four were stored at No 169 Rly Wkshp Sqn. At least three, WD 34/7/8, returned to the UK in 1947 and were sold out of WD service in that year or early 1948. Disposal of WD 35/6 is not known.

The remaining fifteen (29-33/9-48) were concentrated at Longmoor, for use in the invasion of Europe, by February 1944. Three were in daily use, the remainder undergoing overhaul or being in store, those mostly in use being 33, 41/2/5. Invasion preparations with these locomotives commenced at Longmoor in April 1944. Arrangements were made to load them on to adapted tank-transporter vehicles and, from time to time, two or three of them would be driven away to the port of shipment for testing their clearances on tank landing craft.

Plate 16   WD 30 at a depot in the UK (Photo: R. Tourret Collection)

WD 29, 30/2/3 were shipped from Southampton to Normandy in July 1944, each mounted on a tank-transporter road trailer, in tank landing craft, with tracked tractors in front to enable the locomotives to be hauled off. These were the first WD locomotives to land on the Continent of Europe after D-Day. WD 32 (military histories say WD 42 but this is believed to be wrong) was the first to be re-railed on to the coast line Chemin de Fer du Calvados which then existed between Bayeux, Arromanches and Ouistreham. The three other WD 0-4-0Ds were similarly placed into service, bringing landed stores to depots set up at Bayeux, Luc-sur-Mer and later St Martin des Entrees near Bayeux. Depots were soon also established at Ouistreham and Arromanches. As the battlefront advanced, by August 1944

Plate 17   WD 45 shown mounted on a tank-transporter vehicle at Longmoor during training for loading for the invasion (Photo: R. Tourret Collection)

these WD 0–4–0Ds were at work as follows: 29 Courseulles, 30 Bayeux and 32/3 Caen.

The remaining eleven locomotives WD 31/9–48 were shipped by conventional means from Southampton to Cherbourg during September 1944 but there was little work for them. WD 39 and 40 were put to work at Caen and 41 at Bretteville, while WD 42–8 went into 102 Transportation Stores Depot at Bayeux. Apart from these duties, these small diesels were never used much on the continent, and spent most of their time at various military dumps.

WD 70030 was repaired by No 155 Railway Workshops Coy shops at Mechelen (Malines) in March 1945, after which it went to Nijmegen. WD 70031 was at SNCB Vilvoorde for a while in August 1945. WD 70032 worked at Ostend for the period July to September 1945. WD 70039 was in No 155 Rly Wks Coy shops from March to August 1945 ex Schaerbeek awaiting spares. WD 70040 acted as works shunter for No 155 Rly Wks Coy briefly in January/February 1945. WD 70042 was allocated to Merelbeek (Ghent) in August 1945.

In 1945, a further batch of twenty were built, WD 2220–31 by DC 2175–86 who subcontracted to Vulcan 5256–67; and

Plate 18   WD 32 being unloaded by tractors on the British Second Army beachhead in Normandy on 26 July 1944 (Photo: R. Tourret Collection)

Plate 19 WD 72222 at Highbridge Depot in October 1946 (Photo: R. Tourret)

2235–9 by AB 368–72 respectively. Requirements changed because of the end of the war and the small degree of usefulness of these engines in practice, and the last three Drewry locomotives which would have been 2232–4 were cancelled. The remaining seventeen engines (2220–31/5–9) were used at various military depots in the UK. These engines were numbered in the 722XX series when built.

Early in 1946, five of the original locomotives, WD 29, 33, 40/1/5, were hired to various Dutch tramways to see if they would effectively perform the work of the diminutive steam tram engines, but without much success. Eventually, towards the end of 1947, they became the property of the NS who numbered them in their diesel series NS 161–5 of Class 160. NS 163 was withdrawn in 1949 to provide spares, and NS 161 was withdrawn about 1950/1.

The other three locomotives were used on the light railway branch from the NS railway station at Steenwijk to Oosterwolde, but were replaced by new locomotives in 1957, the branch itself closing in 1962. Ns 165 (WD 70045) was sold to the oil depot at Pakhuismeesteren at Pernis near Rotterdam and became number 801, but replaced by a new locomotive in 1962. NS 162/4 (WD 70033/41) were purchased by the colliery Willem-Sophia in Spekholzerheide and were renumbered WS II and III. When this colliery closed in 1971, the two locomotives were sold to Frans van den Bossche in Belgium. NS 162 was dismantled and cut up to provide spare parts for NS 164, which was then used on a rubbish dump. When the dump closed, the locomotive was returned to the yard of Frans van den Bossche in Aartselaar and offered for sale. It was still there two years later.

Eight locomotives (30–2/9, 42–4/6–8) returned to the UK about June 1946, but 43/8 were employed for a time on the Detmold Military Railway and did not return until January 1947. WD 72220 took part in the Victory Parade in London on 8 June 1946, and went on tour round Britain afterwards. WD 72225 also went on tour. All remained in WD service, except 39 which appears to have been sold to Sentinels about 1949.

In early 1952, the locomotives remaining in WD service were renumbered into the new WD series: 70030–2/42–4/6–8, 72220–31/5–9 becoming WD 820–45. In February 1952, six locomotives (70032/42/3/6–8) were sent to the Middle East, where on arrival they were named after some of the dwarfs in "Snow White". In early 1955, however, they were returned to the UK and concentrated at Bicester Central Ordnance Depot.

According to observations, not reflected in official records, there were some exchanges of identities in the 1960s, as follows. The original 823 (70042 AB 357/41) had its number painted out in December 1960 and became WD 859 around June 1961. Its place as WD 823 was taken by AB 359/41 in December 1960 and this engine was renumbered WD 220 in 1968. WD 825 (70044 AB 359/41) was renumbered WD 823 as mentioned above. WD 70039 (AB 354/41) was not included in the 1952 general renumbering, being derelict but it seems that its chassis was used as a basis for a

Plate 20 WD 826 (ex 70046) "Sleepy" at Fanara in March 1952 (Photo: S. R. Clark)

Plate 21 WD 842 (ex WD 2236) at Bicester, just out of shops, in May 1959 (Photo: H. D. Bowtell)

rebuilt locomotive incorporating spare parts and some new platework at Bicester circa 1957, which was numbered WD 825, and subsequently WD 221. The new WD 859, ex WD 823, became WD 202. It was restored as WD 42 and named "Overlord" in October 1992. The renumbered WD 823/5 were subsequently sold out of service.

Surprisingly, eight of these locomotives were still in military service in 1991, albeit renumbered yet again. As just stated, WD 823/59 which became WD 202 was restored as WD 42 and named "Overlord". This locomotive was intended for the Army Transport Museum at Beverley but was still at Burton Dassett WD Depot, now known as CAD Kineton, in 1992/3. WD 70043 (AB 358/41) had become Army 200 and was awaiting disposal as RNAD Dean Hill, WD 72222 (DC 2177/45) had become Army 249 allocated to Hessay, WD 72225 (DC 2180/45) had become Army 226 and was still operational at Inchterf, WD 72229 (DC 2184/45) had become Army 230 at Long Marston WD Depot but was destined for the Royal Engineers Museum at Chatham, WD 72237 (AB 370/45) had become Army 234 and was allocated to RNAD Dean Hill, WD 72238 (AB 371/45) had become Army 235 which was also at Long Marston but destined for the RE Museum at Chatham, and WD 72239 (AB 372/45) had become Army 236 located at RNAD Trecwyn.

Chapter 19

Ex-LNE Class J69 0–6–0Ts, WD 78–91

In October 1939, the WD took over thirteen LNE J69 0–6–0Ts and one J68 (7041) of almost identical dimensions. LNE (pre-1946 numbering) 7274, 7272, 7081, 7197, 7168 and 7058 went to the Melbourne Military Railway; and 7388, 7041, 7054, 7056, 7344, 7362, 7088 and 7271 went to Longmoor. LNE 7271 was returned to the LNE in May 1940 and was replaced by 7167. In October 1940, they were written off the LNE books. In March 1942, 7041 (WD 85) was sent to Bicester Central Ordnance Depot.

In early 1942, they were given numbers 78–91 in the WD series, in the same order as given above, 7167 being interposed as WD 90. Details were as follows:

Plate 22 LNE J69 0–6–0T 7054 at Longmoor before being renumbered into the WD series (Photo: H. N. James)

Plate 23 LNE 0–6–0Ts WD 89 and 91 at Longmoor before being sent to Cairnryan (Photo: H. N. James)

Plate 24 WD ex LNE J69 class 0-6-0T 70091 (ex 7088) at Kinnerley on the Shropshire and Montgomeryshire Railway in February 1946 (Photo: R. Tourret)

After the war, they were sold to various private companies. At Faslane, WD 70086/7 were in poor condition but were sold to Metal Industries Ltd who had taken over the Port. WD 70078/9/83/5/90 were subsequently also bought by MIL but were little more than scrap. WD 70086/7/78/83/90 became MIL Nos 1 to 5 respectively, while WD 79 was sold on to George Wimpey. WD 85 was scrapped around 1952. MIL 5 (ex WD 70090) was later renumbered MIL 3 sometime after 1955 when MIL 3 original was scrapped. WD 80, 91 and 84 went to John Lysaght Ltd, Scunthorpe Nos 25–7; WD 81/2 went to British Industrial Solvents Ltd, Margam Nos 1 & 2; WD 88 went to Steel Breaking & Dismantling Co Ltd, Chesterfield and WD 89 was last seen at Cairnryan in July 1947. They were all scrapped between 1949 and 1962.

	0	1	2	3	4	5	6	7	8	9
7X	–	–	–	–	–	–	–	–	7274	7272
8X	7081	7197	7168	7058	7388	7041	7054	7056	7344	7362
9X	7167	7088	–	–	–	–	–	–	7362	–

In May 1942, there was a general move away from Melbourne and Longmoor, 13 out of the 14 engines being allocated to the two Military Ports in Scotland. WD 79, 80/3/6/7 and 90, followed by WD 85 from Bicester, went to Military Port No 1 (Faslane); and WD 78, 81/2/8/9 and 91 went to Military Port No 2 (Cairnryan). The remaining locomotive, WD 84, went to Long Marston. There were some reallocations later, for instance WD 78 went from Cairnryan to Faslane in exchange for WD 80, WD 91 went to Longtown by February 1943, while by 1945 WD 84 and 91 had reached the Shropshire & Montgomeryshire Railway.

Plate 25 Wimpey 75 (ex WD 79 and LNE 7272) (Photo: J. M. S. Roberts)

Chapter 20

Ex–GWR "DEAN GOODS" 0–6–0's, WD 93–200

The famous GWR 23XX "Dean Goods" standard goods locomotives were amongst the first engines to be transferred to the WD, a total of 108 out of the then 180 survivors being taken over. These were GWR 2392/3/9, 2400/2–5/10/ 2/3/5/6/8/9/22/3/5/7–30/2–43/6/7, 2451/4–7/9/61/3/5–7/9–73/5–81/5–90, 2511/2/4/7–22/4/6–9/31/3/6/9/40/4–50/2/ 3/5/7–62/5–7/71/4/6/7/80. It is interesting to note that 32 of these engines had gone overseas for the military authorities in the 1914–18 war. Of these engines, twenty-four (WD 101/4/11/6/33/6/9/40/2/ 4/6–8/51/61/3/5–7/82/4/6/92/4) went abroad again in the 1939–45 war, whereas eight (WD 95/8/9, 177/8/80/95/6) stayed in the UK.

WD 101–200 were handed over to the WD in late 1939 and early 1940, although officially shown as sold to the WD in October 1940. The official date is evidently merely the date at which they were finally written off from GWR stock. Similarly, WD 93–100 were handed over to the WD in October 1940, although the official date is December 1940.

Before being put into use by the WD, they were passed through works. They were all dealt with by Swindon, except

Plate 26 Dean 0–6–0 WD 101 (ex GWR 2533), the first Dean 0–6–0 to be taken over by the WD. (Photo: R. Tourret Collection)

fourteen of them (WD 181–94) which were handled by Eastleigh. The ATC equipment was removed, Westinghouse brake gear fitted, a direct-acting steam-brake valve fitted in place of the original valve worked from the vacuum ejector, and other minor alterations carried out. Ten of the engines, WD 177–80/95–200, were equipped with condensing gear and pannier tanks, carried on each side of the boiler, into which exhaust steam could be directed. Two reservoirs were placed at the left-hand side of the smokebox and the Westinghouse pump was placed on the right-hand side. They were painted dull black with pale yellow Gill Sans lettering.

For the record, the GWR numbers of WD 93–200 are given below:

WD	0	1	2	3	4	5	6	7	8	9
9X	–	–	–	2433	2399	2470	2425	2442	2415	2528
10X	2521	2533	2439	2486	2518	2539	2419	2512	2436	2585
11X	2561	2480	2524	2393	2456	2547	2567	2427	2490	2418
12X	2441	2471	2412	2544	2562	2481	2400	2455	2447	2560
13X	2553	2429	2526	2454	2432	2416	2577	2413	2546	2571
14X	2520	2443	2489	2477	2519	2423	2522	2566	2457	2555
15X	2527	2557	2405	2550	2459	2428	2529	2475	2467	2487
16X	2438	2469	2465	2476	2434	2549	2574	2463	2548	2479
17X	2536	2545	2478	2485	2451	2511	2558	2430	2446	2466
18X	2514	2402	2403	2410	2461	2440	2580	2392	2435	2472
19X	2404	2437	2473	2422	2488	2531	2576	2540	2559	2517
20X	2552	–	–	–	–	–	–	–	–	–

A total of 79 locomotives, WD 101–55/7–66/81–94, were shipped to France from October 1939 to April 1940, probably all of them via Harwich. The dates of shipment were as follows:

October 1939	WD 101–8
November 1939	WD 109–18/81–4
January 1940	WD 119–26
February 1940	WD 127–35
March 1940	WD 136–48/53–5/7–60/85–94
April 1940	WD 161–6 and probably 149–52

Two engines, painted green and named "Troy" and "Casabianca" in white lettering, were observed being landed at Brest in October 1939. The identities could not be noted at the time because they had been obliterated for security, but WD 108 came back to the UK carrying the name "Casabianca" and this locomotive was shipped in October 1939 as noted above.

The locomotives shipped to France were shortly either destroyed in the retreat or captured. Little is known of their wartime activities but many went into service on the SNCF. Some may have been dismantled to provide spares. Those that stayed on the former Chemin de Fer du Nord retained their WD numbers. These 21 engines were WD 115/9–26/8–31/53/4/8/61/3/4/6/82. The 35 locomotives that went to the former Etat, WD 101–5/8–10/2–4/6/27/34/6–40/3/4/7/50–5/9/62/81/3/4/7/9/90/2/3, were renumbered in accordance with SNCF standard practice. The SNCF style was at first "030-0XX" and then later "030W0XX". Sometimes the "0" before the actual number was omitted like "030WXX". The numbers were usually painted on, although plates were occasionally fitted. The LMS 0–6–0Ts were grouped in the same series, although a "T" was inserted to give "030TW0XX". The "Deans" on the Nord may have been treated differently owing to being under a different German command.

Some observations made after the Allies liberated France may indicate some of the work carried out by these locomotives during the war, as follows. WD 102 was at Batignolles depot, Paris, in August 1945. WD 115/20/4/5/58/64 were used for carriage and other shunting duties at Lille Fives depot in June 1946. WD 112/4/83/4 were at Brest out of use in December 1947.

Many tenders became interchanged during the course of the war, particularly on the SNCF. Those known are as follows:

Engine	Tender
104	134
105	190
115	130
116	136
136	143
140	152
149	186?
158	125
164	120
190	114

The official SNCF position at 29 December 1947 was as follows. Of the 35 locomotives that had been on the former Etat system, only three SNCF 030W018/31/45 (WD 190 & 104/10 respectively) remained in service, twelve had been sent to China (WD 102/3/13/34/9/43/7/51/9/62/81/7) and the other 20 had not been in service for a long time. Of the 21 that had been on the former Nord system, WD 115/26/30/64 were allocated to Lille Fives depot, ten had been sent to China (WD 119–21/4/5/9/53/4/8/61), WD 123/8/31/63 were war damaged, WD 166 was damaged and without its boiler and WD 122/82 had been scrapped in Belgium. Thus, 22 of the

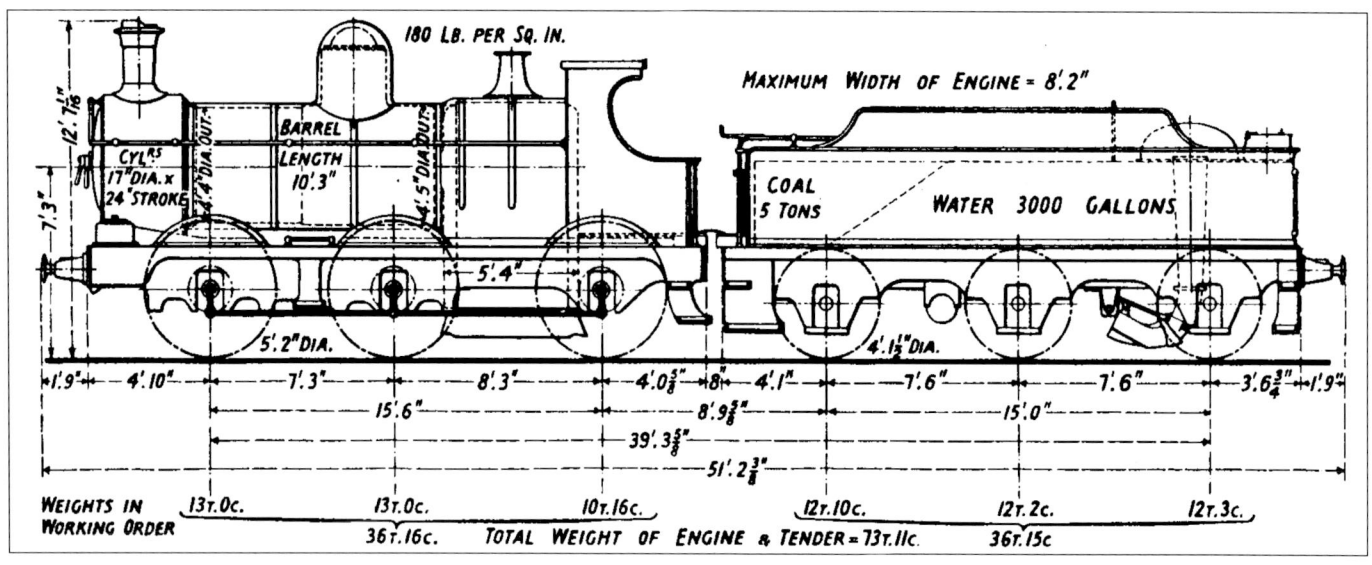

Fig 4 GWR "Dean Goods" 0–6–0 (Courtesy Railway Gazette)

For the record, the SBCF numbers are listed below in order:

SNCF	0	1	2	3	4	5	6	7	8	9
030W00X	–	114	127	134	136	139	149	143	144	147
030W01X	150	151	152	159	162	181	187	189	190	192
030W02X	138	–	–	–	–	–	(12)	(14)	101	102
030W03X	103	104	105	108	109	112	113	116	137	183
030W04X	184	193	(9)	(10)	(11)	110	–	–	–	–

56 locomotives were sold to China. The remainder, except WD 122/66/82, were returned to the UK and scrapped.

A total of 29 Dean Goods remained in WD service in Britain, WD 93–100/56/67–80/95–200. WD 156, in the middle of one of the batches which went to France, was sent to Longmoor for instructional purposes and thus avoided capture. It had reached Longmoor by April 1940,

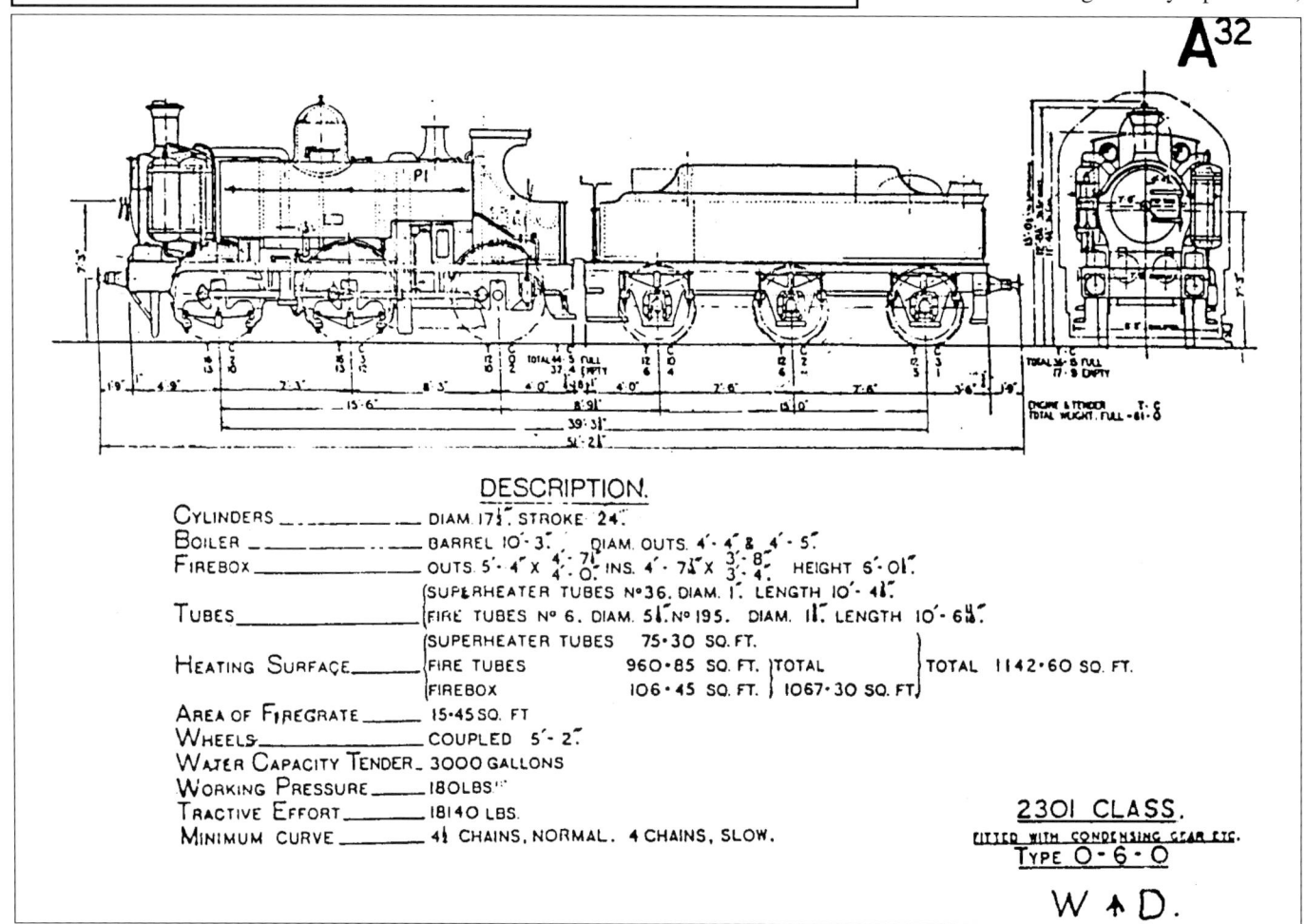

Fig 5 GWR "Dean Goods" 0–6–0, as fitted with pannier tanks and condensing gear

Plate 27 Dean 0–6–0 WD 156 official photograph. Fitted with Westinghouse brake (Photo: British Rail)

but was back at Swindon by July 1940, before returning to Longmoor.

With no immediate military use for all of them, many Dean 0-6-0s were temporarily returned to the GWR, their old GWR numbers being painted on the cab side. WD 167–76 were officially returned, but WD 93–100/56/77/8/96/7/9 were also observed carrying GWR numbers in the Summer and Autumn of 1940.

To defend Britain against a possible German invasion, many rail-mounted artillery guns and howitzers from World War One were brought out of store and deployed in the south, from March to October 1940. The Dean 0-6-0s were used for these guns, except for the units in the Dover area (see Chapter 43). With the deployment of these rail guns, by September 1940 all the Dean 0-6-0s had returned to the WD.

The 4th Super Heavy Battery (SHB) was formed at Felixstowe in March 1940 and was equipped with two 9.2 inch railway guns built in 1918, later named "S. M. Cleeve" and "E. E. Gee" after two senior officers at the School of Heavy Artillery at Catterick. Also in March 1940, the 5th SHB was formed at Dover and took over two 12 inch howitzer rail guns, later named "Sheba" and "Cleo". These guns were originally intended for France, but in July 1940 the 4th SHB moved to Kirton near Boston and the 5th SHB to Stallingborough near Grimsby. With the fall of France changing the likely direction of attack, in September 1940 4th SHB moved to Kent, "S. M. Cleeve" to Hythe and "E. E. Gee" to Folkestone West Junction sidings. The howitzers of 5th SHB went to the East Kent Light Railway, "Sheba" at Eythorne and "Cleo" at Shepherdswell. It is hardly necessary to say that some work was necessary to the track on the EKR before the guns arrived!

The 7th SHB brought two 12 inch howitzers to Elham Station on the EVMR. The 8th SHB brought two more 12 inch howitzers to Eythorne in October 1940, "Sheba" joining "Cleo" at Shepherdswell. Also in October 1940, the 12th SHB deployed 12 inch howitzers at Staple Halt and Ash, Poulton Farm, on the EKR. The 13th SHB brought one 12 inch howitzer to a siding near Ruckinge, Holly Bush Farm, on the Ashford to Hastings line, and another to Sellinge, Grove Bridge, on the Ashford to Folkestone line. The Royal Canadian Artillery had two 9.2 inch guns at Calves Wood at Kingsnorth on the Ashford to Hastings line, soon moved to Ruckinge Golden Wood, as well as single 9.2 inch guns at Grove Ferry and Canterbury West station.

These guns were moved occasionally. By March 1941, the 4th SHB had moved their 9.2 inch guns to Rolvenden station and Wittersham Crossing on the Kent and East Sussex Light Railway, 5th SHB's 12 inch howitzers were still at Shepherdswell, 7th SHB's two 12 inch howitzers had moved to Elham on the EVMR, 8th SHB's two 12 inch howitzers remained at Eythorne, 12th SHB had moved both of its 12 inch howitzers to Poulton Farm, 13th SHB's 12 inch howitzers remained at Ruckinge and Sellinge, the Canadian personnel had moved on but

Plate 28 WD 179 at Canterbury East in September 1940. The engine is fitted with pannier tanks, with two Westinghouse reservoirs placed in front of the pannier tank (Photo: A. G. Wells)

15th SHB had taken over the two 9.2 inch guns at Ruckinge Golden Wood, 16th SHB had installed two 9.2 inch guns at Adisham station and 17th SHB had installed one 9.2 inch gun at Kingsnorth Calves Wood and another at Sevington Spur. Most of these guns remained in these locations until December 1943, although 13th SHB moved its 12 inch howitzers to Lyminge Spur and Midley Crossing.

These guns were mounted on well wagons modified to have a platform which folded down with steadying feet on the ground, so that the gun could fire in any direction relative to the railway track, for example see the photograph of the GWR C22 Crocodile G wagon on page 25 of "A History of GWR Goods Wagons". When firing, the platforms were also lashed down to the ground.

In the event, these 9.2 inch guns and 12 inch howitzers remained concealed in their sidings and, with one exception, only fired a very few practice rounds for calibration. The exception was "E. E. Gee" which fired one shot at German E-boats on 18 October 1940, and jumped sideways off the rails due to the holding-down arrangements not proving adequate!

Virtually all of the 29 Dean Goods 0–6–0s WD 93–9, 100/56/67–80/95–9 and 200, served these rail-mounted guns. They stood by in steam most of the time, but occasionally did some shunting and at rare intervals took their trains and guns about the country. The allocation in the middle of 1940 was as follows: WD 169–72/9/80/95–7 in Kent, WD 173–6 in Essex and WD 198/9 in Lincolnshire. At the end of 1940, they were joined by the extra engines from the GWR as follows: WD 94/5 and 100 in Kent, and WD 93/6–9 in Essex.

In the autumn and winter of 1940/1, the engines in Kent were WD 94/5/8/9, 100/56/67–72/9/80/95–7, WD 156 from Longmoor having turned up in Kent in November 1940. The others were mostly attached to batteries elsewhere in Eastern England. WD 175/6 were on the Felixstowe branch in January 1941. WD 173/4 appeared in Kent in 1941 on transfer from Essex. In later years, WD 93, 175–8/98/9 and 200 came to Kent. Thus, all but two (WD 96/7) are known to have served with the railway batteries in Kent at one time or another. While on SHB duty in Kent and East Sussex, the Dean Goods were serviced at Ashford and Faversham.

While in Kent, names were put on four engines, WD 169 "Gert", 171 "Betty", 172 "Wavell" and 197 "Daisy". WD 170/1 were on the East Kent Railway in

Plate 29   Dean 0–6–0 WD 167 alongside the briquette stock at Algiers (Agha) shed in 1943. The name "Margaret" is just visible painted on the middle wheel splasher in the original print (Photo: R. Tourret Collection)

Plate 30   WD 70198, fitted with pannier tanks, at Longmoor in November 1945. The Westinghouse pump is fitted in front of the pannier tank (Photo: R. Tourret)

Plate 31   WD ex GWR Dean Goods 0–6–0 70099 at Kinnerley on the Shropshire and Montgomeryshire Railway in February 1946 (Photo: R. Tourret)

Plate 32   WD 70200 Dean Goods 0–6–0 at Stonor in June 1946, showing tender and footplate fittings
(Photo: A. G. Wells)

November 1940, while WD 93/5 and 177/97 were recorded at Eythorne in 1944. Engines were noted on the Kent & East Sussex Railway by 1941, including WD 197 in August 1943. In 1943, WD 95 and 175/80/99 were shedded at Canterbury West, serving the guns stationed at Bishopsbourne on the Elham Valley line. WD 180 was still there in November 1944. Engines were also to be found at Appledore and Hythe, and on the Eridge to Polegate Junction line.

Two of the engines at Canterbury by a combination of military spit-and-polish and natural engineman's pride were kept in a beautiful condition in 1941. Paint was carefully scraped off all the brass work that could be found, the coupling rods were touched up in scarlet, and a daily clean made everything glitter in the sun. Alas, the glitter attracted the attention of higher authority, who held that it could attract the enemy, and so a dull coat of camouflage paint had to be spread over everything.

By July 1942, some of the non-condensing engines had reverted from Westinghouse to vacuum brake for working ordinary British rolling stock. These included WD 100/67–72/4.

In October 1942, an empty forces coaching stock train was machine-gunned on the Elham Valley Railway between Bishopsbourne and Barham. The fireman died and the locomotive 171 was damaged. In November 1942, the tender of 167 was damaged slightly by enemy action at Elham. In December 1942, engine 168 was machine-gunned at Staple on the EKR, fortunately without casualties or damage. As the risk of invasion decreased, the engines were gradually drafted to other duties at various military establishments. The advent of D-Day allowed the rest to be

Plate 33   WD 123 at Bethune in June 1946, having suffered from the attentions of the RAF (Photo: R. J. Tredwell)

Plate 34 WD 128 at Bethune in June 1946 (Photo: R. J. Tredwell)

collided at Bicester on 30 December 1944 due to a wrongly set point and were sent to Swindon for heavy repair on 24 February 1945. They returned to Bicester on 27 April and 8 May 1945 respectively.

Some locomotives in the UK were given names temporarily from time to time, as follows:

WD 94	"Monty"
WD 108	"Casabianca"
WD 156	"Flying Fortress"
WD 169	"Gert"
WD 173	"Alexander"
WD 178	"Fagan"
WD 197	"Daisy"
WD 200	"City of Birmingham"

The names "Flying Fortress" and "Alexander" were unusually placed, being painted on the top half of the smokebox door, in a curved manner to follow the periphery, while at Bicester.

At the end of the war, all except WD 70195 (the re-railing practice locomotive at Longmoor) were quickly disposed of, most being scrapped during 1946–8.

Six of the class, WD 100/67/8/71/2/4, were sent from No 1 Military Port Faslane to Algiers in North Africa in February 1943. They were used as shunting engines and also ran trips from Algiers to the marshalling yard at Maison Carrée. They were named in white letters on the centre splasher, "Virginia", "Margaret", "Rosemary", "Voiara", "Wavell" and "Jean Ann", although these names did not survive after the engines had passed through shops in Africa.

By the end of March 1943, two were sent on loan to the American forces, WD 172 to Phillipville and WD 174 to Ouled Rahmoun. They did not stay long but went further on to the British at Bône. The

released, several going to Longmoor to replace standard WD locomotives being shipped to Europe.

WD 93 went to Cairnryan in November 1941, then Old Dalby in 1942, Melbourne and the SMR in 1943 and the EKR and back to the SMR in 1944. WD 94 went to Faslane by April 1941, then to Cairnryan in 1941, Bicester Central Ordnance Depot in August 1942 and the SMR in December 1946. WD 95 went to Cairnryan in 1941, then Kent in 1943, Bicester in 1943, EKR and Longmoor, then Bicester in 1944, and SMR in 1946. WD 96 went to Longmoor in 1940, SMR in 1941, Longmoor in 1945 and back to the SMR in 1945. WD 97 went to the SMR in 1941. WD 98 went to the SMR in May 1942. WD 99 went to Burton Dassett WD Depot in January 1943, then Melbourne in July 1943 and SMR in 1944. WD 156 went to Bicester in December 1941.

WD 169 went to Burton Dassett in July 1942, Long Marston WD Depot in September 1943 and SMR in 1944. WD 170 went to Burton Dassett in October 1942, SMR in March 1944 and Cairnryan in 1945. WD 173 went to Bicester in April 1942. WD 175 went to the SMR in 1942. WD 176 went to the SMR in 1942, and after an accident in October 1943 was scrapped in January 1944. WD 177 was at Longmoor in 1940, Cairnryan in 1941, then to Kent and back to Longmoor in 1945. WD 178 was at Melbourne in 1940, Cairnryan in 1941, Burton Dassett in August 1942, then to Kent, Longmoor in April 1944, Bicester in November 1945 and back to Longmoor in July 1946. WD 179 went to Longmoor in April 1944. WD 180 went to the SMR in 1946.

WD 195 went to Longmoor in 1945 and was subsequently used for re-railing practice. WD 196/7 went to the SMR in 1946. WD 198 went to Longmoor in 1945. WD 199 went to Longmoor in May 1944, then Cairnryan in 1946. WD 200 went to Longmoor in 1940, SMR in 1941, then to Kent for 1942/3 and was stored at Richborough WD dump ca. 1946/7, then at Ramsgate April to August 1947.

WD 156 received heavy repairs at Swindon in March 1943. WD 70094/5

Plate 35 WD 188 (ex GWR 2435) was captured by the German Armed Forces when the British Forces retreated from Dunkerque. Under the handrail on the cab side, the inscription "German Armed Forces OKH" can be seen on the original print. After a general repair in Cottbus, it went with German troops to Austria where it fell into disuse. It was captured by the Russian Forces and was given Soviet markings. It was photographed at Wien Huttldorf shed in 1948. (Photo: F. Kraus)

Plate 36 Dean 0-6-0 WD 157 at Dover in June 1949, having gathered a more sheltered cab (Photo: A. G. Wells)

remaining four were sent east into Tunisia in June 1943 and went on banking duties at Medjez-el-Bab and on the Mastouta to Mateur line. WD 168 went to Bône in November 1943 and was joined by the other three in January 1944 after they had spent a period working from Mateur to Bizerta and Ferryville.

In March 1944, the six engines were shipped from Bône to Taranto, being the first WD engines to be landed in Italy. They were sent to Bari for work on the harbour branch, and shortly afterwards to Barletta, again for use on the harbour branch and other local duties. At the end of August 1944, the six engines were sent north to Falconara where a wagon repair shop was in use as an engine shed. As the railhead was pushed forward, WD 171/2 went with it, first to Pesaro in the beginning of October 1944, and then into Rimini a week or two later. In March 1945, they were joined by WD 100. Work was hard and the condition of the engines deteriorated.

However, by July 1945, all had been overhauled at Foligno and repainted in the FS livery of unlined black with red-brown wheels and frames. From mid-1945, the six engines were manned by Italian crews and at least one was fitted with an extended cab roof and supporting pillars. In July 1946, the FS took them over and they were allocated FS numbers 293.001-6. Shortly afterwards, the engines were laid aside. In March 1947, three were stored at Rimini and three at the reopened shed at Ancona. All were officially withdrawn in 1953.

Some of the locomotives that went to France, other than those which served on the SNCF as already discussed, probably served initially in Belgium and Holland. For example, WD 106 was seen at Bruxelles Sud in 1942. A GWR Dean Goods was said to have hauled a works train in Holland on an exercise for the German Army to see how easily Russian 1524mm (5'0") gauge track could be converted to 1435mm (4'8½"). Others were found after the war. WD 111/57/91 were noted at Minden in 1945. WD 160/88 were used by the German forces on the Eastern Front. WD 188 was captured by the Russians and worked for a few years in the Soviet Zone of Austria, ending her days as scrap iron in an Austrian steel works. WD 149 was noted stored at Roosendaal in Holland in June 1946 and presumably had been working in Holland for the German forces since its WD number had been reapplied in Deutsche Reichsbahn style numerals. It had been fitted out to supply steam heating. Sometime during 1948/9, it moved to Tilburg Works and by the end of 1949 it had been scrapped.

Some of the locomotives that went to France, both those serving on the SNCF and others, had the cab roof extended, with vertical support rails. This was presumably both for greater comfort and to reduce the light from the firebox doors which might attract the attention of Allied aeroplanes! So far as is known, the following engines were so treated; WD 101/2/4/5/10/3/5/6/20/5/7/8/30/1/5-7/49/57/8/60/4/88/90.

Some of the engines in better condition of those rescued in France were sent to China under UNRRA auspices. There were 22 of these locomotives, WD 102/3/13/9-21/4/5/9/34/9/43/7/51/3/4/8/9/61/2/81/7. Officially, all these locomotives were regarded as having been sent to China in 1946 but only those from SNCF Regions 1 (Est) and 3 (Etat) actually went that year; the engines on SNCF Region 2 (Nord) not leaving until the following year, being shipped from Antwerp about Christmas time. The ex-Nord engines were WD 119-21/4/5/9/53/4/8/61, ten in

Plate 37 WD 70195 Dean 0-6-0 during a re-railing demonstration at Longmoor in September 1949 (Photo: B. M. Barber)

all; the others were ex-Est and Etat. In late 1945, three engines at Longmoor, WD 177/9/98, had their pannier tanks removed and in late 1947 these engines together with WD 178 were sent abroad from Birkenhead Docks, it is believed to China.

The Dean Goods 0-6-0s were allocated class XK3 in China, with two groups of numbers, 61-5 and 66-90. This information does not altogether match with the disposal information from

Plate 38 Another view of WD 188, this time on Breitenlee dump in Austria in 1951. The British did not want to repatriate this locomotive, so the Soviet HQ sent it to a blast furnace at Enzesfeld an der Triesting, south-west of Wien (Photo: Othmar Bamer)

Europe, and there is no apparent reason for the split into two groups. One possible explanation is that 61–5 were some other class of small 0-6-0s, and only 66–90 were ex-WD locomotives. This would make a total of 25 engines, whereas so far as is known, 26 were actually sent to China. Possibly one engine was regarded as a source of spare parts, and so did not enter service as such? Unfortunately, no information is available on either their work or withdrawal dates in China, but in view of their small size, it is probable that they were used in industry and not on the main line.

Most of the remaining engines in Europe were in bad condition, some having been damaged by aircraft cannon fire for instance. Many were returned to Britain in late 1948 and early 1949 via Dover for scrap, a few on the spot at Dover when not fit to travel any further, but mostly at various private scrap yards. These were WD 101/4/5/8–11/4–6/23/6–8/30/1/5–7/40/52/7/63/4/83/4/9–92. Those remaining on the Continent had mostly been scrapped but WD 106/32 are known to have passed to Eastern Europe. After the war, all the engines remaining in Britain were scrapped except for WD 195 which lingered on at Longmoor until 1959 in derelict state used for re-railing practice.

The only "Dean Goods" in preservation is GWR 2516 at the Great Western Railway Museum in Swindon town, but this engine was never in WD service.

Chapter 21

STANIER LMS CLASS 8F 2-8-0s, WD 300–449, 500–24/40–623

In 1939, it was considered that many freight locomotives would be required for service in Europe. The Director of Transport Equipment for the War Department happened to be Mr R. A. Riddles, the LMS Vice-President, so it is perhaps not surprising that the Stanier 8F design was selected, but it was certainly the most modern design available and had a good track record. Indeed, for the first three years of World War II, the LMS 8F was adopted as standard for new construction by the WD.

Orders were placed by the Ministry of Supply for the WD in December 1939 for 240 of these engines, 100 each from the North British Locomotive Co (WD 300–99) and Beyer Peacock & Co (WD 400–99) and 40 from the Vulcan Foundry (WD 500–39). Some modifications were made to the LMS design as it stood then, partly to avoid using materials likely to be in short supply and partly to suit operation under conditions likely to be experienced in war. The 1in thick high tensile steel frames were changed to 1¹/₁₆ in mild steel. The connecting rods were shortened by 5in, with piston rods and slidebars lengthened to correspond, to make it easier to change piston rings. The manganese molybdenum steel coupling and connecting rods were changed to mild steel. Plain bearings were used instead of needle roller for the motion bushes. Silicon manganese steel springs were changed to carbon steel. Two live steam injectors were fitted, together with Westinghouse air brake (steam brake was retained for the engine and tender), wheels turned to a European profile and the water scoop was not fitted. Steam heating was fitted and side chains on the buffers.

The first engine, WD 300, appeared on 24 May 1940 from Hyde Park Works, Glasgow, in grey livery with large lettering in either white or yellow (reports vary). Within a week, Dunkirk had occurred and the need for large numbers of freight engines for Europe disappeared, so the orders were cut back. Details of the orders at this stage were as follows (see below).

None were shipped to France, where they would almost certainly have been lost in the retreat to Dunkirk. Vulcan had produced 20 boilers and these were passed over to the other two builders so that in the event, none were built by Vulcan.

WD 300–18 and some BP locomotives were completed to the full "European" specification. It was decided that these WD 8Fs should be loaned to the LMS. Non-standard fittings were removed at Crewe and the tyres turned as near as possible to the British ARLE "A" profile. The LMS combined vacuum/steam brake valve was substituted for the dual brake valve and the

Maker	Order No	No of Locos	Works No	WD Nos	Delivered	Notes
NBL	L932	100	24600–99	300–99	5/40–3/41	Reduced to 60
BP	1544	10	6980–9	400–9	7/40–10/40	—
BP	1545	15	6990–7004	410–24	10/40–4/41	—
BP	1546	25	7005–29	425–49	4/41–11/41	Reduced to 15
BP	1547	25	(7030–54)	(450–74)	—	Cancelled
BP	1548	25	(7055–79)	(475–99)	—	Cancelled
VF	2267	10	(4855–64?)	(500–9)	—	Cancelled
VF	2268	30	(4865–94?)	(510–39)	—	Cancelled

Plate 39 WD 300 Stanier 8F 2–8–0 official photograph in grey livery, the first Stanier 8F to be built for the WD. Note the air brake equipment, air reservoir on the running plate, and the side chains on the buffers (Photo: British Rail)

live steam injector on the right-hand side replaced by the standard Davis & Metcalfe exhaust steam injector. The locomotives were repainted in the LMS 1928 black goods livery with 12 in yellow letters shaded vermillion.

Further locomotives were built as LMS locomotives, although WD 319–24 were originally completed in WD livery. In all, 53 locomotives were loaned to the LMS. In this way, WD 300–37 became LMS 8226–63 and WD 400–14 became LMS 8286–8300 at the end of 1940. LMS 8251–5 (WD 325–9) spent a couple of weeks working from Feltham, but the SR did not like these engines and they were soon transferred away; the longer term disposition being LMS 8226/37–44/52/3/7/61/86–96 and 8300 being loaned to the GWR, the others remaining on the LMS. It may be mentioned here that LMS 8226–8325 were allotted to WD 300–59 and 400–49.

At the end of 1940, military demand increased again but this time for service in the Middle East. Locomotives from the manufacturers were taken from the production line, in preference to those in service on the LMS and GWR. WD 415, which had been sent to Crewe and ran trials as LMS 8301, was sent back to Beyer Peacock and never worked as 8301 on the LMS. Seven locomotives, which had been chosen for despatch to Egypt early in 1941, were returned to the LMS for a few months while awaiting shipping, and these operated in WD livery as WD 312/6/7/24/6/7 and 405.

In December 1940, further orders were placed for 62 locomotives from North British (WD 360–99 and 500–21) (increased by three as described below) and ten from Beyer Peacock (WD 440–9).

At this time, the available amount of shipping was the limiting factor regarding the number of locomotives that could be sent to the Middle East. Engines were taken direct from the manufacturers and, if enough shipping was available, those on loan to the LMS and GWR were recalled for shipment. The earliest engines went to Egypt, with some to Turkey, but by September 1941, Persia (as it was then) took priority for supplies to Russia.

Recall started in January 1941 and 19 had been taken back by March. Further recalls took place with ten in June and 20 in July. The last 12 were taken back in September. Thus WD 300–37 and 400–14 were taken back by the WD and sent to the MEF. The sole exception was WD 407 which as LMS 8293 was involved in an accident at Slough in July 1941 while at work on the GWR. When others of the batch were shipped it was still awaiting repair. It was returned to the LMS on loan in February 1942 and was taken back into LMS stock in July 1943.

Three locomotives were lost en route to Turkey. Accordingly, the North British order was increased by three (NBL 24730–2) to compensate. The three engines sent to Turkey were numbered WD 522–4 although in order of construction they should have been WD 362–4. To

Plate 40 WD 358 prepared for shipment to Turkey and carrying Turkish insignia. Note right hand drive. Air brake equipment was mounted on the left-hand side. Photographed at NBL Hyde Park Works in photographic grey in 1941 (Photo: Mitchell Library)

balance this, the last three were turned out as WD 362–4.

The number of engines available for the military being insufficient, fifty-one LMS locomotives (one extra to compensate for the loss of LMS 8293/WD 407 awaiting repair) were requisitioned in 1941. Those in shops were selected, and others were taken out of service and overhauled. Some had boiler changes. All were converted to oil firing, six at Swindon, four at Eastleigh, and the rest at Crewe Works. They were renumbered WD 572–622 as follows: 572–86 at Crewe, 587–9 at Swindon and 590/1 at Eastleigh all in September 1941; 592–601/7–11/6 at Crewe and 605/6 at Eastleigh in October 1941 and 602–4 at Swindon and 612–5/7–22 at Crewe in November 1941.The overhaul included fitting cowcatchers and air brakes. They were repainted plain black with very small WD numbers on the front buffer beam and on the tender sides. Renumbering details were as follows:

WD	0	1	2	3	4	5	6	7	8	9
57X	–	–	8041	8045	8019	8021	8015	8012	8013	8020
58X	8022	8030	8018	8025	8031	8032	8047	8023	8039	8091
59X	8014	8016	8028	8034	8038	8040	8042	8043	8044	8046
60X	8048	8052	8079	8024	8080	8086	8094	8051	8066	8072
61X	8049	8077	8058	8059	8061	8069	8078	8071	8085	8087
62X	8088	8093	8068	–	–	–	–	–	–	–

All the WD 572–622 series were despatched to Persia, being loaded at Birkenhead, Hull, Stobcross (Glasgow) and Swansea docks. One of the last shipments, on SS "Pembridge Hall", experienced a severe storm, soon after departure from Swansea. Four engines that were on board, WD 608/17/9/22, had to be cut loose and let go overboard. The ship managed to reach Glasgow, where the other eight engines, WD 602–4/15/6/8/20/1, and all 12 tenders, were unloaded. The eight engines were observed at Balornock shed in December 1941 and certainly bore evidence of their experience in the way of stoved-in cabs, etc. They were sent to St Rollox Works for repair. By the time they were ready again for shipment, locomotives were no longer being sent to Persia, so they were put back into LMS service. The four spare tenders were repaired and attached to WD 553–6.

Although WD 572–622 were taken out of LMS service in 1941, they were not officially withdrawn until later. WD 608/17/9/22 were deleted from LMS stock in June 1942. WD 611 was officially withdrawn in December 1943, to balance taking WD 407 into LMS stock as 8293, so that nominally only 50 locomotives were requisitioned as originally planned. It was intended to send 8293 as well when it was repaired and compensate the LMS with a locomotive at the end of the WD 540–71 series, but 8293 was retained and the latter series had to be extended by one and had to take the next number available, WD 623. The remainder of the series were officially withdrawn from LMS service in December 1944.

A further order L937 was placed on North British in August 1941 for 33 locomotives (WD 540–71 and 623). The LMS also ordered 50 engines under L938 (LMS 8176–8225). These two orders were delivered concurrently. After 11 WD engines had been completed (WD 540–50), the next two became LMS 8176/7, followed by WD 551, then LMS 8178/9 and so on until all 33 WD locomotives had been delivered, leaving six at the end for the LMS. Two other orders L940/3 were placed for 100 (WD800–99) and 50 locomotives respectively, but these were later converted to orders for WD Standard 2–8–0s.

Nos "496–9" appeared outside the North British Hyde Park Works in 1941 but since nothing further was heard of these engines, it was considered that they appeared as 496–9 in error and that they were renumbered WD 500–3.

A total of 208 of these engines was built by North British and Beyer Peacock, the WD numbers, maker and works numbers being as follows (see below).

In addition to new construction, as described, fifty-one older engines of the same design were taken over by the WD from the LMS stock, making a total of 259 of the class which were at one time or another in WD service. Many of the locomotives were either built for or converted to oil fuel. Orders were also placed by the Ministry of Supply for these engines for use on British railways and the GWR, LNE and SR all built engines of this class. However, since these did not enter WD service, they are not considered here.

For service on the LMS and GWR, the locomotives were, of course, modified back to British standards. Locomotives destined for Turkey were right-hand drive and had the compressor and reservoir on the left-hand side. Air brakes and oil burning were found desirable for Persia. At least WD 362–4/73–7/84–7/96–9, 437–49 and 500–21/40–8 were built as oil burners or converted at St Rollox or Crewe before despatch, while further sets of equipment were sent to Persia for local conversion. WD 387 was based at Crewe for a week of trial running as an oil burner in September 1941. WD 360–99, 430–49, 500–21/40–7 and 623 appear to have been built with both air and vacuum brakes. Electric headlights were fitted to the later deliveries to Persia. All the locomotives sent overseas were fitted with cowcatchers.

WD 421 was sent to the Longmoor Military Railway in February 1941 for instructional purposes, before being sent to the Middle East via Crewe in October 1941. While at Longmoor, it was named "Wolfe".

The supply of locomotives to Turkey, when such supplies were limited in Britain, may seem strange now but was made for political and strategic reasons. Nominally it was to partially fulfill pre-war orders that had not been met, but maintaining Turkish friendship was considered important.

Twenty-two of the engines (WD 338–59) were sent to Turkey in 1941 as follows. WD 343–51 left NBL in January 1941, 343–5 being loaded at Hull on to SS "Jessmore" and 346–51 at Liverpool on to

WD	Maker	Works Nos	Built
300–37	North British	24600–37	1940
338–59	North British	24538–59	1941
360/1	North British	24668/9	1941
362–4	North British	24730–2	1941
365–99	North British	24673–24707	1941
400–16	Beyer Peacock	6980–96	1940
417–39	Beyer Peacock	6997–7019	1941
440–9	Beyer Peacock	7034–43	1941
500–21	North British	24708–16/9/7/8/20–9	1941
522–4	North British	24670–2	1941
540/1	North British	24733/4	1941
542–50	North British	24735–43	1942
551–71	North British	24746/9/52/5/8/61/4/70/3/6/9/82/5/8/91/4/7, 24800/3/6	1942
623	North British	24809	1942

Plate 41 WD 387 Stanier 8F 2–8–0 official photograph. This was one of the first oil-burning 8Fs, completed by NBL in August 1941. It ran trials from Crewe to Shrewsbury and Wigan to test the oil-burning equipment in September 1941. Note the cow-catcher and the very small lettering used on the sides of the locomotive, but it carried a standard LMS smokebox numberplate. It was fitted with both air and vacuum brakes (Photo: British Rail)

SS "City of Manilla". WD 339–42/52/3/7–9 left NBL in March 1941, being loaded at Hull, 339–42/52/3 on to SS "City of Newcastle" and 357–9 on to SS "Aliphant". WD 338/54–6 left NBL in April 1941 and were loaded at Hull on to SS "Berhala". Seven (WD 338/43–5/54–6) were unfortunately lost en route. WD 343–5 were lost on the SS "Jessmore" when it collided with the SS "Baron Pentland" on 19 February 1941 in the Atlantic west of Ireland, and WD 338/54–6 were lost on the SS "Berhala" when it was torpedoed near Freetown on 23 May 1941. It was to make up for the loss of WD 343–5 that the North British order was increased by three in April 1941.

Five replacements were sent, WD 522–4/52/4. Actually, in view of the urgent need for immediate replacement the first available new engines, which would have been WD 362–4, were despatched under the numbers WD 522–4. The locomotives which would have carried the latter numbers then became WD 362–4 on delivery. WD 522–4 left NBL in June 1941, being loaded at Hull, 522 on to SS "Allioth" and 523/4 on to SS "Benalder". WD 552/4 were sent later, in 1943. The twenty Turkish engines became TCDD 45151–70.

All were supplied as coal burners, painted in plain black livery, with a star-and-crescent emblem on the tender and plates on the cab sides to indicate TCDD ownership. The WD number was on a small plate below the TCDD plate. They were used for local and shunting work. All twenty were still in service in 1975, but by 1986 most had gone.

The TCDD numbers are given below:

TCDD	0	1	2	3	4	5	6	7	8	9
4515X	–	524	523	357	358	359	346	351	350	349
4516X	348	522	347	339	342	353	341	352	340	552
4517X	554	–	–	–	–	–	–	–	–	–

TCDD 45160 was shipped back to the UK in 1989 and went to the Swanage Railway.

In the period January to April 1941, twenty-two LMS 2–8–0s were shipped to Egypt. Four (WD 304/22 and 428/9) were lost en route. Engines received in Egypt were given MEF numbers originally derived by adding 9000 to the WD numbers, so as to avoid any confusion with Egyptian State Railway (ESR) locomotives. By June 1941, the 18 engines that arrived safely (MEF 9302/9/10/5/9/23/5/7/9/33 and 9411/7–20/2/4/5) were used on the Alexandria to Mersa Matruh line, on hire to the ESR, bringing stores up to the WDER, and by Railway Operating Companies working the WDER. Two were usually allocated to El Hadra for working Western Desert line passenger trains, and MEF 9319 on a passenger train was shot up by enemy aircraft near Fuka on 8 July 1941.

Between August 1941 and February 1942, a further 24 LMS 2–8–0s arrived and were put into service. This made a total of 42 engines, WD 302/9/10/2/5–7/9/23–7/9/33/60/1/5–8/79–83 and 405/11/7–20/2/4–7/30–2/5/6. All the LMS 2–8–0s arrived as coal burners but were later converted to oil firing. Shortly after arrival in Egypt, two locomotives were involved in a collision. WD 316 was never repaired and WD 422 had to wait until summer 1944

Plate 42 WD 441 Beyer Peacock 8F 2–8–0 built in 1941 as an oil burner. Note the air reservoir for the Westinghouse brake. This engine was sent to Persia, and then to Italy (Photo: North Western Museum of Science & Industry)

Plate 43 WD 317 near Market Harborough on 7 June 1941, still in WD livery but on temporary loan to the LMS (Photo: A. G. Wells)

Plate 44 WD 555 on Motherwell shed in August 1942 (Photo: H. N. James)

Plate 45 Because of enemy air attack, several 8Fs on the Western Desert Extension Railway in Egypt were fitted with reinforced-concrete armour plating. Later, this was extended to cover the front of the tender, and the photograph shows an 8F with this extended armour (Photo: R. Tourret Collection)

before being repaired. To form a tidy continuous series MEF 9301–42, when the total reached 35, those from 9360 upwards (9360/1/5–8 and 9405/11/7–20/2/4/5/30–2/5/6) were renumbered into the blanks in the series 9301–35, the seven later engines (WD 426/7 and 379–83) becoming 9336–42. Full details are given later in this Chapter. By the end of 1941, sixteen locomotives were on the WDER (MEF 9302–5/7/8/11/2/7/23–5/7/35–7), and the rest on hire to ESR.

In January 1942, two 8Fs WD 366 (MEF 9305) and 436 (MEF 9335) were transferred from the WDER to Palestine. These were returned in May 1942. Also in May 1942, the ESR purchased seven (MEF 9314/5/9/20/8/30/1) and renumbered them ESR 850–6. In July 1942, five locomotives WD 317/61/81/2 and 427 (MEF 9317/03/40/1/37) were similarly transferred from the WDER to Palestine, being returned in October 1942. The 35 engines under WD control were all on the WDER at the end of 1942, except MEF 9316/21 (WD 316 and 422) both damaged and 9318 (WD 419). For protection against enemy air attack, seven engines had armour plating or concrete slabs fitted to cover the boiler and cab. The steel plates added 8 tons to the weight and the concrete slabs 11 tons.

For the build-up for the new offensive in late 1942, the Whitcomb diesels were preferred on the WDER because they needed much less water and because they did not show tell-tale smoke and steam. The LMS 2–8–0s were allocated to Gabbary and used for long-distance heavy freight and various military trains. Early in 1943, all 35 were hired to the ESR who purchased twenty in August 1943 (MEF 9301/4/8–11/3/22/5–7/9/32/3/6–40/2) and renumbered them ESR 857–76. Thirteen more (MEF 9302/3/5–7/12/7/8/23/4/34/5/41) were purchased in March 1944 to become ESR 877–89. This left the two damaged ones. MEF 9321, then WD 70422, was given the boiler off MEF 9316 and went to the ESR in April 1945 to become ESR 890, while WD 70316 was purchased in May 1946 as a source of spare parts. A complete list is given later in this Chapter. ESR 850/65 were specially overhauled in April 1945 for working the Cairo-Haifa express, and both had the legend "The Orient Express" painted in Arabic letters on the cabside above the number.

A total of 155 locomotives were sent to Iran, the first batch sailing in September 1941 and reaching Iran in the first week of December, and the last batch reaching Iran in March 1942. Twelve locomotives, WD 370/1, 415/6/33/4/44/5 and 608/17/9/22, were lost en route. The 143 locomotives that arrived in Iran were WD 300/1/3/5–8/11/3/4/8/20/1/8/30–2/4–7/62–4/9/72–8/84–99, 400–4/6/8–10/2–4/21/3/37–43/6–9, 500–21/40–8/72–99 and 600/1/5–7/9–14.

The first engines to arrive were transhipped at Basra in Iraq on to barges for the 60 mile trip up river to reach the railway jetty at Ahwaz, where it is said that the crane consumed so much electricity that the electrical supply to the whole town had to be cut off during unloading. Later, the locomotives were landed at Abadan and sent by rail to Ahwaz. At Ahwaz, the

Plate 46 A WD 8F being unloaded at Ahwaz in Persia by the Anglo-Iranian Oil Co's crane. This operation was said to use so much electricity that the supply to the town had to be cut off! (Photo: R. Tourret Collection)

engines were made ready for service. Components like coupling rods and connecting rods, which had been removed for shipment, were replaced. The 143 locomotives became IrSR 41.100–45/50–246, the Iranian numbers being allocated in the order that they were put into service, in two batches, the first coal-burners and the second oil-burners.

The first forty-six of these were coalburners, of which thirty-two were built by North British and fourteen by Beyer Peacock. The remaining ninety-seven were oilburners, forty-seven being built by North British, eleven by Beyer Peacock, while the other thirty-nine were ex-LMS locomotives. The coal burners were equipped with vacuum and steam brakes only and were therefore restricted to working in station yards or on the flat sections on the line in the Southern Division and between Bandar Shah and Polesafid. The vacuum brake gear from the last eight was removed before they went into service. The oilburners were all fitted with Westinghouse brake in addition to vacuum and steam brake.

Locomotives IrSR 41.100–27 were put into service from December 1941 to February 1942. The remaining coalburners were then left aside while the newly arrived oilburners were dealt with since the latter were more suitable for conditions on the IrSR. IrSR 41.150–246 were turned out between February and August 1942. IrSR 41.128–45 went into traffic, not exactly in order, between May and December 1942 in the intervals between batches of oilburners. By the end of 1942, six coalburners (IrSR 41.103/14/5/23/4/7) had been converted to oil-firing with various types of burner. IrSR 41.115 was fitted with Westinghouse brake at the same time. Twenty-three locomotives in the last batches were fitted with electric headlights when received, while headlights were fitted later to some of the earlier locomotives. IrSR 41.196 was fitted with a snifting valve behind the chimney in an effort to obviate burning the firebox ends of the superheater elements.

The IrSR numbers are given below:

In December 1942, the distribution was as follows: 36 at Tehran, 38 at Ahwaz, 20 at Arak, 17 at Andimeshk, 15 at Do-rood, eight at Bandar Shah, six at Polesafid (near Chirja near the Caspian Sea), two at Bandar Shahpur and one at Khorramshahr.

The overseas military needs for the 8F 2–8–0s were virtually satisfied by early 1942, leaving 33 locomotives in Britain consisting of WD 549–71 and 623, the eight engines from SS "Pembridge Hall" WD 602–4/15/6/8/20/1 and LMS 8293. The last engine was the only one not to have ever carried a WD number in service. It was put to work on the LMS in March 1942. WD 549–62 and 602–4/15/6/8/20 went to the LMS in May 1942, followed by WD 563–71 and 621/3 in the next four months. After about a year, most were taken out of service and many stored at Derby. In June and July 1943, the eight ex-LMS engines were de-requisitioned and returned to LMS ownership; 8293 finally became LMS stock as well. WD 552/4 were sent to Turkey during 1943. WD 566/7/9 and 623 had not been taken out of service and these were subsequently handed over to the LMS, together with the remainder.

In summary, in 1943, WD 549–51/3/55–71 and 623 were taken into LMS stock as 8264–85, conveniently filling the gap left in 1940 between the North British and Beyer Peacock locomotives when 20 engines were diverted to Turkey. Also, the requisitioned locomotives WD 602–4/15/6/8/20/1 were returned to the LMS and resumed their original numbers.

After a year or two, the arrival of the American 2–8–2s and the 1500hp diesels in Iran rendered many of the 8F 2–8–0s redundant. Therefore, in January 1944, thirty of the class were sent by sea to MEF Egypt. At the end of July 1944, twenty

IrSR	0	1	2	3	4	5	6	7	8	9
41.10X	337	305	413	412	408	330	306	331	320	307
41.11X	389	313	308	372	410	402	300	318	404	334
41.12X	314	301	403	421	328	336	409	400	369	311
41.13X	393	321	332	401	394	395	378	414	388	303
41.14X	423	406	335	392	390	391	–	–	–	–
41.15X	374	373	575	576	580	387	376	396	503	504
41.16X	502	587	585	582	375	377	441	384	579	578
41.17X	577	440	385	581	439	574	572	437	573	438
41.18X	442	443	594	600	583	589	508	588	587	505
41.19X	507	592	595	597	601	612	598	599	609	593
41.20X	614	516	515	513	512	613	607	596	611	610
41.21X	514	511	510	399	386	397	506	509	584	544
41.22X	545	546	547	548	543	398	500	446	501	591
41.23X	606	605	590	518	520	517	540	364	521	519
41.24X	447	449	448	363	362	542	541	–	–	–

more arrived by sea. These fifty locomotives were WD 305/8/31/4/6/7/69/74/5/ 88/9/91/3/7, 400/6/8/10/2/4/37/41/2, 508/ 13–6/9–21/41/2/6/8/72/4/9/83/5/6/9/94– 6/8 and 605/7/9/12. Of these fifty locomotives, thirty-five were overhauled at Suez and Jaffa. The other fifteen were withdrawn but put aside for attention later. They were meanwhile used a source of spare parts for the other engines. These engines were renumbered in a series starting at MEF 9350. This series had reached 9383 when the 7XXXX numbering scheme was introduced and from November 1944 all the engines remaining in WD service were renumbered by the addition of 70000 to the *original* WD numbers. This renumbering scheme included locomotives with MEF or IrSR numbers but not locomotives which had by that date been acquired by railways such as the ESR and the TCDD. Although the numbers for MEF 9377–83 were allocated, some of these were never actually carried but the engines were renumbered directly into the 7XXXX series.

Details of the earlier MEF 9301–42 and the later 9350–83 are given below:

Plate 47 WD 547 being unloaded at Ahwaz (Photo: R. Tourret Collection)

MEF	0	1	2	3	4	5	6	7	8	9
930X	–	360	302	361	365	366	367	368	405	309
931X	310	411	312	417	418	315	316	317	419	319
932X	420	422	424	323	324	325	326	327	425	329
933X	430	431	432	333	435	436	426	427	379	380
934X	381	382	383	–	–	–	–	–	–	–
935X	414	589	612	548	397	595	308	388	605	515
936X	305	369	441	520	521	412	410	391	514	572
937X	594	598	375	609	437	336	400	586	585	596
938X	334	408	541	374	–	–	–	–	–	–

Plate 48 IrSR 41.218 (ex WD 584) in Persia (Photo: R. Tourret Collection)

Of the overhauled engines from those returned in January 1944, WD 305/8/88, 414/41 and 589 were transferred to the Army in Palestine in February 1944, WD 410/2 in March 1944, WD 369/91 in April 1944 and 521 in July 1944. Some went to the PR, WD 397 in April 1944, 515 in May 1944, 605 in June 1944, 572 in July 1944 and 586 in March 1945. In January 1945, WD 336, 400 and 596 were sent to the HBT.

There were, of course, some exchanges from time to time. WD 305 went to the PR in April 1944. WD 308 went to the PR in April 1944, back to the Army in Palestine in May 1944, the HBT in February 1945, PR in March 1945, the Army in Palestine in April 1945 and to the PR in May 1945. WD 336 returned to the Army in Palestine in April 1945 and then the PR in June 1945. WD 369 went to the PR in July 1944. WD 388 went to the PR in April 1944, back to the Army in May 1944, HBT in February 1945 and back to the PR in March 1945. WD 391 went to the PR in March 1945. WD 400 went to the Army in Palestine in June 1945 and to the PR in July 1945. WD 410 went to the PR in June 1944, 412 in July 1944, 414 in April 1944 and 521 in August 1944. WD 441 went to Italy in November 1944. WD 589 went to the PR in June 1944, the Army in Palestine in July 1944 and to Italy in November 1944. WD 596 went to the Army in Palestine in April 1945 and to the PR in June 1945.

Of the overhauled engines from those returned in July 1944, WD 374 went to the PR in March 1945, 513 to the Army in Palestine in April 1945 and PR in June

Plate 49 IrSR 41.235 (ex WD 517) at Teheran in Persia (Photo: R. Tourret Collection)

1945, 541 to PR in March 1945 and 583 to the Army in Palestine in November 1945 (awaiting repairs in June 1946).

Summarising, WD 308/36/88, 400 and 596 worked on the HBT until transferred to the PR in 1945. Thus, twenty were on the PR by 1946, WD 305/8/36/69/74/88/91/7, 400/10/2/4, 513/5/21/41/72/86/96 and 605, of which early in 1946 WD 308/36/88/91/7 and 513/5/41/86/96 were allocated to Haifa and the remainder to Lydda.

The other fifteen overhauled engines, WD 334/75, 408/37/41, 514/20/48/85/9/94/5/8 and 609/12, were sent to Italy, thirteen in November and December 1944 and two more in April 1945, being unloaded at Taranto and working to the Army Workshops at Naples. Here, those that were not already oil-burners were converted to oil. WD 334 and 408 were converted at Rimini. The engines worked from Falconara (near Ancona) to Fabriano, Faenza and Rimini. After the war, all fifteen were taken over by the FS and renumbered FS 737.001–15 in order of their WD numbers. In 1950, all were moved to Bari shed in southern Italy and used on the Adriatic lines until 1956. After this date, they were rapidly withdrawn due to lack of spares.

Of the fifteen remaining MEF locomotives, four, WD 331/7/89 and 406, were scrapped in 1946 but the others, WD 393, 442, 508/16/9/42/6/74/9/83 and 607, were gradually overhauled even though WD 508/83 had to wait until 1952!

When the war ended, there were 93 8F 2-8-0 locomotives in Persia. It was decided to bring some back in an erected state but because shipping was short, an overland route through Iraq and Syria was used. The journey started with a barge trip across the River Euphrates to Basra in Iraq. In Iraq, part of the route was narrow gauge and wagons were specially built with four metre-gauge bogies close-coupled together to carry the locomotives without exceeding the maximum axleload of the line. The tenders were carried on ordinary bogie wagons which also acted as match trucks. At the end of the narrow-gauge section, near Baghdad, the engines were re-railed and went via Syria and Palestine to Jaffa and Suez. The first batch of four arrived in Baghdad in December 1945 and 71 engines travelled over the narrow-gauge line.

Twelve remained in Iraq and 59 went on to Egypt and Palestine, leaving 22 in Persia.

The 22 in Persia were WD 306/62/77/85, 409/23/39, 506/11/2/43/5/78/80/1/7/90/2/7 and 600/1/10 (506 being formerly 584). By May 1957, twelve were in service and ten awaiting spare parts before undergoing general repairs but they all appear to have been withdrawn by 1963. Six, IrSR 42.169/73/220/4/32/44, were derelict on a dump at Ahwaz in 1977.

Of the 59 locomotives that went to Egypt and Palestine in 1946, 48 went to Palestine, WD 301/7/11/3/4/8/20/1/8/32/5/63/72/6/8/84/6/7/90/2/4/5/8, 403/13/21/38/40/7/9, 501/3–5/7/10/8/44/73/5–7/88/91/9 and 606/11/13, while eleven carried on to Egypt, WD 300/73/96, 401/2/43/6, 582/4/93 and 614. The Egyptian engines went to the MEF Workshops at Suez, while the Palestine engines mostly went to the MEF Workshops at Jaffa or into store at Azzib and Sarafand.

IrSR 41.216 (506) and 41.218 (584) had exchanged identities, so that the "584" that returned was actually 506. IrSR 41.131 (321) and 41.135 (395) had also exchanged identities, although 41.135 reverted to 395

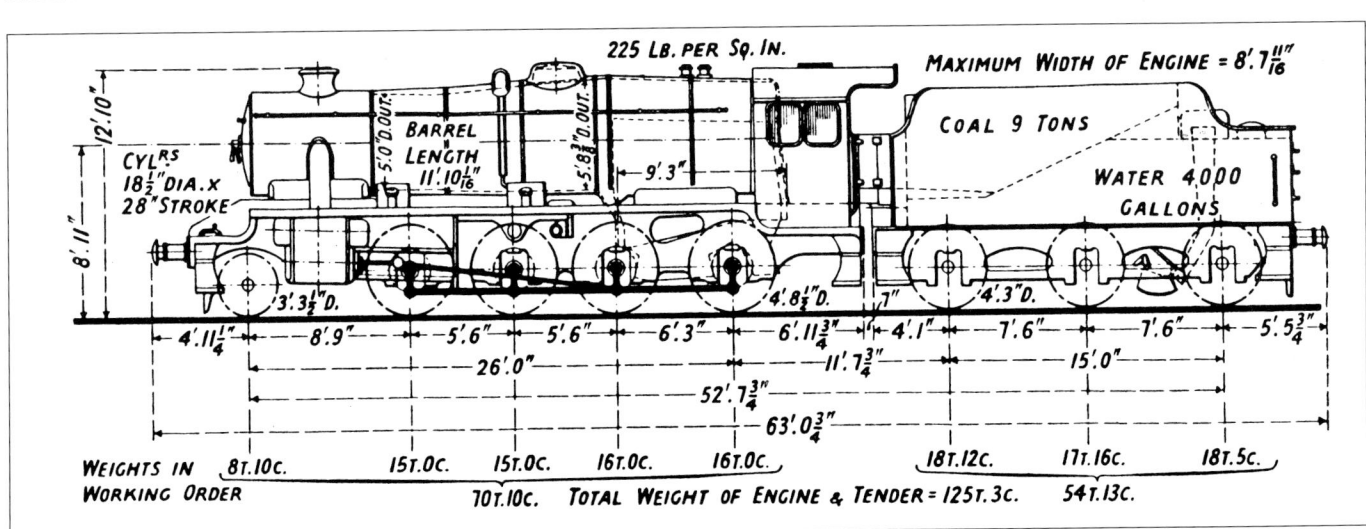

Fig 6 LMS Stanier Class 8F 2-8-0 (Courtesy Railway Gazette)

Plate 56   WD 70521 at Lydda shed on the PR in September 1945 (Photo: R. E. Tustin)

Railways, who renumbered them 48773–5. Both the Cairnryan locomotives were scrapped in 1959.

All the sixteen locomotives were renumbered in the post-war series as follows:

The ESR have stated that ESR 832–93 were withdrawn from service in 1963.

The final ownership of the 259 locomotives was as follows:

1952 WD	0	1	2	3	4	5	6	7	8	9
50X	307	320	607	387	392	393	395	501	508	516
51X	574	575	583	593	373*	613	–	–	–	–
* Ex 576										

WD 502 was given to a combination of the frames of 607 and the boiler that that engine had received off 373 which still carried smokebox numberplate 373. WD 574, the bomb damaged engine, was simply marked 510 on the cab side and was probably scrapped around 1954. By coincidence, 508 retained its original number. WD 373 was originally LMS 8015 which became 576 which exchanged numbers with 373 in Persia. In summer 1952, the frames of this engine were fitted with the boiler off 320 and the combination renumbered 514, out of sequence because "502" was taken.

The ten remaining locomotives in the Middle East were sold to the ESR in 1954 and became ESR 832–40/93. A complete list of the 62 ESR numbers is given below:

73	British Railways
20	Turkey
62	Egypt
15	Italy
23	Israel
22	Persia
12	Iraq
23	Lost
9	Not sold

It is pleasant to record that 48773, ex WD 307, survives on the Severn Valley Railway under its original number LMS 8233, after service on six railways in three continents!

Plate 57   WD 501 in the postwar series at Derby Works in April 1954 (Photo: R. Tourret)

ESR	0	1	2	3	4	5	6	7	8	9
83X	–	–	516	607	387	392	393	501	593	576
84X	613	390	313	328	386	396	505	507	519	542
85X	418	315	319	420	425	430	431	360	365	405
86X	309	310	411	417	424	325	326	327	329	432
87X	333	426	427	379	380	381	383	302	361	366
88X	367	368	312	317	419	323	324	435	436	382
89X	422	546	421	395	–	–	–	–	–	–

Plate 58   TCDD 45161 (ex WD 522) at Irmak in May 1972 (Photo: C. R. Miell)

Chapter 22

LOCOMOTIVES OF THE ITALIAN NORTH AFRICAN COLONIES, WD 70624–44

During the Italo-Turkish war of 1911/2, short narrow-gauge railways from Tripoli and Benghazi were built for military purposes. In 1913, the Italian State Railways assumed control, but turned the railways over to the Colonial Government in 1922. By the end of 1939, the combined route mileage was nearly 250 miles. Both lines were 0.95 metre gauge and all the engines (except 70639–42) were of standard Italian State Railway classes.

The Benghazi, Barce and Soluch Railway was based in Benghazi. One line ran to Barce (67 miles) and one to Soluch (35 miles), while there was also a harbour line at Benghazi (1 mile), giving a total route mileage of 103 miles. The Barce line possessed severe gradients up to 1:50 to 1:80, with an average of 1:100, but the Soluch line was comparatively level. The original plan had been to build the narrow-gauge railway from Tobruk via Benghazi to Tripoli. The German forces started to extend the Barce route to Tobruk but built only the track foundations, no tracks being laid.

The railway came under British control after the final occupation of Benghazi. It was operated by the British Military Administration but the operating personnel were mainly Arab. The line closed in September 1946 and was put on a care-and-maintenance basis, but it was reopened in March 1948. On 1 April 1949, the name was changed to the Cyrenaica Government Railway when the British Foreign Office took over the administration from the military. On 1 June 1949, the Government of Cyrenaica

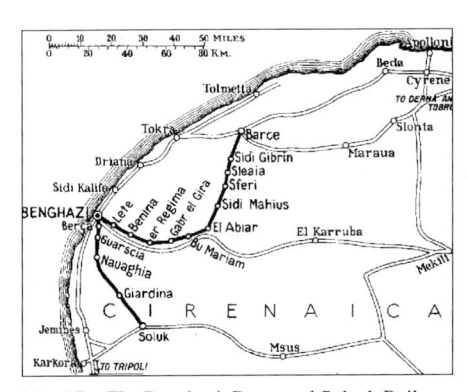

Map 17   The Benghazi, Barce and Soluch Railway (Courtesy Railway Magazine)

Plate 59   Tripolitanian Railway 2–6–0T trying to sort out the debris after the battle (Photo: R. Tourret Collection)

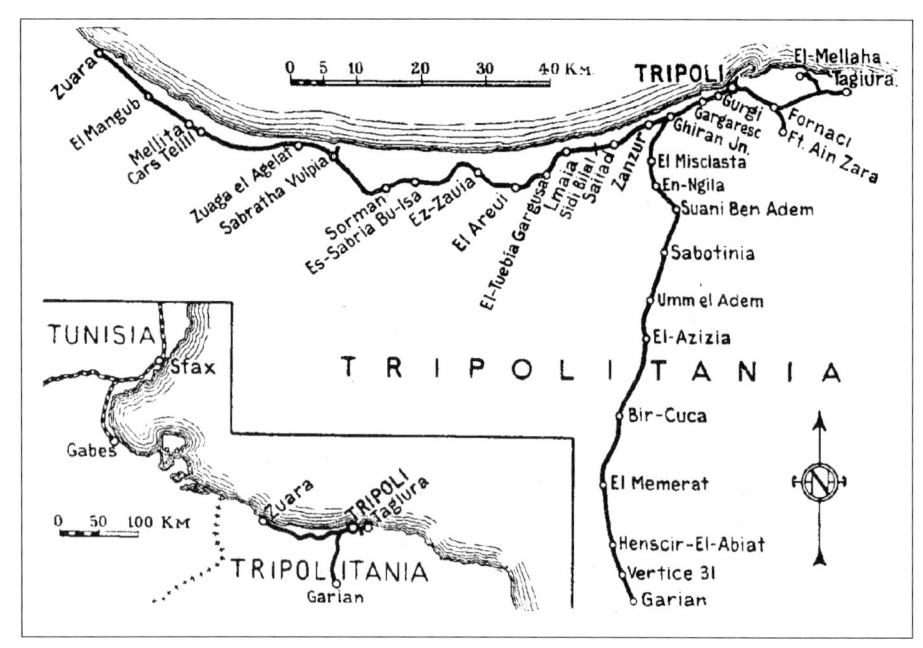

Map 18 The Tripolitanian Railway (Courtesy Railway Magazine)

Another line ran from Tripoli to Taguira (13 miles) with a purely military branch from Fornaci Junction to Ain Zara fort and another branch further along the main line to El Melbaha aerodrome. Another short branch served Tripoli docks. Tripoli had two stations, Centrale and Riccardo, the works being at the former. Gradients on the Zuara and Taguira lines had only negligible proportions, but the line to Garian had gradients up to 1:50 or more.

In January 1943, these lines came under British control. By mid-February, WD freight traffic was being worked to and from the docks and dispersal areas outside the city. Two steam locomotives were transferred from the BB & SR. Most of the Zuara branch was altered to metre gauge with a view to extending the line on metre gauge into Tunisia. Much of the Garian line was lifted to provide track, but in the event, the Mediterranean was fully opened and the work was suspended. By was set up, and in October 1949 the railway became the responsibility of the Public Works Department of the new government. Later, the new Libyan Government took over, but the line ceased operation in 1966.

During the wartime, the track consisted of 30ft flat-bottomed rail coach-screwed via bearing plates to wooden sleepers. Signalling was practically negligible; old fashioned disc signals had been used at approaches to stations but these had fallen into disuse and trains were telegraphed from station to station. Repairs were handled at the works at Benghazi, and about one locomotive per month was overhauled.

The BB & SR coaching stock used to consist of about ten wooden coaches, but only three of these survived into WD ownership. The diesel railcar, which used to operate the express Benghazi-Barce service, but from which the engine had been removed, was also used as a coach. There were about 240 wagons, all fitted with hand brakes in small compartments at the end of each wagon. These were mainly of two 10-ton types, open and covered, but there were also ten 2200gl petrol tankers.

After intensive military use, a passenger service was inaugurated which consisted of one train on five days of the week to Barce called to "Barce Belle", and two trains a week to Soluch called the "Soluch Bint". Freight wagons were attached to the passenger trains as required.

The Tripolitanian Railway was based on Tripoli and had one line along the coast to Zuara (73 miles) with a branch from Ghiran to Garian (52 miles) extended to Tegriana (2 miles) just before the war.

Plate 60 WD 70629 2–6–0T "Jessie Madden" in July 1948 (Photo: A. J. Knight)

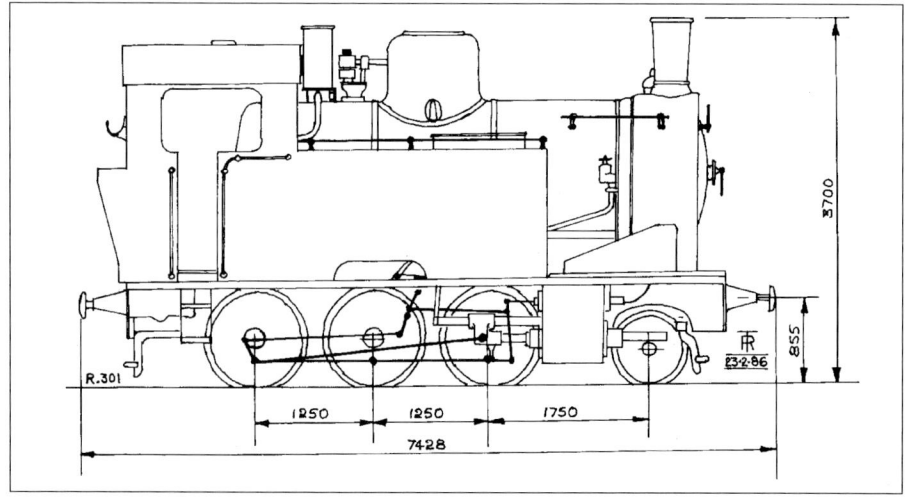

Fig 8 Class R301 2–6–0T as used in North Africa

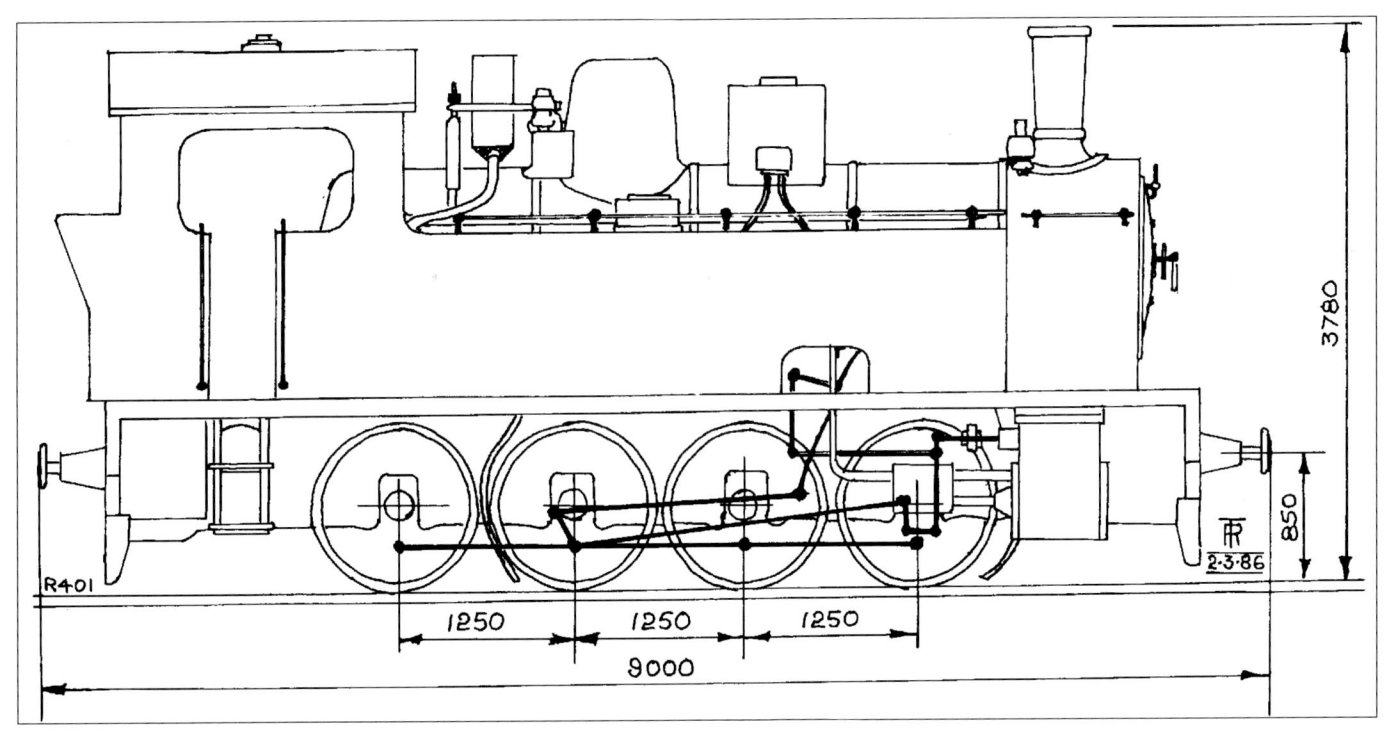

Fig 9 Class R401 0-8-0T as used on the Tripolitanian Railway

the end of 1943, the tracks were reconverted and relaid.

The line was reopened to the public on 1 June 1944 as the Tripoli Military Railway. It was operated by RE personnel under the Directorate of Transportation, MEF. Shortly afterwards, it became the Tripolitanian Railways. The end of the Garian branch was closed, making El Azizia the terminus. After a similar process of change of responsibility as the BB & SR, the Tripolitanian Railways became under the control of the Libyan Government. Trains ceased operating in 1962.

The British military authorities numbered all the usable engines on both railways into one series, WD 70624–44, and they may be conveniently considered together. The locomotives still carried Italian State Railway numbers although the Colonial railway administration had been broken off in 1929. The works numbers quoted are those allotted when the locomotives were built, but these often did not correspond with the works plates carried later, since exchanges were frequent. On some of these locomotives, the works plates were fixed to the combined dome-and-sandbox, which led to especially frequent exchanges. On both railways, a number of semi-derelict locomotives reposed about the works, and these were used as a source of spare parts.

WD 70624–9, the 2–6–0Ts, had two outside cylinders, 15in by 17½in for 70624–7 and 16in by 17½in for 70628/9, and 3ft 1¼in diameter driving wheels. The boiler pressure was 165psi for 70624–7 and 170psi for 70628/9. The water capacity was 992gl and the coal capacity 1½ tons. The length was 24ft 4in, width 8ft 6in and height 12ft 2in. The weight in working order was 35 tons. Walschaerts valve gear was fitted. WD 70624–7 had no superheaters and were fitted with slide valves, while 70628/9 had superheaters and were fitted with piston valves. WD 70627 was named "Christine" and 70629 "Jessie Madden".

WD 70630–3/43/4, the Schwartzkopf 0–8–0Ts used on the Tripolitanian Railways, had Walschaerts valve gear and slide valves. No superheaters were fitted.

WD 70634–6, the 0–4–4–0DE locomotives, were built by Brown-Boveri in 1940 and were powered by 550hp Fiat V-type diesel engines numbered 2595–7 in order, generating 800 amps at 500 volts. Three hundred gallons of diesel fuel were carried. Westinghouse brakes were fitted. The weight in working order was 42 tons. Four of these locomotives were originally intended for the Ferrovie Eritrée but when Eritrea was captured by the British, the locomotives were diverted to the BB & SR. Here, DE 204 was destroyed in 1942, leaving DE 201–3 to be captured by the British and renumbered WD 70634–6. These locomotives were chiefly used to Barce.

Little is known about WD 70637/8, the Brown-Boveri 0–4–0DEs used on the Tripolitanian Railway.

WD 70639–42, the 0–4–4–0Ts, had four outside cylinders and 2ft 11½in driving wheel diameter. The boiler pressure was 190psi. The water capacity was 1100gl, which was often increased in

Plate 61 Class 301 locomotive in 1949 (Photo: BB & SR)

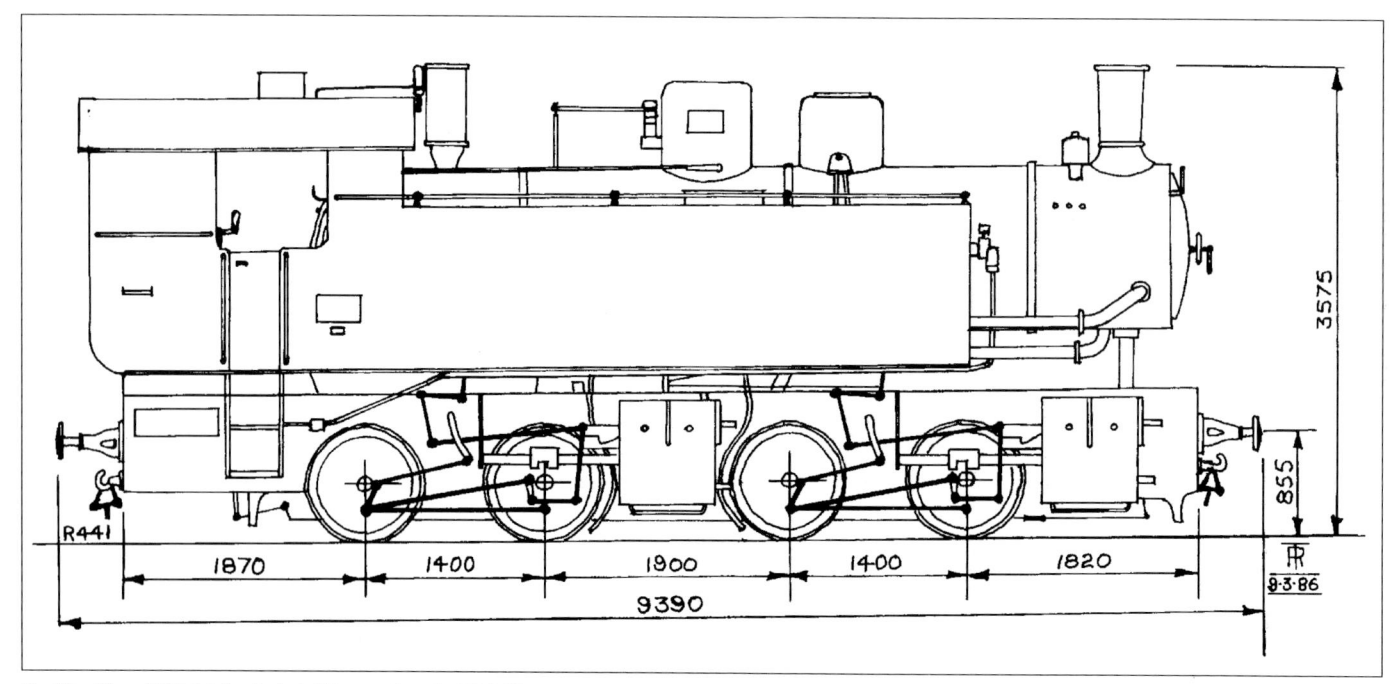

Fig 10   Class R441 Mallet 0–4–4–0T as used on the BB&SR

Plate 62   WD 70636 at Benghazi shed in November 1945 (Photo: F. Saville)

Plate 63   BB & SR Brown Boveri 0–4–4–0D WD 70636 at Benghazi shed. Steam Mallett 0–4–4–0T WD 70639 is in the right background and the Deutz 0–4–0DM on the left. The time is November 1945 (Photo: F. Saville)

Plate 64   Mallett 0–4–4–0T locomotive in January 1945 before shipment from Eritrea to Benghazi for service on the BB & SR (Photo: F. Saville)

Plate 65   Class 441 locomotive WD 70641 "Giuliana" fitted with Caprotti valve gear, photographed in 1949 (Photo: BB & SR)

Plate 66   Brown Boveri 0–4–4–0D WD 70634 at Benghazi in July 1948 (Photo: A. J. Knight)

Plate 67   Tripolitanian Railway 0–8–0T R401.7, which later became WD 70630 (Photo: R. Tourret Collection)

practice by a water wagon "tender". Coal capacity was 1½ tons. The length was 30ft 9in, width 8ft 10in and height 12ft 2in. The wheelbase was 15ft 7in, while the weight in working order was 44 tons. WD 70639/40 were fitted with Walschaerts valve gear and WD 70641/2 with Caprotti valve gear. Superheaters were fitted to all four engines. WD 70640 was named "Susan" and WD 70641 "Giuliana". These four engines were sent to the BB & SR from the Ferrovie Eritrée in January or February 1945 by the WD.

An 0–4–0D locomotive was repaired for use as an inspection and general yard duties locomotive at Benghazi Works using a 45hp Spa V8 engine from an Italian tank. The length was 20ft 9in, height 9ft 4in and width 8ft 2in. The old number was FS-M1 and it carried a plate Deutz 7761. It was renumbered 70637 locally although this number clashed with another locomotive on the Tripolitanian Railway. It was capable of hauling about 75 tons on the level.

Six Garratt 2–8–2+2–8–2 locomotives were ordered from Ansaldo for the Chemin de Fer Franco-Ethiopien de Dijbouti á Addis Ababa by the Italians after they conquered Ethiopia. Three were delivered to Dijbouti where they were seized by the Free French forces and lay disused until after the end of the war. They became nos 501–3 when placed in service. Two were shipped to Tripoli but being metre gauge were of no use on the 0.95 metre gauge Tripolitanian Railways. They were then damaged in air raids and subsequently scrapped in 1945. The last locomotive of the six is unaccounted for and presumably was sunk en route to Tripoli.

Plate 68 Class 401 0–8–0T 401.6, later to become WD 70644, on Tripolitanian Railways. This was left damaged by retreating axis troops and was rebuilt by a detachment from No 199 Rly Wkshps Co whose corporal had a girl friend in the Women's Land Army – hence the name "The Land Army Girl" (Photo: K. R. M. Cameron)

Plate 69 Fiat Spa diesel in the yards at Benghazi in March 1949. The locomotive is in full working order as shown in the photograph (Photo: A. G. Knight)

WD No	Type	Maker, Works No & Date	Former No	Railway
70624	2–6–0T	Construsione Meccaniche Saronno 471/12	R301.12	Tripolitanian
70625	2–6–0T	Construsione Meccaniche Saronno 473/12	R301.14	Tripolitanian
70626	2–6–0T	E. Breda, Milan 1531/14	R301.21	BB & SR
70627	2–6–0T	Officine Meccaniche Milan 613/14	R301.33	BB & SR
70628	2–6–0T	Nicola Romeo Saronno 674/22	R302.22	BB & SR
70629	2–6–0T	O. M. Navale di Napoli 116/27	R302.35	BB & SR
70630	0–8–0T	Schwartzkopf 4013/08	R401.7	Tripolitanian
70631	0–8–0T	Schwartzkopf 4014/08	R401.8	Tripolitanian
70632	0–8–0T	Schwartzkopf 4016/08	R401.10	Tripolitanian
70633	0–8–0T	Schwartzkopf 4018/08	R401.12	Tripolitanian
70634	0–4–4–0DE	Brown-Boveri 4217/40	FE DE 201	BB & SR
70635	0–4–4–0DE	Brown-Boveri 4218/40	FE DE 202	BB & SR
70636	0–4–4–0DE	Brown-Boveri 4219/40	FE DE 203	BB & SR
70637	0–4–0DE	Brown-Boveri 4066/35	A 11	Tripolitanian
70638	0–4–0DE	Brown-Boveri 4068/35	A 12	Tripolitanian
70639	0–4–4–0T	Reggiane 136/33	FE 441.101	BB & SR
70640	0–4–4–0T	Reggiane 146/36	FE 441.106	BB & SR
70641	0–4–4–0T	Reggiane 139/33	FE 441.201	BB & SR
70642	0–4–4–0T	Reggiane 142/33	FE 441.204	BB & SR
70643	0–8–0T	Schwartzkopf 4011/08	R401.5	Tripolitanian
70644	0–8–0T	Schwartzkopf 4012/08	R401.6	Tripolitanian

Chapter 23

ROBINSON LNE (GCR) CLASS O4 2–8–0's, WD 700–91

During World War I, when locomotives were urgently required by the Railway Operating Division, the GCR class 8K 2–8–0, designed by Robinson, was chosen as a standard type and 521 were eventually constructed by various contractors and by the GCR itself. Whilst many of the locomotives were sold to other British lines after the war, and some went as far afield as China, more than half of them eventually found their way to the LNE. The LNE numbers were allotted without regard to the date of building or to the makers or the ROD numbers. Full details were given in the RCTS books "Locomotives of the LNER, 1923–37" and "Locomotives of the LNER" Part 6B, so they will not be repeated here.

When World War Two broke out, it was presumed that military requirements for locomotives on the continent would arise as in World War One. In October 1939, an order was issued to requisition 300 Class O4 locomotives from the LNE. In November 1939, after 57 had been prepared, the order was cancelled and the engines returned to service in Britain. In 1940, thirty O4s were loaned to the GWR, being returned during 1941–3.

In September 1941, locomotives were again urgently needed, this time for railway lines in the Middle East and to help transport supplies to Russia. Accordingly, 92 of the LNE locomotives were requested by the Ministry of War Transport. The basis of selection was that mileages since the last general repair were not to exceed 20,000, boilers to be fit for at least two years service and coupled wheel tyres not to be less than 2 inches (preferably 2¼in). The engines were painted grey and numbered WD 700–91 in the order that they were dealt with, with numbers on front and rear buffer beams only, in 1¼in high golden yellow figures. LNE number plates were left on the cab sides. Preparatory work was handled at Gorton Works and two O4s, Nos 6234 and 6635, were set aside to be stripped to provide spare parts.

These 92 locomotives were all fitted with Belpaire fireboxes and Diagram 15 boilers. Sixty-one had originally been built for the ROD in World War One and 31 were ex Great Central engines. Although these engines were transferred to the WD in 1941/2, they were not officially taken out of LNE stock until December 1943 and the sale price of £5,700 per engine was not agreed with the British government until February 1947.

The LNE numbers (pre-1946) of WD 700–91 were as follows:

After preparation, and as shipping became available, the engines travelled to the ports of embarkation, usually in pairs with one engine in steam and with wagons with spare parts. WD 700 hauled 701 to Birkenhead Docks on 11 September 1941. The first locomotives sent to Glasgow were WD 711 hauling 714/6 on 15 September. By the end of the first week in October 1941, WD 700–21/3–5 had left Gorton. By the end of October, WD 722/6–61/3/5/7 had also been sent. None were sent in November. WD 766/8–74/81/2 were sent in the first half of December and WD 783/7 in the second half. During January 1942, WD 762/4/75–9/84–6/8–91 left Gorton and finally 780 left for Swansea on 3 February. The delay in despatching engines in November was due to the requirement to fit vacuum brake equipment for train braking. The locomotives went from the following ports; 27 from Birkenhead (700–6/12/

WD	0	1	2	3	4	5	6	7	8	9
70X	6549	6196	6557	6279	6509	6239	6497	6597	6560	6565
71X	6301	5383	6499	5382	6183	6368	6623	6339	6600	6212
72X	6355	5019	6607	6520	5354	6514	6517	6530	6587	6610
73X	6185	6345	6225	5420	6599	6504	6217	6204	6547	6202
74X	6335	6551	6569	6369	6330	6593	5392	6233	6537	6613
75X	6508	6541	6322	6348	6340	6332	5271	6346	6585	6315
76X	6570	6238	6377	5376	6605	6580	5017	5346	5375	5402
77X	5413	6197	6230	6235	6247	6260	6273	6266	6312	6362
78X	6602	5421	6251	6563	6317	6297	6628	5014	6327	6603
79X	6373	6527	–	–	–	–	–	–	–	–

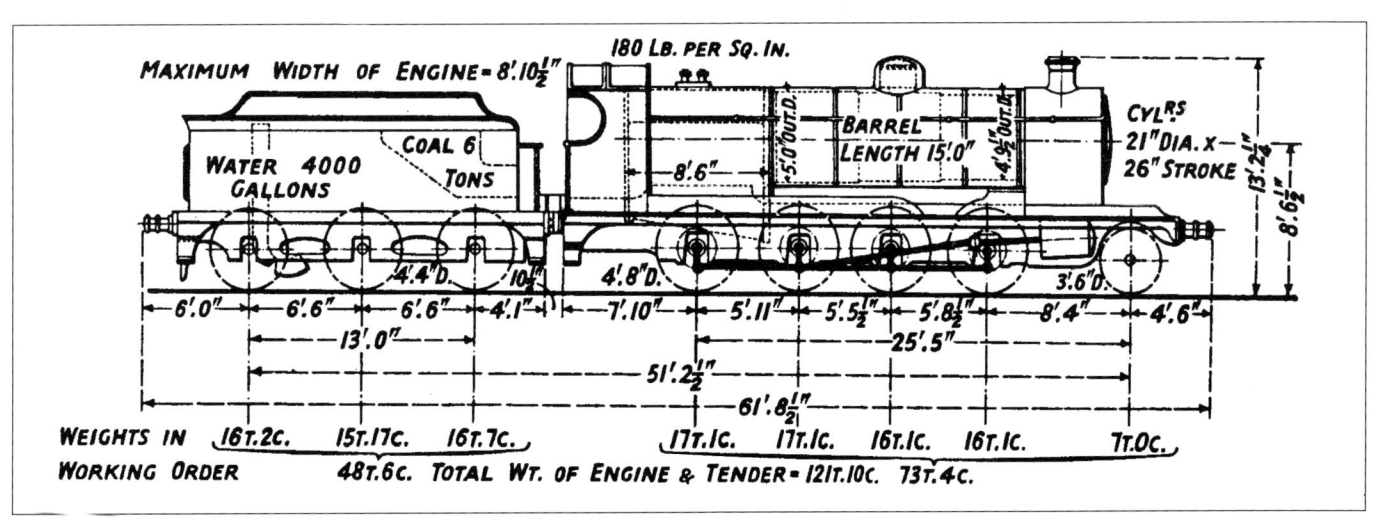

Fig 11   Robinson LNE (GCR) Class O4 2–8–0 (Courtesy Railway Gazette)

Plate 70   Class O4 2–8–0 repainted for War Department service in 1942 (Photo: British Rail)

5/8–20/3–5/37–42/53/4/9/60/84/91), 26 from Glasgow (707–11/3/4/6/22/6–8/49–52/5/6/62/71–4/83/5/7), 21 from Swansea (735/6/43/4/63–6/8–70/5/6/9–82/6/8–90), six from Ellesmere Port (731/2/45–8), four each from Greenock (729/30/3/4) and Hull (717/21/77/8) and two each from Cardiff (757/8) and Penarth (761/7).

All 92 engines were sent to the Middle East and arrived during 1941/2, apart from two (WD 739/40) which were lost en route in October 1941. They were generally loaded in pairs on the ships and most of them were landed at Port Said, although a few were unloaded at Alexandria. WD 741/2 were originally delivered to Persia in error about February 1942. They were sent back to the MEF without ever going into service in Persia. As with other classes in the MEF, the original WD numbers were prefixed with a "9" to avoid confusion with ESR locomotive stock.

By December 1941, 25 had arrived and were put into service on the ESR hauling heavy freight trains. In January 1942, six more arrived, one of which was sent to the Palestine Railway (PR). In February 1942, 16 more arrived, but one was sent direct to the PR and another five were transferred from the ESR to the PR. In March 1942, seven more arrived, of which three went direct to the PR and two were transferred from the ESR to the PR. In April 1942, four more arrived, of which two went direct to the PR. In May 1942, 14 more arrived, of which 12 went to the PR and two to the HBT.

Eighteen of the O4s were unusually all loaded on to one ship, SS "Belray". This ship was probably accidentally diverted to Bombay, from where it was brought through the Suez Canal in April 1942 and sent up to Tripoli in Lebanon, where they were unloaded in May 1942 by a floating crane on to landing craft which beached on a ramp specially built on the south beach near the railway. These locomotives were too heavy for the Syrian lines which had a 13 to 14 ton axleload limit, so little use was made of them until the HBT was completed, although two were used on the works for the HBT. Once the through route was complete, they were put into use and transfers were fairly frequent, particularly between the PR and HBT.

Thus, the arrival of all 90 locomotives had been accomplished by May 1942. In July 1942, 20 engines on the PR were to be converted to oil firing. In September 1942, five PR locomotives went to the HBT and three were exchanged between the ESR and PR. In October 1942, one locomotive was transferred from the ESR to the PR. The allocation in October 1942 was 53 to Egypt with many on loan to the ESR, 22 to the PR, 14 to the HBT (WD 719/21/8/9/32/3/41/4/5/8/56/61/79/88) and one (WD 749) whose whereabouts was not known. This totals 90, but leaves the 18 at Tripoli unaccounted for. However, the 14 mile section from Tripoli to Cheka was opened in July 1942, and since other official statistics record 43 locomotives on loan to the ESR in October 1942, 22 on the PR, 7 on the HBT, and 18 at Tripoli, it seems probable that ten of the 53 "Egypt" and seven of the "HBT" and the one unaccounted for make up the 18 locomotives at Tripoli.

Plate 71   MEF 9789 (ex WD 789) in service in Egypt (Photo: R. Tourret Collection)

Plate 72   MEF 9781 (ex WD 781) at Bulaq shed on the ESR in April 1945 (Photo: R. E. Tustin)

In November 1942, four engines (9722/7/43 and one other) went into service on the Chemin de Fer Damas, Hamah et Prolonguements (DHP) in Syria, it presumably having been decided that the track could take the weight! In the same month, one PR locomotive went to the HBT. In December 1942, five locomotives ex ESR went into service at Army depots. These would include 9713/48 at Jaffa in Palestine and 9738/61 at Haifa in Palestine. Also in December 1942, the whole HBT line opened from Beirut to Tripoli, and five locomotives ex store at Tripoli were brought into service on the HBT.

In January 1943, three returned from the Army to the ESR, and seven more came out of store at Tripoli into service on the HBT. In February and March 1943, there were further transfers, probably including 9743 from the DHP to the HBT, and 9722/7 to the ESR. The four engines on the DHP were now 9731/2/55/6. In April 1943, most HBT engines went into store. By May 1943, 70 engines were oil-fired and only 20 remained coal-fired. In June 1943, three locomotives went from the HBT to the Army and store. Also, 9738 went from the Army in Palestine (Jaffa) to the Army in Egypt (Suez), and 9772 from the PR to the Army in Egypt (Suez). In July 1943, 9743 went from the HBT to the ESR, and 9713/48/61 from the Army in Palestine (9713/48 at Jaffa and 9761 at Haifa) to the ESR. In August 1943, 9744 went from the HBT to the Army in Palestine, this bringing out the last O4 from the HBT. Also, 9727 went to the Army in Egypt (Suez).

In September 1943, 9783 was transferred from the ESR to the Army in Egypt, and 9726/8/41/9 from the Army in Palestine to the DHP. In November 1943, 9783 went from the Army in Egypt to the PR. In December 1943, 9721 moved from the Army in Egypt to the ESR, and 9705/37 from the Army in Egypt to the PR.

As at 31 December 1943, the official allocation was 50 to the ESR (WD 700/2–4/6–10/2/3/5–8/20–3/5/30/4/5/42/3/8/51–4/7–62/4–8/70/4/6/80–2/4/5/7), 24 to the PR (WD 701/5/11/4/9/24/33/6/7/46/7/63/9/71/3/5/7/8/83/6/8–91), eight to the DHP (WD 726/8/31/2/41/9/55/6), four with the Army in Egypt (WD 727/38/50/72) and four with the Army in Palestine (WD 729/44/5/79). The PR locomotives presumably also operated over the HBT.

In April 1944, 9731/56 moved from the DHP to the Army in Palestine, in May 1944, 9732 moved from the DHP to the Army in Palestine, and in July 1944, 9755 also moved from the DHP to the Army in Palestine.

The position of the 15 coal-burning and 75 oil-burning locomotives at 1 August 1944 was as follows. In service on the ESR were four coal-burners (WD 727/38/50/72) and 44 oil-burners (WD 702–4/6/8–10/3/5–8/20–3/5/30/4/5/42/3/8/51/3/4/7–62/4–6/8/70/4/6/80/2/4/5/7). One coal-burner (WD 707) was put aside and five oil-burners (WD 700/12/52/67/81) were under repair. In service on the PR was one coal-burner (WD 705) and nine oil-burners (WD 711/9/46/7/73/7/8/83/90). Under repair were coal-burner WD 737 and oil-burners WD 701/33/6/75, while nine oil-burners (WD 714/24/63/9/71/86/8/9/91) were awaiting repair. Four coal-burners (WD 726/8/41/9) were in service on the DHP. The Army had coal-burners WD 729/45/79 and oil-burners WD 732/55 stored serviceable, coal-burner WD 744 and oil-burner WD 756 awaiting repair and oil-burner WD 731 under repair.

In September 1944, 9729/45/79 moved from the Army in Palestine to the HBT.

As from November 1944, all other than those working on the ESR were renumbered by the addition of 70,000 to their original WD numbers. For example, 709 became first 9709 and then 70709. The engines on the ESR were also given these 707XX numbers but only in small figures, the 97XX numbers being retained as the main identity presumably to avoid unnecessary alteration to the ESR records. It may be as well to mention here that, like the ex-LMS 8F 2–8–0s, parts of locomotives were frequently exchanged in a cannibalisation process for want of spare parts.

In November 1944, there were several changes. WD 705/37/69 moved from the PR to the ESR, 711/4/33/63/71 from the

Plate 73   Ex LNE O4 2–8–0 on a southbound freight train at Geneifa on the ESR in April 1947 (Photo: G. Horsman)

Plate 75 Official photograph of WD 7000 built by NBL in 1943. Note the very small 2 inch lettering (Photo: Mitchell Library)

insulation against heat loss being provided by the air space between these plates and the boiler shell proper.

Plain bearings were used throughout the valve-operating mechanism, the bushes being of cast iron. Mechanical lubrication was deleted. The tender was an all-welded eight-wheeled non-bogie type with a self-trimming coal bunker. The tender wheels were disc-type, braked by steam and hand. Westinghouse and vacuum brakes were provided for train operation. Provision was made for fitting a water scoop if required.

Dimensions, additional to those shown on the diagram, were as follows:

Boiler heating surface	
Tubes & flues	1512sq ft
Firebox	168sq ft
Total evaporative	1680sq ft
Superheater	310sq ft
Combined total	1990sq ft
Grate area	28.6sq ft
Tractive effort at 85% BP	34,215lb
Adhesive weight	61¼ tons

It may be mentioned here that the original intention had been to use superheater elements that were 10in longer than actually fitted, and this would have given a superheater surface of 338sq ft. The GWR issued this figure on its engine diagram in error.

A total of 935 of these engines were built in 1943–5, the second largest class of one type of locomotive ever built in Britain, 545 by the North British Locomotive Co (Glasgow) and 390 by Vulcan Foundry Co of Newton-le-Willows. The North British engines were built under two orders; L943 for 430 engines to be numbered WD 800–79, 7000–49 and 7150–7449, and order L943A for 115 engines WD 8510–8624. Works numbers 24891–25435 were allotted to the 545 engines. Both Hyde Park and Queens Park Works were employed on these orders, the latter works not having built any locomotives for the previous three years having been busy on contracts for armoured fighting vehicles.

As it was expected that construction of the engines would probably have to be transferred from one works to another at short notice, to meet wartime demands, a design of works plate common to both works was adopted. The traditional circular plate of Hyde Park Works gave place to the diamond-shaped plate hitherto associated only with Queens Park Works, although no mention was made on the new plate of the works at which the engine concerned had been constructed. WD 7000 with works No 24971 was the first engine to appear with this type of plate.

Order L943 was in three parts. In August 1942, 50 (WD 7000–49) were ordered, replacing 50 LMS 8F type 2–8–0s ordered in July 1942, which were delivered in the period January to May 1943; and 300 (WD 7150–7449) which were delivered in May 1943 to March 1944. In May 1943, 80 more were ordered

Plate 76 Cab of a WD 2–8–0 (Photo: Mitchell Library)

Plate 77   WD 7195, the armoured WD 2-8-0 (Photo: Mitchell Library)

(WD 800–79) still under Order L943, which replaced 80 LMS 8F type 2–8–0s ordered in March 1942, hence their apparently curious numbering. WD 800–79 were delivered from March to September 1944. In July 1943, a further 115 were ordered under Order L943A (WD 8510–8624), which were delivered from September 1944 to March 1945. Actually, Hyde Park Works built 200 of the 430 engines comprising Order L943, these being WD 7000–49 and 7150–7299, while Queens Park was responsible for WD 7300–7449 and 800–79.

WD 800–79 were originally ordered as LMS 8F type 2–8–0s under NB Order L940 of March 1942 but construction was delayed to give priority to start building the Standard 2–8–0s. Not unnaturally, the order was subsequently changed to Standard 2–8–0s as part of Order L943, but the running numbers allocated (800–79) were not changed, nor were the works numbers allocated (24891–24970). This explains why the first WD 2–8–0 built WD 7000 had the later works number 24971, and why 800–79 although built later mostly had the earlier works numbers.

WD 7300 appeared from Queens Park Works about two months after WD 7000 from Hyde Park, and the batches were turned out simultaneously until to meet an urgent order from the Ministry of Supply for one hundred 2–10–0s, Hyde Park Works suspended work on 2–8–0s at WD 7262 to build 2–10–0s WD 3650–3749, before finishing off 2–8–0s WD 7263–99. Meanwhile, Queens Park Works had built 7300–7449 and 800–79, and had commenced work on Order L943A for 115 engines, WD 8510–8624. Fifty of these, 8510–59, were to have been built at Queens Park, but in fact only 8510–30 were constructed there, 8531–59 being transferred to Hyde Park Works, following completion of the latter's batch 8560–8624.

Of the total of 545 2–8–0s constructed by North British, therefore, Hyde Park Works built 294 and Queens Park Works 251. With a few exceptions the engines built at the former works carried their correct works numbers, but the Queens Park Works numbers were not allotted in sequence, being fitted as they came to hand from stores, and some engines left the works without any plates.

The 390 Vulcan engines were built under nine orders; 2289 of 1942 for ten engines WD 7050–9 delivered May to June 1943, 2290 of 1942 for 50 engines WD 7060–7109 delivered June to October 1943, 2291 of 1942 for 50 engines WD 7110–49 and 7450–9 delivered October to December 1943, 2292 of 1942 for 50 engines WD 7460–7509 delivered December 1943 to March 1944, 2299 of 1943 for 47 engines WD 8625–71 delivered March to June 1944, 2300 of 1943 for 47 engines WD 8672–8718 delivered June to September 1944, 2307 of 1944 for 43 engines WD 9177–9219 delivered September to November 1944, 2308 of 1944 for 43 engines WD 9220–62 delivered November 1944 to February 1945, and 2313 of 1944 for 50 engines WD 9263–9312 delivered in February to May 1945. They were built in four series in correct works number sequence; WD 7050–7149 (works numbers 4866–4965), WD 7450–7509 (4966–5025), WD 8625–8718 (5026–5119) and WD 9177–9312 (5120–5255). WD 9312 was the last "Austerity" 2–8–0 to be built and was named "Vulcan" on leaving the works.

The complete list of works numbers is shown in the following table.

800–12	NB 25308–20	1944
813–20	NB 24891–8	1944
821–8	NB 25163–70	1944
829–41	NB 24899–24911	1944
842	NB 24914	1944
843–8	NB 24916–21	1944
849/50	NB 24923/2	1944
851–4	NB 24912/24/13/5	1944
855–67	NB 24925–37	1944
868	NB 25411	1944
869	NB 24938	1944
870	NB 25412	1944
871–9	NB 24939–47	1944
7000–18	NB 24971–89	1943
7019	NB –	1943
7020–49	NB 24991–25020	1943
7050–7149	VF 4866–4965	1943
7150–6	NB 25021–7	1943
7157	NB 25088	1943
7158–7280	NB 25029–25151	1943
7281–99	NB 24952–70	1944
7300	NB 24990	1943
7301–5	NB 25171–5	1943
7306–10	NB 25186–90	1943
7311–20	NB 25176–85	1943

Plate 78   WD 79305 somewhere on the LNER in March 1945 (Photo: K. A. C. R. Nunn, Courtesy British Rail)

7321–9	NB 25191–9	1943
7330/1	NB 25208/9	1943
7332–9	NB 25200–7	1943
7340–51	NB 25210–21	1943
7352	NB –	1943
7353/4	NB 25223/4	1943
7355–7	NB 25230/2/22	1943
7358–62	NB 25225–9	1943
7363	NB 25231	1943
7364–74	NB 25235–45	1943
7375–80	NB 25247–52	1943
7381–3	NB 25254/5/3	1943
7384–7	NB 25256–9	1943
7388	NB 25233	1943
7389	NB –	1943
7390–7407	NB 25260–77	1943
7408–16	NB 25279–87	1943
7417	NB 25278	1944
7418–23	NB 25288–93	1944
7424–7	NB 25152–5	1944
7428	NB 25234	1944
7429–35	NB 25156–62	1944
7436–49	NB 25294–25307	1944
7450–64	VF 4966–80	1943
7465–7509	VF 4981–5025	1944
8510	NB 25415	1944
8511–4	NB 24948–51	1944
8515–7	NB 25414/5/25	1944
8518–26	NB 25416–24	1944
8527–30	NB 25426–9	1944
8531–59	NB 25386–25414	1945
8560–8611	NB 25321–72	1944
8612–24	NB 25375–85	1945
8625–8716	VF 5026–5119	1944
9177–9243	VF 5120–86	1944
9244–9312	VF 5187–5255	1945

It will be noticed that WD 868/70, 8510/5 carried the same works numbers as WD 8556–9 respectively. This anomaly was caused as follows. Works plates 25411–4 were damaged while the bolt holes were being drilled and replacements were ordered from the Paisley firm which cast them. Before they came to hand it was decided to use the damaged plates after all, and these were fitted to engines WD 868/70, 8510/5 respectively. When the replacements were received, Queens Park were finishing off their current batch of engines at 8530, and as construction of 8531–59 was transferred to Hyde Park, all available works plates were sent along, including the four replacements. The actual plates sent were 25386–25414/30–5; of these 25386–25414 were fitted to the remaining twenty-nine locomotives, WD 8531–59, the replacement plates being fitted to WD 8556–9. As these were the last 2–8–0s of this design built by North British, works plates 25430–5 were left over.

Works number 25246 was also unallotted as this plate was damaged and scrapped, and no replacement made. These seven blank numbers were balanced by the four duplicate works numbers (25411–4), plus WD 7019, 7352/89 which had no works plates fitted. WD 7019 at one time carried works number 25170, which should have gone on WD 7300. This works number was later allotted to engine WD 828.

Early in 1944, there was a temporary shortage of works plates at Queens Park, and plates 25152–70 were borrowed from Hyde Park and fitted to WD 7424–7/9–35 and 821–8 respectively. These were repaid by plates 24952–70, which were fitted to WD 7281–99. With regard to the batch WD 8510–8624 which should have had works numbers 25321–25435 in sequence, Hyde Park were allotted the first 65 works numbers, although their engines bore the last 65 WD numbers, WD 8560–8624.

These WD 2–8–0s had been ordered "off the drawing board" without development experience, but they were found to work well on the whole. The air compressor was lowered ten inches to improve visibility on the right-hand (fireman's) side, from 7027 onwards. The original tender wheels of chilled cast iron did not take kindly to the British practice, with semi-fitted or un-braked trains, of using the tender hand brake when descending an incline, and were changed to rolled forged wheels. The Ministry of Supply vacuum relief valves were troublesome. Tenders had a tendency to derail when running tender first. As to performance, they were good starters, moving up to 80 four-wheeled wagons with 50% cut-off and a third-open regulator, and rolled along at an adequate speed.

The earlier engines were painted a light khaki-brown colour. The prototype WD 7000 had very small 2in numerals on the cab sides but the other engines had 4in numbers on the cab sides, and "WD" and the typical WD broad arrow emblem between the "W" and the "D" on the sides of the tenders, all painted in matt golden yellow. From March 1943, the size of the cab numerals was increased to 6in for clarity, and then from December 1943 to

Plate 79 Loading trials being carried out with WD 79250 on board a landing barge (tank), probably at Marchwood, preparing for shipment of WD 2–8–0s to Europe. In the event, WD 79250 was one of the few WD 2–8–0s that did not go to Europe! (Photo: R. Tourret Collection)

8in. From March 1944, the general livery was changed to an "army" green, the numbers on the cab side increased to 12in and the "WD" on the tender sides enlarged to 12in with a 10in broad arrow. Numbers were also painted on the front buffer beam but this varied with the two builders, Vulcan Foundry using 2in figures, while North British used full-sized figures. In the 8625 and 9177 series, Vulcan Foundry used bright yellow painted figures on the cab sides.

All WD numbers were increased by 70,000 as from August 1944, WD 78518 and 78560 being the first North British locomotives to be out-shopped with five-figure numbers from Queens Park and Hyde Park Works respectively, and WD 78715 the first from Vulcan. Existing engines in WD hands were quickly renumbered, but those on loan to British railways were renumbered only when passing through works or after being handed back to the WD.

In case of enemy attack during the forthcoming invasion of the Continent, three Schemes for protecting the WD 2–8–0s against 20mm armour-piercing ammunition were drawn up. Scheme 1 employed armour plate, 1in thick round the cab and ½in thick elsewhere, and was calculated to weight a total of an extra 7.38 tons. Scheme 2 employed mild steel, 1½ and 1in round the cab and ½in thick elsewhere, and was calculated to weight 7.88 tons. Scheme 3 employed various thicknesses of plastic armour and mild steel and was calculated to weight 7.16 tons. Similar Schemes were prepared for the USA/TC 2–8–0s. WD 7195 left works in September 1943 experimentally fitted with plating over the cab and top of the boiler as a prototype but not following exactly any of the three Schemes drawn up. WD 7195 went to Melbourne and then to Longmoor. In the event, the Allied air superiority made such armour plating unnecessary and it was removed from this single locomotive before it was shipped to France. Just as well, as it would have been too heavy for most lines.

The first of the "Austerity" 2–8–0s were built well before they were needed on the Continent, so they were naturally put to work in the UK to help the British railways. The first locomotive to be completed, WD 7000, went to St Rollox shed for evaluation trials on the LMS, from 30 January to 27 February 1943. This trial period was not regarded as a loan to the LMS, and on 6 March 1943 WD 7000 passed to the LNE on loan.

In all, 450 of these engines were loaned to the main line railways in 1943 and 1944. These were WD 7000–14/6–99, 7100–28/30–67/9–94/6–9, 7200–22/4–40/2–62, 7300–68/70–99, 7400–45/50–97. Those built by North British Locomotive were run-in from Eastfield shed, and those built by Vulcan from Gorton shed. After the engines were run-in, most were transferred to other sheds on the LNE. In addition, Eastfield sent six engines to the WD, 7015 to Longmoor, 7168 to Faslane (in June 1943) and then Longmoor, 7195 to Melbourne and then Longmoor, 7223 to Faslane and then Cairn Ryan, 7241 to Cairn Ryan and 7369 to Faslane; and twenty-four (7422–45) to the SR. Subsequently, another 169 went to the WD for store. Other engines built by North British were run-in by the LMS from St Rollox (Hyde Park engines) or Polmadie (Queens Park engines). Of the Vulcan engines run-in by Gorton, 106 were sent to other sheds on the LNE, 26 (7472–97) to the SR and one (7129) to Longmoor, followed by 14 to the WD for store (7498/9, 7500/1/8/9 and 8625/6 to Longmoor and 7502–7 to Melbourne). Other Vulcan engines were dealt with by the LMS at Springs Branch and Patricroft sheds, the LMS taking 50 on loan in all. Thus, in total the LNE had 350 engines and the LMS and SR 50 engines each. WD 7226/7/34 were originally intended

Plate 80 WD 2–8–0 WD 78627 at Woodford shed in February 1946 (Photo: R. Tourret)

to go to Faslane, but in the event went to the LNE.

The 350 engines going on loan to the LNE between February 1943 and January 1944 were 7000–10/2–4/6–41/65–99, 7100–28/30–49/62–7/9–94/6–9, 7200–22/4–40/2–62, 7300–9/24–68/70–99 and 7400–21/50–71. The LNE had so large a number of these engines that they were used over virtually the whole system; Aberdeen 7171–4, Carlisle 7253–6 and 7387/8/94–7, Colwick 7107–16, 7261/2 and 7402/5–11/62–71, Dundee 7175–7, 7226 and 7330–3/67/8, Dunfermline 7219/27–9 and 7362–5, Eastfield 7000–5/13/6–8/39–41, 7206/8/9 and 7308/9/34–6/56/7, Haymarket 7390–3, Hull Dairycoates 7184–6/9–94/6, 7231–4 and 7339/40/3–5/77, March 7095–9, 7100–6/17–28/30–2/97/8, 7200–2/13, 7346–50/60/1 and 7452–61, New England 7006–12/9–22/9/30/5–8/80–94 and 7300/4/5/7, Newport 7133–49, 7240/2/59, 7383–6/9 and 7400/1/3/4/12–4/50/1, Parkhead 7243–6 and 7372–4/89, St Margarets 7230/47–52 and 7324–9/75/6, Stratford 7075–9, 7180–3/7/8 and 7337/8/41/2, Thornton Junction 7178/9, 7205/7/14–8/20/1 and 7353–5/66, Tyne Dock 7199, 7203/4/10–2/22/4/5/35/6/57/8/60, 7351/2/8/9/70/1/8–80/98 and 7415–21 and York 7014/23–8/31–4/65–74, 7162–7/9/70, 7237–9 and 7301–3/6/81/2.

As mentioned, the WD 2–8–0s were used over almost all of the LNE system, the exceptions being the rural branches, the Wrexham lines and the Cheshire lines, while they rarely worked over the Great North of Scotland section. The first engines allocated to the LNE worked mainly between Glasgow and Edinburgh. Some went over the West Highland line to Fort William, but at first they could not be turned on the turntable without separating the tender from the engine.

The New England (Peterborough) engines mainly worked to Ferme Park in North London. The Colwick engines worked freight trains to New England. The March and Stratford locomotives worked ammunition and petrol trains to East Anglia to service the airfields from which American and British aeroplanes set out to bomb Germany. While engaged on this work, WD 7337 was considerably damaged in the munitions train explosion at Soham in Cambridgeshire on 2 June 1944. It was rebuilt by North British at Queens Park Works in September 1944, where a new boiler was fitted. Another engine which required heavy repairs while at Stratford Works was WD 7095, whose boiler was returned to Vulcan for repair in 1944, but was condemned by the Ministry of Supply inspector, thus requiring a replacement to be fitted.

Occasionally a passenger train was hauled, known examples being 31 July 1943 WD 7337 Ipswich to Yarmouth, 14 December 1943 WD 7117 March to Ely and 11 January 1944 WD 7084 replacing a failed locomotive from Offord to Kings Cross.

There were many transfers of WD 2–8–0s between LNE sheds, especially when the USA/TC 2–8–0s left the LNE, and in September and November 1944 when 72 WD 2–8–0s were moved to the GWR (see later), as follows; Carlisle to March 7256 in November 1944, Dundee to March 7367 in November 1944, Dunfermline to Dundee 7329, Dunfermline to Eastfield 7362–4, Eastfield to Aberdeen 7039–41 and 7309, Eastfield to Dundee 7000, Eastfield to Parkhead 7162–5 in November 1944 and 7169/70, Eastfield to St Margarets 7308/34–6/56/7. Hull Dairycoates to Hull Springhead 7234 and 7324 in February 1944 and 7066–8 and 7184/6 in December 1944, Hull Springhead to Hull Dairycoates 7066–8 in November 1944, Hull Springhead to York 7068, March to Mexborough 7452–61, March to Neasden 7075–9/97–9 in June 1944, Mexborough to Colwick 7452, New England to Neasden 7092 in June 1944, Neasden to New England 7300/5/7, Newport to New England 7133/4/49/99 and 7351 in September 1944, Parkhead to March 7244–6 and 7272/89 in November 1944, St Margarets to Dunfermline 7327–9, St Margarets to Thornton Junction 7324–6, Stratford to March 7075–9, 7180–3/7/8 and 7337/8/41/2, Thornton Junction to Eastfield 7214/21, Thornton Junction to Parkhead 7353/5, Tyne Dock to Heaton 7235/6/60, 7358/9/71/8–80/98 and 7417 in September 1944, Tyne Dock to Newport 7199, 7203/4/10–2/22/4/5/57 and 7351/2/70, and York to Hull Springhead 7066–74 and 7381/2.

A third WD 2–8–0, 77406, received a new boiler at Stratford Works in May 1945 due to a damaged firebox on the original boiler, which was returned to North British.

The fifty engines loaned to the LMS in May and June 1943 were 7011/42–64, 7150–61 and 7310–23. Route restrictions were the same as for the LMS 8F 2–8–0s. A few of these (7057/64, 7160 and 7322) were painted black at that company's works, with lettering and numerals of the standard LMS type and size. These engines were allocated as follows; Kingmoor 7011/42–9, 7150–2 and 7311–7, Polmadie 7310, Shrewsbury 7050–64 and Wellingborough 7153–61 and 7318–23. The Wellingborough engines worked south to Cricklewood and north to Leeds. The Shrewsbury engines worked on the Central Wales line. In May 1943, WD 7310, after only two weeks at Polmadie, was moved to Kingmoor. In June and July 1943, WD 7050–4 were moved to Swansea. In November 1944, WD 7046, 7151/2 and 7310–7 and moved to Wellingborough.

The fifty engines loaned to the SR in January, February and March 1944 were WD 7422–45/72–97. The SR treated the "Austerity" 2–8–0s as equal to their 2–6–0s for operating purposes. The WD 2–8–0s were allocated as follows; Bricklayers Arms 7422–30/72–80, Eastleigh 7436–45, Feltham 7488–97, Hither Green 7481–7 and New Cross 7431–5.

After the first 450 engines went into service on the main line railways, others were put into store ready for the forthcoming invasion of Europe. Longmoor received 7263–80 in late 1943; 7281–99 in early 1944; 7498 & 7500/1 in March 1944; 800/1/8/9, 7499, 7509 & 8525/6 in

Plate 81   WD 2–8–0 WD 77180 at Bricklayers Arms shed in April 1947 (Photo: A. G. Wells)

Plate 82   WD 2–8–0 WD 77214 on down Western Region goods train between Teignmouth and Newton Abbot in June 1949 (Photo: E. D. Bruton)

April 1944; 806/7/10/21–4/8–32, 7508 and 8639/41–4/51/2 in May 1944; and 811/33/41/2 and 8653/4/9–64 in June 1944. WD 7446–9 had also arrived at Longmoor by mid-1944. Between March and May 1944, Melbourne received 7502–7. By early August 1944, Melbourne had received others of the 8XX and 8625 series.

Later in 1944, further engines were put into store at Longmoor; 8524/6–30/75/7–84/6–8/90 and 9201/3–17 in November 1944; 8585/9/91–9, 8600–5 and 9200/18–23 in December 1944; and 844/9–52/74, 8513–6/23/63/5/7/8/70–3, 8682/3/7–94/6/8/9, 8700–3/5/6/8–18 and 9178/82/8/91/2/5/7 in late 1944 but month not known. Some of these engines stayed for only a month or so before shipment.

When the American S160 class 2–8–0s at work on loan to British lines were recalled for USA/TC service towards the end of 1944, some transfers were made of the WD 2–8–0s in compensation. The GWR received eight from the LMS (WD 7011/42–5/7–9). 72 from the LNE (WD 7040/1/87–9/91–4, 7111/3/4/6/35–8/40–2/4/6/8/50, 7215–20/9/31/3/40/3/4/58/9/61/2. 7354/66/77/83/5/6/99 and 7400/1/3/4/8/9/12–6/8–21/50/1/3–61/5) and nine from the SR (WD 7489–97), eighty of these arriving in September 1944 and nine more (WD 7040/1 and 7215–20/43 from the LNE) in November 1944. They were used all over the GWR system, being allocated to Banbury 7049, 7244/62, 7354 and 7416/20, Bristol St Philips Marsh 7261, 7385/99 and 7453/5/6. Cardiff Canton 7114/6 and 7408, Croes Newydd 7045, Didcot 7219 and 7490, Neath 7259 and 7401/13/54/9/60, Newport Ebbw Junction 7087, 7113/36, 7383/6 and 7414/5/50, Old Oak Common 7094, 7217/8/31, 7377 and 7465/92, Oxford 7215/6 and 7491/6, Oxley 7011/42/4/7/8, 7150, 7366 and 7403, Pontypool Road 7111/37/42, 7240 and 7451, Reading 7040/1, 7220 and 7489/94/5/7, Severn Tunnel Junction 7088/9/91 and 7135, Shrewsbury 7146 and 7421, Southall 7493, Stourbridge 7140/1 and 7419, Swindon 7138 and 7409/57, Tyseley 7144 and 7258, Westbury 7412 and Worcester 7043, 7148, 7229/33/43 and 7400/4/18/58/61. Someone with a sense of humour sent five (7136, 7383/6 and 7414/50) from Newport LNE to Newport GWR!

On the GWR, the "Austerity" 2–8–0s were regarded as "Blue" engines for route restriction purposes, and group "E" for power rating. There were a few changes in the initial shed allocations as follows; Croes Newydd to Oxley 7045, Didcot to Reading 7490, Oxley to Stourbridge 7150, and Severn Tunnel Junction to Newport Ebbw Junction 7091 and 7135.

In the invasion of Europe, the USA/TC 2–8–0s were the first to be sent, going to Cherbourg. It was not until September 1944 that shipment of the WD 2–8–0s and 2–10–0s started, presumably so that they could help British railways for as long as possible. Removal of stored locomotives from Longmoor started in September 1944, being hauled in batches via Havant to Eastleigh where they were serviced. Most were temporarily stored in the north yard, but a few were taken to Southampton so as to be ready for shipment. Others went to Dover. The second load of WD locomotives delivered to Dieppe on 2 October 1944 included two 2–8–0s, and in that month 38 arrived at Dieppe, and were put to work in France and Belgium. In November 1944, 200 engines were delivered to Cherbourg for use in Belgium.

In November and December 1944, sixteen WD 2–8–0s were transferred to the SR (WD 7068/73, 7156–9, 7210/37/9 and 7301/18/9/21–3/44) to help with movement of traffic to the southern ports. Between October 1944 and February 1945, all the "Austerity" 2–8–0s at work on British railways were transferred back to the WD and, together with those in store in WD dumps at Longmoor and Melbourne, were gradually shipped to France. The engines returned to the WD in 1944 were sent to Longmoor to await their turn for shipment, preference being given to new engines. Longmoor serviced 573 2–8–0s, of which 150 had been on loan to British railways. Some 300 were checked over in railway workshops, and had their "7" prefix added to their running numbers. Some of the new engines needed attention on their way to Southampton or Dover and were dealt with at Eastleigh or Ashford respectively, which works also serviced most of the engines off loan. Crewe and Gorton also handled many engines off loan, and Swindon a few. All the WD 2–8–0s were sent to Europe, except three, WD 7223 and 7369, and 9250 of January 1945 which was sent direct to Longmoor and stayed there.

The first WD 2–8–0s were also landed at Cherbourg and were allocated to Caen. However, after 30 September, they were landed at Dieppe and were worked to Antwerp. From 21 November, they were also brought into Calais by ferry, augmented from December by rail-fitted landing craft. The locomotives were shipped with coupling rods removed and carried in their tenders, because of probable excessive vertical movement of the driving wheels when run on and off the ships. Later locomotives were allocated to Aalst, Aarschot, Ghent, Leopoldsberg, Mechelen and Ostend.

The first supply of WD locomotives for service on the SNCB were twelve 2–8–0s to Ostend and seven 2–8–0s (and eleven 2–10–0s) to Merelbeke in November 1944. In December, eight 2–8–0s went to Hasselt followed by 15 more in February 1945, while Aarschot received 14 2–8–0s in December followed by six more in January. Tournai was allocated 23 in December and a further four in January. The largest allocation was 44 to Schaerbeek in January and February 1945, while 16 went to Muizen and seven to Aalst. The total by February 1945 was thus 156. During the German Ardennes attack, the WD 2–8–0s based at Hasselt were temporarily withdrawn to Aarschot.

Shipment to France was as follows. In September 1944, 855 and 7264/6/7; in October 1944, 801/8/9/56/7/9–64/6–8/70/3/5, 7263/73/8/82–5/8/93/5/7, 7446/7 and 8511/2/9/60/1/4; in November 1944, 806/7/10/1/21–4/8/9/31/3/41/2/4/9–52/8/69/72/4/6–8, 7095/9, 7106, 7241/61/5/8–71/6/9/81/9–91, 7430/48/9/54/7–61/72/3/5/8/83/5–7/9/91/5/7–9, 7500/8/9, 8513/5/6/20/2/3/9/30/63/5/7/8/70–3/80–4/6/7, 8625/6/9/82/3/7–94/6/8/9, 8700–18, 9177/8/81–8/91/2/4/5/7 and 9205/8/9–11/3–5; in December 1944, 7000–5/8/12–8/23–8/31–4/40/58/9/64/9/76/7/9/93/6–8, 7101/21–30/49/67/8/88/95/6/9, 7206/60, 7310, 7402/4/5/7/23/36/7/9/40/1/5/52/3/5/6/63/5–71/4/6/7/9–81/4/8/90/4, 8510/4/24–8/69/74–8/85/8–99, 8600–5, 9190/6/8/9 and 9200–4/6/7/12/6–34; while in late 1944 but exact month not known:800/2–5/12–20/5–7/30/2/4–40/3/5–8/53/4/65/71/9, 7286/94, 7501–7, 8521/62/6/79, 8627/8/30–81/4–6/95/7 and 9179/80/9/93.

Further locomotives were shipped to France in 1945 as follows. In January 1945, 7006/7/9–11/9–22/9/30/5–9/41–63/5–8/70–3/5/8/81/6–8/90/2/4, 7102/3/5/7/9/12/4–8/20/37–9/42/3/5/7/50/2/5–9/62/4–6/9–73/5–82/4–7/9–94/7/8, 7200–5/7/10–2/4/21/6–8/31/2/5/7/9/42–4/7–55/72/4/5/7/80/7/92/6/8/9, 7300–2/4–7/9/12/8/9/21–30/2–7/9/40/3–7/50/1/3/5/6/8–60/2/7/70/1/7–82/7/8/91/2/5/8/9, 7400/1/3/9–11/3/4/8/9/22/4/5/7–9/32–5/8/42–4/51/62/4/82/92/3 and 8607/12; in February 1945, 7074/80/3–5/91, 7100/4/10/3/9/31–3/5/6/40/4/6/8/51/3/4/60/1/3/74/83, 7213/5–8/20/2/4/5/9/30/3/4/40/5/6/56–9, 7311/3–7/20/31/8/41/2/8/52/4/7/61/3–6/8/72–6/83–6/9/90/3/4/6/7, 7412/5/6/20/1/6/31/50, 8614–6 and 9239/42–4/7; in March 1945, 7082/9, 7108/11/34/31, 7208/9/19/36/8/62, 7303/8/49, 7408/17/96, 8534/6–8, 8617–20 and 9240/6/8/51/4–6/8/64; in June 1945 7406 and 9308; and some time in early 1945 but exact month not known, 8517/8/31–3/5/9–59, 8606–8–11/3/21–4, 9235–8/41/5/9/52/3/7/9–63/5–99 and 9300–7/9–12.

Some of the last to arrive were not needed for the war effort and so went into storage, for example WD 79301–12 at Calais in May 1945.

There were a few German air attacks on the WD 2–8–0s, such as on 78686 at Dendermonde engine shed in Belgium on 31 December 1944, 70862 near Eindhoven on 1 January 1945, 70851 near Louvain sometime in January 1945, and 79197 near Geldrop in Holland on 6 February 1945. To prevent Allied air attacks in error, some locomotives had a white star painted on the cab roof.

There was concern that the destruction of all the Rhine bridges would hinder the rail supply of military freight. In the event, as described in Chapter 10, temporary rail bridges were rapidly built, but the WD experimented with WD 79250 at Southampton Water (Marchwood) successfully loading her on to a converted tank landing craft in March/April 1945, as a back-up technique.

In the Spring of 1945, 222 of these engines were loaned to the USA/TC who were temporarily short of motive power. The first to go were 8513 and 8640 in January 1945. In February 1945, 191 went as follows, 802–4/6/7/10–54/65/72/8, 7265–70/2/6/7/9/80/7/90/8/9, 7448/9/98/9, 7500–9, 8515/20/2/62/5/71/2/80, 8622/5–39/41–61/3–99, 8700–4/6–18 and 9177/8/80/5/7/8/91/2/4. In March 1945, 805/69/79, 7275, 7472/5, 8518/29/66/7/73/9/86, 9183/96 and 9217 were transferred. In April 1945, 7143 and 8611; and in June 1945, 7281 and 8662. Nine engines were loaned sometime in 1945 but exact months not known, 800, 7477/83/95/7, 8576, 9179/89 and 9201. While on loan to the American authorities the engines carried "Transportation Corps, USA" on their tenders. The USA/TC operated them from Brussels Midi, Landon, Ans, Ottignies, Ronat, Muysen, Louvain, Renary, Charleroi St Martin and Antwerp Dam in Belgium; Le

Plate 83   BR 90527 (ex WD 7056) at Nine Elms shed in July 1949 (Photo: E. D. Bruton)

Havre (some being loaned in turn to the SNCF at Le Havre), Le Mans, Aulnoye, Troyes, Tergnier and Laon in France; and Maastricht in the Netherlands. All locomotives were returned to the WD by August 1945. The American engine crews preferred the WD screw reverser to their USA/TC lever reverse, but did not like the lack of a rocking grate, especially with the low quality coal which was all that was available.

As the war progressed, and further ports were put back into Allied service, the locomotives were moved forward, and some of those used in France moved on to Belgium and Holland. When shipment to Europe effectively ceased in May 1945, the 932 engines were used by the British Army Groups in France, Belgium, and Holland. In France, 180 operated from Boulogne, Hazebrouck, Calais, Le Mans, Lille, Bethune, Acheres and Dieppe. In Belgium, 470 were allocated to Antwerp South and Antwerp Dam, Mouscron, Muysen, Ostend, Merelbeke, Bruges, Aalst, Hasselt, Schaerbeek and Tournai. In Holland, 232 saw service from Heerlen, Nijmegen, Amsterdam, Roosendaal, Eindhoven, Maastricht, Den Bosch, Rotterdam, Hengelo, Groningen, Roermond, Zwolle, Utrecht, Amersfoort and Leewarden. Fifty engines reached Germany and were stored at Goch and Cleves for a while.

When the war finished in May 1945, military traffic naturally decreased considerably. Dumps of WD 2–8–0s were formed, the two largest in Belgium being Tournai with 114 locomotives and Ostend with 78, followed by Mouscron with 38 and Aalst and Merelbeke each with 27. Another large dump was at Calais with 54 engines. In Germany, the dumps just over the border at Goch and Cleves now held 58.

Hitherto, the locomotives which had previously been on loan during the war were officially regarded as for use only on trains of military importance, but as peace-time conditions returned and with it the need for civilian traffic, the "Austerity" 2–8–0s were divided into two groups, those to be used solely for military traffic and those that could be allocated to the national railways for use on any services that the railways wished. Many engines were put into service on the SNCF, NS and SNCB, and by October 1945, most of the dumps were cleared.

By September 1945, a total of 127 engines were allocated to the WD in the Netherlands, 35 at Roosendaal, 33 at Nijmegen, 28 at Maastricht, 17 at Heerlen and 14 at Eindhoven, while 100 were on loan to the NS. By October 1945, a total of 170 engines were allocated to the SNCB, 36 at Schaerbeek, 30 at Merelbeke, 23 at Hasselt, 22 at Muysen, 17 at Antwerp South, 15 at Tournai, 13 at Antwerp Dam, 9 at Ostend and 5 at Aalst. The SNCB often painted the locomotive number on the smokebox door in large ornamental figures, an example illustrated is 78627 at Woodford after its return to the UK (Plate 80). A total of 373 locomotives were on loan to the SNCF, while 72 were stored at Ostend. A total of 61 engines were in Germany, most, if not all, stored at Goch and Cleves. Some locomotives required repairs and 70 2–8–0s were dealt with at the Belgian Mechelen Royal Engineers Central Workshops up to July 1945, the first having been 77286 in October 1944.

Plate 84 WD 400 (ex WD 7337) "Sir Guy Williams" at Longmoor shed in April 1957 (Photo: M. T. McHatton)

WD 78678 was severely damaged in June 1945 in the south of Belgium while on loan to the USA/TC and was immediately withdrawn from service. It was subsequently scrapped at Mechelen (Malines) Works. WD 77125 and 77238 were involved with a British Army leave train in a head-on collision near Cleves on 16 August 1945. Both engines were severely damaged. They remained at Goch for a while but since both engines had been intended for the NS, they were later sent to Tilburg Works for examination. They were condemned in September 1945 and scrapped at Mechelen Works.

Considering the Nederlandsche Spoorwegen, by December 1944 there were 12 WD 2–8–0s working on the NS, and 54 by June 1945. In July 1945, the NS asked for 75 and by August 1945 these 75 engines working on the NS were allocated NS 4401–75. They were allocated 25 to Amsterdam, 20 to Utrecht, 15 to Roosendaal, 10 to Eindhoven and 5 to Nijmegen. In October 1945, another 25 WD 2–8–0s were loaned to the NS, taken from the dump at Ostend, and became NS 4400/76–99. As already mentioned, there were then also 127 WD 2–8–0s working under WD control in Holland. In November 1945, these were handed over to the NS and became NS 4301–99 and 4500–27. This made a total of 227 engines and these were initially allocated as follows; 39 to Nijmegen, 30 to Roosendaal, 27 to Maastricht, 26 to Utrecht, 22 to Heerlen, 21 to Eindhoven, nine each to Amsterdam, Hertogenbosch and Zwolle, eight to Feijenoord, seven to Hengelo, six to Rietlanden, five each to Groningen and Leeuwarden, three to Amersfoort and one to Roermond.

The NS numbers were allotted in strict order within the three batches, except for NS 4526/7 at the end of the 4500–27 batch. Presumably this was because WD 77125 and 77238, originally intended for the NS, had been withdrawn due to collision damage, and were replaced by WD 77376/7. The delay caused them to be tacked on to the end of the batch for the renumbering.

In January 1946, three not fitted with steam heating, NS 4504/9/11 (WD 8677 and 9189/96) were exchanged with three fitted with steam heating (WD 77193/4/7) that had been working on the NSM (see later), which became NS 4530–2. Of the three withdrawn from NS, 79196 (NS 4511) went to the NSM, and 78677 and 79189 went back to the WD. In February 1946, seven more 2–8–0s were received ex store in Belgium (7009–11/38, 7188/90 and 7358) in replacement for seven 2–10-0s taken back for work in Germany, making a total of 234 WD 2–8–0s, the highest number ever in NS service. These seven 2–8–0s became NS 4528/9/33–7. In June 1946, because of receiving 50 WD 2–10–0s from Germany, 50 WD 2–8–0s (77003/9/10/2/8/21–3/ 6/8/31/6/7/40/2/67/80/9, 77104/28/38/ 51/62/5/7/74/5/87, 77202/21/5/30/4/52, 77303/15/23/38/53/8/64/5/72/90/2 and 77407/8/10/67/9) were returned to the WD and UK. Towards the end of 1946, the 184 "Austerity" 2–8–0s remaining on the NS were purchased.

Meanwhile, two engines had been in collisions, NS 4485 (WD 77183) on 6 November 1945 at Kranenburg just over the border into Germany, and NS 4505 (WD 78693) on 28 January 1946 at Ravenstein. Both were extensively damaged. They were at Malines Works for repairs in August 1946, but in the end they were withdrawn officially in January 1947. Usable parts were retrieved and the remainder scrapped at Tilburg Works. Their boilers were retained for further use. The tender from NS 4485 found its way to NS 4491, and the other tender became a spare.

For convenience of reference, the WD Nos of the NS series are listed below:

Plate 85 BR 9000 (ex WD 7009) (Photo: R. Tourret Collection)

79284) at Gouda. The locomotive was repaired, using the tender from NS 4491, and its own tender became a spare. On 8 April 1949, NS 4302 (WD 70806) was left as an unattended light engine at Meppel at a signal stop when both enginemen incorrectly left the footplate without handbrakes being applied or the engine set in mid-gear, and the locomotive set off by itself through the station, head-shunt buffers and into a river! The engine was cut up on the spot, but the tender was retrieved to become a spare.

They were given an olive green livery with black lining on the cab and tender sides. The NS number, prefixed by "NS", was painted in white on the cab sides and the rear of the tender. The bufferbeams were painted red, with "No" on the left of the coupling and the number to the right. Frames, smokebox, running gear and buffer shanks were all black. Locomotives retained the WD number as well until actual purchase by the NS. One or two engines were repaired in Belgium due to lack of adequate workshop capacity in Holland. NS 4410 (WD 77159) was overhauled at Mechelen in June 1946 and had Belgium features in its new livery, such as reversed radius corners on the cab and tender lining, an extra yellow line on the inner side of the lining, the white numerals being placed on a black oval, edged in white, and elaborate figures on the smokebox door.

The NS made various modifications, the most noticeable being a 550mm stovepipe-style extension to the chimney to cure drifting smoke. Small smoke deflectors on top of the smokebox were tried on NS 4482 (WD 77162) and large sheet deflectors sitting on the running plate on NS 4444 (WD 78539), but the chimney extension was considered the best cure. A ladder was fitted, usually on the right-hand side, giving easier access to the clack valves. Steam heating was fitted, where not already present, and the vacuum brake equipment changed for air brake. The exhaust pipe of the air compressor was directed into the blast pipe. To prevent firing irons inadvertently touching the overhead electric wires, the cab roof was extended back towards the tender. For running tender first, the footplate was fitted with narrow partitions with small windows behind each seat, and the cab was fitted with folding doors. The cabs were also fitted with a sliding ventilator in the roof and sliding side windows.

As from 1 January 1950, the tenders were given their own numbers prefixed by a "T", each tender having a numberplate fixed to the rear bufferbeam to the left of the coupling. Initially, the WD 2–8–0 tenders were numbered by the addition of 800 to the numbers of the locomotives, but the tenders attached to NS 4301–3 were allotted special numbers 5115, 5117 and 5116 respectively to avoid clashing with WD 2–10–0 tender numbers.

These WD 2–8–0 locomotives were

NS	0	1	2	3	4	5	6	7	8	9
430X	–	803	806	812	819	835	855	856	861	862
431X	863	868	869	873	879	7003	7012	7018	7021	7022
432X	7023	7026	7028	7031	7036	7043	7045	7065	7067	7069
433X	7080	7082	7089	7104	7105	7117	7128	7138	7143	7167
434X	7168	7172	7174	7177	7202	7252	7264	7266	7267	7273
435X	7282	7287	7293	7295	7303	7304	7308	7315	7323	7331
436X	7338	7341	7353	7364	7365	7372	7390	7392	7407	7408
437X	7410	7438	7446	7467	7469	7472	7495	7500	8511	8517
438X	8518	8523	8524	8529	8530	8536	8555	8557	8567	8571
439X	8573	8574	8576	8579	8593	8617	8620	8622	8631	8636
440X	7037	7084	7109	7114	7132	7134	7137	7139	7140	7158
441X	7159	7187	7216	7221	7224	7230	7234	7240	7244	7245
442X	7246	7262	7275	7301	7345	7346	7347	7349	7361	7366
443X	7383	7384	7387	7389	7400	7403	7405	7409	7417	7475
444X	7477	7483	8533	8535	8539	8545	8548	8549	8552	8558
445X	8566	8586	8611	8613	8618	8623	9179	9201	9217	9230
446X	9231	9248	9249	9252	9257	9258	9260	9267	9270	9277
447X	9284	9287	9289	9290	9291	9300	7040	7042	7151	7153
448X	7154	7156	7162	7165	7175	7183	7189	7191	7217	7219
449X	7225	7333	7344	7396	8519	8547	8569	8619	9238	9246
450X	8640	8647	8657	8669	8677	8693	8701	9183	9188	9189
451X	9193	9196	9197	9212	9218	9222	9223	9255	9256	9286
452X	9292	9293	9295	9296	9297	9299	7376	7377	7009	7010
453X	7193	7194	7197	7011	7038	7188	7190	7358	–	–

Shortly after the NS purchase, two more locomotives were involved in accidents. On 30 November 1946, a passenger train ran into the tender of NS 4470 (WD

Plate 86   BR 90386 (ex WD 8592) ex works at Darlington Works in October 1964 (Photo: David Mills)

widely used on both passenger and freight trains, and acquired the nicknames of "Dakota" and "Little Jeep" due to their simplicity and general usefulness. A major electrification scheme was completed in May 1949, after which they were less frequently used on passenger trains and were more often used on local and pick-up work. In April 1949, some 28 were withdrawn (NS 4308/11/38/50/61/77/ 87/90/2, 4408/9/21/4/5/7/38/47/57/91–3/6/9 and 4500/20/1/3/6) in anticipation of the completion of the electrification scheme, but it was found to be premature and they were all reinstated in August 1949. However, in November 1949, all 28 but two (NS 4438 and 4520) were again withdrawn, plus another six (NS 4302/59 and 4414/26/70/81). By March 1954, their work on passenger trains ceased, and in 1954 another 37 were withdrawn. On 5 April 1955, NS4331 (WD 77082) had an accident at Zevenaar and was scrapped at the end of the month. In June 1955, NS 4310 (WD 70863) was the last steam locomotive to be overhauled at Tilburg Works. In 1955, another 27 were withdrawn, 30 in 1956, 19 in 1957 and the last four in 1958. Nine boilers were retained for stationary use (WD 77153/77, 77216/6/67, 77366, 78530/5 and 79238) and one (WD 77043) was used for a month at the end of 1954 as a stationary boiler at the Philips Works at Eindhoven. Three tenders were retained for use with the NS PO3 Class 4–6–0s.

Two of the NS 2–8–0s, NS 4383 and 4464 (WD 78529 and 79257) were sold to the Statens Järnvägar (Swedish State Railways) in June 1953 and became SJ class G11 1930/1. They were too big for Swedish turntables so that the tender had to be shortened to six wheels! Other alterations were fitting headlights, fully enclosed cab and a chimney extension. Oval brass number plates of Statens Järvägar design were fitted to the cab sides and the tenders were lettered "SJ". These two locomotives worked in the Falun area. It was understood that they were on trial with a view to purchase of other 2–8–0s from the NS but further sales did not materialise, perhaps because of the modifications found necessary. In 1958, they were placed in store as strategic reserve. When the storing of these two engines was decided to be no longer necessary, SJ 1931 returned to England in January 1973 and went into service on the Keighley and Worth Valley Railway.

In late 1944, WD 7192–4/7 were loaned to the Nederlandsche Staatsminen (Dutch State Mines) at Limberg where they became NSM 61–4. The NSM engines worked southwards from South Limberg to Liége in Belgium, crossing the Maas River by a temporary bridge, the only one available at the time, and then northwards to join the NS at Lutterdale. These NSM trains carried coal for use by Belgian industries, and also military and civilian traffic for Holland. Sometime in late 1945, WD 70825 ex repair at Mechelen Works was also loaned to the NSM where it became NSM 70. In January 1946, WD 7193/4/7 (NSM 62–4) were passed to the NS, and WD 79196 loaned from the NS (4511) to the NSM where it became NSM 77. These moves were to allow locomotives fitted with steam heating to pass to the NS. WD 70825 and 77192 returned to the WD in early 1946, followed by 79196 in April 1946.

As mentioned earlier, in October 1945 there were 170 WD 2–8–0s allocated to the SNCB. By November 1945, the number had increased to 181, but by the end of 1945, 23 locomotives were taken out of service and returned to the UK, as part of the 150 returned from Europe between November 1945 and January 1946. A further seven were sent to Holland in February 1946 as already mentioned, while another 92 were returned to the UK between February and July 1946, leaving 59 in Belgium in 1947 by which time they had ceased work and had been put into store, some of them in France.

In September 1945, there were 113 WD 2-8-0s working in France, but by October 1945 they had been joined by 54 locomotives ex store at Calais and 206 ex store in Belgium, making the total of 373 WD 2-8-0s mentioned earlier. While in France, some of them were painted in the chocolate-brown livery of the SNCF. Between February and July 1946, 177 were returned to the UK, while the rest were returned in 1947.

Sixteen WD 2-8-0s were stored in Germany at January 1946. Ten WD 2-8-0s were put to use in Germany, probably starting at the beginning of 1946 until early 1947. These are believed to have been WD 70814/49, 78580, 78626/38/44/52/8/81 and 78704, which returned to the UK in 1947. The other six probably went to the Detmold Military Railway.

The Detmold Military Railway, a single-track line 25 miles long, officially opened on 23 April 1946, running from Himminghausen (with running powers to Altenbeken) to Bad Salzuflen (with running powers to Herfold). Detmold itself was roughly at the centre of the line. Six WD 2-8-0s, 70845/51, 77299 and 78672/5/89, plus some German locomotives, worked the line. Freight trains generally loaded from 1000 to 1600 tons, and there were also daily passenger trains. WD 78675 was named "The Sapper" and 78689 was known as the "Lance Corporal" because it had been given a white chevron chalked below each cab window. WD 78672 was named "Sir Guy Williams" on 5 May 1947. WD 77299 and 78672/5/89 returned to the UK in the autumn of 1947, WD 78672/5 losing their names, although the name "Sir Guy Williams" was transferred to 77337 at Longmoor. WD 70845/51 returned to the UK in 1948.

In January 1946, the overall position was that 150 WD 2-8-0s had been returned to the UK, 373 were in France, 227 in Holland, 158 in Belgium, 16 stored in Germany and five were on the NSM. During 1946, a further 320 were repatriated and the position in Europe at December 1946 was 258 stored in Belgium and France, 184 in Holland, ten in Germany and six on the Detmold Military Railway. One, WD 79189, disappeared from the records in 1946 and is believed to have gone to the USA in exchange for USA/TC 2-8-0 3257 which went to Longmoor.

Some unofficial names have been reported for when these engines were working in Europe, such as 77138 "Lisa" and 79286 "Bertha". WD 77337 was also reported as carrying the name "La Deliverance" but this was probably because it was allocated to Lille La Deliverance shed. WD 77325 carried on its smokebox door the inscription "Je suis la 100m machine sortie de l'Annexe Dujardin" (I am the 100th engine coming out of the Annex Dujardin).

In October 1945, the Railway Executive Committee was informed that the WD had locomotives surplus to their requirements and it was decided that 250 should go to the LNE. Later that month, the Railway Executive Committee agreed to accept 460, provided that they were fit for immediate service, of which 310 would go to the LNE (60 extra so that the LMS 8F 2-8-0s 8500-59 could go to the LMS), 100 to the GWR (to allow the 8Fs 8400-79 to go to the LMS) and 50 to the SR. The Ministry of War Transport advised that return from the Continent was about to start, then two weeks later the War Office said that only 260 WD locomotives could be released, which must include the 103 WD 2-10-0s! There were further discussions on this point, and on the way that hire charges would be calculated and when they would start.

The SR train ferries were used to bring back the locomotives, the first eight returning to Dover on 17 November 1945 being WD 70818/48, 77279, 77504, 78645/51/61 and 78716. Returned later in November were WD 70823/4/8/31, 77146, 77276/81/98, 77507, 78534, 78628/39/42/8/9/53/67/80/6/99, 78710/2/8, 79180/5 and 79237/88. In December, the following were returned 70800/13/5/6/21/6/7/32/7/40-2/6/7/72, 77136, 77213/20/33/6/43/65/8/9/72/7/90, 77354/7/67/73, 77450/98, 77501/2/5/6/9, 78513/5/27/8/62/5/70/7/84/91, 78625/30/3-5/46/54/5/9/60/2-5/8/70/3/4/6/9/91/4/6, 78702/3/7-9/11, 79177/91 and 79236/51/85. In January 1946, the following came back 70805/10/20/2/30/44/52/4, 77422/30/7/48/58/73/8/86/7/90/1/3, 78516/20, 78608/27/41/56/87/90/7/8 and 79200/40/1.

In the period up to January 1946, a total of 150 locomotives came back, 108 from Belgium and 42 from Germany. The 42 from Germany, returned in December 1945 and January 1946, were WD 70800/5/10/3/20/2/32/41/2/4/52/72, 77243/68/9/72, 77448, 77502/6/9, 78515/65/70, 78627/41/55/6/9/60/73/6/9/90/7/8, 78709/11, 79191 and 79236/7/40/1. The LNE accepted 130 and these were allocated to Aberdeen, Colwick, Dundee, March, New England, Newport, St Margarets, Thornton Junction, Woodford and York. The remaining 20 (WD 70805/20/46, 77268/9, 77422/50/8/78/90/3, 77509, 78516, 78649/59/60/7/76/94 and 79237) went to Longmoor for storage. At Dover, the arrivals were handled by Army personnel, but the LNE complained of the lack of engine tools and lamps.

In early 1946, it was agreed that following the first 150 locomotives, another 320 would be returned to the UK, consisting of 270 from France and 50 from Belgium, and shipments resumed on 11 February 1946. In June and July 1946, the 50 WD 2-8-0s were returned from Holland, and these were included in the 320. The last shipment in this second series arrived at Dover on 12 July 1946. In fact, 177 came from France, 92 from Belgium and 51 from Holland.

The proportion of locomotives considered fit for immediate service was much smaller in this second batch, and the LNE accepted only 56 into traffic. Storage became a problem. Initially, engines were held in sidings around Dover while they were inspected and their immediate future decided. Almost all of those rejected by the LNE and needing repair were then moved elsewhere, and the SR set up a large dump in the old port area of Richborough (also known as Stonor). By May 1946, there were 110 locomotives at Richborough and it was agreed that the LMS would accept 30 for storage, the GWR 35 and the LNE 30 (increased to 35 in June).

From this second batch, 96 went into service. The SR took 20 into service in March 1946 at Bricklayers Arms (WD 77086/90/4, 77101/80, 77205/26/56/9, 77311/21/55, 77481/5, 78569, 78688 and 79203/10/62/81) and five in September 1946 at Feltham (WD 77052/6/9/62 and 77359). The LNE took another 60 into service (making a total of 190), 37 in March 1946 and the rest between April and November 1946 (WD 70804/58/70, 77002/9/21/33/83/91, 77100/10/3/31, 77211/23/50/1/4/84, 77300/16/8/22/36/9/43/60/3/9/70/82/5/97, 77410/2/20/3/7/35/74/96, 78516/40/50/82, 78603/76/7/92, 78706/13, 79187/92, 79211/6/45/7/53 and 79305/8), allocating them to Aberdeen, Dunfermline Upper, Eastfield, Heaton, March, New England, Hull Springhead, Woodford and York. Two of these, WD 78516 and 78676, were actually out of store from Longmoor from the first batch, and two more, WD 77223 and 77369, came from the WD at Cairnryan and Faslane respectively. Four of these, WD 77100, 77254 and 78603/77, were second batch engines initially taken into store at Richborough but then taken into LNE service. The GWR took 15 into service in September to December 1946 at Bristol St Phillips Marsh and Oxley (WD 70801/36/76, 77012/40/9, 77116/51/65, 77200, 77326, 77508, 79261 and 79301/9). Ten of these were second batch engines initially taken into store, WD 70801/36, 77116, 77200, 77326, 77508, 79261 and 79301 at Richborough and 70876 and 79309 at Kingham.

The remaining 236 of the February to July 1946 intake went into store. They returned to the UK as follows, in February WD 70817, 77061, 77108/22/9, 77222, 77362/95, 77402/11/24/6/84, 78588 and 78637; in March 77005/14/70/5/6/81/ 93/8, 77100/6/12/6/20/4/33/42/81/5, 77200/1/7/18/35/70, 77326/34/40/79/91, 77419/33/4/44/53/6/7/70, 77508, 78522/94, 78677/82 and 79301/9; in April 70836/53/78, 77030/46/53/64/74/7, 77103/18/23/70, 77254/5/7/96, 77307/ 10/25/37/78/80, 77418/21/5/60/1/80/9, 78587/96/7, 78603/66/95, 78714/7, 79184 and 79207/20/5/6/61; in May 70801/8/11/43/76, 77001/4/6/7/15/58/63/ 97/9, 77102/15/50/96, 77203/14/41/7/86/ 8/94/7, 77314/42/51/88, 77404/29/54/94, 78531/64, 78632/71, 78705, 79199 and 79219/24/32; in June 70871/7, 77003/ 16–8/22/4/6/8/31/4/6/42/50/5/67/71/9, 77104/21/8/30/8/47/9/61/4/75/84/7, 77202/4/6/10/21/52/60/1/3/71/4/8/83/9, 77303/6/23/38/53/8/72/92, 77413/41/65/7–9/92, 78561, 78600/4/10 and 79229/34; in July 77010/23/37/44/ 78/85/9/95, 77162/7/74/8, 77230/4/92, 77309/15/64/5/71/90 and 77407/8; and some time in this period but month not known 77047.

In February 1946, Hither Green received for storage 70817, 77362, 77424 and 78637 and in March 1946 two more 77201/7. However, in June 1946, 77362 moved to Blisworth and 70817, 77201, 77424 and 78637 to March, while 77207 was taken by the LNE and went into service in January 1947. One engine 79309 stored at Dover in March 1946 moved on to Kingham in June 1946. WD 77225 arrived in July 1946 but was taken by the LNE to Stratford Works and then to Darlington Works. It was eventually repaired and put into service in February 1948! Similarly WD 77080 which arrived in July 1946 was taken by the LNE in August 1946 but did not enter service until May 1948.

Arising from the above movements, 235 locomotives from the second intake went into storage at the following dumps. The SR had 134 in store, 21 at Dover (WD 77010/23/37/85/9/95, 77129/62/74/8. 77222/30/92, 77309/64/5/71/90/5, 77426 and 78588), three at Pluckley Station sidings near Ashford (77234 and 77407/8) and 110 at Richborough (70801/8/11/ 36/53/76, 77005/7/14/ 30/46/7/53/61/ 4/70/4–7/81/93/7–9, 77100/3/6/8/12/ 5/6/8/20/2–4/33/42/50/70/81/5, 77200/ 18/35/54/5/7/70/86/96, 77307/10/4/ 25/6/34/7/40/51/78–80/91, 77402/11/ 8/9/21/5/9/33/4/44/53/4/6/7/60/1/70/80/ 4/9, 77508, 78522/31/87/94/6/7, 78603/66/77/82/95, 78705/14/7, 79184/ 99, 79207/19/20/4–6/61 and 79301).

The GWR had 37 stored at Kingham (70843/76, 77001/4/6/15/58/63/79, 77102/30/61/7/84/96, 77203/6/ 10/4/41/7/88/94/7, 77315/42/88, 77404/94, 78564, 78604/31/71, 79229/32/4 and 79309). The LMS had 30, nine at Blisworth (77031/6/44/67/78, 77128/87 and 77338/62) and 21 at Northampton (77003/18/22/42/50, 77104/21/38/75, 77221/52/60/83, 77303/23/53/8/72 and 77465/7/8). The LNE had 34, two at Annesley (77149 and 77469), six at Colwick (70871/7, 77016, 77147/64 and 77392), five at Leicester (77017/34, 77204/74 and 78610), two at Lincoln (77055 and 78600), four at March (70817, 77201, 77424 and 78637), six at Staveley (77028, 77261/71/89, 77413 and 78561), three at Tuxford (77024/71 and 77441) and six at Woodford (77026, 77202/63/78, 77306 and 77492).

In February 1947, the Railway Executive Committee was informed that there were 71 available in France and 29 in Belgium, but that the ten in Germany were still required there (WD 70814/49, 78580, 78626/38/44/52/8/81 and 78704). In March 1947, a total of 240 were offered to the Railway Executive Committee, and accepted subject to the engines being in good order, but the ten in Germany were still not on offer. In the event, in 1947 and early 1948, all the remaining 275 (excluding only the 184 purchased by the NS and the three scrapped) were returned, including the ten from Germany. This time, they came back via Harwich as well as Dover. Amongst the last were the six from the Detmold Military Railway (WD 70845/51, 77299 and 78672/5/89). In fact, 59 came from Belgium, 196 from France, 16 from Germany and the remaining four probably from Holland.

Only a few shipping dates are known for this batch. In July 1947, 70802, 77155, 77209, 77324, 77406, 78553, 78683, 79186 and 79209/43 were returned; in August 1947, 70839, 77060/88, 77145, 77291, 77320, 77436, 78578, 78614 and 79244/78; in September 1947, 77280, 77398, 79283 and 79311. Returned some time in 1947, but the exact month not known, the following, 70807/9/25/9/ 33/4/8/49/50/7/9/60/4–7/74/5, 77000/8/13/9/20/5/7/9/32/5/9/41/8/51/4/7 /66/8/72/3/87/92/6, 77107/11/9/26/ 7/35/41/8/52/7/60/3/6/9/71/3/6/9/82/6/ 92/5/8/9, 77208/12/5/27–9/31/2/7/9/42/ 9/53/8/85/99, 77302/5/12/3/7/9/27–30/ 2/5/48/50/2/6/68/74/5/81/6/93/4/9, 77401/14–6/28/31/2/9/40/2/3/5/9/51/2/5/ 9/62–4/6/71/6/9/82/8/97/9, 77503, 78510/2/4/21/5/6/32/7/8/41–4/6/51/4/6/9/ 63/8/72/5/85/90/2/8/9, 78601/2/ 7/9/12/5/6/21/4/6/9/38/43/4/50/2/8/72/5/ 81/4/5/9, 78700/4/15, 79178/81/2/ 90/4–6/8, 79202/4–6/8/13–5/21/7/8/33/5/ 9/42/54/9/63–6/8/9/71–6/9/80/2/94/8 and 79302–4/6/7/10/2. In 1948, the stragglers came home, 70814/45/51, 77447, 78560/80/1/3/95 and 78605/6.

Most of the engines were ready for service, or only required minor attention, but 108 went into store as follows. There were 75 stored on the GWR, 42 at Kingham (70825/33/65/75, 77029/48/72/92, 77126/60/71/9/92, 77212/29/39/42, 77330/2/48, 77451/63/6/71/9, 78541/4/6/51/4/6/63, 78602/15/85, 79190 and 79215/21/72/5/82/98) and 33 at Marston sidings near Swindon (70809/14/29/38/64/6, 77025/54/60, 77141/5/8, 77280, 77335/98, 78590/5, 78621/4/81, 79195, 79214/44/54/66/8/ 9/73/94 and 79302/4/7/11). The other 33 were stored on the LNE, six at Colchester (70849/59, 77285, 77482 and 78581/3), two at Dovercourt Bay (77299 and 78689), 18 at Parkestone (70845/51/7/60, 77447, 78560, 78606/12/26/9/38/44/ 52/8/72, 78704, 79196 and 79213) and seven at Stratford Works (70867/74, 78580, 78605/75 and 79205/33).

The LNE was keen to obtain more "Austerity" 2–8–0s and on 7 May 1946, it said that it would accept 86 of the locomotives stored at Richborough for repairs. Then on 25 June 1946, the GWR agreed to take 25 that only needed light repairs so as to be able to release 20 8F 2–8–0s to the LMS. At a meeting on 15 January 1947, it was agreed that the LMS would overhaul 50 locomotives, the LNE ten and the SR twelve. By this time, the LNE had purchased 200 (see later) and the LNE decided to take another 210, which were allocated for overhaul as follows;

LNE, Cowlairs	9
LNE, Darlington	5
LNE, Gateshead	5
LNE, Gorton	4
LNE, Stratford	1
LNE depots	21
LMS, Crewe	50
SR, Brighton	19
SR, Eastleigh	16
R. Stephenson & Hawthorn, Darlington	18
Vickers Armstrong, Scotswood	19
Belgium, Couillet, La Croyere, De Tubize, Haine St Pierre & Marcinelle	43
	210

Presumably the Belgian companies overhauled locomotives stored in Europe, prior to return to the UK, whereas the British works handled the engines already stored in the UK. The Ministry of Supply provided seven spare boilers in 1947 to facilitate these repairs, one to Swindon, two to Brighton and four to Scotswood.

As already mentioned, the SR put 25 "Austerity" 2–8–0s into service in February and September 1946. Another 25 were taken from the Richborough dump, overhauled and put into use in 1947, as follows. In May 1947, two at Fratton (77108 and 79207) and one at Hither Green (78597); in June 1947, three at Ashford (70811, 77296 and 78705), two at Bricklayers Arms (78531/96) and two at Hither Green (70853 and 77103); in July 1947, one at Ashford (78666), two at Feltham (77379 and 77444) and one at Hither Green (79199); in August 1947, one at Feltham (77460); in September 1947, two at Feltham (77030/74); and in December 1947, five at Brighton (70878, 77007, 77270/86 and 77340) and three at Feltham (77098 and 77122/50). Naturally, they were mainly used for freight trains, but for a few weeks in the summer of 1946, a WD 2–8–0 worked the 07.40 Ashford to Folkestone passenger train, and on one occasion one even piloted the "Golden Arrow" from Tonbridge to Victoria!

Again, as already mentioned, the GWR put 15 WD 2–8–0s into service between September and December 1946. All through 1947, another 74 were taken from Kingham dump (23), Richborough dump (26), one or two from LNE dumps and the later ones direct from the 1947 arrivals, overhauled either by the GWR (presumably they overhauled 24 or 25) and by the LMS at Crewe (presumably they overhauled the remainder, either 49 or the full 50 agreed in January 1947). They were introduced as follows, in January 1947, one at Newton Abbot (77001) and one at Oxford (77058); in February 1947, one at Laira (77161) and one at Old Oak Common (77015); in March 1947, one at Banbury (78604), two at Bristol St Phillips Marsh (77142 and 77289), one at Didcot (70843), two at Exeter (77288 and 77388), one at Laira (77196), one at Newton Abbot (77214), two at Old Oak Common (78632 and 79234) and five at Oxley (77026/8/79 and 77202/97); in April 1947, one at Bristol St Phillips Marsh (77247), four at Cardiff Canton (77053, 77106/23 and 77380), two at Gloucester (77203 and 79232), six at Laira (77255/94, 77325, 77421, 78671 and 78717), two at Llanelly (77310 and 77489), two at Newton Abbot (77210/41), three at Old Oak Common (77005 and 77130/84), three at Oxley (77408 and 79224/5) and two at Reading (77387 and 78522); in May 1947, one at Birkenhead (79226), two at Llanelly (77407/29), one at Newport Ebbw Junction (77102), nine at Oxley (70808, 77014/64, 77115, 77234/57, 78695, 78714 and 79219), one at Pontypool Road (77099), one at Taunton (77077) and one at Tyseley (77097); in June 1947, one at Banbury (78512), one at Newport Ebbw Junction (78510) and one at Pontypool Road (77443); in July 1947, one at Cardiff Canton (77000), one at Old Oak Common (78521) and one at Pontypool Road (79235); in August 1947, one at Didcot (79303); in October 1947, one at Cardiff Canton (78543), one at Reading (77368) and one at Severn Tunnel Junction (79274); in November 1947, two at Gloucester (78542 and 79278) and in December 1947, one at Old Oak Common (77291) and one at Reading (77393). Normally, the GWR did not accept loan charges until the locomotives were actually in service, but since all the loans had to be in place officially by the end of 1947, ready for the formation of British Railways, six engines (77291, 77368/93, 77407, 78542 and 79278) were officially regarded as present on loan despite still being in the workshops.

Turning to the LNE, as discussed already, the LNE took into service 130 of the first batch of WD 2–8–0s to be returned in late 1945 and early 1946, and another 60 from the second batch in the first half of 1946, making 190 in all. In January and February 1947, the LNE took a further ten into service, making 200 in all. These were WD 70846, 77046/93, 77112, 77391, 77422/93 and 78649/67 in January and 77133 in February.

Between November 1945 and July 1946, the LNE acquired 184 WD 2–8–0s of which 178 went straight into traffic but the other six (WD 70826/42, 78641/98, 78703 and 79240) required minor attention at Ashford Works before entering service. The last sixteen engines required overhaul. Stratford Works dealt with WD 70846, 77422/93, 78516, 78649/67/76; Darlington with WD 77100, 77254, 77391 and 78603/77; R. Stephenson Hawthorns with 77093 and 77112/33; and Eastleigh with 77046. Five of these, WD 70846, 77422/93 and 78649/67, came out of the twenty from the first batch sent to store at Longmoor, while another five, WD 77046/93, 77112/33 and 77391, came from the second batch out of store at Richborough. They then entered LNE service between October 1946 and February 1947, being allocated to Heaton, Immingham, March and New England.

In November 1946, the LNE decided to purchase 200 WD 2–8–0s and the 190 in service on loan were taken into stock on 28 December 1946, and the other ten were recorded as LNE stock in January and February 1947. The price was £4500 each. The LNE classified them as O7 and they were to be lettered "LNER". Between February and April 1947, they were renumbered LNE 3000–3199 in order of construction, 3000–3100 being those built by North British (irrespective of which of the two works they had been built at) and 3101–99 being those built by Vulcan Foundry. However, there were two anomalies, WD 77002 (3001) was placed after 77009 (3000) although both were built in February 1943; and 70852 (3071) was shown as built in July 1944 instead of June, which thus placed it after 77265 (3070).

The LNE coded the boiler as type 119 and allotted them its own numbers 10151–350, not related to the former WD numbers. They also purchased 17 spare boilers, one from North British (previously on 77406), one from Vulcan Foundry (previously on 7095), six from Longmoor, and nine from Belgium (including two that had been on 78533 and 78657). The tenders were numbered 3000–3199 in the LNE series, the same as the locomotive numbers.

By 1947, many of the LNE O7 2–8–0s needed general repairs. To help the LNE, 35 locomotives were repaired by Vickers Armstrong at Scotswood Works in 1947, with another 17 in hand at the end of the year.

The LNE requirements for freight engines were still not satisfied, and all through 1947, more and more WD 2–8–0s were loaned to the LNE. In September 1947, the number of WD 2–8–0s allotted to the LNE was increased by 68 so that the LMS 8F 2–8–0s on the LNE could be transferred to the LMS. By the end of December 1947, the LNE had 270 WD 2–8–0s on loan (in addition to the 200 purchased). These went into service as follows; nine in January 1947, WD 77061, 77201/7/35 and 77411/53/4/8/84; 32 in February, 70817, 77003/10/22/42/50/70/89/95, 77175, 77260/3/78/83, 77303/23/72/90/2, 77418/24/39/41/5/65/7/8/92/7, 78601/10 and 79220; 57 in March, 70871, 77004/6/16–8/31/4/6/44/63/7/75/8, 77104/20/1/8/9/38/49/64/7/74/85/7, 77204/6/18/21/32/52/61/74/92, 77315/38/42/53/8/62, 77402/4/13/26/33/69/70/94, 78537/59/64/94, 79182 and 79227/9/42; 17 in April, 77051/85, 77124/95/9, 77230/7, 77334/56/71, 77414/9/59, 78561/75 and

Plate 87 BR 90265 (ex WD 7375) on Goole shed in April 1966 (Photo: David Mills)

79259/64; 14 in May, 77057, 77118/70, 77271, 77314/51/64, 77434/61, 78525/68/72, 78609 and 79208; 13 in June, 70834, 77047/55/81, 77147, 77307/28, 77401/80, 78587/92 and 79181/98; twelve in July, 70877, 77169/86, 77208, 77305, 77488, 78600/16/37 and 79202/6/63; 29 in August, 70802/39, 77035/41/66/76, 77127/55, 77222/48, 77309/13/20/4/75/81/95, 77406/25/40, 78553/78/88/99. 79184/6 and 79209/39/43; 35 in September, 70807, 77019/32/7/9/71/3/87/96, 77107/19/78/81/98, 77209/31, 77302/12/7, 77431/42/55/7/62/76, 78514/32/85, 78614/82/3, 79204/65 and 79306/10; 32 in October, 70850, 77008/13/23/88, 77111/35/44, 77215/58, 77319/29/52, 77416/28/36/49/52/99, 77503, 78526/38/98, 78643/50/84, 78715, 79178/94 and 79271/6/80; and twenty in November, 77020/68, 77152/7/63/6/73/6/82, 77227/8/49, 77350/86/94, 77415/32/64, 78700 and 79312. These engines were allocated all over the LNE system.

One of the January 1947 engines, WD 77458, was out of store at Longmoor from the first batch. Others were received direct from Europe, or out of store, or from Belgium. All these engines needed repair before being placed in service, and were dealt with at Brighton, Crewe or Eastleigh, or else by R. Stephenson & Hawthorns or Vickers Armstrong, while no less than 111 were overhauled in Belgium before being sent back to the UK.

As mentioned earlier, WD 77080 and 77225, which arrived in July 1946, stood at Darlington Works for a long period, and by the end of 1947, they had been joined there by 77024 (June 1946 return stored at Tuxford), 77162 (July 1946 return stored at Dover), 77306 (June 1946 return stored at Woodford), 77365 (July 1946 return stored at Dover) and 77465 (June 1946 returned stored at Northampton). All these engines were by now cannibalised for spare parts. WD 77253, which returned in 1947, was under repair at Stratford Works. Thus, at the end of 1947, eight engines officially awaited going on loan to the LNE.

The LNE made some detail changes to the WD 2–8–0s. Even before the locomotives had been purchased, in July 1946, they started removing the air compressors. Following purchase, the cabs were fitted with doors, sliding side windows and sliding roof ventilators. The right-hand side arms of the regulator handles were removed. Steam heating, if fitted, was removed. A new type of water gauge was fitted. An anti-glare screen was fitted to the left side of the firebox door. By July 1947, it was agreed that these alterations could also be made to the locomotives on loan. In September 1947, replacement superheater elements were made 9 SWG (Standard Wire Gauge) instead of 11 SWG (that is, 0.144in instead of 0.116in), the thicker tube walls reducing the heating surface from 310 to 298sq ft. The vacuum relief valves gave trouble and so a new type was designed based on LNE practice.

Both R. Stephenson & Hawthorn and Vickers Armstrong continued their work of overhauls and modifications. In 1947/8, RSH dealt with 33 locomotives, but most work went to Vickers Armstrong who between July 1947 and April 1949 dealt with 475 locomotives, some individual locomotives making a second or even third visit. One, WD 77418, went there four times! Most of the spare boilers went to VA for this work. An LNE boiler was put on 77071 in September 1947, and WD boiler 7071 was put on LNE 3147 in October 1947, but both were identified as LNE boiler 10355, whereas the second should have been numbered in the separate LNE series for boilers of locomotives on loan.

After the war, there was a short-lived scheme to convert some of the British railways locomotives to burn fuel oil instead of coal. The LNE included 111 class O7 locomotives in this scheme, but only one, LNE 3152 (WD 78670), was actually converted, at Doncaster in January 1947. A Weir type burner was fitted in the firebox, and the superheater elements were shortened by 1ft 6in and the firebox stays protected by steel caps. This engine went to March for trials hauling 400 ton freight trains between Whitemoor Yard and Peterborough. Trouble was experienced initially in maintaining steam pressure but this was overcome later by various modifications. In June 1947, conversion started on another locomotive, LNE 3012 (WD 77211) at Vickers Armstrong, but was abandoned. In 1948, the oil burner, by then 63152, was sent to work on the Western Region and was allocated to Old Oak Common, but in October 1948 it was converted back to coal burning at Swindon Works, and returned to the Eastern Region.

On 1 January 1948, the four main line companies in Britain were merged into British Railways. In 1948, the eight WD 2–8–0s 77024/80, 77162, 77225/53, 77306/65 & 77465 at Darlington and Stratford Works went on loan to BR, plus eight others all 1947 returns, as follows; in January 1948 to Mexborough 77253; in February 1948, 77225 to Hull Dairycoates and 77306 to Eastfield; in March 1948, 77027 to Cardiff and 79279 to Severn Tunnel Junction; in April 1948, 77162 and 77456 to Eastfield; in May 1948, 77237 and 77365/99 to Aberdeen, 77080 and 77374 to Eastfield, 78607 and 79228 to Newport Ebbw Junction and 79283 to Old Oak Common; and in July 1948, 77024 to Aberdeen (that is, eleven to ex LNE sheds and five to ex GWR sheds).

Thus, by this time, British Railways owned 200 (ex LNE) and had 425 WD 2–8–0s on loan, consisting of the following:

GWR, September to December 1946	15
GWR, 1947	74
LNE, 1947	270
SR, March 1946	20
SR, September 1946	5
SR, 1947	25
	409
BR, 1948	16
	425

From March 1948, 60,000 was added to the running numbers of the ex LNE O7s.

Plate 88   WD 70805 awaiting shipment to Hong Kong at the Royal Albert Docks in October 1946 (Photo: R. E. Tustin)

The modifications which the LNE started to carry out in 1946/7 as discussed earlier were continued by all Regions of British Railways. Water gauges were largely replaced by LMS or BR standard fittings. The crossheads were altered to take gudgeon pins held by nuts. However, some Regional variations started to appear. Western Region locomotives overhauled at Swindon Works were usually fitted with GWR pattern top feed which increased the height to 13ft 2 3/4in and so restricted their route availability off the Western Region. The Western Region also added a compartment for the firing irons on the right-hand side of the running plate. Some engines overhauled in Scotland received another type of top feed with the clacks further apart. From 1951, the Eastern and North Eastern Regions made some detailed changes to the boiler design, and adopted a new tube arrangement of 161 tubes of 2in diameter instead of 193 tubes of 1 3/4in diameter, reducing the heating surface by 50sq ft. Doncaster pattern inspection doors replaced the washout plugs on the firebox sides. About a third of the boilers were so modified, mostly at Darlington but some at Crewe and Gorton. The spare boilers built at Crewe also had these changes. On the other boilers, the number of tubes was reduced from 193 to 189, reducing the heating surface by 22sq ft.

Other changes made were from June 1954 onwards the blastpipe orifice was reduced in diameter, from 1955 onwards fibreglass mattresses were used for boiler lagging to reduce heat losses, from January 1959 onwards British Railways type Automatic Warning System was fitted to many locomotives, and also from 1959 the London Midland Region decided to fit a glass screen on the driver's side of the cab.

Some trial modifications were made. One engine, BR 90527, was rebalanced to take account of 40% of the reciprocating masses, and the fore-and-aft movement was considerably reduced, but no further engines were re-balanced although rough riding remained a source of complaints. In 1949/50, New England engines BR 90169, 90253, 90659/65 and 90730 were temporarily fitted with Automatic Warning System for trials on the East Coast main line between Barnet and Peterborough. Because of trouble with tender derailments when running tender first, in 1953/4 BR 90184 and 90473 were fitted with larger springs on the third and fourth axles on their tenders. The results were sufficiently good for the London Midland Region to obtain authority to alter 310 tenders, but the other Regions were not convinced and did not alter their tenders.

The first locomotive to be withdrawn from British Railways was 90083 in December 1959. Two more went in 1960, 80 in 1962, 97 in 1963, 125 in 1964, 201 in 1965, 104 in 1966 and the last 123 in 1967. The last 2-8-0s to work on British Railways were those allocated to Normanton in what was then Eastern Region, and they were withdrawn in September 1967, the last being 90632.

After the war, locomotives were required on the British Section of the Kowloon-Canton Railway to replace those taken away during the war (See Chapter 38). Accordingly, in 1946 twelve WD 2-8-0s in store at Longmoor were purchased by the Crown Agents and overhauled at Woolwich Arsenal. They were also fitted with centre knuckle-type couplers, electric headlights and cowcatchers. Vacuum brake equipment was replaced by air brake. The first six, which became KCR 21-6, were sent from King George V Dock in London in October and November 1946, and the other six, which became KCR 27-32, followed in 1947 from Tilbury Docks, as shipping became available. They were given a grey livery before despatch, with their WD numbers in large figures on the cab sides and smokebox door.

On arrival in Hong Kong, they were renumbered KCR 21-32 and soon repainted green with white smokebox doors, with their new KCR numbers on the cab sides, smokebox doors and tender sides. In service, they were used for both passenger and freight trains up to the Chinese border. However, their narrow fireboxes were not satisfactory with the low grade of coal available. Five of them, KCR 21-5, were converted to burn oil fuel, with satisfactory results, but subsequently "Hulson" grates, with narrow gaps between the firebars and so particularly suitable for low-grade coal, were fitted to the remainder and their performance was greatly improved. In 1951, over 9000 tons of railway equipment for

Plate 89   KCR 32 (ex WD 79237) at Kowloon, Hong Kong, in April 1957 (Photo: C. S. Small)

China was worked over the KCR, the WD 2–8–0s easily working 700 ton trains up the 1 in 100 incline to Beacon Hill Tunnel. By August 1954, only four remained as oil burners, KCR 21–4.

The first diesel locomotives arrived in August 1955 and left little work for the WD 2–8–0s. Six were put into store, and the others used solely on freight workings. On 27 April 1956, the firebox crown on KCR 22 collapsed, the explosion leading to six deaths. In 1957, more diesels were acquired and seven WD 2–8–0s were withdrawn, leaving three (KCR 23/6/9) in traffic and two (KCR 27 and 32) retained as spares. By 1960, only 3500 train-miles were operated by steam, and KCR 26 was the last engine to work on 2 September 1962.

The original numbers, delivery dates and withdrawal dates are given opposite.

Two of the WD 2–8–0s, WD 77337 and 79250, remained allocated to the Longmoor Military railway and were named "Sir Guy Williams" and "Major General McMullen" respectively. WD 79189 (ex NS 4509) was returned to the WD and almost certainly went to the USA in the post-war exchange of specimen locomotives, WD for USA/TC 2–8–0s and 0–6–0Ts. Thus the post-war disposal of the 935 WD Standard 2–8–0s was 733 to British Railways, 184 to the NS, 12 to the KCR, three scrapped, two to Longmoor and one to the USA.

It is a pity that there is only one WD 2–8–0 in preservation, which is WD 79257 (ex NS 4464 and SJ 1931) on the Keighley & Worth Valley Railway. This has been modified in some ways, in particular the tender shortened and changed to six-wheeled, so does not represent the WD 2–8–0s very well but it is nevertheless good that one survives. At the time of writing (1991), there are plans to convert this engine back to its original WD appearance.

KCR No	WD No	Despatched	Landed Kowloon	Out of service	Withdrawn
21	78660	1946	1/47	5/56	8/57
22	77268	1946	12/46	5/56	8/57
23	70805	1946	12/46	6/58	8/59
24	77509	1946	12/46	4/57	8/57
25	77490	1946	2/47	8/57	8/57
26	77478	1946	2/47	9/62	5/63
27	77269	1946	8/47	12/60	3/62
28	70820	1946	8/47	9/55	8/57
29	78694	1947	3/48	9/62	3/63
30	77450	1947	3/48	6/56	8/57
31	78659	1947	3/48	5/55	8/57
32	79237	1947	3/48	12/56	8/59

Chapter 25

WHITCOMB 650hp DIESEL LOCOMOTIVES USED IN THE MIDDLE EAST & ITALY
WD 1200–51 & 1537–96, MRS 1200–8/32–71

In May 1941, twenty-five diesel locomotives were ordered from America under Lease-Lend for service in the Middle East. They were built by the Whitcomb Locomotive Co of Rochelle, Illinois under Extra Order 3096 (WD 1200–24). In October 1941, a repeat order for 27 locomotives was made, the two extra being to replace two of the first batch lost at sea, and they were built under Extra Order 3132 (WD 1225–51). Their Whitcomb designation was type 65DE14. In May 1942, 40 more were ordered; and in June 1942 another sixty. These were generally similar to WD 1200–51 but incorporated certain modifications, including an improved braking system, which increased the weight slightly. The first 40 were type 65DE14a and were numbered WD 1537–76. In the event, only 20 were made of the second lot. These had some further modifications and were type 65DE14b, being numbered 1577–96. The cancelled 40 would have been numbered 1597–1636. The running numbers of these locomotives, 1200–51 and 1537–96, were included in both the WD and the USA/TC stock lists.

Details of the differences between the three types are given in the following table.

Nos	1200–51	1537–76	1577–96
Specification	65DE14	65DE14a	65DE14b
Weight in WC, tons (short), no armour	65	73	73
Type of starter	Motor	Generator	Generator
Top spectacles fitted above engine covers	Yes	No	No
Cab side windows	Large	Large	Small
Auxiliary contactor gear cabinet inside cab	No	Yes	Yes

The works numbers were as follows:

WD	Whitcomb	
1200–24	60130–54	1942
1225–51	60167–93	1942
1537/8	60236/7	1942
1539–76	60238–75	1943
1577–96	60302–21	1943

The design was conventional by American standards. The locomotives weighed some 67 tons in working order and were powered by two Buda diesel engines giving a total power output of 650hp, so that the power/weight ratio was nearly 10:1. Each axle had its own nose-suspended electric traction motor. The cab was in the centre of the locomotive. A number of special features were provided for high-temperature desert service. The radiators, fans and air ducts were designed to provide adequate cooling. To prevent sand entering the engine compartments, all the air was passed through oil-bath filters as well as through conventional cleaners. They were fitted with vacuum brakes for use with ESR rolling stock and straight air-brake equipment for the locomotives themselves.

WD 1208/9/41/3/5 and 1552/3 were lost at sea en route to the Middle East. The others all arrived safely. In November 1944, they all had 5000 added to their numbers to bring them into the MEF series 6200–51 and 6537–96. Locomotives 1577 onwards were renumbered immediately on arrival. The fifty-

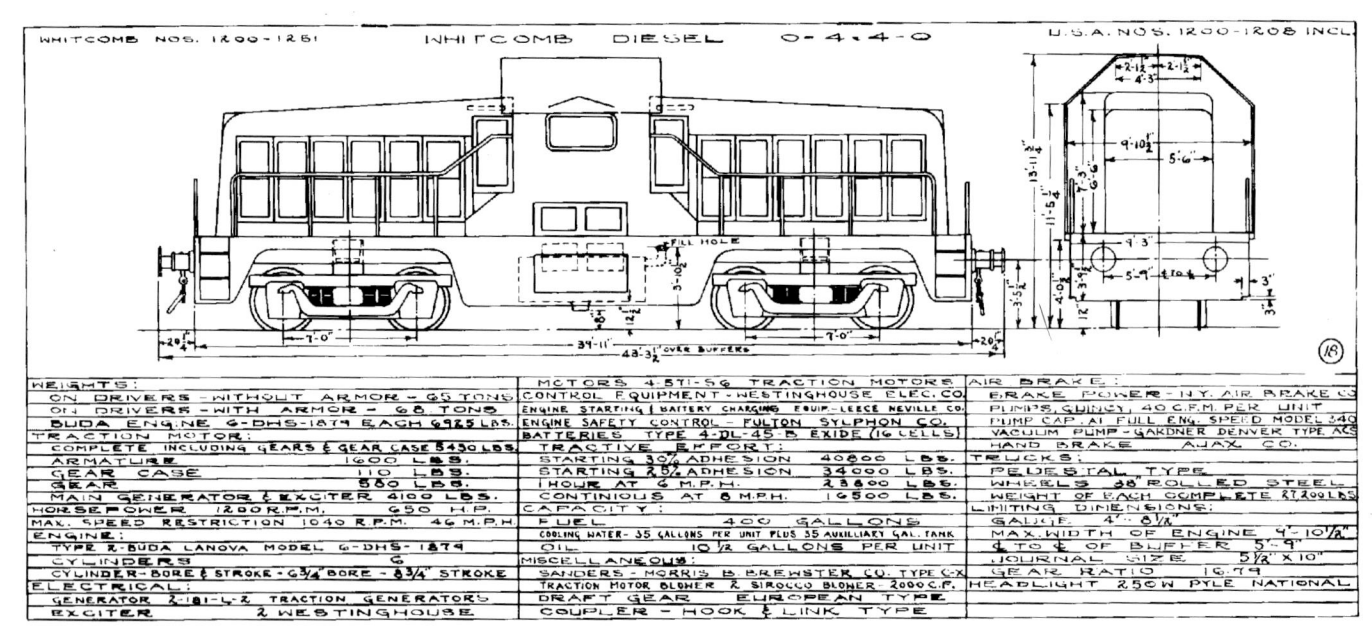

Fig 13   Dimensions and details of the Whitcomb 0–4–4–0DE WD 1200-51

six locomotives which remained in the MEF area were duly renumbered into the WD 71200–51 and 71537–96 series when the 7XXXX series numbering scheme came into force.

The first of the locomotives, WD 1200, arrived at Suez in June 1942 and such was the urgency of military requirements that the locomotive was in running order within four hours of the chassis being set on the tracks. By the end of October 1942, twenty-one of these locomotives had arrived in the Middle East. A further twenty arrived shortly afterwards and the remaining five of the first series WD 1200–51, apart from the five sunk en route, slightly later.

These diesels were naturally most suitable for the Western Desert Extension Railway. By the end of 1942, nineteen were there, WD 1200–4/6/7/10–21. Early in 1943, another seventeen had arrived, WD 1222–8/30–3/5/44/8–51. Most of the first series were thus available for the second offensive in the Western desert as detailed in Chapter 3. For this, many were armour-plated for a time, having the entire cab fabricated from case-hardened steel. In addition, special end plates of case-hardened steel were fitted and the top of the engine compartment hood was armour-plated. Sufficient sets of armour plating for fifty-two locomotives were delivered from Whitcomb but it is not know if all these sets were used. In some instances, the locomotives were camouflaged as box cars. They were then often used in the middle of the train, a relatively inconspicuous position.

Later, when the enemy were on the retreat, and speed rather than caution became the need, the customary manner

Plate 90   MEF 6557 on Haifa to Azzib train in the loop at Manshia station on the HBT. This locomotive still has the armoured-plated cab and plates of case-hardened steel (Photo: F. Saville)

Plate 91   WD 71240 (Photo: R. Tourret Collection)

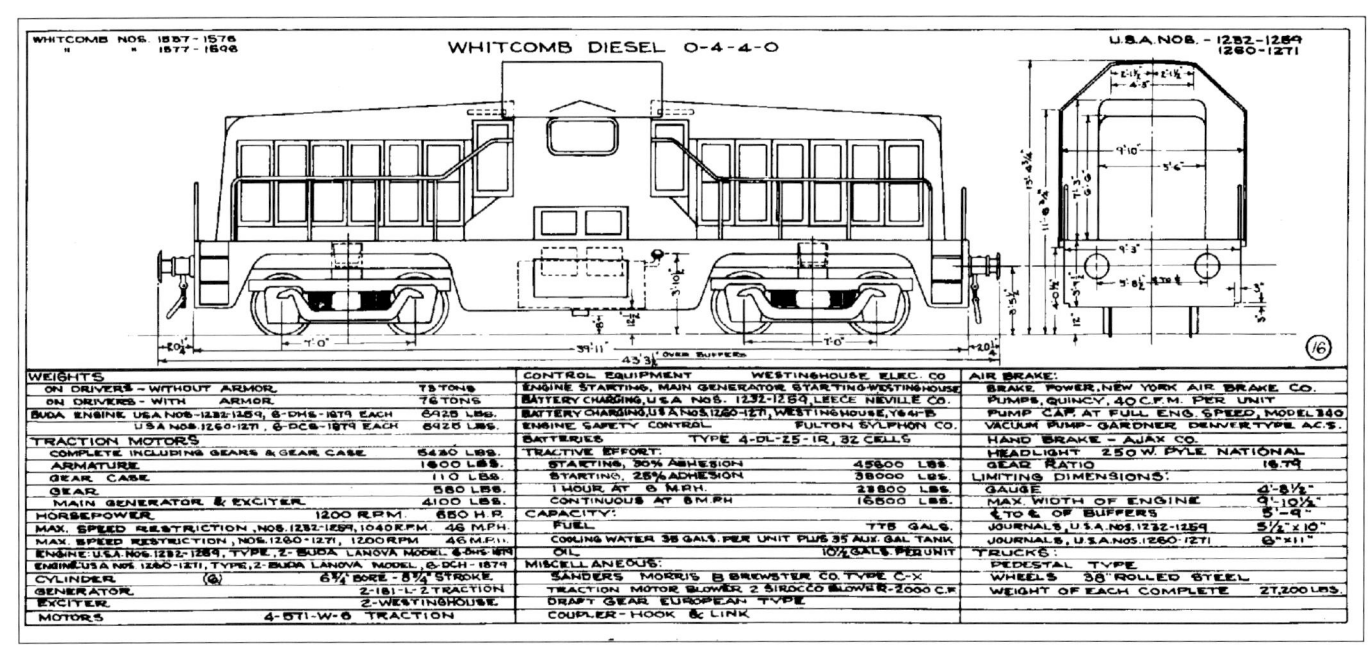

Fig 14   Dimensions and details of the Whitcomb 0–4–4–0DE WD 1537–96

Plate 92   One of the Whitcomb diesel locomotives pulling Egyptian freight wagons out of the yard at Similla Junction, near Mersa Matruh, in July 1943 (Photo: R. Tourret Collection)

Plate 93   WD 71555 at the army depot at Azzib on the HBT in June 1945 (Photo: R. E. Tustin)

of operating over the single line was to use two locomotives at the head of the train, which was then made as long as possible. The first batch suffered somewhat from inadequate braking power and this, rather than insufficient hauling power, was the reason for the double-heading. The later series, WD 1537–96, incorporated an improved braking system.

As the number of locomotives in service increased, some were sent to Kantara (East) for working transfer freights

Plate 94   MRS 1238 (ex WD 1547) on war service in Italy crossing a temporary bridge (Photo: R. Tourret Collection)

between there and Nefisha marshalling yards about two miles west of Ismailia, via the El Firdan Swing bridge across the Suez Canal. They also began to work on the newly-constructed line running parallel to the Canal down its east bank to El Shatt, opposite Port Tewfik. ESR had ten on loan for this duty. By the end of March 1943, 41 locomotives had been erected.

From then on the requirements of the WDER lessened and it was decided to operate the HBT with these diesels. In April 1943, four arrived and eight more in May (WD 1201/3/4/14/5/8/20/2/31/5/49/51). They were normally used in pairs. Six more were transferred in July (WD 1205/37/9/40/6/7), one more (WD 1575) in October and four more in November (WD 1542/55/71/91), bringing the total to 23. In December, WD 6595/6 arrived as a replacement for WD 6218/22 (which went to Italy).

They worked most, if not all, of the traffic on the HBT until about the middle of 1944, when they were replaced by steam locomotives. For a time, the PR used them on the Qantara to Gaza section, where two diesels coupled together could haul a 1000 ton load, provided that there were at least seven vacuum-fitted wagons at the front for adequate braking. Eight diesels were transferred there in August 1943 and a further eight in October 1943. Four these went on to the HBT in November 1943, leaving 12 on hire to the PR until June 1944.

Between August and September 1943, four units, WD 1200/12/36/8, were transferred to North Africa. In 1944, these four were sent on to Italy. Between November 1943 and January 1944, forty-five were sent directly to Italy, these being MEF 6210/8/9/22/5 and 6538/40/1/3–5/7–9/51/4/6/8–61/3–70/2–4/6–83/5–7/9/93.

At January 1944, 23 were on the HBT (WD 6201/3–5/14/5/20/31/5/7/9/40/6/7/9/51 and 6542/55/71/5/91/5/6), twelve on the PR (WD 6228/9/33/42 and 6537/9/46/50/7/62/90/2) and five probably with the Army in Egypt (WD 6206/34 and 6584/8/94). In January 1944, WD 6546 moved from the PR to the Army in Palestine, and in February 1944 back again to the PR. In February 1944, three diesels went from the HBT to the Army in Palestine (WD 6203–5) and five from the Army in Egypt to the Army in Palestine (WD 6206/34 and 6584/8/94). In March 1944, three moved from the HBT to the Army in Palestine (WD 6237/49 and 6595), and two (WD 6584/94) back from the Army in Palestine to the HBT. In April 1944, WD 6588/95 moved from the Army in Palestine to the HBT. In May

Plate 95   MRS 1239 and 1203 hauling a freight train past a war-damaged yard near Rome. Although these locomotives are marked "USA", the numbers belong to the MRS series (Photo: R. Tourret Collection)

Plate 96   MRS 1266 (ex WD 1593) at Rome Littorio in 1946 (Photo: R. S. Savill)

1944, WD 6240 moved from the HBT to the Army in Palestine. In June 1944, seven moved from the PR to the Army in Palestine (WD 6228/9/33/42 and 6539/46/92), one (WD 6249) from the Army in Palestine to the HBT, and five (WD 6537/56/7/62/90) from the PR to the WDER. In July 1944, WD 6214 moved from the HBT to the Army in Palestine, and WD 6228/40 from the Army in Palestine to the HBT.

The stock position on 1 August 1944 of the 105 units was as follows. Thirteen locomotives (WD 1207/11/6/21/3/4/32/ 44/50/7/62/88/90) were on the Western Desert Extension Railway. In Egypt under repair were WD 1227/50 and 1537; awaiting repair were WD 1226/30/49 and 1595; and put aside were WD 1202/ 13/7/48. In Palestine stored serviceable were WD 1233/42 and 1529/46; awaiting repair were WD 1214/29 and 1592; and put aside were WD 1203–6/34/7. Fourteen units were in service on the HBT, WD 1201/15/20/8/31/40/2/6/7 and 1571/5/84/91/4 and under repair on the HBT were WD 1235/9/51/5 and 1596. The remaining 49 units were in Italy.

In the Middle East, trouble began to be experienced with cracked cylinder heads, so it was decided to concentrate these diesels on the WDER, maintained by No 169 Railway Workshops Co at Suez.

In November 1944, WD 6592 moved from the Army in Palestine to the HBT and WD 6247 the reverse. In January 1945, WD 6214 moved from the Army in Palestine to the Army in Egypt. In February 1945, WD 6201/15/20/8/31/ 5/46/51 and 6542/55/71/5/84/91/2/4/6 moved from the HBT to the Army in Palestine, and WD 6239/40 from the HBT to the Army in Egypt. In April 1945, WD 6201/5 moved from the Army in Palestine to the Army in Egypt. In July 1945, WD 6571/96 moved from the Army in Palestine to the Army in Egypt. In September 1945, WD 6203–6/20/ 8/35/7/42/6 and 6542/75/84/92/4 moved from the Army in Palestine to the Army in Egypt, and WD 6229/31/3/51 and 6539/46 from the Army in Palestine to the WDER. In October 1945, WD 6234/47 and 6555/91 moved from the Army in Palestine to the Army in Egypt.

By December 1945, thirty-two locomotives were on the Western Desert Extension railway, although a number has been withdrawn to supply spares for the others. The remainder were "sided" or under repair at Suez RE workshops. Five of the last, 1215/26/42/6 and 1555, were repaired, polished up and used for the Returned Allied Prisoners of War and Internees traffic between Adabiya and Suez in November and December 1945. The RAPWI traffic consisted of carrying the ex-POWs etc from Adabiya where they were landed, to Suez on their way to the United Kingdom.

In the years immediately after the war, several locomotives were named, as follows:

1215	Doreen
1228	Kathleen
1239	Kiwi
1244	Ivy
1539	Susan
1555	Christine
1592	Shirley
1594	Irene, later Hilda
1596	Mary Ann

Forty-nine locomotives were shipped to Italy in January 1944 and came under USA/TC control. They were renumbered into the MRS series 1200–8/32–71, in order of their arrival in Italy, in three batches as follows: 1200 upwards, 1259 downwards and 1260 upwards. Locomotives from MEF 6200–51 became MRS 1200–8, from MEF 6537–76 became MRS 1232–59 and from MEF 6577–96 became MRS 1260–71. These numbers were frequently referred to as USA/TC numbers, even in Italy at the time, but they were in fact MRS numbers.

Details of the renumbering are as follows:

Plate 97 WD 71217 undergoing repair at No 169 Rly Wksp at Suez in autumn 1947 (Photo: H. Sanderson)

The first units in Italy arrived at Brindisi in January and February 1944 for use from there to Foggia. They were used only at night, being kept inside the shed during the day. Later, 1200–8/32–71 were all allocated to Naples (where most of them except the first few had been unloaded) or Caserta. They stayed at these sheds until the line was opened to Rome, when half of them were sent to Rome. As the advance continued, all the diesels were moved up until Florence was taken, by which time the 1300–67 series had arrived directly from the United States (See Chapter 61).

At the end of the war, all the diesels were allocated to Florence depot and at January 1946 all were in fact at Florence except for 1202/6/50 which were in store at Littorio (Rome). By summer 1946, although all the locomotives were still officially allocated to Florence, many were in store or under repair at Littorio. In June 1946, 1240/5/8 were taken out of store and sent to Trieste to operate transfer freights from the docks to the marshalling yard. Nos 1200–8/32–71 were taken into stock by the FS as Nos Ne 1200.001–49 in order, probably in 1947. From 1952 or so, they were renumbered Ne 120.001–49.

After acquisition by the FS, the rather unsatisfactory Buda engines were taken out and replaced by a pair of 250hp Fiat engines in 1947–50. The locomotives were still considered not very satisfactory for their size, so in 1966, sixteen were withdrawn for rebuilding by Tecnomasio Italiano Brown Boveri (TIBB). They were given a single 570hp OM engine and a TIBB generator, as well as having all the electrical systems renewed except for the original Westinghouse traction motors. The same external outline was retained, although the Whitcomb works plates naturally vanished. The sixteen came out

MRS	0	1	2	3	4	5	6	7	8	9
120X	1200	1212	1236	1238	1219	1218	1210	1225	1222	–
123X	–	–	1586	1563	1565	1589	1568	1564	1547	1556
124X	1576	1559	1541	1572	1544	1574	1558	1561	1560	1538
125X	1543	1545	1548	1567	1573	1549	1551	1570	1554	1540
126X	1585	1581	1586	1578	1580	1577	1593	1583	1589	1582
127X	1579	1587	–	–	–	–	–	–	–	–

Two of the Middle East locomotives, WD 1232/3, were brought back to the UK and went to Longmoor by April 1948, where they were subsequently named "Tobruk" and "Algiers". They were renumbered WD 890/1 in the postwar scheme in 1952. WD 891 was withdrawn in March 1953 and some parts were used to keep WD 890 operational until this locomotive was scrapped in 1957.

Plate 98   WD 71539 "Susan" in Suez Farz on goods train from Ataku to No 169 Rly Wksp Suez in January 1948 (Photo: H. Sanderson)

with TIBB 1966 works plates but no works numbers, as FS D143.3001–16, in 1966 and 1967. Another sixteen were withdrawn and similarly treated, coming out as TIBB 6874–89 dated 1970, being D143.3017–32 and appearing during 1970–2. The remaining seventeen were withdrawn in 1972 and reappeared as D143.3033–49 during 1972–4. No effort was made to allot numbers corresponding to the previous Ne 120 class numbers as is usual on the FS on these occasions, but new numbers were allocated to the locomotives as they were rebuilt.

Details of the renumbering are as follows:

Plate 99   WD 71233 at Longmoor in October 1952 (Photo: E. W. Fry)

D143	0	1	2	3	4	5	6	7	8	9
300X	–	039	002	036	006	009	047	030	018	016
301X	040	033	031	005	015	022	008	038	012	021
302X	042	026	017	027	023	034	028	019	035	004
303X	043	003	044	029	048	041	007	025	046	014
304X	010	045	011	013	001	020	024	037	032	049

Plate 100   FS Whitcomb diesel Ne 120.030 at Turin Smistamento depot (Photo: R. Tourret Collection)

Chapter 26

STANDARD WD 0–6–0STs, WD 1437–56/62–1536, 5000–5199, 5250–5331

As mentioned in Chapter 24, the origin of these engines dates back to 1942 when it was decided to prepare for an invasion of the Continent, for which a heavy shunting locomotive was required, and that Hunslet Engine Co should proceed with the design and construction. Initially, it was considered that the LMS 3F 0–6–0T should be taken as the basic design but in view of the short delivery required and the need to economise in manpower, the Ministry of Supply accepted Hunslet's proposal that the design should be based on their industrial 0–6–0STs, this decision being taken in July and August 1942.

There were three chief reasons for this change. Fewer man-hours were needed to build this engine. It had simpler forging and machining requirements, for instance. Indeed, it was claimed that at least three Hunslet 0–6–0STs could be built for every two LMS-type 0–6–0Ts. Less drawing office work would be required to incorporate the changes in design necessary to suit the material available. Finally, the shorter wheelbase and greater compactness generally gave a greater availability.

The original Hunslet design may be traced back to 1923 when a short-wheelbase 38¾ ton inside cylinder 0–6–0ST was built for a Yorkshire colliery. This was developed in 1930 when a heavy 0–6–0ST with 48in wheels was built for the Pontop & Jarrow Railway of the Bowes colliery group, and further developed in 1937 when an even larger engine, known as the 48150 class, with 48½in wheels weighing 46¼ tons on an 11ft wheelbase was built for a steel works. Finally, in 1941, a batch of engines, known as the 50550 class, was built with the same wheel and wheelbase dimensions but with a weight of 49¼ tons, for Stewarts and Lloyds Minerals Ltd for use between a planned new ironstone quarry at Islip and the company's Corby steel works. However, this project was abandoned and of the eight locomotives built, only one went to Stewarts & Lloyds. Three were taken over by the WD in 1942, becoming WD 65–7. This 50550 design first introduced the distinctive full-length saddle tank, so that the appearance of WD 65–7 is very similar to that of the WD Standard 0–6–0STs.

The WD Standard 0–6–0STs were designed to give a minimum of two years hard work irrespective of the state of the track. It was accepted that the locomotives were to be essentially for war-time use and need not be designed to last as long as normal peace-time locomotives. Changes were made in detail design therefore to economise in production time and to use available materials.

The weight of steel castings had to be reduced to a minimum and cast-iron wheel centres were used instead of cast steel. Steel castings were eliminated from the motion plates and frame stays. Lower quality steel was accepted for the tyres and this was used in the "as rolled" condition without annealing to save production time and costs. Despite this, the tyres have given good service. Cast-iron bushes were tried in the coupling rods and valve-spindle guides of the first few locomotives but these were soon substituted by phosphor-bronze bushes. Cast-iron slide valves were fitted.

To suit the changed operating conditions, the wheel diameter was increased by 2½in to 4ft 3in to give greater wheel clearance and to make the engines more suitable for short-journey military trains. The tank capacity was increased by 200gl to 1200gl, and the bunker capacity was increased slightly. All the other changes were made either to assist production or to suit available materials. A comparison of the various designs is given below.

The first locomotive was built in about 4½ months, and was first steamed on 1 January 1943. Hunslet built forty-nine more engines in the next ten months. Because of the large numbers needed, orders were also given to Robert Stephenson & Hawthorns, Hudswell Clarke, Bagnall and later to Andrew Barclay and Vulcan Foundry. Hunslet supplied all the drawings and general instructions, and ordered some of the materials, such as copper plates, in bulk for all the builders. To expedite production, other builders supplied certain components, such as firebox front and back plates, for all the locomotives.

Eventually, 377 of these locomotives were built in the years 1943–7 as follows; 120 from Hunslet, 90 from Robert Stephenson & Hawthorns, 52 from Bagnall, 50 from Hudswell Clarke, 50 from Vulcan Foundry and 15 from Andrew Barclay. Five more, which would have been 1457–61 from Hunslet, were cancelled. In late 1951, the Ministry of Supply ordered fourteen more 0–6–0STs, so that construction started again with WD (post-war series) 190–203 in 1952/3.

The works numbers were as follows:

1437/8	HE 3201/2	1944
1439–56	HE 3203–20	1945
1462–5	AB 2211–4	1946
1466	AB 2215	1947
1467–74	HC 1785–92	1945
1475/6	HC 1793/4	1946
1477–86	RSH 7286–95	1945
1487–96	HC 1763–72	1944
1497–1502	HC 1774–9	1944
1503–6	HC 1780–3	1945
1507–26	RSH 7161–80	1944
1527	AB 2181	1944
1528–35	AB 2182–9	1945
1536	AB 2190	1946
5000–49	HE 2849–98	1943
5050–79	RSH 7086–7115	1943
5080–4	HC 1737–41	1943
5085–9	HC 1744–8	1943
5090–4	HC 1751–5	1943
5095	HC 1758	1943
5096–9	HC 1759–62	1944
5100–36	HE 3150–86	1944
5137–46	HE 3188–97	1944
5147	HE 3187	1944

	LMS Class 3F 0–6–0T	Hunslet 18in 0–6–0ST 1937	Hunslet 18in 0–6–0ST 1941	"Austerity" 0–6–0ST
Cylinders, in	18 x 26	18 x 26	18 x 26	18 x 26
Wheel dia, ft in	4'7"	4'0½"	4'0½"	4'3"
Wheelbase, ft in	16'6"	11'0"	11'0"	11'0"
Boiler pressure, lb/sq in	160	170	170	170
Heating surface, sq ft	1064	960	970	960
Grate area, sq ft	16.0	16.8	16.8	16.8
Weight in WO, tons	49.5	46.35	49.35	48.2
Max. axle load, tons	17.7	15.9	17.0	16.35
Weight of lightest rail, lb/yd	90	80	85	80
Minimum curve, ft	450	180	180	180
Tractive effort at 85% BP, lb	18,400	26,280	26,280	23,870

Plate 101   WD 75108 at Stonor in June 1946 (Photo: A. G. Wells)

5148/9	HE 3198/9	1944
5150–73	WGB 2738–61	1944
5174–9	WGB 2762–7	1945
5180–99	RSH 7130–49	1944
5250–71	WGB 2773–94	1945
5272–81	RSH 7202–11	1945
5282–5331	VF 5272–5321	1945
190/1*	HE 3790/1	1952
192–203*	HE 3792–3803	1953

*Post-war series

The frame structure, main frames and buffer beams, were built up of 1¼in thick plates strongly braced by welded vertical and horizontal frame stretchers and by a big inside-cylinder casting. There was a good depth between the tops of the horns and the top of the frames, and the horn stays were of a deeper and stronger section than normal. This was all intended to give a strong structure which would not deflect under service stresses. The axlebox and crankpin bearing surfaces were ample.

The adhesion factor of 5:1 in full working order and about 4.7:1 in normal working conditions, in conjunction with a pilot-valve regulator, rendered these engines generally immune from slipping. Indeed, they were capable of starting and hauling at low speed a freight train of 1000 to 1100 tons weight on the level, 550 tons up an incline of 1 in 100, and 300 tons up an incline of 1 in 50. The boiler proportions were chosen to give quick steaming without being uneconomical during standby periods. The boiler had a cylindrical barrel 4ft 3in in external diameter by 10ft 2in long, the contours being continued over a round-top firebox. The firebox was shallow but there was a fair ashpan capacity. Asbestos mattresses were used for the boiler lagging and only the firebox back-plate was not lagged. Two 2 in Ross pop safety valves were fitted together with two Gresham & Craven hot-water injectors below the cab feeding through internal pipes. There was a wire-net spark arrestor in the smokebox. A welded saddle tank was fitted, extending to the front of the smokebox.

Stephensons link motion actuated ordinary cast-iron slide valves located between the cylinders, which were placed directly under the smokebox and which drove the middle axle through strap-end connecting rods. The motion was controlled by a hand reversing lever on the right-hand side of the cab. All wheels were fitted with brakes. Braking power was obtained from a steam brake cylinder under the bunker end of the cab, supplemented by a hand-screw brake. The regulator and the steam brake valve were arranged for control from either side of the cab. Two sanding boxes with steam-sanding equipment were fitted at each end of the locomotive for sanding the leading and trailing wheels for each direction of running. The cab was welded, and fitted with hinged windows back and front and a ventilator in the roof. It was designed so that its upper part could be easily removed.

The first locomotives, WD 5000–44/80–94, were turned out with 2in high numbers, while later ones had 6in high figures. From WD 1489 and 5126 onwards, the khaki livery was changed to the later green colour. Most locomotives had 70,000 added to their numbers after the engine left works; those that were given the five-figure numbers when built were WD 71437–56/62–86/94–1536, 75134–49/64–79 and 75250–331. The "7" prefix is generally omitted here to avoid unnecessary repetition.

The first two engines built were temporarily loaned to the LMS, probably to afford an opportunity of comparing the performance of the design with that of the LMS 0–6–0T on which they might easily have been based. The LMS classified them 3F. As further engines were built, they were allocated to various military establishments, dumps, depots, docks, etc, while some were loaned to industrial concerns, collieries and to the Ministry of Fuel & Power for working at open-cast coal-mining sites. These allocations are unfortunately too complicated to record in detail here.

A few of the locomotives were fitted with Westinghouse brake control gear for use with air-braked stock. WD 75028/41/2/79, for instance, were fitted at Brighton Works in September 1944. The pump was mounted on the right-hand side of the platform in front of the smokebox, steam being provided from a stop valve on top of the dome, controlled by a rod running horizontally from the valve to bearings mounted on the cab roof. The exhaust pipe from the pump ran forward and then looped back to the smokebox. The main reservoir was on the platform on the right-hand side above the driving wheels and the

Plate 102   WD 71483 at Longmoor in January 1947 (Photo: J. B. Latham)

Plate 103 Port of London Authority 88 (ex WD 75116) at Tilbury in May 1947 (Photo: R. Tourret)

PLA	0	1	2	3	4	5	6	7	8	9
7X	–	–	–	–	–	–	(70)	(71)	5089	(66)
8X	5027	5032	5067	5068	5069	5071	5077	5029	5116	–

auxiliary reservoir was on the same side, in front of the cab. The driver's brake valve was mounted on the right-hand cab side sheet, and usual Westinghouse pipe connections were provided on the front and rear buffer beams. A few others of the class had vacuum ejectors and train pipes for working vacuum-fitted stock. Most, if not all, of the locomotives with air or vacuum brake equipment were stationed on the Longmoor Military Railway or the Shropshire and Montgomeryshire Railway.

Some locomotives were loaned to sites important to the war industry, such as coal mine systems. Details are too complicated to be given here. However, it may be mentioned that ten engines found their way to the Port of London Authority in 1944 and 1945 (5116 in May 1946), and became PLA 78, 80–8 as detailed above. They went to the "Royal" docks, except PLA 87/8 which went to Tilbury Docks. While not WD Standard 0–6–0STs, it might be mentioned that the very similar 0–6–0STs WD 66, 70/1 went on loan to the PLA circa 1943 and were numbered PLA 79, 76/7 respectively in May 1946.

As the war in Europe came to a successful conclusion, there were still some outstanding orders for WD 0–6–0STs. These engines were nevertheless manufactured, but the pace of construction slowed and the engines went straight into store at Longmoor at the dates shown below.

June 1943	1480, 1532, 5256/7/91–8 and 5300/2
July 1945	1478/9/81–4, 1533, 5255/99 and 5301/3–6/8–20/2/3
August 1945	5259–61 and 5307/21/4–31
September 1945	1467/85/6 and 5258/62
October 1945	1468/9 and 1534
November 1945	1470/1 and 5263–5
December 1945	1472/3, 1535 and 5266–8
January 1946	1474 and 5269
March 1946	1475 and 5270/1

As will be detailed later, many of these engines subsequently went to the LNER.

After the invasion, 90 were sent to the Continent in late 1944 and early 1945, as follows. The first to go were 18 in November 1944, 5004/5/8–10/3/4/6/8/22/5/51/2/7–9/65/85. Thirty-two went in December 1944, 1489–91/6, 5001/7/12/20/1/3/4/50/5/74/81/6/8 and 5123/7/8/30–2/55–7/9/60/96–9. In January 1945, six were sent 5000/2/3/11/26/82. In February 1945, ten were sent 5053/4/66/80/98 and 5104–6/15/36. There was then a gap until May 1945, when 24 were sent 1439/92, 1502–4/13/8–22/6, 5120/45/6/63/72/5/7/8/85/7 and 5273/9.

In Belgium, in Autumn 1944, there was a shortage of shunting locomotives, in particular for Antwerp Docks. To overcome this, fifty WD 0–6–0STs were sent to Belgium and most of them hired to the SNCB. They were allocated as follows, Antwerp Dam had 75008/21/3/5/50/65 and 75127/8/30/1/59, Antwerp South had 71489, 75010/6/8/22/58/88 and 75132/56/96/7, Merelbeke had 75001–3/7/24/53–5/9/74/82/5/98 and 75105/36/98, and Ostend had 75081. Some were stored as follows, Merelbeke had 71490, 75011/4/51/66 and 75157 in store and Ostend had 75026 in store.

WD 75199 became the No 155 Rly Wksp Co shunter at Malines for a while, and then went to SNCB Muizen as shed pilot for leave train locomotives. WD 71491 and 75020 were used at Brussels Schaerbeek for shunting leave train coaches. WD 71496 is unaccounted for and may well have worked at the dumps of Austerity 2–8–0s at Ostend, Brughes and Ghent, as may have some of the stored locomotives from time to time. It was the original intention to allocate some WD 0–6–0STs to Ghent Zeehaven docks but on carrying out trials, problems were encountered with some sharp curves, so no WD 0–6–0STs were allocated in the event.

By Spring 1946, the locomotive position had improved and the WD 0–6–0STs were returned to the WD. They went into store at Calais and Antwerp where they lay idle for a year or so prior to disposal. As will be discussed shortly, some went to

Plate 104 WD 180 in the post-war series, previously WD 75280 and still showing this number on the frame below the bunker, at Shoeburyness in May 1953 (Photo: A. G. Wells)

Plate 105 WD 181 (ex WD 5282) "Insein" just out of workshops at Longmoor Sheds in May 1953, painted blue (Photo: M. T. McHatton)

NS	0	1	2	3	4	5	6	7	8	9
880X	–	5000	5001	5012	5013	5020	5025	5051	5054	5059
881X	5066	5080	5082	5085	5098	5105	5106	5123	5155	5157
882X	5160	1490	5026	5053	5086	5104	5115	5199	–	–

Holland, while others returned to the UK.

In the Netherlands, the WD 0–6–0STs were distributed fairly evenly throughout the southern half of the country; Roosendaal, Nijmegen and Maastricht having four or five each. Fifteen of these engines were operating on the Nederlandsche Spoorwegen during 1944 and 1945. By early 1945, some allocations were WD 75057 at Eindhoven, 75000/13 and 75160 at Nijmegen, 75012 at Roosendaal, 75009/80 and 75106 at s'Hertogenbosch, and 75086 and 75104/15 at Tilburg. In July 1945, four were returned to the WD authorities and the remainder came under the control of the NS. In August, ten more were loaned to the NS and in November 1945 they were joined by six more, making 27 engines in all. They were renumbered NS 8801–27 as shown in the table above.

These engines were officially sold to the NS in 1947. They were constantly interchanged between sheds, but up to 1952 they all remained in service, although the intention was to replace them by diesel shunters. They were all withdrawn and sold for scrap or further use between 1953 and 1957.

Three of the first WD 0–6–0STs to go to France in November 1944, WD 75004/5/52, remained in a dump at Calais, WD 75004 being used as a shunter. They were joined there by all the May 1945 arrivals. The SNCF preferred the USA/TC 0–6–0T to the WD 0–6–0ST, so none of the WD tanks officially saw service on the SNCF, although one or two at Calais were sometimes used for shunting the leave trains.

WD 71439 was sold to Peugeot and 71492 to Simca in early 1946. WD 71502/13 were sold to the Compagnie Generale de Voies Ferees d'Interet Local St Quentin and became VSTQ 512/3, while 75279 became Compagnie Generale de Voies Ferees d'Interet Local BM 511, also in early 1946. WD 71503 and 75273 went to the Forges et Ateliers du Nord et de Lorraine at Uckange in June 1946. WD 71504 is believed to have been sold to a steelworks near Longuyon in France. WD 75120/87 returned to GB in January 1947, and the remaining locomotives WD 71518–22/6, 75004/5/52 and 75145/6/63/72/5/7/8/85 in May 1947.

In October 1945, eleven WD 0–6–0STs were loaned to the Dutch State Mines at Limburg and renumbered NSM 65–9 and 71–6 as shown in the table on the opposite page.

WD 5009 and 5057 were previously on loan to the NS, but the others were all ex loan to the SNCB. WD 5002/3 and 5198 reverted to WD control in 1946, but the others were sold to the NSM. WD 5002 went to the USA in 1947, 5003 returned to GB in 1947, 5198 was sold by the WD to an opencast brown coal mine near Heerlen, and later in 1948 it was sold to Oranje Nassau Mijnen and became ON 28. It was rebuilt with a larger coal bunker and sliding windows to the cab, which was fitted with doors. Seven of the eight remaining NSM locomotives went to Krupps of Essen for repair in 1950. They were withdrawn in 1957–9.

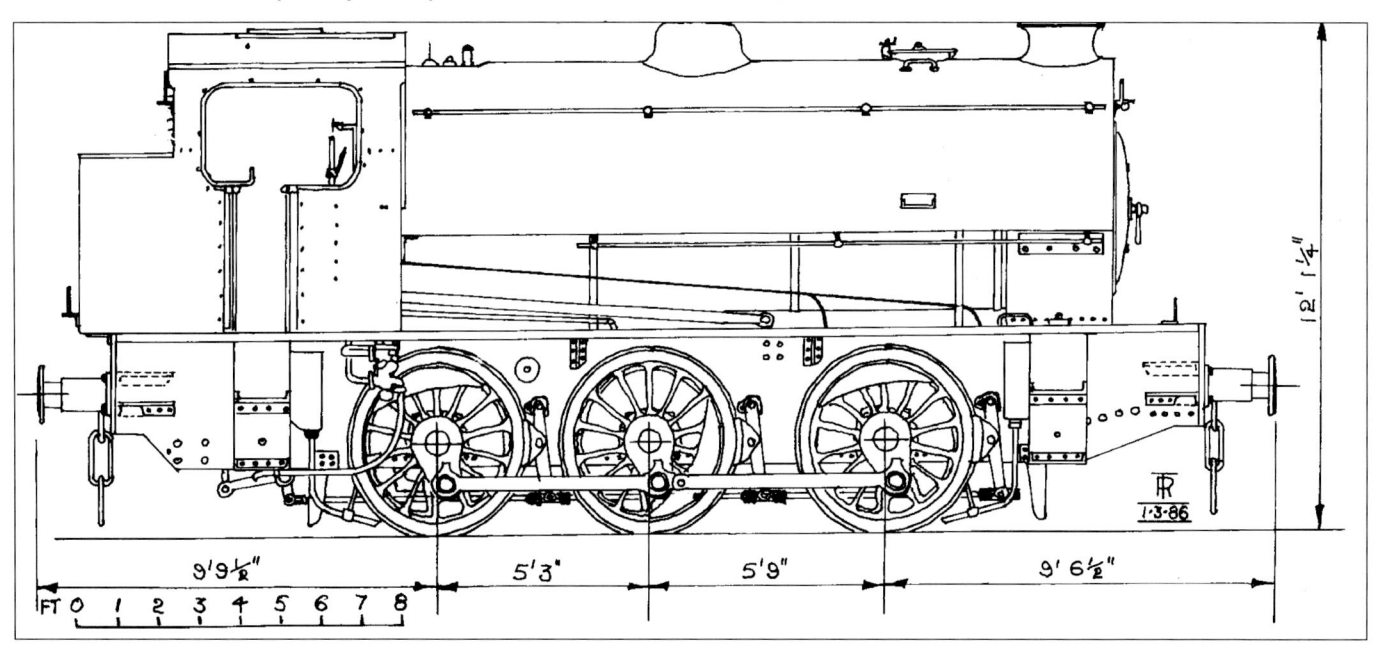

Fig 15 Side elevation of the WD Standard 0–6–0ST. Note that double gussets on the buffer beams were fitted on locomotives built after 1950 or on earlier WD locomotives returned to Hunslet for repair after that date. Thus, no LNE J94 had double gussets, since none were returned to Hunslet for repair.

NSM	0	1	2	3	4	5	6	7	8	9
6X	–	–	–	–	–	5007	5074	5009	5057	1496
7X	–	5011	5014	5136	5002	5003	5198	–	–	–

Three engines from the SNCB, WD 71489/91 and 75197, were sold to the NV Koninklijke Nederlandsche Hoogovens en Staalfabrieken (KNHS or Royal Dutch Steelworks) at Ijmuiden in May/June 1946 and became KNHS 31–3. They were fitted with two-way radio, but were withdrawn and scrapped in 1958–60.

The Belgian company Laura en Vereeneging at Eygelshoven, some five miles from Heerlen, owned the Laura and Julia mines, for which they acquired WD 5024 from the WD ex SNCB in August 1945. They later bought other 0–6–0STs from the NS.

The remaining 21 WD locomotives ex SNCB returned to GB as follows: 5050 in February 1946, 5018 in May 1946, 5008 at the end of 1946, 5016/23/55/8/81/8 and 5130–2/56 in January 1947, 5159 in February 1947, 5022 in March 1947, 5010 and 5127 in May 1947, 5065 in June 1947, 5021 sometime in 1947, and 5128/96 in July 1947, 5196 being the last WD 0–6–0ST to return to GB.

The bulk of the WD 0–6–0STs were disposed of in 1946 and 1947. Overseas disposals have already been discussed. One engine stored in England, 5291, went abroad. The main disposals in the UK will be discussed now.

In November 1945, WD 71486 was allocated to Doncaster for trials, as a result of which the LNER purchased 75 engines, including 71486, on 22 May 1946. Of these 75, 29 were in service at various military establishments, 40 were new (including 71486) in store at Longmoor and the remainder were still under construction by Andrew Barclay. The used engines nearly all needed repairs and, indeed, most of the "new" engines needed attention to their bearings.

Most of the engines were handed over to the LNER in June and July 1946 and usually worked light to the nearest LNER shed, being recorded as added to stock on that day although many were not fit to enter traffic. WD 71535 broke down at Immingham on 9 July 1946 and was sent to Barclays for "light repair" from which it did not return until 30 January 1948. The last six engines still being built were not delivered until January 1947.

These engines formed the LNE Class J94 with freight load classification 3, and were allocated Nos 8006–80 more or less in order of date of construction. 8006–34 were the engines already in use by the WD, 8035–74 the forty new engines and 8075–80 the six still under construction. Details are given in tabular form below:

In most cases, the engines were renumbered at the shed to which they were allocated, soon after arrival. In the North Eastern area, shaded numerals and letters were used on the side of the saddle tanks, Gorton engines received plain unshaded numerals and letters again on the side of the saddle tanks, while those at Immingham simply received numbers only, usually on the bunker sides. At first shopping, they were painted unlined black. LNE 8077 should have been WD 71463 but 8077 could not be used immediately being carried by an F3 2–4–2T which was involved in a legal case which prevented it from being renumbered. Accordingly, 71463 became 8078, so that 8077 was eventually taken by the final locomotive 71466 in January 1947.

To make the locomotives more suitable for duties on the LNER, new cab seats, cab side doors and LNER lamp irons were soon fitted. In November 1946, bigger changes were proposed; increase in capacity of the coal bunker, provision of a ladder and steps at the rear, and the rear cab windows altered from round to a narrow vertical rectangular shape. LNE 8006 was the first engine dealt with in August 1947 at Gorton, followed by 8012 in November. Others were altered by BR between 1948 and 1951. Starting in February 1947, an additional handrail was fitted at an angle on the tank side to facilitate access to the tank filling hole. An extra footstep was fitted under the tank. Many engines had an extra footstep fitted halfway along the running plate. From October 1948 onwards, the cast-iron slide valves were replaced by phosphor-bronze. BR classified them 4F.

Some J94s were allocated to the Cromford and High Peak line. These were fitted with oval buffers to prevent bufferlocking on the sharp curves. Nos 68006/12/3/30/4/79 had the bunker extension removed because it was difficult to coal these engines by hand at Middleton Top. Nos 68012/3/34 also lost the ladders. Full details of the LNER J94 class may be found in the RCTS publication "Locomotives of the LNER" Part 8B, but it may be said here that withdrawals started in 1960 and were completed in 1967. Six were sold out of service to collieries or open-cast sites, and the remainder scrapped.

Six engines were sold to the Chemins de Fer Tunisiens in March and April 1946, WD 1478/81, 5255/99 and 5300/2 becoming CFT 3.51 to 3.56 respectively. These locomotives were loaded on to SS "Bir Hakeim" at Southampton on 10 April 1946. They were used for shunting at Ghardimaou, Mateur and Tunis Duboisville in place of the CFT 2–6–0Ts used previously. Two engines, CFT 3.53 and 3.54, were scrapped at the Sofomeca Foundry in November 1962; two more CFT 3.51 and 3.52 were scrapped by Sofomeca in September 1968; and one more CFT 3.56 scrapped by Sofomeca in July 1971. The remaining engine, CFT 3.55, was preserved at Tunisville.

One WD 0–6–0ST, WD 5002, went to the USA in the post-war exchange of specimen locomotives. This engine arrived at Fort Eustis in 1947 but was scrapped in 1952.

Many of the WD 0–6–0STs were used by the coal-mining industry in the UK and these may be divided into four categories:
  (a) engines loaned to various collieries when built
  (b) engines purchased by various collieries from store in Britain in 1946
  (c) engines purchased by the National Coal Board from store abroad in 1947
  (d) engines operated by the Directorate of Opencast Coal Production of the Ministry of Fuel and Power. These were frequently transferred from one site to another, and were sometimes housed in engine sheds belonging to collieries.

Those loaned or sold to the various collieries came under the control of the NCB

LNE	0	1	2	3	4	5	6	7	8	9
800X	–	–	–	–	–	–	5094	5097	5101	5108
801X	5117	5119	5124	5125	5134	5139	5148	5149	5150	5153
802X	5164	5183	5184	5190	1509	1498	1506	1440	1447	1451
803X	1452	5272	5281	5287	5297	5320	5321	5322	5323	5324
804X	5325	5326	5327	5328	5329	5330	5331	5258	5259	5260
805X	5261	5262	5263	5265	5266	5267	5268	5269	5270	5271
806X	1467	1468	1469	1470	1471	1472	1473	1474	1475	1476
807X	1486	1532	1533	1534	1535	1536	1462	1466	1463	1464
808X	1465	–	–	–	–	–	–	–	–	–

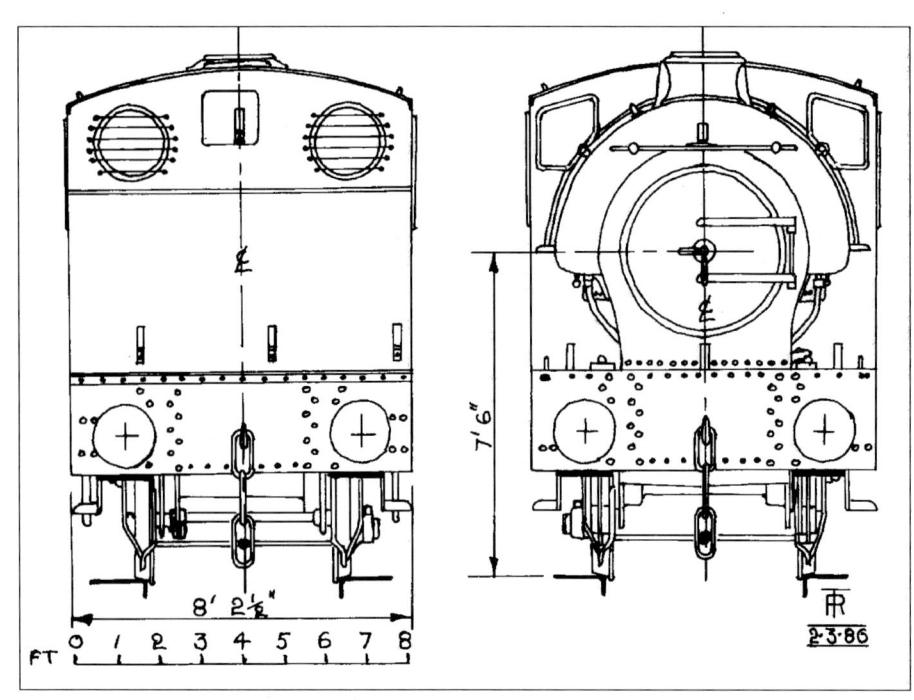

Fig 16   Front and rear elevations of the WD Standard 0–6–0ST.

on its formation on 1 January 1947. The collieries using WD 0–6–0STs were mainly in the Northumberland and Durham fields, while the outcrop coal sites were mainly in the Nottinghamshire and Derby areas. Other engines were sold to various industrial concerns, steelworks, dock authorities, such as the Port of London Authority and the Manchester Ship Canal Co etc in Britain.

In late 1951 and early 1952, the 90 engines remaining under WD control were renumbered into the post-war WD series as WD 100–189. Details are given in Chapter 15. In 1952/3, fourteen new 0–6–0STs were built for the WD and these became WD 190–203. Many of the locomotives serving for long periods at military establishments such as Longmoor, Bicester, etc were named. Sometimes the same name was used on different locomotives at different times. Bicester, who used brass plates with Corps badges, rightly regarded the nameplates as their property, and removed them from departing locomotives for use on another of their own.

1438	Sapper, then Tobruk and McMurdo
1443	Arnhem, then Constantine
1444	Greensleeves
1505	Brussels
5028	Ahwaz
5035	Caen
5039	Sapper
5040	Spyck
5041	Foggia
5042	Jullundur
5078	Royal Pioneer
5079	Sir John French, then Lisieux
5100	Black Knight
5113	Sapper
5118	King Feisal
5133	King Feisal of Iraq, then King Feisal
5151	The Craftsman
5162	The Storeman
5176	Sapper
5186	Royal Pioneer
5189	Rennes
5191	Black Knight
5199	Old Yek
5250	Black Knight
5275	Matruh
5277	Foligno
5282	Insein
5290	Manipur Road
191	Black Knight
192	Waggoner
195	The Storeman, then King Feisal
196	Errol Lonsdale
197	Sapper
198	Royal Engineer
202	Sapper
203	Ahwaz

By 1968, there were only a few WD 0–6–0STs remaining in the service of No 1 Railway Group. In the 1968 renumbering, WD 190–4 became WD 90–4, WD 200–2 became WD 95–7 and WD 198 became WD 98. WD 196 "Errol Lonsdale" and WD 197 "Sapper" were then both intended for preservation and so were not renumbered.

It is noteworthy, that when these engines were used for lengthy service instead of the short military service originally contemplated, it was mainly the wartime modifications to the original design which required most maintenance. For instance, in bad water districts the lack of the manhole on the bottom of the barrel just behind the smokebox tube-plate led to fouling at the front of the barrel, despite the number of washout plugs on the front tubeplate. Similarly, the change in the dome design from that of the earlier 18 in Hunslet tanks, a flat cover instead of the deep dished type, made it a lengthy process to dismantle the regulator, its operating links and swan neck. Early locomotives had a single triangular gusset between the frame and the buffer beam but it was found that heavy shunting could result in the buffer beam being bent and so later locomotives had two gussets fitted.

Despite such defects, the Austerity 0–6–0STs gave a very satisfactory performance. The frames and running gear were very sturdy. On at least two occasions, locomotives were back in service only a few hours after falling down embankments. One batch of eight locomotives worked for more than four years, in 16 or 24 hour shifts, on loads up to 750–800

Plate 106   WD 5154 at Stanlow, Cheshire, while working at the oil refinery there. "SCP/SB3" means Shell Chemical Plant Steam Boiler 3 (Photo: R. Tourret Collection)

tons, without being lifted off their wheels or even having their tyres trued.

Civilian interest in these locomotives first arose during the war when production and allocation of materials was tightly controlled by the government. In March 1943, Rothervale Collieries, a branch of United Steel Co Ltd, asked Hunslet if they could supply them urgently with an "Austerity" 0–6–0ST similar to the 50 being built for the WD. Unfortunately, the government required priority for their 50 locomotives and it was not until February 1944 that Hunslet 3134/44 was delivered to Orgreave Colliery.

The next civilian locomotive was ordered by Garswood Hall Collieries in July 1944, again for urgent delivery. On 28 August 1944, Hunslet sent a locomotive to Garswood, nominally works number 3302 but actually 3187 from the second WD batch which had not been accepted by the government inspector. However, the government did not like this diversion and put a stop to it, so that this locomotive was returned to Leeds and eventually became WD 75147, out of sequence. The Garswood order was cancelled and the real Works No 3302 was left on the maker's hands until it was supplied to Manchester Collieries in August 1945.

Shortly afterwards, the National Coal Board came into existence and adopted the WD 0–6–0ST as its standard design. Post-war civilian construction may be summarised as (see table opposite).

Thus, there were 377 built for the WD in 1943–7, 14 more for the WD in 1952/3 and 94 for civilian orders (one in wartime), making a total of 485 built in 22 years by seven separate firms. The eight built by the Yorkshire Engine Co differ in detail from the others, for example they had 12-spoke wheels instead of the usual 14-spoke type, and also had oval buffers.

In 1961, Hunslet rebuilt one, their 2876/43, with underfeed mechanical stoker, modified grate, brick arches and blast pipes to make a gas producer system which greatly reduced the amount of smoke produced as well as increasing thermal efficiency. The last three new ones were built in the same way, the external evidence being a distinctive shape to the chimney.

In 1954/5, W. G. Bagnall rebuilt two locomotives for the WD, and in 1961-9, Hunslet rebuilt some old engines for resale. In all these cases, new works numbers were allocated when rebuilt. Details are as follows (see table opposite).

All the Hunslet rebuilds, except HE 3877–9/81/93, were fitted with mechanical stokers upon rebuilding.

The details of industrial service are too

Plate 107   WD 107 (ex 75041) "Foggia" at Longmoor Sheds in October 1958 (Photo: E.A.S. Cotton)

Year	Builder	Works No	Built for	Total
1945	Hunslet	3302	Manchester Colliery	1
1948	Hunslet	3685	NCB	1
1949	Hunslet	3686–9/91	NCB (4), Guest Keen & Baldwin	5
1950	Hunslet	3692–3701/17/8	NCB (10), GKB (2)	12
1951	Hunslet	3767/8	NCB	2
1952	Hunslet	3760/1/9–72/6–81	GKB (2), NCB (10)	12
1955	Hunslet	3784–9, 3806/7	NCB	8
	Stephenson Hawthorns	7751/2	NCB	2
1954	Hunslet	3808–11/6–27	NCB	16
	Yorkshire	2566–73	United Steel Co	8
1955	Hunslet	3828–37	NCB	10
1956	Hunslet	3838–43/5/6/8/9	NCB (8), GKB (1), NCB (1)	10
1957	Hunslet	3844/7	NCB	2
1958	Hunslet	3850	Stewart & Lloyds Minerals	1
1962	Hunslet	3851	NCB	1
1964	Hunslet	3889/90	NCB	2
				93

New works No	Old Works No	WD No
WGB 7077/55	RSH 7111/43	75075
WGB 7079/54	WGB 2740/44	75152
HE 3877/61	AB 2185/45	71531
HE 3878/61	VF 5280/45	75290
HE 3879/61	VF 5272/45	75282
HE 3880/61	RSH 7139/45	75189
HE 3881/62	HE 2893/43	75044
HE 3882/62	HE 2890/43	75041
HE 3883/63	HE 2868/43	75019
HE 3884/63	RSH 7204/45	75274
HE 3885/64	HE 3163/44	75113
HE 3886/62	HE 2897/43	75048
HE 3887/64	HE 3193/44	75142
HE 3888/64	HE 3192/44	75141
HE 3891/65	HC 1763/44	71487
HE 3892/69	RSH 7136/44	75186
HE 3893/65	WGB 2774/45	75251

Plate 108 WD 118 (ex 71505) "Brussels" at Longmoor Sheds in October 1958. Note the different ways of mounting Westinghouse brake equipment (Photo: E. A. S. Cotton)

Plate 109 WD 132 (ex 5113) "Sapper" at Bicester in May 1959 (Photo: H. D. Bowtell)

Plate 110 WD 0–6–0STs at Bicester Central Ordnance Depot in May 1959. WD 201, 148, 192, 170 & 154 on right, WD 123 on left (Photo: H. D. Bowtell)

complicated to discuss here, but interested readers are referred to the book "Continent, Coalfield and Conservation" by A. P. Lambert and J. C. Woods, published by the Industrial Railway Society in 1991. It may be mentioned, however, that in industrial service, all sorts of individual variations were made, such as tankside ladders, electrical headlights, additional footsteps, cab weatherboards, mechanical lubricators, Giesl chimneys, flangeless centre driving wheels, etc. Other items were removed or fell off, such as lamp irons, guard irons, steam sanding gear, etc. Locomotives working on the NCB Philadelphia system were given rounded cabs to fit the restricted loading gauge. All sorts of colourful liveries were applied.

There are quite a few WD 0–6–0STs in preservation, the design being a handy size for small lines and/or the initial stages of railway preservation. The situation is complicated, in so much as the post-war industrial series were never in WD service, and in some cases locomotives which have never been in LNE service have been given spurious LNE/BR numbers! The preservationists often gave these engines brake equipment for passenger trains and painted them in more colourful liveries.

Some of the preserved locomotives are currently located as follows:

WD Nos

1463	Southall Railway Centre LNE 8078
1466	Keighley & Worth Valley Railway LNE 8077
1480	Keighley & Worth Valley Railway
1505	Keighley & Worth Valley Railway
1515	East Somerset Railway "LNE 68005"
1516	Gwili Railway
5006	Nene Valley Railway "LNE 68081"
5008	Bodmin & Wenford Railway
5015	Strathspey Railway
5019	Rutland Railway Museum
5030	Brechin Railway
5031	Scottish Railway Preservation Society
5041	South Devon Railway
5050	Kent & East Sussex Railway 27 "Rolvenden"
5061	Strathspey Railway
5062	Tanfield Railway
5080	Stoom Stichting Nederland, Rotterdam
5091	Crewe Heritage Centre
5105	Southport Steam Centre
5113	Swanage Railway
5118	Embsay Steam Railway
5130	North Yorks Moors Railway

Plate 111 BR J94 68050 (ex WD 5261) hauling a transfer freight train through Darlington in June 1954 (Photo: R. K. Evans)

Plate 112 BR J94 68011 (ex WD 5119) at Darlington Works in October 1964 (Photo: David Mills)

5133	South Yorks Railway Preservation Society
5141	South Yorks Railway Preservation Society
5142	Lavender Line, Isfield "LNE 68012"
5158	Peak Rail
5161	Brechin Railway
5171	Brechin Railway
5178	South Devon Railway
5186	Peak Rail
5189	Blaenavon Railway Society
5254	Scottish Railway Preservation Society
5256	Tanfield Railway
5282	Caerphilly Railway Society
5300	CFT, Tunisville, 3.55
5319	Colne Valley Railway "LNE 68072"

Post-war WD

190	Colne Valley Railway "Castle Hedingham"
191	Kent & East Sussex Railway 23 "Holman F. Stephens"
192	Museum of Army Transport, Beverley "Waggoner"
193	East Lancashire Railway "Shropshire"
194	Lakeside Railway "Cumbria"
196	South Devon Railway "Errol Lonsdale"
197	Kent & East Sussex Railway 25 "Northiam"
198	Ministry of Defence, Long Marston "Royal Engineer", on loan Isle of Wight Steam Rly
200	Kent & East Sussex Railway 24 "William H. Austen"

Industrial

WE 3810/54	Bodmin & Wenford Railway "Glendower"
HE 3825/54	Great Central Railway "LNE 68009"

Of note is that parts such as the cylinders of one WD 0–6–0ST 75185 were used as a basis for the broad-gauge replica of "Iron Duke"!

Chapter 27

HUDSWELL CLARKE 2–8–2T, WD 2200

Plate 113   IqSR 1015 at Beirut shed on the HBT in August 1945, standing in front of an 04 2–8–0 fitted with oil burning equipment (Photo: R. E. Tustin)

In 1937 Hudswell Clarke built a standard-gauge 2–8–2T (HC 1678/37) to the order of the Eagle Oil & Shipping Co Ltd for use at oil refineries in Mexico. The boiler was of the Belpaire type, fitted with steel firebox, and two Ross pop safety valves. The cylinders drove the third pair of coupled wheels, via piston valves actuated by Walschaert's valve gear. The engine burnt oil as fuel, using Holden's patent oil fuel apparatus. Pyle National electric lighting equipment was used and the central couplers were of the MCB type. The locomotive had steam brakes in conjunction with Westinghouse air brakes for operating the train.

Owing to financial difficulties in Mexico the locomotive was not delivered and it remained at the works until 1942 when it was sold to the War Department as WD 2200, the date on the maker's plate being altered to 1942. It was sent to Basra and thence by barge up the river to Baghdad, arriving in October 1942. It was loaned to the Iraqi State Railways and became 1015 in their list, being put into service in December 1942 for shunting at Baghdad. An old tender was attached to act as an auxiliary water tank.

Plate 114   IqSR 1015 at Haifa. For a long time this locomotive was listed as "missing", but it turned up at Haifa one day, quite unannounced! The black accessory apparently hanging from the rear buffer is a hole in the negative! (Photo: K. R. M. Cameron)

In February 1943, it was returned to shops for alterations to the fuel-burning arrangements, and later that year it was handed back to WD control and sent (without tender) to the Haifa-Beirut-Tripoli Railway where it was used for shunting at Beirut. Although it should have become WD 72200 it was still at Beirut as No 1015 in August 1946. It was noted stored at Azzib in 1947 and later it was in the RE Railway Workshops at Suez from about September 1951 to March 1952 under repair. It survived long enough to become 014 in the post-war (1952) series.

The dimensions as built are given below, although some modifications may have been made in 1942.

Cylinders, two outside	20in x 24in
Wheels, coupled	3ft 9in
Wheels, leading and trailing	2ft 2in
Wheelbase, coupled	13ft 6in
Wheelbase, total	27ft 0in
Boiler heating surface,	
tubes	1150sq ft
firebox	112sq ft
total	1262sq ft
Grate area	24sq ft
Boiler pressure	160psi
Tractive effort at 85% boiler pressure	29,013lb
Weight of engine in working order	66 tons
Water capacity	1750gal
Oil capacity	3 tons

Plate 115   WD 72200 2–8–2T at the Railway Workshops Suez in September 1951. By now it had been given its WD identity, also its headlight had been returned (Photo: S. Clark)

Chapter 28

Ex LB&SCR ATLANTIC TANKS, WD 2400/1

These two locomotives were part of the LB&SCR I2 class 4–4–2T numbered LB&SCR 13/9 and were built at Brighton in 1908. When absorbed by the SR they were eventually renumbered 2013/9, and were withdrawn in January 1939 and December 1937 respectively. They were not scrapped immediately, however, but went to Eastleigh Works and were still intact at the outbreak of war. After lying derelict for about a year, they were both sent to Bournemouth, where they were placed over one of the pits in the shed and covered with sandbags for use as an air-raid shelter.

They returned to Eastleigh in early 1941 and were dumped on the scrap road until later in the year, when they were superficially overhauled, repainted unlined black, renumbered WD 2400/1 respectively and sold to the War Department for service on the Longmoor Military Railway. They arrived there in April 1942.

WD 2400 assumed the name "Earl Roberts", once carried by WD 206, in late 1945 or early 1946. They were both officially withdrawn from service in October 1946 and were sold to Abelson & Co

Plate 116   WD 2401 at Longmoor (Photo: H. N. James)

(Engineers) Ltd, Sheldon, Birmingham in 1948, who advertised them for sale during 1948 and 1949. In July 1949, they appeared at Guildford shed, where they were stored until July 1951. They were then moved to Godalming Goods station for a period. They left in February 1952, for Belgium, presumably for scrap.

Plate 119 Cab and footplate fittings of WD 2600–5 (Photo: Mitchell Library)

141/4 had left Suez. All six were converted to 1.050 metre gauge and taken over by the Jordan Royal Hashemite Railways, which has its headquarters in Amman, and was formerly part of the Hedjaz Railway. Some slight modifications were made but all six locomotives remained in operation until about 1962. Officially they were all broken up by 1970 but at least two, 141/5, were still in existence in January 1972, lying derelict in a scrap yard a few miles out from Amman.

Dimensions, additional to those shown on the drawing, were as follows:

Cylinders, two outside	15in x 22in
Boiler heating surface	
Small tubes	412sq ft
Large tubes	260sq ft
Arch tubes	9.5sq ft
Firebox and combustion chamber	127sq ft
Total evaporative	808.5sq ft
Superheater elements	180sq ft
Combined total	988.5sq ft
Grate area	28sq ft
Boiler pressure	250psi
Tractive effort at 85% boiler pressure	19,840lb
Adhesive weight	37tons 8cwt
Weight, empty	56 tons 19cwt
Weight in working order (coal fuel)	74 tons 19cwt
Weight in working order (oil fuel)	75 tons 14cwt
Maximum axleload	12 tons 10cwt
Fuel capacity, coal	4 tons
Fuel capacity, oil	930gal
Water capacity	2000 gal

Plate 120 MEF 144 at No 169 Rly Wksp Suez in 1946 (Photo: J. D. Blythe)

Plate 121   Hedjaz Railway 144 at Ma'an in March 1954 (Photo: A. Quayle)

Chapter 30

SUDAN TYPE 4–6–2s, WD 2800–54

When the war in the Middle East theatre began to develop, it was soon realised that additional locomotive power would be needed on the various 3ft 6in gauge lines in Africa, and in particular in the Sudan. This was to cope with the extra military traffic, and as a precaution in case these lines had to cope with still greater traffic over the Nile Valley route in the event of access to Egyptian ports being lost, either by German land advances in Egypt or by the Germans preventing ships reaching Egyptian ports.

To avoid delay, an existing design built by the North British Locomotive Co for Sudan Railways was chosen, namely the "220" class 4–6–2 locomotives of the Sudan Government Railway, sixteen of which had been built by the North British some years previously. This design was chosen because it represented a modern design with a moderate axle load, for which all drawings, dies and patterns were readily available, so that building could be begun with a minimum of delay. Features of the design included bar frames with outside cylinders and Walschaerts valve gear, a boiler having a wide firebox with a combustion chamber, and a high-capacity double-bogie tender. Although the original "220" class engines had burnt coal, the new engines were equipped for burning oil fuel, but provision was made for rapid conversion to coal burning, should it be necessary to do so.

It was intended that these new WD locomotives should be available also for use on the Nigerian, Gold Coast, Belgian Congo, French Ocean Congo and Rhodesian Railways, with only minor alterations. To permit this, the height of the chimney, dome and cab roof were reduced from that of the original engines to enable them to clear the most restrictive loading gauge of the above railways. It was necessary to remove the foot-steps, and to cut holes in the foot-step plates as a substitute for steps, in order to clear the Nigerian and Gold Coast loading gauges. Different types of couplers could be fitted, as favoured by the various railway systems.

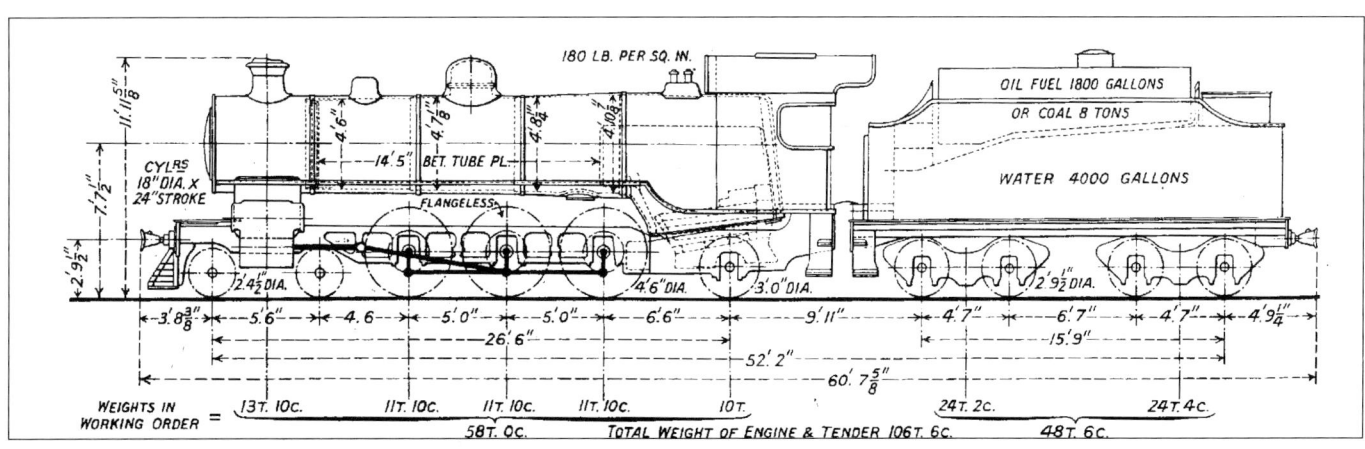

Fig 19   Sudan type 4–6–2 WD 2800–54 (Courtesy Railway Gazette)

Plate 122 WD 4-6-2 2807 at Abu Hamid on the Sudan Railways in 1946 (Photo: P. J. Bawcutt)

In the event, 55 locomotives of this type were built by the North British Locomotive Co in 1942 with works numbers 24816–70 under Contract L939.

The boiler barrel was constructed of three rings, and the inner firebox was copper. The wide firegrate extended over supplementary frames, and hand-operated rocking and drop grate was provided in case of conversion from oil to coal fuel. A spark arrestor was housed in the smokebox. Two Ross pop safety valves were fitted. Valve gear was Walschaerts and cylinder lubrication effected by a British Detroit sight-feed lubricator.

The works numbers of WD 2800–54 were N 24816–70 as mentioned earlier, but there was a minor mixup in that WD 72834–9 were N 24851/2/0/3/5/4. All works plates showed 1942, except the last two 24869/70 which showed 1943.

WD 2800–24 were delivered by North British to various ports during November and December 1942. WD 2830–4 were sent overseas in September 1943. The balance of the order, that is WD 2825–9/35–54, were sent to the Melbourne Military Railway near Derby for store, starting in February 1943 and completing about August 1943, although WD 2850–4 were delivered in June 1943.

Although the design of the locomotives was an excellent one, it did not in the event satisfy the requirements of any railway other than the Sudan Government Railway, owing to the limited adhesion obtainable with six-coupled wheels, an eight-coupled locomotive being required elsewhere. Consequently only 25 engines of the class saw duty during the war, all these being used in the Sudan. WD 72800–9/15–24 arrived in the Sudan in 1942, followed by 72829/51–4 ex store MMR. These became SGR 236–60 in order. They were chiefly used between Atbara and Wadi Halfa. These WD locomotives were erected and went into service as oil burners. The existing "220" class locomotives 220–35 were converted to oil burning at the same time, and the Sudan Railways treated them as being all in the same class.

The remainder were stored in an unassembled condition for the duration of the war, 72825–8/35–50 remaining at Melbourne, while in the Middle East, 72810–4 were at the Transportation Stores Depot at Azzib in Northern Palestine, and 72830–4 at Suez. In 1946, the twenty locomotives at Melbourne were disposed of, fourteen, 72825–8/39/41/3–50 going to the Western Australian Government Railway and becoming WAGR 664/3/0/1/51/6/2/62/59/4/5/3/7/8 respectively and six, WD 72835–8/40/2, to the Trans-Zambesia Railway and becoming TZR Class F 25–30 in the order 29, 30, 28, 25, 26 and 27. The ten remaining in the Middle East were transferred to the Sudan Government Railway, 72830–4 in 1946 and 72810–4 in 1947.

The locomotives of the SGR were officially on loan from the WD but after the arrival of 72810–4/30–4, they were taken into SGR stock, so that the whole series was numbered SGR 236–70. WD 72830–4 became SGR 266–70 and 72810–4 became SGR 261–5.

Observation in Sudan in January 1983 showed that six were still in service at Sennar, two at Atbara and two at Ad Damazin. Fifteen were out of use at Sennar and eight at Atbara, one (probably 245) was lying wrecked on the Damazin branch and one (possibly 241) existed as frames only at Atbara. NBL plates on the boilers and the works numbers, so far as it was possible to decipher them, showed that considerable boiler changes had occurred, and indeed plate changes as well since several boilers carried plates off boilers of other NBL classes on the SGR!

Plate 123 Sudan Railways 246 (ex WD 72815) in 1983 (Photo: B. J. Ashworth)

Plate 124 Sudan Railways 251 (ex WD 72820) at Sennar Junction in September 1981 (Photo: J. L. Alexander)

The locomotives sent to the Trans-Zambesia Railway required very little alteration, the principle change being the fitting of American-type knuckle couplers instead of the original drawgear. The oil fuel equipment was retained when the engines were despatched, but, although oil fuel has been used during temporary coal shortages, coal was the normal fuel used by them on the TZR. TZR 26 was involved in a collision in July 1948 and was damaged beyond repair. The remaining five locomotives were still in service in 1958, but most were dumped at Inhamiuga by 1969.

The locomotives which went to the Western Australian Government Railway became Class U on that railway and the most obvious alteration was the provision of a sand dome on top of the boiler barrel in front of the steam dome. Although it was intended that these locomotives should burn coal on arrival in Australia, it was found more convenient to burn fuel oil when they first arrived, and the oil fuel equipment was retained. They were placed in service as follows, WAGR 651 in November 1946, 652–4 in December 1946, 655 in January 1947, 656–9 in February 1947, 660–3 in March 1947 and 664 in April 1947.

WAGR 664 was converted to coal burning in December 1954 until withdrawn in November 1956. It was converted to an oil-burning 4–6–4 side tank

Plate 125 Sudan Railways 257 (ex WD 72851) at Sennar Junction in September 1981 (Photo: J. L. Alexander)

engine in July 1957 and was then used for metropolitan passenger services. It was withdrawn again in December 1959. The other thirteen engines were in store by August 1957. As a result of a serious coal shortage in early 1961, WAGR 664 and five U class locomotives were returned to service. WAGR 656 was withdrawn in July 1969, and the remainder, except for two, in October 1969. The two remaining, WAGR 655/64 were officially written off in September 1970 and both passed to the ARHS Bassendean Museum in June 1972.

Dimensions, additional to those shown on the drawing, were as follows:

Heating surface	
Small tubes	627sq ft
Large tubes	356sq ft
Firebox	142sq ft
Total evaporative	1125sq ft
Superheater	260sq ft
Combined total	1385sq ft
Grate area	26sq ft
Tractive effort at 85% BP	22050lb

Plate 126 Western Australian Government Railway Class UT 4–6–4T rebuild (ex WD 72825), withdrawn December 1959 but put back into service for a few months in 1961. It was finally withdrawn in September 1970 but was preserved in the ARHS Bassendean Rail Transport Museum, where it was photographed in May 1981 (Photo: J. L. Alexander)

Chapter 31

STANDARD WD 2–10–0s, WD 3650–3799

It is remarkable that although only two isolated examples of ten-coupled locomotives had previously appeared on British railways, the Great Eastern "Decapod" 0–10–0T and the Midland Lickey banker, both somewhat restricted in their activities, the WD was able to introduce the 2–10–0 wheel arrangement, the logical development of the 2–8–0, in a light design which was able to work over the most important sections of the British railway network.

This class of engine was designed by Mr R. A. Riddle, the Deputy Director General, RE Equipment, who was previously Works Manager at St Rollox, LMS. The most noteworthy differences between these engines and the WD 2–8–0s were that the 2–10–0s had a lighter axleload, a larger lagged boiler and a wide steel firebox, and a rocking grate similar to that on the USA/TC 2–8–0s. The cylinder dimensions were the same as for the eight-coupled engines. The firebox was equipped with three arch tubes, an innovation on British locomotives, which probably helped to provide the excellent steaming qualities of the engines. The middle pair of driving wheels was flangeless and this feature, together with the side play allowance and slight flexibility of the frames, enabled 4½ chain curves to be traversed.

As in the case of the 2–8–0s, these engines had two cylinders driving the third pair of coupled wheels and Walschaerts motion actuating inside-admission piston valves working above the cylinders. Hand-screw reversing gear was fitted for left-hand drive. The economies effected in the construction of the 2–8–0s were applied to the 2–10–0s, and the tender was of identical design.

Below are given comparative details of the main dimensions and weights of the 2–10–0 and 2–8–0 "Austerity" locomotives.

	2–10–0	2–8–0
Cylinders (2), dia	19in	19in
Cylinders, stroke	28in	28in
Piston valves, dia	10in	10in
Piston valves, max travel	6⅝in	6⅝in
Wheels, coupled, dia	4ft 8½in	4ft 8½in
Wheels, leading truck, dia	3ft 2in	3ft 2in
Wheelbase, coupled	21ft 0in	16ft 3in
Wheelbase, total	29ft 8in	24ft 10in
Boiler heating surface		
Large tubes	589sq ft	451sq ft
Small tubes	1170sq ft	1061sq ft
Firebox	192sq ft	168sq ft
Total evaporative	1951sq ft	1680sq ft
Superheater	423sq ft	310sq ft
Combined total	2374sq ft	1990sq ft
Grate area	40sq ft	28.6sq ft
Boiler pressure	225psi	225psi
Tractive effort at 85% BP	34,215lb	34,125lb
Adhesive weight	67¼ tons	61¼ tons
Weight of engine in WO	78½ tons	70¼ tons
Weight of tender in WO	55½ tons	55½ tons
Total weight of engine and tender	134 tons	125¾ tons
Max axle load	13½ tons	15½ tons

A point of interest to operators was that these 2–10–0 locomotives were readily adaptable to altered conditions. The boiler could be converted to oil burning without removal from the frames. It was necessary only to fit a false bottom in the ashpan and to fit front oil burners. The slides normally occupied by the two halves of the firedoor served to hold in position a firehole blanking plate provided with a firedoor having a small opening for furnace observation. Bolt holes on the front of the engine were provided to allow a cowcatcher to be fitted if needed. The tender was also readily adaptable and could be provided with a water scoop if required. The narrow bunker gave good visibility when running tender first, and left a conventional ledge to accommodate fire tools.

In all, 150 2–10–0s were built by the North British Locomotive Company all at

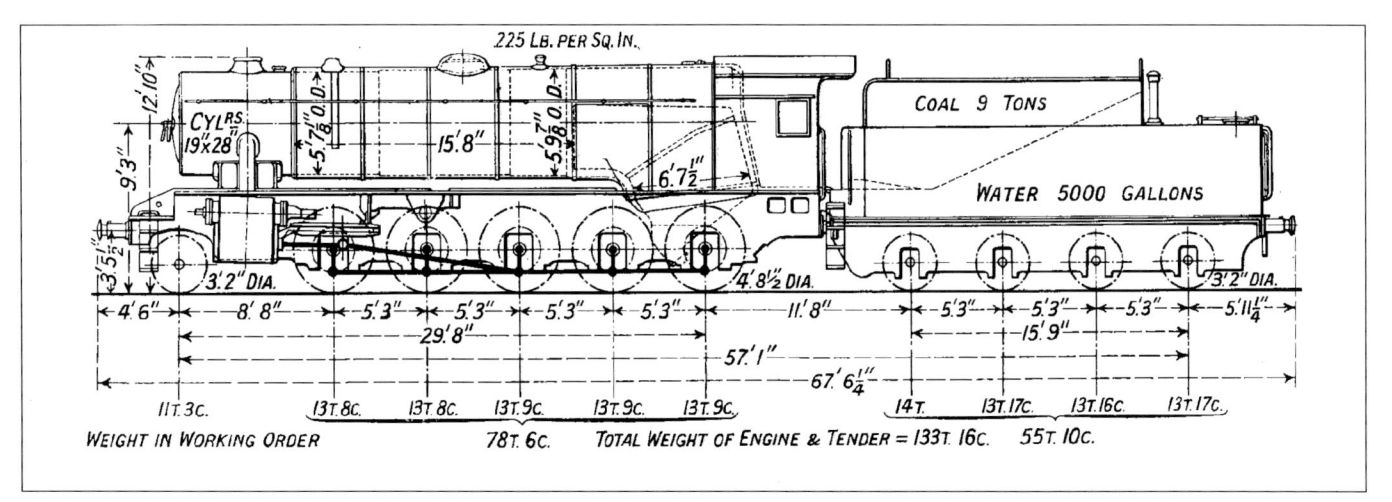

Fig 20 Diagram giving the principal dimensions and axleloads of the WD 2–10–0 "Austerity" locomotive (Courtesy Railway Magazine)

Plate 127 Official photograph of the first WD 2–10–0, WD 3650, at Hyde Park Works (Photo: Mitchell Library)

Hyde Park Works, under two order numbers, L945 of June 1943 (WD 3650–3749) delivered between December 1943 and June 1944, and L948 of March 1944 (WD 3750–99) delivered between March and September 1945 after the last 2–8–0s had been completed. Although NB works numbers 25321–420 were originally alloted to order L945, they were later altered to 25436–535 to follow the 2–8–0s, and the latter appeared on engines 3650–3749 in order; up to 3661 (NB 25447) being 1943 built and the rest 1944. The engines built under order L948 were given works number 25596–645 in sequence, all built in 1945.

The first batch, WD 3650–3749, were painted khaki-brown. WD 3650 originally had 6in numerals on the cab sides, but the rest of the batch had 8in high numerals, all in matt golden yellow. The tender was marked "WD" in 2in high letters with a broad arrow between the letters. The second batch, WD 3750–99, were painted "army" green, with 8in numerals on the cab sides and 12in letters on the tender with a 10in broad arrow. With both batches, 2in high numbers were painted on the front buffer beam. All WD numbers were increased by 70,000 as from August 1944, WD 73750 being the first to be out-shopped with the five-figure number. Some of the earlier engines of the second batch left works carrying the 21st Army Group flash of a blue cross on a red shield on the cab side above the number. The last two, 73798/9, were both named "North British", as a parting gesture by the makers.

The first engine, WD 3650, was completed about 5 December 1943. Since they were not yet needed overseas, it was intended to put them to use on British railways, then short of locomotive power, but some of the Chief Mechanical Engineers were wary about the long coupled wheelbase and the LMS CME stated that these 2–10–0s would not be allowed to operate over his company's lines until tests over 1 in 8 crossings alongside station platforms had been conducted. By this time, the second engine, WD 3651, was at Longmoor where by chance there was such a crossing. Trials were carried out satisfactorily that weekend and the results reported to the CME Monday morning, who could no longer object to the 2–10–0s. As soon as the first 2–10–0 went to St Rollox shed, its flexibility on sharp curves was amply demonstrated on his own track!

Between December 1943 and March 1944, fifty-one 2–10–0s, WD 3650–61/7–99 & 3700–5, were delivered new to Eastfield where they were run-in on mainline freight trains, chiefly Glasgow to Edinburgh, via Polmont and via Bathgate. Afterwards they were retained for a while. By mid-March 1944, thirty 2–10–0s had been despatched, 3651 to Longmoor (where it stayed throughout the war), 3652–60/72/4/7/8/82–5 to the Middle East, 3661/7 to Stratford LNE, 3668–71/3/5/6/9/80/1 to New England, leaving 3650 at Eastfield. While at New England, the WD 2–10–0s worked to Ferme Park and all were seen in London. The LMS received WD 3662–6 direct from the makers and then agreed to take the remaining engines from the LNE, on loan until required overseas. Between 26 March and 2 April 1944, WD 3686–99 and 3700–5 were transferred to the LMS from Eastfield and all subsequent new engines were delivered direct to the LMS. On 28 March 1944, the two Stratford engines were transferred to the LMS, followed on 29 March 1944 by eight of the ten New England engines. WD 3650 at Eastfield was transferred on 7 April 1944

Plate 128 Cab and footplate fittings of a WD 2–10–0 (Photo: Mitchell Library)

Plate 129 Official photograph of WD 3726 (Photo: Mitchell Library)

and the last two, WD 3669/70, which had been under repair at New England, were transferred on 3 May and 25 April 1944 respectively. This made a total of 79 in all on loan to the LMS, WD 3650/61–71/3/5/6/9–81/9–99 and 3700–49. These were stationed at various sheds on the Western and Midland divisions as follows: Crewe South 3689/91/3/5–9, Leeds 3716–25, Royston 3666, Rugby 3690/2/4 and 3700–5/15, Toton 3662–5 and 3726–49, Wellingborough 3668–71/3/5/6/9–81 and Willesden 3650/61/7 and 3706–14.

The route restrictions applied to the WD 2–10–0s on the LMS were the same as for the LMS 8F 2–8–0s. The locomotives allocated to Crewe South, Rugby and Willesden worked chiefly on the southern part of the Western Division, including Bletchley to Oxford, but less often north of Crewe. The Toton engines worked mainly to Willesden, at first being prohibited south of Wellingborough on the Midland main line, and also to Bristol.

In the Spring of 1944, a Crewe South 2–10–0 was tried on the Central Wales line but was evidently not favoured and it returned within a week. In May 1944, WD 3666 was moved from Royston to Leeds, the only change made to the original shed allocations.

The seventy-nine which were on loan to the LMS were taken back by the WD between August and November 1944, and sent to Longmoor for checking over and servicing. They were then shipped to the Continent, the last leaving Longmoor by late November 1944. In September 1944, 3670/80 and 3706/24, and probably 3668/93 and 3707–9/11–3/25/30 went to France. In October 1944, 3650/61/6/7/71/3/6/9/81/9/90/2/4/9 and 3700/1/3–5/10/4–7/9/21/3/6–8/32/41/2 and probably 3675 were shipped. In November, the following went, 3663/5/91/8 and 3702/18/20/2/9/34/5/8–40/3–9; and in December 1944, 3662/4/9/95–7 and 3731/3/6/7.

The second batch of 2–10–0s, WD 73750–99, appeared between March and September 1945 and were all delivered to Eastfield for running in. The first 24 were sent to the Continent, 73750–64 probably in May 1945 and 73765–73 in June 1945. WD 73755 was the 1000th British-made locomotive sent to Europe, when it was shipped on 9 May 1945, and was named "Longmoor" with commemorative plates to that effect. On arrival, it was not needed for the war effort and joined the other 2–10–0s, WD 73750–73, in storage at Calais.

The ending of hostilities reduced the need for locomotives in Europe and the remaining engines stayed in the UK, 73774–93 being loaned to the LNE allocated to March shed (73774–84 in June 1945, 73785–91 in July and 73792/3 in August), and the final six going into store at Longmoor. The engines at March were chiefly used on freight trains to Temple Mills, but they also appeared at other places on the GE, such as Ipswich.

Several WD 2–10–0s saw service on the Nederlandsche Spoorwegen in

Plate 130 Official photograph of WD 73798, one of the last two built, both carrying the name "North British" and the 21st Army Group flash of a blue cross on a red shield (Photo: Mitchell Library)

Plate 131 WD 2–10–0 73777 running light near Cambridge in July 1945 (Photo: E. R. Wethersett, courtesy British Rail)

1944/5, working ammunition, fuel, rations, ambulance and leave trains. In December 1944, there were nine allotted to the NS, 33 by April 1945 working from Eindhoven, Nijmegen and Roosendaal, but down to 22, and of these only 17 operational, by June 1945. There were a few German air attacks on the WD 2–10–0s, such as on 73711/27 on the Turnhout-Tilburg line in Holland on 2 January 1945 in which 73727 had its boiler and firebox pierced by shells, 73673 between Roosendaal and Breda on 10 February 1945, and 73664 at Haps in Holland on 2 March 1945. As with the WD 2–8–0s, some of the WD 2–10–0s had a white star painted on the cab roof to try to prevent inadvertent Allied air attacks. Mechelen Royal Engineers Central Workshops repaired 24 2–10–0s between October 1944 and July 1945.

Seven were returned by the NS to the WD in July 1945 and the remaining 15 in September 1945. At the end of 1945, all the 103 WD 2–10–0s on the Continent were in store. Roosendaal had 45, WD 73650/61/4/6/7/9–71/3/6/9–81/9–93/6/7/9 and 73700/5–7/9/11–3/5/7–22/7/9/33/4/6/9/41/4/8; Antwerp South had 19, 73663/94 and 73702/3/8/10/4/6/23–6/8/30/1/5/42/3/6; Tournai had 24, 73750–73; and Eindhoven had 15, 73662/5/8/75/95/8 and 73701/4/32/7/8/40/5/7/9. The NS did not like them because they were too long for some turntables, and they had no steam heating. Some unofficial names have been reported for their European service, such as 73681 "Flying Dutchman" and 73722 "Good Old Ranger".

However, in January 1946, sixty locomotives were taken out of store and loaned to the NS, receiving NS No 5001–60. In February 1946, a shortage of locomotives arose in the part of the Deutsche Reichsbahn in the British Zone and fifty 2–10–0s were sent to the DR. This number was made up from the 43 locomotives remaining in store, plus seven (73703/11/7–21) taken back from loan to the NS. The locomotives were allocated to two sheds in the Ruhr as follows: Krefeld Hohenbudberg 73663/94 & 73702–4/8/10/4/6/23–6/8/30/1/5/42/6/51 –3/6/7/60/1/3/6–71 and Krefeld Main 73707/11/7–21/50/4/5/8/9/62/5/72/3. In June 1946, the 50 locomotives on the DR were released and transferred to the NS so that all 103 locomotives were on that railway. They were given NS Nos 5001–5103, the seven that had been in NS stock previously taking back their original NS numbers, while the other 43 became NS 5061–5103. They were purchased by the NS towards the end of 1946.

The details are shown below:

NS	0	1	2	3	4	5	6	7	8	9
500X	–	3650	3661	3662	3664	3665	3666	3667	3668	3669
501X	3670	3671	3673	3675	3676	3679	3680	3681	3689	3690
502X	3691	3692	3693	3695	3696	3697	3698	3699	3700	3701
503X	3704	3705	3706	3707	3709	3711	3712	3713	3715	3717
504X	3718	3719	3720	3721	3722	3727	3729	3732	3733	3734
505X	3736	3737	3738	3739	3740	3741	3744	3745	3747	3748
506X	3749	3663	3694	3702	3703	3708	3710	3714	3716	3723
507X	3724	3725	3726	3728	3730	3731	3735	3742	3743	3746
508X	3750	3751	3752	3753	3754	3755	3756	3757	3758	3759
509X	3760	3761	3762	3763	3764	3765	3766	3767	3768	3769
510X	3770	3771	3772	3773	–	–	–	–	–	–

WD 73669 (NS 5009) was given a temporary plaque "Major Constant Mertens" on the side of the cab, for the purpose of obtaining a photographic souvenir!

Similar modifications were made to the WD 2–10–0s as to the WD 2–8–0s on the NS, as discussed in Chapter 24, and a similar livery was adopted. Like the 2–8–0s, the 2–10–0s were widely used on passenger and freight trains and earned the nicknames "Dakota" and "Big Jeep". After the electrification scheme of 1949, they were mainly used on heavy freight trains. As from 1 January 1950, the tenders were given numbers which in the case of the WD 2–10–0s were the same as the NS locomotive numbers. When mass withdrawal of ex-WD locomotives became possible in 1949, it was decided to withdraw all the 2–10–0s by October 1951. Three were scrapped in 1948, eight in 1949, 24 in 1950, 64 in 1951 and the last four by April 1952, although one of these, WD 73755 "Longmoor", was not scrapped but preserved in the NS Railway Museum at Utrecht. In June 1950, the boilers off WD 73756/7 were sold to the Orange-Nassau mines in South Limberg for use as stationary boilers. Sixty tenders were retained, and slightly modified, for use with 59 NS PO3 Class 4–6–0s and one NS PO4 Class 4–6–0. Other components, such as injectors, air compressors and smokebox doors, were also used on the 4–6–0s.

Twenty locomotives of the first batch, WD 73652–60/72/4/7/8/82–8, went to the Middle East in late 1943. They were erected, then run-in on the PR, and then put into store at Suez. One, at least, was recorded as working a freight train from Beirut to Lydda "on trial".

Four of them, WD 73685–8, were hired to the Chemin de Fer Damas, Hamah et Prolonguements (DHP) in Syria in July 1944. They were worked through from Suez to Haifa by No 193 Rly Op Co, arriving 21/2 June 1944, and were then run in on trains between Haifa and Azzib and between Haifa and Lydda before being taken up to Tripoli and handed over to the DHP on 10 July 1944. They were sold to the DHP in April 1946 and around 1956 were renumbered 150.685–8. Minor modifications were made, such as fitting small smoke deflectors alongside the chimney, large headlamps and a cow-catcher. The whistle was changed from a horizontal to vertical position for better audibility. One engine frequently hauled the Taurus Express from Aleppo to the Turkish border. They were still at work in 1972, but by 1976 all steam working had ceased in Syria.

The other sixteen engines remained in store at Suez until shipped to Salonika in Greece in January 1946 to meet the urgent

Plate 132   WD 2–10–0 73799 "North British" stored at Longmoor in November 1945. The 21st Army Group flashes have now gone (Photo: R. Tourret)

Plate 133   WD 2–10–0 73755 "Longmoor" in storage sidings at Tournai in Belgium in October 1945 (Photo: E. A. S. Cotton)

Plate 134   Nameplate "Longmoor" on WD 73755, the 1000th British-built freight locomotive to be ferried to Europe since D-Day (Photo: E. A. S. Cotton)

Plate 135   WD "Austerity" 2–10–0 73730 at Hook of Holland, on loan to Nederlandsche Spoorwegen and fitted by them with a stovepipe chimney, photographed in June 1946 (Photo: F. W. Goudie)

Plate 136 NS 5097 (ex WD 73767) on a freight train (Photo: Photomatic)

Plate 137 WD 2-10-0 3685 at Homs on the DHP Railway in Syria. The baskets of coal ranged alongside the footplating are for coal consumption tests (Photo: K. R. M. Cameron)

need for locomotives on the Greek Railways, where they became HSR Class Lb Nos 951–66 in order. Renumbering details are shown below:

HSR/OSE	0	1	2	3	4	5	6	7	8	9
95X	–	3652	3653	3654	3655	3656	3657	3658	3659	3660
96X	3672	3674	3677	3678	3682	3683	3684	–	–	–

Some minor modifications were made, such as change to right-hand drive, fitted with headlamps and a second roof to the cab. The chimney was lengthened and a small smoke deflector placed behind it. They were put to work in the Thesalonika Division and were divided up between the sheds at Salonika, Drama, Alexandroupolis and Pithion (on the Turkish frontier). They worked the international services to Istanbul over the line through Thrace, much of which was heavily graded, and over the former Chemin de Fer Franco-Hellenic line from Alexandroupolis to Pithion. They were maintained in good condition and carried large oval brass CEH number plates with the class letter in Greek. It may seem strange that this class of locomotive was used for important international services but speeds were low and in fact they appeared to have been well suited for these duties. By 1967, some diesel locomotives arrived and the WD 2-10-0s were concentrated in the eastern part of the Division where there were some light axle-load lines.

Locomotives Nos 953/4/8/9/61–4 were withdrawn in June 1973, 951/2 in January 1974, 955–7 in May 1974 and 960/5/6 in October 1976. However, they were not scrapped. HSR 962 (ex WD 73677) was put back into service in April 1980 for a special LCGB Tour of Greece. In August 1984, HSR 951/60 returned to England, the former for the Mid-Hants Railway and the latter for the Lavender Line (soon afterwards moved to the North Yorkshire Moors Railway). These were ex WD 3652/72. In June 1989, OSE said that 958 was reserved for their railway museum, while 962/4 had been repaired for use on special trains.

Twenty-seven locomotives were left in Great Britain, one in service and six stored at Longmoor, and twenty in service at March. However, as the WD 2-8-0s came back into service on the LNE, and since the 2-8-0s had a wider route availability than the 2-10-0s, the WD 2-10-0s were returned to the WD and went into store at Longmoor, 73774/6/80/2/4/9/91/3 in September 1946; 73775/7–9/81/6–8/90 in October 1946 and 73783/5/92 in November 1946. Three other 2-10-0s that had been in store at Longmoor were put into service in 1946, WD 73797 at Longmoor and 73798/9 at Cairnryan.

In March 1947, WD 73798/9 went into service on loan to the LMS in the Scottish area, working from Carlisle Kingmoor. In September 1947, the SR started overhauling the 23 engines, WD 73774–96, that had been stored at Longmoor.

Plate 138 WD 2-10-0 3688 hauling the DHP Syrian Taurus Express from Aleppo to Medain Ekbese just over the border into Turkey. Note the upright position of the whistle; this was to enable freight train brakemen to hear it during the frequent gales which blew on the Surian Plain (Photo: K. R. M. Cameron)

machinery at the newly-completed Rugby Test Station, to enable all the brake rollers to be tested simultaneously, after which it returned to Carlisle. During the later part of 1949, WD 73788 went to Crewe Works and then spent 1950 at the Rugby Test Station, and did not re-enter service in Scotland until March 1951.

In 1952, British Railways tested a WD 2–10–0 (90772) against a WD 2–8–0 (90464), each of which had been given a general repair and run in for 500 miles, on the G&SW line between Carlisle and Hurlford. Some 3500 miles each were run, using two grades of coal, hard coal 2B Blidworth Cobbles and soft coal 3B Blackwell B Winning. The hard coal was better. BR 90772 gave 27,000 lb/hr of steam and 90464 gave 19,500, whereas on the soft coal 3B, 90772 gave 23,500 lb/hr and 90464 gave 13,000. Thus, the WD 2–10–0 was markedly superior in steam production to the 2–8–0, perhaps not surprising in view of the wide firebox and arch tubes. However, both gave inferior results to the results normally obtained from the more expensive LMS Stanier 8F 2–8–0s.

The details of the British Rail renumbering are given in the table.

In BR service, these locomotives

BR	0	1	2	3	4	5	6	7	8	9
9075X	3774	3775	3776	3777	3778	3779	3780	3781	3782	3783
9076X	3784	3785	3786	3787	3788	3789	3790	3791	3792	3793
9077X	3794	3795	3796	3798	3799	–	–	–	–	–

stayed in the Scottish Region and at the four sheds to which they were initially allocated, with only an occasional change between the four sheds. However, there was one exception, in May 1952 when BR 90763 (ex 73787) was transferred to Doncaster. In August 1952, it was exchanged for BR 90757 (ex 73781). BR 90757 was soon transferred to Banbury on the Western Region and then to Ashford on the Southern Region, before returning to Scotland in October 1952. Presumably these movements were in connection with the forthcoming introduction of BR Standard 2–10–0s instead of the originally planned 2–8–2s and may have been to allay fears that a 2–10–0 would not negotiate tight curves or intricate pointwork.

Three 2–10–0s (90752–4) were withdrawn by BR in 1961 and the rest in 1962, mostly in December, the last being 90773.

WD 73651 stayed at Longmoor during the war. In October 1946, WD 73797 which had been in store at Longmoor, was put into service there. WD 73651 was named "Gordon", while WD 73797 was first named "Sapper" and then "Kitchener". They were renumbered WD 600/1 respectively in 1952. WD 601 was on loan to BR from May 1957 until February 1959. WD 600 is now on the Severn Valley Railway.

The final disposition of the 150 locomotives of this class was thus 103 to the NS, 25 to BR, 16 to Greece, 4 to Syria and 2 to Longmoor.

Three WD 2–10–0s are preserved in the UK, WD 600 (ex WD 73651) "Gordon" on the Severn Valley Railway, WD 3652 (ex HSR 951) as WD "601" "Sturdee" on the Mid Hants Railway and WD 3672 (ex HSR 960) "Dame Vera Lynn" on the North Yorkshire Moors Railway. In Holland, WD 73755 (ex NS 5085) "Longmoor" is at the Dutch Railway Museum in Utrecht. In Greece, WD 3659 (OSE 958) is reserved for their railway nuseum, while WD 3677/82 (OSE 962/4) are retained for use on special trains. Others exist in scrap condition.

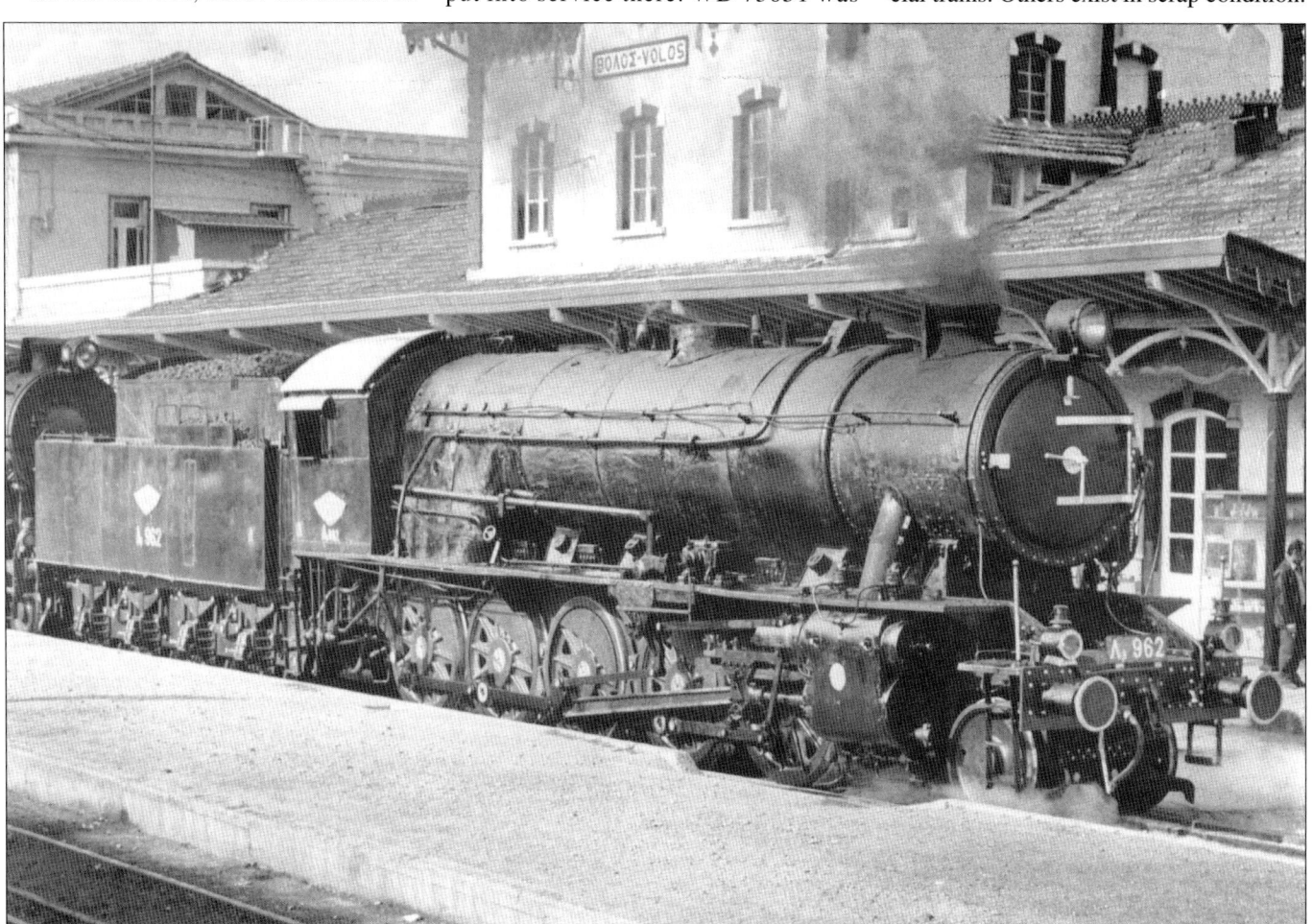

Plate 145   HSR 2–10–0 962 (ex WD 73677) on LCGB special train at Volos in 1980 (Photo: B. J. Ashworth)

Chapter 32

60cm GAUGE 2–8–2s, WD 4000–4

When the eventual result of the North African campaign was in some doubt and the shipping available for sending supplies to the Middle East via the Cape was barely adequate, steps were taken to provide alternative overland routes across Central Africa to the Sudan and Egypt.

One of these routes involved the use of the Chemins de Fer Vicinaux du Congo in the Belgian Congo, a 60cm gauge line over 300 miles long, which spanned a large part of the distance separating the River Congo from the River Nile. The existing locomotive stock of the railway would have been inadequate to deal with a great volume of through military traffic, and therefore the Ministry of Supply ordered eighteen 2–8–2 locomotives for the line from Messrs W. G. Bagnall Ltd in 1943. Only five of these locomotives were completed, however, although a considerable amount of material for the remainder had been made, when the order for the last ten was cancelled. The unassembled parts of the next ten were sent to WD Sinfin Lane depot, Derby.

The design appears to have been based on an existing one of Continental origin and had a maximum axle-load of only eight tons. It was unusual in that side tanks were provided in addition to a tender, the side tanks providing useful additional adhesive weight, and at the same time leaving more tender space available for the bulky wood fuel which was used. The cylinders and frames were outside the wheels, the former being provided with slide valves operated by Walschaerts valve gear. The leading and trailing Bissel trucks had outside axleboxes.

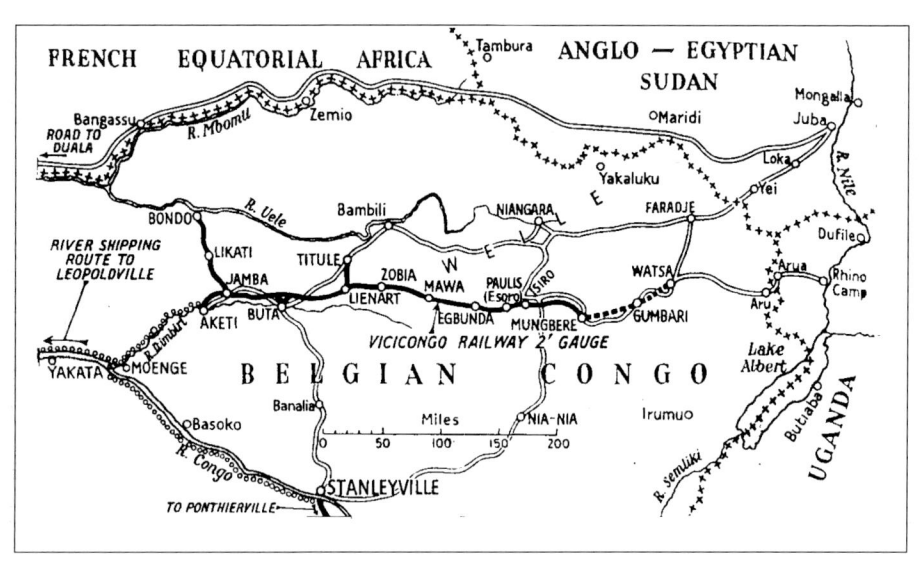

Map 19   Sketch map showing the Vicicongo Railway and its relationship to the lines of communication between the valleys of the Congo and the Nile (Courtesy Railway Gazette)

The boiler had a steel firebox with a wide grate and a combustion chamber, but was unusual in being unsuperheated. The ample grate area was required to suit the wood fuel used, and a conical spark-arresting chimney was provided for the same reason. Two live steam injectors were provided and arrangements were made for these to take water from the tender until this was empty and then from the side tanks. This avoided reducing the adhesive weight sooner than was necessary. The tender was of the double-bogie type with four-wheeled bogies. Westinghouse air brakes were provided on the engine only, and the centre buffers and couplings were of Belgian design. Other fittings included complete electric light equipment with a turbo-generator.

The eighteen engines ordered were allocated works numbers 2683–2700 by Bagnall but only 2683–7 of 1943 were completed. These five engines were allocated WD Nos 4000–4, although it is not known if these numbers were actually carried on the locomotives. They were put into service in 1944, with Vicicongo Nos 56 to 60, for both passenger and goods work, and were still in service in 1958.

The dimensions were as follows:

Plate 146   WD 4000 narrow-gauge 2–8–2 official photograph. This is a bit of a fake photograph, since it is actually two photographs joined together, one of the locomotive and one of the tender, the scale and perspective being slightly diffcrent. Also, the gap between the locomotive and tender is filled in (Photo: W. G. Bagnall)

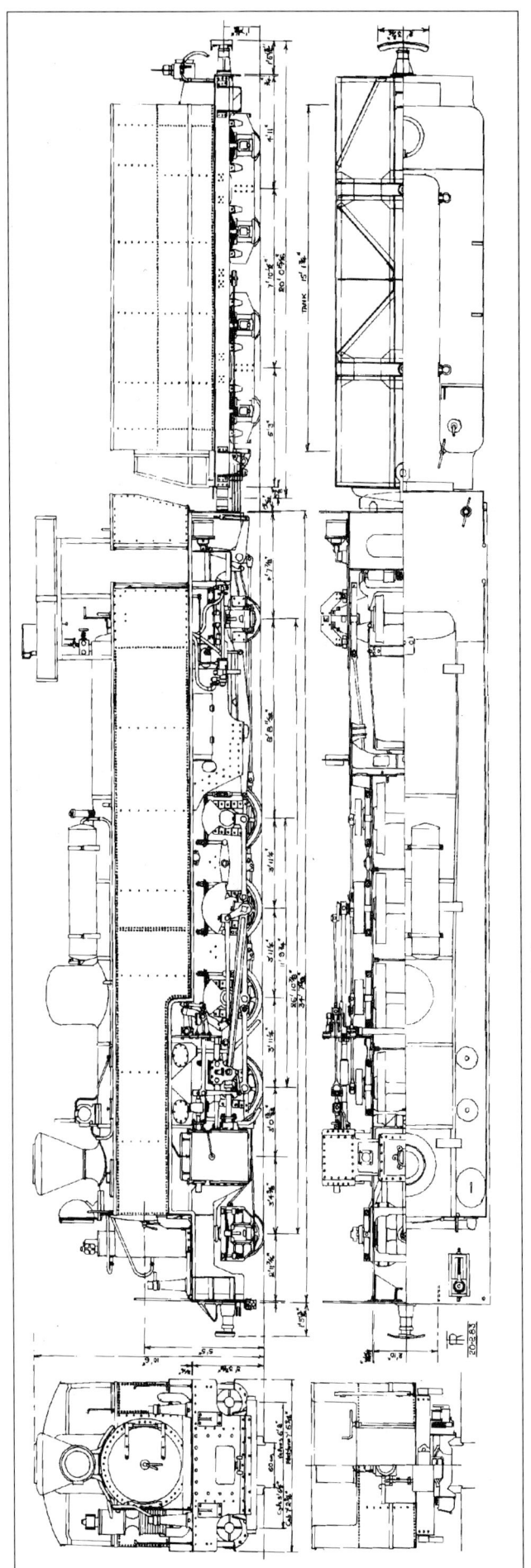

Cylinders, two outside	15¾in x 17¾in
Wheel diameter, coupled	3ft 1¹³/₃₂in
truck	1ft 11⅝in
Boiler heating surface	
tubes	870sq ft
firebox	98sq ft
total evaporative	968sq ft
Grate area	24.2sq ft
Boiler pressure	170psi
Tractive effort at 85% boiler pressure	17,000lb
Adhesive weight	31t 10cwt
Weight in working order, engine	42tons 6¾cwt
Water capacity	
engine	1122gal
tender	1100gal
total	2222gal
Fuel capacity, wood	247cub ft
Tender wheel diameter	1ft 5¾in
Tender wheelbase	11ft 7¾in
Weight of tender, full	13tons 6cwt
Weight of engine & tender in working order	55tons 12¾cwt

Fig 21 Narrow-gauge 2–8–2 WD 4000–4 used on the Chemins de Fer Vicianaux du Congo

Chapter 33

2ft 6in GAUGE 2–8–0s, WD 4005–10

When preparations were being made for an increased offensive against the Japanese in Burma, troops were trained in jungle warfare at various parts of the coast of West Africa. As a result, a heavy traffic developed on the Sierra Leone Railway. To provide additional locomotive power, six 2–8–0 locomotives were transferred from the South Indian Railway early in 1943, these becoming WD 74005–10 and SLR 111–6. They had been SIR class W, and were numbered W1–6 on that railway. They had outside cylinders with Walschaerts valve gear, and the frames were inside. The boilers had round-topped fireboxes. The engines were built by the Swiss Locomotive Company and the works numbers given below are the correct ones for the locomotives as originally built. Observation of these engines has shown some discrepancies, possibly due to boiler exchanges.

Unfortunately, when they arrived on the SLR in March 1943, they were found somewhat too heavy. Consequently, they were restricted to the Freetown and Clinetown areas, where they were employed on shunting and banking duties. The change of ownership from SIR to SLR was initially indicated on the engines by the simple addition of a horizontal line at the base of the "I" on the lettering of the tender. All six locomotives were scrapped at the end of the war.

The dimensions were as follows:

WD No	Builder, works No & date	SIR No	SLR No
74005	Swiss Locomotive 2313/13	W2	111
74006	Swiss Locomotive 2314/13	W3	112
74007	Swiss Locomotive 2312/13	W1	113
74008	Swiss Locomotive 2738/20	W5	114
74009	Swiss Locomotive 2737/20	W4	115
74010	Swiss Locomotive 2739/20	W6	116

Gauge	2ft 6in
Cylinders, two outside	14¼in x 16½in
Wheel diameter, coupled	2ft 10in
truck	1ft 11in
Wheelbase, total engine	18ft 10⅜in
Boiler heating surface	
tubes & flues	667sq ft
firebox	56sq ft
total evaporative	723sq ft
superheater	230sq ft
total	953sq ft
Grate area	14.4sq ft
Boiler pressure	175psi
Tractive effort at 85% boiler pressure	14,567lb
Adhesive weight	23.5 tons
Weight in working order, engine	27.5 tons
Tender wheelbase	8ft 10¼in
Water capacity	2400gal
Coal capacity	2½ tons
Tender weight, full	15.5 tons
Wheelbase, engine & tender	34ft 6in
Weight of engine & tender in working order	43 tons

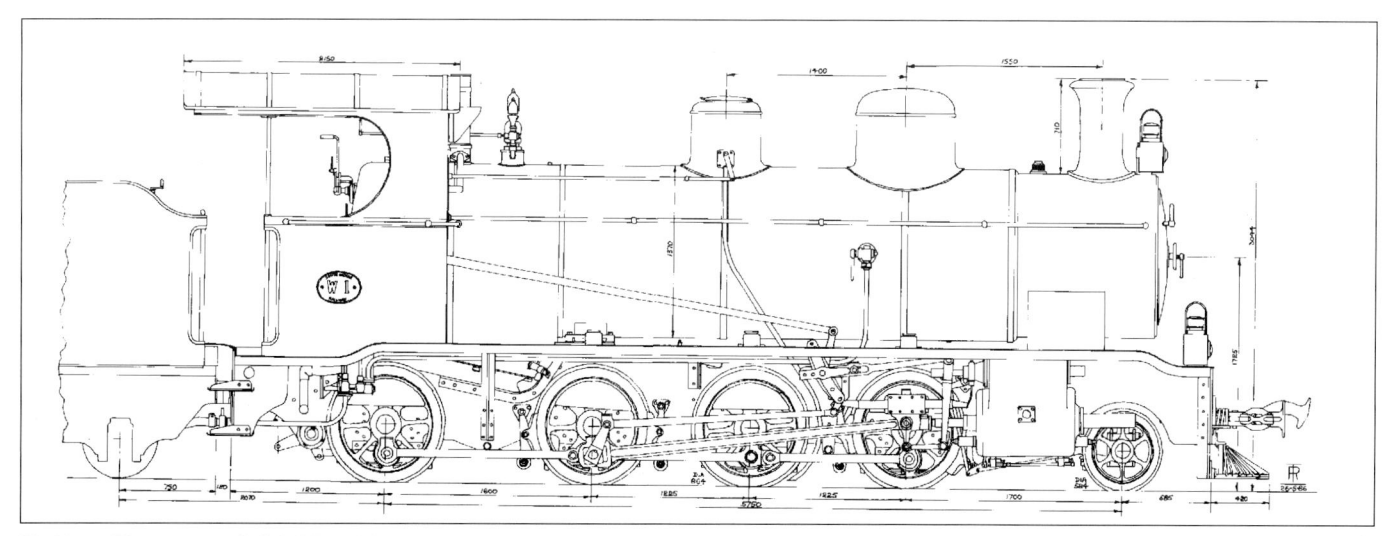

Fig 22   Narrow-gauge 2–8–0 WD 4005–10 used on the Sierra Leone Railway

Plate 147   SIR W2 (later WD 4005) official photograph (Photo: SLM-Winterthur)

Chapter 34

LIGHT BEYER-GARRATT LOCOMOTIVES, WD 4200–43

The Light Beyer-Garratt locomotives fall into three groups with different wheel arrangements.

2–8–0+0–8–2

When the campaign against the Japanese in Burma was beginning to develop, it was realised that additional locomotive power would be required at an early date on the metre-gauge lines serving the north-eastern corner of India and in 1943 the Ministry of Supply placed an order with Beyer Peacock (Order 11122) for the supply of ten metre-gauge Beyer-Garratt locomotives, WD 4200–9, with a light (10^1/$_2$in ton) axleload, for delivery in four months.

This meant that exceptional efforts were needed to produce ten engines of this type in so short a time, and an existing design of 2–8–0+0–8–2 was therefore adopted. This type had previously been built for the Burma Railways in 1927, but advantage was taken of the opportunity to modernise the design, and new features included an all-welded steel inner firebox and improved bogie centres. All the usual features of Beyer-Garratt locomotives were incorporated, and the design presented a very massive appearance owing to the short chimney and other boiler mountings, which had to clear the somewhat restricted loading gauge of the Indian metre-gauge lines. These engines, together with the subsequent 2–8–2+2–8–2 light Garratts, had Belpaire fireboxes, whereas all the other WD Garratt designs had round-top fireboxes. BP works nos were 7112–21, all built in 1943.

On arrival in India, these engines were re-erected by the Bengal Assam Railway and were put into traffic between February and June 1944. The WD numbers allocated to these engines, 4200–9, do not appear to have been used in India, as the BAR renumbered them BAR 702–4/1/5–10. Later, they were again renumbered in a separate series allocated to WD engines in India, the new numbers being 411–3/0/4–9. The BAR classified these engines "MWGL". They were used on the plains section between Akhaura and Badarpur, several being shedded at the latter place.

At the end of 1945 the whole class was transferred to Burma, being shipped via Calcutta Docks. On arrival in Burma, they were put into Burma Railways stock as class "GB", with numbers shuffled again, being BR 822–4/1/5/6/9/30/27/8 in order of the original WD nos and works nos. Most of them were allocated to Thazi shed during 1946.

2–8–2+2–8–2

Following the 2–8–0+0–8–2 engines, a further order (11123) was placed for fourteen additional Beyer-Garratts, WD 4210–23, for use in the same area, and as more time was available for revising the design of this later series, it was decided to provide additional pony trucks at the inner ends of the engines units, thus improving the ability of the locomotives to negotiate the severe curvature of the Bengal Assam Railway, and at the same time increasing the coal and water capacity. In other respects, the 2–8–2+2–8–2 engines were almost identical with the earlier engines. BP works nos were 7122–35, all built in 1943.

Two engines of this series, WD 4210/1, were lost at sea. Although originally intended for Burma, the remainder were re-erected and put into service on the Bengal Assam Railway between May & October 1944. Only two of this series

Plate 148   Official photograph WD 4200 Light Beyer-Garratt 2–8–0+0–8–2 for Burma Order No 11122 (Photo: North Western Museum of Science & Industry)

Plate 149 Official photograph WD 4210 Light Beyer-Garratt 2–8–2+2–8–2 for Burma Order No 11123 (Photo: North Western Museum of Science & Industry)

received BAR numbers, WD 4214/5 becoming BAR 711/2, but these were shortly renumbered in the WD (India) series, together with the rest of the series, which became WD (India) 420/07/0–5/21/09/6/8. These twelve engines were used on the hill section between Badarpur and Lumding, a section which included eleven miles of almost continuous gradient of 1 in 37. They were officially classified "MWGH" by the BAR. Several also carried unofficial names, 4213 "Goliath", 4215 "Jatinger Flyer", 4216 "Irish Molly" and 4217 "Bridal Blush".

At the end of 1945 and the beginning of 1946, the whole class was shipped to the Burma Railways and all were in stock on the latter system by September 1946. On the BR they were classified "GC", and were renumbered 831–42 in the same order as the WD (India) numbers.

4–8–2+2–8–4

As the war in the Far East developed, further increases in locomotive power were required on the metre-gauge lines of India, and a completely new design was evolved under Order 11124. This was not only suitable for use in India, but also in Burma, Malaya, Siam and Indo-China, in view of the impending campaign for the liberation of the latter countries from the Japanese. Eventually, twenty locomotives of this type were built, WD 4224–43 which were BP 7140–59, the first two built in 1944 and the rest in 1945. WD 74240 was completed by Beyer Peacock on VE-Day, 7 May 1945, and carried a plate to commemorate this, and in addition it was named "Beyer Peacock", the nameplates being attached to the cab sides.

The design was intended to be more suitable for general use than the earlier 2–8–0+0–8–2 and 2–8–2+2–8–2 types, which had been designed for use on very heavy grades, and had not proved entirely satisfactory on more level routes. The wheel arrangement of the new design was 4–8–2+2–8–4, with a maximum axle-load of ten tons to permit operation on 50lb/yd rail. The coupled wheel diameter was increased to 4ft 0in to permit higher speeds. The tractive effort, 43520lb, was the highest figure for any metre-gauge locomotive in the Far East.

The boiler had a diameter of 6ft 0in with a round-top firebox having an inner steel box, fitted with arch tubes and providing a grate area of 48¾ square feet. Plate frames were used for the engine units and the cylinders followed the best modern practice in providing an easy steam flow. The Walschaerts valve gear was designed to give very consistent valve events, and reversing was by a geared wheel and screw.

Owing to the climatic conditions for which the engines were designed, it was essential that the cab should be as spacious and well ventilated as possible, and this was done as far as the rather restricted Indian loading gauge for metre-gauge lines would permit. As, however, it was expected that many of the class would be used on lines having a less restricted loading gauge, the cab was provided with a removable strip along the top of the front, back and side plates, 6in deep, which allowed the roof to be raised by that amount, where the loading gauge permitted. Fittings included electric-lighting equipment and soot blowers mounted on the sides of the firebox. The coal and water capacity was considerably greater than that of the earlier light Garratts, a great advantage for engines working under war-time conditions.

The Ministry of Supply code-word for these engines was "STALIG" (Standard Light Garratt) and of the twenty engines of the class, sixteen were originally allocated to the Bengal Assam Railway, and two to the Burma Railways, while the two remaining were delivered far away from the area for which they were designed, namely to the Kenya and Uganda Railway.

The sixteen engines, WD 4224–37/40/1, allocated to the Bengal Assam Railway started arriving in November 1945 and replaced the 2–8–2+2–8–2 and 2–8–0+0–8–2 WD Garratts which were being transferred to Burma. They were shedded at Badarpur for working the Badarpur to Lumding "Hill" section. These engines were classified "MWGX" by the BAR and were allocated numbers 680–93/6/7 in order. Subsequently, seven of the class, WD 4230–5/41, were transferred to the Burma Railways, probably in 1946.

After the partition of India, the metre-gauge section of the Bengal Assam Railway was divided up, the western part which came within the new India going to the Oudh and Tirhut Railway, and the

Plate 150 Official photograph WD 74224 Light Beyer-Garratt 4–8–2+2–8–4 for general use Order No 11124 (Photo: North Western Museum of Science & Industry)

Fig 23 General arrangement drawing of the 4-8-2+2-8-4 Light Beyer-Garratt locomotives WD 4224-43 (Courtesy Modern Transport)

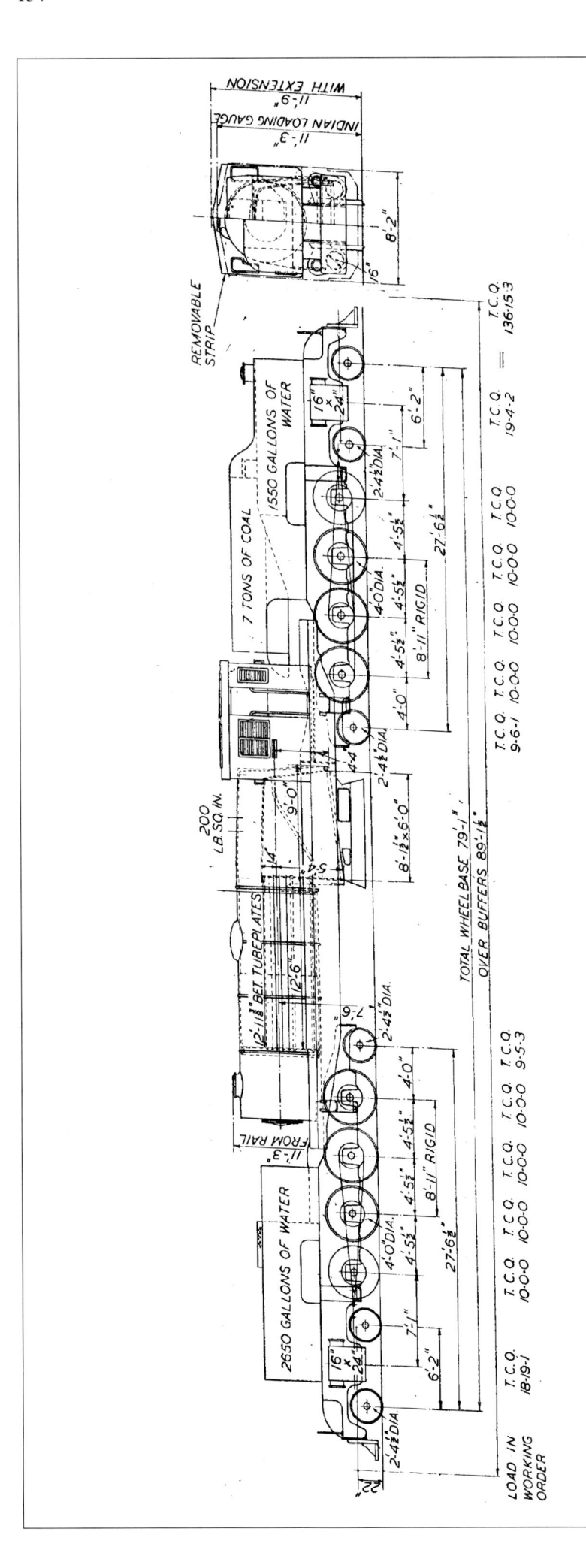

remaining part in India being incorporated into a new railway, the Assam Railway. The part coming within Pakistan formed yet another line, the Eastern Bengal Railway. This division took place on 15 August 1947, and the remaining nine 4-8-2+2-8-4 Garratts, WD 4224-9/36/7/40, became Assam Railway stock. Their numbers initially remained unchanged as AR 680-5/92/3/6. They later became Class GX Northeast Frontier Railway 975-83, and in the all-India renumbering scheme of 1958 they became 32082-90.

Nine engines were sent to Burma, two direct and seven from the BAR. These were WD 4230-5/8/9/41. Two were noted at Madras, not fully erected, in October 1945, carrying WD (India) Nos 422/3 (BP 7150/1), but no other engines of the class were reported with numbers in this series. In Burma, the class was classified "GD" and was numbered 854-7/1/2/8/9/3.

In March 1948, BR 851-4 were sold to the Tanganyika Railways. Between July 1946 and June 1947, the five remaining engines were renumbered 865-9 to make room for six new class "GE" Garratts then expected but not in fact delivered because the order was taken over by the KUR.

The last two engines of the class, WD 4242/3, went to the Kenya and Uganda Railways in October 1945. They differed from the other engines in having Westinghouse brake equipment for both engine and train, whereas the other engines of the class had steam brakes on the engine with vacuum ejectors and train pipes. These two formed class "EC5" of the KUR and were numbered 120/1. They were used on the 50lb/yd rail section west of Nairobi and were shedded at Nakuru. They mainly operated between Nakuru and Kisumu, on Lake Victoria, a section which included a climb in the eastward direction of 52 miles at an average gradient of 1 in 73 to Mau Summit, the altitude of which is 8322ft above sea level.

As already mentioned, in March 1948, four of the BR engines, 851-4, were transferred to the Tanganyika Railways. These engines were required in connection with the East African Ground Nut Scheme which was expected to make a substantial increase in the traffic on the Tanganyika Railways. The TR classified them "GB" and numbered them 750-3 in order. They were used on the section between Dar-es-Salaam and Morogoro. In May 1948, the KUR and the TR were combined to form the East African Railways and Harbours, so that the combined administration had six engines of this class which became EAR class 55. KUR 120/1 became 5501/2 and TR 750-3

Plate 151   Official photograph WD 74242 Light Beyer-Garratt 4–8–2+2–8–4 for KUR Order No 11129 (Photo: North Western Museum of Science & Industry)

became 5503–6, in order.

EAR 5501/2 were converted to vacuum brake and transferred to the Central line in Tanganyika, and all were eventually converted to oil-burning in the general changeover to oil firing. In 1952, the EAR purchased the five remaining engines of this type in Burma, BR 865–9. These were numbered EAR 5507–11 in the order in which they came into shops to be prepared for service. BR 865/6 became 5510/1 or vice versa, 867 became 5509, 868 became 5508 and 869 became 5507. EAR 5507 went to the KUR section and 5510/1 to Tanganyika.

EAR 5507–9 were fitted with Westinghouse brake, extended water tanks and oil-firing, and were used on the main line between Eldaret and Kampala (Uganda) and on the Uganda branch lines. In 1954/5, it became necessary to provide Garratt motive power for the Tanga-Arusha line in Northern Tanganyika and the connecting link with the main KUR line. Owing to the very light ex-German track still in use on part of those sections, the 55 class, with reduced water and oil tanks, were the only Garratts the axle-loading of which could be reduced sufficiently. Accordingly, all eleven on the 55 class on the Tanganyika Central line were gradually shipped to Kenya and modified for work on the Tanga line. They were still in service in 1960, ten at work on the Voi-Moshi and Tanga-Arusha lines and one stationed at Kampala for work on the Western Uganda extension. They were equipped with Giesl ejectors and chimneys. Scrapping started in the mid-1970s, and by 1975 only 5501–3/5/6/9/10 were still in service.

The dimensions were as follows:

WD Nos	**4200–9**	**4210–23**	**4224–43**
Wheel arrangement	2–8–0+0–8–2	2–8–2+2–8–2	4–8–2+2–8–4
Gauge	Metre	Metre	Metre
Cylinders, four	15$\frac{1}{2}$in x 20in	15$\frac{1}{2}$in x 20in	16in x 24in
Wheel diameter, coupled	3ft 3in	3ft 3in	4ft 0in
bogies truck	2ft 4$\frac{1}{2}$in	2ft 4$\frac{1}{2}$in	2ft 4$\frac{1}{2}$in
Wheelbase, coupled	11ft 0in	11ft 0in	13ft 4$\frac{1}{2}$in
total	60ft 2in	67ft 6in	79ft 1in
Boiler heating surface			
Tubes & flues, sq ft	1555	1555	1813
Firebox, sq ft	187	187	183
Total evaporative, sq ft	1742	1742	1996
Superheater, sq ft	313	313	399
Combined total, sq ft	2055	2055	2395
Grate area, sq ft	43.7	43.7	48.75
Boiler pressure, psi	200	200	200
Tractive effort at 85% boiler pressure, lb	41890	41890	43520
Adhesive weight	83 tons 15cwt	83 tons 9cwt	80 tons 0cwt
Weight in working order	103 tons 7cwt	117 tons 17cwt	136 tons 16cwt
Length over couplers	70ft 7in	78ft 0in	89ft 1$\frac{1}{2}$in
Maximum axleload	10 tons 10cwt	10 tons 10cwt	10 tons 0cwt
Coal capacity, tons	5	6	7
Water capacity, gal	2000	3600	4200

Plate 152   EAR 5503 (ex WD 4234) Light Beyer-Garratt 4–8–2+2–8–4 (Photo: EAR)

Chapter 35

HEAVY BEYER-GARRATT LOCOMOTIVES, WD 4400–24

The Heavy Beyer-Garratt locomotives fall into two groups with different wheel arrangements.

2–8–2+2–8–2

This class was the first of the five types of Beyer-Garratts that were eventually built for the War Office, and was constructed by Beyer Peacock and Co for use on the 3ft 6in gauge lines of Africa. Many of these lines were laid with 60lb rail, yet the traffic on them had increased considerably as a result of the Middle East campaign. The engines were intended for use in the Gold Coast, Rhodesia and the French and Belgian Congos, and were given the code-word "SHEG" (Standard Heavy Garratt). The locomotives, WD 4400–17, were of the 2–8–2+2–8–2 type. The design was based to some extent on earlier ones for the Rhodesia Railways and for South African Railways (GE class), but a number of improvements were incorporated to bring the design up to date, and the overall dimensions were modified to enable the locomotives to clear the loading gauges of all the railways over which they were likely to operate.

The boiler was a large one with a round-top firebox and a large grate to enable the engines to burn low-grade coal or even wood. The inner firebox was of steel, with welded joints, and was provided with four arch tubes. The smokebox had self-cleaning baffle plates and was provided with a short stovepipe chimney. The engine units had plate frames, these being used instead of bar frames, which represented more modern practice for Garratt locomotives, owing to the easier availability of steel plate when the engines were built. Outside cylinders, of course, were used and the valve gear was Walschaerts type, operated by steam reversing gear. A roomy cab was provided with provision for adequate ventilation, an important point for engines operating in the tropics. Fittings included steam brakes on both engine units, top feed clackboxes, and electric lighting equipment.

The first six of the class, WD 4400–5 built BP 7057–62 in 1943, were sent to the Gold Coast Railway under Order 11125, on which line they were numbered 301–6. These were the first Garratt locomotives to be used in the Gold Coast. These engines had vacuum brakes and "Takoradi"-type central buffers, with separate screw couplings above. They were received in July 1943 and were employed hauling manganese ore trains between Nsuta and Takoradi Harbour, a distance of 38 miles. When the Gold Coast achieved independence, the railway system became part of the Ghana Railway and Harbours Administration. They were withdrawn in June 1960.

The next three, WD 4406–8 built BP 7063–5 in 1943, were sent to the Congo-Ocean Railway of French West Africa also under Order 11125, where they were the first British engines to be used. They were placed in service in November and December 1943, numbered COR 100.401–3, and used for hauling freight trains. They were withdrawn from service in November 1950 and stored until 1954, when they were sold to the Caminhos de Ferro de Mocambique, leaving on the SS "Sofala" in August 1954 bound for Beira. They were numbered CFM 990–2 and were used for working goods and mixed trains over the Gondola-Umtali line on the Beira system. They were still in service in 1975.

The remaining nine engines of the class, WD 4409–17, were built by BP 7066–74, up to 7070 in 1943 and the rest in 1944, under Order 11126. They were used on the Rhodesia Railways, where they went into service between October 1943 and June 1944. They were numbered 281–9, forming the "18th" class. These engines had vacuum brake equipment, and the "MCB" type of knuckle coupler. They were chiefly used on heavy coal trains on the Wankie-Dett section, a

Plate 153   Official photograph WD 4400 Heavy Beyer-Garratt 2–8–2+2–8–2 Order No 11125 (Photo: North Western Museum of Science & Industry)

Plate 154   Official photograph WD 4418 Heavy Beyer-Garratt 4–8–2+2–8–4 for KUR Order No 11127 (Photo: North Western Museum of Science & Industry)

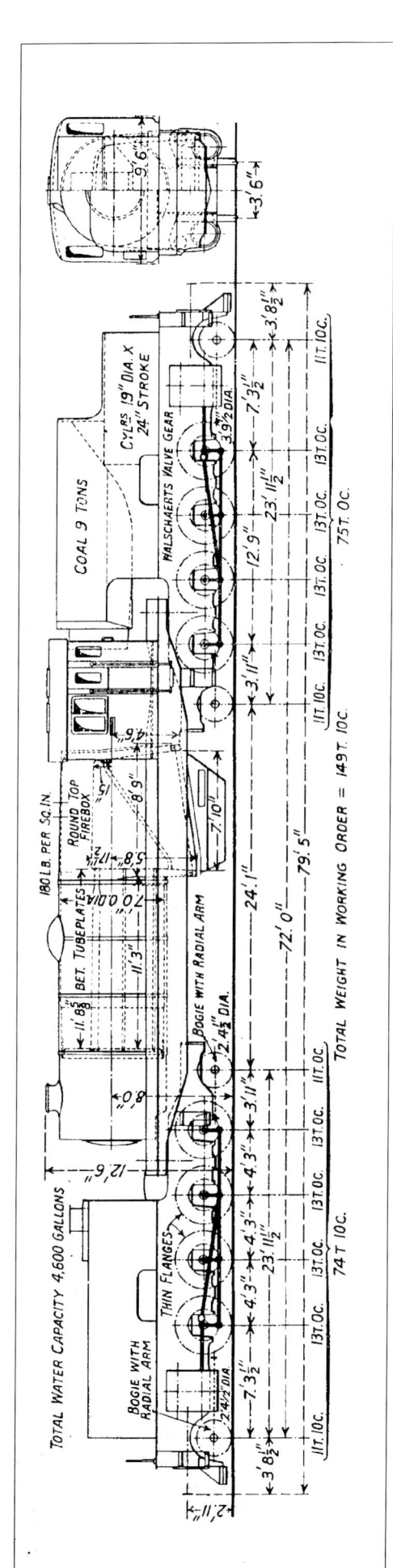

Fig 24 General arrangement drawing of the 2–8–2+2–8–2 Heavy Beyer-Garratt locomotives WD 4400–17 (Courtesy Railway Gazette)

Plate 155 EAR 5402 (ex WD 4419) Heavy Beyer-Garratt 4–8–2+2–8–4 (Photo: EAR)

heavily-graded run of some 51 miles. After the war, they were transferred to the Vila-Machado section. In 1949, when 200 miles of line from Beira to Umtali were taken over by the Mozambique authorities to form the Caminho de Ferro da Beira, these nine locomotives, with others, were sold to the Portuguese authorities for £30,000 each to operate this section. They became Caminhos de Ferro de Mocambique 981–9 and were still in service in 1975.

4–8–2+2–8–4

When the 2–8–2+2–8–2 Beyer-Garratts were being built, it was decided that additional locomotive power would also be required for the metre-gauge Kenya and Uganda Railway. This railway already had a number of Garratt locomotives in use, and experience had shown that for the conditions of curvature existing, two-wheeled pony trucks were not entirely suitable, four-wheeled bogies being preferred. In addition, the water capacity of the 2–8–2+2–8–2 engines was rather small for conditions on the KUR.

As the gauge of the KUR precluded the use of Standard Heavy Garratts on this line, a modified design was adopted which complied more closely with the requirements of the railway. The wheel arrangement was altered to 4–8–2+2–8–4, which permitted larger water tanks to be used owing to the increased frame length of the engine units. The braking system was changed to Westinghouse air brakes for both engine and train, the standard system on the KUR. The boiler was interchangeable between the two classes and so were many detail parts, but the motion was different in some respects, owing to the cylinders on the KUR engines being further forward to clear the trailing bogie wheels.

Seven engines, WD 4418–24, of this type were built in 1944, BP 7075–81, under Order 11127. They arrived in Kenya about the middle of 1944. On arrival, they carried numbers 89–95, in addition to their WD numbers 4418–24, which were shown in small figures beneath the KUR number on the cab side, but they appear to have been renumbered 100–6 after reassembly (no doubt to leave room for further EC3 class engines whose numbers finished at 88), and the WD numbers were soon deleted. The KUR classified these engines "EC4".

They were used on the Mombasa-Nairobi section of the KUR, a heavily-graded section which climbs from sea level at Mombasa to an altitude of 5450ft at Nairobi, 330 miles away. The section was laid with 80lb rail and the EC4 class was restricted to this section owing to its relatively high axle-loading. Following the amalgamation of the KUR and the Tanganyika Railways in May 1948, these locomotives became part of the stock of the East African Railways and Harbours, and were classified "54" class and renumbered 5401–7. They were still in service in 1960, but all except 5402 were scrapped by the mid 1960s, since the small coupled wheels and plate frames did not stand up to the pounding which they received.

The dimensions were as follows:

WD Nos	4400–17	4418–24
Wheel arrangement	2–8–2+2–8–2	4–8–2+2–8–4
Gauge	3ft 6in	Metre
Cylinders, four	19in x 24in	19in x 24in
Wheel diameter, coupled	3ft 9½in	3ft 3in
bogie and truck	2ft 4½in	2ft 5in
Wheelbase, coupled	12ft 9in	12ft 9in
total	72ft 0in	77ft 9in
Boiler heating surface		
Tubes & flues, sq ft	2328	2328
Firebox, sq ft	212	212
Total evaporative, sq ft	2540	2540
Superheater, sq ft	470	470
Combined total, sq ft	3010	3010
Grate area, sq ft	51.3	51.3
Boiler pressure, psi	180	180
Tractive effort at 85% boiler pressure, lb	58260	58260
Adhesive weight	103 tons 14cwt	105 tons 17cwt
Weight in working order	151 tons 16cwt	171 tons 10cwt
Length over couplers	79ft 5in	88ft 5in
Maximum axleload	13 tons 2½cwt	13 tons 5cwt
Coal capacity, tons	9	12
Water capacity, gal	4600	6000

Chapter 36

LNE ARMOURED 2–4–2Ts, WD A–M (& SPARES)

In 1940, several LNE F4 2–4–2Ts, and one F5, were taken out of normal service and fitted with armour plate so that they could be used for hauling armoured trains, distributed at various strategic centres around the country. With the armour, the locomotives weighed nearly 60 tons. In some cases, armoured tenders were supplied by the LMS to increase their radius of operation. The locomotive was usually flanked by two 3 or 5 plank wagons and two LMS steel 20 ton coal wagons reinforced with armour and fitted with naval six-pounder guns. They were given a mottle camouflage of grey, green and khaki.

LNE 7172, 7072, 7214, 7178, 7244, 7077, 7189, 7071, 7180, 7573, 7173 and 7784 (the F5) (all pre-1946 numbering, of course) became WD A to N in order (omitting I), which were the letters of the armoured trains that they were to haul. LNE 7071 went to the WD in March 1940; LNE 7180, 7573, 7173 and 7784 in July 1940; and the rest in June 1940.

The main purpose of the armoured trains was to counteract Britain's shortage of conventional armoured vehicles in the aftermath of Dunkirk and, in particular, to help repel any possible invasion. For this purpose, WD A–M and their trains were officially stationed (in order) at Hitchin, Canterbury, Canterbury, Mistley,

Plate 157 WD armoured LNE 2–4–4T working an armoured train (Photo: R. Tourret Collection)

Plate 156 WD "H" 2–4–2T (ex LNE 7071) armoured and camouflaged for service hauling armoured trains (Photo: British Rail)

Ashford, Tilbury, Heacham, Canterbury, Stirling, Longniddry, Aberdeen and Spalding. However, WD A made occasional appearances hauling an armoured train at and around Heathfield and Torquay during 1941, and it was probably this train which sometimes appeared on the Helston Branch and at Wadebridge. WD G was also used on the Melton Constable to Cromer Beach line. WD H (7071) was named "Auld Reekie". LNE 7174/7 and 7586 were also armoured as spare locomotives and went to the WD in January 1941, and 7111 in February 1941. They were not allocated permanently.

Plate 159 WD armoured LNE 2–4–2T working an armoured train said to be near Wadebridge in Cornwall (Photo: R. Tourret Collection)

According to some reports, 7174 was WD N and 7177 WD O.

Fortunately, the invasion never happened. The locomotives, therefore, were never very busy apart from the occasional exercises. After a year or two, some locomotives were put to use at various WD depots, and for this purpose the military authorities used their LNE numbers because the locomotives no longer had their armoured trains with them. WD A (7172) went to Burton Dassett and Long Marston, WD B (7072) was also at Long Marston, WD F (7077) went to Bicester, 7111 also to Bicester and 7177 to Burton Dassett.

With the arrival of the new WD 0–6–0STs, the need for old shunting locomotives decreased and the locomotives were returned to the LNE. WD F was returned to the LNE in March 1943; WD A, B and G in May 1943; LNE 7111/77 and 7586 in June 1943; WD C, D, E, H and M in July 1943 and finally WD J, K, L and 7174 in January 1945.

The LNE restored them to their original condition. In 1947, brass plates were fitted to the sides of the bunkers above the number plates inscribed "LNER. During the war of 1939–45 this locomotive was armoured and hauled defence trains on the coast lines". The engines did not survive long afterwards, the majority being withdrawn in April 1948.

According to observation, L was 7573 and not 7173 for at least some of the period under WD control. The Eastern Region of the Railway Executive, however, have confirmed the numbers given above and also stated that these locomotives had the same lettering as put on originally when handed back to the LNE. There remains the possibility of a temporary change while the engine was on loan to the WD.

Plate 158 Posed photographed of an armoured train with troops at the ready (Photo: R. Tourret Collection)

Chapter 37

INDIAN CLASS YD (MODIFIED) METRE-GAUGE 2–8–2s, WD (INDIA) 1 & 2

The two engines of this class were built by W. G. Bagnall 2625/6 of 1942 to the order of the Sao Paulo – Parana Railway of Brazil, but owing to the war, they were diverted to India, where they became WD (India) Nos 1 and 2. The numbers allocated to them by the SPPR were 28 and 29, but these numbers were never carried. A works photograph shows No 21.

The engines appear to have been a repeat order of two engines of the same design built by Bagnall 2528/9 of 1935 (see the Railway Gazette, 13 December 1935). The design seems to have been based on the standard Indian YD type, but

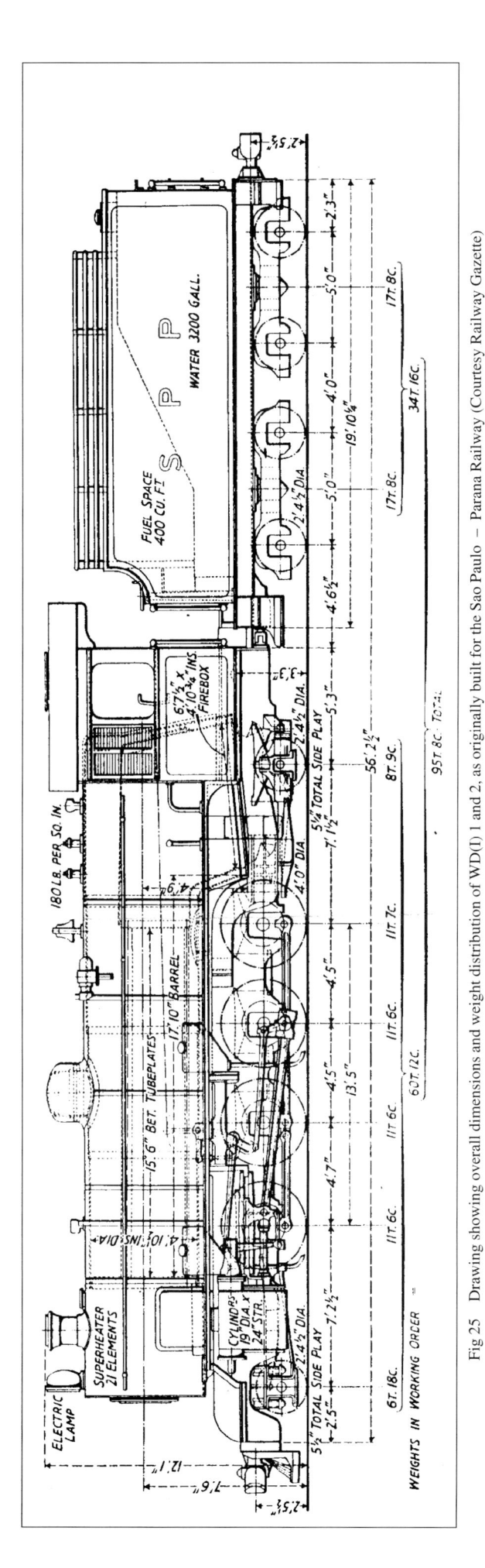

Fig 25 Drawing showing overall dimensions and weight distribution of WD(I) 1 and 2, as originally built for the Sao Paulo – Parana Railway (Courtesy Railway Gazette)

with 19in cylinders instead of 17in, and a larger firebox with a round top instead of the Belpaire type. The frames underneath the firebox were somewhat different also, the extension frames being attached to the main frame in front of the trailing coupled wheels instead of behind them, as for the YD. The cabs of the SPPR engines were larger and higher, and the chimney and dome were also higher, because the SPPR loading gauge was larger than the Indian one.

These metre-gauge locomotives were designed to run on 60lb rails and to negotiate minimum curves of 333ft radius, hauling trains of 400 to 500 tons on gradients of 1 in 55 at 15 mph. The boiler was large with a wide firebox and a large grate was provided for burning wood fuel. The interior firebox was steel and the boiler was fitted with a superheater. The smokebox was self-cleaning with a system of deflector plates and wire netting forming a spark arrestor. Ross pop safety valves were mounted on the firebox and a warning bell carried on top of the boiler. The ashpan was self-dumping hopper type with bottom discharge door operated by a lever from the footplate.

The main frames were 1 in thick plate, stayed by steel castings and widened behind the trailing wheels by a supplementary rear frame 1½in thick to accommodate the wide firebox and trailing two-wheeled truck. Oil lubrication was provided for the truck and main axleboxes and the spring gear was compensated throughout in two groups; the leading truck, leading and intermediate coupled wheels forming one group and the driving and trailing wheels with the trailing truck forming the other group. Steam distribution was effected by piston valves of the inside admission type, working above the cylinders. Walschaerts valve gear was fitted.

The cab was wide and spacious. Seats were provided on each side and the regulator could be operated by the driver while sitting down with a clear vision ahead. Vacuum brake was fitted and graduable steam brake valve arranged for operating the steam brake on the engine and vacuum brake on the tender and train. The bogie tender was also provided with a hand brake. A Stone turbo-generator supplied current to a 14in diameter headlamp with tail cab and inspection lamps. The Sharon top operating type of central coupler was fitted.

Their original dimensions, additional to those shown on the drawing, were as follows:

Boiler heating surface,	
Tubes	1290sq ft
Firebox	154sq ft
Total evaporative	1444sq ft
Superheater	322sq ft
Combined total	1766sq ft
Grate area	32.33sq ft
Tractive effort at 85% BP	27,616lb

To adopt the locomotives for use in India, the cab roof had to be lowered and a shorter dome and chimney provided, and the headlamp moved to a lower position. The original American-type knuckle couplers were replaced by the Jones-Watson type of combined central buffer and hook coupling. The locomotives originally had vacuum brake equipment, and this required no alteration. Owing to their similarity to the Indian Standard YD class, they were classified YD (Modified).

These two locomotives were erected on arrival in India at the Ajmer workshops of the Bombay, Baroda and Central India Railway. WD (India) 1 entered service on the BBCI in December 1943, and WD (I) 2 in February 1944. In November 1946, WD (I) 1 was sold to the Jodhpur Railway on which line it became No 100. In February 1947, WD (I) 2 was sold to the Mysore Railway. JR 100 became South Central Railway No 99 in the 1951/2 regrouping, and then 30289 in 1958 when the all-India numbering system was adopted. WD(I) 1 on the Mysore Railway became SCR 161 and then all-India 30253. In 1975, both engines were at Donakonda shed on the SCR and they were both still in service in 1977.

Chapter 38

LOCOMOTIVES FROM CHINA

Towards the end of 1941, it was decided to evacuate some standard-gauge locomotives from China that were at Hong Kong, and use them to relieve the motive-power shortage in the Middle East. In addition, there was a desire to remove most of the engines in case the Japanese over-ran Hong Kong. Nine engines went to Egypt, four to Iraq and nine to Iran.

The nine engines that went to Egypt were four class A 2–6–4Ts from the Kowloon-Canton Railway (British Section) numbered KCR 1–4; three 2–6–0s from the Canton-Kowloon Railway (Chinese Section) numbered CKR IV, V and X; another 2–6–0 probably also from the CKR; and a 2–8–0 from the Canton-Hankow Railway numbered 104. The four 2–6–4Ts were built by Kitson & Co 4698/9 in 1909 and 4874/81 in 1912. The CKR 2–6–0s IV, V and X were built by North British Atlas Works 18994/09, 19557/11 and 20645/14. The other 2–6–0 was also built by North British but the works number was unidentifiable. The 2–8–0 was built by Baldwin 43653/16.

They arrived at the Abu Za'abal works of the Egyptian State Railways in late 1941 and were apparently allotted MEF numbers from 801 (later 9801) upwards. Most of these engines were in so poor a condition that they were not put into service. When Ein Shams stores was opened about 1943, most of the parts went there although the frames and boilers lay at the ESR shops until all were evacuated to Suez by 1945 where they were noted in a dismantled and derelict condition, except for the boilers of KCR 2–4 which were sold to the ESR in January 1944 for use in a stationary capacity. Doubtless the rest of the parts were ultimately scrapped.

Only two, KCR 1 and the unknown 2–6–0, were actually erected and put into service as MEF 9801/5 in August and May 1942 (later WD 70220/19 respectively). This means that KCR 2–4 could have been allocated MEF 9802–4. The 2–8–0 was believed to have been allocated MEF 9808, but this leaves only 9806/7 to cover the three CKR 2–6–0s.

The big tank MEF 9801 shunted at Rafa and El Jiya until it eventually required shops attention, when it was brought to Jaffa in 1943. It was reconditioned by No 199 Rly Workshop Coy, and was used for shunting for a while but proved too cumbersome. The Palestine Railway did not like it because of the Westinghouse brake, so it was sent back to El Jiya.

The 2–6–0, MEF 9805, was used at Fanara in Egypt to start with and later Beirut, but then it came to Jaffa shops for

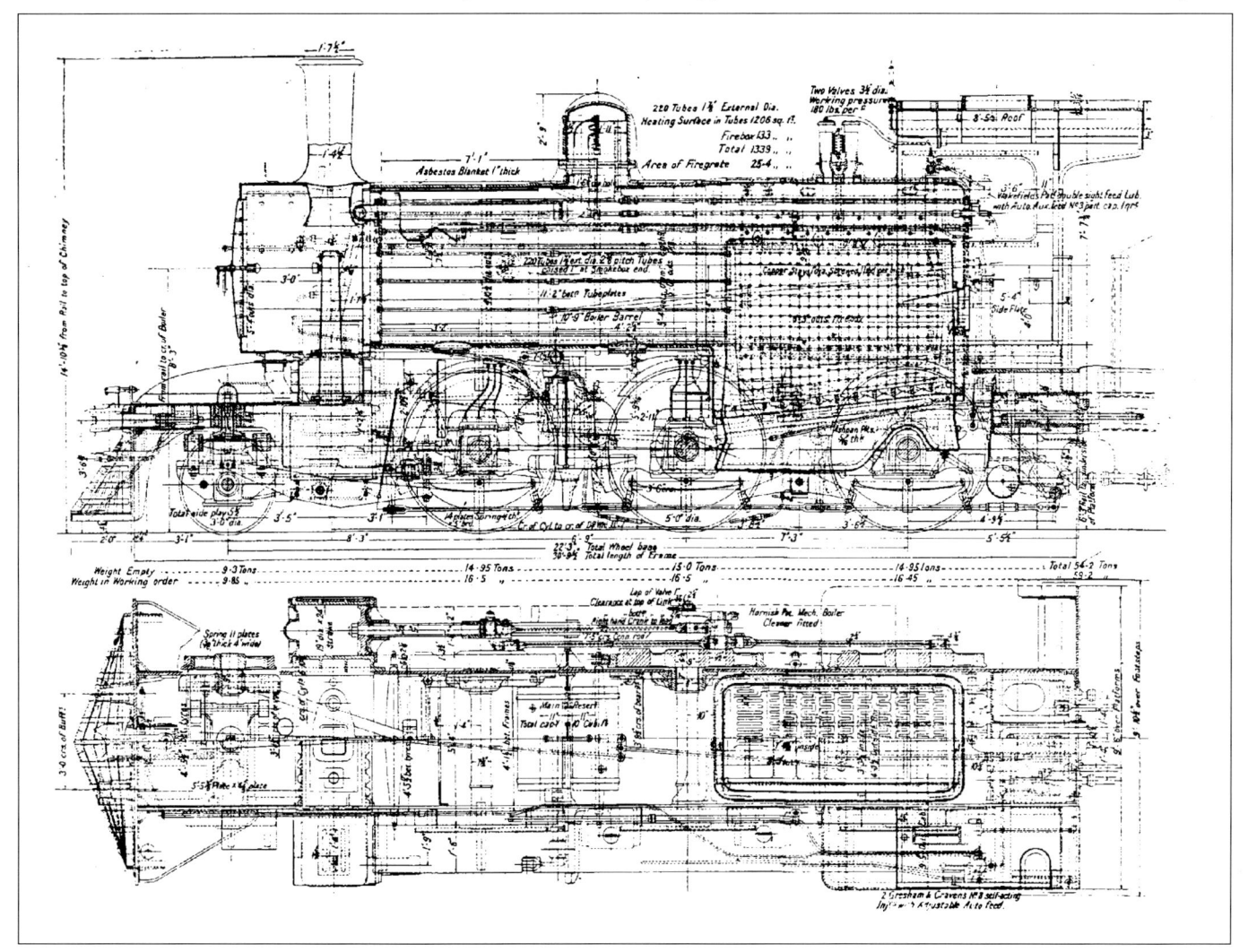

Fig 26   Elevation and plan of Canton-Kowloon Railway 2–6–0s built by North British (Courtesy The Locomotive)

Plate 160 MEF 9801 ex KCR No 1 2–6–4T at Jaffa Workshops in 1943 (Photo: K. R. M. Cameron)

repairs, being worked from Lydda without any brakes, including the final 1 in 50 descent into Jaffa! There it was the first engine to be lifted on the newly-installed Whiting electric beam jacks. The injectors continually gave trouble and were eventually replaced by LNE "below-footplate" injectors doubtless cannibalised from an LNE O4 class locomotive. MEF 9805 was retained at Jaffa, since the officer-in-charge Mr K. R. M. Cameron developed a liking for it, because of which it was sometimes known as "Clan Cameron". The tender had the tank-filling lids at the front or cab end, which seemed an excellent idea which saved climbing over the coals. However, a rapid stop just after filling the tender showed that it also had a disadvantage since water poured out of both lids and soaked the footplate personnel! Finally, MEF 9805 went to Azzib as a permanent shunting and ballast engine with No 193 Rly Operating Coy. Both 9801/5 were still in existence in 1954 when they were at Haifa East, but were probably cut up around 1955/6.

The four engines that went to Iraq were a 2–6–0 numbered 61 from an unknown railway: 2–6–0 No 143 from the Pekin-Mukden Railway built Tongshan 35/09; 2–8–0 No 255 from the Kiao-Tsi Railway built by Baldwin in 1917; and a 2–8–0 numbered 511 from an unknown railway. These four engines arrived at the Schalchiyah works, near Baghdad, of the Iraqi State Railway early in 1942 and received IqSR Nos 1011–4. IqSR 1012 was erected and put into traffic by March 1943 and IqSR 1013 entered service later that year. The other two were not erected and remained in a derelict condition in the works yard. IqSR 1012/3 did only a small amount of useful work and were withdrawn by March 1944. IqSR 1012 had a round-top firebox, while IqSR 1013 appeared to be one of the standard 2–8–0s built by Baldwin for war service in 1917.

It had outside cylinders, Walschaerts valve gear, piston valves and a side-window cab. These four engines were allocated WD Nos 73606–9, 73606 being IqSR 1012, 73607 the other 2–6–0, 73608 IqSR 1013 and 73609 the other 2–8–0.

All nine of the engines that went to Iran arrived on SS "Belpareil" in February 1943. Three of the nine engines were three KCR engines, class A 2–6–4T 5 and class B 4–6–4Ts 9 and 10. KCR 5 was built by Kitson 5038/14 and KCR 9 and 10 were built by Kitson 5375/6 in 1924. These arrived by 1943, 2–6–4T KCR 5 being renumbered IrSR 33.300 and 4–6–4Ts KCR 9 and 10 being renumbered IrSR 34.600/1. The engines were erected at Ahwaz in April 1943 and were originally used at Andimeshk on shunting duties. By July 1943, they were stored, but by September 1943 they were transferred to Teheran works for shunting purposes. Apparently neither WD nor MEF numbers were ever allocated. The remains of all three were on a dump at Ahwaz in 1977.

The other six engines that went to Iran were six large 2–10–2 locomotives built by Krupp 1708–10/30–2 in 1937 for the Chung Hsing Coal Mines in Tsao-chuang (or Tsai-er-chuang) in North China, in the southern border of Shan-tung Province. These six engines were practically duplicates of six locomotives delivered from Krupp in 1936 to the Chinese National Railways for working on the Tientsin-Pukow line, from which the branch line to Chung Hsing Mines diverges at Lin-cheng, about 45 miles north of Hsu-chow. It is believed that the Chung Hsing locomotives were numbered 61–6 but on completion these locomotives could not reach their destination, since in July 1937, the Sino-Japanese War had broken out. They were therefore landed – and

Plate 161 MEF 9805 (later WD 70219) 2–6–0 at Jaffa Workshops in 1943 (Photo: K. R. M. Cameron)

stranded – at Hong Kong.

These six engines were taken over by the British Government, numbered WD 3600–5, and modified in India to suit conditions in Iran. The alterations included new cabs, oil-burning equipment and different buffing and drawgear equipment. On arrival in Iran in 1943, they were given IrSR Nos 52.500/1/3/2/5/4 which was the order of re-erection at Ahwaz in April 1943. They were used, under Russian control, on the heavy 1 in 36 gradients between Teheran and the Caspian Sea. They were subsequently renumbered IrSR 52.01–6. Five were still in service on the IrSR in October 1951, and some at least in 1962.

Knowledge of dimensions of these engines is not complete. The Canton-Hankow Railway 2–8–0 No 104 had 4ft 2in driving wheels and 160psi boiler pressure. It is interesting to note that its works number, Baldwin 43653/16, relates to a 4–6–0 which was, in fact, built for the Canton-Hankow Railway. Evidently the boiler, which carries the works plate, was transferred to a 2–8–0 chassis at some time. The Pekin-Mukden Railway 2–6–0 No 143 had 19in by 24in outside cylinders and 5ft 0in driving wheels.

Dimensions of the classes for which fuller details are available are given below.

The KCR Class A 2–6–4Ts Nos 1/2 had inside cylinders with slide valves actuated by Allan's straight-link motion. The boiler barrel was 11ft 6in long and 5ft 4in outside diameter, containing 260 tubes of 2in diameter. The total length of frames was 41ft. Further information on the CKR 2–6–0s is given in the elevation and plan.

Civil Railway Nos	KCR Class A 1/2	KCR Class A 3–5	KCR Class B 9 & 10	CKR Class A IV, V & X	CHC 61–6
Later Railway Nos	MEF 9801 WD 70220	IrSR 33.300	IrSR 34.600/1	MEF 9805 WD 70219	WD 3600–5 IrSR 52.500–5
Cylinders, in	19 x 26	19 x 26	22 x 28	19 x 24	22 x 28
Wheel diameter, coupled	5ft 1½in	5ft 1½in	5ft 1½in	5ft 0in	4ft 6in
leading	3ft 7in	3ft 7in	3ft 7in	3ft 0in	?
trailing	3ft 7in	3ft 7in	3ft 7in	–	?
Wheelbase, coupled	13ft 0in	13ft 0in	14ft 9in	14ft 0in	14ft 3¼in
total engine	35ft 9in	35ft 9in	40ft 9in	22ft 3in	37ft 1in
Heating surface, sq ft					
Tubes	1623	1623	1520	1206	?
Firebox	187	187	205	133	?
Total evaporative	1810	1810	1725	1339	2325
Superheater	–	–	372	–	753
Combined total	1810	1810	2097	1339	3078
Grate area, sq ft	32	32	34	25.4	54
Boiler pressure, psi	180	180	180	180	200
Tractive effort at 85% BP	23350	23350	33700	22093	42548
Water capacity, gal	2500	1900	2500	?	5500
Coal capacity, tons	3½	3½	4	?	10
Adhesive weight, tons	50.9	51	60	49.45	75
Engine weight in WO, tons	87.75	91	106	59.2	101.5
Tender weight in WO, tons	–	–	–	?	59.5

Chapter 39

THE LONGMOOR MILITARY RAILWAY

The earliest railway activities at Longmoor took an unusual form. The camp there consisted of corrugated iron huts, about sixty-eight of which had to be transported to Bordon, five miles away, after the South African War. To save the expense of dismantling and re-erection, they were moved bodily. For this purpose, starting in May 1903, two lines of 1ft 6in gauge tramway were laid through Woolmer Forest to Bordon, parallel to each other and one hut's width, 20ft 6in apart. The huts were supported on cross-beams of old rails resting on trollies along each side of the building.

Motive power was provided by mobile steam winches which were carried, complete with boilers, on an old-rail framework spanning the gap between the trollies on the parallel tracks. After the winch rope had been pulled forward by horses and secured to a convenient tree (or to an anchor in some cases), the winch carriage worked itself forward and made fast. The rope was next dragged back to the hut in transit, which was then hauled forward to the winch. Downhill movement was controlled by a tail rope, eased round a tree used as a checking bollard. A steam ploughing engine was also used for haulage for a part of the journey. Some huts completed the five-mile trip in twenty-four hours at an average speed of 0.2mph.

This project was completed in 1905, by which time a start was made on surveying and constructing a standard-gauge (4ft 8½in) line from Bordon, the terminal of the then recently-completed (1905) branch of the London and South Western Railway, to Longmoor. The alignment departed considerably from the direct route used by the "hut" tramway but was nevertheless selected to reduce earthworks to the minimum and entailed sharp bends (minimum radius 500ft) and severe gradients (up to 1 in 40). It was greatly improved later.

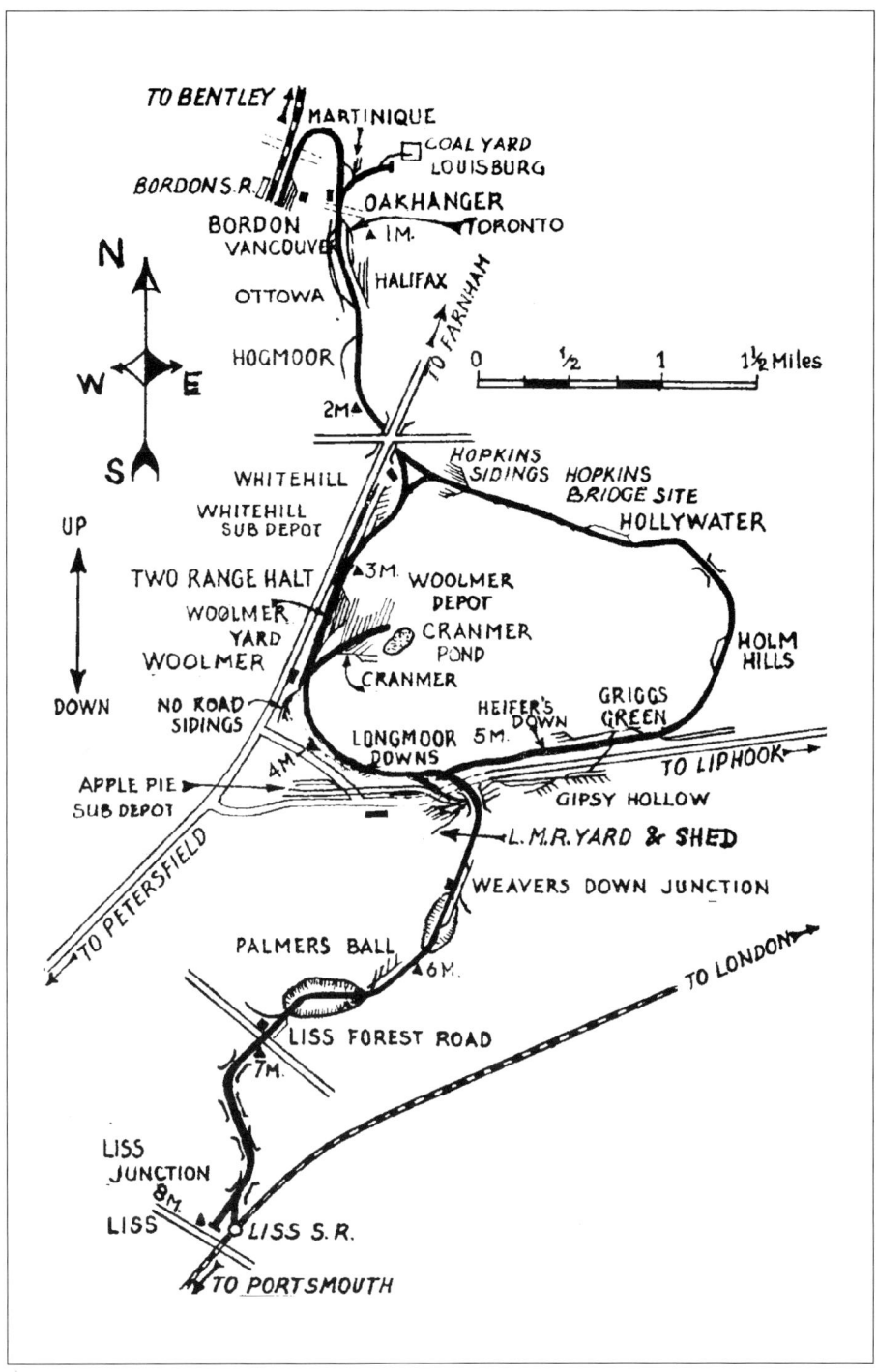

Map 20 The Longmoor Railway system, showing the principal stations and depots, as well as connections to the Southern Railway

To transport working parties and stores between Longmoor and the standard-gauge railhead, the 1ft 6in gauge tramway was regraded, with a single track, and equipped in 1906 with three old narrow-gauge 0-4-2T locomotives named "Mars", "Venus" and "Flamingo". They were acquired from the Admiralty Dockyard at Chatham, who had in their turn obtained them from the Royal Engineer operated Royal Arsenal Railway at Woolwich. These locomotives passed out of use in late 1907, the boiler of "Mars" however being preserved in the diesel shed at Longmoor, as a cut-away instructional aid until after World War 2.

The Longmoor Military Railway gave all its permanent locomotives a serial number for internal reference purposes. These numbers not carried on the engines, at least not in any form normally visible, but are the key to LMR locomotives which spanned at least three series of WD numbers, World War 1, World War 2 and the Postwar WD series. At the time, it provided a useful guide as to whether an engine was officially regarded as permanent or merely on loan – a matter often difficult to decide when engines could remain on loan for two or three years.

The three narrow-gauge locomotives were LMR 1-3, "Mars", "Venus" and "Flamingo" respectively. LMR 1/2 were 0-4-2WTs built by Vulcan Foundry 1160 and 1161 of 1885, while LMR 3 was an 0-4-2T built by John Fowler 585/85.

An unforeseen difficulty was encountered when the line reached Whitehill, halfway between Bordon and Longmoor. The narrow-gauge line crossed the main Farnham-Petersfield road on the level but permission for similar facilities for a standard-gauge crossing was refused. Platelaying continued during the summer of 1907 by using narrow-gauge engines and rolling stock to carry standard-gauge materials across the road and for construction onwards, the track being laid with three rails to give mixed-gauge facilities. By this expedient, the line reached Longmoor in 1907, although available for narrow-gauge through traffic only.

In 1906, the first standard-gauge locomotives arrived, two 0-6-0STs LMR 4/5 "Bordon" and "Hampshire" built by Avonside 1505 and 1520 in 1906; followed in 1908 by an unusual 0-4-4T "Longmoor" from the St Ives branch of the Great Western Railway. This was LMR 6 built by Swindon 1179 in 1890 as an 0-4-2ST GWR 34 and subsequently rebuilt as an 0-4-4T. A workshop, engine shed and stores building were erected at Longmoor and equipped. The last was one of the "portable" store sheds originally supplied for shipment to the Suakim-Berber Railway twenty years earlier. Another such shed was used as a carriage shed.

In the beginning, the line was known as the "Longmoor Military Railway" but the title "Woolmer Instructional Military Railway" was substituted in 1906 to stress that its primary object was training and not transport in the usual sense. The original title was resumed in 1935, possibly because WIMR was achieving an undesirable connotation of "Will It Move Railway"!

In 1908/9, the gap at Whitehill was closed by a temporary level-crossing on a better alignment, permitting through running to Bordon on the standard gauge. Meanwhile, the present bridge passing the railway underneath the road, and its approach cuttings, were constructed.

In 1910, an 0-6-0ST identical to "Bordon", LMR 7 named "Woolmer" was delivered by Avonside, having been built 1572/10. This particular engine replaced "Bordon" which was needed at Shoeburyness. Passenger rolling stock at this time consisted of two ancient saloons from the Kent & East Sussex Railway and there were various goods vehicles.

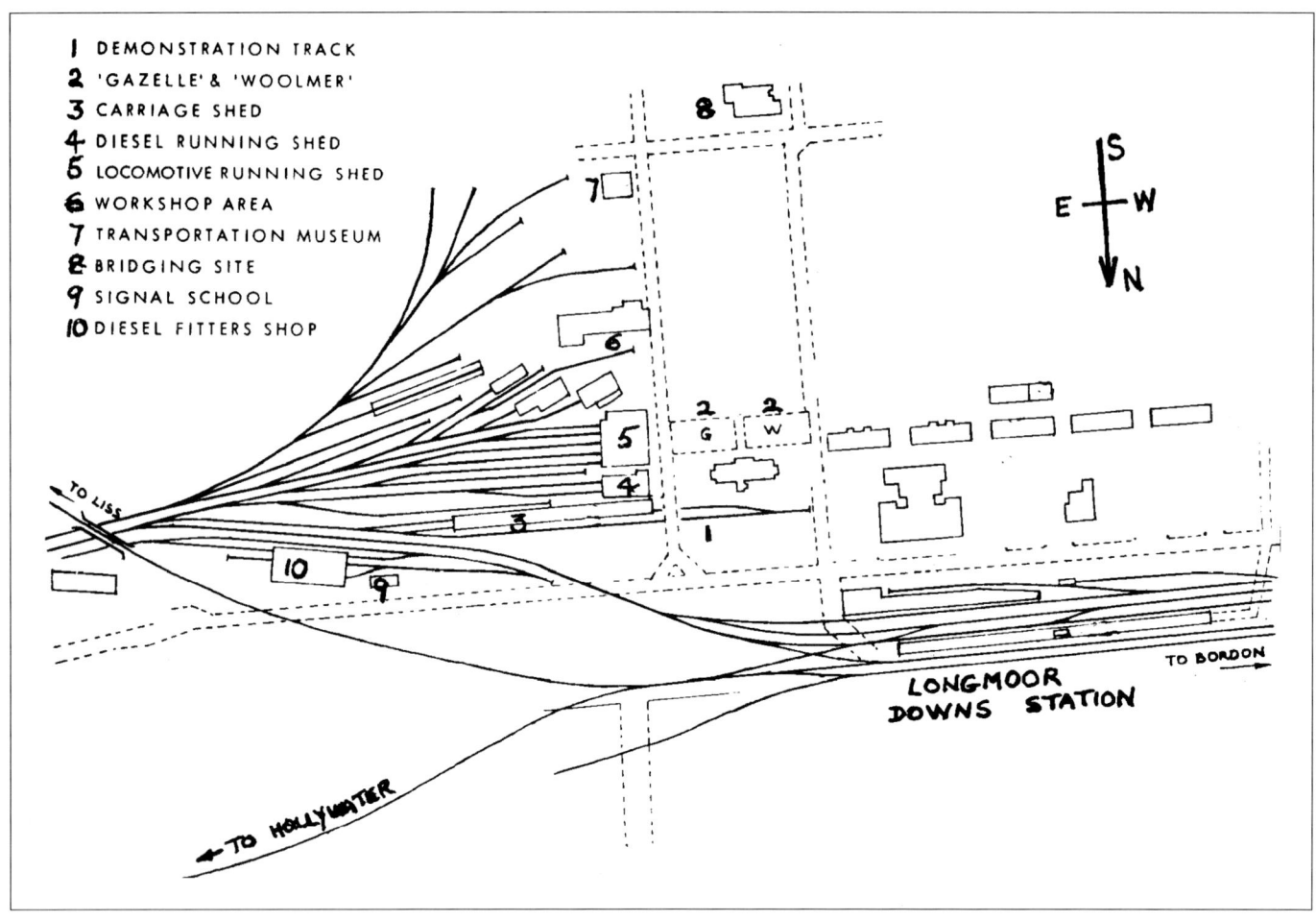

Map 21   The layout of the depot and station at Longmoor Downs

Training continued normally until 1914. An instructional branch leading to a bridging site, the so-called Hollywater line, was built out from Whitehill, capable of being demolished or dismantled and relaid without interfering with main-line operations.

During World War 1, Longmoor became a depot and training establishment for all railway troops, including the newly-formed Railway Operating Division (ROD). Another newcomer, the Inland Waterways and Docks, was also based on Longmoor at first until its own depot was completed at Richborough in Kent. Working lines were extended to serve several widely-spread training camps and depots and, at peak, reached a total of over 100 miles in length. It may be noted in passing that the WD Nos then in use did not belong to the ROD list.

To give additional motive power, an 0–6–2T "Sir John French" was delivered by Hawthorn Leslie in 1914, works number 3088, which became LMR 8. Also, an 0–6–2T from the Shropshire and Montgomeryshire Railway named "Thisbe" was bought in 1914. This engine was built by Hawthorn Leslie 2879/11 and became LMR 9.

Another purchase was a 4–4–0T from the Midland & Great Northern Joint Railway named "Kingsley" which became LMR 10. This engine had been built by Hudswell Clarke & Rodgers 224/80 for the Lynn & Fakenham Railway as "Norwich", then became Eastern & Midland Rly 10, them M&GN 10. It was rebuilt by the M&GN in 1896. It went to Longmoor in 1916, was rebuilt by Yorkshire Engine Co in 1923, withdrawn in 1931 but lingered on for many years being used for re-railing practice

Plate 162   LMR 8 (later WD 203) Hawthorn Leslie 0–6–2T "Sir John French" (Photo: H. N. James)

Plate 163   LMR 10 ex Midland & Great Northern Joint Railway 4–4–0T, as used for rerailing practice (Photo: H. N. James)

Plate 164   LMR 18 (later WD 204) Hawthorn Leslie 0–6–0T "Selborne" (Photo: H. N. James)

Plate 165   LMR 19 (later WD 205) Taff Vale 0–6–2T "Gordon" (Photo: H. N. James)

until eventually scrapped in October 1952.

Various other engines were taken into stock in 1914. LMR 11 was originally on the East & West Junction Rly, then S&MJ 5; a 2–4–0T built by Beyer Peacock 2466/85. LMR 12 was L&SWR 424, a 4–4–2WT built by Beyer Peacock 2176/82. LMR 13 was built by Robert Stephenson 2242/75 as NER 0–6–0ST 973, renumbered 1799 in 1889, rebuilt as 0–6–0T and renumbered 968 in February 1893. LMR 14 was originally old Brecon & Merthyr Rly 4 "Caerleon" 0–6–0 built by Sharp Stewart 1587/65, which was rebuilt as an 0–6–0ST. LMR 15 was an 0–6–0ST "Monmouth" built by Hunslet 397/86. LMR 16 was an 0–6–0T "Salisbury" built by Hudswell Clarke 1069/14. LMR 17 was an 0–6–0ST "Westminster" built by Pecket 1378/14. Many of these engines carried WD Nos of World War 1, LMR 5 being WD 12 and LMR 8–17 being WD 110, 84, 51, 94, 424, 103, 102, 86, 3 and 13 respectively.

In addition, many locomotives were loaned to Longmoor, LB&SCR "Terriers" 673, 647, 681, 667, 673 and 655, in that sequence, worked there between 1916 and 1920. A Brecon & Merthyr double-framed 0–6–0ST (WD101), an L&SWR A12 623, an NER 0–6–0ST and a Beyer Peacock 2–4–0T built for the Stratford-on-Avon and Midland Junction Rly, were others to work at Longmoor during and after World War 1.

About 1920, nine GWR elliptical-roof bogie coaches were returned from the Continent after service as an ambulance train. These became the standard passenger stock, and most were still in service at Longmoor or Marchwood years after World War 2. Later, two London & South Western bogie family saloon coaches and an LNWR 6-wheel inspection saloon were acquired.

HMT (His Majesty's Train?) "Alice" and "Norma", armoured GNR 0–6–2Ts Nos 1590/87, Doncaster Nos 1335/2 respectively of 1912 (later LNE 4590/87) were at Longmoor in 1922, but returned to the GNR during 1923.

In 1921, "Woolmer" was sent to Hilsea Ordnance Depot. To replace this and many other of the earlier locomotives which were sold around 1922/3, several replacement engines were obtained. LMR 18 was a rare treat, a new 0–6–0T "Selborne" delivered from Hawthorn Leslie 3531/22. LMR 19 0–6–2T "Gordon" was a Taff Vale Class O1 No 78 built TV 306/97, which became GWR 450 and was rebuilt in December 1923. Another TV 0–6–2T was taken over in March 1927, TV Class M No 168, later

Class M1, which became GWR 579 and was built by Kitson 2977/86. This was named "Kitchener" and then "Wellington" in 1938. It was scrapped in 1940 and for some unknown reason was never given an LMR Serial No. LMR 20 "Marlborough" was an NSR Class New L 0–6–2T No 158 which became LMS 2253, was rebuilt in 1925 and came to Longmoor in April 1936. LMR 21 "Kitchener", the second locomotive of that name, was another new locomotive, an oil-burning 0–6–2T built specially for Longmoor by Bagnall 2587/38. LMR 22 and 23 were two LNWR 2–4–2Ts, LNWR 658 LMS 6613 coming to Longmoor in August 1930 and becoming "Earl Haig"; and LNWR 608 LMS 6610, which was rebuilt in 1923 and came to Longmoor in May 1931 to become "Earl Roberts'. These two were Crewe 3160/5 respectively, built 1891.

In February 1936, Longmoor received a new 4w Drewry railcar which could seat 20 people. It was intended both for training drivers and fitters, and for carrying passenger traffic when it was specially light. It was fully enclosed and was the size of an average guards van. It had windows in the sides and ends, and a central sliding door. It was powered by a 62hp Gardner 4LW diesel engine and the drive line was a Wilson-Drewry gearbox, Voight-Sinclair coupling and chain drive to a single axle. It was numbered 941, renumbered 9111 in the 1952 renumbering and finally withdrawn and scrapped around 1959.

After World War 1, a considerable amount of constructional work was undertaken to rehabilitate and improve the railway and workshops, both of which had been hard worked during the war. Much of the material required was recovered from France. The original 60lb/yd track to Bordon, worn by wartime traffic, was relaid with 75lb/yd track. The sidings, which had been originally laid with 40lb/yd rail, were relaid with 60lb/yd rail. The track layout at Longmoor was improved. The workshops were extended and a lifting shed with beam jacks and a wheel drop were added. Later, a portion of the line to Bordon was doubled, and a short branch to Cranmer Pond was laid to allow pile-driving and bridging instruction to take place there. The 3½ mile extension south to Liss was begun in 1924 and completed in 1933. In general, lines were, and for that matter always have been, laid and lifted from time to time as exercises and to provide storage as required.

There was naturally a big expansion in World War 2. Longmoor was supplemented in late 1939 by a similar establishment, the Melbourne Military Railway. This is described in Chapter 40. Training in port operations took place at Penarth and later at Barrow and Stranraer. There were also two training centres in India, one for railway and one for Port and Inland Water Transport work respectively. Longmoor itself became an important Transportation Stores Depot. Camps sprang up all along the line, together with quickly-expanding Stores Depots. Such names as Toronto, Vancouver and Halifax bear witness to the large Canadian Camps and Stores near Bordon. Other store depots and sidings were constructed at Whitehill, Woolmer, Applepie, Gypsy Hollow, Heifers Down and Palmers Ball. The Hollywater line was extended in a large curve round to Gypsy Hollow and Longmoor Downs in June 1942, forming a six-mile circuit with the main-line from Longmoor to Whitehill, so that engine crews could be trained in continuous running. Exchange sidings and a connection with the SR at Liss were provided in 1942.

In October 1939, eight LNE J69 0–6–0Ts LNE 7041/54/6/88, 7271, 7344/62/88 (See Chapter 19) came on loan. They stayed until May 1942. In March 1940, four LMS (ex Caledonian) non-corridor six-wheel bogie coaches arrived from Melbourne to help carry the

Plate 166   LMR 20 (later WD 207) NSR Class New L 0–6–2T "Marlborough" (Photo: H. N. James)

Plate 167   LMR 21 (later WD 208) oil-burning 0–6–2T "Kitchener" built specially for Longmoor (Photo: H. N. James)

Plate 168 WD 70208 0–6–2T "Kitchener" at Longmoor in later days, in August 1946 (Photo: H. C. Casserley)

passenger traffic. Ten passenger trains a day were operated over the eight miles from Bordon to Liss. No fares were charged! Passengers were mainly soldiers, of course, but civilians, most of whom had some connection with Longmoor, were also allowed to travel. Passenger coaches, and most of the very miscellaneous freight stock, were painted a grey-green colour. Around 1940, WD 2, a 150hp Fowler 0–4–0DM, was the resident shunter for the Applepie sub-depot. At the end of May 1940, LNE 7271 went back to the LNE and was replaced by LNE 7167. Shortly afterwards, three GWR Dean Goods WD 156/77 and 200 arrived, the latter two fitted with condensing gear and pannier tanks, where they were used on passenger trains. By early 1942, WD 2 had been replaced by the similar Fowler diesel WD 28.

It should perhaps be mentioned that at the end of 1940, Longmoor purchased LMS 27384, an old 0–6–0ST built for the LNWR as 2306 in 1878, which had been withdrawn by the LMS. It arrived at Longmoor in March 1941 and was broken up by Longmoor in September 1942 for sake of the boiler which was used for instructional purposes to train men in changing boiler tubes, renewing stays, etc.

There were two German air raids, the first on 13 August 1940 on Apple Pie Sub-Depot during which three men were killed, and the second two days later on Longmoor itself, but without any further casualties. An interesting coach was destroyed in one of these raids. This was former K&ESR coach 19, acquired by the WIMR in 1912 and rebuilt around 1922 to become No 110 used as a saloon/brake and believed to have carried HM King George V on a visit to Longmoor in the late 1920s.

The track mileage operated rose from 18 in 1939 to a maximum of 70. At peak periods, twenty-seven engines were in steam and 850 loaded wagons were despatched on one particular day. Engine miles run during the war years totalled 1¾ million, while 6½ million passengers were carried. In the busiest year, 1944, 602,000 tons of traffic were exchanged with the SR at Bordon and Liss.

The permanent Longmoor locomotives, which were then LMR 8 "Sir John French", LMR 18 "Selborne", LMR 19 "Gordon", LMR 20 "Marlborough", LMR 21 "Kitchener" and LMR 23 "Earl Roberts" (LMR 22 "Earl Haig" having been scrapped around 1939) were given WD Nos in the World War 2 series, WD 203–5/7/8/6 respectively.

In 1941, the first large locomotive reached Longmoor. This was WD 421, an ex-LMS Stanier 2–8–0 which was named "Wolfe" and became LMR 24. Later in the year, however, it was sent to Iran. The next large engine did not arrive until April 1943 when WD 7015 of the standard WD "Austerity" design arrived. This was the first of 573 2–8–0s which came to Longmoor, practically all of which were stored and prepared for shipment at Longmoor and then despatched overseas. The armoured 2–8–0, WD 7195, arrived at Longmoor in February 1944 and stayed for some months. In addition, WD 2–10–0s started to arrive and a total of 79 passed through Longmoor. The second of the class to be built, WD 73651, came to Longmoor and became part of the permanent stock as LMR 25.

To cope with the increasing internal traffic, three standard WD 0–6–STs and some USA/TC 0–6–0Ts arrived. Eventually, by 1946, the LMR had two WD 2–10–0s, two WD 2–8–0s, one USA/TC 2–8–0, one USA/TC 0–6–0T, twelve WD 0–6–0STs, two Whitcomb 0–4–4–0DEs, three LMS-design 0–6–0DEs, two 0–4–0DMs and four railcars (acquired before the war), giving a total permanent stock of eighteen steam and seven diesel locomotives and four railcars. Many engines were fitted with Westinghouse brake gear for operating passenger trains. The old "Selborne", "Sir John French", "Kingsley", etc had become worn out and were sold, mostly as scrap.

The following engines were evidently regarded as permanent, having been given LMR serial numbers. LMR 26 was 2–10–0 3797 and named "Kitchener",

Plate 169 LMR 23 (later WD 206) LNWR 2–4–2T "Earl Roberts" (Photo: H. N. James)

Plate 170 LROD 3239 narrow-gauge 4–6–0T at Longmoor in November 1945 (Photo: R. Tourret)

LMR 27 was 2–8–0 7337 and named "Sir Guy Williams" and LMR 28 was 2–8–0 9250 and named "Major General McMullen". LMR 29–40 were all WD 0–6–0STs as follows; 1443 "Constantine" (late "Arnhem"), 1505 "Brussels", 5028 "Ahwaz", 5040 "Spyck", 5041 "Foggia", 5042 "Jullundur", 5079 "Sir John French" (later "Lisieux"), 5275 "Matruh", 5189 "Rennes", 5277 "Foligno", 5282 "Insein" and 5290 "Manipur Road".

LMR 41 was USA/TC 2–8–0 3257 "Major-General Carl R Gray, Jr" (who was Director General of the US Military Railway Service 1942–5 and who subsequently wrote an interesting book on his wartime experiences "Railroading in Eighteen Countries"). LMR 42 was USA/TC 0–6–0T 4382 "Major General Frank S. Ross", LMR 43/4 were Derby-built 0–6–0DEs 271/2 "Bari" and "Chittagong" (later "Basra"). LMR 45/6 were Whitcomb 0–4–4–0DEs 1232/3, the former of which was named "Tobruk". LMR 47 was Armstrong Whitcomb 0–6–0DE D58/35 WD 213. LMR 48 was 0–4–0D WD 2220 named "Basra" (later "Chittagong") and LMR 49 was 4wD WD 2214 named "Caen". Details of all these engines are given in other Chapters.

During the war, especially the first year or so, the locomotive stock was strengthened by various locomotives received on loan. The following lists most of the engines concerned: WD "Dean" 0–6–0s 70095/6, 70156/77–9/95/8/9 and 70200; WD 0–4–0D 28; SR A12 0–4–2s 599, 614/8/25/38; SR 01 0–6–0 1046; SR D1 0–4–2Ts 2233/40/86; LMS 0–6–0Ds 7058/9, USA/TC 0–6–0Ts 1255/60/6/82/3/6 and 1417; SR O2 0–4–4Ts 213/25, WD ex-LNE J69 0–6–0Ts 84–91 and LNE 7271; and USA/TC 2–8–0s 2292 and 2639. (SR 225 also served at Bicester around 1942/3 and SR 625 during 1944/5.)

LROD 3239, a 1ft 9in gauge 4–6–0T built by Hunslet 1355/19 too late for use in France in World War 1, came to Longmoor in September 1934 as a museum/instructional engine. WD 195, ex-GWR 2531 "Dean" 0–6–0 built at Swindon in 1897 came back to Longmoor in 1945 and was used for re-railing practice. WD 2400/1, for details of which see Chapter 28, served at Longmoor for a period. None of these locomotives were given LMR Serial numbers.

After World War 2, Longmoor continued to be the headquarters of the Transportation Centre, Royal Engineers.

Training in port operation and inland water transport, controlled by Longmoor, moved from Stranraer to Marchwood on Southampton Water. Thus, the locomotives at Marchwood were supplied from Longmoor and were sometimes frequently exchanged with those at Longmoor. Many locomotives used on WD service in Great Britain became surplus to requirements and were stored at Longmoor for a period prior to being sold or scrapped. Track mileage at Longmoor was reduced from 70 to 64 by taking up some of the sidings. Both WD 2–8–0s were converted to oil-firing.

In November 1945, two German 130hp 0–6–0DHs built Gmeinder & Co of Mosbach 4147/77 in 1944 and numbered HFM 13.906/15 and some 750mm (2ft 5½in) gauge track were acquired. These locomotives were at one time used for hauling V2 rockets. After storage for some while, about 3/4mile of track was laid on Weaversdown and this new line was operated on Public Days in 1949 and 1950 as the Weaversdown Light Railway. After three years disuse, in 1953 the then newly-formed Longmoor Railway Club took over the line and recommenced operations. To commemorate Longmoor's first two locomotives, the two diesels were named "Mars" and "Venus". These engines weighed about 16 tons each and had a maximum speed of about 16mph. They were given LMR Serial Nos 50/1, believed to have been the last issued. The second was rebuilt with a Gardner engine in 1953, but both were scrapped in 1959.

At the end of 1947, Longmoor was the only military railway to have 2–8–0 and 2–10–0 locomotives working on it. These were WD 73651, 73797, 77337 (a new-

Plate 171 German Gmeinder 750mm diesel locomotive HFM 13.915 (Photo: R. Tourret)

comer and the only one to have seen overseas service, also the survivor of the Soham explosion of 2 June 1944) and 79250, as well as USA/TC 3257. During 1946, 79250 was repainted in a livery of dark blue and red, with red lining, and named "Major General McMullen". WD 73651 and 73797 were named "Gordon" and "Kitchener" respectively, and 77337 took the name "Sir Guy Williams" previously used on 78672 on the Detmold Military Railway. USA/TC 3257 was named "Major General Carl R Gray". In 1952, the post-war renumbering scheme led to 73651 and 73797 becoming 600/1 respectively, 77337 and 79250 becoming 400/1 respectively, and USA/TC 3257 becoming WD 700.

In August 1949, the BR Executive presented an unusual 0-4-2T named "Gazelle" to Longmoor. This famous locomotive, built by Dodman in 1893, which is claimed to be the smallest standard-gauge locomotive in the world, came from the Shropshire & Montgomeryshire Railway, an independent railway taken over and given a new lease of life by the WD. "Gazelle" never ran at Longmoor, but in view of the long association between the SMR and the WD, the Railway Executive, who nominally possessed the SMR, presented "Gazelle" to Longmoor on indefinite loan. It was mounted on display as a museum engine, together with LMR 7 "Woolmer" which returned to Longmoor in June 1953, for several years.

Normally the locomotives were repaired at Longmoor for sake of instructional purposes, but in the post-war period, locomotives were sent away for heavy overhauls, such as 73651 to Brighton in 1947/8, 77337 to Swindon in 1951, 601 to Eastleigh in 1952, 600 to Bagnall of Stafford in 1953–5, 601 to Polmadie for a few weeks working on BR before overhaul by North British from which it emerged as an oil-burner and with two air compressors for further trials on BR based on Kingmoor shed before return to Longmoor in February 1959, and 600 to Eastleigh in 1962. WD 700, the USA/TC 2–8–0, was scrapped in October 1957.

LROD 3249 was, for some unknown reason, renumbered 4530 about 1952, by which time it had been brought indoors into the fitters' school and mounted on concrete blocks fore and aft, so that the driving wheels could be turned and the action of the Walschaerts valve gear studied. It survived until about July 1961, when it was scrapped on site by W. H. Arnott.

On 13 October 1956, there was a head-on collision between an 8F 2–8–0 WD 512

Plate 172   Captured German track-ripper device at Longmoor in September 1947 (Photo: R. Tourret)

Plate 173   WD 77337 2–8–0 on Liss to Longmoor passenger train at Forest Road Halt (Photo: E. C. Griffith)

Plate 174 LMS 45021 six-wheel inspection saloon coach at Longmoor in August 1952. This vehicle, subsequently renumbered WD 3005, was built at Wolverton in 1910 and is believed to have been used by Mr George Whale, then CME of the LNWR. After the closure of the LMR, this coach went to the Severn Valley Railway in September 1971 (Photo: A. G. Wells)

Plate 176 "Woolmer" 0–6–0ST on exhibition at Longmoor in October 1958. This engine was LMR 7 (Photo: H. D. Bowtell)

Plate 175 Collision on the Longmoor Military Railway between Stanier 8F 2–8–0 WD 512 and an LMS-type diesel. This occurred near Liss Forest Road on 13 October 1956, and was then the LMR's only fatal running accident. In the impact, the diesel-electric locomotive was forced back over the brake van of the permanent way train, reducing the vehicle to matchwood. The 8F was fitted for oil burning. The oil heater is visible alongside the firebox, as is the linkage for the manual blow-down fitted to many WD 8F locomotives (Photo: E. C. Griffith)

and an 0–6–0D in heavy mist on the single line between Liss and Longmoor Downs. Six soldiers who were travelling in a covered van behind the diesel were killed and several others injured. This is believed to have been the first fatal accident since the line commenced operations.

WD 400 stopped working in 1965 but was retained for two years for instructional purposes before scrapping in 1967. Similarly, WD 401 and 601 remained out of use for a while before being scrapped in 1958 and 1967 respectively. The final survivor of the big engines was 600. On 30 April 1966, it ventured out on BR's lines to Woking to pick up an enthusiasts' train to bring it to Liss and then over the Longmoor line.

Since World War Two, the tremendous changes in military and transport technology have made railways of less importance, and so the Longmoor line closed on 31 October 1969. There followed a withdrawal of WD engines, with some going into preservation. WD 600 fortunately found a home on the Severn Valley Railway. There was also an influx of preserved engines, since it was hoped that Longmoor would become a combination museum and running track for preserved engines. To the onlooker, Longmoor seemed to be an excellent place for such a purpose, with a continuous running line and a shed complex. It is a great pity that the scheme met difficulties, and that Longmoor is now without track, locomotives or rolling stock. It is bare indeed.

The locomotive livery before World War 2 was green lined out with black and white, but since the war most locomotives have been painted in the Royal Engineer colours of blue lined out in red, with gold lettering and numbering. There were,

Dimensions

The dimensions given are generally those appertaining to the locomotive as originally built. Engine types dealt with in detail in other Chapters are not included here. All engines had two cylinders.

Serial No	**1,2**	**4**	**5**	**6**	**7**	**8**	**9**	**10**	**11**	**12**	**13**	**14**	**15**	**16**	**17**	**18**	**19**	**20**	**21**	**22,23**	**W**	**LROD 3209**
Cylinder, bore, in	7½	14	15	16	14	16	14	15	17	17½	16	17½	15	16	12	16	17½	18½	18	17	17½	9
stroke, in	12	20	20	24	20	24	22	20	24	24	22	24	22	20	20	24	26	26	24	24	26	12
Wheel dia, leading, ft in	–	–	–	–	–	–	–	–	–	3'0"	–	–	–	–	–	–	–	–	–	3'9"	–	1'6½"
driving, ft in	1'8¼"	3'3"	3'4"	4'8½"	3'3"	4'0"	3'6"	4'6"	5'6"	5'7"	4'0"	–	–	3'6"	–	4'0"	4'6½"	5'0"	4'3"	5'8½"	4'6½"	2'0"
trailing, ft in	1'8¼"	–	–	2'8"	–	3'0"	2'9"	–	–	3'0"	–	–	–	–	–	–	3'8¾"	4'0"	2'9"	3'9"	3'8¾"	–
Wheelbase, rigid, ft in	3'0"	–	–	20'2"	–	11'0"	–	6'9"	–	8'6"	–	–	–	–	–	11'0"	13'5"	–	10'6"	–	–	5'6"
total, ft in	–	–	–	–	–	17'0"	15'6"	17'7½"	–	27'5"	–	–	–	–	–	11'0"	19'3"	23'0"	17'0"	22'5"	19'3"	13'0"
Boiler pressure, psi	100	–	–	150	–	170	170	140	140	160	140	140	160	160	160	170	170	175	180	160	140	160
Total heating surface, sq ft	225	498	–	1235	–	1017	724	822	–	1059	–	–	–	–	–	860	1148	1019	1074	1074	1022	205
Grate area, sq ft	4.0	8.0	–	14.8	–	17	11.3	11.3	–	18	–	–	–	–	–	14.5	19.1	17.7	16.3	17.1	18.3	3.9
Tractive effort at 85% BP, lb	3000	13300	–	16765	–	18500	14800	8000	–	14900	–	–	–	–	–	18496	21110	21060	23325	13771	17380	5415
Length	–	–	–	–	–	31'10½"	–	–	–	–	–	–	–	–	–	26'10½"	32'10"	37'2"	31'3½"	–	32'10"	–
Coal capacity, tons	–	1	1	–	–	2½	3	1½	–	1	–	–	–	–	–	1½	1¾	3½	1¾	2½	1¾	¾
Water capacity, gal	200	750	750	–	–	1330	720	690	–	1000	–	–	–	–	–	1100	1400	1700	1500	1350	1400	375
Weight in WO, tons	7¾	30	33	40	30	58½	43½	37¾	–	53	40	45	29	33	30	42¾	60	59¾	58½	50½	52	14

Note: "W" is "Wellington"

however, a few exceptions. For instance, in 1954, "Woolmer", 177 "Matruh", 191, 601, 700 and 877 were black, and 186 "Manipur Road" and 931 were green. The Weaversdown Light Railway livery was Indian red with black and yellow lining in 1953/4.

Chapter 40

THE MELBOURNE MILITARY RAILWAY

Early in World War 2, it was realised that the Longmoor Military Railway would not provide enough facilities to train all the military railwaymen required and a site for a second depot was sought. The choice fell on the Melbourne branch of the LMS. Military occupation was obtained on 19 November 1939 from Chellaston East Junction (on the Trent to Repton line) 9¾ miles southwards to a mile north of Ashby-de-la-Zouch, where barbed wire was drawn across the railway on top of the Ashby-Smisby road bridge. The military occupation was not extended right into Ashby because two level crossings would have complicated operation.

For the first seven months, civilian freight traffic continued to be worked by LMS engines, thereafter the military took over all responsibility. Civilian passenger services had been withdrawn in 1930. At first, the railway was used for training military railwaymen individually, but towards the end of 1941 the line was used for the training of complete Railway Operating Companies, so that their personnel could have experience of working together. Each company took over the line for a month or two, and among companies trained in this way were two of the Canadian Army. By 1944, requirements for the additional training facilities lapsed and the railway handed back to the LMS from 1 January 1945.

The army made considerable additions to the traffic facilities on the line. Railway headquarters were established immediately south of Chellaston East Junction, and exchange sidings laid in known as Quarry yard. A locomotive shed was opened in an old wagon repair shop, and army huts for offices and lecture rooms were erected. A mile down the line, across the 1868 iron bridge over the River Trent, was Kings Newton military blockpost where access was obtained to extensive Transportation Stores sidings laid down in 1940. Two shunting engines were always at work here and a water column was provided. The signal box at Melbourne continued in use. The station at Tonge was largely demolished, but a passing loop and extra sidings to serve a tank depot were installed. At Newbold were the exchange sidings of the New Lount colliery and at Ticknall the military authorities laid several sidings which later in the war were used for loading the output of some new open-cast coal workings. Beyond the tunnel was a new blockpost named Smisby Road and a new passing loop.

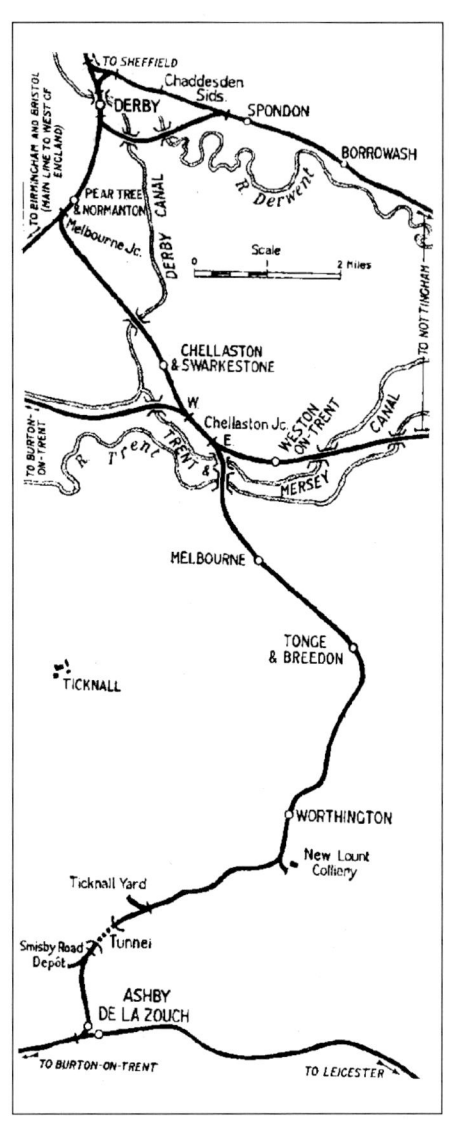

Map 22 The Melbourne Military Railway (Courtesy Railway Magazine)

The major traffic handled consisted of military stores to and from Kings Newton and Tonge, and coal from New Lount colliery. There was some lime from Breedon & Cloud Hill Limeworks siding at Worthington and the odd wagon or two for Melbourne. In fact, the traffic was heavier than that at Longmoor until the peak 1944/5 period. After the regular train services instituted for individual training ceased in 1940, there was little use of the line beyond Newbold until the open-cast workings started at Ticknall in 1943.

Eight or more engines were in steam daily. This was more than would normally be required for a line of this nature, but the bad condition of the engines necessitated the employment of larger numbers than usual. Indeed, a round trip from Quarry locomotive shed to Newbold and back frequently occupied eight hours. Water at Quarry, Kings Newton and Worthington was pumped out of the Trent or neighbouring streams for the locomotive boilers. In spite of the addition of scale-remover compounds, boiler troubles were common. Military "flagboard" signalling and telephone-and-ticket working were employed. The idiosyncrasies of the line caused visiting civilian railwaymen, who sometimes took LMS engines up to New Lount with empties when power was particularly short, to view the military railway with some amazement. Nevertheless, the line offered good training for conditions later met with overseas.

The first locomotives to work on the line when the WD took over were six LNE Class J69 0-6-0Ts 7274/2, 7081, 7197/68 and 7058 (later WD 78-83, see Chapter 19), and these worked from 1939 to 1941. The backbone of the permanent stock were six LMS Class 1F 0-6-0Ts 1666, 1708/51/88, 1839/90, which arrived in 1940 and worked until the end in 1944, except that 1839 was replaced by 1773 in the latter half of 1944. These were ex-Midland engines with steam brake, but as training was required in the handling of Westinghouse brake they were fitted with the necessary pumps and gear at Derby, each pump carrying the lettering LT&SR and one or two retaining the red livery of the Tilbury tanks from which they came. Other steam locomotives used were ex-GWR "Dean" 0-6-0s WD 178 (1940/1) and 99 (1943), SR Class A12 0-4-2s 614/8 (1942/3) and WD Standard 0-6-0STs 5060/1 (1943/4). Ex-LNWR 0-6-0ST LMS 27477 was purchased and placed on an isolated piece of track at Quarry for training purposes.

Some interesting diesel locomotives were employed. One was of French manufacture with a 90hp Junkers engine, which was renumbered WD 76 later. It worked on the MMR in 1941. Vulcan Foundry diesel-mechanical works No 4564/36, later WD 75, worked on the line from 1941-4. Two LMS diesels were used, 7062 (later WD 215) from 1941-4, and 7054 as WD 26 in 1941.

Apart from the permanent stock, several locomotives were received on temporary loan from the LMS. These included Class 1F 0-6-0Ts 1695 (1942/3), 1726

Plate 177 LNE J69 0-6-0T 7274 and ex-GWR Dean Goods 0-6-0 WD 178 on the Melbourne Military Railway in the early days, sometime in 1940/1 (Photo: R. Tourret Collection)

(1941) and 1727 (1940); Class 1P 0-4-4Ts 1267 (1940 and 1943) and 1429 (1940); and Class 2F 0-6-0s 22979 (1942/3), 22982 (1942), 3083 (1942/3) and 3123/41 (1942).

The most numerous class to work on the line, although not permanent stock, was the USA/TC Standard 0-6-0T (see Chapter 49) on Lease-Lend to the WD (and lettered "WD"). Quarry shed was a depot for the reception of these engines in England and some small alterations were made there prior to running-in on the military railway. The USA/TC 0-6-0Ts thus dealt with at Quarry included 1252-4/7/9/62/5/77-81/4/5, 1387-99, 1403/4/7/10/2/23-9, 1937-40/2-4/52/3/5-60/6/8-71 and 6006. It is believed that 1405/6 and 1941 were also dealt with.

WD 1254 was the only USA/TC 0-6-0T permanently allocated to the MMR but as the class became more numerous in 1943 certain engines were used for six weeks or more while awaiting allocation to other duties. The six of the class at Sudbury WD Depot ran over the LMS to and from Quarry for six months in 1942/3 until suitable facilities were made available at their own depot.

Rolling stock allocated to MMR at first included a set of Tilbury "Ealing" stock which was replaced by a set of ex-Caledonian six-wheel bogie coaches. Both sets were dual-fitted and during their service at Melbourne were in LMS livery. Both later saw service on the Shropshire and Montgomeryshire Railway. There was also a set of ex-GWR coaches, ex-ambulance train coaches off the LMR, a six-wheeled ex-LNWR inspection coach (later to go to the LMR), and several wagons and brake vans ex-LMR and ex-LMS.

In individual training days, there was a free passenger service for military personnel from Quarry to Smisby Road. Later, there was a week-end passenger service from Quarry to Derby, manned by RE crews. Trains left Quarry at 18.00 hours on Friday and Saturday, to return at 23.00 hours. On Saturday, there was an extra train at 14.00 hours which returned as empty stock. The LMS charged a fare for these trains, tickets being sold at Quarry and elsewhere.

In this area, but not part of the MMR, was a WD establishment in an old factory south-east of the main line between Derby and Melbourne Junction. At the end of 1943, this was shunted by WD 211 and 223, which locomotives were serviced at Derby LMS shed. In 1944, they were joined by WD 73 from the Shropshire and Montgomeryshire Railway.

Chapter 41

WD TRAMWAY, SHOEBURYNESS

The garrison at Shoeburyness and the gun ranges and other government establishments north and east of that town were served by an extensive railway system. This line was known as the "WD Tramway, Shoeburyness", a rather misleading title, since the tracks and equipment used there were more substantial than those usually associated with the word "tramway", and included sections laid with 100lb/yd rails, while rolling stock of up to 280 ton weight has been in use.

Land was first purchased for experimental artillery ranges at Shoeburyness in 1849, while a separate school of gunnery was opened in 1859. By 1873, there was a large military establishment, with the railway forming an integral part of it. Since the line did not cross any highway, the Tramways Act of 1870 was not applicable, and by the time that the first extension was required, the Military Tramways Act of 1887 had been passed. In 1890, the tramway was extended to the so-called New Ranges, and the whole line was brought within the scope of the 1887 Act. In 1905, the line was extended to Havengore Point, an extension which does not seem to have been made to conform to the 1887 Act. In 1919, the tramway was carried across to Havengore Island, by a bridge over Havengore Creek, and in 1925 the line was completed to its present terminal.

In later years, the railway was as follows. The southern extremity of the tramway was at Shoebury Ness, on the shore of the Thames Estuary, about three miles from Southend. From here, the line ran northward ³/₄ mile to the town of Shoeburyness, where it served the barracks, and there was a connection with the former London Tilbury & Southend Railway. Beyond this, the line came close to the shore again at Pig's Bay, and entered the area of WD installations.

Within the WD establishment, the line divided into two main branches. One ran more or less parallel with the shore, but about 1/4 mile inland, and terminated at the mouth of Havengore Creek, about two miles from Pig's Bay. The other line ran further north, crossed Havengore Creek and eventually reached New England Creek, where it turned south-east to terminate near the mouth of the creek. This point was about 5¹/₄ miles from the southern terminus. A connecting line from this line joined the other line near Wakering Stairs. There were also numerous sidings, especially near the engine sheds and repair shops at New Ranges.

There was also a subsidiary railway at Yantlett Creek, Isle of Grain, Kent. The WDTS was responsible for it and provided the locomotives.

Plate 178   WD 806 (ex WD 2213) Ruston 0–4–0D at Shoeburyness in May 1953 (Photo: A. G. Wells)

At the same time, small diesel and petrol railcars which had carried local numbers were given "Eastern Command Numbers" in the same list as other rolling stock, these numbers all being prefixed "3/".

Rolling stock on the tramway consisted of both goods and passenger vehicles. The passenger stock was varied, and ranged from ex-main-line bogie corridor coaches to four-wheelers, possibly acquired from the neighbouring LTSR. Two vehicles were of special interest. One was No 3/932 "X. P. Pullman", a former London Transport Metropolitan Line bogie coach, which was used by Sir Winston Churchill when he visited the ranges during World War 2. The other was No 3/2189, a coach which had formerly run on the Suakim and Berber Railway. It was an 8-wheel rigid wheelbase saloon, with open-end platforms, screw couplers, and no continuous brake, the only brake being a single level on one side only.

Locomotives were first used on the WDTS in 1885, but there do not seem to have been any records preserved of the original stock. It is believed, however, that the first locomotives were a series of Manning Wardle 0–6–0s that had been built for a campaign overseas, possibly the Suakim and Berber Railway since coaching stock from this railway came to Shoeburyness. Before about 1919, the entire locomotive stock was steam, but afterwards internal-combustion and electric locomotives were introduced.

The locomotive stock of this railway was numbered in a separate Shoeburyness list of local numbers. This has caused confusion with the ROD and WD lists of World War 1 and with the WD list of World War 2. Further confusion arises from the fact that these local numbers were reused when the original locomotives were scrapped or sold. For instance, there were no less than five No 7's! Full details of the entire locomotive stock, so far as is known, were given in the Railway Observer 1955 p7, and will not be repeated here.

During World War 2, to augment the remaining Shoeburyness locomotives, both standard and non-standard WD locomotives were sent there. These carried their WD numbers, but were also given local numbers. WD 1660 0–6–0ST became WDTS 1 and later 12; WD 2212/3 0–4–0Ds became 3/4; WD 238 0–4–0D became 7; WD 1687 0–4–0D became 8; WD 1677/8 0–6–0STs became 9 and 11; and WD standard 0–6–0STs 1449, 5285, 5176, 5099, 5019, 1450, 5252/80/4 became WDTS 12, 22–9 respectively. WD 0–4–0Ds 28, 232 and 2211 also worked on the WDTS but were not given WDTS Nos, also WD 236 0–6–0T.

Plate 179   WD 813 0–4–0D at Shoeburyness in May 1953 (Photo: A. G. Wells)

In 1952, when all the WD locomotives were renumbered, these new numbers were painted on the engines without removal of the 7XXXX numbers. As the local number was also carried, it was general to see locomotives carrying three different running numbers at the same time. However, early in 1953 the use of local numbers was officially discontinued, and as locomotives were repainted, only the 3-figure postwar WD number was displayed.

Plate 180 Coach 3/2189, an eight-wheel rigid wheelbase saloon which formerly ran on the Suakim and Berber Railway (Photo: A. G. Wells)

Chapter 42

SHROPSHIRE & MONTGOMERYSHIRE RAILWAY

The full history of the Shropshire & Montgomeryshire Railway has been ably recounted by E. S. Tonks in his books of that title. This period piece railway had become defunct by 1941, at which time it was requisitioned by the WD – an unlikely saviour of period pieces. The WD also requisitioned some 23 square miles of land in the vicinity of the railway for ammunition storage. They laid out numerous storage depots all connected to the S&MR which was mostly relaid usually with 75lb/yd track. An extensive marshalling yard was provided at Hockagate near Shrewsbury, a connection to the Welshpool line was put in, a reversing triangle between Nesscliff and Edgerley, extra sidings at various places, new signalling and five new halts for passengers. At Kinnerley, the main locomotive depot, the track was relaid and a new locomotive shed built.

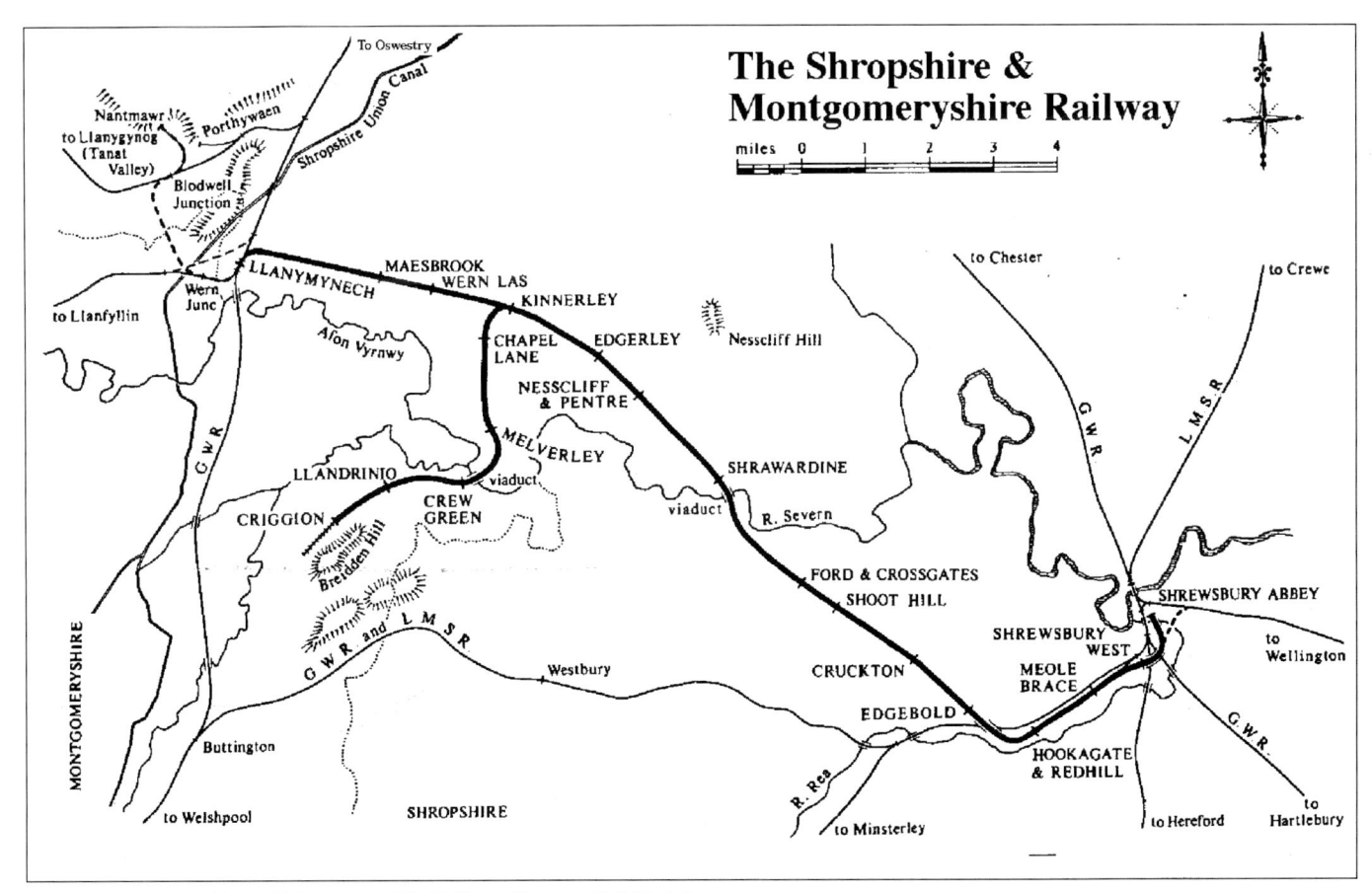

Map 23 The Shropshire and Montgomeryshire Railway (Courtesy E. S. Tonks)

The S&MR was also regarded as a training railway, so partly as a relic of S&MR methods and partly to provide military personnel with wider experience, a variety of operating methods were used, such as Staff and Ticket, Ticket and Telegraph, Miniature Staff and one engine in steam.

Military requirements were heavy in World War 2 and a dozen locomotives were in steam daily. Over a million tons of military traffic were carried. Civilian traffic was handled by a daily goods between Shrewsbury and Llanymynech. There were also workmens' trains and leave trains at weekends. The Criggion branch remained outside WD control.

The WD took over five locomotives, the little 0–4–2T "Gazelle", an old 0–6–0 "Hesperus" and three ex-LNWR 0–6–0s 8108/82 and 8236. The last three were painted in camouflage green by the WD.

These were obviously inadequate for WD purposes and were reinforced by WD locomotives. One popular type was the ex-GWR Dean Goods 0–6–0, of which the following worked on the S&MR for the periods shown; 93 (1943/4–8), 94 (1946–8), 95 (1946–8), 96 (1941–8), 97 (1941–8), 98 (1942–8), 99 (1944–8), 169 (1948), 170 (1944/5), 175 (1942–8), 176 (1942–4), 180 (1946), 196 (1946–8), 197 (1946–8) and 200 (1941–3). In 1943, one or two were painted dark green, but in general their livery was black, sometimes with red lining. WD 70094 was named "Monty".

Miscellaneous engines were 0–6–0PT WD 73 (1941–4), LNE 0–6–0T WD 84 (1945–8), LNE 0–6–0T WD 91 (1944–8), 0–6–0ST WD 92 (1942–5), 0–4–0ST WD 202 "Tartar" (1942/3), LNE J15 0–6–0s WD 212/21 (1942–4) and 0–6–0ST WD 71872 "Ashford" (1942–9). WD 0–4–0Ds 32, 40/4/5/8 worked on the line when new in 1941/2 but left 1942/3 not being considered very suitable. LNE Y7 0–4–0T 982 and LMS 0–4–0WTs 3014/5 were on loan 1942/3 for shunting the ammunition store sheds sidings but did not have enough braking power. USA/TC 0–6–0Ts 1395/9 and 1427 were on loan 1944/5.

For passenger stock there were eight ex-LTSR centre-corridor bogie coaches painted grey-green, four ex-GWR clerestory bogie coaches and one ex-LMS (Caledonian Railway) six-wheel bogie coach painted brown. The four-wheel ex-L&SWR Royal Train coach, inherited from the S&MR, was not used. Goods wagons were ex-LMS, LNE, L&Y, LSWR, MMR etc plus a few new items such as brake vans.

Curiously, a weekday civilian S&MR freight train from Hookagate to Llanymynech and back survived, worked by civilian S&MR crew using LMS 8108, until it packed up and was replaced by LMS 28204 on hire. The WD worked an early morning passenger train from Shrewsbury Abbey station to Kinnerley, returning when the day's work had finished. There were also weekend military passenger trains from Kinnerley into Shrewsbury, the return service leaving Abbey station at 23.00 hours.

On 26 July 1943, there was a head-on collision between Shrawardine and Ford Quarry between two passenger trains, Dean Goods WD 176 hauling six coaches and WD 212 (LNE J15 7835) hauling two brake vans. Eighteen soldiers were injured, coaches WD 3070, 3967 and 6399 were judged not repairable and 212's tender was also considered not repairable and to be broken up on site.

Plate 181 Shropshire & Montgomeryshire Railway 0–4–2T "Gazelle" at Kinnerley in February 1946 (Photo: R. Tourret)

After World War 2 had finished, traffic rapidly dropped and many locomotives were withdrawn and stored at Kinnerley or Hookagate yard. Most of these were scrapped in 1948. The rebuilding of Shrawardine viaduct allowed the axle-loading limit to be raised and this permitted the use of the standard WD 0–6–0ST. The following are known to have worked on the S&MR; 75171 (1947–9), 75193 (1949/50), 103 (1949–54), 120 (1950–3), 121 (1954–57?), 124 (1948–53?), 125 (1957–60), 130 (1954), 135 (1951–3), 139 (1947–52), 141 (1955?–60), 143 (1947–53), 146 (1948–50/1–?), 151 (1947–53), 153 (1947–54), 154 (1950–4), 167 (1948–56?), 185 (1952–7), 188 (1957–60), 189 (1954–6) and 193 (1955–60). The first specimens were camouflage green or brown, but later arrivals from Cairnryan were black with yellow figures.

In 1959, the WD decided to finish its use of the S&MR, which had in the meanwhile officially become part of British Railways. The last military depots were closed and tracks lifted. The Criggion branch closed in December 1956 and civilian traffic on the main line in February 1960. The SLS ran a farewell trip on 20 March 1960 and the line was formally handed over to BR on 31 March 1960. Dismantling took place in 1962.

Chapter 43

MARTIN MILL MILITARY RAILWAY

During the early part of the 1939–45 war, one of the main diesel centres was Martin Mill on the Martin Mill Military Railway. The origin of the MMMR was a line built in 1897 by the contractor S. Pearson & Son for the construction of the Eastern Blockyard followed by the Eastern Arm of the Admiralty Harbour at Dover. This line ran from Martin Mill about five miles north of Dover, to the top of the East Cliff near Dover Castle above the Harbour. A balanced rope-worked incline was used to lower materials to the foreshore. This work was finished in 1904, but the line appears to have been

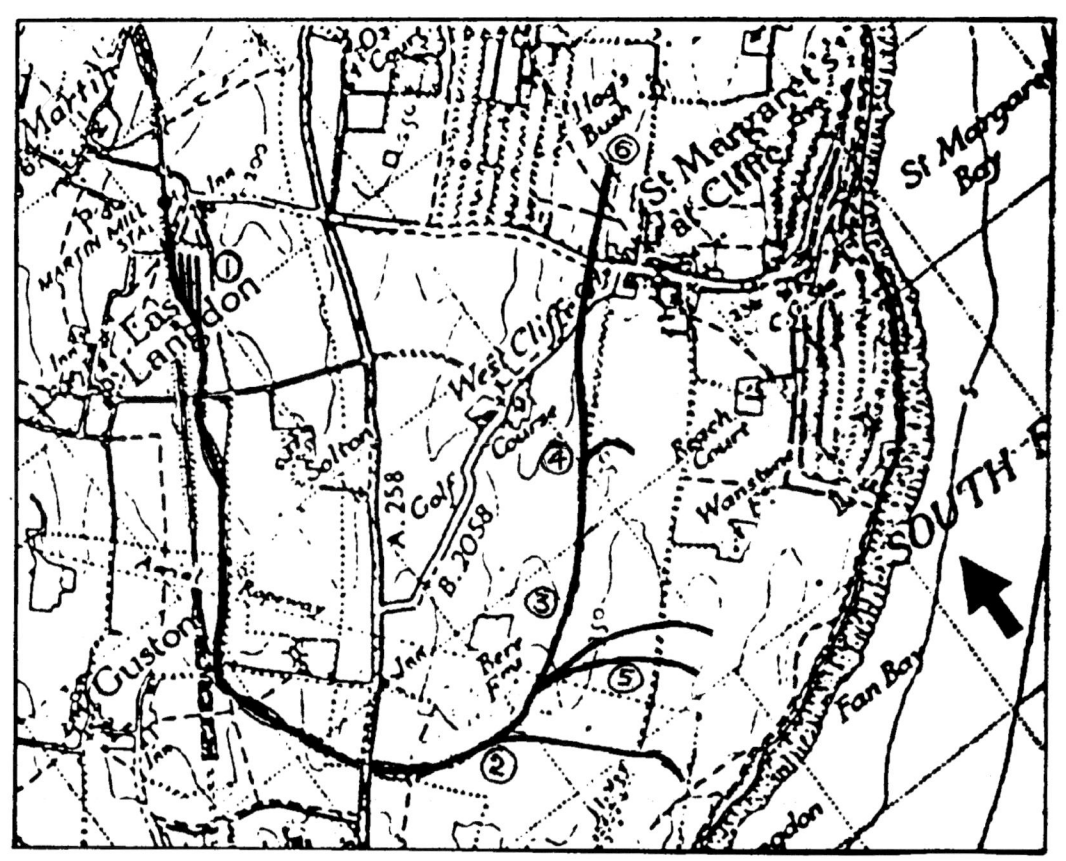

Map 24 The Martin Mill Military Railway. The items marked are as follows: 1 WD yard, 2 Decoy Junction, 3 "Pooh", 4 "Winnie", 5 the first two firing spurs for the mobile 13.5in guns, &6 the dummy gun "Clem".

acquired by the War Office. The cliff top end was lifted in 1917/8 to supply track for the construction of the railway along the seafront, and the rest was lifted by the Army in 1937.

When France fell, a site was required from which to operate long-range guns to counter German long-range guns being installed in the Pas de Calais area, and accordingly rails were relaid over the first part of the contractor's line. The military railway trailed into the down SR line to Dover. The MMMR then ran more or less parallel to the SR line to near Guston Tunnel, where it swung away to the left towards the sea, passing under the Dover to Deal A258 road. From this point, a new alignment was taken with the line running back parallel to the SR and to the coast, as far as St Margarets-at-Cliffe. The new section left the old formation at a point which became known as RDF Junction. The name came from 'radio direction finding', an early name for what was later called radar, because there was then a prominent RDF station on South Foreland. There was no junction as such, in so much as the track had been lifted from the original line, but there was blockpost and passing loop. This was 1¾ miles from Martin Mill. The next blockpost and loop was at Decoy Junction (2¼ miles), so called because it was originally fitted with a dummy gun barrel which deceived the German airmen for at least one day! They are said to have dropped a wooden bomb at one stage!

Work started on the MMMR line in June 1940. The first gun to arrive was a static one with a 14 inch barrel weighing 97 tons. This was a new gun designed for the "King George V" class battleships, mounted in an existing trial mounting. It took three railway cranes, two 50 ton and one 45 ton, to assemble the mounting and barrel. It was named "Winnie" after Winston Churchill. It was first fired on 22 August 1940, to counter German fire on a convoy passing through the Channel. Static guns were considered vulnerable to air attack and had a slow rate of fire, so two 13.5 inch rail-mounted naval guns were next obtained, "HMG Scene Shifter" in September 1940 and "HMG Piecemaker" in November 1940. They were accompanied by a rake of SNCF ferry vans. These guns were followed by another static gun which also used a 14 inch barrel and which became operational on 9 February 1941. It was named "Pooh" as an accompaniment to "Winnie". This was followed by another 13.5 inch rail-mounted gun in May 1941, which was named "HMG Gladiator". These 13.5 inch guns dated back to the First World War. Several dummy guns were erected, to give the impression that our defences were stronger than they actually were, and to confuse air attacks.

The rail-mounted 13.5 inch guns were 250 ton units on fifteen axles, two eight-wheel bogies in front and an eight-wheeled and a six-wheeled bogie at the rear. The gun barrel was mounted between two large plate girders which had a well between the pairs of bogies. Each unit was accompanied by a 70 ton armoured ammunition wagon on a pair of six-wheeled bogies, and various coaches and vans. Westinghouse brakes were fitted later to the gun units. The 13.5 inch rail-mounted guns, unlike the 9.2 inch guns and 12 inch howitzers discussed elsewhere, could only be fired with the barrels in line with the track, so in order to be able to aim them, two curved spurs were laid out on the cliff top on the MMMR in August and September 1940. These firing spurs were laid in a specially smooth curve, and the degrees (of aiming, that is) were marked off on the sleepers. The gun was moved to the required degree mark and the final adjustment made using the limited traverse that the gun barrel could make inside its support girders. They could fire a distance of over 22 miles. Later, another firing spur was laid in near Swingate RDF station and a fourth at Cold Blow Farm, Ripple, near Walmer Station.

From Decoy Junction, two long sidings reached well out on to South Foreland to serve as firing spurs as discussed. The main line continued north to serve the two fixed guns "Winnie" and "Pooh". The guns were close to the railway, which had a loop at each gun. A third siding was added in October 1941. The line continued across the Martin Mill to St Margarets road where there was a dummy fixed naval gun "Clem" on the other side with a loop. This was, at 3¼ miles, the end of the railway. The railway was signalled with military flag boards. When the guns were firing, it was closed beyond Decoy Junction.

Near Lydden Halt between Kearsney and Shepherdswell on the Dover to Canterbury line, extra sidings were laid on the site of Stone Hall Colliery, and a gantry assembled for changing gun barrels, so that gun maintenance could be carried out here. A short spur for firing from in an emergency was also constructed.

Three LMS Armstrong Whitworth diesel shunters LMS 7059/63/4 arrived in September 1940, in time to help with some of the construction work. At that time, they were named "Old Joe", "Flying Scotsman" and "Ubique" (meaning everywhere, the motto of the Royal Engineers) respectively, in neat white letters at the top of the radiator. In November 1940, LMS 7062 arrived on the MMMR and LMS 7061 arrived at South Canterbury on the Elham Valley Military Railway with another rail-mounted gun to be discussed later. In March and April 1941, SR diesel shunters Nos 1–3 arrived on the MMMR. The arrival of the SR diesels freed LMS 7059 to go to Longmoor and LMS 7062 to go to Melbourne. However, in July 1941, LMS 7059 replaced LMS 7061 at South Canterbury and LMS 7061 went to the MMMR. LMS 7063 failed due to a burst armature due to being driven too fast. It was sent to Derby for repair, and LMS 7067 received in its place in July 1941. The LMS stood ready to replace any diesel locomotive that failed, the out-of-service locomotive being sent to Derby who sent a temporary replacement.

Diesel locomotives were preferred to steam for operating trains on the MMMR, since steam from the latter might have given away the position of the guns. However, a diesel locomotive was shot at on at least one occasion. The diesel locomotives were serviced and repaired at Martin Mill, but in the open. On one occasion, condenser Dean Goods WD 180 and 197 were tried at Martin Mill, but were unable to surmount the first incline of 1 in 50 with a gun! They were not tried again!

Other rolling stock was limited. The SNCF vans were of little use. There was a prototype Warflat wagon intended for transporting tanks but on the MMMR used for rails. There were four SR brake vans. One was a bogie van used for Mr Churchill when he visited the line in 1940. The other three were half van and half low-sided open vehicles from the Folkestone Harbour branch.

As discussed in Chapter 16, the LMS locomotives were eventually purchased and taken into WD stock so that they could be used elsewhere, but the SR locomotives remained SR property and were not renumbered, although 1 and 3 were painted dull khaki and 2 dark green, all with red coupling rods and white buffer beams. They were overhauled by the SR in 1943 and again in 1944, and returned to the SR in February 1945 when the need for long-range guns had passed and overseas service was not contemplated for them.

Normally, two of the rail-mounted guns were kept inside Guston Tunnel. Single track working was in force over the eastern (down) line and the guns occupied the western (up) line. The spur from Kearsney East Junction to Kearsney West Junction was used for gun movements, as well as light engine trips, to and from Martin Mill to Lydden Halt. One or two guns were kept at Lydden sidings, covered in camouflage netting. For moving a gun and ammunition wagon, it was normal practice to have a diesel locomotive at each end because of braking capacity, since the locomotives had no continuous brakes. This sometimes involved complicated movements, specially when extricating a gun from Guston Tunnel. Also, guns had to be reversed on the triangle at Kearsney Junction if moving from Martin Mill to Lydden because the firing spurs faced in opposite directions. To further complicate matters, these movements usually took place when it was dark.

Regarding the Elham Valley Military Railway, in October 1940, loop sidings were installed at Canterbury South, Barham and Elham. At Bourne Park, the old "up" line was relaid as a loop through the tunnel with a siding at the south end. On 1 December 1940, the WD officially took over the line north of Lyminge. Various bridges and the track were strengthened, ready for the arrival of a rail-mounted gun of 18 inch calibre, which was named "HMG Boche Buster". It could fire a 1¼ ton shell over 12 miles and was intended to fire at any invasion fleet. The gun was aimed by using the twists and turns of this branch line! A short spur was installed at Kingston to cover Pegwell Bay. It was fired for the first time in February 1941. Churchill visited it on 20 June 1941. In May 1943, the WD took over the whole line, and for a short time the EVMR took on a training function as an overflow from Longmoor. At the end of 1943, the railway guns were withdrawn. In 1944, the WD handed the line back to the SR.

Heavy guns in Kent and Essex were the responsibility of the No 195 Rail Mounted Batteries Company of the Royal Engineers, with headquarters at Great Chart near Ashford in Kent. While the static cross-Channel guns on the MMMR were the responsibility of the No 195 Company Super Heavy Detachment of the RE, the 13.5 inch mobile guns were operated by the Royal Marines Siege Artillery. "HMG Boche Buster" was operated by 12th SHB.

Chapter 44

THE KOWLOON-CANTON RAILWAY

Kowloon is a town on the mainland of China opposite Hong Kong and is a British possession sited on the leased "New Territories". The KCR was built by the British and completed in 1910. It is standard 4ft 8½in gauge and is operated in two sections, from Kowloon 22 miles to Lo Wu on the border of the New Territory with China, and from thence on to Canton. The locomotive sheds and works of the British section are at Hung Hom. Westinghouse brake is used and automatic couplers are fitted.

The locomotive stock in 1925 consisted of ten engines, KCR 1/2 being inside-cylinder 2–6–4Ts, KCR 3–8 being outside-cylinder 2–6–4Ts and KCR 9/10 being the first two of four 4–6–4Ts (all dated 1924) to be numbered 9–12. It would appear that 11/2 were not delivered until 1925.

By the early 1930s, the locomotive stock consisted on eight Class A 2–6–4Ts KCR 1–8, the four Class B 4–6–4Ts KCR 9–12 and three Class C 4–6–0s KCR 20–2. All these engines were built by Kitson. Class A 1–8 were built 4698/9 of 1909, 4874/81 of 1912, 5038 of 1914 and 5127–9 of 1915; Class B 9–12 were built 5375–8 of 1924; and Class C 20–2 were built 5435–7 of 1930. Both inside and outside cylinder types of 2–6–4Ts were now regarded as one class, and indeed the basic dimensions, 19in by 26in cylinders, 5ft 1½in driving wheel diameter and weight about 90 ton, were the same. The 4–6–4Ts were an enlargement of the design, using the same size driving wheels but with outside cylinders 22in by 28in and a weight of 106 ton. Further dimensions of both classes are given in Chapter 38. The three Class C 4–6–0s were quite large machines, with 6ft 0in driving wheels, 21in by 28in outside cylinders with Walschaerts valve gear, and large bogie tenders. The locomotive weight was 76 ton 17cwt and the tender 61 ton 17cwt in working order.

Originally, through trains ran the 113 miles between Kowloon and Canton but by 1931 the British section locomotives, especially the 4–6–4Ts, rarely if ever worked through to Canton, but were replaced by Chinese section ones such as 2–6–0s. On at least one occasion a 4–6–4T was retained by the Chinese and recovered only after prolonged protests and negotiations. The British section kept its locomotives in good order compared with those on the Chinese section, and the temptation to appropriate one was evidently too strong to resist.

Shortly after 1931, through working was resumed, probably soon after the delivery of the Class C 4–6–0s, since these three locomotives were intended for through working over the Chinese section. Indeed, in May 1936, they were handed over to the Chinese authorities. Through working of Chinese locomotives into Kowloon commenced, although the through working of British locomotives over the Chinese section continued with both Class A and Class B tanks. At the end of 1936, Chinese locomotives were hauling the four daily express trains between Kowloon and Canton, while British locomotives hauled the two daily "fast" trains. In the summer of 1937, through working of rolling stock was extended to Hankow (Wuchang) via the Canton Hankow Railway, a distance of 791 miles, whilst in the following year a bi-weekly passenger service, using Chinese locomotives and rolling stock, was operated between Kowloon and Hankow.

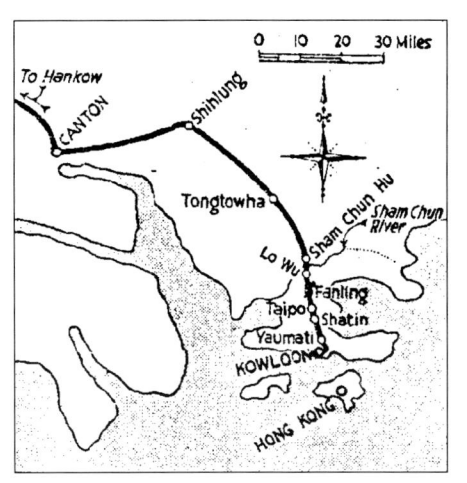

Map 25 The Kowloon-Canton Railway. The border between Hong Kong territories and mainland China is between the stations of Lo Wu and Sham Chun Hu (Courtesy Railway Magazine)

To cope with the increased freight traffic resulting from the through traffic to Hankow, two Bagnall 0–4–0ST locomotives works Nos 2503/4 of 1934 were added to stock in November 1937 as the S class. They were purchased from the Shing Mun Water Works for shunting duties. The S class locomotives had 12½in by 18in cylinders, 3ft 0in diameter wheels and they weighed 24½ tons. They were numbered KCR 15/6.

All through running ceased in October 1938, when the Japanese invasion of China made this impossible. In 1942, there was a general retreat before the advancing Japanese forces, and several Chinese locomotives were held in or worked through into the British section. As many engines as possible were shipped away. As recounted in Chapter 38, five 2–6–4Ts KCR 1–5 and two 4–6–4Ts KCR 9/10 were shipped to the Middle East as well as three or four 2–6–0s from the Chinese section and a few 2–6–0s and 2–8–0s from other Chinese railways.

During the Japanese occupation of Hong Kong of 1942–5, the international boundary was abolished and the two halves of the railway were operated as one. When the war ended, the original KCR 2–6–4Ts 6–8 and 4–6–4Ts 11/2 were returned. Separate working was resumed in May 1946, although through running was also resumed.

There was naturally a shortage of locomotive stock, since the Middle East locomotives were not returned, and the S class 0–4–0STs had disappeared. In May 1946, the Ministry of Supply sent five American 2–8–2s, WD 1034/58, 1129/33/68 (see Chapter 48) to the Far East and these were used on the KCR as an interim measure. They were renumbered 701/3–6, although these numbers were not KCR but belonged to some unknown series.

In October 1946, the two 2–6–0STs WD 2001/1 built by Robert Stephenson & Hawthorn 7017/8 of 1942 arrived and were taken into stock as Class S KCR 15/16. These had 17½in by 24 in cylinders and 3ft 6in driving wheels. In 1946/7, twelve ex-WD "Austerity" 2–8–0s arrived and became KCR 21–32 (see Chapter 24). Class A 2–6–4Ts 7/8 and Class B 4–6–4T 11 were withdrawn in 1948/9.

In October 1949, Canton fell to the Communist forces. This resulted in services being terminated at the border, 22 miles from Kowloon. Passengers had to change trains, while goods wagons were loose-shunted across.

In 1951, a renumbering took place. The two 2–6–0STs became KCR 1/2, and the sole remaining 4–6–4T No 12 and 2–6–4T No 6 (possibly renumbered 13 in the meanwhile) became KCR 3 and 4 respectively. In August 1954, KCR 1/2 were out of service, while KCR 3/4 were relegated to shunting duties at Kowloon Station and the adjacent marshalling yard. In 1955, diesel locomotives started arriving.KCR 3/4 were disposed of in January 1957 and the two 2–6–0STs in August 1959. The WD 2–8–0s were withdrawn about the same time, as detailed in Chapter 24.

SECTION 3

Chapter 45

USA/TC LOCOMOTIVE STOCK LIST

The United States Army Transportation Corps developed, in collaboration with American locomotive builders, four basic steam and four basic diesel locomotive designs. Details such as precise gauge, buffers, brakes, coupling arrangements, etc were varied to suit the needs of the railway or theatre of war to which it was intended to send the engines. Some designs incorporated British experience. These basic designs consisted of:

(a) Steam standard-gauge 2–8–0 (see Chapter 50)
(b) Steam narrow-gauge 2–8–2 ("MacArthur", see Chapter 47)
(c) Steam standard-gauge 0–6–0T (see Chapter 49)
(d) Steam standard or broad-gauge 2–8–2 (see Chapters 48 and 64)
(e) Diesel 65 ton 650hp 0–4–4–0DE (Whitcomb, see Chapters 25 and 61)
(f) Diesel 45 ton 380hp 0–4–4–0DE (GE, see Chapter 60)
(g) Diesel 127 ton 1000hp 0–4–4–0DE (Alco-GE, see Chapter 62)
(h) Diesel 25 ton 150hp 0–4–0DE (GE, see Chapter 59)

The diesel designs were all standard or broad gauge. A steam narrow-gauge 0–6–0T reached the design stage but was not proceeded with owing to the end of the war.

In view of the adverse comments which have been made in certain quarters regarding the life of these locomotives, the following American semi-official comment from "Mechanical Engineering" (Vol 66, No 12, December 1944, p783) may be of interest: "The relative life of railroad equipment is generally governed by two factors, operation and maintenance. These factors are usually adverse in military operation and consequently, it is unnecessary to provide refinements to extend the life of this equipment over a four or five year period". In fact, many USA/TC locomotives were successfully used for a much longer period.

Apart from these engines, there were many miscellaneous engines, mostly diesels, used internally in the United States at various depots. In all probability, the following list is incomplete in this respect, since the USA/TC locomotives appear to have been numbered consecutively in one series. The MRS in Italy used their own series, and many captured Italian locomotives were given numbers in it (see Chapter 65), as well as some USA/TC engines.

The main USA/TC list is given following these introductory notes. When classes are dealt with in detail, reference is made to the appropriate Chapter, otherwise brief details of the locomotives are given.

UNITED STATES ARMY TRANSPORTATION CORPS LOCOMOTIVE STOCK LIST

USA/TC Nos	Maker, Works No & Date	Type	Notes
1–7	–	4–6–0	See Chapter 46
10	L 7881/42	2–8–0	See Chapter 46
11	L 7882/42	2–8–0	See Chapter 46
20	B 47032/17	2–8–0	See Chapter 46
22	A ?/?	2–8–0	See Chapter 46
100	V 4419/42	0–6–0T	
101	C 1248/14	0–6–0ST	Ex Baldry, Yerburgh & Hutchingson 26
102	P ?/?	2–6–2ST	
130–249	Standard	2–8–2	See Chapter 47
250–6	A	2–8–2	See Chapter 66
257–890	Standard	2–8–2	See Chapter 47
500–4	A 69736–40/41	2–8–2	Later Newfoundland Rly 1009–13, CNR 309–13
1000–1199	WD	2–8–2	See Chapter 48
1200–51	Whitcomb	0–4–4–0DE	See Chapter 25
1252–1316	Standard	0–6–0T	See Chapter 49
1387–1436	Standard	0–6–0T	See Chapter 49
1537–96	Whitcomb	0–4–4–0DE	See Chapter 25
1600–1926	Standard	2–8–0	See Chapter 50
1927–2001	Standard	0–6–0T	See Chapter 49
2032–2382	Standard	2–8–0	See Chapter 50
2383–99	–	0–4–0P	See Chapter 51
2400–59	Standard	2–8–0	See Chapter 50
2460–89	B 72173–202/45	0–6–6–0DE	USSR 20.71 to 20.100
2490–7	–	–	See USA/TC 7942–9
2500–2989	Standard	2–8–0	See Chapter 50
2990–7	–	0–4–0P	See Chapter 51
3000–29	Standard	2–8–2	See Chapter 47
3030–9	–	0–4–0ST	See Chapter 52

USA/TC Nos	Maker, Works No & Date	Type	Notes
3040–59	–	0–6–0ST	See Chapter 52
3060–75	–	0–8–0	See Chapter 52
3200–3749	Standard	2–8–0	See Chapter 50
3750–3914	Standard	2–8–2	See Chapter 64
3925–95	–	2–10–0	See Chapter 53
4000–79	Standard	0–6–0	See Chapter 54
(4080–4102)	V	0–6–0	Narrow gauge, Cancelled order
4103–42	–	2–8–2	See Chapter 64
4143–4280	–	2–10–0	See Chapter 53
4281–4305	Standard	2–8–2	See Chapter 47 (USA/TC 764–88)
4313–41	Standard	0–6–0T	See Chapter 49
4372–4401	Standard	0–6–0T	See Chapter 49
4402–83	Standard	2–8–0	See Chapter 50
4500–4999	–	2–10–0	See Chapter 53
5000–60	Standard	0–6–0T	See Chapter 49
5061–5120	Standard	2–8–2	See Chapter 64
(5121–54)	–	0–8–0	Narrow gauge. Cancelled order
5155–99	Standard	2–8–0	See Chapter 50
5200–5699	–	2–10–0	See Chapter 53
5700–5859	Standard	2–8–0	See Chapter 50
5860–5999	–	2–10–0	See Chapter 53
6000–23	Standard	0–6–0T	See Chapter 49
6024–78	Standard	2–8–0	See Chapter 50
6080–6103	Standard	0–6–0T	See Chapter 49
6104–54	–	2–10–0	See Chapter 53
6160–83	Standard	0–6–0T	See Chapter 49
(6184–6233)	–	0–8–0	Narrow gauge. Cancelled order
6240–6739	–	2–10–0	See Chapter 53
6740–63	–	0–6–0ST	See Chapter 55
6800–2	B 30676–8/07	0–6–0	Ex Oregon Rly & Navigation 28–30
6803	B 33789/90	0–6–0	Ex Oregon Rly & Navigation 32
6813	B 38965/12	2–8–2	Ex Smith Lumber & Mfr 102
6814	B 43344/16	2–8–0	Ex Sierra Rly 20
6817	P ?/18	0–6–0	
6818	P 6229/18	0–6–0	
(6824–63)	Standard	2–8–0	Cancelled order
6900	B 31912/07	0–6–0T	Ex Balaklala Copper Co 1
6905	GNR ?/06	0–6–0	Ex GNR Class A9 17
6908	B 42102/15	2–6–2	Ex Algoma Lumber Co 2–6–2T 2, Rbt 2–6–2 1942
6913	A-S 47512/10	0–6–0	Ex Escabana & Lake Superior RR
6917	L ?/16	0–6–0	Ex Arthur Mining Co 201–210 series
6919	B 31322/07	0–6–0	Ex Mahoning Ore & Steel Co 10
6920	A–R 53517/13	0–6–0	Ex Chicago, Rock Island & Pacific 231
6923	B 24554/04	4–6–0	Ex Southern RR 7533?
6924	B 30190/07	2–6–0	Ex ICC Panama RR 321
6926	B 50622/18	0–6–0	Ex US Army 1 (of WW1)
6928	P 6149/18	0–6–0	Ex US Army OD (of WW1)
6929	P 6153/18	0–6–0	Ex US Army OD (of WW1)
6931	B 30052/07	2–6–0	Ex ICC 302, Panama RR 302
6932	B 58797/25	2–6–0	Ex Veterans Administration Hospital, Perry Point
6936	B 30141/07	2–6–0	Ex ICC 311, Panama RR 311
6938	V 2824/18	0–4–0ST	Ex US Ordnance Dept 13
6939	V 2753/17	0–4–0ST	Ex USA 4928 (of WW1)
6943	CM&StP ?/03	0–6–0	Ex Chicago, Milwaukee & St Paul RR 1168
6944–50	?	?	Ex Chicago, Milwaukee & St Paul RR ?
6951	A-S 3049/90	0–6–0ST	Orig 0–6–0, Rb 0–6–0ST 1920s, SP-MW 1199
6952	A 50931/12	0–6–0	Ex Chicago, St Paul, Minneapolis & Omaha RR 12
6953	A 50122/11	0–6–0	Ex Chicago, St Paul, Minneapolis & Omaha RR 34
6955	A–B 67189/26	2–8–2ST	Ex Chas Nelson Lumber Co 7
6956	V 1759/11	0–6–0	Ex State Belt Rly of Cal 4
6957	D ?/18	2–6–2T	60cm gauge. Ex US Army 52XX, Rbt with tender

USA/TC Nos	Maker, Works No & Date	Type	Notes
6961	B 31899/07	0–6–0	Ex Atlanta, Birmingham & Atlantic 58
6963	A 61580/20	0–6–0	Ex Worth Steel Co 3
6966	A 30130/04	2–8–0	Ex Georgia & Florida RR 406
6967	B ?/?	2–6–0	Ex ICC, Panama RR
6969	P 6237/18	2–8–0	
6970	B 30262/07	2–6–0	Ex ICC 332, Panama RR 332
6971	B 30218/07	2–6–0	Ex ICC 326, Panama RR 326
6973	B 30053/07	2–6–0	Ex ICC 303, Panama RR 303
6974	B 49365/18	0–6–0ST	Ex USA 2 (of WW1)
6975	B 30123/07	2–6–0	Ex ICC 309, Panama RR 309
6977	? ?/?	2–6–2	
6979	B 47565/18	2–8–0	Pershing, Ex USA 448 (of WW1), Rn USA/TC 765, Korea/48, USA Museum
6981	B 50624/18	0–6–0	Ex USA 3 (of WW1), "Gen Holabird"
6982	A–B 38141/05	0–6–0	Ex Illinois Central RR 71
6983	A–B 38136/05	0–6–0	Ex Illinois Central RR 66
6984	? ?/?	0–4–0ST	Camp Fannin
6987	L 7882/42	2–8–0	Ex USA/TC 11, see Chapter 46
6988	A–C 39156/06	2–6–0	Ex ICC 245, Panama RR 245
6989	A 40112/06	0–6–0	Ex Alco Schen Works loco "A. J. Pitkin"
6990	B 9030/88	2–6–0	Ex BR&P 82
6991	A–B 44363/07	0–6–0	Ex Manufacturers Rly 2, St Louis & O'Fallon Rly 1
6992	A–R 53881/15	0–4–0ST	Ex Remington Arms Co 6
6993	B 58131/24	2–6–2	Ex Caddo River Lumber Co 12
6994–9	L 7875–80/42	2–8–0	See Chapter 56
7000	EMD ?/?	B–B DE	
7001	EMD 1990/42	B–B DE	ARR 1203
7002	EMD 2012/42	B–B DE	ARR 1204
7003	EMD 2000/42	B–B DE	ARR 1201
7004	EMD 2001/42	B–B DE	ARR 1202
7007	GE 15669/42	B–B DE	Hanford Engineering Works, Wash
7008	GE 15263/42	B–B DE	Holston Ordnance Works 8
7010	GE 13073/41	B–B DE	Hoosier Ordnance Works 1
7011	GE 13074/41	B–B DE	Hoosier Ordnance Works 2
7012	GE 15655/42	B–B DE	Picatinny Arsenal 3
7013	GE 15656/42	B–B DE	Picatinny Arsenal 4
7014	V 4306/41	B–B DE	Indiana Ordnance Works 602–207
7015	V 4307/41	B–B DE	Indiana Ordnance Works 602–208
7016	GE 15267/42	B–B DE	Sacramento Signal Depot
7017	GE 15268/42	B–B DE	Wingate Ordnance Depot
7018	GE 15269/42	B–B DE	Seneca Ordnance Depot
7019	GE 15270/42	B–B DE	Milan Ordnance Depot
7020	GE 15271/42	B–B DE	Portago Ordnance Depot
7021	GE 15628/42	B–B DE	Hanford Engineering Works, Wash
7022	P 7423/42	B–B DE	Red River Ordnance Depot
7023	P 7424/42	B–B DE	Red River Ordnance Depot
7024	P 7425/42	B–B DE	San Jacinto Ordnance Depot, ARR 1104
7025	V 4389/42	B–B DE	Seneca Ordnance Depot
7026	V 4390/42	B–B DE	Milan Ordnance Depot
7027	Atlas 2320/42	B–B DE	South Carolina Port Authority 105
7028	Atlas 2321/42	B–B DE	
7029	P 7382/42	B–B DE	Raritan Arsenal
7030	GE 15661/42	B–B DE	Edgewood Arsenal
7031	GE 15662/42	B–B DE	Edgewood Arsenal
7032	P 7391/42	B–B DE	
7033	P 7392/42	B–B DE	Sierra Ordnance Depot, ARR 1102
7034	P 7403/42	B–B DE	Toledo Ordnance Works, ARR 1103
7035	P 7375/42	B–B DE	Umatilla Ordnance Depot
7036	V 4399/43	B–B DE	Pueblo Ordnance Depot
7037	V 4400/43	B–B DE	Pueblo Ordnance Depot
7038	V 4401/44	B–B DE	Pueblo Ordnance Depot

USA/TC Nos	Maker, Works No & Date	Type	Notes
7041	GE 12967/40	B–B DE	Indiana Ordnance Works 1
7042	GE 12968/40	B–B DE	Indiana Ordnance Works 2
7044	Whit 60157/42	B–B DE	Kansas Ordnance Plant 3
7045	GE 15241/42	B–B DE	New York Air Command, Newark
7046	GE 15242/42	B–B DE	Louisana Ordnance Plant 2
7047	GE 15246/42	B–B DE	Casad Ordnance Depot
7048	GE 15249/42	B–B DE	Savanna Ordnance Depot
7049	GE 15247/42	B–B DE	Watertown Arsenal
7050	GE 15248/42	B–B DE	Curtis Bay Ordnance Depot
7051	GE 15863/42	B–B DE	Edgewood Arsenal
7052	V 4349/42	B–B DE	Southwestern Proving Ground 1
7053	V 4350/42	B–B DE	Southwestern Proving Ground 2
7054	GE 17815/43	B–B DE	Charleston Ordnance Depot
7057	GE 17816/43	B–B DE	Nensemand Ordnance Depot
7058	GE 17836/43	B–B DE	Kankakee Ordnance Works
7059	Whit 40246/42	4wDM	Dickson Gun Plant 1
7060	P 7399/42	B–B DE	Lake Ontario Ordnance Works 1
7061	GE 15147/42	B–B DE	Jayhawk Ordnance Works 1
7064	GE 15113/42	B–B DE	Pine Bluff Arsenal
7065	GE 15155/42	B–B DE	Pine Bluff Arsenal
7066	GE 15156/42	B–B DE	Pine Bluff Arsenal
7067	GE 15057/41	B–B DE	Louisiana Ordnance Plant 1
7068	GE 15058/41	B–B DE	Louisiana Ordnance Plant 2
7069	GE 15757/42	B–B DE	Deseret Chemical Warfare Depot
7070	Whit 40264/42	4wDM	Camp Fannin
7071	GE 15872/42	B–B DE	Kelly Field
7072	GE 13147/41	4wDE	Kingsbury Ordnance Plant C2
7074	GE 13011/41	B–B DE	Kingsbury Ordnance Plant B1
7075	GE 13012/41	B–B DE	Kingsbury Ordnance Plant B2
7076	GE 13013/41	B–B DE	Kingsbury Ordnance Plant B3
7077	GE 13051/41	B–B DE	Kingsbury Ordnance Plant B4
7078	GE 13052/41	B–B DE	Kingsbury Ordnance Plant B5
7079	GE 13035/41	B–B DE	Kingsbury Ordnance Plant A1
7080	GE 13036/41	B–B DE	Kingsbury Ordnance Plant A2
7081	GE 13037/41	B–B DE	Kingsbury Ordnance Plant A3
7083	Whit 60158/42	B–B DE	Illinois Ordnance Plant
7084	Whit 60159/42	B–B DE	Illinois Ordnance Plant
7085	GE 15771/43	B–B DE	Deseret Arsenal
7086	GE 15772/43	B–B DE	Deseret Arsenal
7087	GE 15773/43	B–B DE	Deseret Arsenal
7088	GE 15774/43	B–B DE	Deseret Arsenal
7089	GE 17722/42	B–B DE	Ozark Ordnance Plant
7091	GE 13191/41	B–B DE	Picatinny Arsenal 2
7092	Atlas 1986/36	4wDE	Picatinny Arsenal 1
7093	Atlas 1987/36	4wDE	Picatinny Arsenal 2
7094	D 2377/42	B–B DE	Red River Ordnance Depot
7095	GE 15126/42	B–B DE	Kentucky Ordnance Works 1
7096	GE 15285/42	B–B DE	Kentucky Ordnance Works
7097	GE 15286/42	B–B DE	Kentucky Ordnance Works
7099	GE 17785/43	4wDE	Camp Hahn
7100	A 70224/43	B–B DE	Navajo Ordnance Depot
7101	A 70223/43	B–B DE	Pueblo Ordnance Depot
7102	A 70220/42	B–B DE	QM Depot, Richmond
7103	A 70225/43	B–B DE	Pueblo Ordnance Depot
7104	A 70221/42	B–B DE	Blue Grass Ordnance Depot
7105	A 70219/42	B–B DE	Letterkenny Ordnance Depot
7106	A 70222/43	B–B DE	Letterkenny Ordnance Depot
7107	A 70266/43	B–B DE	Benecia Arsenal, ARR 7107
7108	A 70267/43	B–B DE	Raritan Arsenal
7109	A 70257/43	B–B DE	Benecia Arsenal, ARR 7109
7110	A 70258/43	B–B DE	Blue Grass Ordnance Depot

USA/TC Nos	Maker, Works No & Date	Type	Notes
7111	A 70080/43	B–B DE	Letterkenny Ordnance Depot
7112	A 70081/43	B–B DE	Tooele Ordnance Depot, ARR 7112
7113	A 70082/43	B–B DE	Letterkenny Ordnance Depot
7114	A 70155/43	B–B DE	Columbus General Depot
7122	A 70189/42	B–B DE	GB 44/5
7123	A 70190/42	B–B DE	Benecia Arsenal, ARR 7123
7124	A 70191/42	B–B DE	
7125	A 70192/42	B–B DE	Black Hills Ordnance Plant
7126	B 64741/43	B–B DE	Memphis
7127	B 64744/43	B–B DE	Anniston
7128	B 64745/43	B–B DE	Ogden
7129	B 67710/43	B–B DE	Rock Island
7130	B 67711/43	B–B DE	Fort Lewis
7132	A 69812/42	B–B DE	Illinois Ordnance Plant GO 40
7133	A 69813/42	B–B DE	Illinois Ordnance Plant GO 41
7134	A 69684/42	B–B DE	I M Service Corps 1
7135	A 69860/43	B–B DE	Aberdeen Proving Grounds
7136	A 69861/43	B–B DE	Navajo Ordnance Depot
7137	B 67718/43	B–B DE	Romulus, NY
7138	B 67719/43	B–B DE	Red River Arsenal
7139	B 67726/43	B–B DE	Hill Field
7140	B 67727/43	B–B DE	Kendia, NY
7141	A 69486/41	B–B DE	Proctor & Gamble Co 1
7142	A 69680/42	B–B DE	Proctor & Gamble Co 501
7143	B 67739/43	B–B DE	Anniston
7144	GE 15896/43	B–B DE	Twin City Ordnance Plant
7145	GE 15740/42	B–B DE	Nebraska Defence Corp
7146	GE 15886/43	B–B DE	Nebraska Ordnance Works
7147	GE 17895/43	B–B DE	Construction Quartermaster, Baldwin
7148	GE 17898/43	B–B DE	Louisiana Ordnance Plant
7149	GE 17908/43	B–B DE	Army Service Forces Depot, Schenectady
7150	P 7404/42	B–B DE	Lake Ontario Ordnance Works
7151	GE 15731/42	B–B DE	Raritan Arsenal
7152	GE 15732/43	B–B DE	Rossford Ordnance Depot
7153	GE 15733/43	B–B DE	Army Ordnance Depot, Herlong
7154	GE 15734/43	B–B DE	Sioux Ordnance Depot
7155	Atlas 2343/43	B–B DE	Ordnance Depot, Anniston
7156	Atlas 2344/43	B–B DE	Ordnance Depot, Anniston
7157	P 7438/43	B–B DE	Navajo Ordnance Depot, ARR 1100
7158	P 7439/43	B–B DE	Navajo Ordnance Depot, ARR 1101
7159	P 7479/43	B–B DE	Raritan Arsenal
7160	P 7480/43	B–B DE	Raritan Arsenal
7161	GE 15882/43	B–B DE	Portage Ordnance Depot
7164	GE 15887/43	B–B DE	Casad Ordnance Depot
7165	GE 15889/43	B–B DE	Curtis Bay Ordnance Depot
7166	GE 17744/43	B–B DE	Blue Grass Ordnance Depot
7167	GE 17746/43	B–B DE	Letterkenny Ordnance Depot
7168	GE 17745/43	B–B DE	Ogden Arsenal
7169	GE 17740/43	B–B DE	Lima Tank Depot
7170	GE 17741/43	B–B DE	Tooele Ordnance Depot
7171	GE 17742/43	B–B DE	Sioux Ordnance Depot
7172	GE 17743/43	B–B DE	Sioux Ordnance Depot
7173	GE 15629/42	B–B DE	Louisiana Arsenal
7174	GE 13157/41	B–B DE	Arkansas Ordnance Plant 1
7175	GE 13197/41	B–B DE	Arkansas Ordnance Plant 2
7176	GE 15631/42	B–B DE	Pine Bluff Arsenal
7177	GE 17891/43	B–B DE	Brooklyn Army Base
7178	GE 17861/43	B–B DE	Camp Holabird
7179	GE 17882/43	B–B DE	Edgewood Arsenal
7180	GE 17883/43	B–B DE	Warner-Robins Air Depot
7181	GE 17887/43	B–B DE	Camp Campbell

USA/TC Nos	Maker, Works No & Date	Type	Notes
7182	GE 17886/43	B–B DE	
7183	GE 17884/43	B–B DE	San Antonio Ordnance Depot
7184	GE 17885/43	B–B DE	Charleston Ordnance Depot
7185	GE 15881/43	B–B DE	Louisiana Ordnance Plant
7186	D 2274/39	4wDE	Consolidated Builders Inc
7187	P 7317/41	B–B DE	Jefferson Proving Ground 1, ARR 1106
7188	P 7318/41	B–B DE	Jefferson Proving Ground 2, ARR 1107
7189	GE 18009/43	B–B DE	Langley Field
7190	GE 17841/43	B–B DE	Camp Holabird
7191	GE 17846/43	B–B DE	Delaware Ordnance Depot
7192	D 2372/42	B–B DE	Umatilla Ordnance Depot
7193	D 2376/42	B–B DE	San Jacinto Ordnance Depot
7195	GE 13162/41	B–B DE	Savannah Ordnance Depot 05
7196	Midwest Loco 1073/33	B–B DE	Ex CB&Q RR 9121, Sacramento Signal Depot
7198	GE 15059/41	B–B DE	San Jacinto Ordnance Depot 1
7199	GE 15060/41	B–B DE	San Jacinto Ordnance Depot 2
7200	GE 15743/42	B–B DE	Lincoln Ordnance Depot
7201	GE 15262/42	B–B DE	Arkansas Ordnance Plant
7202	Whit 60323/42	B–B DE	Curtis Bay Ordnance Depot
7203	Whit 60322/43	B–B DE	Kankakee Ordnance Works
7204	GE 15744/42	B–B DE	Pine Bluff Arsenal
7205	GE 18070/43	B–B DE	Pine Bluff Arsenal
7207	GE 15055/41	B–B DE	Curtis Bay Ordnance Depot
7208	GE 12969/40	B–B DE	Raritan Arsenal
7209	GE 13004/41	B–B DE	Raritan Arsenal
7210	GE 13038/41	B–B DE	Raritan Arsenal
7212	GE 15014/41	4wDE	Ogden Arsenal
7215	D 2332/41	4wDE	Atlanta Ordnance Depot
7218	D 2371/42	B–B DE	Anniston
7219	D 2373/42	B–B DE	Wingate Ordnance Depot
7220	D 2374/42	B–B DE	Milan Ordnance Depot 1
7221	D 2375/42	B–B DE	Seneca Ordnance Depot
7222	V 4385/42	B–B DE	San Antonio Ordnance Depot 1
7223	V 4333/41	B–B DE	Ogden Ordnance Depot 3
7224	Whit 60034/40	B–B DE	Fort Wingate Ordnance Depot
7225	B 70856/44	B–B DE	Henford, Wash
7226	B 70871/44	B–B DE	Fort Belvoir
7227	B 70885/44	B–B DE	New Brunswick, NJ
7228–37	GE 27528–37/44		See Chapter 57
7238	GE 15278/42	B–B DE	Ogden Arsenal 1818
7239	GE 15279/42	B–B DE	Ogden Arsenal 1819, South Korea 53/4, USA
7242	GE 13060/41	B–B DE	Wolf Creek Ordnance Plant 502
7243	GE 13132/41	B–B DE	Wolf Creek Ordnance Plant 503
7245	GE 13140/41	B–B DE	Wolf Creek Ordnance Plant 505
7246	GE 15056/41	B–B DE	Wolf Creek Ordnance Plant 506
7247	GE 15289/42	B–B DE	Cornhusker Ordnance Plant
7248	GE 15290/42	B–B DE	Cornhusker Ordnance Plant
7249	GE 15713/42	B–B DE	Cornhusker Ordnance Plant
7251	GE 15717/42	B–B DE	Camp Bowie
7252	Whit 60207/42	B–B DE	Nebraska Ordnance Plant
7253	GE 15758/42	B–B DE	Fort Clark
7254	GE 17733/42	B–B DE	West Virginia Ordnance Works
7255	GE 17734/42	B–B DE	West Virginia Ordnance Works
7256	Whit 60108/41	B–B DE	Iowa Ordnance Plant 7–44
7257	Whit 60226/42	B–B DE	Oak Ordnance Plant 101
7258	GE 15716/42	B–B DE	Savanna Ordnance Depot 104
7259	GE 15657/42	B–B DE	Savanna Ordnance Depot 651
7260	GE 13158/41	B–B DE	Huntsville Arsenal 1
7261	GE 13198/41	B–B DE	Huntsville Arsenal 2
7262	GE 15632/42	B–B DE	Huntsville Arsenal 3
7263	GE 17860/43	B–B DE	Huntsville Arsenal 7

USA/TC Nos	Maker, Works No & Date	Type	Notes
7264	GE 15667/42	B–B DE	Huntsville Arsenal
7265	GE ?/?	B–B DE	
7266	? ?/?	B–B DE	Watervliet Arsenal
7270	GE 12998/41	B–B DE	Aberdeen Proving Grounds
7271	P 7341/42	B–B DE	Aberdeen Proving Grounds 5
7272	GE 13154/41	B–B DE	New River Ordnance Plant
7274	A 70191/42	B–B DE	
7275	B 62411/41	B–B DE	Iowa Ordnance Plant 1–120
7276	B 62495/41	B–B DE	Iowa Ordnance Plant 2–100
7277	A 69469/41	B–B DE	Iowa Ordnance Plant 3–100
7278	GE 17858/43	B–B DE	Picatinny Arsenal
7279	GE ?/?	B–B DE	
7282	GE 18091/44	B–B DE	Lima Tank Depot
7283	GE 27518/44	B–B DE	Lima Tank Depot
7284	GE 15738/42	B–B DE	Nebraska Defense Corp 653
7285	GE 17892/43	B–B DE	New River Ordnance Plant
7286	GE 17893/43	B–B DE	Fort Knox
7288	GE ?/?	B–B DE	
7290	GE 15188/42	B–B DE	Volunteer Ordnance Works 1
7291	GE 15741/42	B–B DE	Volunteer Ordnance Works 1002
7299	Ply 4252/41	4wP	Erie Proving Ground
7302	Whit 50009/32	4wDE	Raritan Arsenal 3
7304	Whit 13175/39	4wP	Ogden Ordnance Depot 1
7305	Ply 3559/30	4wDE	Aberdeen Proving Grounds 1
7306	V 4144/31	B–B DE	Aberdeen Proving Grounds 2
7307	Whit 60105/41	B–B DE	Iowa Ordnance Plant 4–44
7308	Whit 60106/41	B–B DE	Iowa Ordnance Plant 5–44
7310	GE 13098/41	B–B DE	Iowa Ordnance Plant 8–44
7311	GE 13099/41	B–B DE	Iowa Ordnance Plant 9–44
7312	GE 15119/42	B–B DE	Iowa Ordnance Plant 11–44
7313	GE 15277/42	B–B DE	Cactus Ordnance Depot
7314	GE 15864/42	B–B DE	Green River Ordnance Depot R1
7315	GE 15866/42	B–B DE	Green River Ordnance depot
7316	GE 17729/42	B–B DE	Green River Ordnance Depot AL3
7317	GE 17812/43	B–B DE	Holston Ordnance Depot 3
7318	GE 17813/43	B–B DE	Hercules Powder Co 4
7319	GE 17814/43	B–B DE	Cornhusker Ordnance Plant 5
7320	GE 12981/41	B–B DE	Elwood Ordnance Plant
7321	GE 12980/41	B–B DE	Elwood Ordnance Plant
7322	GE 13005/41	B–B DE	Elwood Ordnance Plant
7323	GE 13006/41	B–B DE	Elwood Ordnance Plant
7324	GE 15244/42	B–B DE	Weldon Springs Ordnance Works
7325	GE 15294/41	B–B DE	Weldon Springs Ordnance Works
7326	GE 15876/42	B–B DE	Gulf Ordnance Plant 502
7327	GE 15877/42	B–B DE	Gulf Ordnance Plant 503
7328	GE 12931/40	B–B DE	Chickasaw Ordnance Depot 1
7329	GE 12934/40	B–B DE	Chickasaw Ordnance Depot 2
7330	GE 12976/40	B–B DE	Indiana Ordnance Works 3
7331	GE 12985/41	B–B DE	Ravenna Ordnance Works 451
7332	GE 15065/41	B–B DE	Ravenna Ordnance Works 452
7333	GE 15066/41	B–B DE	Ravenna Ordnance Works 453, South Korea 50
7334	GE 12977/40	B–B DE	Indiana Ordnance Works 4
7335	GE 13131/41	B–B DE	Wolf Creek Ordnance Plant, South Korea 53/4, USA
7336	GE 17721/42	B–B DE	National Analine Defense Co, NY
7337	GE 15880/42	B–B DE	St Louis Administrative Centre 46, South Korea 53/4, USA
7338	GE 17836/43	B–B DE	Scioto Ordnance Plant
7339	GE 15721/42	B–B DE	Scioto Ordnance Plant
7340	GE 15654/42	B–B DE	Longhorn Ordnance Works 2
7341	GE 15653/42	B–B DE	Longhorn Ordnance Works 1

USA/TC Nos	Maker, Works No & Date	Type	Notes
7342	GE 12966/40	B–B DE	Hercules Powder Co 1
7343	GE 15660/42	B–B DE	Pennsylvania Ordnance Works 3
7344	GE 15235/42	B–B DE	Atlanta General Depot
7346	GE 12965/40	B–B DE	Chickasaw Ordnance Depot 3
7347	GE 15237/42	B–B DE	Mississippi Ordnance Plant 2
7348	GE 15163/42	B–B DE	Edgewood Arsenal 6500
7349	GE 15165/42	B–B DE	Edgewood Arsenal 6501
7350	GE 15730/43	B–B DE	Bluebonnet Ordnance Plant 655
7351	GE 15737/43	B–B DE	Bluebonnet Ordnance Plant 656
7352	GE 15739/42	B–B DE	Bluebonnet Ordnance Plant 654
7353	GE 15234/42	B–B DE	Continental Foundry & Machine Co 2
7354	GE 13072/41	B–B DE	New River Ordnance Plant
7355	GE 13138/41	B–B DE	Plum Brook Ordnance Works 336
7356	GE 13139/41	B–B DE	Plum Brook Ordnance Works
7357	GE 17809/43	B–B DE	Plum Brook Ordnance Works 340
7358	GE 17810/43	B–B DE	Plum Brook Ordnance Works
7359	Whit 60227/42	B–B DE	Oak Ordnance Plant 102
7361	Whit 60212/42	B–B DE	Pennsylvania Ordnance Works 4
7362	Whit 60213/42	B–B DE	Pennsylvania Ordnance Works 5
7364	GE ?/?	B–B DE	
7366	GE 17754/43	B–B DE	Army Service Forces Depot, Montgomery
7367	GE 17755/43	B–B DE	Army Service Forces Depot, Montgomery
7371	A 69464/41	B–B DE	Hunkin-Conkey Construction Co 1002
7372	A 69514/41	B–B DE	Lone Star Defense Corp 100
7373	GE 15265/42	B–B DE	Wabash River Ordnance Depot
7374	A 69594/41	B–B DE	Elwood Ordnance Plant USA 100
7375	A 69595/41	B–B DE	Elwood Ordnance Plant USA 101
7380	GE 15076/41	B–B DE	Oklahoma Ordnance Works 1
7382	GE 15883/43	B–B DE	Oklahoma Ordnance Works
7383	GE 15190/42	B–B DE	Oklahoma Ordnance Works 3
7384	GE 15897/43	B–B DE	Oklahoma Ordnance Works
7385	GE 27568/44	B–B DE	Hanford Ordnance Works
7387	GE 17750/43	B–B DE	Lincoln Ordnance Depot
7388	GE 15743/42	B–B DE	Lincoln Ordnance Depot
7389	GE 15670/42	B–B DE	Sangamon Ordnance Plant
7390	GE 27849/45	B–B DE	Indiana Ordnance Works
7391	GE 27850/45	B–B DE	Kingsbury Ordnance Plant
7392	GE 27851/45	B–B DE	Keystone Ordnance Plant
7393	GE 27852/45	B–B DE	Hoosier Ordnance Plant
7394	GE 27853/45	B–B DE	US Army Air Force Lowry Field
7395	GE 13196/41	B–B DE	Alabama Ordnance Works 2
7401	GE 15284/42	B–B DE	Army Air Base, Orlando
7402	GE 15715/42	B–B DE	Camp Holabird, South Korea 53/4, USA
7403	EMD 1834/42	4wDE	US Army 1
7404	GE 15718/42	B–B DE	Watertown Arsenal
7405	GE 15720/42	B–B DE	Hampton Roads Port of Embarkation
7406	GE 15722/42	B–B DE	Tulalip Ammunition Depot
7407	GE 15724/42	B–B DE	Spokane Air Depot
7408	GE 15726/42	B–B DE	Belle Mead ASF Depot
7409	GE 15862/42	B–B DE	Wellston Air Depot
7410	GE 12912/40	B–B DE	Ex Arkansas Valley Interurban RR 92, Fort Knox
7411	GE 12913/40	B–B DE	Ex AVIRR 93, USAAF Depot San Bernardino
7412	GE 15865/42	B–B DE	Ames Terminal
7413	GE 15868/42	B–B DE	Bever Site Terminal
7414	GE 15869/42	B–B DE	Army Air Field, Douglas
7415	GE 15873/42	B–B DE	New York Port of Embarkation
7416	GE 15875/42	B–B DE	Spokane Air Depot
7417	GE 15878/42	B–B DE	USA Base, Prince Rupert, BC, Canada
7418	GE 15879/42	B–B DE	USA Base, South Boston
7419	GE 17720/42	B–B DE	USA Ordnance Depot, Carteret, South Korea 53/4, USA

USA/TC Nos	Maker, Works No & Date	Type	Notes
7420	GE 17724/42	B–B DE	Oklahoma City Air Depot
7421	GE 17727/42	B–B DE	Port of Embarkation, New Orleans
7422	GE 17732/42	B–B DE	Drew Field
7423	GE 17735/42	B–B DE	Brookley Field
7424	GE 17736/42	B–B DE	Camp Cooke
7425	GE 17827/43	B–B DE	Port Edward Staging Area, BC, Canada
7426	Ply 4069/40	4wDM	QMC-USA 4521, QMD Brooklyn, Camp Claiborne
7427	GE 13165/41	B–B DE	QMC-USA 4546, Fort Mason
7428	GE 13166/41	B–B DE	QMC-USA 4547, Pacific Overseas Air Technical Service Command, Alameda
7429	GE 13167/41	B–B DE	QMC-USA 4548, Pacific Overseas Air Technical Service Command, Alameda
7430	GE 13168/41	B–B DE	QMC-USA 4549, Cumerland
7431	GE 13169/41	B–B DE	QMC-USA 4550
7432	V 4334/41	B–B DE	QMC-USA 4551, Paterson Field
7433	V 4335/41	B–B DE	QMC-USA 4552, Lowry Field
7434	V 4336/41	B–B DE	QMC-USA 4553, Pine Camp, NY
7435	V 4337/41	B–B DE	QMC-USA 4554, Atlanta
7436	V 4338/41	B–B DE	QMC-USA 4555, Richmond
7437	Whit 60301/43	4wDE	Hawaii, 3ft gauge
7438	GE 15762/43	B–B DE	Trinidad Government Rly 52
7439	GE 15764/43	B–B DE	Fort Eustis
7440	GE 17718/42	B–B DE	Maumelle Ordnance Works
7441	GE 17719/42	B–B DE	Rock Island Arsenal
7442	D 2378/42	B–B DE	Edgewood Arsenal
7443	D 2379/42	B–B DE	Edgewood Arsenal
7444	GE 15293/41	B–B DE	AAF Specialised Depot, Los Angeles
7445	P 7399/42	B–B DE	Lake Ontario Ordnance Works 1
7446	P 7402/42	B–B DE	Lake Ontario Ordnance Works 2
7448	GE 15002/41	B–B DE	Utah Depot 5
7449	GE 17910/43	B–B DE	Brooklyn Army Base
7450	A 69669/42	B–B DE	Oakland Army Terminal
7453	B 64407/42	B–B DE	Gallup, NM
7454	B 64413/42	B–B DE	Columbus, Ohio
7455	B 64414/42	B–B DE	Atlanta, Ga
7456	B 64420/42	B–B DE	Marietta, Ga
7457	B 64421/42	B–B DE	Anniston, Ga
7459	A 69408/41	B–B DE	Ex QMC 10041, Holabird QMD
7460	A 69407/41	B–B DE	Ex QMC 10042, Oakland Army Terminal
7461	B 64436/42	B–B DE	Umatilla Ordnance Depot
7462	B 64727/42	B–B DE	Romulus, NY
7463	B 64728/42	B–B DE	Navajo Ordnance Depot
7464	B 64742/43	B–B DE	Watertown, NY
7465	A 69673/43	B–B DE	Bell Aircraft, Marietta
7466	B 67720/43	B–B DE	Columbus, Ohio
7467	B 67738/43	B–B DE	Tullahoma, Ala
7469	? ?/?	B–B DE	
7480	GE 17739/43	B–B DE	GE Nucleonics Project, Richmond
7481	GE 17859/43	B–B DE	McChord Field
7482	GE 15658/42	B–B DE	Savanna Ordnance Deport 652
7483	Ply 4425/42	B–B DE	Pennsylvania Ordnance Works
7484	Ply 4426/42	B–B DE	Pennsylvania Ordnance Works
7485	GE 13155/41	B–B DE	Plum Brook Ordnance Plant
7486	GE 15867/42	B–B DE	Utah QM Depot
7487	Whit 60235/43	B–B DE	Oak Ordnance Plant 108
7488	GE 17730/42	B–B DE	Army Air Force Supply Depot, Memphis
7489	Whit 60208/43	B–B DE	Nebraska Ordnance Plant 17094
7490	GE 17932/43	B–B DE	Vernon Field, Jamaica, JGR 70
7491	GE 17931/43	B–B DE	
7492	GE 18149/43	B–B DE	Fort Clark

USA/TC Nos	Maker, Works No & Date	Type	Notes
7493	GE 18150/43	B–B DE	Fort Mifflin Naval Ammunition Depot
7494	GE 17937/43	B–B DE	Pine Bluff Arsenal
7495	GE 17847/43	B–B DE	Whittimore Ordnance Depot
7496	GE 17848/43	B–B DE	Army Air Force Depot, Orlando
7497	GE 17849/43	B–B DE	Camp Roberts
7498	GE 17850/43	B–B DE	
7499	GE 17851/43	B–B DE	McChord Air Field
7500	GE 13141/41	B–B DE	Ex QMC 6041, Fort Knox
7501	GE 13142/41	B–B DE	Ex QMC 6042, Brooklyn Army Base
7502	GE 13143/41	B–B DE	Ex QMC 6043, Langley Field
7503	GE 15094/42	B–B DE	Ex QMC 6007, Fort Eustis
7504	Whit 60330/43	4wDE	3ft gauge, Hawaii
7505	GE 15092/42	B–B DE	Ex QMC 6005, Fort Hancock
7506	GE 15091/42	B–B DE	Ex QMC 6004, Fort Hancock
7507	GE 15093/42	B–B DE	Ex QMC 6006, Fort Hancock
7508	GE 15118/42	B–B DE	Iowa Ordnance Plant 10–44
7509	GE 17731/42	B–B DE	Lexington Signal Depot
7510	Whit 60107/41	B–B DE	Iowa Ordnance Plant 6–44
7511	V 4394/44	B–B DE	Fort Hancock
7512	Whit 60122/43	B–B DE	Ravenna Ordnance Depot
7513	GE 15112/42	B–B DE	Scioto Ordnance Plant
7514	GE 27743/44	B–B DE	3ft gauge, Hawaii
7515	GE 27744/44	B–B DE	3ft gauge, Hawaii
7516	GE 15759/42	B–B DE	Edgewood Arsenal
7547	Ply ?/?	4wD	Williams Field
7550	D 2445/42	4wP	Seattle
7551	D 2446/42	4wP	Newport News
7552	D 2447/42	4wP	Drew Field
7553	D 2448/42	4wP	Camp Breckinridge
7554	D 2449/42	4wP	Camp Atterbury
7555	D 2450/42	4wP	Camp Campbell
7556	D 2451/42	4wP	Greenville Air Base
7557	D 2452/42	4wP	Fort Sill
7558	D 2453/42	4wP	Richmond Army Air Base
7559	D 2454/42	4wP	QM Depot, Mira Loma
7560	D 2455/42	4wP	Lincoln Air Force Technical Training School
7561	D 2456/42	4wP	Madison Air Force Technical Training School
7562	D 2457/42	4wP	Fort Wayne Ordnance Motor Base
7563	D 2458/42	4wP	Camp Chaffeé
7564	D 2459/42	4wP	Camp Gruber
7565	D 2460/42	4wP	Army Air Force Technical Training School, Goldsboro
7566	D 2461/42	4wP	New Cumberland
7567	D 2462/42	4wP	Camp Maxey
7568	D 2463/42	4wP	Fort McClellan
7569	D 2464/42	4wP	Camp Pickett
7570	D 2465/42	4wP	Fort Storey
7571	D 2466/42	4wP	Camp Bowie
7572	D 2467/42	4wP	McClellan Field
7573	Ply 4441/42	4wP	La Junta Army Air Base
7574	Ply 4442/42	4wP	Minter Field
7575	Ply 4443/42	4wP	Signal Depot, Avon
7576	Ply 4444/42	4wP	Gulfport Field
7577	Ply 4445/42	4wP	3ft gauge. Syracuse Army Base
7578	Ply 4446/42	4wP	Camp Edwards
7579	Ply 4447/42	4wP	Advanced Flying School, Mariana
7580	Ply 4448/42	4wP	Advanced Flying School, Douglas
7581	Ply 4449/42	4wP	Washington
7582	Ply 4450/42	4wP	
7583	Ply 4451/42	4wP	
7584	Ply 4452/42	4wP	

USA/TC Nos	Maker, Works No & Date	Type	Notes
7585	Ply 4453/43	4wP	
7586	Ply 4454/43	4wP	Alexandria, Va
7587	Ply 4455/43	4wP	Port of Embarkation, Los Angeles
7588	Ply 4456/43	4wP	Fort Sam Houston
7589	Ply 4457/43	4wP	
7590	Ply 4458/43	4wP	
7591	Ply 4459/43	4wP	
7592	Ply 4460/43	4wP	
7593	Ply 4461/43	4wP	
7594	Ply 4462/43	4wP	Army Air Force Base, Las Vegas
7595	Ply 4463/43	4wP	
7596	Ply 4464/43	4wP	Port of Embarkation, Boston
7600	Ply 4481/43	4wP	
7601	Ply 4482/43	4wP	
7602	Ply 4483/43	4wP	
7603	Ply 4484/43	4wP	Camp Gordon Johnson
7604	Ply 4485/43	4wP	Ephrata, Wash
7605	Ply 4486/43	4wP	
7606	Ply 4487/43	4wP	Camp Ellis
7607	Ply 4488/43	4wP	George Field
7608	Ply 4489/43	4wP	Sioux City Army Air Base
7609	Ply 4490/43	4wP	
7610	Ply 4491/43	4wP	Lexington Signal Depot
7611	Ply 4492/43	4wP	Pueblo, Colo
7612	Ply 4493/43	4wP	
7613	Ply 4494/43	4wP	Alaska. Named "Julia"
7614	Ply 4495/43	4wP	
7615	Ply 4496/43	4wP	
7616	Ply 4497/43	4wP	
7617	Ply 4498/43	4wP	
7618	Ply 4499/43	4wP	
7619	Ply 4500/43	4wP	Parcel Supply Depot, Shelby
7620	Ply 4501/43	4wP	
7621	Ply 4502/43	4wP	
7622	Ply 4503/43	4wP	McChord Field
7623	Ply 4504/43	4wP	
7624	Ply 4505/43	4wP	
7625	Ply 4506/43	4wP	
7626	Ply 4507/43	4wP	
7627	Ply 4508/43	4wP	
7628	Ply 4509/43	4wP	
7629	D 2329/41	4wDM	New Orleans
7630	D 2330/41	4wDM	Columbus
7650	Ply 4470/42	4wP	3ft gauge, Oahu, TH
7651	Ply 4471/42	4wP	3ft gauge, probably Alaska/WP&Y 3
7653	Ply 3818/36	4wP	Harrisburg
7654	Whit 13179/40	4wP	Ex QMC 2022, Fort Mason
7655	Whit 13180/40	4wP	Ex QMC 2023, Sacramento Air Depot
7656	Whit 13181/40	4wP	Ex QMC 2024, Langley Field
7657	Whit 13182/40	4wP	Ex QMC 2025, Holabird QM Depot
7658	Whit 13183/40	4wP	Ex QMC 2026, Holabird QM Depot
7659	P 7384/41	4wP	Fort Belvoir
7660	V 3946/28	4wP	3ft gauge. Ravenna, Ohio, Marietta Depot
7663	Ply 4066/40	4wP	Ex QMC, McChord Field
7664	Whit 13189/41	4wP	Ex QMC 2032, 3ft gauge, Schofield Barracks, TH
7665	D 2352/41	4wP	Ex QMC, Camp Haan
7666	D 2353/41	4wP	Ex QMC 2014?, Fort Eustis
7667	D 2354/41	4wP	Ex QMC, Charlotte
7668	D 2355/41	4wP	Ex QMC, Fort Hancock
7669	D 2356/41	4wP	Ex QMC, Gowan Field
7670	V 4310/41	4wP	Ex QMC 2038, Tampa

USA/TC Nos	Maker, Works No & Date	Type	Notes
7671	V 4311/41	4wP	Ex QMC 2039, Alexandria
7672	V 4312/41	4wP	Ex QMC 2040, Tuscon
7673	V 4313/41	4wP	Ex QMC 2041, Camp Livingston
7674	V 4314/41	4wP	Ex QMC 2042, Paterson Field
7675	Whit 13199/41	4wP	Ex QMC 2043
7676	Whit 13200/41	4wP	Ex QMC 2044
7677	Whit 13201/41	4wP	Ex QMC 2045
7678	Whit 13202/41	4wP	Ex QMC 2046
7679	Ply 4140/41	4wP	Ex QMC, Camp Forrest
7680	Ply 4141/41	4wP	Ex QMC, QMC Depot, Atlanta
7681	Ply 4142/41	4wP	Ex QMC 2030?, Camp San Luis Obispo
7682	Ply 4143/41	4wP	Ex QMC, QMC Depot, New Cumberland
7683	Ply 4144/41	4wP	Ex QMC, Brookley Field
7684	Ply 4145/41	4wP	Ex QMC, Camp Bowie
7685	Ply 4146/41	4wP	Ex QMC, Pine Camp
7686	Ply 4147/41	4wP	Ex QMC, West Palm Beach Airport
7687	Ply 4148/41	4wP	Ex QMC, Fort McClellan
7688	Ply 4149/41	4wP	Ex QMC, Selfridge Field
7689	Ply 4156/41	4wP	Ex QMC, Camp Roberts
7690	Ply 4157/41	4wP	Ex QMC, Schenectady General Depot
7691	Ply 4158/41	4wP	Ex QMC, Camp Wheeler
7692	Ply 4159/41	4wP	Ex QMC, QM Depot, Philadelphia
7693	Ply 4160/41	4wP	Ex QMC, Spokane Air Base
7694	Ply 4161/41	4wP	Ex QMC, Salt Lake City Airdrome
7695	Ply 4162/41	4wP	Ex QMC, Gray Field
7696	Ply 4163/41	4wP	Ex QMC, Wright Field
7697	Ply 4164/41	4wP	Ex QMC 2067, Fort Benjamin Harrison
7698	Ply 4165/41	4wP	Ex QMC, Chanute Field
7699	D 2339/41	4wP	Ex QMC 2033, March Field
7700	D 2340/41	4wP	Ex QMC 2034, Fort Custer
7701	D 2341/41	4wP	Ex QMC 2035, Fort Wayne
7702	D 2342/41	4wP	Ex QMC 2036, Holabird Depot
7703	D 2343/41	4wP	Ex QMC 2037, Camp Barkley
7704	D 2357/41	4wP	Ex QMC, Duncan Field
7705	D 2358/41	4wP	Ex QMC, San Antonio
7706	D 2359/41	4wP	Ex QMC, Hammer Field
7707	D 2360/42	4wP	Ex QMC, Holabird Depot
7708	D 2361/42	4wP	Ex QMC, Middleton Air Material Area
7711	V 4351/42	4wP	Ex QMC 2080, New Orleans
7712	V 4352/42	4wP	Ex QMC 2081, 60in gauge, Panama Canal Zone
7713	V 4353/42	4wP	Ex QMC 2082, March Field
7714	V 4354/42	4wP	Ex QMC 2083, Camp Cook
7715	V 4355/42	4wP	Ex QMC 2084, 42in gauge, QMC Depot, Long Island City
7716	Whit 13210/41	4wP	Ex QMC 2085
7717	Whit 13211/41	4wP	Ex QMC 2086
7718	Whit 13212/41	4wP	Ex QMC 2087
7719	Whit 13213/42	4wP	Ex QMC 2088
7720	Whit 13214/42	4wP	Ex QMC 2089
7721	Whit 13215/42	4wP	Ex QMC 2090
7722	Whit 13216/42	4wP	Ex QMC 2091, Binghampton Medical Depot
7723	Whit 13217/42	4wP	Ex QMC 2092
7724	Whit 13218/42	4wP	Ex QMC 2093
7725	Whit 13219/42	4wP	Ex QMC 2094
7726	D 2384/42	4wP	Ex QMC 2095
7727	D 2385/42	4wP	Ex QMC 2096, San Antonio
7728	D 2386/42	4wP	Ex QMC 2097, Fort Benning
7729	D 2387/42	4wP	Ex QMC 2098, Fort Benning
7730	D 2388/42	4wP	Ex QMC 2099, Fort Benning
7731–8	Evans ?/?	6wDH	Roadrail, see Chapter 58
7742	Whit 13205/41	4wP	Ex QMC 2047, Middleton Air Material Area

USA/TC Nos	Maker, Works No & Date	Type	Notes
7747	Evans 137/42	4wP	Roadrail. Voorheesville Sub-Depot
7751	GE ?/?	4wDE	3ft gauge. Hawaii
7752	GE 17912/43	4wDE	3ft gauge. Hawaii
7753	GE 17913/43	4wDE	3ft gauge. Hawaii
7754	GE 17777/43	4wDE	Batista Field, San Antonio de los Bancos, Cuba
7755	GE 17914/43	4wDE	Metre gauge, New Caledonia 8/43, Burma 12/44
7756	GE 17915/43	4wDE	Metre gauge, New Caledonia 8/43, Burma 12/44
7757	GE 15680/42	4wDE	Camp Miles Standish
7758	GE 13028/41	4wDE	Ex Charles City Western Rly 200, Ravenna Ordnance Plant 231, Reno Army Air Base
7759	GE 13145/41	4wDE	Ravenna Ordnance Works 232
7760	GE 18135/43	4wDE	Holabird Signal Depot
7761	GE 18136/43	4wDE	Hamilton Air Field
7762	GE 18137/43	4wDE	In-Transit Depot, Alameda
7763	GE 18138/43	4wDE	Fort Miles
7764	GE 18139/43	4wDE	Salvage Centre, Frederick
7765	GE 18143/43	4wDE	Kelly Field
7766	GE 18144/44	4wDE	TC RR Shop, Fort Benning
7767	GE 18198/44	4wDE	Mitchell Field
7768	GE 27500/44	4wDE	Rocky Mountain Arsenal
7769	GE 27501/44	4wDE	Alaska ARR 51
7770–5	GE 27502–7/44	4wDE	See Chapter 57
7776–9	GE 27607–10/44	4wDE	See Chapter 57
7790	GE 13149/41	4wDE	Ravenna Ordnance Plant 233
7791	GE 13150/41	4wDE	Ravenna Ordnance Plant 234
7792	GE 13151/41	4wDE	Ravenna Ordnance Plant 235
7794	GE 12978/40	B–B DE	Kankakee Ordnance Works 1
7795	GE 12979/40	B–B DE	Kankakee Ordnance Works 2
7796	GE 12982/41	B–B DE	Kankakee Ordnance Works 3
7797	GE 12983/41	B–B DE	Kankakee Ordnance Works 4
7800–29	GE 27656–85/44	B–B DE	5ft 6in gauge. See Chapter 60
7850	Whit 60283/43	B–B DE	St Louis
7851	GE 17751/43	B–B DE	Curtis Bay Ordnance Depot
7852	GE 17753/43	B–B DE	Mount Ranier Ordnance Depot
7853	GE 17757/43	B–B DE	Red River Ordnance Depot
7854	GE 17899/43	B–B DE	Milan Ordnance Depot
7855	GE 17900/43	B–B DE	Sierra Ordnance Depot
7856	GE 17901/43	B–B DE	Red River Ordnance Plant
7857	GE 17902/43	B–B DE	Umatilla Ordnance Depot
7858	GE 17903/43	B–B DE	Navajo Ordnance Depot
7859	GE 17904/43	B–B DE	
7860	GE 17905/43	B–B DE	Tooele Ordnance Depot
7861	GE 17906/43	B–B DE	Blue Grass Ordnance Depot
7862	GE 17907/43	B–B DE	Red River Ordnance Plant
7863	GE 18013/43	B–B DE	Black Hills Ordnance Depot
7864	GE 18014/43	B–B DE	
7865	GE 18015/43	B–B DE	Portago Ordnance Depot
7866	GE 18016/43	B–B DE	Wingate Ordnance Depot
7867	GE 18017/43	B–B DE	Casad Ordnance Depot
7868	GE 18018/43	B–B DE	Sierra Ordnance Depot
7869	GE 18019/43	B–B DE	
7870	GE 18020/43	B–B DE	Black Hills Ordnance Depot
7871	GE 18021/43	B–B DE	San Jacinto Ordnance Works
7872	GE 18022/43	B–B DE	Terre Haute Ordnance Plant
7873	GE 18023/43	B–B DE	Ogden Arsenal
7874	GE 18024/43	B–B DE	Blue Grass Ordnance Depot
7875	GE 15664/42	B–B DE	Huntsville Arsenal 6
7876	GE 17862/43	B–B DE	Raritan Arsenal
7877	GE 17863/43	B–B DE	Tooele Ordnance Depot
7878	GE 17864/43	B–B DE	Savanna Ordnance Depot
7879	GE 17865/43	B–B DE	Curtis Bay Ordnance Depot

USA/TC Nos	Maker, Works No & Date	Type	Notes
7880	GE 17866/43	B–B DE	Keystone Ordnance Depot
7881	GE 17867/43	B–B DE	Umatilla Ordnance Depot
7882	GE 17868/43	B–B DE	Savanna Ordnance Depot
7883	GE 17869/43	B–B DE	Letterkenny Ordnance Depot
7884	GE 17870/43	B–B DE	Raritan Arsenal
7885	GE 17871/43	B–B DE	Pueblo Ordnance Depot
7886	GE 17872/43	B–B DE	Charleston Ordnance Depot
7887	GE 17873/43	B–B DE	Umatilla Ordnance Depot
7888	GE 17874/43	B–B DE	Letterkenny Ordnance Depot
7889	GE 17875/43	B–B DE	Aberdeen Proving Grounds
7890	GE 18025/43	B–B DE	Anniston Ordnance Plant
7891	GE 18026/43	B–B DE	Tooele Ordnance Depot
7892	GE 18062/43	B–B DE	TC Shops Ogden
7893	GE 18065/43	B–B DE	Albany Engineers Depot
7920	GE 17938/43	B–B DE	St Mary's Munition Factory, Dunheved, New South Wales, New South Wales Govt Rly 7920
7921	GE 17939/43	B–B DE	SMMF, NSWR 7921, Commonwealth Rly DE–90
7922	GE 17933/43	B–B DE	SMMF, NSWR 7922, CR DE–91
7923	GE 17934/43	B–B DE	SMMF, NSWR 7923
7924–9	GE 27631–6/44	B–B DE	See Chapter 57
7930	GE 17940/43	B–B DE	Aberdeen Proving Grounds
7931	GE 18147/43	B–B DE	Aberdeen Proving Grounds
7932	GE 18148/43	B–B DE	Aberdeen Proving Grounds
7934	GE 15885/43	B–B DE	Tinkler Field
7935	GE 15728/42	B–B DE	Sangamon Ordnance Plant
7936	GE 15723/42	B–B DE	Sangamon Ordnance Plant
7937	GE 13193/41	B–B DE	Weldon Springs Ordnance Works 1
7938	GE 15729/42	B–B DE	Sangamon Ordnance Plant
7939	Whit 60230/43	B–B DE	Oak Ordnance Plant 105
7940	Whit 60231/43	B–B DE	Oak Ordnance Plant 106
7941	Whit 60234/43	B–B DE	Oak Ordnance Plant 107
7942–9	Whit 80068–75/45	4wE	60in gauge Quencher locomotives for Russia, USA/TC 2490–7 8/45 at the works
7950	D 2468/43	B–B DE	
7951	D 2469/43	B–B DE	
7952	EMD 2284/42	4wDE	Schenectady General Depot
7953	EMD 2285/42	4wDE	
7954	EMD 2286/42	4wDE	
7955	GE 17828/43	B–B DE	Plum Brook Ordnance Works
7956	GE 17829/43	B–B DE	Rapid City Air Base, South Korea 53/4, USA /55
7957	GE 17830/43	B–B DE	Delaware Ordnance Depot
7958	GE 17831/43	B–B DE	Milan Ordnance Depot
7959	GE 17832/43	B–B DE	Erie Proving Grounds
7960	GE 17833/43	B–B DE	Seward, Alaska
7961–90	Whit 60331–60/43	B–B DE	See Chapter 61
8000–56	A various	C–C DE	See Chapter 62
8080	Whit 60220/43	B–B DE	
8081	Whit 60221/43	B–B DE	
8082	Whit 60222/43	B–B DE	Oak Ridge
8083	Whit 60223/43	B–B DE	
8120–47	Whit 60361–88/44	B–B DE	See Chapter 61
8204	Whit 13125/33	4wP	Ex QMC 823, Philadelphia QMD
8205	Whit 13125/33	4wP	Ex QMC 821, 3ft gauge, Schofield Barracks, TH
8206	Whit 13124/33	4wP	Ex QMC 822, Fort Knox
8207	Whit 13126/33	4wP	Ex QMC 824, Fort Sill
8209	D 2228/36	4wP	Ex QMC, Holabird Depot
8210	Ply ?/41	4wP	Ex QMC, 60cm gauge, Fort Dix
8220	Ply 4063/40	4wP	Ex QMC 830, Fort Barrancas
8223	V 4364/42	4wP	Maumelle Ordnance Works "Plant Loco 1"
8225	D 2229/36	4wP	Ex QMC 402, Fort Barrancas
8232	Whit ?/?	4wP	60cm gauge, Fort Dix

USA/TC Nos	Maker, Works No & Date	Type	Notes
8288–95	Brookville 3028–35/44	4wP	Metre gauge, Burma /44, See Chapter 51
8298	Ply 4803/44	4wP	3ft gauge
8299	Ply 4804/44	4wP	3ft gauge
8305	Ply 4810/44	4wP	3ft gauge, Badger Ordnance Works
8312	Ply 4817/44	4wP	3ft gauge, Badger Ordnance Works
8317	Ply 5023/45	4wP	3ft gauge, Sunflower Ordnance Works
8318	Ply 5024/45	4wP	3ft gauge, Sunflower Ordnance Works
8319	Ply 5025/45	4wP	3ft gauge, Sunflower Ordnance Works
8378	Whit 60087/41	B–B DE	Kankakee Ordnance Works 82
8379	Whit 60086/41	B–B DE	Kankakee Ordnance Works 81
8390	GE 27792/45	B–B DE	See Chapter 60
8400–98	Whit 60406–504/44	B–B DE	See Chapter 61
8499–8528	GE 27577-606/44	B–B DE	See Chapter 60
8532–9	GE Var/44	B–B DE	See Chapter 60
8550	Ansaldo ?/?	4wP	Italy ca 5/45
8560–73	GE 27698–711/44	B–B DE	See Chapter 60
8574	GE 27751/44	B–B DE	Trinidad, BWI, McDill Field
8575	GE 27752/44	B–B DE	Trinidad, BWI, Baton Rouge Engineers Depot
8576	GE 27755/44	B–B DE	Trinidad, BWI, ASF Depot, Memphis
8577	GE 27754/44	B–B DE	Trinidad, BWI, ASF Depot, Memphis
8578	GE 27755/44	B–B DE	Trinidad, BWI, ASF Depot, Memphis
8579	GE 27756/44	B–B DE	Trinidad, BWI, Trinidad Rly 53
8580	GE 27757/44	B–B DE	Trinidad, BWI, Pacific Overseas Air Terminal Service Depot, Alameda
8581	GE 27758/44	B–B DE	Trinidad, BWI, Pacific Overseas Air Terminal Service Depot, Alameda
8582	GE 27759/44	B–B DE	Trinidad, BWI
8583	GE 27760/44	B–B DE	Trinidad, BWI, Europe 1945, March Field
8584	GE 27572/44	B–B DE	42in gauge, Philippines 3/45, Japan, Nagoya RR 8584
8585	GE 27573/44	B–B DE	42in gauge, Philippines 3/45, Japan, JNR DD–121
8586	GE 27761/44	B–B DE	42in gauge, Philippines 4?/45, Japan, JNR DD–122
8587	GE 27762/45	B–B DE	42in gauge, Philippines 4?/45, Japan
8588	GE 27763/45	B–B DE	42in gauge, Philippines 4?/45, Japan, JNR DD–123
8589	GE 27764/45	B–B DE	42in gauge, Japan 1946, Nagoya RR 8589
8590	GE 27765/45	B–B DE	42in gauge, Japan 1946, Manila RR 8590
8591	GE 27766/45	B–B DE	42in gauge, Japan 1946, Manila RR 8591
8592	GE 27767/45	B–B DE	42in gauge, Japan 1946, JNR DD–124
8593	GE 27768/45	B–B DE	42in gauge, Japan 1946, JNR DD–125
8600–99	A	C–C DE	See Chapter 62
(8700–89)	B	2–8–0	Cancelled order for standard 2–8–0
8800–11	Whit 60515–26/44	B–B DE	See Chapter 61
(8812–8909)	Whit	B–B DE	Cancelled order
8867–9046	L 8867–9046/45	2–8–2	SNCF 141 R1–180
(8932–9)	A	B–B DE	Cancelled order
(8960–9)	D	2–8–2	Cancelled order for standard ng 2–8–2
(8970–88)	V	0–6–0T	Cancelled order for ng 0–6–0T
(9004–49)	D	2–8–2	Cancelled order for standard ng 2–8–2
(9050–9230)	B	2–8–2	Cancelled order for standard ng 2–8–2
(9231–9306)	A	2–8–2	Cancelled order for standard ng 2–8–2
(9307–53)	P	0–6–0T	Cancelled order for ng 0–6–0T
(9354–83)	V	0–6–0T	Cancelled order for ng 0–6–0T
9400–32	Various	2–8–2	See Chapter 63
10000–86	A 73804–90/46	2–10–0	See Chapter 53
10087–99	A 75158–70/47	2–10–0	See Chapter 53
(10100–249)	A	2–10–0	Cancelled order
10250–509	A 74054–313/45	2–8–2	SNCF 141 R 181–440
10500–609	B 72514–623/45	2–10–0	See Chapter 53
(10610–759)	B	2–10–0	Cancelled order
10760–11019	B 72254–513	2–8–2	SNCF 141 R 441–700

Some time around 1951/2, a post-war series in the 6XX was used for steam locomotives at Fort Eustis, Virginia. By the time that it went into use, the Korean War was almost over, as a result of which the USA/TC had many new diesel locomotives, and the scheme died. The complete list, so far as it is known, is given below. The gaps are believed never to have been filled.

USA/TC No	Type	Maker, Works No & Date	Origin
600	2–8–0	Alco 45772/08	Ann Arbor 150 & 2170, Purchased 7/51
601	2–8–0	Alco 45773/08	Ann Arbor 151 & 2171, Purchased 7/51
602	2–8–0	Alco 45774/08	Ann Arbor 152 & 2172, Purchased 7/51
603	2–8–0	Alco 45779/08	Ann Arbor 157 & 2177, Purchased 7/51
606	2–8–0	Lima 8784/45	USA/TC 5846
607	2–8–0	Lima 8846/45	USA/TC 5187
610	2–8–0	B–L–H 75503/52	New as 610 from Baldwin-Lima Hamilton
611	2–8–0	Baldwin 69856/43	USA/TC 2628, rebuilt with Franklin valve gear /50
612	2–8–0	Baldwin 69858/43	USA/TC 2630
613	0–6–0	Alco 70429/42	USA/TC 4003
614	0–6–0	Alco 70397/42	USA/TC 4018
615	0–6–0	Alco 70400/42	USA/TC 4021
616	0–6–0	Alco 70402/42	USA/TC 4023
617	0–6–0	Alco 70414/42	USA/TC 4032
618	0–6–0	Alco 70420/42	USA/TC 4038
619	0–6–0	Alco 70456/42	USA/TC 4042
620	2–8–0	Lima 7878/42	USA/TC 6997

Plate 182 USA/TC 100 0–6–0T at Fort Eustis, Virginia, in October 1952 (Photo: R. Tourret Collection)

Plate 183 USA/TC 500 official photograph (Photo: R. Tourret Collection)

178

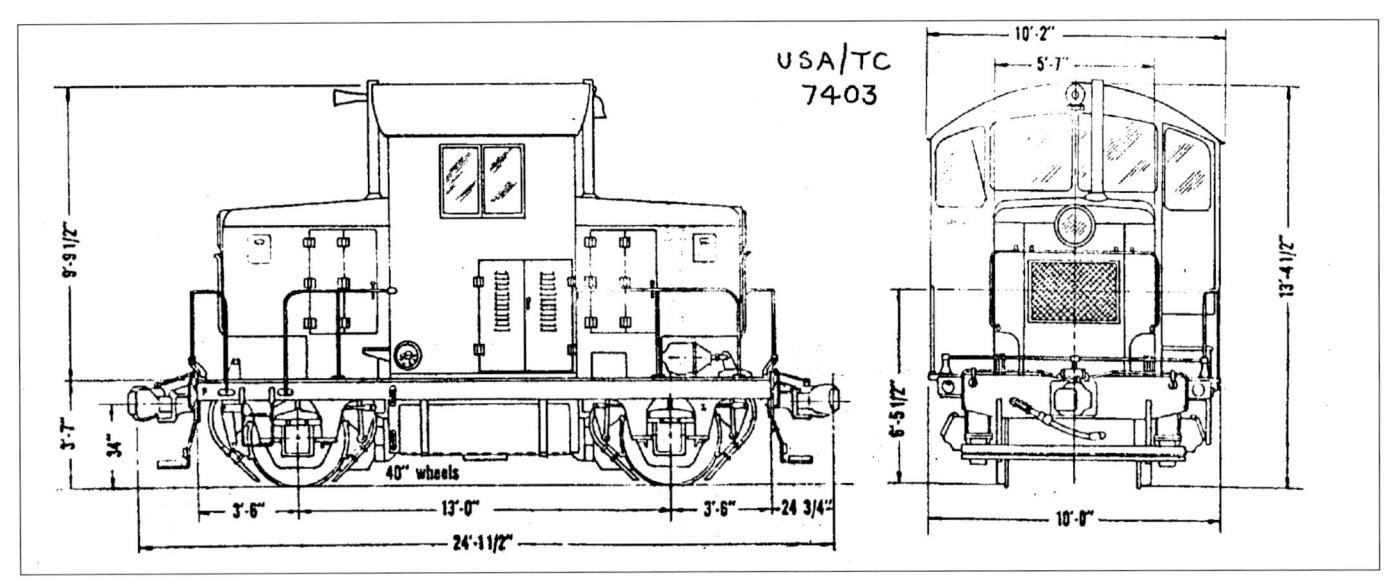

Fig 27   USA/TC 7403 EMD 4wDE

Plate 184   USA/TC 2460 Baldwin Co-Co diesel for Russia (Photo: H. L. Goldsmith Collection)

Plate 185   USA/TC 2497 60in gauge electric quencher locomotive for Russia (Photo: H. L. Goldsmith Collection)

Plate 186   USA/TC 6923 4–6–0 at Camp Stewart, Georgia, in 1942 (Photo: H. L. Goldsmith Collection)

Plate 187   USA/TC 6955 2–8–2ST in 1942 (Photo: H. L. Goldsmith Collection)

Plate 188   USA/TC 6957 2–6–2 60cm gauge at Fort Dix in April 1945 (Photo: R. Tourret Collection)

Plate 189   USA/TC 6971 2–6–0 at Fort Belvoir, Virginia, in August 1947 (Photo: C. W. Witbeck)

Plate 190 USA/TC 6979 Pershing type 2–8–0 of World War One at Oakland, California, in 1948 en route to Korea. Subsequently renumbered USA/TC 756 (Photo: H. L. Goldsmith Collection)

Plate 191 USA/TC 7069 typical General Electric B–B diesel-electric locomotive (Photo: R. Tourret Collection)

Plate 192 Illinois Ordnance Plant locomotive GO 40 (later USA/TC 7132), Alco-built (Photo: R. Tourret Collection)

Plate 193 USA/TC 7402 at work in Korea in 1955 (Photo: R. Tourret Collection)

Plate 194 USA/TC 7498, Nebraska Ordnance Plant 17094, Whitcomb-built B–B DE (Photo: H. L. Goldsmith Collection)

Plate 195 USA/TC 7110 at Fort Knox in April 1956 (Photo: H. K. Vollrath Collection)

Plate 196   USA/TC 7155 Atlas-built B–B DE (Photo: R. Tourret Collection)

Plate 197   USA/TC 7193 (Photo: R. Tourret Collection)

184

Plate 198   USA/TC 7323 at Fort Sheridan, Illinois, in June 1952 (Photo: R. Tourret Collection)

Plate 199   USA/TC 7511 (Photo: R. Tourret Collection)

Plate 200   USA/TC 7555 Davenport 4wP locomotive (Photo: Davenport Locomotive Works)

Plate 201   USA/TC 7730 at Jackson Air Base, Mississippi, in June 1947 (Photo: C. W. Witbeck)

Plate 202   USA/TC 7950 Davenport B–B DE locomotive (Photo: Davenport Locomotive Works)

Plate 203   USA/TC 8081 Whitcomb B–B DE locomotive (Photo: R. Tourret Collection)

186

Plate 204   USA/TC 8232 at Fort Dix, New Jersey, in 1945. Rebuilt from a Baldwin 60cm petrol locomotive of World War One (Photo: R. Tourret Collection)

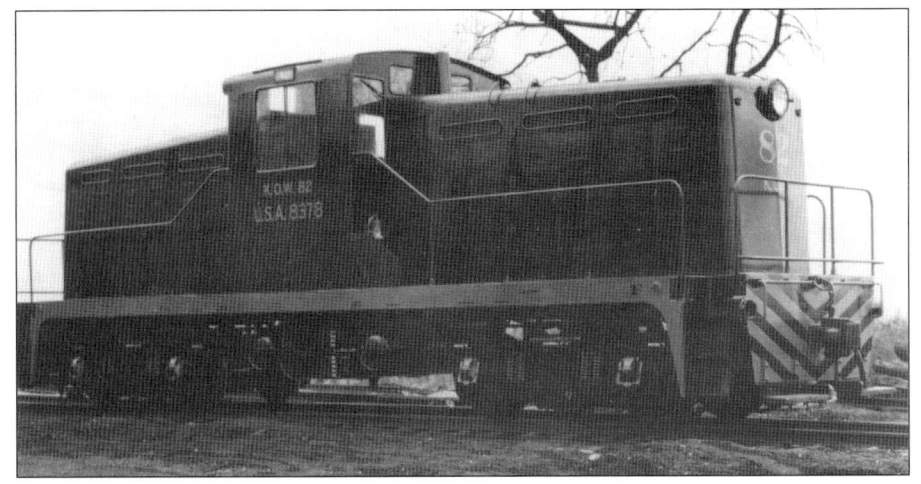

Plate 205   USA/TC 8378 Kankakee Ordnance Works 82 (Photo: R. Tourret Collection)

Plate 206 USA/TC 8586 General Electric B–B DE locomotive, 42in gauge, used in the Philippines and then Japan (Photo: H. L. Goldsmith Collection)

Chapter 46

THE CAMP CLAIBORNE LOCOMOTIVES, USA/TC 1–7, 10/1 & 20/2

In 1941, a large training establishment called Camp Claiborne was set up south of Alexandria, Louisiana, and it was decided to build a railway connecting this with Camp Polk on the Kansas City Southern Railway, about fifty miles away. The line included much of the right of way of an old railway, the Hillyer-Deutches-Edwards Logging Road, which had been abandoned long before. The line was built by No 711 ROB. It was 47½ miles long and had a maximum grade of 2% and curves of 6°. There were 25 bridges, of which the longest was the 2200ft long bridge across the Calcosieu River. The first train passed over this bridge on 19 May 1942. Yards were provided at both Camp Claiborne and Camp Polk, but an engine shed at the former camp only.

The original rolling stock consisted of seven old 4–6–0s, USA/TC 1–7, and two new 2–8–0s, USA/TC 10/1 (all oil-burners), two coaches and various freight wagons.

The seven 4–6–0s were Texas and Pacific Railroad Class D–9 locomotives which had been out of service. They were built by Alco's constituent companies and it may be mentioned that Alco as such did not exist before 1902. Prior to that the plants were independent, but afterwards they kept their own names for a while, as

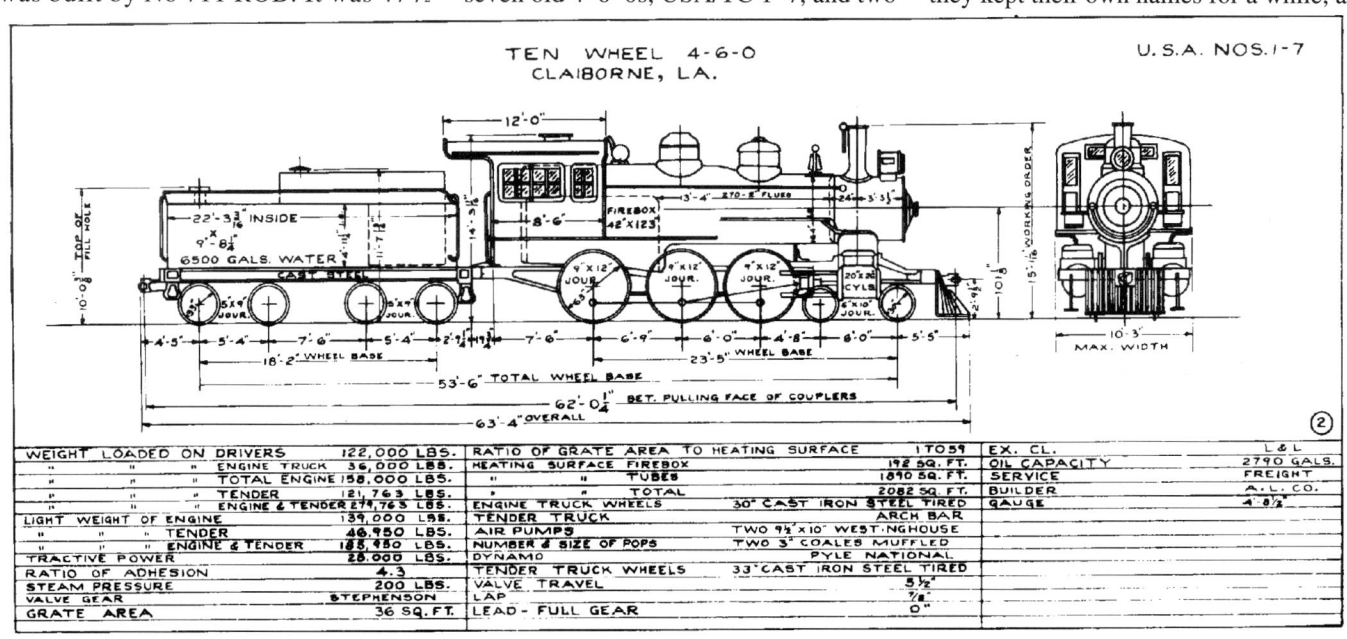

Fig 28 Camp Claiborne 4–6–0 USA/TC 1–7

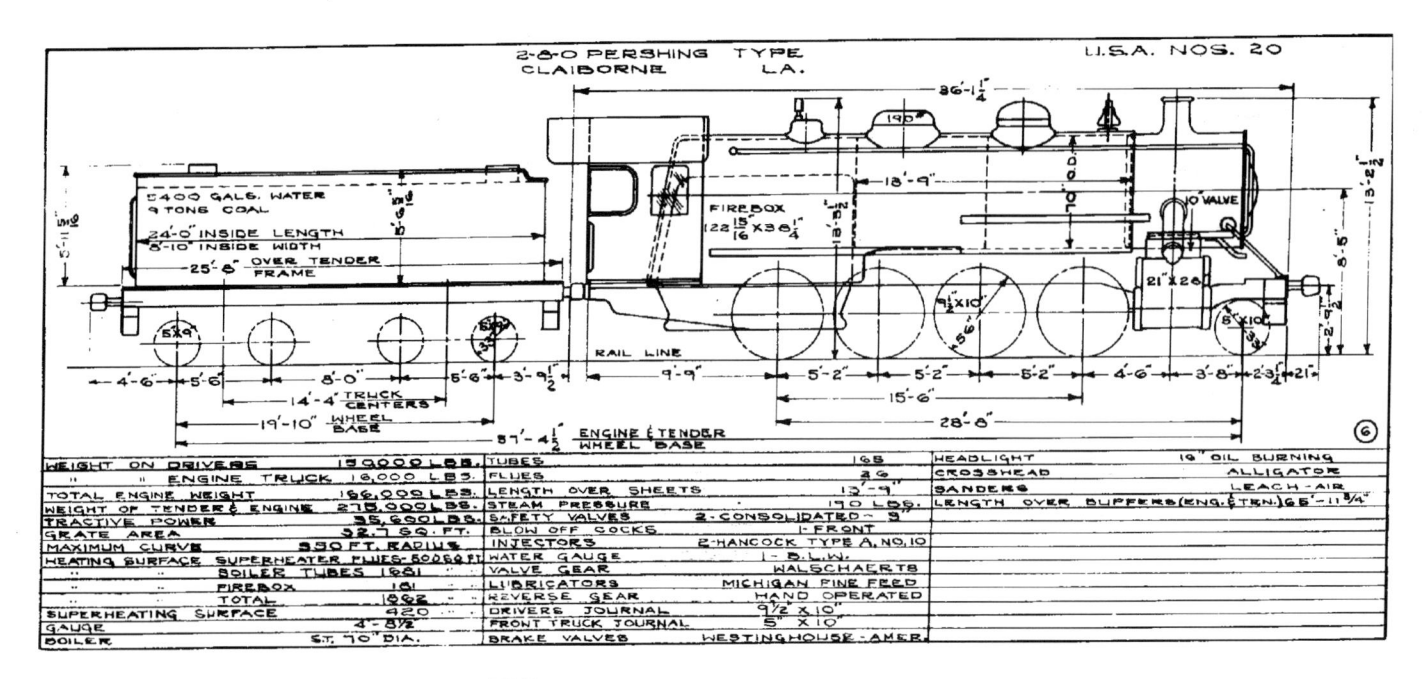

Fig 29 Camp Claiborne Pershing type 2–8–0 USA/TC 20

indicated. These engines were overhauled and painted olive green in the T&P Marshall Shops, and handed over to the USA/TC, No 1 arriving at Claiborne in December 1941 and 2–7 in January 1942. They were written off the T&P books in March 1942. The official sale date shown below is presumed to be the date that they finally settled on the price since only three of the seven had the same value on the T&P books and on two of the seven a supplemental charge was added to the book value, which probably required some discussion.

Details are given below:

USA/TC	T&P	Maker & Works No	Sold date
1	285	Cooke 2688/01	6 Dec 41
2	287	Cooke 2690/01	14 Jan 42
3	357	Alco-Rogers 41496/06	19 Jan 42
4	314	Alco-Cooke 26140/02	25 Jan 42
5	301	Alco-Cooke 25960/02	1 Feb 42
6	310	Alco-Cooke 26132/02	10 Feb 42
7	333	Alco-Cooke 28489/03	5 Mar 42

Plate 208 USA/TC 2 4–6–0 at Camp Caliborne in July 1942 (Photo: R. Tourret Collection)

They were delivered with "US Corps of Engineers" painted on the sand domes but later they became USA/TC property. They were sold or scrapped in 1947.

The new 2–8–0s were USA/TC 10/1, which Lima built 7881/2 in 1942 as USA/TC S.159 class. The design was a typical American steam 2–8–0, apparently very similar to USA/TC 6994–9 discussed in Chapter 56. A feed-water heater was mounted in front of the boiler but this was probably removed later. It was certainly removed from 11 by the time that it was renumbered 6987. USA/TC 10 subsequently went to the Alaska Railroad as ARR 503, while USA/TC 11 remained with the USA/TC. It went to Fort Eustis around 1952 and was cut open for instructional purposes.

The original stock was soon augmented by two old 2–8–0s, USA/TC 20/2. The former was a Pershing 2–8–0, originally US Army 396 of World War 1, built by Baldwin 47032 in 1917. Its movements from 1918 to 1942 are not known

Plate 207 USA/TC 1 4–6–0 at Camp Claiborne in 1941 (Photo: C. W. Witbeck)

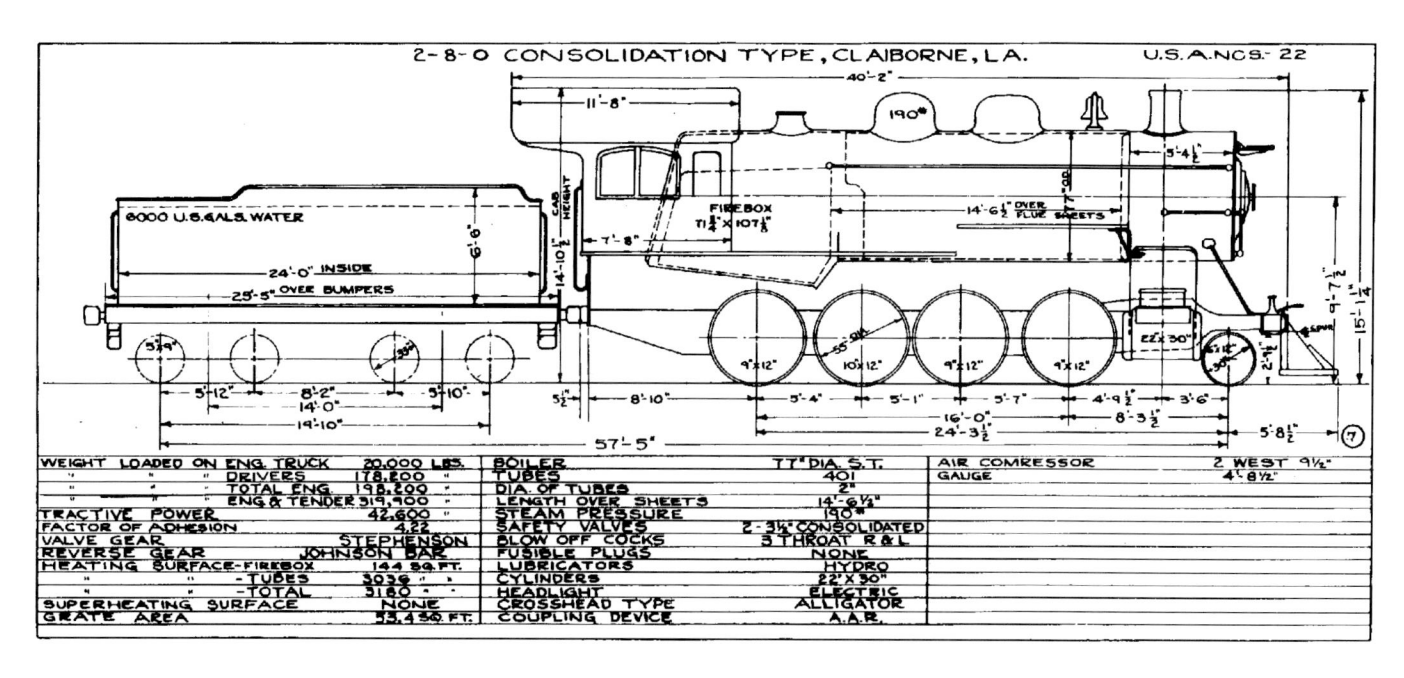

Fig 30   Camp Claiborne Consolidation type 2–8–0 USA/TC 22

but it appeared on the Claiborne line by 1942. USA/TC 22 was built by Alco.

Dimensions, USA/TC 10/1

Cylinders, two outside	21in x 26in
Wheel diameter, coupled	4ft 9in
leading	2ft 9in
Wheelbase, coupled	15ft 6in
total	23ft 3in
Heating surface,	
tubes & flues	1781sq ft
firebox & arch tubes	156sq ft
total evaporative	1937sq ft
superheater	467sq ft
combined total	2404sq ft
Grate area	43sq ft
Boiler pressure	210psi
Tractive effort at 85% BP	35907lb
Adhesive weight	72 ton
Weight of engine in working order	80 tons 14cwt

Plate 209   USA/TC 10 2–8–0 at Camp Claiborne in July 1942 (Photo: R. Tourret Collection)

Plate 210   USA/TC 22 2–8–0 at Camp Claiborne in 1942 (Photo: R. Tourret Collection)

Plate 211   USA/TC 10 Pershing type 2–8–0 in a spot of bother on the Camp Claiborne and Polk RR around 1943/4 (Photo: H. L. Goldsmith Collection)

Chapter 47

STANDARD USA/TC "MacARTHUR" NARROW-GAUGE 2–8–2s, USA/TC 3000–29, 130–249, 257–890, 4281–4312

These 2–8–2 locomotives were designed by the American Locomotive Company for the United States Army as Class S118, and were suitable for use on the majority of metre and 3ft 6in gauge lines throughout the world. Although the design was developed by Alco, the engines were built also by Baldwin Locomotive Works, Davenport-Besler Corporation, H. K. Porter and Vulcan Iron Works.

The USA/TC serial numbers, makers, works numbers and year built are given below:–

USA/TC No	Maker, Works No & Date	
3000–29	A 70328–57	1942
130–59	A 70358–87	1943
160–9	A 70494–503	1943
170–9	A 70484–93	1943
180–9	A 70504–13	1943
190–249	B 69425–84	1943
257–316	A 70689–748	1943
317–46	B 69742–71	1943
347–73	D 2551–77	1943
374–91	V 4504–21	1943
392–401	P 7634–43	1943
402–16	P 7619–33	1943
417–73	A 70889–945	1943
474–505	A 71009–40	1943
506–40	B 69868–902	1943
541–61	A 71335–55	1943
562–7	A 71356–61	1943?
568–614	A 71362–408	1944
615–39	A 73056–80	1945
(640–60	B –	–)
661–763	B 70187–289	1944
764–88	B 71401–25	1945
(789–810	D 2648–69	1944)
811–50	D 2670–2709	1944
851–88	V 4554–91	1944
889/90	V 4592/3	1945

USA/TC 640–60 and 789–810 were cancelled orders.

There seems to have been some confusion regarding the numbering of the "MacArthurs" because the first thirty were numbered 3000–29, and the subsequent ones continued from 130 upwards. Since the majority of these locomotives were constructed for service in British spheres of influence, including the first ones built, it seems probable that originally these engines were intended to fill the 3XXX sequence in the British WD series. After the first thirty engines had been built, the US authorities presumably decided that they would use their own USA/TC series and subsequent locomotives therefore continued at 130, leaving 100–29 in the series vacant for possible future renumbering of 3000–29. In 1945, USA/TC 764–88, which were stored at

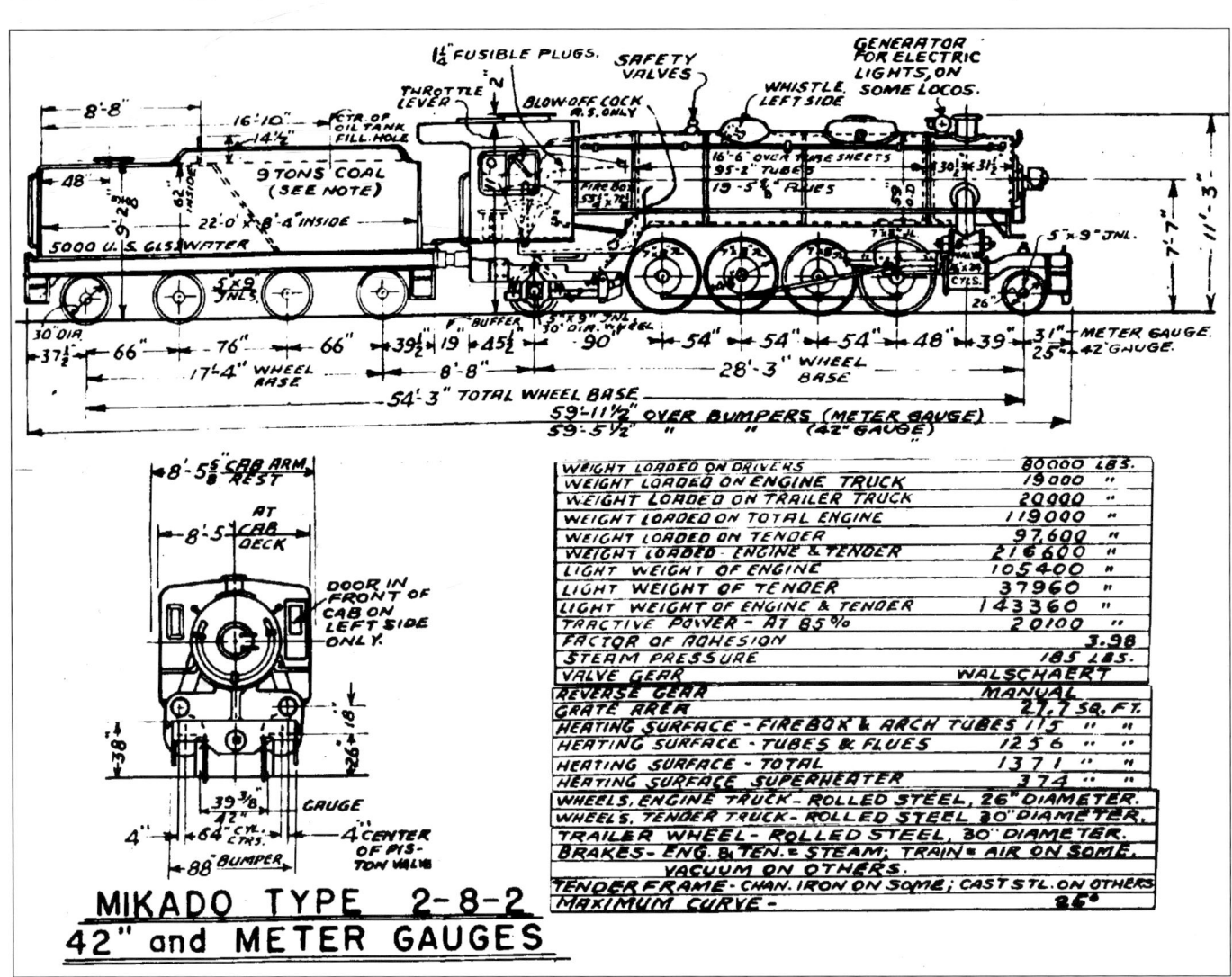

Fig 31   Standard USA/TC "MacArthur" narrow-gauge 2–8–2

Plate 212   USA/TC 3017 official photograph, Alco-built (Photo: R. Tourret Collection)

West Yermo TC Depot in December 1945, were renumbered USA/TC 4281–4305 in order.

These locomotives were probably the nearest approach to a "universal" locomotive that had yet been built, and it is doubtful if any other single design has ever been used on so many different railways or in so many different countries. To achieve this the maximum axle-load was limited to nine tons to permit them to operate over lightly-laid tracks, and their external dimensions were sufficiently small to enable them to clear most of the more restricted loading gauges. The proportions of the design were excellent, with ample boiler capacity and well designed cylinders and valve gear. As the locomotives were primarily intended for military use, the fittings were as simple as possible, and as the life of the locomotives was expected to be fairly short, refinements in detail design were omitted.

The differences between the locomotives of different gauges were not very great, but conversion from one gauge to another after the locomotives were completed was not anticipated, and no special provision was made for this.

The design could be adapted to suit most types of drawgear, including side buffers with screw couplings, central buffers combined with a hook, central knuckle couplers, and various other types of automatic centre couplers. The brake gear could be varied also to suit the requirements of the various railways, engines fitted with vacuum train pipes being fitted with steam brakes and an automatic steam brake valve, while those having Westinghouse train pipes had Westinghouse engine and tender brakes also. Provision was made for the use of either coal or oil fuel; equipment for using oil could be fitted without any major alteration being required.

The design was typically American, with bar frames, two outside cylinders with Walschaerts valve gear, and a large high-pitched boiler with a round-top firebox and a wide shallow grate. The cab and side platforms were carried from the boiler, which had a short chimney of the usual American stove-pipe design. Other typical American features were the sandbox on top of the boiler, the whistle at the side of the dome and the safety valves mounted side by side on the back ring of the boiler barrel. The inner firebox was of steel, with welded joints, and contained two arch tubes. The superheater was of conventional design and the smokebox had self-cleaning baffle plates. To suit the badly-laid tracks over which the locomotives were to be capable of operating, the spring gear was compensated throughout. The large cab had sliding side windows and provision was made for ample ventilation. The tender was of simple design, carried on two cast-steel four-wheeled bogies, and the tank, when viewed from above, was U-shaped.

Owing to the preoccupation of British locomotive builders with other work, this American design was adopted for use on the 3ft 6in and metre gauge lines within British theatres of war for which the WD Garratts were too large or otherwise unsuitable. They were commonly known as the "MacArthur" class, particularly by the British authorities. They were also used in various American theatres of war.

North Africa

A number of the metre-gauge "MacArthurs" were used in North Africa. The original estimate of requirements for the campaign included 175 of these 2–8–2s. By March 1943, it was possible to reassess the situation, and requirements were reduced to sixty locomotives. These appear to have been USA/TC 144–50/2/4/6/8–69 and 257–94. Locomotives were received at Oran knocked down in crates. They were assembled at Sidi Mabrouk and then despatched by well wagon to the metre-gauge track at Ouled Rhamoun in Algeria. Twenty-five were erected by July 1943, plus another seven in October 1943, making thirty-two in all. Owing to the end of the campaign in North Africa, no more were needed and since metre-gauge locomotives were not needed in Europe, the rest were reshipped to India without having been erected in North Africa.

It is not clear if they were allocated to the any particular railway at first, but USA/TC 144/54/6/8/9 were noted at Ouled Rhamoun in June 1943 operating on the line thence into Tunisia, and all of

Plate 213   USA/TC 240 official photograph, Baldwin-built (Photo: R. Tourret Collection)

these eventually became the property of the CFT. USA/TC 154 was the first narrow-gauge 2–8–2 to enter Tunis. In mid-July 1943, USA/TC 145/62/7 were noted at Ouled Rhamoun, USA/TC 147/63/6 between Ouled Rhamoun and Ain Beida and USA/TC 152/68 between Kasserine and Sousse in Tunisia.

In 1943, twelve "MacArthurs", USA/TC 144/8–50/4/6/8/9/63 and 277–9, were taken over by the CFT. Eight more, USA/TC 615–22, were obtained in 1946 and were delivered new, direct from the United States. These engines appear to have been numbered CFT 19.901–20 originally and to have been subsequently renumbered 141.901–20, in the same order. The first twelve were 141.901–12, while the second batch was 141.913–20. Nine of the locomotives, 141.912–20, were converted to burn heavy fuel oil. In July 1961, eighteen were withdrawn, leaving two in store for emergencies.

The Algerian Railways (CFA) acquired six "MacArthurs", USA/TC 145/7/61/6–8, in 1943 which were renumbered 141 XU 1 to 6 in order, when formally taken over in 1946. They were withdrawn and scrapped when the railway was turned over to diesel operation. Other engines which had been used on the system by the USA/TC were sent on to India, but it is believed that USA/TC 152 was sunk en route.

Indian State Railways

By far the greatest number of "MacArthur" locomotives were delivered to the Indian railways, the first of them being delivered early in 1943. They were shipped in parts and re-erected at the shops at Ajmer (Bombay, Baroda and Central India Railway), Jodhpur (Jodhpur Railway), Goraghpur (Oudh Tirhut Railway), Saidpur and Kanchrapara (Bengal & Assam Railway). A few were also erected by the North Western Railway at Karachi "Field Workshops". They were all metre gauge and were provided with combined centre buffers and couplers, vacuum ejectors and train pipes, and steam brakes on the engine. The locomotives delivered to India were USA/TC 3020–9, 151/3/5/7/70–89, 201–15/36–49/95–9, 300–99, 400–36/57–95, 506–30/41–61/8–85/91–6, 603–7/61–6/83/6/8/90–9, 700–7/12–26/36–40.

The majority of those delivered up to the end of 1944 were used on the Bengal and Assam Railway and were numbered in two series. One hundred and ten of them received numbers 3–112 in the WD (India) series, and the remainder had BAR numbers between 801 and 1104. On arrival in India in crates, they nearly all

Plate 214 USA/TC 272 loaded on standard-gauge wagons somewhere in North Africa in 1943 (Photo: US Army)

carried US Army numbers in white stencilled figures on the cab sides and on the back of the tender. In addition, this number was shown on one of the builder's plates, that normally attached to the right-hand side of the smokebox. This plate, however, was occasionally lost or omitted on re-erection. In most cases, engines were allowed to go into traffic with these numbers only and the WD (India) or BAR numbers were added on arrival at the sheds to which they were allocated. A few arrived in India with WD stencilled on the cab sides in place of the US Army number.

The WD (India) locomotives carried the WD number on the cab sides with the letters "WD" above it and/or on the tender sides. The BAR locomotives carried the BAR number in large figures on the cab sides, with the Indian State Railways classification "MAWD" (metre gauge, American War Department) painted below it, and large initials "B&A" on the tender sides. The number was usually painted on the back of the tender also.

The title of the Bengal Assam Railway was 'Bengal and Assam Railway" before 1946, and the "&" was deleted from the tenders after the name was changed. There were various styles of painting and lettering which differed in detail, and the locomotives operated by the US Army Transportation Corps were often smartly lined out in red. The US Army number was usually painted in a small oval panel at the bottom of the cab side in addition to the large BAR number already mentioned. The BAR shed code was normally shown also at the bottom of the cab.

All the WD (India) series were allocated to BAR sheds in 1943/4, as were most of the remainder, but from about April 1945, the war in Burma being nearly won, few more allocations were made to this railway. The BAR had, however, allocated numbers to 304 "MacArthurs", 801–1104, but some of these never arrived on the BAR and the numbers were not used.

In May 1944, a number of "MacArthur" class locomotives, USA/TC 146/60/2/4/5/9, 257–76/80–94, were shipped to India from North Africa. They were surplus to the requirements of the railways in that theatre of war, and many had not been erected in Africa. Some alterations had to be made to them on arrival in India owing to the original drawgear being unsuitable. Many, if not all of them, were dealt with at the Ajmer shops of the BBCI and they were allocated to the BAR, OTR, JR and BBCI for service. Those allocated to the OTR appear to have been renumbered in April 1945 as follows. USA/TC 273/6/80/1/4/7/9/91/3 to OTR 460–8 in order. These engines were noteworthy in being neatly painted and fully lined out, with standard OTR transfers on the tender, in contrast to the majority of the "MacArthurs" in India. Those remaining on the BBCI do not appear to have been put into traffic until 1946, as will be described later.

In view of the large numbers of these locomotives which were renumbered into WD (Indian) and BAR stock, lists are given here for convenience to enable the USA/TC numbers to be readily determined. The numbers given in brackets are those allocated but not used.

At the end of 1944 and during 1945, new locomotives of this class arriving in India were erected at the South India Railway shops at Golden Rock, Trichinopoly. They ran trials on the SIR and then were concentrated at Villupuram, near Madras, in store for shipment to South East Asia Command.

The SEAC locomotives, most if not all of which passed through Golden Rock and many of which were stored at Villupuram, were USA/TC 586–90/7–602/79–82/4/5/7/9, 708–11/27–35/41–3, 811–50. It may be mentioned that little of India was included in SEAC and these locomotives were destined for Burma, Malaya, Siam and elsewhere. USA/TC 587–90, however, were loaned to the SIR for trial in December 1944, but eventually rejoined the remainder and were transferred to Malaya and Burma. These SEAC engines were not renumbered but retained their USA/TC numbers on the cab, with the initials "WD" on the tender in most cases.

A number of them, USA/TC 681, 811/3/5/6/8/24/6–8/30/1/4/42, were not required by SEAC and were loaned to the Indian Railway Board. All of these were allocated to the Madras and Southern Mahratta railway, where they were noted in service, still carrying their USA/TC numbers, in 1945.

In 1945, six "MacArthurs", USA/TC 438/42/3/9/51/3, were transferred to India from Iraq, these differing from the others in having oil-fuel equipment and being numbered in the main WD series 73032/6/7/43/5/7. They were eventually taken into stock by the SIR, by whom they were renumbered by the addition of the prefix "WD" to their USA/TC numbers. Oil firing was retained for these locomotives.

About the end of 1945, it was found that there was a surplus of engines on the BAR, and many of these were transferred to other Indian lines, or were sent to Burma, Malaya or Siam, while others which had been allocated to the BAR, and had been allotted BAR numbers, were diverted elsewhere.

In 1946 and 1947, the BBCI took into traffic 67 "MacArthurs", some of which had been under repair in its own workshops and had not been in traffic previously, while others had been in use on other Indian railways. Ten of these, USA/TC 270/88/71, 169/2, 268, 309, 661, 201 and 426, were renumbered BBCI 917–26 respectively. The others at first retained their original numbers in the WD (India), BAR or USA/TC series, but then were renumbered BBCI 927–79/83–6. One engine, USA/TC 270, which became BBCI 917 in the BBCI series, was transferred to Siam in May 1946 and was replaced by USA/TC 314 (BAR 835) which became BBCI 917.

During the year ending 31 March 1947, the Indian Railway Board purchased 351 "MacArthurs" from the Directorate of Disposals. Some excess locomotives were taken over subse-

WD (Indian)

	0	1	2	3	4	5	6	7	8	9
0X	–	–	–	3021	3022	3020	3023	3024	3025	3026
1X	3027	3028	3029	178	173	180	172	176	170	183
2X	177	171	181	182	179	174	175	151	157	189
3X	153	155	184	187	186	185	188	241	243	242
4X	246	249	247	244	245	248	236	237	238	239
5X	240	207	208	209	201	205	206	202	203	204
6X	295	296	297	298	300	301	302	299	213	214
7X	215	324	325	327	328	329	303	304	305	306
8X	311	312	313	352	354	356	404	406	407	408
9X	409	348	349	350	351	489	492	493	511	494
10X	495	527	528	360	412	413	415	353	355	357
11X	359	392	410	–	–	–	–	–	–	–

BAR

	0	1	2	3	4	5	6	7	8	9
80X	–	210	211	212	323	326	319	320	321	322
81X	315	316	317	318	331	334	336	332	335	423
82X	422	467	468	337	339	459	465	338	457	466
83X	461	345	462	463	458	314	340	346	460	464
84X	341	342	343	344	484	521	523	486	522	487
85X	485	470	471	488	490	514	516	491	469	425
86X	472	473	333	428	330	430	431	427	429	432
87X	307	308	309	310	417	418	419	420	421	433
88X	434	435	436	474	475	476	424	426	512	513
89X	517	519	518	477	478	481	482	483	506	507
90X	508	509	510	515	525	520	524	526	402	479
91X	480	374	376	361	529	411	414	347	416	403
92X	405	(164)	(165)	(259)	(262)	(270)	(273)	(276)	(281)	(284)
93X	(289)	(287)	(290)	(291)	292	(293)	(294)	(146)	(169)	(258)
94X	(268)	(269)	(271)	(162)	267	282	283	257	260	263
95X	266	275	(280)	285	286	(288)	541	542	543	544
96X	545	551	552	553	554	555	556	557	558	559
97X	560	546	547	548	549	550	383	385	381	386
98X	363	365	366	378	375	379	395	398	400	530
99X	661	358	362	364	377	393	(160)	(274)	(272)	(261)
100X	382	388	391	396	399	401	394	397	662	663
101X	390	575	380	384	389	387	571	574	579	580
102X	568	569	572	573	577	578	664	665	666	585
103X	591	592	593	594	595	596	367	368	369	686
104X	688	694	695	(264)	(265)	570	700	701	702	703
105X	704	705	706	707	(735)	603	604	606	607	721
106X	722	740	581	582	583	(608)	(609)	(610)	561	576
107X	(829)	(835)	(836)	370	371	372	373	690	691	692
108X	693	683	696	697	698	699	584	(733)	(734)	(687)
109X	717	(689)	(611)	(612)	(613)	(614)	712	713	714	715
110X	716	723	724	725	726	–	–	–	–	–

Plate 215   USA/TC 581 at Schenectady, New York (Photo: R. Tourret Collection)

quently by the Indian Railway Board, as a revised total of 358 was officially given in the first half of 1947.

By 15 August 1947, the date of the partition of India, there were 168 "MacArthur" locomotives on the BAR. On this date, these locomotives were divided between the three railways into which the BAR was split up; 16 to the Oudh Tirhut Railway which incorporated the western metre-gauge section of the BAR into its existing system, 65 to the Assam Railway which was a new railway incorporating the northern part of the BAR, and 87 to the Eastern Bengal Railway which was another new railway formed to incorporate the remainder of the BAR which came within the Dominion of Pakistan, later renamed the Pakistan Eastern Railway.

The OTR's stock of "MacArthurs', including ones it already had, consisted of USA/TC 3021/5, 153/83, 204/6/14/36/40/4/5/61/4/5/9, 317/20/2/31/2/6/40/6/50/5/7, 404/62/8/90, 522/7/8, 686/8/92/5, 700/3/7/12–4/6/24, plus OTR 460–8 already referred to. The 65 which passed to the Assam Railway were USA/TC 3024, 155/7/75/88, 242/99, 301/15/35/8/42/4/59/61/70/3/4/6/85/6/91/3, 402/10/4/8–21/5/7/34/69/79–82/6/7/93/4, 506/8–10/5/7/9/20/6/52/4/69/75/9/82/3/91, 690, 702/4/5/25/6. The EBR locomotives were USA/TC 3020/2/3/6/8, 151/70/4/7–80/2/4/9, 208/10/1/3/5/37/8/47–9, 302/4/6–8/16/25/6/34/43/7/9/56/8/60/9/77/82/8/9/92, 406/12/3/5/6/24/31/3/59–61/3–6/72/3/5/95, 514/6/29/42/3/50/1/3/6–60/94, 603/4/6/96/9, 715/23. Actually, the EBR say that they received 86, not 87, and the disposal of USA/TC 472 (BAR 860) is not certain.

After the partition, ex-BAR engines continued to carry their original BAR or WD numbers. In this connection it may be mentioned that locomotives from the BAR which were transferred to Siam were all lettered "BA", whether they carried BAR or WD numbers, so that it would seem that no distinction was made between the WD and BAR locomotives after the end of the war, although they retained their original numbers. On the Assam Railway, the "MacArthurs" were known as Class WD and this designation was probably used elsewhere in India where the ISR classification MAWD was not used.

Ten "MacArthurs" were transferred to the Mysore State Railway from the BAR. Four of the class, USA/TC 380, 411, 512/41, were noted at Bangalore during the latter half of 1947, working on the MSR. These retained their BAR numbers and livery, and USA/TC 411 retained the BAR lettering also. Three later went to the BBCI, while the other seven became MSR 171–7.

In addition to the six "MacArthurs" from Iraq, the South Indian Railway also acquired twenty engines of the class from the BAR before partition. These were USA/TC 3027/9, 171, 202/3/9/41/6/96/7, 403/32/70/7/83, 507/18/24/45 and 693. These were renumbered by the SIR by the addition of the prefix "WD" in front of their BAR or WD numbers, thus differing from those received from Iraq, for which the USA/TC numbers were used. These were included in the 358 locomotives mentioned above. The SIR later received ten more of the class from the Assam Railway, the last of which was transferred in 1949. These were USA/TC 370/93, 421/69/82, 517/26, 690 and 702/5.

By the time of Zoning, Western Railway had 67 locomotives with the BBCI numbers 917–79/83–6, Southern Railway had 34 engines, Northern Railway had ten engines, North Eastern Railway had 81 and the Northeast Frontier Railway had 79, making a total of 271. These were USA/TC 3021/4/5/7/9, 146/53/5/7/60/2/9/71–3/5/6/81/3/6–8, 201–7/9/14/36/9–46/58/9/61/4/5/8/9–74/6/80–4/7–93/5–9, 300/1/3/9–15/7/8/20/2–4/7/30–2/5–8/40–2/4–6/8/50/2–5/7/9/61–3/5/6/70–6/9/83/5–7/91/3/4/7, 400–4/7/9/10/4/7–22/5–8/30/2/4/5/8/42/3/9/51/3/7/8/62/7–9/70/4/6–90/3/4, 506–11/3/5/7–24/6–8/44/5/52/4/5/68–70/2–5/7–80/2–5/91–3/5, 661–3/6/81/6/8/90–5/7, 700/2–7/12–4/6/24–6/36 and 811/3/5/6/8/24/6–8/30/1/4/42 plus two others not known.

In 1948, a further thirty-three locomotives, almost identical with the original "MacArthurs", were supplied by Baldwin to the Indian Government Railways. These were Baldwin 73990–74022 and were presumably built specially for the IGR. Assam Railway took ten, Assam 1–10 being Baldwin 73990/1/5/4, 74004/2, 73992/9 and 74000/6 in order. The BBCI took 18, BBCI 989–1006 being Baldwin 74003, 73993, 74001/7, 73998/6, 74009/8/5, 73997 and 74010–4/6/5/21 in order, and the OTR took the remaining five Baldwin 74017–20/2.

Assam Railway 1–10 became NFR 1801–10 in order, BBCI 989–95/7/8 and 1000 became NFR 1811–7/9/20/2 in order, BBCI 996/9 and 1001–6 became WR 1818/21/3–8 in order and the OTR engines became NFR 1829–33 in Baldwin works numbers order. In the All-India renumbering, WR 1818/21/3–8 became 1567–74 and NFR 1801–17/9/20/2/9–33 became 1779–1803 in order.

By the time of the All-India renumbering of 1957/8, there were 271 ex-wartime WD 2–8–2s, plus the 33 postwar 2–8–2s. The general scheme was to allot number blocks according to the different railways on which they were running in 1958. The Western Railway was given 1500–66 for WD and 1567–74 for postwar locomotives, the Southern Railway 1575–1608 for WD locomotives, the Northern Railway 1609–18 for WD locomotives, the North Eastern Railway 1619–99 for WD locomotives and the Northeast Frontier Railway 1700–78 for WD locomotives and 1779–1803 for postwar locomotives. Later, the 1609–18 series moved to the North Eastern Railway and some of the 1619–99 series were transferred to the NFR. Full details of the renumbering follow, although it should be mentioned that many boilers and other parts have now been interchanged.

By 1975, there were 76 on the NER, 116 on the NFR, 34 on the SR and 75 on the WR, while presumably three had been withdrawn.

PW indicates post-war construction locomotives, dealt with elsewhere. Four of the six unknowns are 270, 391 and 527/91.

As stated earlier, 86 (or possibly 87) engines came to Pakistan. By 1978, Bangladesh had 69, the allocation being 13 at Chittagong, 28 at Dacca and another 28 at Lalmanirhat.

Burma Railways

Owing to the great damage incurred by the rolling stock of the Burma Railways during the Japanese occupation, locomotives were needed as soon as part of the railway was freed, and a large number of "MacArthurs" were sent to Burma in addition to a number of standard Indian types. The first three to be sent were despatched from India in the "Completely knocked down" condition, and were carried on tank transporters over the Kohima-Imphal-Tamu road to Kalewa. They were then loaded on to barges and were taken down to Chindwin river and up the Irrawaddy to Myingyan, a distance of 210 miles. At Myingyan they were erected in the engine shed and were put into service on the Myingyan-Thazi-Tatkou section of BR, the first part of the line to be reopened. These three engines, USA/TC 733–5, were allocated BAR Nos 1087/8/54 respectively, but it is doubtful if these numbers were carried, since it seems probable that these engines were never erected in India.

Fifty-seven "MacArthurs" in all were sent to Burma, 35 of them on WD account and 22 to the requirements of Lord Killearn's Commission through civil channels. There were USA/TC 212/60/3/6/7/75/85, 321/67/8/78/81/4/95/6/8, 436, 576/88–90/8, 600–2/5/64/5/85/8?, 708–10/27/33–5/42 and 812/4/7/9–23/5/32/3/43–50. All of them came from India, those on WD account having been erected by the SIR and shipped in the erected condition from Madras, without

All India	0	1	2	3	4	5	6	7	8	9
150X	314	288	271	169	162	268	309	661	201	426
151X	663	584	666	323	318	467	205	592	387	736
152X	428	186	662	337	330	409	365	363	397	400
153X	523	239	366	290	274	298	593	595	422	362
154X	691	272	521	258	295	243	513	345	585	372
155X	430	511	830	834	697	826	570	442	443	842
156X	438	?	176	469	421	517	518	PW	PW	PW
157X	PW	PW	PW	PW	PW	3027	3029	171	241	209
158X	202	297	407	259	449	451	453	681	811	813
159X	815	816	818	824	827	828	831	470	432	483
160X	524	403	544	545	379	401	702	705	706	203
161X	296	477	342	236	?	478	690	246	526	181
162X	153	245	240	206	300	303	352	404	350	489
163X	527	353	355	359	146	160	?	?	?	?
164X	261	264	265	269	322	317	331	336	332	338
165X	457	346	484	487	485	488	310	419	435	474
166X	476	507	374	273	276	281	284	289	287	291
167X	292	293	282	283	554	383	375	393	574	580
168X	572	573	577	578	688	695	703	704	707	582
169X	370	371	373	692	713	714	716	724	725	726
170X	3021	3024	3025	173	172	183	175	157	155	187
171X	188	242	244	207	204	301	299	214	324	327
172X	311	312	313	354	348	493	494	528	357	410
173X	320	315	335	468	462	458	340	341	344	486
174X	522	490	425	427	417	418	420	434	519	481
175X	482	506	508	509	510	515	520	402	479	480
176X	376	361	414	280	552	555	385	386	394	575
177X	579	568	569	686	694	700	583	693	712	PW

Plate 216 USA/TC 876 at work in the Philippine Islands (Photo: H. L. Goldsmith Collection)

having been used in India, whilst most of the remainder had previously been in service on the Indian railways. They were allocated Nos 1001–57 in the BR list, as follows (see table opposite):

When first renumbered, USA/TC 589 became BR 552 following a sequence of YD class 2–8–2 locomotives, but shortly afterwards was renumbered BR 1005. Their BR classification was "D" and several of them which were put into service while the railway was under military control, were named after various Army, Corps and Divisional Commanders whose units had served in Burma. These nameplates were of polished brass, curved in shape, and were mounted on brackets on the side platform. The names included the following:

BR	0	1	2	3	4	5	6	7	8	9
100X	–	733	734	735	588	589	590	598	600	601
101X	602	605	685	708	709	710	817	819	820	821
102X	822	843	844	849	850	812	814	823	825	833
103X	845	846	847	848	742	576	727	832	378	395
104X	212	321	436	267	263	381	398	664	665	368
105X	688?	260	266	275	285	396	384	367	–	–

1001	"Snelling"
1002	"Rees"
1003	"Cowan"
1004	"Nicholson"
1005	"Slim"
1006	"Roberts"
1007	"Warren"
1008	"Messervy"
1009	"Stopford"
1011	"Evans"
1012	"Gracey"
1013	"Wingate"
1015	"Festing"
1016	"Stockwell"
1018	"Dyer"
1019	"Scoones"
1021	"Symes"
1023	"Dimaline"

While the railway was under military control, the tenders were lettered "WD" and the engine number was prefixed "WD" but after the civil authorities took charge on 1 January 1946, the tenders were lettered "BR" and the "WD" prefix to the number was discontinued. The class was used on all types of trains on the Rangoon-Mandalay and Rangoon-Prome lines. Their performance was good although they were less popular with their crews than the considerably larger British 2–8–2 locomotives of the YD class.

Malayan Railway

Twenty-eight "MacArthur" class locomotives USA/TC 364/99, 561/86/7/97/9, 607/79/80/2–4, 717/8/21/2/30/1/7–40 and 837–41 were transferred from India to the Malayan Railway between November 1945 and April 1946. Most of them had been erected by SIR and had been at Villupuram dump before being sent to Malaya, but USA/TC 683, 717/21/2/40 had previously been in service on the BAR, USA/TC 683 and 740 having been erected by the Jodhpur Railway. The last four to arrive, USA/TC 364/99, 561 and 607, had been on the BAR for some time before being transferred to Malaya, and these carried their BAR numbers on arrival, all the others being numbered in the USA/TC series. Eventually the class was renumbered in accordance with the system introduced by the Malayan Railway after the war, their numbers being 901.01–28. The locomotives formed the 901 class, the "90" being the general class number and "1" representing the first batch of the class.

The USA/TC numbers were as follows:

MR	0	1	2	3	4	5	6	7	8	9
901.0X	–	586	587	597	599	679	680	682	683	684
901.1X	717	718	721	722	730	731	737	738	739	740
901.2X	837	838	839	840	841	364	399	607	561	–

When they first arrived in Malaya these engines worked nearly all the traffic, both passenger and freight, but after the arrival of the "564" class 4–6–2 locomotives built by the North British Locomotive Co in 1946/7, they were largely relegated to freight traffic only. There were then more locomotives of this class than could be fully employed and in 1948, eight of them were transferred to the Tanganyika section of the East African Railways and Harbours, whilst a further eight of them followed in 1949. A further one, MR 901.08, was withdrawn in July 1947 as a result of accident damage. The remaining locomotives were then used on the Prai-Kelantan through goods trains running via South Siam but when the East Coast line of the Malayan Railway was reopened, this service was no longer required. These eleven locomotives were still in stock in March 1965, however. Some were scrapped in 1971, the remainder being moved to the Tapah area.

Royal State Railways of Siam (Thailand)

Sixty-eight "MacArthur" locomotives were supplied to the Royal State Railways of Siam, these being divided into three batches. One batch consisted of twenty engines which had first been to India and then had been reallocated to the Malayan Railway, but which were surplus to that system's requirements. They were shipped, in parts, from India to Fort Swettenham in Malaya in August 1946 and were erected at the Sentul workshops of the Malayan Railway between August and November of that year. They were subsequently despatched by rail to Siam, through running being possible between the two systems. The USA/TC numbers of these locomotives were 608–14/87/9, 711/9/20/8/9/32/41/3 and 829/35/6, and all arrived in Siam by April 1947 with the exception of USA/TC 611, which was still at Sentul awaiting missing parts. USA/TC 612 and 743 were out of service at this time, however, having been damaged in a collision. After spending some time at Sentul in a damaged state, they appeared at Thing Sand, South Siam, in April 1947.

Another batch comprised thirty locomotives obtained second-hand from the Indian Railways. These USA/TC 164/5/85, 257/62/70/86/94, 305/19/29/33/9/51/90, 405/8/23/9/71/91/2, 530/46–9/96, 698 and 701. They were shipped to Malaya and sent to Siam by rail, the first arriving in January 1947.

These two batches of locomotives were allocated RSR numbers 380–429, in the order that they crossed the Rama Ferry in Bangkok, but a number of locomotives were in service for a time in South Siam still carrying only their USA/TC numbers. In October 1947, RSR 393–6/8–400/17 were renumbered in order to give the 380–99 series to the ex-Malayan locomotives erected in Malaya, and series 400–29 to the ex-Indian locomotives.

The last batch of eighteen locomotives, USA/TC 629/30/6, 754–63 and 4301–5, were obtained new direct from the United States and became RSR 430–47 but not in sequence. They were delivered in the "completely knocked down" condition and were erected at Makasan workshops, Bangkok, from March 1947 onwards. USA/TC 4301–5 were originally USA/TC 784–8 built for metre-gauge service in India but by the time that they were ready for shipment, the need for metre-gauge engines had passed so they were converted to 3ft 6in gauge for the war against Japan, being renumbered on conversion. The rest of the engines shipped direct from the US had been built for 3ft 6in gauge for use in Japan but due to the war ending before they were shipped, they were stored for sale as surplus with the ex-metre gauge engines and were offered for sale by the War Assets Administration at the TC Depot at West Yermo, California, between December 1945 and February 1946. The Davenport works probably converted these engines from 3ft 6in gauge to metre gauge as they had performed similar conversion work for the USA/TC.

The RSR numbers given to the USA/TC 2–8–2s were as follows:

RSR	0	1	2	3	4	5	6	7	8	9
38X	732	835	741	719	687	829	689	836	720	728
				701	164	185	423		471	262
39X	614	608	729	(610)	(613)	(743)	(612)	711	(609)	(611)
	613									
40X	(164)	351	305	257	492	286	549	596	547	270
								609		
41X	491	548	698	408	530	405	294	(423)	(701)	(185)
42X	(262)	(471)	546	333	339	429	165	319	390	329
43X	784	787	763	755	761	759	786	758	629	630
44X	756	754	785	757	762	636	788	760	–	–

The numbers in brackets are after the October 1947 renumbering.

Twenty-six "MacArthurs" were sent from Bangkok to Japan for overhaul in March 1953. Lot A, USA/TC 294, 339, 408, 612/3/87/98 and 701/11/9/20/57/61, were overhauled by Kisha Seiijo Kuisha at Oasaka, and lot B, USA/TC 165, 270, 329/33, 405/23/71/92, 546/9, 762 and 836 by Hitachi Ltd, Yamaguchi. These locomotives were in bad condition and at least one, USA/TC 408, had never been put into service after being hauled from Singapore (ex-India) in 1947. The many missing parts, such as lighting and brake equipment, were replaced by Japanese fittings.

RSR 395 and 447 were condemned, the former due to damage received in a collision, while the remainder of the class were overhauled at Bangkok. It was hoped to have all sixty-six locomotives back in service by the end of 1953. All these locomotives were still in service in 1965, and most in 1970.

In 1970, five MacArthur 2–8–2s were sold to Cambodia (Kampuchea), these being RSR 386/8 & 408/11/35. Meanwhile, RSR 383/7 and 403/6/14/6 had been withdrawn, thus decreasing the class total from 66 to 55. As at February 1972, the allocation of MacArthur 2–8–2s was 27 at Thonburi, 13 at Thung Song, nine at Paknampo, three at Bang Sue (actually sub-shedded at Ban Paji), two at Nakkon Ratchasima and one at Kaeng Khoi. By the end of 1976, 17 MacArthur 2–8–2s were dumped at Thonburi shed.

It may be realised from the various transfers that occurred that the "MacArthur" locomotives in India, Burma, Malaya and Siam had the same drawgear and brake equipment as described previously in connection with the Indian locomotives.

Cambodia (Kampuchea) Railways

The five MacArthur 2–8–2s bought by Cambodia Railways in 1970 became Nos 141.501–5, in the order ex RSR 408/11/35 and 386/8. They were all allocated to Battampang. Within a year, two of the MacArthurs had been damaged in accidents!

Iraqi State Railways

Thirty metre-gauge "MacArthurs", USA/TC 437–56 and 496–506, were delivered to the Iraqi State Railways between October 1943 and January 1944, and were erected at the Schalchiyah workshops, Baghdad. Twenty-six were put into traffic by March 1944, the remaining four being stored. These engines were fitted for burning oil fuel. The brake equipment and drawgear were the same as those used for the Indian "MacArthurs". On arrival in Iraq, they ran with their USA/TC numbers, but during 1945 they were renumbered into the British WD series as WD 73031–60 in order. These appear to have been the only engines of the class to have been renumbered in this series. They became IqSR class "W", the class letter being shown above the numbers on the cabside when USA/TC or WD numbers were carried. They represented a considerable advance in motive power on any previous metre-gauge locomotives in Iraq, and they were used for all classes of trains on the main Baghdad to Basra line, including the Mail trains.

Six engines, USA/TC 438/42/3/9/51/3, were taken out of stock by March 1945 and were transferred to India, being observed at the Golden Rock works of the South Indian Railway in December 1945. On arrival at Golden Rock, USA/TC 442/53 appeared to be in new condition and presumably had not been in service in Iraq. At the end of 1946, the remaining twenty-four of the engines were taken into stock by the IqSR and these were again renumbered, becoming Nos 41–64 in order in the IqSR list.

In March 1965, all 24 "W" class locomotives were still in service, but it was expected that twelve would become surplus to requirements when the standard-gauge line between Baghdad-MaquilumQassir was completed. At least three still existed in 1988.

Nigerian Railway

The first twenty "MacArthurs" to be built, USA/TC 3000–19, were supplied to the Nigerian Railway arriving from December 1942 to September 1943. These were not operated by the War Department at any time, but were delivered direct from the United States and carried "United States Army" plates on the smokeboxes. The Nigerian "MacArthurs" were 3ft 6in gauge and were fitted with steam brakes, vacuum control for the train, and central combined buffers and couplers, these being of a different design and at a different height from those used on the Indian locomotives of this class. The headlamps on the Nigerian locomotives were fitted after arrival in Nigeria and were mounted in front of the chimney, whereas later "MacArthurs" had them mounted on the smokebox door. They were renumbered NR 651–70 in order, and were known as the "651" class.

Between March & June 1946, six more were transferred to Nigeria from the Gold Coast railway, USA/TC 131/2/6–8/40. The additional six became NR 681–6 in order, and were also regarded as "651" class. A number of detailed modifications had to be made before they became entirely reliable in service whilst a more noticeable alteration was the provision of a lipped chimney of typical British design.

The "651" class was allowed to work over the whole of the 3ft 6in gauge lines of the Nigerian Railway, with the exception of the Baro-Minna branch. They were insufficiently powerful for the majority of duties in Nigeria, however, and in 1950 it was decided to withdraw most of them,

United Fruit Company

Twenty Baldwin-built "MacArthurs", USA/TC 764–83, were purchased in 1946 by the United Fruit Co of Boston, Mass for use on their estates at Golfito, Costa Rica and at Tela, Honduras. These locomotives were 3ft 6in gauge and burnt oil fuel. They were fitted with American knuckle couplers and Westinghouse air brakes.

These engines were part of a batch of twenty-five, USA/TC 764–88, which had been stored at West Yermo TC Depot, and for some unknown reason, renumbered USA/TC 4281–4305 (but for convenience here the original USA/TC Nos will be used). USA/TC 764–78 became Tela Railroad 150–64 in order, USA/TC 779/80 became Ferrocarril Nacional de Honduras (FCN) 40/5 respectively and USA/TC 781–3 became Ferrocarril del Sor (Costa Rica) 90–2 respectively. FCN 40/5 were later renumbered 50/1.

In 1951, TRR 152/3 went to the FCN and became FCN 52/3 respectively and in 1954 TRR 163/4 became FCN 56/7 respectively. In 1958, Ferrocarril del Sor 90/2 were sold and transferred from Costa Rica to the FCN where they became FCN 58/9 respectively. All these locomotives appeared to be still in service in 1965.

United States Navy

Metre gauge USA/TC 633/4 were rebuilt from metre gauge to 3ft 6in by Davenport for service with the USN at some unknown location, and were allocated USN numbers 65–00459/60. USA/TC 633/4 were noted in store at Fort Eustis around 1952, but their subsequent disposal is not known.

West Yermo TC Depot

Towards the end of the war, newly built engines were stored at West Yermo TC Depot awaiting despatch or disposal. Thirteen engines, USA/TC 623–30/5–9, were stored at West Yermo in December 1945 after being built. Three of them, USA/TC 629/30/6 went to Siam, as discussed under that country, and USA/TC 635/7–9 went to E. F. Nazareth in Brazil as Nos 32–5 in 1947. The disposal of USA/TC 623–8 is not known.

Another ten engines, USA/TC 744–53, were also stored at West Yermo in December 1945. These went to the French Cameroons, after gauge conversion, as discussed under that country.

Twenty-five further engines, USA/TC 764–88, which were renumbered USA/TC 4281–4305, were also at West Yermo. USA/TC 764–83 went to the United Fruit Company as discussed under that heading, and USA/TC 784–8 (4301–5) went to Siam as discussed under that heading.

Unaccounted For

A few of the "MacArthur" class have not been accounted for. These are USA/TC 531–40/62–7 and 623–8/67–78. However, 22 Baldwin MacArthurs were supplied to the French origin Dakar to Niger line in 1944–6 and it is probable that these were USA/TC 531–40 and 667–78.

Similar Locomotives

Two engines, Porter 7644/5 built 1943, were never USA/TC but went to the Chemins de Fer des Grands Lacs, a 3ft 6in gauge system in the Belgian Congo, as Nos 70/1. By July 1973, both were at Kabalo, 70 dumped and 71 under repair.

Apart from the thirty-three locomotives already mentioned as built for the IGR, some very similar engines were supplied to the Peloponnesus Railway in Greece, but these were supplied directly by the locomotive builders, Vulcan Ironworks, and were not part of the USA/TC stock. These were the only engines of the class known to have operated in Europe.

A further batch of six locomotives almost identical with the "MacArthurs" was delivered by the Davenport Besler Corporation in February 1947 for the Chemin de Fer Franco-Ethiopien de Djibouti à Addis-Ababa. The only important difference was that these locomotives had a boiler pressure of 200psi, whereas the pressure of the original locomotives was 185psi. The tractive effort was thus increased to 21,800lb at 85% boiler pressure. These locomotives were Davenport 3070–5 of 1946 and became Nos 421–6 in Ethiopia.

Plate 220   Tela RR 161 (ex USA/TC 775) at Puerto Cortes, Honduras, in October 1956 (Photo: R. Tourret Collection)

Chapter 48

STANDARD USA/TC STANDARD-GAUGE 2–8–2s, WD & USA/TC 1000–1199

Towards the end of 1941, the British Government ordered two hundred standard-gauge 2–8–2s from the United States, under Lease-Lend arrangements, for service in the Middle East, Iraq and Iran. These locomotives were built to British specifications but were of typical American design. The WD laid down a broad outline of their requirements which the American authorities elaborated into a complete specification as the components, details, etc were decided. They were built to the American Engineer Board Composite Equipment Diagram No C–43090 and to US Army Specification No T.1546, being US Army Class S.200.

They are curious in so far as their running numbers, 1000–1199, appear to figure in both the Main WD series and the USA/TC series.

They were all constructed in 1942, by the American Locomotive Co, the Baldwin Locomotive Works and the Lima Locomotive Works, and minor items dif-

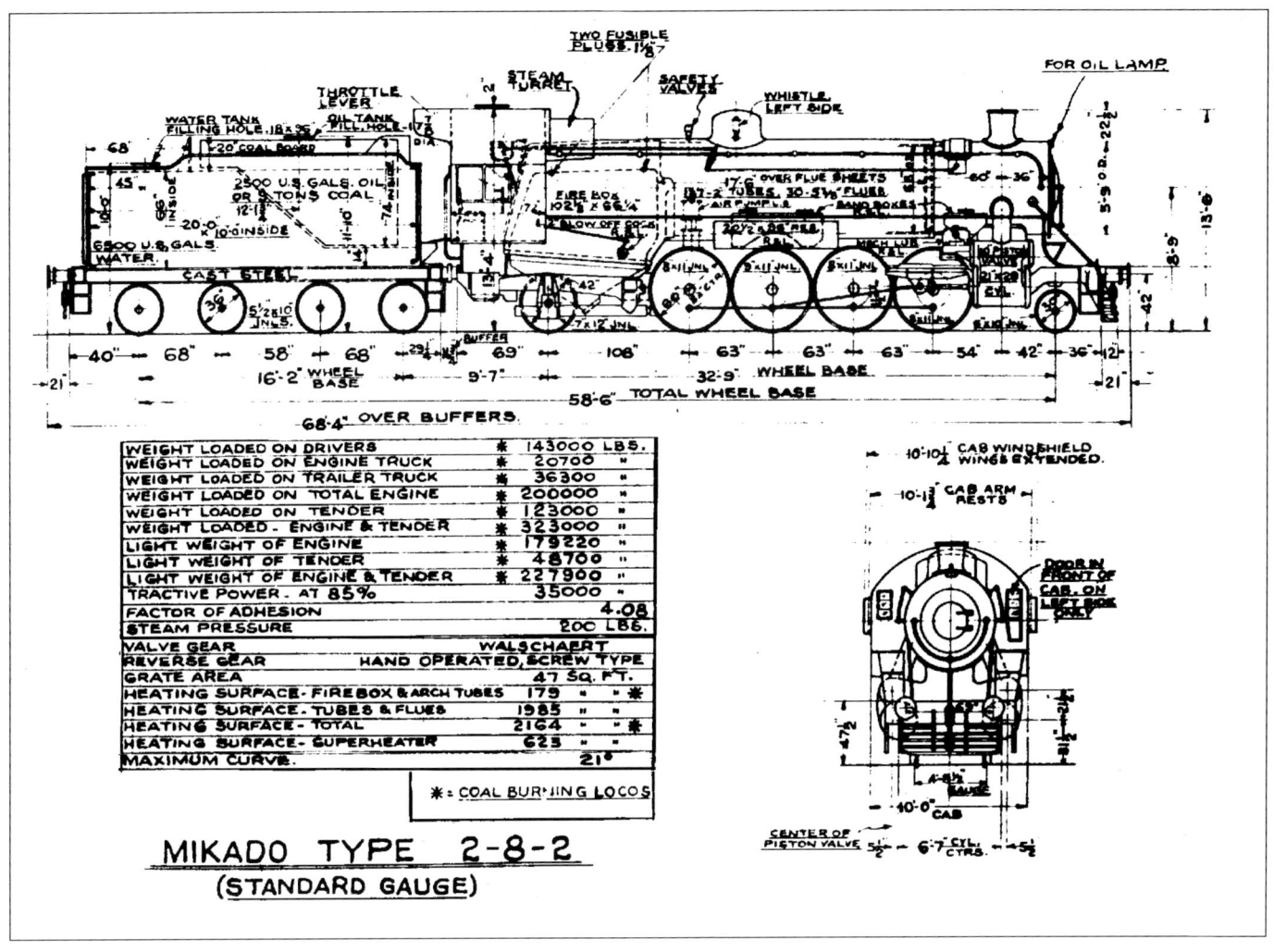

Fig 32   Standard USA/TC standard-gauge 2–8–2

fered slightly according to the maker. The Lima locomotives were built against Order No 1492, the Baldwin locomotives against Order No 1493 and the Alco locomotives against Order No 1494.

Their works numbers were as follows:

1000–12	Baldwin	64503–15
1013–8	Lima	7893–8
1019–24	Alco	70032–7
1025–32	Baldwin	64516–23
1033–45	Baldwin	64537–49
1046–58	Baldwin	64524–36
1059–81	Baldwin	64550–72
1082–90	Lima	7899–7907
1091–1110	Lima	7913–32
1111–5	Lima	7908–12
1116–45	Lima	7933–62
1146–9	Alco	70038–41
1150–99	Alco	70083–132

They had steel fireboxes and could be fitted for either coal or oil fuel. Nos 1000–24 and 1154–62 were originally built for coal firing, although the engines were designed for easy conversion from coal to oil or vice versa. All engines were fitted with Hennessy journal lubricators on all axles. The engines were equipped with oil lamps as originally built but ninety-five locomotives were subsequently equipped with Pyle-National electric head-lights. The tenders of all engines were fitted with a hand brake, a vertical handwheel being located on the inside corner of the right-tank leg. Nos 1000–31/82–90 and 1111–5/46–9 had steam heating equipment fitted. Nos 1000–18/25–31/82–90 and 1111–5 were equipped with air and steam brakes on the engine and tender, while the remainder had steam brakes only. All the locomotives were equipped for vacuum and air train brake operation.

The original allocation of the 200 actually built, 1000–1199, was 56 to the Middle East, 69 to Iraq and 75 to Iran. A further 70 were ordered and allocated the numbers 1317–86, but these were cancelled. In fact, 121 were shipped to the Middle East, of which 20 were lost en route. Sixteen were forwarded to Iran and 20 to Iraq. Seventy-nine were shipped directly to Iran of which four were lost en route. The twenty-four missing locomotives were 1006/7/12/20/1/33/5/48/ 56/92/3 and 1104/8/17/8/23/32/60/1/4/5/ 80/4/99.

Middle East

A total of 101 engines arrived in Egypt mostly during the second half of 1942, although others arrived in 1943 and the last two (1130/1) did not arrive until September 1943. They were mostly shipped in pairs, but a few ships carried four, and "Seatrain Texas" arrived in September 1942 with ten on board. They were unloaded at Port Said or Suez.

The first engines were erected at Port Said. Later engines were erected at El Shatt, on the east bank of the Suez Canal opposite Suez, by a detachment from the Royal Engineers No 199 Railway Workshop Company, who were then based at the PR Qishon Works at Haifa. Later still, the engines were merely made fit to travel to various points, such as Haifa, Jaffa and Kantara East, for complete assembly. The first locomotives to be dealt with by No 199 Rly Wksps Co in Palestine were 1095 and 1157 at Haifa and 1089/90 and 1100/46 at Jaffa, all in September 1942.

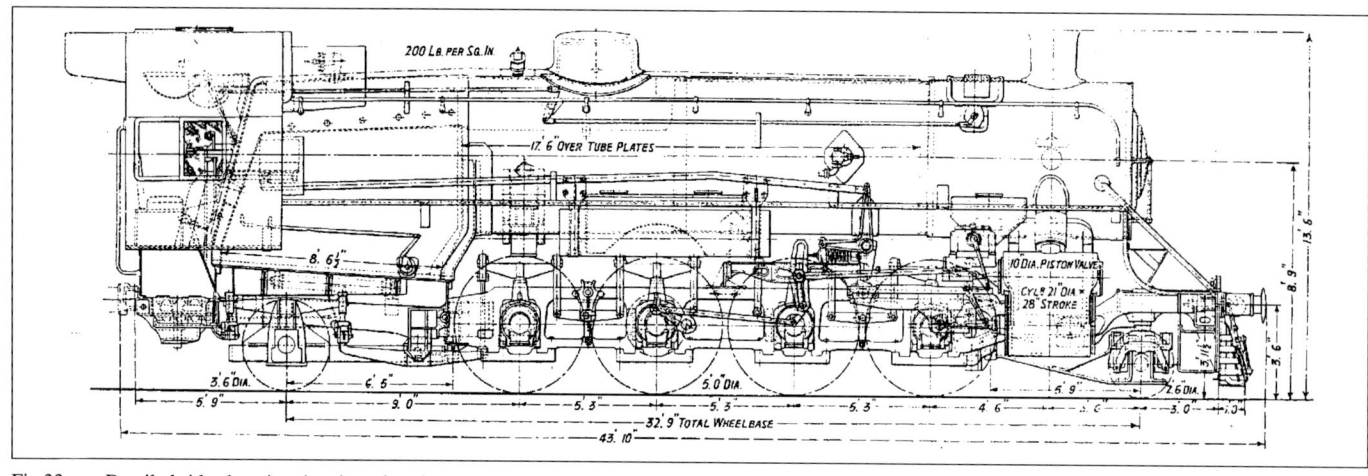

Fig 33 Detailed side elevation drawing of engine only of standard USA/TC standard-gauge 2–8–2 (Courtesy Railway Gazette)

From these 101 locomotives, 65 were put into service in Egypt and Palestine from June 1942 to December 1942. These were 1000–5/8–11/3–9/22–4/8/37/8/83/6–9/95–8 and 1100/3/9/10/3/4/6/9–22/30/1/46–9/51/4–9/62/6/7/74/8/9/88/90/2. None of these engines were fitted with electric headlights, the British purchasing authorities having stated that it was not the custom to use lighting in England!

The engines went into service immediately they were assembled. In July 1942, 16 went to the Palestine Railway (PR) and one into Army service. In August 1942, four more went to the PR and in September 1942, two more went to the PR.

In October 1942, 34 more were put into service, three more on the PR, one sent to the HBT, 14 more into Army service and 16 sent to Iran. The Army locomotives were used in Egypt working from Gabbary (Alexandria) westwards to Mersa Matruh over the Western Desert line (see Chapter 3). The 16 sent to Iran were probably 1025–7/9/31/2/90/1/9 and 1101/11/2/5/53/72/83, of which 1090 and 1115 were prepared at Jaffa.

No 1086 was destroyed by fire in October 1942 at El Mazar after running only about three or four hundred miles. The driver had left the engine in charge of the fireman when they stopped for water. The fireman turned on the oil flow, but did not turn on the steam to feed it up the firebox to ignite it from the heat of the firebox. The oil flowed and filled the ashpan until eventually it exploded. The heat was sufficient to weld the wheels to the rails. The axleloads were solid and the springs lost their temper and drooped! The wreck was made fit to move and then hauled to Haifa where it lay at Qishon Works for about a year, after which it was stripped for spare parts. For instance, the left-hand cylinder casting went on to 1016 which had been standing at Jaffa for almost a year awaiting repair.

In November 1942, 25 more were put into service, two more on the PR, 18 on the Western Desert line, one more on the HBT and three more for the Army, and one counting as a replacement for 1086. By November 1942, there were eighteen 1000–5/8/10/4/6–9/22 and 1155–7/9 allocated to the Gabbary to Mersa Matruh duty.

In December 1942, six more were put into service. Ten were sent to Iraq, presumably the six new locomotives plus one from the HBT and three from the Army. These were 1030/47/85/94 and 1105/52/63/89/91/6.

In January 1943, eight of the Western Desert locomotives were transferred to the control of the Egyptian State Railways (ESR). These were 1000/4/14/7/22 and 1156/7/9. Thus these engines began to appear more frequently in Lower Egypt, presumably because of the arrival of the Whitcomb diesels which were more suitable for service in the Western Desert. They also replaced Stanier 2–8–0s over the Gaza to Kantara section across the Sinai Desert over which exceptional traffic was passing owing to the war operations in the Western Desert. They were allocated to Gaza, Kantara, Lydda and Haifa. Also in January 1943, ten more locomotives went to Iraq, probably composed of two from the PR and eight from the Army. These engines were 1040/6/82/4 and 1106/50/73/85/93/5.

At first in Egypt and Palestine, the WD numbers were retained, but around December 1942 to February 1943, these were increased by 8000 to avoid confusion with ESR locomotive stock and the series became 9000 upwards. Those known to have been renumbered were 9000–5/8–11/3–9/22–4/8/30/7/8/40/6/82–5/7–9/95–8 and 9100/3/5/6/9/10/3/4/6/9–22/30/1/46–52/4–9/62/3/6/7/74/8/9/85/8–93/5/6.

Plate 221 Official photograph of Baldwin-built USA/TC 1000 (Photo: R. Tourret Collection)

Plate 222 Official photograph of Lima-built 2–8–2 (Photo: R. Tourret Collection)

Initially, those of the class in Egypt were overhauled by the No 199 Rly Wksp Co at Jaffa, but later they were handled by the No 169 Rly WKsp Co at Suez. Those in Palestine were maintained at the PR Qishon Works at Haifa, as well as at Jaffa.

In February 1943, there was one new locomotive in service, but some transfers were made so that the 25 on the PR was reduced to 22, the ten on the Western Desert line to eight, while the Army total increased from eight to 14.

In March 1943, there were six new engines 9037/8 and 9103/9/10/6. The last eight came off the Western Desert line, three left the PR but seven went to the HBT, making eight in all, and two more went to the Army. Eight were sent to Turkey, 9002/9/11/3/5/24 and 9158/62.

In April 1943, there were two new locomotives 9119/20. Four returned from the ESR, one left the PR and five went to the Army. Two locomotives went to Turkey 9023 and 9154.

In April 1943, two oil-burners, 9087 and 9174, were transferred to the ESR to work the regular passenger train, the "Orient Express", running between Haifa and Kantara which, with the opening of the El Firdan Swing Bridge across the Suez Canal, went on to Cairo. The 2–8–2s worked this train right through (415km), taking just over thirteen hours. The through running arrangements did not last long, however, because the fuel oils used at Cairo and Haifa had different viscosity and other characteristics which led to trouble when they were mixed together. The operating arrangements for these trains were therefore brought into line with those of other trains, and engines were changed at Kantara East. Nos 9087 and 9174 spent nearly two years (until they left the ESR) regularly working this train between Cairo and Kantara, for which purpose they were stationed at Bulac Anaber (Cairo). At times, the engine spare from this turn worked over the Upper Egypt line to El Wasta, the only known occasions when this class worked down this line.

In May 1943, there were again two new locomotives, 9121/2. Two more left the ESR, four joined the PR probably from the HBT which lost four. Four engines went to Turkey 9000/1/8/14.

In June 1943, six engines went from the Army to Turkey, 9004/10/7–9/22. In July 1943, three Army engines and two HBT engines went to the ESR making a total of seven on the ESR. In August 1943, two HBT engines rejoined the Army leaving none on the HBT.

In September 1943, the last two new engines arrived, 9130/1. One went to the PR and one to the Army. About September 1943, five engines 9095/7 and 9100/90/2 were loaned to the ESR for working freight trains from Cairo to Suez, being allocated to El Taudib. This arrangement lasted until June 1945.

In October 1943, five Army engines in Palestine (AP) went to the PR 9088 and 9103/19/21/2. In November 1943, six engines 9082/4/5/94 and 9105/6 were returned from Iraq to the MEF for Army service.

In December 1943, five more engines 9003/5 and 9131/55/9 were sent to Turkey, depleting PR stock by two, ESR by one and the Army by two. This left the PR with 26 locomotives which were 9028/82/3/5/8/9/98 and 9103/9/10/3/4/6/9–22/46–9/51/67/78/9/88. There were 14 allocated to the Army, of which nine were with the Army in Palestine (AP) 9016/37/8/94/6 and 9105/30/56/7, four with the Army in Egypt (AE) 9084/97 and 9106/66, and one (1086) written off.

In January 1944, three engines 9094/6 and 9130 were sent from AP to Turkey. One engine 9097 was sent from AE to AP. In February 1944, 9105 went from AP to Turkey, while three 9084 and 9106/66 went from AE to AP.

In April 1944, four engines 9098 and 9110/51/88 went from the PR to AP. In May 1944, three engines 9037 and 9106/56 went from AP to the HBT, and one engine 9167 from PR to AP. In June 1944, 9016 moved from AP to the HBT.

The position of the nine coal-burners and 33 oil-burners in the Middle East at 1 August 1944 was as follows. In service with the ESR were six oil-burners 1087/95 and 1100/74/90/2. The PR had all oil-burners, six in service 1028 and 1116/20/1/47/79, five 1082/3 and 1103/19/78 under repair and ten 1085/8/9 and 1109/13/4/22/46/8/9 awaiting repair.

Plate 223 Coal-burning 2–8–2 MEF 9019 at Jaffa Workshops in 1942 (Photo: K. R. M. Cameron)

Plate 224 WD 1105 in Jaffa Yard after preparation for storage circa 1944. The outside connecting rods have been removed and fastened on the running boards (Photo: K. R. M. Cameron)

The HBT had three coal-burners 1016 and 1106/56 in service and one coal-burner 1037 under repair. The army had five coal-burners 1038/84/97 and 1157/66 stored for transfer, one oil-burner 1188 stored serviceable (whatever that fine distinction means!) and four oil-burners 1098 and 1110/51/67 under repair. WD 1086 had been written off.

In August 1944, 9113 moved from the PR to AP. In September 1944, 9083 went from the PR to AP and 9113 from AP to the PR in exchange. In October 1944, two engines 9089 and 9114 went from the PR to AP.

In November 1944, the 41 engines remaining in the MEF were again renumbered with 70,000 added to their original WD numbers, thus becoming the 71XXX series. In November 1944, thirteen engines were sent to the Central Mediterranean Force, that is, Italy. These were 71038/83/4/9/97/8 and 71114/51/7/66/7/88 from AP and 71148 from the PR. Also, 71110 moved from AP to AE, and 71113 from the PR to AE. In December 1944, these two engines 71110/3 moved on to Italy.

In February 1945, four engines 71016/37 and 71106/56 moved from the HBT to AP. In March 1945, these four engines moved from AP to AE. Four engines, 71085 and 71109/19/46, moved from the PR to AE and two engines 71116/20 from the PR to AP.

In April 1945, two engines 71028/88 moved from the PR to AE, one 71120 from AP to AE, and one 71149 from the PR to AP. One engine 71085 was the first

Plate 225 MEF 9174 backing down on to a Palestine train at Cairo Main Station ESR in February 1945 (Photo: R. E. Tustin 4291)

of a second batch to move to Italy. In May 1945, 71082 moved from PR to AE, and two engines 71116/49 from AP to AE.

Between April and July 1945, twelve more engines were sent to Italy, these being 71016/28/37/85/7/95 and 71100/6/9/19/20/46. These locomotives for Italy first went to the No 169 Rly Wksp Co at Suez for light overhaul and preparation for shipping. All were oil-burning, except 71016/37/8/84/97 and 71106/57/66. Some of these were converted from oil to coal-burning prior to shipment. A further eight engines, 71082/8 and 71116/49/56/74/90/2, were sent to Port Said in 1945 and made ready for shipment but in the event were not required owing to the successful conclusion of the campaign. After a short period in store, they were returned to service in the MEF.

In August 1945, 71122 moved from the PR to AP. In November 1945, 71156 moved from AE to AP, and in April 1946, 71156 moved on from AP to the HBT.

In August and September 1945, six 2–8–2s were received from Iraq in exchange for six ex-LNE O4s (see Chapter 23). These were 71030/46 and 71152/63/95/6. This made a total of twenty 2–8–2s in MEF at the end of 1945, all then being oil burners.

By July 1946, fourteen locomotives (71030/46/82/8 and 71116/22/49/52/63/74/90/2/5/6) were in store at Azzib, Sarafand and Suez, one (71156) was on the Haifa-Beirut-Tripoli Railway and five (71103/21/47/78/9) were on loan to the PR. In 1946, these were all sent to Turkey, those from store being moved to Azzib where the engines were concentrated for a final examination prior to shipment.

A peculiarity in some of the Lima-built engines was brought to light one day at an enquiry following a mishap in which a military driver who had reversed into another engine claimed in his defence that his engine was in forward gear and not in reverse. On investigation, it was found that this engine had the reverse the opposite way round from the others, that is, instead of the reversing screw nut being right forward and the valve rod in the bottom of the link for fore-gear, this engine had the nut right back and the valve rod at the top of the link for fore-gear! Further investigation showed that several engines exhibited this peculiarity and that they were all Lima-built, although not all Lima engines were like it. It was decided that these engines had been incorrectly assembled and it was suggested, only half seriously, that all that was required was to change the driving axle round left for right! After much discussion, one of these engines was taken to the wheel drop at Lydda and the driving axle turned left for right on top of a jack in the wheel drop pit and replaced in the frames. The gear then reversed in the way intended and the half-a-dozen or so similar locomotives were soon dealt with.

Iraq

Twenty locomotives arrived in Iraq in December 1942 and January 1943, all being oil burners. These were 1030/40/6/7/82/4/5/94, 1105/6/50/2/63/73/85/9/91/3/5/6. Many, if not all, of these had been on the PR first briefly, probably for erection. They were loaned to the IqSR and the letters "ISR" were painted on the tenders. The original WD Nos were used until the end of 1944 when they were increased by 70,000. Six were transferred to the MEF in November 1943, four (71040, 71189/91/3) to the CMF (Italy) in February/March 1945 and a further six to the MEF later in August/September 1945, leaving four (71047, 71150/73/85) in service in Iraq. These went to Turkey in October 1946.

Iran

All the ninety-one locomotives sent to Iran (1025–7/9/31/2/4/6/9/41–5/9–55/7–81/90/1/9, 1101/2/7/11/2/5/24–9/33–45/53/68–72/5–7/81–3/6/7/94/7/8) were oil burners, the first being erected there in October 1942. They were erected by American and British engineers at Ahwaz Workshops and were renumbered in the IrSR list from 42.400 to 42.490 in order of erection, those up to 42.424 being completed by the end of 1942. By end May 1943, 75 were erected and the remainder were completed by November 1943. They were immediately put to work on the mountainous main line between Ahwaz and Teheran, replacing the LMS-type

Plate 226   IrSR 42.456 (ex WD 1073) at Durad in Iran in May 1945 (Photo: H. C. Hughes)

It may be noted that the first series, 1252–1316/87–1436, were ordered by the WD authorities and this series fits into the Main WD Stock list. However, since most of them reverted to USA/TC control, it is convenient to consider them with the remaining, and far larger, portion of the class which were always USA/TC.

USA/TC 6104–59 would have been built by Porter as Works Nos 7684–7739 but the order was cancelled at the end of the war. Similarly, Davenport received an order for USA/TC 6000–79, which was cancelled from 6024 onwards.

These locomotives were of typical American design, although on a small scale, with bar frames, parallel boiler-barrel, round-top firebox, a steel inner-firebox and a rocking grate. The whistle and safety valves were mounted on the dome, while two sandboxes were also placed on top of the boiler. Piston valves and steam brake gear were fitted. This design was available as either coal or oil fired and, for instance, 1252–66/77–86 as built were equipped for coal burning and 1267–76/87–1301 were equipped for oil burning. The valve gear was Walschaerts type with level reverse. A twin-feed "Nathan" mechanical lubricator was fitted above the right-hand piston-valve chest. Two "Sellers" non-lifting injectors and two "Lonergon" safety valves were fitted.

The first 20 or so of the 5000–60 series appear to have been used in the USA at various military depots and industrial complexes. Little is known about the whereabouts of the last 40 during 1943/4. Possibly they were in store. However, in 1945 many, if not all, from the 5023–60 series were sent direct to France.

When these engines were first operated in England in July 1942, it became apparent that several features of the design could be improved. Accordingly, various alterations were made to the engines at Longmoor and Melbourne, the work being shared between the two establishments. Most of these modifications were soon incorporated into the design on the production lines at the works, so that later engines did not require alteration. The main modifications were as follows. Wooden floorboards were fitted to cover the slippery steel footplate. Rails were added to the coal bunker to increase its capacity from 2000lb to 2240lb nominal. Drop sliding doors were also fitted. The spectacle glasses in the rear weather board of the cab were raised. Larger cylinder cocks were fitted. After the first fifty engines, 1252–1301, the width of the firebox was reduced from 42½in to 40in, consequently reducing the grate area from 19.4sq ft to 18.3sq ft.

Many of the engines arrived in Great Britain from July 1942 onwards. Those arriving in 1942 and early 1943 came under WD control, and, while some were stored, many entered service on military railways and WD Depots, and a few were loaned to the Ministry of Fuel and Power, who allocated them to various collieries. The official allocation of the first batches was 1252–66/77–86, 1400–2/4–11/7–20/5–7 on loan to the WD, 1413–6/21/2/30–6 on loan to the M of F & P, and 1387–99, 1403/12/23/4/8/9 stored. These engines were lettered "WD" as they passed through Longmoor or Melbourne, although in one or two cases if they went to depots which were subsequently handed over to the American authorities (such as Ashchurch and Sudbury Depots), they reverted to USA/TC control and the "WD" was soon deleted perhaps only staying on a week or two.

As far as can be ascertained, the following were lettered "WD", 1252–66/77/86, 1387–99, 1400–12/7/23–9, 1937–44/52–75, 6006. USA/TC 1252–4/7/9/62/5/77–81/4/5, 1387–99, 1403/4/7/10/2/23–9, 1937–40/2–4/52/3/5–60/6/8–71 and 6006 were treated at Melbourne and USA/TC 1255/6/8/60/1/3/4/6/82/3/6, 1400–2/17, 1954/61–5/72/3 at Longmoor (the latter establishment using smaller letters), USA/TC 1405/6 and 1941/67 were probably dealt with at Melbourne and USA/TC 1409/11 and 1974/5 were probably dealt with at Longmoor.

Later arrivals, USA/TC 1302–16, 1932–6/45–51/67/76–91/7–2001, 4313–39/72–4401, 6000–9/15/6 and 6162–6, entering the UK from November 1943 to June 1944, remained under USA/TC control. USA/TC 1945/6 were landed at London, the rest at Newport, Cardiff and Swansea. Most, probably all, passed through Newport GWR USA/TC shops for the weather boarding to be removed, and for steam trial, which was carried out in and around the shop yard, on pilot duty as far as possible. Some were loaned to the GWR in the South Wales area. Although some had already been on loan to the GWR for a short time, the official loan date was 7 June 1944. USA/TC 1945/6/76/8/81/3/5 were working in the Cardiff Valleys Division, shedded at Cardiff East Dock, Barry and Radyr; USA/TC 4381/3–5/8–90/2/3/5/7/8 in the Newport Division, shedded at Ebbw Junction and Pill; while USA/TC 1307 and 1987 were at Dyffryn Yard and 4399 and 4401 were at Danygraig, both sheds being in the Neath Division. USA/TC 4385 and 4398 were transferred to the Victoria and Albert Docks, London, on 6 July 1944.

Apart from one or two retained at Ebbw Junction for shunting purposes, the USA/TC 0-6-0Ts not out on loan, were despatched to Duffryn Isaf sidings for storage. These sidings were sited between Bedwas and Maesycwmmer on the former Brecon and Merthyr section. These were redundant exchange sidings, between the Barry and B&M Railways, on the west side of the B&M line, sited at the eastern end of the former Llanbradach Viaduct. It is thought that around 116 engines were stored there at one time or another, including USA/TC 1302–16, 1932–6/45–51/67/76–87, 2000/1, 4313–39/4372–4401, 6000–9/15/6 and 6162–6. It will be seen that some were taken out of store for loan.

The engines on loan were returned to the USA/TC at Ebbw Junction between 29 August and 8 September 1944, from where, after inspection, they and the stored engines were despatched to embarkation ports for service in Europe. Several were loaned to various docks for a period. These included USA/TC 1302–5/13/5, 1933/48–50/67/79/80, 4326/9/34/7/8/72/5–7/82/96, 4400, 6001/2/6 and 6163/5/6. USA/TC 4326/72 and 6006 remained in the UK, but the rest were shipped to France, mostly from Cardiff Docks but some from Southampton.

Most of the earlier locomotives were also shipped to the Continent when they then reverted to USA/TC control. Some of the earlier arrivals passed through Newport GWR USA/TC shops for attention prior to despatch via Cardiff Docks. These included USA/TC 1257/60/2/3/5/78/81/3/6, 1389/92/5/7, 1401/6/9/23/6 and 1939/42/3/54/6/8/62/3/7/70/2.

The first six to arrive in France, USA/TC 6000/3–5/7/9, came in June 1944 and were doubtless destined for Cherbourg. In August 1944, another 35 were sent to France, 1306/9–12/4–6, 1932/4–6/47/78/82/6, 2000, 4314/5/7–9/21/33/5/6/73/4/8/80/6, 6015/6 and 6162/4. In September, nineteen were sent, 1308, 1977, 2001, 4313/6/20/3/4/7/8/31/81/3/4/7/8/90/1 and 6008. In October 1944, 21 were sent 1307, 1423, 1943/6/63/72/6/9/81/3–5/7 and 4322/5/30/2/89/92/7/9. In November 1944, 45 were sent 1257/60/2/3/5/78/81/3/6, 1302/4/5/13/89/92/7, 1401/9, 1933/9/42/5/8/50/3/4/6/62/7/70/80, 4329/76/9/82/5/93–6/8, 4400/1 and 6165/6. In December 1944, there was a single straggler 1997. In January 1945, another 46 were sent to France 1303/95/6, 1406/10/3–22/7/30–6, 1958/88–91/8/9, 4337–9/75/7 and 6163. In February 1945,

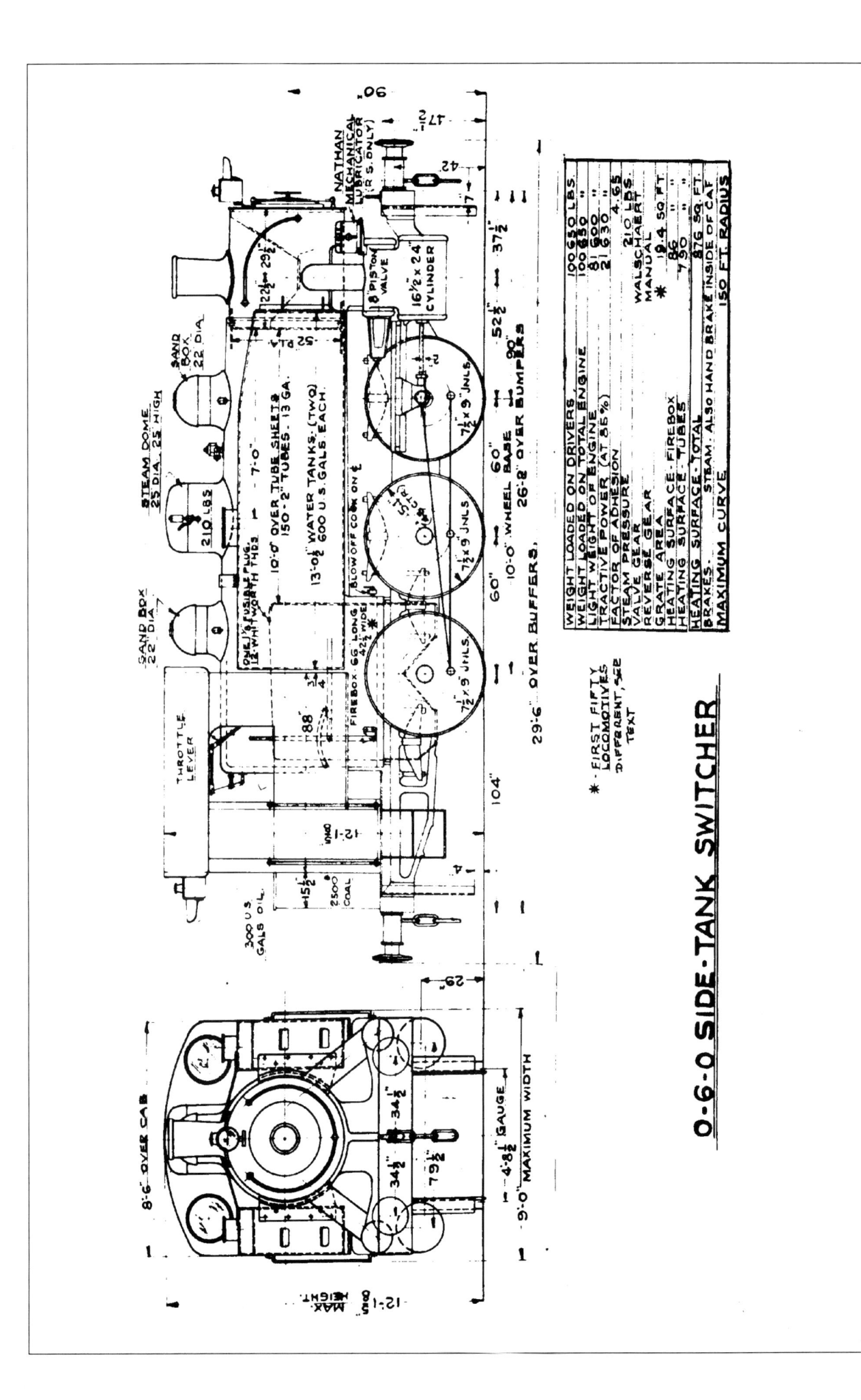

Fig 34 Standard USA/TC standard-gauge shunting/switching 0–6–0T

Plate 228 USA/TC 5001 in the United States in November 1942 (Photo: R. Tourret Collection)

eleven more were sent 1391/9, 1405/24, 1955/64/5/9, 4334 and 6001/2. In March 1945, two were sent 1426 and 1937 and finally in May 45 another nine were sent 1255/85, 1394 and 1941/9/51/7/61/75.

Apart from most of the USA/TC 0–6–0Ts in Great Britain, further locomotives were sent direct from the United States to the Continent in late 1944 and 1945. These included 5017/23–8/35/8/9/41/4/5/7/8/51–6/9/60, 6010–3/7/20–3/80/1/4–9/91–8 and 6100–3/69/70/2/5–83 and possibly others in these series.

In Europe, the USA/TC 0–6–0Ts provided a considerable proportion of the motive power in and around Antwerp docks but worked only from Antwerp Dam and not from Antwerp South (up to March 1946, at least). Antwerp South had WD 0–6–0STs and Dam also had a number to support the USA/TC stud. Early in 1946, the WD engines went into store at both sheds. An influx of USA/TC 0–6–0Ts took over at Dam but Belgian types moved into South shed.

In the early part of 1945, USA/TC 0–6–0Ts also worked from Brussels Schaerbeek, mostly in and around the shed and adjacent yard, although USA/TC 1987 was the regular station pilot and 4386 appeared regularly on a workmens train. Later arrivals to Schaerbeek were usually for store and of short duration. USA/TC 0–6–0Ts at Brussels Midi were never noted at work, nor those at Louvain except when the dump was being sorted for UNRRA when one or two were put into steam for shunting.

After the war, 42 UK locomotives, WD 1252–4/6/8/9/61/4/6/77/9/80/2/4, 1387/8/90/3/8, 1400/2–4/7/8/11/2/25/9, 1938/40/4/52/9/60/6/8/71/3/4, 4372 and 6006, were concentrated in store at Newbury WD Depot during 1945, ready for disposal, where some remained until 1947. Many of these went to Yugoslavia under the auspices of UNRRA or were bought by the Southern Railway for use at Southampton Docks.

On the Continent, the following were noted stored at Ronet in Belgium in April 1945; 5034, 6088/9/91/6–8 and 6100–3/71. The following were noted on Louvain storage dump in May 1945; 1420/2; 1976/88, 4316/8/33/8/9/82, 5041, 6003/11/2/6/20–3/84–7 and 6162/76–83. Some were stored at Brussels Forest Midi shed in July 1945; 1431/4, 1946, 4324/75 and 5038/9.

The process of disposal of the USA/TC 0–6–0Ts began about February 1946 and took most of 1946/7. The "USA/TC" on the tank sides was obliterated and replaced by "UNRRA".

Middle East and Iraq

Thirty of these engines, all oil-fired, were sent to the Middle East and Iraq, arriving in late 1942 and 1943. Twenty-two were intended for the MEF of which two, 1288/9, were lost en route. USA/TC 1267/70/2–6/87/90/4–9 arrived in late 1942 and early in 1943, followed by USA/TC 1992–6 in September 1943. The first two to arrive were USA/TC 1267/70 which the ship "Thompson Lykes" brought into Suez in September 1942. They were hired to the PR in November 1942. Next to arrive in January 1943 were USA/TC 1287/90 which were allocated to the HBT in February 1943, followed by USA/TC 1276/94–6 in March 1943 which were given to the Army in Palestine. WD 1296 became the shunter at the WD depot at Wadi Sarar from April 1943. USA/TC 1297–9 arrived in April 1943, 1298 going to the PR and 1297/9 to the Army in Palestine in May 1943. By July, 1276/94 were shunting at Rafa, 1295 at Azzib and 1297–9 were on hire to the PR. USA/TC 1272–5 arrived shortly afterwards, and were used in Egypt.

The remaining eight from the initial 30, USA/TC 1268/9/71/91–3 and 1300/1, went to Iraq where they were sent up the river from Basrah to Baghdad and put into service from the Iraqi State Railways works at Schalchiyah. After a few months three of the Iraqi locomotives, 1268/9/71, was transferred to the MEF and probably used in Egypt. The remaining five were renumbered WD 71291–3 and 71300/1 in 1944 and then sold to the IqSR becoming their Class SA Nos 1211–5 in order, probably in 1948.

Reverting to the MEF locomotives, in June 1943 USA/TC 1297–9 were hired to the PR. In November 1943, 1290 came off the HBT for service with the Army in Palestine. The position at 1 August 1944 was that eight locomotives 1268/9/72–4 and 1993/5/6 were in service with the ESR; 1275 and 1992/4 were in service with the Army in Egypt and 1271 was stored serviceable by the Army in Egypt. Five locomotives 1267/70/97–9 were in service with the PR, 1276/90/6 were in service with the Army in Palestine and 1294/5 were stored serviceable by the Army in Palestine. One engine, 1287, was in service on the HBT. All 23 units were still oil-burners at this date.

WD 1271/5/94 and 1992/4 worked on the Ataka and Adabiya Bay Military

211

Plate 229   WD 1255 at Longmoor in 1943 (Photo: H. N. James)

Plate 230   WD 1286 at Longmoor in March 1943 (Photo: H. N. James)

Railway in 1944, during which time 1994 was named "Sapper". Towards the end of 1944, the numbers of the MEF locomotives, which were treated as WD numbers, were increased by 70,000. WD 1992–6 were renumbered WD 71302–6 to bring the MEF engines into one series.

In October 1944, WD 1290 was transferred from the Army in Palestine to the Army in Egypt and allocated as shunter to the army ammunition depot at Gilbana in the Sinai, 15km from Kantara East. In April 1945, WD 1297 was transferred to the Army in Palestine, in May 1945 WD 1296 was moved to the Army in Egypt for shunting at Gilbana, in June 1945 WD 1267/99 were transferred from the PR to the Army in Palestine, in August 1945 WD 1270 was also shifted from the PR to the Army in Palestine and in December 1945 WD 1287 moved from the HBT to the PR.

In February 1946, WD 1298 moved from the Army in Palestine to the PR, and in March 1946 WD 1296 moved from Gilbana to the ESR on hire. By June 1946, WD 1267/70/6/94/5/7/9 were with the Army in Palestine, WD 1270/99 being in store at Sarafand. WD 1287/98 were on hire to the PR. WD 1290 was with the Army in Egypt (Gilbana) and 1296 on hire to the ESR. Soon afterwards, WD 1270/99 were brought out of store and loaned to the PR.

Plate 231 WD 1417 on a freight train at Oakhanger on the Longmoor Military Railway in June 1943 (Photo: H. N. James)

By 1946, four USA/TC 0–6–0Ts WD 1270/87/98/9 remained on loan to the Palestine Railways. To their consternation, the PR found out somewhat indirectly that ownership of these engines, formerly officially on lend-lease to the WD, had reverted to the US Army, who were considering sale to the Turkish State Railways! There was, not surprisingly, a lot of correspondence on the subject of these engines and the many other items of military rolling stock now essential to the well-being of the PR, during the course of which the four locomotives became two and then seemed to disappear entirely! Nevertheless, all four locomotives remained in Palestine. WD 1287/98 were purchased in 1946 and became PR 20/1. The other two were probably deemed to be only worth scrap value. PR 21 was reputedly used as a battering ram against

Plate 232 USA/TC 1940 as repainted WD 1940 shortly after arrival in the UK, photographed in September 1943 at a GWR shed (Photo: R. Tourret Collection)

Plate 233   WD 1396 at Westbury shed in January 1944   (Photo: R. Tourret Collection)

the SR looked favourably on their experience with them, and USA/TC 4326 remained in the UK and became officially on loan to the SR from April 1946.

Tests at Southampton confirmed the basic suitability of the USA/TC 0–6–0Ts, so 13 locomotives mostly ex store at Newbury were purchased for £2500 each at the end of 1946. The SR originally bought 1264/77/84, 1388/96, 1402/18/9, 1952/60/6/73/4 and 4326 but later changed Porter-built 1388/96, 1402/18/9 for Vulcan-built 1279/82, 1959/68/71 so that, with the one exception of 1264, all were made by the same builder. This was to facilitate the interchangeability of parts.

Thus, USA/TC 1264/77/84, 1959/68, 1279/82, 1971/52/60/6/73/4 and 4326 became SR Nos 61–74 in order, being put

Arab fortifications at Lydda in May 1948 during Israel's War of Independence.

WD 1270, which was out of service at the end of WW2, was surprisingly put back to work by the Israeli Railways about 1956/7 as IR 22. One of the USA/TC 0–6–0Ts, number unknown, was said to have been used as a stationary boiler in Haifa port for a time in the late 1950s. On 27 February 1959, IR 21 hauled a special passenger train to commemorate the passing of steam in Israel and was officially the last steam engine in service. (However, Baldwin 4–6–0 901 was retained in traffic for another six months). IR 20–2, plus WD 1299, were all scrapped around 1960.

In 1946, WD 1268/9/72–4/96 and 1995/6 were sold to the ESR and became ESR 1151–8. The remaining MEF locomotives, WD 1267/71/5/6/90/4/5/7 and 1992–4 (WD 71302–4) continued in service after the war, becoming WD 301–11 in order in 1952 in the post-war renumbering scheme. These engines congregated at Suez, WD 71304 (311) still being named Sapper", and were subsequently sold or scrapped.

North Africa and Italy

Five locomotives, USA/TC 1927–31, were sent to North Africa in 1943 and from there on to Italy in 1944. USA/TC 1928 was subsequently sold to a private firm but 1927/9–31 were sold to the Ferrovie dello Stato and became FS 831.001–4. They were withdrawn in 1953.

Jamaica Government Railway

Two engines, USA/TC 4340/1, were supplied to the Jamaica Government Railway in 1943 where they became JGR Class C Nos 10 and 11. In 1945, a further two engines were supplied through the auspices of the British Colonies Supply Mission to Washington. These were Vulcan 4626/7 built in 1945 specially for the JGR under Vulcan Shop Order No 2300–44. These two were never USA/TC stock, even nominally. They became JGR Nos 14/5 respectively.

Southern Railway and British Railways

In 1945, the cost of replacement boilers for the SR B4 0–4–0Ts used for shunting at Southampton Docks was estimated at £1580 each and over 14 months delivery. When the war finished, surplus WD and USA/TC 0–6–0Ts became available cheap. The SR preferred the 10ft wheelbase of the USA/TC 0–6–0Ts to the 11ft wheelbase of the WD locomotives. Also, some USA/TC 0–6–0Ts had been on loan to various ports used to embark troops and equipment for Europe. These included USA/TC 4326. It is probable that

Plate 234   USA/TC 4384, with cab boarded up, being unloaded at Cardiff Docks in December 1943   (Photo: R. Tourret Collection)

into service between April and November 1947, although the locomotives had gone to Eastleigh some months earlier for modifications and repainting. They were officially taken into stock in December 1946. An extra locomotive, No 1261, also arrived at Eastleigh in September 1947, presumably for spare parts since it was officially scrapped in November 1950.

The modifications made by the SR consisted of fitting vacuum brake equipment with a Gresham ejector in the right-hand side of the cab over the reversing lever, fitting steam-heating connections, addition of sliding side windows, as well as minor alterations such as additional lamp irons. Because these engines were wider than the B4 0–4–0Ts which they replaced it was necessary to paint a notice on the bunker sides "When standing on this footstep, you are not within the loading gauge". Later, the engines were also fitted with a new centre window in the front of the cab, a different and larger bunker similar to that on the LNE J50/4 class and regulator handles of conventional pattern in the usual position instead of the US pull-out type. In April 1951, 30062 was fitted at Eastleigh with a hinged flap over the front buffer beam on which a man could stand when clearing out smokebox ashes. The remainder were similarly modified as they passed through Eastleigh in 1951/2.

A decade later, many of them were fitted with radio-telephone, with turbo-generators and whip aerials. During 1962, diesel locomotives were brought into the docks. During 1962–4, seven USA/TC 0–6–0Ts BR 30061–3/5/6/70/4 left the docks. BR 30063 was withdrawn due to collision damage but the others entered Departmental Stock as DS 233/4/7/5/8/6 respectively. The remaining locomotives worked for only a few more months in the docks before being transferred elsewhere. Three more were withdrawn in 1964–6, before Southern Region abandoned steam altogether in July 1967.

Happily, some survive on preserved lines, 30064 on the Bluebell Railway, 30065/70 as No 22 "Maunsell" and 21 "Wainright" on the Kent and East Sussex Railway, and 30072 on the Keighley & Worth Valley Railway.

For convenience, details of the SR engines are listed here, in order.

Plate 235 USA/TC 0–6–0Ts being loaded in the UK for shipment to France in 1944. WD 1975 and USA/TC 1255 are the two nearest locomotives, and it can be noted that 1255 was previously lettered "WD" (see Plate 229) but had been relettered "USA/TC" before loading, whereas 1975 had not been relettered (Photo: R. Tourret Collection)

SR No	USA/TC No	Date into service	BR No	Date renumbered	Hinged flap fitted	Withdrawn
61	1264	11/47	30061	5/51	5/51	3/67
62	1277	5/47	30062	8/48	4/51	3/67
63	1284	11/47	30063	1/51	–	5/62
64	1959	6/47	S64 30064	2/48 ?	3/52	7/67
65	1968	11/47	30065	5/48	2/52	9/67
66	1279	5/47	30066	5/48	6/51	8/65
67	1282	5/47	30067	6/48	–	7/67
68	1971	10/47	30058	6/51	7/51	3/64
69	1952	11/47	30069	6/51	–	7/67
70	1960	4/47	30070	8/51	8/51	9/67
71	1966	11/47	30071	11/51?	11/51	7/67
72	1973	4/47	30072	7/48	9/51	7/67
73	1974	6/47	S73 30073	3/48 12/51?	12/51	12/66
74	4326	On Loan 4/46	30074	10/48	4/52	8/65

Société Nationale des Chemins de Fer Français

Many of the locomotives that went to the Continent were used by the SNCF (French State Railways). By June 1945, a total of 38 were in use, all on the Western Region. By January 1946, a total of 77 were in use, 25 on the Eastern Region, two on the Northern, 40 on the Western and ten on the South Eastern. By September 1946, 11 of the Eastern ones had left, ten to the Northern Region and one to the South Eastern. All 77 were purchased by the SNCF in January 1948 and renumbered into SNCF stock as is shown on the following page.

Engines 030TU 1–14 were originally on the Region Est, 030TU 15–26 on Region Nord, 030TU 27–66 on Region Ouest and 030TU 67–77 on Region Sud-Est. Having neither continuous brake nor speed indicator, they were used only as depot shunters. These engines survived to the last of French steam in 1970/1 and came to be regarded as French engines, unlike the big postwar 141R 2–8–2s. Indeed, the writer well remembers unsuccessfully trying to convince a retired Rouenais cheminot in 1970 that a derelict USA/TC 0–6–0T standing outside his house was in fact American! Unfortunately, it lacked its works plate!

Osterreichische Bundesbahnen (OBB)

After the war, many of the engines were disposed of to Central European countries. Ten went to Austria (OBB) in May 1946 and were renumbered in May 1953 in three batches according to the maker; USA/TC 1961/5/75, 6169/70 becoming OBB 989.01–5, USA/TC 6007/15/7 becoming OBB 989.101–3 and USA/TC 5017/47 becoming OBB 989.201/2. They went into use in 1946 in the Linz division and were still in service in 1961, but have now been withdrawn. OBB 989.01/4 were later in industrial service.

SNCF	0	1	2	3	4	5	6	7	8	9
030TUX	–	1427	1962	4317	4322	4335	4336	4380	6001	6088
030TU1X	6089	6096	6101	6102	6166	1308	1392	1417	1432	1939
030TU2X	1943	1976	4383	6091	6098	6100	6103	1286	1302	1305
030TU3X	1306	1309	1312	1315	1389	1409	1435	1934	1935	1945
030TU4X	1953	1954	1978	1979	1980	1982	1983	1984	1997	2000
030TU5X	4313	4315	4319	4327	4373	4376	4378	4381	4388	4390
030TU6X	4392	4394	4395	4399	6000	6009	6164	5023	5024	5025
030TU6X	5026	5028	5048	5051	5052	5054	5056	5060	–	–

rying its "correct" works plate Porter 7547 of April 1943, USA/TC 1433.

Hellenic State Railways

Twenty engines, USA/TC 1303/99, 1415, 1970/99, 4385, 4400/1, 6013, 6172, 1310, 1405, 6008, 1436, 1987, 4384/6/20/8/9, went to Greece in 1947 and became Hellenic State Railways Class Da Nos 51–70 respectively.

In April 1980, on the occasion of the

Jugoslav Railways

One hundred and six went to Jugoslavia in 1946, many from store at Newbury, where they became JZ series 61.001–106 and were used in Slovenia and Croatia. It is believed that 120 locomotives were received and the rest used for spare parts. They were renumbered into JZ stock as shown in the table opposite.

More locomotives were built new locally by Djuro Djakovic, Slavonski Brod, based on the USA/TC 0–6–0Ts but with slight changes in minor external details. Information is far from complete, but it seems likely that about 80 were built and that they were originally intended for industry such as coal mines and factories. Industrial locomotives seem to be numbered 62.3XX, 62.5XX and 62.6XX, often operating with their works numbers as running numbers. Examples known are as follows: 62.314–6 of 1952, 62.317–24 of 1953, 62.361–83 of 1953/4, 62.520/1 of 1954, 62.644/5/50 of 1958, 62.669, 62.673 of 1960 and 62.677 of 1961.

Twenty-three such locomotives, built by Djuro Djakovic during 1956/7, went to the JZ as 62.107–29, but the fact that their works numbers around 614–39 were not in order and there were some gaps, suggests that these were taken up by JZ from locomotives not required by industry. Known details are shown in the table below.

Most of the locomotives were still in service in 1971, and some, such as 62.064/88 and 62.107/21, were still in use in 1989. Five examples were observed during the LCGB Tour to the northern part of Jugoslavia in May 1990. JZ 62.121 was stored at the Ljubljana Railway Museum. It carried a works plate Industria Lokomotiva Strojeva Imosbova without any works number or date. JZ 62.037, carrying its "correct" works plate Vulcan 4494/43, was observed at Zagorje shunting and put up a stirring performance lifting coal wagons up to the coal mine. JZ 62.199 and 62.324 from a local

JZ	0	1	2	3	4	5	6	7	8	9
62.00X	–	1257	1260	1262	1263	1283	1285	1307	1391	1394
62.01X	1406	1413	1420	1421	1422	1423	1424	1426	1431	1433
62.02X	1936	1947	1949	1955	1957	1958	1967	1969	1985	1988
62.03X	1991	1998	4316	4318	4321	4325	4333	4332	4338	4339
62.04X	4375	4396	5022	5030	5035	5038	5041	5042	6010	6011
62.05X	6012	6016	6020	6021	6022	6023	6081	6082	6083	6084
62.06X	6085	6086	6087	6090	6092	6093	6094	6095	6162	6163
62.07X	6171	6173	6174	6175	6176	6177	6178	6180	6181	6182
62.08X	6183	1388	1390	1393	1396	1398	1400	1402	1412	1418
62.09X	1419	1387	1256	1280	1429	1404	1258	1407	1254	1259
62.10X	1266	1408	1252	1253	1403	1411	1425	–	–	–

Plate 236 USA/TC 1976 shunting a military train into the yards at Cherbourg in March 1945. The locomotive carries a marking for No 710 RGD. The vehicles were British Bren carriers for the French Army (Photo: R. Tourret Collection)

factory were displayed for the LCGB party at Kidrivevo, with one in steam and the other complete but not in steam. The works plates were uninformative but appeared to indicate class "62+". The motion parts were stamped with the JZ numbers. Finally, JZ 62.019 was seen plinthed at Maribor near the works, carrying its "correct" works plate Vulcan 4494/43, was observed at Zagorje

LCGB Tour of Greece, they all still existed and appear to have retained their original identities, but few were in service. HSR 53 (USA/TC 1415) was static for supplying hot water, while HSR 55 (USA/TC 1999) had its tanks removed and was coupled to a tender.

China

It appears that twenty of the class went to China, becoming Class XK2. Around twenty passed through the Suez Canal in 1947 on board the ship "Belpareil" and these were presumably the shipment

JZ	0	1	2	3	4	5	6	7	8	9
61.10X	–	–	–	–	–	–	–	?	637/56	639/56
62.11X	619/56	?	?	?	?	?	?	622/56	?	?
62.12X	?	?	625/56	630/57	?	614/57	626/57	620/57	618/57	?

bound for China. Of those on board, USA/TC 4324/79 and 6165/79 were identifiable. Two have been identified in China so far, No 22 V 4496/43 (USA/TC 4334) being works shunter at Zhu Zhon in October 1981 and No 57 (USA/TC 1416) at Anshan Steel Works in September 1985, plus two others not identified.

Miscellaneous Disposals

Other disposals were USA/TC 1938 to the Austin Motor Co at Longbridge in July 1947 where it was named "Ada II". USA/TC 1940 went to Metal Recovery and Produce Co at Eaglescliffe in 1947 and in 1949 to Austin at Longbridge. USA/TC 1944 went to Hartley Main Colliery as No 35. USA/TC 4389 and 1948 became Oranje Nassau Mijnen 26/7. USA/TC 4372 went to Wallsend & Hebburn Colliery in April 1947. USA/TC 4382 was returned from France to Great Britain in July 1946 and went to Longmoor in August where it was named "Major-General Frank S Ross". It was renumbered WD 300 in the postwar WD series in 1952 and finally scrapped in April 1959. USA/TC 5053/5/9 became Regie des Chemins de Fer et Tramways Electrique des Bouches du Rhone Nos 40–2 respectively. USA/TC 6006 went to Hartley Main Colliery No 36 in 1947.

According to Mr W. A. Rakov's book "Russische und Sowjetische Dampflokomotiven" published by Transpress of Berlin in 1986, one or more Davenport 0–6–0Ts were used in industry in Russia. A photograph shows what appears to be a more or less standard USA/TC 0–6–0T, but no details are given of either works numbers or running numbers, and there is no other knowledge of any batch of 5ft 0in gauge USA/TC 0–6–0Ts.

Plate 237   USA/TC 1948 shunting in France circa 1944 (Photo: H. L. Goldsmith Collection)

Plate 238   WD 1269 at Bulaq shed ESR in February 1945 (Photo: R. E. Tustin 4293)

Plate 239   WD 71293 (ex USA/TC 1293) on loan to the Iraqi State Railway in September 1945 (Photo: H. C. Hughes)

Plate 240   WD 6006 in store at Newbury WD Depot in December 1945 (Photo: R. Tourret)

Plate 241   WD 1279 in store at Newbury WD Depot (Photo: C. Turner)

218

Plate 242 USA/TC 4326 in store at Newbury WD Depot prior to loan to the Southern Railway (Photo: C. Turner)

Plate 243 USA/TC 6103 at Lille La Delivrance in June 1946 (Photo: R. J. Tredwell)

Plate 244 A later view of USA/TC 5001, previously shewn in Plate 228, now in Los Angeles, California, in April 1947. Note that this locomotive apparently was fitted with twin Westinghouse compressors, one each side of the smokebox (Photo: C. W. Witbeck)

219

Plate 245 USA/TC 1974 at Eastleigh Works in April 1947 (Photo: W. Gilbert)

Plate 246 WD 71302 (ex USA/TC 1992) in Ataku Yard in December 1947 (Photo: H. Sanderson)

Plate 248 WD 300 (ex USA/TC 4382) "Major-General Frank S. Ross" on Commanding Officer's inspection train (ex LNWR 6-wheel inspection saloon) at Longmoor in May 1953 (Photo: M. T. McHatton)

Plate 247   British Railways (Southern Region) 30061 (ex USA/TC 1264) at Southampton Old Docks in May 1953 (Photo: E. D. Bruton A891)

Plate 249   HSR ex USA/TC 0–6–0T at Larissa in Greece in August 1954. The tank wagon is ex USA/TC (Photo: N. N. Forbes)

Plate 250   JDZ 62.070 (ex USA/TC 6171) at Maribar in July 1958 (Photo: Hellmuth Frohlich 894)

Plate 251 OBB 989.103 (ex USA/TC 6017) at Bischofshofen shed in September 1958 (Photo: E. A. S. Cotton)

Plate 252 SNCF 030TU18 (ex USA/TC 1432) at Lille Fives shed in June 1959 (Photo: E. A. S. Cotton)

Plate 253 SNCF 030TU56 (ex USA/TC 4378) at Rouen Sotteville shed in February 1964. On the original print, "Transportation Corps U.S. Army" is still partly visible (Photo: E. A. S. Cotton)

Plate 254   SNCF 030TU47 (ex USA/TC 1984) at Thouars in June 1968 (Photo: David Mills)

Plate 255   Chinese Railways XK2.22 (ex USA/TC 4334) works shunter at Zhu Zhon in October 1981
(Photo: H. N. James)

Chapter 50

STANDARD USA/TC STANDARD-GAUGE 2–8–0s, USA/TC 1600–1926, 2032–2382, 2400–59, 2500–2989, 3200–3749, 4402–83, 5155–99, 5700–5859 & 6024–78

The standard-gauge steam 2–8–0s were one of the standard designs developed by the US Army for world-wide service. As far as can be ascertained, 2120 engines of this class were built, thus making it one of the world's largest classes. Apart from a few stragglers, all were built in four years. Most of the engines were to the basic USA/TC S160 design which was suitable for European service, although there were a few variants which were designated with different numbers. Class S162 and S166 were supplied to Russia and S161 to Jamaica for example. The engines were built by the American Locomotive Co, the Baldwin Locomotive Works and the Lima Locomotive Works.

Their works numbers were as follows:

These engines were designed to give good route availability, reasonably high power-to-weight ratio, rugged construction and easy maintenance. The design was typically American with bar frames, high-pitched boiler barrel, round-top wide firebox and a steel inner firebox. They complied with the British as well as European loading gauges. The driver's controls were arranged for right-hand drive. In front of the cab on the left side was a door giving access to the high running platform which ran the full length of the boiler on each side of the engine. This door was so small and inaccessible, however, that it was rarely used and was perhaps only intended for ventilation purposes when the locomotive was used in the tropics. Steam braking was used on the engine, while Westinghouse brakes were fitted for train operation. Air reservoirs were placed under the running platforms on either side of the engine. The spring gear, which utilised both laminated and coil springs, was compensated throughout the locomotive. The smokebox front had a small door hinged on the right and offset on the smokebox front to allow room for the air compressor on the left. A long combined dome and sandbox was placed on top of the boiler.

The steel inner firebox was electrically welded, while the outer firebox was rivetted. High degree superheating, 30 flues in four rows, was provided. Two safety valves were fitted, a muffled valve set to 225psi and an open valve set 3psi higher. The two 19 in dia cylinders were supplied with steam by 10 in dia piston valves with inside admission. Lever reverse was fitted. The cylinder and smokebox saddle were cast integrally in American fashion, and were designed to be interchangeable left to right. Driving wheel bearings were 8 in dia and 11 in length.

Locomotives with outside Walschaerts valve gear normally have the radius rod in the lower half of the expansion link when in forward gear. Unusually, the USA/TC 2–8–0s have the radius rod in the upper half of the expansion link when in forward gear. The exception to this rule is the last batch of Lima-built locomotives 5770–5859, which are also exceptional in having screw reverse and a stepped running plate on the right-hand side. Surprisingly, no cylinder cover relief valves were fitted to the S160s, but this did not appear to cause any problems.

The S160s were all fitted with rocking grates, hopper ashpans and self-cleaning smokeboxes, all useful features new to Britain but later incorporated into the British Railways standard locomotives, and even today being retro-fitted into some preserved steam locomotives! Most of the S160s were coal-burners, but some of those built later were fitted for oil-burning.

The engines and tenders were painted a matt dark bluey grey, with lettering in white. However, variations occurred. Probably the different plants manufacturing these locomotives differed in their practice. Also, a matt paint is more likely to change colour in service than a gloss or varnished paint, depending on weathering,

1600–24	Alco	70431–55	1942
1625–49	Alco	70278–302	1942
1650–76	Alco	70457–83	1942
1677–1701	Baldwin	67661–85	1943
1702–26	Baldwin	64641–65	1942
1727–1826	Baldwin	67561–660	1942
1827–70	Lima	8058–8101	1942
1871–1926	Lima	8102–57	1043
2032–49	Alco	70514–31	1942
2050–8	Alco	70532–40	1942
2059–2151	Alco	70541–633	1943
2152–2241	Lima	8158–8247	1943
2242–2331	Baldwin	69485–574	1943
2332–82	Baldwin	69589–639	1943
2400–59	Alco	70749–808	1943
2500–59	Lima	8317–76	1943
2560–89	Lima	8262–91	1943
2590–2639	Baldwin	69818–67	1943
2640–2775	Baldwin	69903–70038	1943
2776–2803	Lima	8429–56	1943
2804–53	Alco	70959–71008	1943
2854–2989	Alco	71051–186	1943
3200–4	Alco	71455–9	1943
3205–3379	Alco	71460–634	1944
3380–3559	Baldwin	70337–516	1944
3560–3699	Lima	8473–8612	1944
3700–49	Alco	71895–944	1943
4402–83	Alco	73394–475	1945
5155–99	Lima	8814–58	1945
5700–39	Lima	8623–62	1944
5740–61	Lima	8678–99	1944
5762–9	Lima	8700–7	1944
5770–5859	Lima	8708–97	1945
6024–78	Baldwin	72058–112	1945

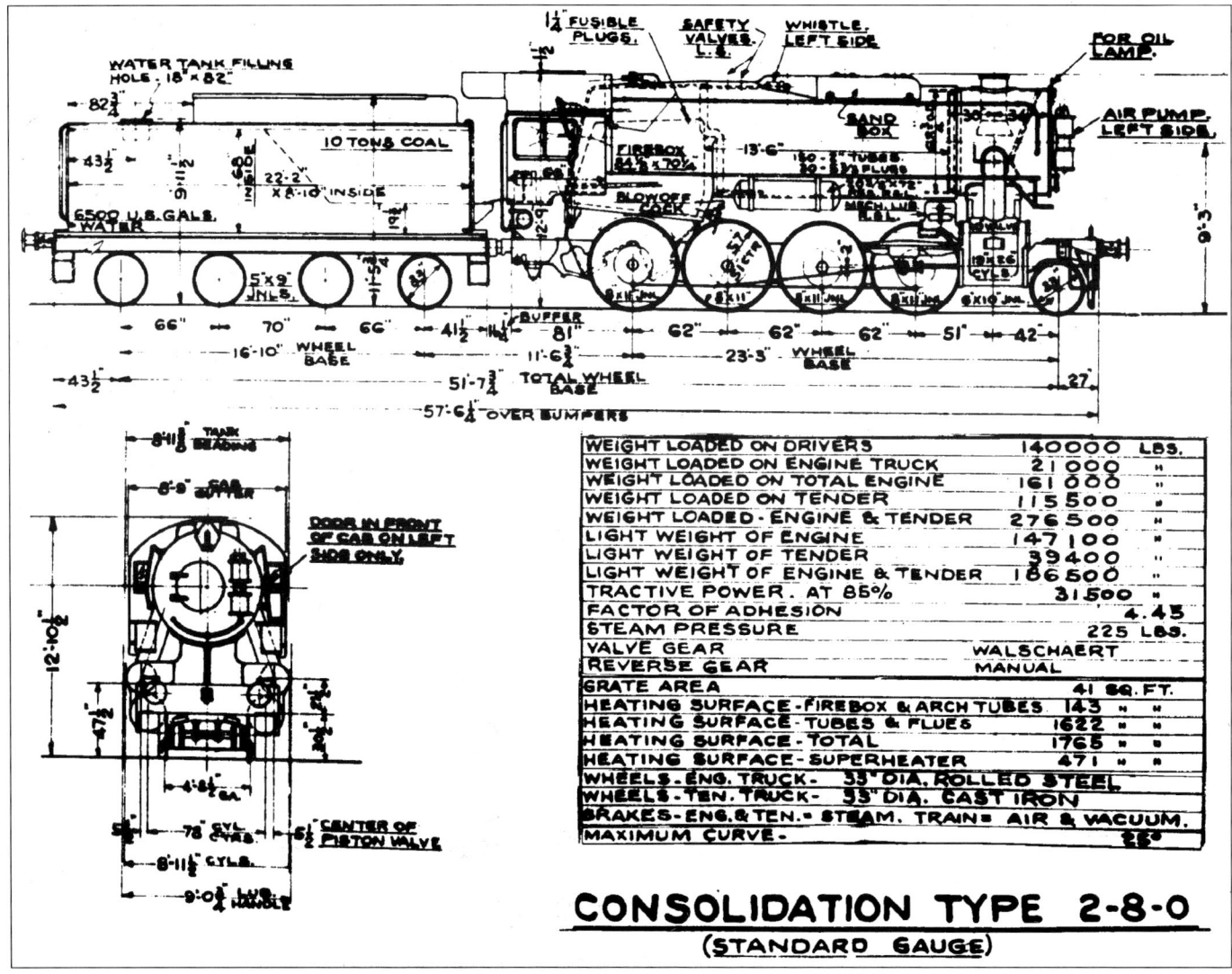

Fig. 35   Standard USA/TC standard-gauge S160 class 2–8–0

wiping with oily rags, etc. Thus, the general colour was also recorded at the time as matt black, dark grey and medium grey. Buffer beams were not red but were the same colour as the rest of the locomotive.

The tenders mostly carried "U.S.A." placed centrally, with letters either 10in or 12in high. Both sizes could have either long or short spacing, the distance apart can be judged from photographs knowing that the vertical rows of rivets are 2ft 5in apart. A few tenders also carried "Transportation Corps" in smaller capital letters 6in high immediately above the "U.S.A." and midway between the "U.S.A." and the top of the tender side, the length matching the length of "U.S.A." exactly. The locomotive numbers were of "square" format 6in by 6in, although a few engines had 9in high figures. Sometimes the engine number was also carried centrally on the back of the tender. All lettering and numbering was painted, that is transfers were not used.

Great Britain

Engines of this class started to arrive in Great Britain on 27 November 1942, when MV "Pacific Enterprise" brought USA/TC 1604/7/9/24 to Cardiff. USA/TC 1609 is believed to have been the first landed, but the first to be put into service officially on a British Railway (GWR) was 1604 and this engine was formally handed over by Col N. A. Ryan of the US Army to Lord Leathers, Minister of War Transport, at Paddington Station on 11 December 1942.

USA/TC 1601–3/6 were landed from MV "Santos" at Liverpool in November 1942 and 1605/8/11/7 at Birkenhead. By the end of December 1942, 26 had arrived. Six more came in January 1943 and twelve more in February. By May 1943, 184 2–8–0s had arrived and eventually 402 had arrived and were on loan to various British railways. Examples of later arrivals were MV "Devis" landing 2082/4/93/5 at Manchester, the tanker "Empire Heritage" landing 1891–4 and 1901/2 at Liverpool in May 1943, 2323/4 landed by Liberty Ship "Robert F. Hoke" at Liverpool, 2352/4 landed by Liberty Ship "Frederick Douglas" at Glasgow in July 1943. Ships usually carried these locomotives in pairs, one on each side of the ship, but MV "Sea Train Texas" brought in no less than 40 S160s in July 1943, by far the largest single consignment.

These USA/TC S160s were sent to Britain at the time of the submarine war in the Atlantic and inevitably some were lost at sea. It is believed that 18 in all were lost. Known examples were 2034–8/40 on the Norwegian whaling factory ship "Svend Foyn" which hit an iceberg on 19 March 1943 and sank the following day, four S160s went down with MV "Southern Princess" sunk by submarine U600 on 17 March 1943 (these were probably four from 2058/61/5, 2189/90 and 2332 which are known to have been lost en route to the UK), 2087/90–2 on MV "Pacific Grove" sunk by submarine on 12 April 1943, and 2248/9 on MV "Robert Gray" sunk by U-boat U306 on 22 April 1943.

Plate 256   USA/TC Class S160 2–8–0 1604 built by Alco (Photo: British Rail)

The S160s were all transported across the Atlantic as deck cargo, fully assembled and many with even their coupling rods fitted, but tenders separate. They were chocked on wooden baulks and secured by heavy chains. The cab windows and back were boarded over. The wheels and valve gear, being made in bright steel, were all painted to protect these parts from salt spray. The normal method of lifting a locomotive is by chains and hooks slung underneath the buffer beams, but this was not possible with the S160s. Accordingly, a special design of balanced lifting beam was produced to lift these locomotives off the ships. This was bolted to the circular rim of the boiler dome cover (twenty studs) and to the special lifting plate fitted to the front of the smokebox.

All these engines were first passed through workshops in the UK for stripping the weather protection away and for adjustments before being put into traffic. This work was carried out at Cowlairs, Crewe, Danygraig, Darlington, Derby, Doncaster, Eastleigh, Gorton, St Rollox, Stratford, Swindon and Wolverhampton. Although the engines were shipped already assembled, in some cases the coupling rods and valve gear had been removed and stored in the tenders. This had to be re-assembled.

Although they were designed to operate with steam braking on the engine and tender, and with Westinghouse on the train, pipes were supplied for vacuum brake if required. Accordingly, a Gresham and Craven solid jet ejector, a vacuum reservoir and a G & G compressed air and vacuum graduable steam brake valve were fitted to ensure that when either the Westinghouse or vacuum brake was applied on the train, the steam brake would be applied to the engine with corresponding force.

The smokebox was partially stripped to permit alteration to the spark-arrestor plates, and on the engines loaned to the GWR, to allow the front tubeplate to be drilled for wash-out plugs. A stop-valve was placed in the top left-hand side of the boiler and a pipe led to the smokebox front for the steam lance cock. The thickness of the flanges of the tyres was slightly reduced by facing the inside. This was accomplished on a ground wheel-lathe so that it was not necessary to remove the axles. An improved hand-brake was fitted to the fireman's side of the tender in place of the original rather unsatisfactory type which did not comply with British regulations. Finally, the pistons and motion were assembled and British lamp irons fitted in place of the American type supplied.

Some features of the engines which were then strange to British crews included sandboxes on top of the boiler, hopper ashpans and lack of dampers on the ashpans. The original design included arch tubes in the firebox. In service, these soon proved to be a source of weakness and by the middle of 1943, they had been removed from all the engines, both in the

Plate 257   Official photograph of USA/TC 1702 built by Baldwin (Photo: R. Tourret Collection)

UK and in North Africa. Later batches, again from about mid-1943 onwards, were built without them.

Although intended for operation in Europe by the USA/TC, it was agreed that prior to the invasion of Europe it would assist the war effort if the first 400 engines could be loaned to British railways. As will be described, in the event, these locomotives were distributed as follows:

GWR	174
LNE	168
LMS	50
SR	6
WD	4
	402

On the LNE, USA/TC 1623 was the first engine to be loaned for service on 30 December 1942, followed by 1616/9 and 1835/6. These engines went through Cowlairs Works, and presumably had been landed at a Scottish port. In all, 58 locomotives were prepared at Cowlairs Works. USA/TC 1835 was allocated to Thornton Junction shed and the others to St Margarets. It was then decided to concentrate the class in South Wales for the time being and these five engines were transferred to the GWR in the last week of January 1943. As well as Cowlairs, all the main LNE works, Darlington, Doncaster, Gorton and Stratford, commissioned S160 2-8-0s. A further 38 engines were prepared for service by the LNE before being handed over to the GWR, LMS and SR, although they were first run-in from LNE sheds. These 43 engines were 1616/9/23, 1771. 1835/6/77, 1900, 2100/2/12/35-8/ 64/5, 2244/5, 2314/5/26/7/39/49/54/8/ 75/7 and 2400/1/7/8/10/9/21/3/7-9/ 33/4/9.

By March 1943, the policy of concentrating these engines on the GWR had changed, and between March 1943 and January 1944, the LNE acquired 168 S160s and retained them on loan until after D-Day. These engines were 1697–9, 1700/3–10/2–4/20–3/7–31/68/9/72/3/80/ 8/92, 1827–34/6/9/40/2–50/79/82/5–90, 1903/4/8/11/2/9/22–6, 2032/3/41/3/5/ 7–51/7/83/5/6/94/7/9, 2101/4–8/11/3–5/ 7/9–21/3–8/46, 2242/6/7/50–3/73/4/ 82–7/9/91/3/5–9, 2300–11/6/7/28/9/48/ 55/61–7/70/1/3/4 and 2418/20/36/7/44–7.

LNE policy was to concentrate its USA/TC 2-8-0s by allocating large batches to only six major depots, but nevertheless they worked to all parts of the LNE system, except the GNofS and the West Highland lines. Gorton had ten, but none for more than two months. Five were re-allocated to other LNE sheds, while the other five went on to other railways. Darlington had ten, eight of which went on to the GWR after running-in, and the other two went to March. Doncaster kept its seven engines for one to three months before transfer elsewhere. March received 50 between April and May 1943 to help with the extra traffic to the RAF and USAAF bases in East Anglia, one engine later being transferred to Ipswich. Woodford received 25 by March 1943. Stratford had 22 allocated which arrived between August 1943 and January 1944. St Margarets received 22 which were transferred elsewhere, and then 21 between July and October 1943 which it retained. Heaton received 25 in the same period. Neville Hill received 25 between June and October 1943.

The USA/TC 2-8-0s worked heavy goods trains, particularly between Newcastle and Edinburgh, March to Temple Mills, and on the Great Central line south of Annesley. However, quite a few failures were experienced such as hot axleboxes (due to lubrication by grease instead of oil), firebox arch tubes leaking and dropped lead plugs (see discussion on boiler explosions at the end of this Chapter).

The GWR works at Swindon and Wolverhampton both commissioned S160 2-8-0s until October 1943, when the work was transferred to the USA/TC at Newport Ebbw Junction works (as will be discussed in more detail later). Thereafter, running repairs were concentrated at Wolverhampton.

The GWR eventually had 174 engines on loan, arriving all through 1943 and early 1944, USA/TC 1601–24/8/32/9/ 41–9/51/4–6/8–65/81–4/7–9, 1749/57, 1 8 3 5 / 4 1 / 7 7 / 8 0 / 1 / 3 / 4 / 9 1 – 9, 1900–2/9/10/3–5, 2096/8, 2100/2/3/9/10/ 2/6/8/22/9–45/7–51/9/64/5/7, 2267/9/ 70/9/80/90/4, 2312–5/8/9/23/4/6/7/38/ 9/49–54/7–60/8/9/75/7 and 2403–5/ 7/8/10/22–4/30–5/8–43/8/50. These were allocated all round the system, to at least 28 depots, and were quite often transferred from one shed to another. Around 24 were at Newport, 20 at Oxley, 17 at Bristol, 13 at Old Oak Common, 12 at Oxford, 11 at Pontypool Road, 11 at Newton Abbot, 9 at Cardiff, 8 at Banbury and so on. In addition, the GWR had the temporary use, for running-in purposes, of locomotives being commissioned at Newport by the USA/TC. One of these saw some service from Laira, who said that they "thought it had been allocated to them"! The locomotives on loan to the GWR were used everywhere allowed by their route availability. Some even reached Gresty Lane, Crewe. They were widely seen between Swindon and London, Swansea and Cardiff, and on the South Wales mineral trains. On one day in February 1944, no less than 17 were on Old Oak Common.

On the LMS, Crewe, Derby and Horwich works commissioned the 2-8-0s, USA/TC 1704 being one of the first handled by Crewe. Fifty engines were allocated to the LMS on loan, namely 1762, 1871–6/8, 1907/17/8/21, 2039/42/4/6/52–6/82/4/8/9/93/5, 2152/3, 2243–5 and 2400–2/6/9/11–7/9/21/5–9.

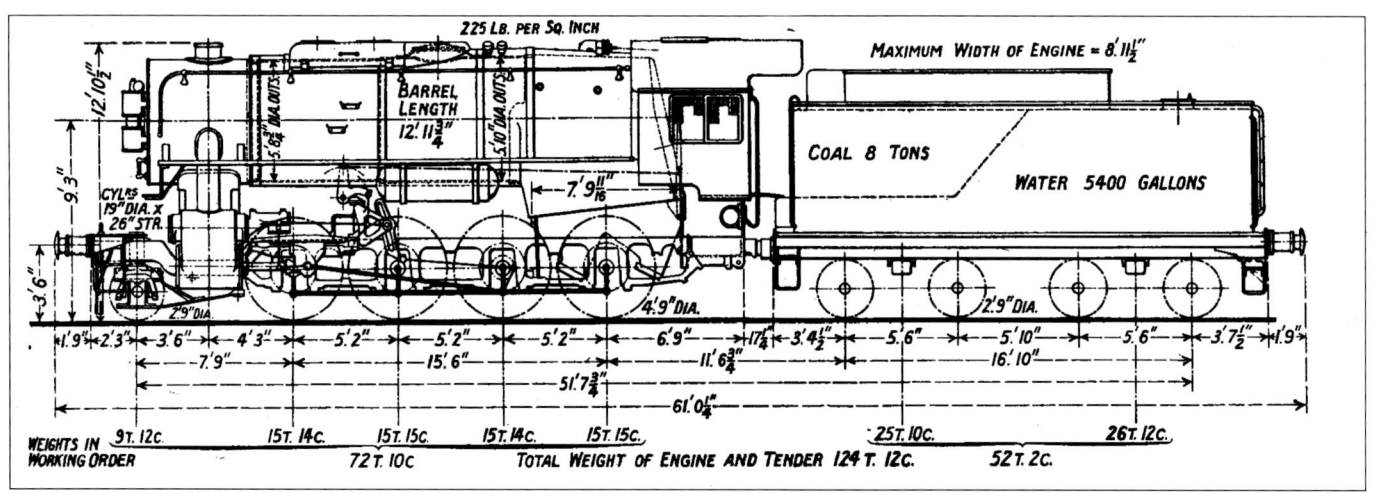

Fig. 36   Diagram giving principal dimensions and weights of USA/TC S160 class 2-8-0 (Courtesy Railway Magazine)

227

Plate 258   USA/TC 1707 in Britain during the war, built by Baldwin (Photo: C. Turner)

Plate 259   USA/TC Class S160 2–8–0 1870 built by Lima (Photo: H. L. Goldsmith Collection)

Plate 260   USA/TC 2108 before service on the LNER in the war, built by Alco (Photo: British Rail)

Plate 261   USA/TC 2217 built by Lima in 1943 (Photo: H. L. Goldsmith Collection)

They were shared between three sheds, Toton receiving 26 (1762, 1871–6/8, 2039/42/4/6/52–6/82/4/8/9/93/5 and 2243–5) from May to July 1943, with one (1762) in October 1943; Crewe South 13 (1917 and 2400–2/9/11–3/5/9/21/6/8) in August 1943, with one (1917) in September 1943; and Mold Junction 11 (1907/18/21, 2152 and 2406/14/6/7/25/7/9) in September 1943, with one (2429) in October 1943. One of the Toton engines (2044) was transferred to the WD Depot at Sudbury in July 1943 and was not replaced, and one Crewe South engine (2412) was re-allocated to Shrewsbury in December 1943.

The Toton engines worked to Leeds and then over the Settle route to Carlisle, south with coal trains via the LNWR line to Willesden and via the Midland line to Brent, and then in both cases sometimes through to Norwood Junction on the SR. West from Toton they worked to Birmingham, Burton, Coventry, Derby and Gloucester. Crewe South engines worked to Birmingham and Willesden, as well as north. Mold Junction locomotives worked along the North Wales coast line, to Lancashire and to Leeds. None of these engines worked on the Barrow Whitehaven line, nor the Midland line to Bath, nor the S&DJR.

On the SR, Eastleigh works commissioned over 30 S160 2–8–0s after arrival at Southampton Docks. The first, USA/TC 1843, went to Waterloo Station on 21 April 1943 for inspection by the SR Directors. The second engine, 1850, was run-in on a Salisbury freight train before being sent to March on the LNE. Because of the loss of its Continental traffic, and some of its seaside holiday traffic, the SR had no great need of freight locomotives and it was not until September 1943 that any were allocated to the SR, four (1771, 1916/20 and 2356) being allocated in that month, followed by 2378 in November 1943 and 2590 in January 1944. All these engines went to Exmouth Junction shed, and worked mainly between Exeter, Salisbury and Southampton.

So far as the WD was concerned, USA/TC 2292 and 2639 were allocated to the Longmoor Military Railway in June 1943 and February 1944 respectively. USA/TC 2044 went to Sudbury WD Depot in July 1943, after service on the LMS as already mentioned. USA/TC 2638 went to Faslane and 2640 to Cairnryan, probably both around January 1944.

After the first 400 or so engines to arrive in the UK had been loaned to British railways, later arrivals were placed in store. Cowlairs Works dealt with USA/TC 1625/31, 1756/97/8, 1805, 2180/1/93/4, 2256/7/72/5/6/8, 2337/40/3/4, 2601/3–5/15/6 and 2838/40–2/58/68, and these engines were then sent to South Wales for store.

Engines intended for storage for use in Europe started arriving at Newport, South Wales, about July or August 1943 and were temporarily stored in West Mendalgief and other sidings in the vicinity of Ebbw Junction shed, Newport. On 14 September 1943, by which time 104 2–8–0s were in store, No 756 Railway Shop Battalion, US Army, under Major E. C. Hanley, started work in the repair shops at Ebbw Junction. The wood protecting the cabs and motion during shipment was removed and the engines prepared for use, after which they went for a trial run to Risca or Rogerstone, with a GWR crew. After this trial, the locomotives were temporarily loaned to the GWR Ebbw Junction shed, to make a 300-mile round trip under actual working conditions, after which they were returned to the repair shops for US Army engineers to board the cabs up again, make any minor adjustments, and grease for storage.

They were then hauled "dead" to sid-

Plate 262   Official photograph of USA/TC 2589 built by Lima (Photo: H. L. Goldsmith Collection)

Plate 263 USA/TC 2626 official photograph. Built by Baldwin and used in the United States (Photo: R. Tourret Collection)

ings at Treforest, Penrhos or Cadoxton, for storage, in batches of three or four. The dump at Treforest (Tonteg) was the first to be formed, locomotives arriving from 11 October to 8 December 1943. Penrhos was the next dump to be formed, locomotives arriving from 9 December 1943 to 26 February 1944. Cadoxton was the last of the three dumps to be formed, locomotives arriving from 1 March to early May 1944. There was certainly 119 locomotives at Tonteg, there was probably 151 at Penrhos and it is believed that there were 83 at Cadoxton, plus two at Ebbw Junction, making a total of 355 in all which agrees with an official but naturally unpublished GWR record of the time.

The Treforest (Tonteg to the USA/TC) site was the up line of the old Barry line to Pontypridd and the Rhondda, and stretched from "round the corner" from Tonteg Halt to just outside the south end of Treforest Tunnel. Just about halfway along this line was the old Barry station at Treforest, closed to passengers in May 1930 but then reasonably intact. The Penrhos site were the Barry/Rhymney exchange sidings between the old Penrhos Lower and Upper Junctions, which had mainly fallen into disuse. The sidings consisted of four double-ended sidings on each side of the double track Barry's Rhymney branch, the sidings being just over a quarter of a mile in length. The Cadoxton site was almost immediately east of Cadoxton Junction, where two sets of dead-end sidings fanned out each side of the main line, terminating at the embankment for the Palmerston Road bridge, just west of Biglis Junction with the Taff Vale's Penarth branch.

The locomotives at Treforest were 2154–8/60–3/6/8–88/91–3/5–9, 2232–7/40/56/62/8/71/2/5/6/8/81, 2320/72/6, 2449/51–9, 2500/72/4/8/9/81/3–5/91/3–9, 2600–14/8, 2804/6–10/2–21/7/8. This dump was notable in that it consisted of 119 locomotives in one long line all facing the same way except one! At Penrhos were 1625/6/9–31/3–8/40/52/3/66/77–9/90/1, 1701/81/90/3/8/6/7, 1804–8, 1906, 2071/2, 2194, 2200/1/3–5/8/9/11/3/4/8/30/1/41/54/5/7/8/60/1/6/77, 2336/41/2/7, 2501–5/7–9/12/26/38–45/60–7/9/70/3/5/80/2/6/8/9/92, 2615–7/20/2/3/5/32/4/6–8/40–4, 2805/11/22–5/9/31–3/5/7–45/62/3/6/7/9–72/92/3 and 2901/8/9/17/24/8/9. At Cadoxton reposed 1627/80/5/6, 1756/89/91/5/8, 2202/6/7/10/5/59/63/5, 2330/1/3–5/7/40/3–6, 2506/10/1/3–9/33–7/46–9/68/71/6/7/87, 2619/24/33/5/45, 2778–81, 2830/4/47/68/94–7 and 2900/2–7/10–3/20/3/6/7.

USA/TC 2264 and 2858 arrived at Newport Ebbw Junction March 1944 and then left for overseas 2 May 1944. They may have gone to Cadoxton but it is considered more likely that they stayed at Ebbw Junction.

Some engines only just arrived in the UK before being sent on to France, in some cases moving on within a month. These were 2522/7, 2638/40, 2797/8, 2858/80/9, 3250/61/7/74, 3398, 3400/93–6, 3513–8/24–9/34/8/56–9/64–7/76/7/9–87/93/6–9, 3600/2/6, 5706/7/9/10/20–3/7/92/3/8, 5803/38–40 and 6051/3/4/6/60/2/4.

In June 1944, the second phase of the 756 RSB operations at Ebbw Junction started, namely the release from storage of the locomotives under their control, with spot checks to ensure that all was well prior to despatch to the embarkation ports. The 355 engines stored in South Wales were the first to go. In June, there was an initial shipment of 14 engines from Penrhos, presumably for Cherbourg. These were 1781/93, 2072, 2211/66, 2342, 2507/12/43, 2636, 2835/67 and 2917/29. Of these, 2507/12/43 and 2867 paused a while at Cadoxton en route.

In August, large scale shipments started. The engines from Penrhos were sometimes used to refill the Cadoxton

Plate 264 Official photograph of USA/TC 5724 built by Lima in 1944 (Photo: H. L. Goldsmith Collection)

Plate 268 USA/TC 1645 at Kennington on a train of USA/TC bogie oil tank wagons in July 1944 (Photo: R. G. H. Simpson)

6–10/3–21/7/8/34/6/8/68/95–7 and 2902–7/10–3/23/6/7. In October 1944, the following came 1601/3–20/2/4/32/9/41–5/54–6/8/61/2/4/5/81/2/9, 1710/29/49/57/62, 1841/71/2/81/3/4/91/3/5/6/9, 1900/2/9/10/3/21/6, 2043–6/54, 2103/9/11/2/4/6/8/22/9/31–3/5–7/40–2/5/7/53/9/64/5/7, 2267/9/70/9/80/92/4, 2312/4/5/8/9/23/4/6/7/39/50/1/3/7–60/5/7–71, 2401/3/7/8/10–2/22–4/30–4/8–40/2/3/8/50 and 2638/9. There were two stragglers, USA/TC 2378 in November 1944 and 1707 in February 1945.

Following the invasion of Southern France, 2–8–0s from North Africa were shipped to Europe. By the middle of 1945, engines were being shipped in to Europe directly from the United States. These were 1809–12/4–26, 1905, 2062–4/73/4, 2212/6/7/9–29/38/9/88, 2321/2/5, 2520/1/3/5/8–32/50–9, 2621, 2751–65/76/7/82–96/9, 2800–3/26/46/8–57/9–61/4/5/73–9/81–8/90/1, 2914–6/8/9/21/2/5, 3200–49/51–60/2–6/8–73/9–82, 3321/7/30/1/3/8/40/1/3–7/9/51–79/97/9, 3401–4/29/31/2/97–9, 3500–12/9/20/30–5/5–7/9–55/60/1/3/73–5/8/88–92/4/5, 3601/3–5/7–10/2–6/20/1/4–39/42–59/72–84, 4402–17/9/20/2–36/8–83, 5155–86, 5700/3–5/8/11–9/24–6/8–30/2–4/7–9/59/62–91/4–7/9, 5800–2/4–24/6–8/30–3/6/7/41–3/7–59 and 6024–50/2/5/7–9/61/3/5–78 (although 6030/2/5/40/5/59 were transhipped at Royal Victoria Docks in London in April/May 1945). Hitherto, all the engines had been coal-burners, but amongst the later arrivals were some, from the series USA/TC 3275–3396, 3610–99 and 5759/62–4, that were oil-burners.

The USA/TC 2–8–0 locomotives were used extensively between the time of the big "break-through" in the autumn of 1944 and the end of that year, during which period long lines of communication were being maintained to keep the front line forces supplied. The engines were used to operate military freight trains on the old "Etat" system to the Paris area where they were then remarshalled for the various front line areas. The locomotives used were chiefly those which had been stored while in England. They were then based largely on Cherbourg, which had a large allocation because it was then the only large port in use by the Allied forces, and to a lesser extent on Dreux where the American forces had established a large military depot. However, these engines did not carry a "Dreux" allocation, doubtless for security reasons. The trains were worked by a complicated route round the North Western suburbs of Paris to Batignolles; from which extensive depot and the Paris "Ceinture" line they were distributed in all directions but principally via La Chapelle and La Villette towards the East. The American locomotives worked to Batignolles only, where they were turned, serviced and returned to the Cherbourg and Dreux area. SNCF locomotives then worked the trains forward.

By the middle of November 1944, the

Plate 269 USA/TC 2134 at Shrewsbury shed in August 1944 (Photo: R. E. Tustin)

Plate 270 USA/TC S160 2–8–0 believed to be 2313 hauling a freight train in the UK (Photo: H. N. James)

traffic had reached such proportions as to be beyond the capabilities of the available S160 class locomotives (and the few USA/TC diesel locomotives also present) and British WD "Austerity" 2–8–0s were drafted in to help in quite large numbers. By December, the S160 class engines which had been on loan to the British railways began to arrive in quantity and they gradually replaced the WD locomotives, which were not popular with the American crews because they were not fitted with a rocking grate, a refinement especially desirable because of the poor quality of the coal available. After the beginning of 1945, Antwerp was reopened as a port and naturally the amount of military traffic from Cherbourg decreased.

The locomotives which left Britain to go to the Continent came under the 2nd MRS, which was responsible for operations on the SNCF and on the American-controlled sections of the SNCB and the NS. The locomotives which went to North Africa and then Italy came under the 1st MRS and it was not until the 1st MRS extended its activities to Southern France that any exchange of locomotives took place, a few 2–8–0s being transferred from the control of the 2nd MRS to the 1st MRS.

Ambulance trains were initially monopolised by S160 2–8–0s, although occasionally USA/TC diesel locomotives or WD "Austerity" 2–8–0s appeared. To deal with these ambulance trains, some S160 engines were fitted with steam carriage-heating connections. The trains were routed via Paris and many of these locomotives were allocated to work the trains (a) from the northern front to Paris, (b) from the eastern front to Paris and (c) from Paris to Cherbourg. At the end of November 1944, however, the electrification was restored on the Le Mans line and consequently SNCF electric locomotives took over most of these ambulance trains using this line. Steam locomotives still appeared, however, and since the bulk of the ambulance trains were destined for the Batignolles/St Lazare line, the electric locomotives were replaced at Chantiers Station by steam locomotives of whatever type happened to be available.

The USA/TC 2–8–0s were at first manned exclusively by American crews, French pilots being provided from Chantiers to Batignolles and return, but not between Dreux and St Cyr. Soon, however, French crews took over, at first with an American on the footplate. This phase was only a temporary one for instructional purposes, the locomotives being driven solely by French crews shortly afterwards.

By March 1945, a few 2–8–0s were on loan to the SNCF operating from Le Havre, but in April arrangements were made to assign over 200 locomotives of this class to the SNCF. Later on, because

Plate 271 USA/TC 2318 hauling an oil train at Reading West Junction on the GWR (Photo: M. W. Earley)

the SNCF was still short of engines, further 2–8–0s were loaned. The following table gives some idea of how the distribution varied in course of time.

All these engines were coal-burning except for 106 of those on the Sud-Est. The peak period was late in 1945, after which the number of engines on loan decreased until eventually none were left in service on the SNCF by the end of 1946. When 121 were left on the SNCF, they were temporarily renumbered 140 U 1–121.

Locomotives known to have worked on the SNCF were as follows:

Date	Est	Nord	Ouest	Sud-Est	Total
June 1945	–	50	221	–	271
November 1945	199	50	182	127	558
December 1945	178	50	182	150	560
September 1946	51	2	43	98	194

1601/6/8/10/2/4/6/9/24/7/9/31/40/2–4/51/4/9/63/5/6/79/82–4/7/9/91/5, 1706/7/9/20–2/30/1/6/44/5/54–8/62/4/8/9/73/6/9/89/93, 1806/8/13/20/1/8/30/3/4/9/42/3/5/7/8/54/5/9/71/3/5/6/8/92–4/6/7/9, 1900/9–12/5/24–6, 2033/42–4/8–51/7/62/71/6/7/86/9/93/4/9, 2111/2/4/8/9/25/7/32–4/7/8/42/6/9/50/4/6–8/65/7/9/70/3/83/4/8, 2206/9–14/6/7/9–25/8–30/2–5/8/9/41/3/4/7/56–8/61/3–6/9/71/6/83/5/7/9–91/4, 2300–3/5/8/11/2/5/6/8/20–2/4/31/6/7/40/4/7/9/51/3/8/66/9/71/5/7, 2410/2/6/8/20/1/3/4/6/8/33/7/40/1/3/5/8/56/7, 2504/6/8/10/4/6/7/20/1/3–5/7/8/31/2/4/46–8/50/3/9/68/70/3/80/7/91/5/9, 2602/6/12/3/20/2/32/41/3/4, 2751–65/76–8/80/90/3/7/8, 2801–3/5/9–11/3/9/21/31/2/7/9/40/4/50/2/4/5/8/63/9/76–9/85/7/93, 2904/5/12/4–9/21–3/5–7, 3209/10/4/24/5/7/35/9/44/8/50/55/6/8/9/65/6/74/9–82, 3321/7/30/1/3/8/40/1/3–7/9/51–79/98, 3400/31/94/6, 3516/8/24/6/9–31/4/6/8–40/52/63/5/73/4/84/5/94/5/8, 3602/10/2–6/20/1/4–39/42–59/72–84, 4442–77, 5710/7/8/22/39/59/62–4/8/85/9/90/6/7, 5801/26/8/32/6/43/7–53, 6024/33/9/46/9.

The engines on Region Est were allocated to Châlons-sur-Marne, Mohon, Thionville, Hausbergen, Reding, Chalindrey, Metz, Nancy, Blainville and Saint Dizier; those on Region Nord to Aulnoye, Tergnier, Laon and Hirson; those on Region Ouest to Paris-Batignolles, Dreux, Trappes, Le Havre, Cherbourg, Mézidon, Lisieux, Argentan, Caen, Sainte-Gauburge and Lison; those on Region Sud-Est to Lyon-Mouche, Marseille-Blancarde and Chalon-sur-Saône; and the oil-fired engines on Region Sud-Est to Dijon, Lyon-Mouche, Miramas, Marseille-Blancarde and Marseille-Arenc.

In Belgium, the main sheds from which these 2–8–0s operated were Antwerp Dam and Louvain. There was an allocation to Antwerp Dam in January 1945, but from then until July 1945, this shed was used by the WD 2–8–0s. In July 1945, the USA/TC 2–8–0s started to take over the duties and by December 1945, very few WD 2–8–0s remained. The line to Roosendaal in the Netherlands, however, continued to be operated by WD 2–8–0s and USA/TC engines were very rare even at the close of 1945. In the early months of 1945, WD 2–8–0s were allo-

Plate 272 USA/TC 2–8–0s being prepared for service at Newport Ebbw Junction shed in South Wales ion March 1944 (Photo: R. Tourret Collection)

cated to Louvain but about March 1945, USA/TC 2–8–0s started to arrive and by June 1945, the only WD 2–8–0s to be seen were from other sheds. Muizen had a few USA/TC 2–8–0s, together with its WD 2–8–0s. Antwerp South had a few USA/TC 2–8–0s on loan for a time but otherwise used WD 2–8–0s. A large number of USA/TC 2–8–0s were allocated to Liège.

Around February 1945, eighteen of the locomotives were named after Transportation Corps men who had been killed in the line of duty. Amongst these were 1609, 2039/52, 2171/4/81/2, 2208, 2327/60, 2582, 2603/15, 2792 and 2913. USA/TC 2582 was named "Pvt H. J. O'Brien", 2792 "Pvt John M. McGillis" and 2913 "Pvt C. J. Anderson".

Towards the end of hostilities and afterwards, many of the locomotives which saw service in Belgium and the Netherlands, together with some of the French ones, were gathered together at Louvain. The main dump and a secondary one were in various sidings near the station. The first engines to arrive were 3213/5/9 at the end of March 1945 but the bulk of the engines arrived in April and May 1945. The following USA/TC 2–8–0s were present in May 1945; 3202/4–6/13/5/9/26/9–34/6–8/41/2/5–7/62, 3403/4, 3509–11/32/3/7/41–3/6–51/75/87/8, 3603/7, 4402–8/10–4/27–9/31–6/41, 5706/7/24/70–2/88/91/4/5 and 5804/5/7.

The position in Belgium at 28 September 1945 was that 217 USA/TC 2–8–0s were on loan to the SNCB as follows. There were 35 at Antwerp Dam 1602/38, 1749/91/8, 1817/26/40/4/85/9, 1913/7, 2073/4, 2325/45/6/8/57/62/4/7/72, 2402/13/9/36/8/54/5/90 and 2826/36/65; 27 at Louvain 1874, 2116/22/59/61/77, 2231/80/1/4/93/5/6/8, 2306/7/9/30/68, 2575, 2618, 2825/61/73, 2902/7 and 3503; 26 at Ronet 1723, 1805/16/80/95, 1904/7, 2110, 2227/62, 2363, 2400/18/31, 2529/90, 2603, 2864, 3200/23, 3429 and 3500/1/76/7/81; 23 at Renory 1634/90, 1819/35/46, 1921, 2055, 2136/43/62/78, 2414/7/27/9/46, 2501/18/49/52/85, 2604 and 2901; 22 at St Martins 1609/53/97, 2083, 2106/24/80, 2288, 2338, 2435, 2519/56, 2640/2. 2779/86, 2808/17/62, 3201, 3497 and 3502; 15 at Ans 1685, 1825, 2131/76/9/91, 2215/46, 2530/40/83, 2608/33 and 3504/5; 15 at Herbesthal 1649/64, 2108/81/6/97, 2237/68/73, 2304/19/28/42, 2567 and 2615; 15 at Landen 1647/56/8/60, 1700/1/27, 2350/9/76, 2452, 2526/71 and 2833/41; nine at Bruxelles Midi 1729/96, 2047/72, 2121/66/82, 2557 and 2886;

Plate 273 Dump of stored USA/TC 2–8–0s at Treforest in 1944, consisting of 119 locomotives in one long line! (Photo: R. Tourret Collection)

eight at Liége 1633, 2126/55, 2267/82, 2365, 2535 and 2913; seven at Aarschot 1680, 2082 and 2208/42/53/5/70; seven at Hasselt 1781, 2056, 2129, 2401, 2872 and 2909/10; six at Ottignies 1615/61, 2075, 2272/8 and 2906; and two at Muizen 1626/52.

At the same date, 52 were to be sent to store at Louvain 1607/18/28/30/5/9/99, 1788, 1815/24/41/84/6, 1908/20/3, 2085, 2100/2/17/20/3/60/3/8/74/5/94/9, 2218/40/51/4/60/5, 2313/43, 2408, 2505/15/39/64/6/76, 2610/4 and 2800/4/30/4/47/91. Nine were to be stored and put at the disposal of the USA/TC 1604, 1823, 2104, 2310, 2418, 2542/82/6 and 2639. USA/TC 3397 was not officially allocated to the SNCB at the time, but was used as the Liége/Ans banker, and probably came to Ans from Germany.

By October 1945, a considerable number of engines ex service had arrived at Louvain dump, but only a few more from the higher-numbered series, so that all the higher series probably came to the dump by June or July 1945. The influx of engines ex service required a secondary dump to be established in sidings around the station about July or August, and this was complete by October 1945.

There was also a storage dump at Ronet in Belgium. In April 1945 this held the following USA/TC 2–8–0s, 2889, 3207/17/8/20–2/49/50/2/4/61/3/5/7/9/74/98/9, 3400/93/5, 3525–9/36/44/5/52/3/5/7–60/6/7/85/6/96, 3604/8/9, 4423, 5710/20/1/3/65/7/9/73–5/80/1/3/6–8, 5806/8/12/3/6/7/23 and 6030/2/5/45/55/7/61/7/9/72.

At the end of 1945, the SNCF were considering acquiring 140 of the S160 locomotives, and decided to test two of them, one coal burner and one oil burner, at their test station at Vitry-sur-Seine. The purpose of these tests was to determine the power and riding characteristics at different speeds and the combustion efficiency and fuel consumption at the same conditions. The first locomotive tested was coal-burner USA/TC 6033 from Thionville depot, which was operated at 20, 40, 60 and 80 km/hr and fed with coal at 200, 300 and 400 kg/sq m/hr. As well as water and coal consumption, boiler pressure, smokebox vacuum, superheater temperature, exhaust gas, etc were measured. In view of the low steam capacity of 7.5 ton/hr at 20 km/hr, the exhaust system was modified twice and it was even considered to try a Kylchap exhaust. The maximum power obtained was 1405hp at 40km/hr, with 60% cylinder admission. Water was consumed at 12.5 ton/hr and coal at 1970 kg/hr.

The second locomotive tested was oil-burner USA/TC 3675 from Blainville depot. Again, the first tests revealed inadequate steam capacity, and the exhaust system was modified in the same way as the previous locomotive, but without any real improvement. The oil burner equipment was not considered satisfactory and some modifications proposed. The maximum power, limited by boiler capacity, was 1300hp.

It was concluded that from a technical point of view, oil-burning did not give any benefit over coal. The proposed modifications, including Kylchap exhaust, were not proceeded with due to lack of finance.

In April 1946, the SNCF decided not to proceed with the purchase of the USA/TC 2–8–0s, and shortly afterwards the massive 141R locomotives arrived under the Marshall Plan.

The process of breaking up the dumps began about February 1946, both the 2–8–0s and the 0–6–0Ts having the letters "UNRRA" painted on the tender and tank sides respectively and the "USA/TC" obliterated. With very few exceptions, all the USA/TC 2–8–0s in Europe were disposed of during 1946 and 1947. USA/TC 3257 returned to Great Britain in July 1946 and went to the Longmoor Military Railway in August 1946, where it was subsequently named "Major General Carl R. Gray". It was renumbered WD 700 in the postwar WD series in 1952 and scrapped in October 1957.

Two locomotives, USA/TC 2245 and 2835, were involved in accidents in Europe in March 1945 and were subsequently scrapped.

North Africa

The original estimate of the number of 2–8–0s required for the North African theatre was 250 but this was later scaled down as described in Chapter 5. The engines were received ready assembled at Oran. By July 1943, 135 had been received. Nine were stored but the remaining 126 were in service. These locomotives came from the series 1651–2081. The identities of 113 of them are known, as follows: 1650/7/67–76/92–6, 1711/5–9/24–6/32–48/50–5/8–61/3–7/70/4–9/82–7/99, 1800–3/13/37/8/51–70 and 2059/60/6–70/5–81. They saw service in Morocco, Algeria and Tunisia, working military freight eastwards from the ports in Morocco and Algeria.

Originally, during the war, the CFM (Morocco) was loaned 15 2–8–0s but as the tide of war passed and shipments came in to Oran and Algiers, the extra traffic on the CFM disappeared and the locomotives were moved eastwards to the CFA and CFT. However, presumably the CFM were appreciative of their performance because after the war, in June 1946, they took delivery of four engines from Europe; 2132, 2233, 2570 and 2641.

In Algeria, as well as working the main standard-gauge line from west to east, they also worked the branches to Philippeville and Bone, and of course from Algiers itself. Sixteen engines, 1657/67–71/3/6, 1726/35/8/42/87 and 1838/61/2, were left behind from the North African military operations in 1943/4 and remained in service on the CFA. Another ten engines, 1608, 2300, 2591, 2760, 3613/55/74 and 4442/3/7, were sent to Algeria from Europe in 1946 or 1947 after the cessation of hostilities. However, the postwar stock of these engines on the CFA was 25 and it is believed that they were numbered 140.U.1 to 25. USA/TC 1657/68/9/71, 1735 and 1838 are known to have become CFA 140.U.1/3/4/6/11/6 respectively and possibly USA/TC 1667/70/3 became CFA 140.U.2/5/7 but the precise identifies of the others are not known.

In Tunisia, to supplement the existing CFT locomotive stock, in June 1943 the British No 189 Rly Op Coy was allocated 18 USA/TC 2–8–0s. In October 1943, these 18 2–8–0s were exchanged for 14 different locomotives of the same type, apparently because the official, but disputed, service life under war conditions was supposed to be only six months! In fact, Tunisian water was so hard that the boilers had to be washed out every three days, until water softening measures increased this to weekly.

Plate 274 Dump of stored USA/TC 2–8–0s at Penrhos in April 1944, at this time guarded by armed US soldiers who had little sympathy towards railway enthusiasts! (Photo: R. Tourret Collection)

They worked the following routes; Tunis-Ghardimaou, Mastouta-Mateur, Djedeida-Mateur-Bizerta and the twice-weekly service to Tabarka, occasionally from Sidi Smail to Dakla, the triangles at Djedeida and Tindja, but not the Ferryville branch.

Some of the engines operated by the British were given names as follows:

1694	La Belle Patrie
1695	The Errant Knight
1759	The Royal Engineer
1760	Queen of the Hills
1763	Stanbury
1864	The Baron
1867	King George VI

"The Errant Knight" was so-called because on one occasion, being driven by L/C Knight, this locomotive was unintentionally diverted into a civil engineer's yard where it demolished some platelayers motor trolleys. L/C Knight was not amused, because the accident was not his fault, since the points were not interlocked with the indicator board!

In Tunisia, seven engines (by chance the named ones 1694/5, 1759/60/3 and 1864/7) were handed over from British operation to CFT operation in July 1943, the ownership of the engines remaining vested in the USA/TC. About mid-July 1944, three other locomotives of this class arrived in Tunisia from Morocco making ten engines in all on loan to the CFT. One was 1751, one was undoubtedly 1746, while the identity of the third is not known. Later, 1695, 1759/60 and the unknown engine were sent away from Tunisia to France, leaving six engines, 1694, 1746/51/63 and 1864/7 to be officially handed over to the CFT in July 1944. These became CFT 140.251–6 in 1946.

The remaining locomotives in North Africa not taken into CFA or CFT stock were stored until Italy was invaded, when many were sent there. Others not required in Italy were used for the invasion of Southern France. The official history of the USA/TC operations overseas mentions with regard to North Africa that approximately 16 locomotives were "lost to the enemy", without explaining the circumstances or the identity of the locomotives. The Kasserine offensive of the German forces seems not to have resulted in any permanent loss of "MacArthur" 2-8-2s on the metre-gauge lines in that area, but there are puzzling gaps in the post-war disposals of the USA/TC 2-8-0s, many of which affect locomotives which went to North Africa, such as the 13 engines 1674, 1715/7/9/33/43/8/66/77/8 and 1856/63/9. Other locomotives not accounted for, and which probably originally went to North Africa, are 1771 and 1850, making a total of 15. Was there a German raid on a locomotive dump somewhere?

Italy

Most of the North African engines were sent on to Italy in the period January to March 1944. Further engines were despatched directly to Italy from the United States, some from the 2736–75 series arriving in the summer of 1944, some from the 3275–3576 series at the end of 1944 and finally some from the 3611–5845 series in early 1945. In all, 244 engines of this class arrived in Italy and in February 1946, 100 were allocated to Rome, 50 to Leghorn, 40 to Florence, 25 to Falconara and 28 to Bologna, while 1869 had meanwhile been withdrawn due to accident damage. All these engines were oil-burners, except 4421/37 and 5825/9/34/5/44/5.

All the engines were taken over by the Italian State Railways (Ferrovie dello Stato or FS) after the war and became FS Class 736.001–243. Details of the FS renumbering follow:

FS 736.244–8 were five of six locomotives which sank in Rimini Harbour in ss Fanning. USA/TC 2093, 2755, 2839, 4469 and 5171 were salvaged and added to FS stock in 1948. The sixth locomotive, USA/TC 5180, was originally intended to become FS 736.249 but was subsequently retained for spares only.

During the last six months of 1959, twenty-five engines, FS 726.011/23/40/55/73/90, 101/2/26/7/31/5/51/8/60/4/6/78/88/90/9, 203/7/9/17, which had been displaced by the electrification of the Ancona-Pescara line, were sold to the Hellenic State Railway and became HSR 571–95 in order.

India

Sixty engines, USA/TC 3433–92, were built to 5ft 6in gauge and with detail fittings suitable for service on the Indian railways by Baldwin 70390–70449 in February to April 1944. They were allocated IGR Nos 6433–92 and went into traffic around August to December 1944 as Class "AWC". The US Army numbers were carried on plates on the right-hand side of the smokeboxes and the Baldwin plates, of the old circular variety, on the left-hand side. The

FS	0	1	2	3	4	5	6	7	8	9
736.00X	–	1650	1675	1693	1696	1711	1716	1718	1732	1734
736.01X	1737	1740	1741	1747	1752	1753	1761	1765	1767	1774
736.02X	1775	1782	1783	1785	1799	1851	1852	1857	1858	1860
736.03X	1865	1866	1868	1870	2059	2060	2066	2067	2068	2069
736.04X	2070	2078	2079	2080	2081	2736	2737	2738	2739	2740
736.05X	2741	2742	2743	2744	2745	2746	2747	2748	2749	2750
736.06X	2766	2767	2768	2769	2770	2771	2772	2773	2774	2775
736.07X	3275	3276	3277	3278	3283	3284	3285	3286	3287	3288
736.08X	3289	3290	3291	3292	3293	3294	3295	3296	3297	3298
736.09X	3299	3300	3301	3302	3303	3304	3305	3306	3307	3308
736.10X	3309	3310	3311	3312	3313	3314	3315	3316	3317	3318
736.11X	3319	3320	3322	3323	3324	3325	3326	3328	3329	3332
736.12X	3334	3335	3336	3337	3339	3342	3348	3350	3380	3381
736.13X	3382	3383	3384	3385	3386	3387	3388	3389	3390	3391
736.14X	3392	3393	3394	3395	3396	3405	3406	3407	3408	3411
736.15X	3412	3413	3414	3415	3416	3417	3418	3419	3420	3421
736.16X	3422	3423	3424	3425	3426	3427	3428	3430	3562	3568
736.17X	3569	3570	3571	3572	3611	3617	3618	3619	3622	3623
736.18X	3640	3641	3660	3661	3662	3663	3664	3665	3666	3667
736.19X	3668	3669	3670	3671	3685	3686	3687	3688	3689	3690
736.20X	3691	3692	3693	3694	3695	3696	3697	3698	3699	4418
736.21X	4421	4437	5701	5702	5731	5735	5736	5740	5741	5742
736.22X	5743	5744	5745	5746	5747	5748	5749	5750	5751	5752
736.23X	5753	5754	5755	5756	5757	5758	5760	5761	5825	5829
736.24X	5834	5835	5844	5845	2093	2755	2839	4469	5171	–

Plate 275 USA/TC 2867 being unloaded at Cherbourg in June 1944. USA/TC 0-6-0T 6009 standing in the foreground had just been unloaded (Photo: R. Tourret Collection)

numbers painted on the cabside were increased, as the engines were erected, by 3000 to bring them into the 64XX series in order to raise them above the highest number of any individual railway's locomotives. The tenders were at first lettered "B&A" or "EIR" but this soon gave place to "ISR" and then "IGR".

The final erection of the locomotives was carried out on arrival in India, the Great Indian Peninsular Railway turning out 28 from their Matunga Carriage & Wagon Shops, near Bombay (these shops having been adapted for the purpose of final assembly of wartime locomotives), between August and December 1944. The remaining 32 locomotives were erected by the Bengal & Assam Railway in their Kanchrapara Shops, near Calcutta. The Indian USA/TC 2-8-0s carried no Westinghouse pumps, reservoirs, brake valves, etc but were equipped with vacuum brakes, this being the usual Indian practice, and solid jet ejectors.

The engines were at first allocated to two of the lines carrying the heaviest volume of wartime traffic, the Bengal & Assam Railway using the ones that they had assembled, IGR 6433-44/57-62/7-73/9-81/3-5/90, and the East Indian Railway receiving the remainder which had been assembled by the GIPR. The EIR used their USA/TC 2-8-0s almost exclusively on the 132-mile stretch of the main line from Asansol into Calcutta and, in fact, mainly on the traffic bound for the BAR system at Naihati via the Jubilee Bridge over the River Hooghly, or from Calcutta Docks over the Willington Bridge to the EIR. The BAR used their 2-8-0s from Calcutta and Naihati Yard northwards to Santahar and Parbatipur, at which points most of the traffic was transferred to their metre-gauge system.

On or before the partition of India (from 15 August 1947), a few of the BAR 2-8-0s, probably 6433-9, went to the South Indian Railway. The EIR retained the 28 that it already had and received another 13 engines, 6441-4/67-70/9/81/3/4/90, from the BAR. This left 12 for the newly-constituted Eastern Bengal Railway (of Pakistan), namely 6440/57-62/71-3/80/5. However, all sixty engines of the class were due to go to the South Indian Railway and, by mid-1949, 25 had been received by that line. The final allocation was 14 to EIR and 46 to SIR, with none to East Pakistan. The EIR engines were 6441/7/9/57/9-61/73/9-81/3/4/90 and when the network was zoned, these engines went to the Eastern Railway.

They subsequently became 22601-14 in the All-India renumbering of 1957/8. The SIR engines were 6433-40/2-6/8/50-6/8/62-72/4-8/82/5-9/91/2 and when the network was zoned, these engines went to the Southern Railway. They became 22615-60 in the All-India renumbering.

Russia

Two hundred of these locomotives, USA/TC 2646-2735, 2930-89 and 3700-49, were built to 5ft 0in gauge and went to Russia in 1943, where they became USSR SZD Nos WA 1-200 respectively. This transliterates to SchA, the "A" standing for American. Some, at least, went by the North Sea route. Six were lost en route, Nos 2697-2700/14/5 while one, 2658 was retained in the USA for testing. Nos 2930-89 were USA/TC class S166 and Nos 3700-49 were USA/TC class S162.

They were not specifically designed for Russian requirements and were soon modified to have a weatherproof cab. By Russian standards, they were light-duty engines and were used for hauling suburban trains, empty stock and dock workings on the October Railway, and between Leningrad, Tallinin and Moscow. Later, they were used near the Baltic and on the Volga system.

In 1959-61, many S160 type locomotives were sent to North Korea from Leningrad and Estonia. They were taken to Ulan Ude works where 50 were rebuilt to 1067mm gauge and reclassified SchU, where the "U" presumably stood for Ulan Ude. They were then shipped to Sakhatin. In 1962, a further 94 locomotives were sent to North Korea. Eighty of these became Nos 3101-80 and the remaining fourteen were retained as spares. They were delivered over the bor-

Plate 276 USA/TC 2-8-0 1789 pilots an SNCF engine with a freight train pulling out of the railway yards at Laon in France. The yards had been damaged by Allied bombing. Photograph taken in October 1944 (Photo: R. Tourret Collection)

Plate 277 Allied train wrecks were not always caused by enemy action. A rear-end collision at Lourches at Christmas 1944 led to a sarcastic GI railroader to letter USA/TC 2845's tender accordingly (Photo: R. Tourret Collection)

United States

A few of these locomotives stayed in the United States throughout the war. USA/TC 1600, 1702 and 2628–31 were at Fort Eustis during the war. USA/TC 1600 subsequently went to Alaska, while 1702 subsequently became Warren and Saline River RR No 1702. USA/TC 2628-31 stayed at Fort Eustis to at least 1952. No 2628 was fitted with rotary-cam poppet-valve gear by Vulcan around 1950, and then was on loan to the Maryland & Penna RR in the same year, for trials. It was renumbered USA/TC 611 in the postwar series in 1953. USA/TC 2631 was similarly renumbered 612, and presumably USA/TC 2629/30 had been disposed of by 1953. USA/TC 5846 was at Fort Eustis, being renumbered 606 around 1952.

USA/TC 5187–99 were stored at Marietta TC Depot in December 1945, 5192/6/8 then being named "Edith Lehman", "Fiorella La Guardia" and "Herbert H. Lehman" respectively. Nos 5188–99 went to China in January 1946 under UNRRA arrangements, but 5187 remained behind and went to Fort Eustis in 1946, where it was renumbered 607 in the post-war series around 1952.

Other Countries

The Jamaican Government Railway purchased two of these engines, Nos 2898/9, in 1943, which became JGR Class P Nos 60/1. In 1945, a further three engines were obtained through the British Colonies Supply Mission to Washington. These were Alco 73749–51 of USA/TC Class S161 and were built under the makers order No S1977. They

(der at Khasan and eventually regauged at Chongjin Works in 1963/4.)

Plate 278 In February 1945, the MRS began operation of the "Toot Sweet Special" (Note the pun on the French word for immediately) to carry top-priority freight at express schedules to the fighting front. The commander of the 728 ROB, Lt Col Carl D. Love, issues orders to the crew of USA/TC 2-8-0 1822 prior to its inaugural departure from Cherbourg on 10 February 1945 (Photo: R. Tourret Collection)

became JGR Class P1 Nos 62–4. The last three were never allocated USA/TC running numbers and none of the five engines saw service with the USA/TC, the JGR obtaining them directly from the makers. These engines were fitted with cow-catchers and headlights.

Two engines built by Alco 71331/2 in 1943 went directly to the Central Railway of Peru to become Class 80 Nos 55/6. These were almost certainly the same design as the USA/TC engines. They were scrapped in 1965.

The Mexican Railway (Vera Cruz to Mexico City) had eleven 2–8–0s Nos 210–20 built by Baldwin 73236–46 in 1946, which appear to have been the same basic design as the USA/TC engines, although of course these were never USA/TC.

Jugoslavia

Sixty-five locomotives went to Jugoslavia, the first 51 between December 1945 and June 1946 under the auspices of UNRRA, and the rest probably a little later. They became JDZ 37.001–65 (Jugoslovenske Drzavne Zeleznica or Jugoslav State Railways). These 65 engines were used at Vinkovci, Doboj Novi etc where they ran on the lines from Slavonski Brod to Beograd, from Vrpolje to Sarajevo and from Sisak to Split. They behaved well, but were eventually taken out of service around the late 1960s due to the boilers becoming defective.

Details of the renumbering, so far as they are known, are given below:

Plate 279 USA/TC 1779 being unloaded at Casablanca in French Morocco in early 1943 (Photo: R. Tourret Collection)

JDZ	0	1	2	3	4	5	6	7	8	9
37.00X	–	3202	3204	3205	3206	3213	3215	3219	3226	3227
37.01X	3228	3229	3230	3231	3233	3234	3238	3241	3245	3246
37.02X	3247	3262	3403	3404	3525	3575	3587	3597	3601	4420
37.03X	4423	4424	5160	5161	5163	5165	5175	5177	5183	5184
37.04X	5185	5186	5706	5707	6036	6050	6053	6054	6057	6058
37.05X	6059	6065	?	6052	?	6026	4426	4422	4419	?
37.06X	?	3527	?	?	?	3232	–	–	–	–

USA/TC 3242 is also known to have gone to the JDZ.

Oesterreichische Bundesbahnen

Thirty engines went to the Oesterreichische Bundesbahnen (OBB or Austrian Federal Railways) in March and April 1946, and were renumbered as follows:

OBB	0	1	2	3	4	5	6	7	8	9
956.0X	–	1655	1672	1802	1809	1832	1853	1882	2130	2536
956.1X	2621	2795	3243	3267	3553	5784	5827	–	–	–
956.11X	–	–	–	–	–	–	–	1811	1914	2063
956.12X	2064	2277	2335	2356	2785	2794	2815	2822	2908	2928
956.13X	5837	–	–	–	–	–	–	–	–	–

Nos 956.01–16 were rebuilt by the OBB with larger cab, larger smoke-box door, air-brake pump at the side, electric lighting, etc., whereas OBB 956.117–30 were left in their original condition and were not used much. OBB 956.01–16 were shedded at Linz, Bischofshofen and Wels. From Linz, they operated light fast freight trains to Vienna and Selzthal. By 1955, 956.03/10/5 were derelict at Wels shed, 956.11 was working at Linz and the remainder were stored at Linz. Apart from 3553 and 5837 which were converted to heating boilers, all were scrapped between June 1955 and January 1956.

Deutsche Bundesbahn

Forty locomotives were operated from Bremen in 1947 by the Deutsche Bundesbahn and it is fairly certain that they were the only USA/TC locomotives operating on the DB at that time. It would also seem that they were the last USA/TC 2–8–0s to operate in Europe other than those sold, or disposed of via UNRRA. On withdrawal in August 1947, all are believed to have been sent to Hungary.

Hellenic State Railways

Twenty-seven engines went to Greece in 1947 and became Hellenic State Railways Class THg Nos 521–37/51–60, the first series being coal burners and the second series oil burners. During the last six months of 1959, twenty-five Italian FS class 736 were sold to the HSR and became HSR 571–95 in order of their FS numbers.

Details of the numberings are as follows (see opposite):

Leastwise, the above is the theory of it. In fact, it is not quite as given above. During the LCGB Tour of Greece in

HSR	0	1	2	3	4	5	6	7	8	9
52X	–	2050	2112	2127	2154	2206	2428	2443	2229	2456
53X	2573	3398	3524	1781	2166	2226	2365	2537	–	–
55X	–	3338	3352	3364	3374	3375	3327	3347	3357	3360
56X	3372	–	–	–	–	–	–	–	–	–
57X	–	1740	1785	2070	2746	3278	3299	3310	3311	3348
58X	3350	3383	3387	3413	3420	3422	3426	3428	3622	3666
59X	3668	3690	3694	3698	4418	5740	–	–	–	–

April 1980, the by then dumped engines were studied in great detail so far as surviving markings allowed, with the following results. It was evident that some exchanges of identity had taken place.

In the list below, details are given as visible on the locomotives. Other details given for convenient reference but not sighted, are placed in brackets.

521	(2050)	A70532/42	Correct
522	2112	A70594/43	Correct
523	2428	A70777/43	2428 A 70777/43 should be HSR 526
524	2443	A70792/43	2443 A 70792/43 should be HSR 527
525	2206	L8212/43	Correct. Hauled LCGB special train
526	2573	L8275/(43)	2573 L8275/43 should be HSR 530
527	3338	A71593/44	3338 A71593/44 should be HSR 551
528	2229	L8235/43	Correct
529	2456	A70805/43	Correct
530	–	–	
531	–	–	
532	3524	B70481/44	Correct
533	(1781)	B67615/(42)	Correct
534	–	–	
535	(2226)	L8232/43	Correct
536	2365	B69622/43	Correct
537	2537	L8354/43	Correct
551	–	A71607/44	A71607/44 should be HSR 552 US 3352. US number on locomotive appeared to be 3?77. 3277 was FS 736.072 A71532/44. 3377 A71632/44 went back to USA/TC but not FS. 3477 was Indian. 3577 was L8490/44. 3677 was L8590/44.
552	2127	A70609/43	2127 A70609/43 should be HSR 523
553	3364	A71619/44	Correct
554	3374	A71629/44	Correct
555	3375	A71630/44	Correct
556	3327	A71582/44	Correct
557	3347	(A71602/44)	Correct
558	3357	(A71612/44)	Correct
559	3360	A71615/44	Correct
560	–	–	

571	736.011	1711	B 64550/42	1711 B64550/42 was FS 736.005
572	736.023	1785	B67619/42	Correct
573	736.040	1740	B67574/42	1740 B67574/42 was FS 736.011
574	736.055	–	B70383/44	B70383/44 was 3426 FS 736.164
575	736.073	3383	B70340/44	3383 B70340/44 should be HSR 581
576	–	–	–	
577	736.101	3278	A71533/44	3278 A71533/44 should be HSR 575
578	736.102	3698	L8611/44	3698 L8611/44 should be HSR 593
579	736.126	3348	B71603/44	Correct
580	736.127	3310	A71565/44	3310 A71565/44 should be HSR 577
581	736.131	–	–	
582	736.135	3293	A71548/44	3293 A71548/44 was FS 736.084
583	–	3571	L8484/44	3571 L8484/44 should be FS 736.172
584	736.158	3413	B70370/44	3413 B70370/44 should be HSR 583
585	–	3422	B70379/44	Correct
586	736.164	3426	A71577/44	3426 is correct for 736.164 but A71577/44 was 3322 FS 736.112
587	736.166	3395	L8607/44	L8607/44 should be US 3694. 3395 was FS 736.143 B70352/44. HSR 587 should be 3428.
588	736.178	–	A70551/43	A70551/43 was US 2069 FS 736.039. FS 736.178 was US 3622 L8535/44. USA/TC No on locomotive appeared to end in a "2"
589	736.188	3666	L8579/44	Correct
590	736.190	3668	L8581/44	Correct
591	–	3690	L8603/44	Correct
592	736.203	3420	B70377/44	3420 B70377/44 should be HSR 584. Accident damage
593	736.207	–	–	
594	–	–	–	
595	736.217	–	–	

Turkey

Fifty locomotives went to Turkey in 1947 and became TCDD (Turkiye Cumhuriyeti Devlet Demiryollari Isletmesi or Turkish State Railways) 45171–220, as follows:

The air pump was repositioned at the side of the smokebox, and the smokebox door was modified, but they otherwise mostly retained their original appearance. The last survivors remained in service until the late 1980s.

Two S160 locomotives had passed to the military MKE at Kirikkale by 1976. These were MKE 45001/2, ex USA/TC 2210 (Lima 8216 TCDD 45215) and 2118 (Alco 70600 TCDD 45210) respectively. Both were noted in use shunting at Kirikkale in 1976, but by 1983 only 45001 was in service and 45002 had been dumped alongside a factory.

Hungary

Five hundred and ten engines went to Hungary and became MAV (Magyar Allamvasutak) 411.001–484, leaving 26 that were used for spares and never renumbered. In 1961, two further locomotives were assembled from the spare parts and put into service as MAV 411.485/6, to replace two lost by collision.

They formed what then appeared to be practically the only freight class on this system, while some were used on passenger services as well. They were fitted with taller chimneys with spark arrestors, and painted black with a red lining. They were still in service in 1965, and some were still in service in 1977.

Details of the renumbering from USA/TC to MAV are as follows:

The following locomotives were also received by MAV but were kept for spares only: 1645/90, 1721, 1828/34/42, 1901/13/25, 2051/95, 2107/14, 2264/84, 2315/9, 2437/41/4, 2586/8, 2811, 3200, 3397 and 3500.

TCDD	0	1	2	3	4	5	6	7	8	9
4517X	–	2837	2524	2919	2879	2759	3595	2416	2223	2247
4518X	1707	2150	2912	1757	2926	2797	2516	2263	5739	1878
4519X	1808	2595	2301	1909	2911	5710	2256	1881	1875	2048
4520X	2355	2135	2852	2813	2922	2157	1892	2238	2137	2547
4521X	2118	1893	2094	2227	2311	2210	2347	2133	3539	2125
4522X	2622	–	–	–	–	–	–	–	–	–

MAV No	0	1	2	3	4	5	6	7	8	9
411.00X	–	1618	1920	2251	2576	1786	2309	1800	1725	2138
411.01X	2286	2074	1776	2546	2352	1894	2320	2454	3203	2925
411.02X	2513	3604	2046	2085	2295	2645	1798	2457	2786	2143
411.03X	2321	1606	2518	2806	2239	1656	1749	2368	2179	1821
411.04X	2272	2905	1840	2324	2102	2865	2176	2506	2305	2123?
411.05X	2758	2521	2821	2421	1617	2345	1833	2459	2354	2330
411.06X	1884	1801	1823	1641	2565	2171	1827	2334	1644	2501
411.07X	2304	1653	1651	1627	2169	3526?	2224	2552	2842	5778
411.08X	2057	2523	2086	2221	2151	2361	2172	2914	1601	2257
411.09X	1614	2639	2503	2159	2231	2131	2357	2182	2436	1662
411.10X	1829	2407	2220	2275	2072	2923	2039	2318	2192	1897
411.11X	1643	3259	2841	3552	2342	2042	1654	2285	3540	2787
411.12X	1759	2113	2526	2350	2915	5712	2139	2840	2921	1818
411.13X	2542	2887	1848	3499	2327	2188	2510	3529	1730	2778
411.14X	2265	2203	2250	2520	6046	2824	2450	1712	2162	3498
411.15X	1739	1847	2854	2757	3580	2298	4453	5733	6076	6070
411.16X	5716	2528	1607	2293	2341	2452	1620	2420	2575	1684
411.17X	1755	1660	1665	2924	1714	2751	1788	1691	2916	2156
411.18X	2225	2222	2790	2878	2271	2082	1640	1706	2367	2212
411.19X	2777	2333	2869	1612	2448	1658	2088	2868	1916	3494
411.20X	2817	2122	2877	3429	4465	2564	2804	2168	2599	2580
411.21X	2243	2458	5705	2043	2155	2242	2913	1803	5815	3583
411.22X	1642	1814	1678	2613	2202	1918	2607	2348	2596	2411
411.23X	2344	2144	6071	2149	2110	2056	2270	1831	6032	2409
411.24X	1773	2812	6047	4473	2756	2269	2530	2185	2830	6034
411.25X	6077	6031	2259	2140	5174	2560	5776	2440	2373	2101
411.26X	2103	6029	6028	2583	2781	6024	2836	2632	2049	1789
411.27X	5181	5167	1683	6033	6030	2779	2316	1822	2805	2543
411.28X	1622	2856	2845	2825	2362	2820	2158	6035	5179	2818
411.29X	2415	2299	1756	1784	2906	2322	4479	6037	4458	2310
411.30X	2832	6040	1843	2602	1663	6045	1879	3250	1745	4450
411.31X	1636	2512	3431	3266	2446	4466	1917	2117	2606	1885
411.32X	2105	2165	1849	2517	1744	1713	2073	2418	1855	1912
411.33X	2449	2826	2240	1854	4467	2281	2289	2364	2363	1819
411.34X	2153	1813	2539	1613	2296	2375	2273	6060	1623	2545
411.35X	1731	2502	1758	1637	2851	1873	1695	2572	6056	2882
411.36X	2055	2892	3402	2862	2793	2810	1723	2237	2422	2455
411.37X	2358	2643	2119	1906	2370	2053	1628	1610	2167	2644
411.38X	2336	1602	1704	1619	1797	1908	2099	2574	1631	1911
411.39X	1709	1904	4457	2509	1791	2617	1639	2888	4475	2104
411.40X	3646	3626	3649	3659	3633	3620	5763	3632	3648	3280
411.41X	3657	3634	3681	5762	5764	3651	3650	3354	3642	3631
411.42X	3629	3351	3281	3676	3682	3330	3610	3627	3615	3340
411.43X	3654	3683	3644	3680	3369	3679	3355	3378	3616	3362
411.44X	3333	3370	3371	3279	3684	3614	3377	3625	3658	3647
411.45X	3321	3358	3630	3637	3636	3331	3678	3345	3346	5759
411.46X	3343	3373	3363	3365	3367	3653	3379	3672	3353	3356
411.47X	3366	3344	3638	3628	3635	3677	3675	3359	3673	3621
411.48X	2429	2071	6039	6043	1689	–	–	–	–	–

Plate 280 USA/TC 1740 coupled to newly converted Italian and German coaches operating as an ambulance train, being loaded with wounded troops at Riardo in Italy in 1944 (Photo: R. Tourret Collection)

Czechoslovakia

The Czechoslovakia State Railways (Ceskoslovenske Statni Drahy or CSD) received eighty of these engines which were numbered 456.101–80. Their cabs and chimneys were increased in height and some were fitted with full-size smoke-box doors. They were used on freight trains and for banking, mainly in the Bratislava and Moravia areas, and from the Austrian to the Polish border, but only on light trains.

Details of the CSD renumbering are given opposite.

CSD No	0	1	2	3	4	5	6	7	8	9
456.10X	–	1621	1630	1705	1872	2147	2187	2207	2403	2430
456.11X	2442	2594	2600	2823	2843	2846	2889	2900	3207	3208
456.12X	3220	3222	3249	3251	3252	3254	3264	3268	3269	3270
456.13X	3272	3273	3493	3495	3514	3517	3528	3535	3554	3555
456.14X	3556	3557	3559	3560	3564	3566	3567	3589	3593	3596
456.15X	3599	3609	4416	4438	4439	4440	5709	5721	5723	5766
456.16X	5767	5769	5773	5780	5781	5786	5787	5792	5798	5799
456.17X	5803	5806	5808	5812	5813	5816	5817	5818	5819	5822
456.18X	5823	–	–	–	–	–	–	–	–	–

Plate 281 USA/TC 2-8-0 3671 in Rome in January 1946 (Photo: R. Tourret Collection)

Poland

The Polish State Railways, Polskie Koleje Panstwowe or PKP, received 575 of these engines from July 1946 to October 1947. The first 75 engines arrived under the auspices of UNRRA and were renumbered Tr 201.1–75, while the remaining 500 apparently came as USA/TC and were renumbered TR 203.1–500. There is little or no external difference between the two classes, and some evidence of interchange between them, so it is now though that the only difference was the original lettering on the locomotives. These engines, which appear to be largely unaltered except for chimney extensions, were used for freight duties.

In the mid-fifties, the PKP were concerned about the deterioration of the boilers of their class OK22 4-6-0s and rather than build large replacement boilers for them, it was decided that a cheaper solution would be to fit Tr 203 (not Tr 201, for some reason) boilers, which were still in good condition as the machines had been mainly confined to light duties, to the OK22s and fit new small boilers to the then surplus 2-8-0 chassis. Three OK22s were thus rebuilt to OK55s, and one 2-8-0 chassis received a new boiler and side tanks to become a TKr55.

By 1969, thirty-two of the USA/TC 2-8-0s had been scrapped but the rest were still in service, but by 1988 few if any remained in service. It is good that PKP Tr 203.474 was bought for the Keighley and Worth Valley Railway and arrived there in November 1977.

The renumbering shown in the table opposite is all nice theory and was probably correct originally, but the few recorded actual observations in recent years generally indicate that much changing around of boilers, which carry the works plates, has occurred. The few details known are shown below.

Tr 201.22	2083	
Tr 201.59	5772	Correct
Tr 203.08	2765	
Tr 203.36	5783	
Tr 203.46	1754	Correct
Tr 203.65	2121	
Tr 203.142	2287	
Tr 203.163	1648	
Tr 203.173	2100	Correct
Tr 203.201	3263	
Tr 203.220	2232	and 2561, the latter not even known as going to Poland
Tr 203.221	2194	
Tr 203.236	5737	
Tr 203.256	1779	
Tr 203.257	4432	
Tr 203.286	2255	Correct

Details of the Tr 201 class are as follows

Tr 201	0	1	2	3	4	5	6	7	8	9
1–9	–	3509	3510	3511	3532	3533	3537	3541	3542	3543
10–19	3546	3547	3548	3549	3550	3551	3588	3600	3603	3606
20–29	3607	4402	4403	4404	4405	4406	4407	4408	4409	4410
30–39	4411	4412	4413	4414	4427	4428	4429	4430	4431	4432
40–49	4433	4434	4435	4436	4441	4482	4483	5157	5158	5159
50–59	5162	5164	5166	5176	5178	5724	5738	5770	5771	5772
60–69	5782	5788	5791	5793	5794	5795	5804	5805	5807	5838
70–75	5839	5840	5841	5842	5857	5859	–	–	–	–

Details of the Tr 203 class are as follows

Tr 201	0	1	2	3	4	5	6	7	8	9
1–9	–	3602	1629	1616	1666	2044	1830	1760	1815	1648
10–19	2511	1632	1625	1837	1770	1762	1812	1805	1722	1624
20–29	1790	1768	1635	1604	1626	1780	1810	1652	1794	2041
30–39	1793	1708	1729	2032	1836	2807	1841	1817	1609	1807
40–49	1615	1816	2047	1792	1845	1835	1754	2033	1806	1839
50–59	1720	1750	1649	1820	1634	1772	1779	1846	2244	2637
60–69	2831	2917	2439	2340	2532	2844	2276	2525	2884	2636
70–79	2829	2507	2551	2550	2412	2819	2780	2349	1910	2366
80–89	2445	2424	2287	2410	2062	2291	2216	2798	2623	2802
90–99	2605	2109	2867	2890	2897	2419	2803	1692	1903	1686
100–109	2447	2453	2868	2314	2297	2434	2152	2569	2624	1824
110–119	2317	2598	2577	2579	2883	2115	2881	2610	2500	2111
120–129	2427	2404	1681	2581	2601	2874	2164	2816	2181	2578
130–139	2235	1700	2331	2880	2796	2857	2638	2329	2788	2782
140–149	2792	2783	2784	2065?	2252	2508	2858	2134	2184	2254
150–159	2853	2619	2559	2351	1887	2584	2553	2855	2274	2514
160–169	2593	2763	2128	2789	2562	2870	2566	2799	2801	1877
170–179	2849	2920	2098	2100	2791	2200	2371	2860	2160	2141
180–189	2328	1677	2425	3201	2904	2531	1899	2146	2918	2827
190–199	2191	2120	2290	2541	2145	2052	2859	2903	2592	2582
200–209	2236	2505	1888	1825	1883	2838	2123?	2401	2108	1886
210–219	2533	2338	2359	1699	2590	2177	2097	2833	2808	2303
220–229	1796	2116	2208	2218	2540	2585	2278	2535	2217	2262
230–239	2313	2800	2402	2902	2548	2563	2194	1697	2214	2260
240–249	2219	2307	2895	2435	2519	2142	2609	2909	2834	1701
250–259	1889	2896	2861	2431	2615	2246	2633	2873	1926	2776
260–269	2515	2433	2083	2847	2261	2612	2587	2283	2406	1880
270–279	2121	2765	2288	2556	2640	2180	1647	2603	2234	2828
280–289	2353	1907	2451	2557	1919	2266	2255	2195	2089	2253
290–299	2809	5821	2529	2282	1898	2199	2438	1921	2554	2175
300–309	2124	2360	2228	2894	2558	2267	2170	2927	2764	2893
310–319	2901	2910	2129	2891	2084	2754	1687	2886	2211	2346
320–329	1915	1896	2400	1844	2616	2642	2302	1900	2871	2850
330–339	2504	1679	2163	2611	2215	2568	6074	1826	1685	2294
340–349	2280	2408	2864	2173	2106	1769	2907	2198	1876	2814
350–359	2544	2372	2534	2232	1924	2077	1682	2567	2369	1698
360–369	2075	2054	2343	2872	3209	3210	3225	5722	3239	3400
370–379	5718	3214	3496	3224	3585	3265	3534	3255	3573	3563
380–389	3558	3217	3244	3211	3212	3218	3513	3591	3590	3221
390–399	3260	3263	3586	5719	3515	3512	3261	3518	3274	3519
400–409	3520	5728	3432	3584	5727	5720	3235	3248	5708	5734
410–419	5732	5703	5717	5730	3578	3258	5711	5715	3271	3501
420–429	3506	3504	3401	3545	3505	3530	3256	3538	3531	3598
430–439	5737	3508	3544	3507	3399	5725	3503	5729	3592	5726
440–449	5704	3576	3223	3577	3700	3502	3497	3581	5789	5849
450–459	5850	5801	5836	5852	5811	5790	5796	5847	5775	5814
460–469	5843	5783	5830	5824	5831	5802	5800	5833	5809	5848
470–479	5779	5810	5851	5828	5820	5826	5797	5853	5777	5765
480–489	5832	6069	4477	4476	4444	5785	6061	5768	6073	6049
490–499	4474	3608	6078	6072	4460	4463	4459	4462	4461	3605
500	6066	–	–	–	–	–	–	–	–	–

Tr 203.302	3586	
Tr 203.305	2814	
Tr 203.327	2032	
Tr 203.341	6069	
Tr 203.348	5807	
Tr 203.376	3239	
Tr 203.415	3258	Correct
Tr 203.418	2145	
Tr 203.428	3531	Correct
Tr 203.437	1836	
Tr 203.439	5726	Correct
Tr 203.474	4435	
Tr 203.486	2901	

USA/TC 5164 Tr 201.51 is preserved in the Warsaw Railway Museum.

South Korea

One hundred and one engines were sent to South Korea in 1947 for service on the Korean National Railroad and were renumbered CS2.1 to CS2.101 in order of their USA/TC numbers. Not all details are known, but the following engines were amongst those sent: 1603/64, 1710/27/64, 1895, 1923, 2045, 2174/96, 2292, 2308/12/25/6/37/9/74/7, 2405, 2571, 2608/14/8/20/34, 2752/3/62, 2863/85, 3516/36/61/5, 3652, 4445/9/51/4–6/64/8/70/2/8/80/1, 5156/68–70/2, 5713, 5855/6/8, 6025/7/38/41/2/4/8/51/62/4/7/8/75.

So far as is known, the engines were renumbered as follows (opposite).

China

Forty S160 engines went to China in 1947 becoming Class KD6 461–500. The following are known to have gone to China: 1646/80, 1724/8/95, 1804, 2178, 2201, 2306/23/76/8, 2597, 2604/25/35 and 5188–99. Around a dozen of the S160 engines were on board SS Belpareil passing through the Suez Canal in 1947 and presumably were bound for China or South Korea. Of these, 2522 and 2875 were identifiable.

These Chinese locomotives were altered in appearance by a taller chimney and larger cab, as well as other minor modifications. It is not known where these engines were used, but a number ended up at the giant opencast coal mine at Fushan, where they were used for various purposes such as construction, demolition and maintenance. The engines at Fushan include KD6 463/73/8/89/90. Engine 473 has been checked and found to be carrying USA/TC 1646. No 490 was also checked but no identification was visible. Recently, KD6 477 has been checked and found to be USA/TC 2178.

Alaska Railroad

After the war, twelve locomotives, USA/TC 2379–82, 2626/7, 3523/1/2, 3410/09 and 1600, went to the Alaska Railroad and became ARR 551–62 in that order. Nos 3409/10 are noteworthy in so far as they are the only two locomotives of this class which are known to have returned from Europe to USA (in 1947) after World War II. Six of the engines, ARR 551/4/6/7/61/2, remained in service by November 1955.

F.C.Langreo, Spain

In February 1958, five engines from the Alaska Railroad, ARR 552/5/8–60 ex USA/TC 2380, 2626, 3521/2 and 3410, were sold to F.C.Langreo in Asturias in Spain and retained the same numbers as on the ARR. This railway had a rope-hauled incline between Florida and San Pedro, which was eliminated by a new avoiding line on which the 2–8–0s were used. USA/TC 3410 thus crossed the Atlantic three times.

Ultimate Disposals

It has not proved easy to account for all the S160 class locomotives, a total of 2120 engines dispersed world-wide. The reasonably definite disposals are as follows:

Plate 282 USA/TC 2–8–0 2255 crossing a repaired viaduct at Stolberg in 1945 (Photo: R. Tourret Collection)

KNR No	0	1	2	3	4	5	6	7	8	9
CS2.X	–	1603	?	?	1664	?	?	?	?	?
CS2.1X	?	?	?	1923	2045	?	2174	?	?	?
CS2.2X	?	?	?	?	?	2292	2308	2312	2325	2326
CS2.3X	2337	2339	2374	2377	2405	?	?	?	?	?
CS2.4X	?	2571	2608	2614	2618	2620	2634	2752	2753	2762
CS2.5X	?	?	2885	?	3516	3536	?	3561	3565	?
CS2.6X	?	?	4445	4449	4451	4454	4455	4456	4464	4468
CS2.7X	4470	4472	4478	4480	4481	5156	5168	5169	5170	5172
CS2.8X	?	?	?	?	?	5855	5856	5858	6025	6027
CS2.9X	6038	6041	6042	6044	6048	6051	6062	6064	6067	6068
CS2.10X	6075	?	–	–	–	–	–	–	–	–

Lost en route	18
OBB	30
Greece	27 (+25)
Turkey	50
Jugoslavia	66
Hungary	510
Czechoslovakia	80
Poland	575
South Korea	101
China	40
Tunisia	6
Algeria	25
Morocco	4
Italy	249 (–25)
India	60
Russia	200
Alaska	12
USA	7
Jamaica	2
Written off	2
	2064

Plate 283 USSR W^a1 (USA/TC 2646) ready for shipment to Russia, mounted on a flat car at Eddystone, Pennsylvania, in 1943 (Photo: H. L. Goldsmith Collection)

A ship-load, say 12, were sunk in a ship going to Antwerp. Finally, the PKP may have had another 30 engines as spare. If these are true, and assuming a modest 10 wrecked, written off etc, then just about all the locomotives are accounted for!

One USA/TC 2-8-0 is preserved on the Keighley and Worth Valley Railway, 5820 imported from Poland as Tr 203.474 in November 1977. Actually, this locomotive is somewhat of a mixture of parts. The locomotive is nominally USA/TC 5820 Lima 8758/45. However, the boiler is Alco 73427 from USA/TC 4435, which had been fitted in March 1975. Further detailed examination has revealed that the left-hand frame casting is Lima dated January 1943 and the right-hand frame casting is Baldwin also dated January 1943. The buffer beam, frame stretcher, both cylinder castings, valve-gear weight shaft and associated castings and the drag box casting are all Alco. Its radius rod is in the normal upper half of the expansion link when in forward gear, suggesting that the motion is from an earlier locomotive, but it has the screw reverse and stepped running plate on the right-hand side characteristic of the last batch of Lima locomotives. It entered service on the K&WVR in March 1978.

Another USA/TC 2-8-0 preserved in the UK is HSR 575, ex USA/TC 3383, which was shipped to the UK in August 1984. It now resides on the Mid Hants Railway. More recently, PKP Tr 203.288, which should be USA/TC 2089, arrived on the NYMR in October 1992; and MAV 411.388 (USA/TC 1631) has been bought by the East Lancashire Railway.

Boiler Explosions

As built, the S160 2-8-0s had only one water gauge-glass, the valves for which were of the wheel-type screw-down variety, unlike the plug cock type usually used in Britain. It was therefore not immediately apparent if the top or bottom valves were open or closed. Further, the valve for closing the top of the gauge-glass was situated on a manifold above the backplate where it was one of a row of similar wheel-type valves. It was thus possible to turn off the top gauge-glass valve in error for another valve, such as that for the Westinghouse

Plate 284 USSR W^a24 (USA/TC 2669) loaded on to a Pennsylvania RR flat car ready for shipment (Photo: R. Tourret Collection)

pump. When the gauge-glass valve was closed, the water level remained stationary in the gauge, irrespective of what happened in the boiler, and false indications of adequate water were given. When the possibility of this error occurring became known, instructions were issued by the USA/TC and British railways that the test-cocks on the other side of the backplate should be used from time to time as a safeguard.

In traffic, the engines gained an unfortunate reputation for collapsed fireboxes, far more than could be attributed to accidental causes. These collapses were experienced in Britain, France, Belgium, Germany, Italy, Tunisia, India, Algeria, Czechoslovakia, Poland and Korea. Typical examples were 1707 at South Harrow on 30 August 1944, 1829 at Louvain in October 1945, 2363 at Thurston on 12 January 1944, 2403 at Honeybourne on 17 November 1943, 3451 on the EIR in November 1944, 3460 on the BAR in February 1946 and KNR CS2.39 at Yongdung-po on 18 September 1952.

The first collapses were put down to the deceptive water-gauge indications as described above, but the explosive nature of the failures went far beyond the "normal" dropping of the fusible plug and scorching that might be expected from operation with too low a water level. Finally, other possible causes were suggested by a Frenchman, Mon M Chan (Chemins de Fer, No 4, 1945) and an Italian, Dr Ing Ugo Cantutti (Ingeneria Ferroviaria, Nos 7 & 8, 1947). As a result of their investigations, it was shown that there was an inherent weakness in the roof stays of the firebox at the point where they entered the inner firebox wrapper plate. The stays were screwed and beaded over on the fire side, but the pitch of the screw was such that only five threads were engaged with the plate, and the stress on these threads appeared to be at the limit of safety under normal conditions. Should the temperature of any individual stay rise unduly, the metal of the threads became weakened, and deformed or broke, with the result that the stay pulled out of the wrapper plate. A temperature rise could be caused by low water or the formation of scale. It was calculated that the formation of less than 3/32in thickness of scale in the boiler would make the firebox highly dangerous. Since these locomotives were working under war conditions, often in districts with hard water, it was fortunate that more collapses did not occur, for military exigencies made regular washouts difficult to obtain.

The SNCF got rid of these engines from their railways as soon as possible but the FS had to use them due to the shortage of other motive power. As immediate action, the FS lowered the boiler pressure from 225 to 200psi. A metal plate was placed over the bottom of the gauge-glass to ensure that sufficient water was carried in the boiler, a minimum level of 1in being given over the firebox roof. New Italian-pattern fusible plugs were fitted in which the lead was at a constant level above the firebox sheet, since the original pattern permitted a variation of this level by as much as 3/8in (the original fusible plugs had also been found unsatisfactory and

Plate 285   USA/TC 2628 built for service in the United States at Fort Eustis. Fitted with rotary-cam poppet-valve gear by Vulcan in 1950. Photographed at Delta, Pa, in August 1950 (Photo: R. Tourret Collection)

Plate 286   USA/TC 2629 at Portland, Oregon, in August 1947. Built for service in the United States at Fort Eustis. Note the steam reversing gear (Photo: H. L. Goldsmith Collection)

replaced in Britain). As the stays came up for renewal, they were replaced with a type that had conical heads and finer screw pitch to allow twelve threads to engage in the wrapper sheet. To ensure adequate washing out and cleanliness of the boiler, two mudholes were fitted at the base of the smokebox tubeplate, a washout plug was fitted at the base of the smokebox tubeplate, and eight existing washout plugs round the firebox were replaced by six mudholes. Finally, as the inner fireboxes came up for renewal, the thickness of the plates was increased from $3/8$in to just under $1/2$in.

Plate 287   USA/TC 2631 also at Portland, Oregon, in August 1947 (Photo: H. L. Goldsmith Collection)

Plate 288   B&A (IGR) 6461 (ex USA/TC 3461) class AWC on 80ft turntable at Ishurdi on the Bengal and Assam Railway in February 1945 (Photo: H. D. Bowtell)

249

Plate 289   FS 736.047 (ex USA/TC 2738) at Milan Smistamento shed in May 1961 (Photo: E. A. S. Cotton)

Plate 290   USSR W^{a}193 at the head of a local train at the October Railway's terminus in Leningrad (now St Petersburg) in July 1956 (Photo: H. D. Quinby)

Plate 291   USSR W^{a}194 at Leningrad Warschauer Station in July 1959 (Photo: Hellmuth Frohlich 1182)

Plate 292   USA/TC 606 in the post-war series (ex USA/TC 5846) at Fort Eustis, Virginia, in 1956. This locomotive is one of the last Lima batch with screw reverse and a stepped running plate on the right-hand side (Photo: H. L. Goldsmith Collection)

Plate 293   JDZ 37.028 (ex USA/TC 3601) at Vinkova in June 1960 (Photo: Hellmuth Frohlich 1768)

Plate 294   USA/TC 2–8–0 in Austria immediately after the war. It appears to carry a temporary number 78.09 and may therefore be ex USA/TC 2536 (Photo: R. Tourret Collection)

251

Plate 295 OBB 956.07 (ex USA/TC 1882) on a freight train at Selzthal in 1953. This engine has been rebuilt as described in the text (Photo: Hellmuth Frohlich)

Plate 296 HSR 536 (ex USA/TC 2365) at Larissa in August 1954 (Photo: N. N. Forbes)

Plate 297   TCDD 45182 (ex USA/TC 2912) at Buyukderbent in August 1955 (Photo N. N. Forbes)

Plate 298   MAV 411.043 (ex USA/TC 2324) at Budapest Haman Kato shed in September 1959 (Photo: Hellmuth Frohlich 1277)

253

Plate 299   MAV 411.174 (ex USA/TC 1714) at Debrecen in September 1959(Photo: Hellmuth Frohlich 1388)

Plate 300   MAV 411.123 (ex USA/TC 2350) at Vac shed in August 1977 (Photo: R. Tourret)

Plate 301   PKP Tr 203.492 (ex USA/TC 6078) at Poznan Glowny Station in June 1958(Photo: Hellmuth Frohlich 792)

Plate 302   PKP Tr 203.144 (Alco 70759/43 ex USA/TC 2410) at Nasielsk in December 1977 (Photo: R. Tourret)

Plate 303   PKP Tr 203.335 (ex USA/TC 2568) (Photo: R. Tourret Collection)

Plate 304   USA/TC 5856 at Seoul, Korea, in July 1947 (Photo: A. Hall)

Chapter 51

METRE-GAUGE 0–4–0P LOCOMOTIVES, USA/TC 2383–99, 2990–7 & 8288–95

There were thirty-three of these metre-gauge 0–4–0P locomotives, twenty-five being USA/TC 2383–99 and 2990–7 built by the Plymouth Locomotive Works Division of the Fate-Root-Heath Co, Plymouth, Ohio, works number FRH 5040–64 all built in 1945. The other eight were USA/TC 8288–95, built by Brookville 3028–35 in 1944.

The driving axles of these locomotives were coupled together by chains. The Plymouth locomotives had Hercules engines developing 35hp at 1125rpm. They were Plymouth/FRH Model FLB, a modification of the original Model FHG which was fitted with a Buda engine. The main drive was by roller chains through a four-speed gearbox mounted behind the engine. Gear changes were made by a gear lever similar to that used in a car. One of the minor troubles was that the knobs on the gear levers were very prone to detaching themselves when the gears were changed. The clutch was operated by a foot-pedal and braking was by hand-lever operating blocks on the inner sides of all wheels. The Brookville locomotives appeared to have Ford V-8 engines but were otherwise very similar.

Twenty-three of the locomotives were sent to South East Asia Command. Six of those built by Brookville, USA/TC 8288–91/4/5, were flown into Central Burma to Myingyan in April 1945, before Rangoon was liberated. The other two, USA/TC 8292/3, went to India. In May 1945, seventeen of the FRH locomotives, USA/TC 2383–5/7–90/2–7/9 and 2990/1/3, were flown from USA to Rangoon via Calcutta. USA/TC 2384/5/7/9/92/4–6/9 and 2990/1/3 were put into service hauling light trains over restricted sections of newly-opened lines, and also on shunting duties. Five were never uncrated but were stored at Insein Works until September 1945, when they were sent to Malaya.

At this time, most of the remaining engines were in use at Waw, except for the six at Myingyan. The eighteen in Burma were taken into stock as BR Class P and allocated BR Nos 493–510, at least sixteen being officially renumbered by the end of 1945. The BR Nos given below are according to an official list:

Observation, however, brought to light some discrepancies. BR 506/8 were USA/TC 2387, FRH 5044 and USA/TC 2991, FRH 5059 respectively, while

BR	0	1	2	3	4	5	6	7	8	9
49X	–	–	–	8289	8291	8295	8290	8288	8294	2384
50X	2385	2387	2389	2392	2396	2399	2990	2991	2993	2394
51X	2395	–	–	–	–	–	–	–	–	–

Plate 305 USA/TC 8292 Brookville 4wP locomotive, metre gauge, near Barpeta Road, Assam, in June 1945 (Photo: R. Tourret Collection)

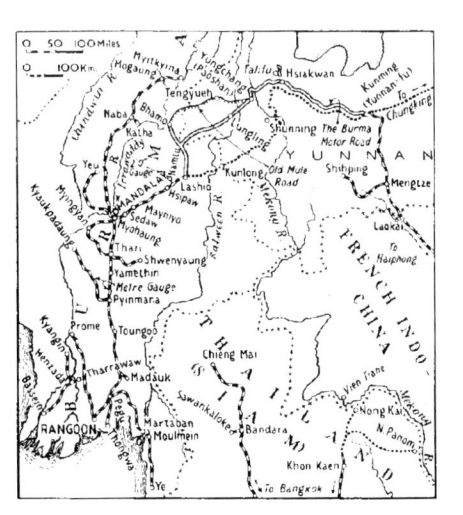

Map 26 Railway map of Burma and adjoining territories (Courtesy Railway Magazine)

USA/TC 8291 was noted as BR 496. Also, USA/TC 2388 carried the body of 2395. It is evident that considerable interchange of parts occurred.

These petrol locomotives, particularly those built by Brookville, were not very suitable for the duties imposed upon them, partly due to inadequate radiator capacity, and were soon replaced by rail Jeeps and three MacArthur 2–8–2s and six BAR Class F 0–6–0s sent over by road from Manipur Road. The locomotive position was later eased by the arrival of the WD Garratts and the repair of damaged locomotives, and the petrol locomotives were withdrawn from service. However, at that time, it was exceedingly difficult to get any locomotives to Burma, and the 0–4–0Ps were probably the largest locomotives that could be flown into the country – a feat equalled only by that of moving the MacArthurs by road in that terrain!

Six locomotives were sent to Malaya, the uncrated USA/TC 2383/8/90/3/7 in September 1945, followed later by 2394. These locomotives were never given FMSR numbers. One, identity unknown, was burnt out at Johore Bahru in late 1945, while the other five were used as service locomotives, USA/TC 2383/8/97 at Singapore and 2390/3 at the Sentul Works, Kuala Lumpur. By November 1947, those remaining on the Malayan Railways were 2388/94/7; 2394 having been transferred from Burma. By 1950, only 2388/97 were in service.

Dimensions (Plymouth/FRH locomotives)

Weight of locomotive in working order	5 tons nominal
Tractive effort, maximum	4000lb (at 2.6 mph using sand)
Fuel capacity	15gl
Wheel diameter	1ft 6in
Wheelbase	4ft 2¼in
Length, over buffer beams	10ft 9¼in
Height, rail to top of hooter	7ft 7⅜in
Width	5ft 5¾in
Number of engines	1
Cylinders per engine, number	4
diameter	4½in
stroke	5in

Plate 306 Burma Railways Plymouth 4wP Class P 500 (ex USA/TC 2385) at Rangoon Station in December 1946 (Photo: R. M. Palmer)

Chapter 52

PORTER STEAM LOCOMOTIVES FOR RUSSIA, USA/TC 3030–75

In 1944, H K Porter Co Inc built forty-six steam locomotives for the Soviet Government Purchasing Commission, the first ten of which were 0–4–0STs (USA/TC 3030–9), the following twenty were 0–6–0STs (USA/TC 3040–59), and the final sixteen were narrow-gauge 0–8–0s (USA/TC 3060–75).

All the engines were fitted with Walschaert valve gear and two Pyle National electric headlights. Westinghouse air brake, acting on all engine and tender wheels, was fitted, with train connections. The 0–4–0STs and the 0–6–0STs were fitted with Russian-type Willison coupling units at 3ft 7⅛in from the top of the rail and additional couplings, height 1ft 9in, to suit ``"customer's ingot cars". Heavy steel buffers were also specified for the tank locomotives, suggesting that these engines were intended for service in steelworks. The 0–8–0s were fitted with equalised drawhook and chain, height 2ft 2½in above the rail. A cab heater was provided for winter conditions and a canopy was fitted to the tender, probably for the same reason.

Nothing is known of any of these engines since shipment to Russia.

Dimensions

USA/TC Nos	3030–9	3040–59	3060–75
Porter Works Nos	7740–9	7750–69	7770–85
Wheel arrangement	0–4–0ST	0–6–0ST	0–8–0
Gauge	5ft 0in	5ft 0in	2ft 5½in
Cylinders	16in x 24in	16in x 24in	13in x 16in
Driving wheel diameter	3ft 8in	3ft 8in	2ft 7in
Wheelbase	7ft 6in	9ft 3in	9ft 8in
Heating surface,			
tubes & flues	996sq ft	926sq ft	620sq ft
firebox	72.2sq ft	110sq ft	52sq ft
total evaporation	1068.2sq ft	1036sq ft	672sq ft
superheater	192sq ft	193sq ft	123sq ft
combined total	1260.2sq ft	1229sq ft	795sq ft
Grate area	16sq ft	30sq ft	13sq ft
Boiler pressure	180psi	190psi	180psi
Tractive effort, 85%BP	21,360lb	26,640lb	13,345lb
Weight in WO, engine	46⅛ ton	62½ ton	24 ton
Height	14ft 0in	14ft 6in	11ft 0in
Width	10ft 2in	10ft 6in	8ft 4in
Length over buffers	27ft 2in	26ft 10in	46ft 2¾in
Water capacity	1500 US gl	2650 US gl	2750 US gl
Coal capacity	2200lb	6000lb	11,000lb
Wheelbase of engine & tender	–	–	36ft 9in

Chapter 53

USA/TC 2–10–0s FOR RUSSIA, USA/TC 3925–95, 4143–4280, 4500–4999, 5200–5699, 5860–5999, 6104–54, 6240–6739, 10000–99, 10500–619

In 1915, Russia ordered four hundred 2–10–0 locomotives from Baldwin, Alco and the Canadian Locomotive Co, all to the same design. Following experience with these engines, Russian engineers suggested certain changes, and a further 475 engines were built. When the need for extra locomotive stock to be supplied to Russia under Lease-lend arose in World War II, this design, although not a modern one, was considered adequate and had the advantages of being suitable for track in poor condition and of being proven by experience under Russian operating conditions. Accordingly, Baldwin and Alco built further units to the modified design, and by the end of the war had built over 2000 new engines of this class.

The engines had bar frames. They were allocated USA/TC Nos but most if not all were painted with their Russian numbers on manufacture. They were carried across America on flatcars and were mostly shipped from Portland, Oregon, to Vladivostok in Russian ships, because Russia was not then at war with Japan. A few were shipped in via Arctic convoys from Britain to Murmansk, but none were landed in Britain. They were set to work in Eastern Russia, the central section of the Trans-Siberian Railway and its branches. None have been seen in Western or Southern Russia, so that these engines are probably still at work in the same Eastern areas.

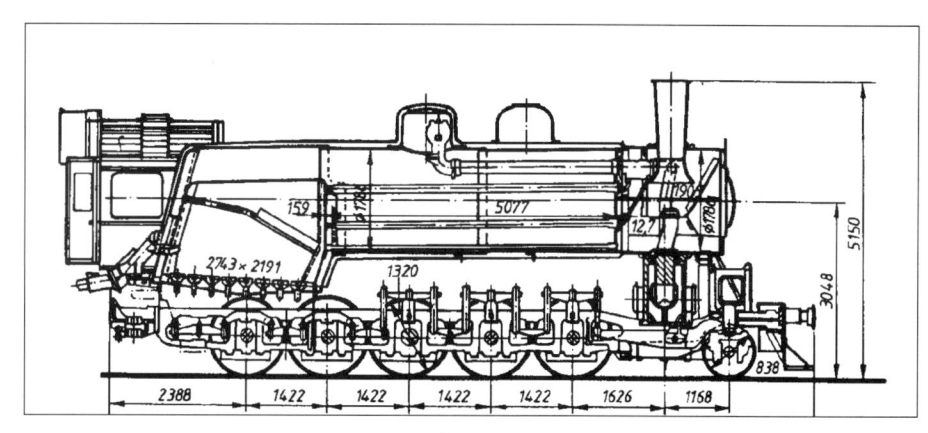

Fig. 37   USA/TC 2–10–0 for Russia SZD Class E^a

The First World War engines from Baldwin, Alco and the Canadian Locomotive Co became classes E^f, E^s and E^k respectively, where the Cyrillic E is pronounced Ye as in "yet". The suffix "f" stood for Filadelphia (sic) ie Baldwin, the "s" for Schenectady ie Alco and the "k" for Kanada (sic) ie Canadian Locomotive Co. The following 475 engines to the modified design became class E^1. The

Plate 307   USSR Class E^1 534, one of the World War One 2–10–0s Alco 57483/17, at Lebyazhe Museum storage yard (Photo: R. Tourret Collection)

Plate 308   USSR Class E^1 1161, one of the World War One 2–10–0s (Photo: F. Moore)

Plate 309   USSR Class E^a 2126 at Schenectady, New York, in May 1944 (Photo: H. L. Goldsmith Collection)

Plate 310   USSR Class E^a 3993 official photograph. This locomotive was nominally USA/TC 10092 but since this is the official photograph it is doubtful if this USA/TC number was ever carried (Photo: R. Tourret Collection)

Plate 311 USSR Class E^m 3635 in store (Photo: R. Tourret Collection)

Second World War engines were class E^a, with the "a" probably standing simply for American. The 1944 engines were modified by strengthening certain moving parts around the leading (driving) axle and the motion, and then became class E^m where the "m" stood for modernised. The 1945 engines were similarly modified and in addition had feed water heaters fitted, with a separate turbo-pump for cold water feed as well as a piston pump for hot water feed. These became class E^{mb}. By 1961, the E^a and E^m engines in the Far East had been modified further to increase efficiency. The main change was the provision of a feed water heater and the application of equipment which decreased or increased the adhesive weight according to requirements.

A few of the later locomotives were not despatched. Forty-six engines, USA/TC 5908/38/40–2/81–93, 6734 and 10060–86, were stored at Voorheesville Depot, New York, for sale in March 1948. USA/TC 10076-86 lacked tenders, evidently tender construction had lagged behind engine construction. In April 1948, the various bidders, including the Finnish Purchasing Commission, were advised that the 46 engines had been withdrawn from sale.

Also, USA/TC 4878 (Baldwin 70695/44, USSR Ea 2379) was damaged in the States and was not shipped. It was sold after the war to the Minneapolis Northfield and Southern RR and became MN&S 506. It was probably scrapped when the railway was converted to diesel operation.

Dimensions

Cylinders	25in x 28in
Driving wheel diameter	4ft 4in
Heating surface, boiler	2605sq ft
Heating surface, superheater	660sq ft
Heating surface, total	3265sq ft
Boiler pressure	180psi
Grate area	64.5sq ft
Tractive effort at 85% BP	51,500lb
Weight on driving wheels	192,500lb
Total weight	218,500lb

The Finnish State Railways (VR) took over twenty of the cancelled locomotives which became Class Tr2 Nos 1300–19 Alco 75195–75214 built 1947. These appeared to be identical to the Russian locomotives except that the VR engines had the sandbox and steam dome combined, and that the headlamp was placed on top of the smokebox.

USA/TC No	USSR Nos	Maker	Works Nos	Built	Number	Notes
3925–95	Ea 3830–3900	Baldwin	71431–71501	1945	71	
4143–4280	Ea 3692–3829	Baldwin	71591–71728	1945	138	a
4500–4699	Ea 2001–2200	Alco	71670–71869	1944	200	
4700–4999	Ea 2201–2500	Baldwin	70517–70816	1944	300	
5200–5699	Ea 2501–3000	Baldwin	70901–71400	1944/5	500	
5860–5999	Ea 3501–3640	Alco	73101–73240	1945	140	
6104–54	Ea 3641–3691	Alco	73241–91	1945	51	
6240–6739	Ea 3001–3500	Alco	72193–72692	1945	500	
10000–86	Ea 3901–87	Alco	73804–90	1946	87	
10087–99	Ea 3988–4000	Alco	75158–70	1947	13	b
10500–609	Ea 4141–4250	Baldwin	72514–72623	1945	110	c
					2110	

Notes
(a) Order for 4278–80 cancelled
(b) Originally ordered up to USA/TC 10249
(c) Originally ordered up to USA/TC 10759

Chapter 54

STANDARD USA/TC 0–6–0s USED IN THE UNITED STATES, USA/TC 4000–79

Eighty standard-gauge locomotives, USA/TC 4000–79, were built for service within the United States for shunting duties at various military depots, etc. They were apparently based on the USRA design of World War One. These were powerful little engines and were capable of high rates of acceleration. No superheaters were fitted. The first forty-three were built by Alco in late 1942. The works numbers were in different batches. All official Alco sources showed them as follows:

4000–3	70426–9
4004–11	70418–25
4012–41	70388–417
4042	70456

Possibly due to inexperienced help in the rush of wartime, the plates were not all applied as intended and recorded, but as follows:

4000–3	70426–9
4004/5	70424/5
4006–8	70393–5
4009–11	70406–8
4012–6	70388–92
4017–26	70396–405
4027–41	70409–23
4042	70456

The building dates also seem to be in some disarray. The error on the part of Alco does not seem to have been reported until many of the engines were sold immediately after the war. The disposal board listed many of them under their official Alco construction numbers. A hassle developed when one dealer found his engine in poor condition, had the wrong construction number on the plate, while another engine, sold to another dealer, had the plate that his should have had! Angry words were exchanged, followed by letters! Meantime similar mixups were being reported from various other disposal offices.

Two years later, thirty-seven more were built to a similar but slightly improved design. The most noticeable external difference from the locomotives of the previous order was the amalgamation of the two sand domes into one. These engines were built by Lima as Order No 1178, USA/TC 4043–71 being coal-burners and USA/TC 4072–9 being oil-burners, and were delivered in the first quarter of 1944. Works numbers were Lima 8377–8413 in order.

Space does not permit a full description of their activities but some of the most interesting items are noted here. USA/TC 4003/18/21/3/32/8 were at the Fort Eustis Military Railroad for some years, including 1950/1. They were joined by 4042 in 1952 and were renumbered USA/TC 613–9 in the post-war series in 1952. Most, if not all, of the others were sold after the war to various concerns in the United States. USA/TC 4043/4/53–5/27/31 were sold in 1947/8 to the Raritan River RR and became Nos 16–22. They were replaced by diesels in 1954 and scrapped at Bethlehem in December 1954. The Norfolk & Portsmouth Belt Line RR of Virginia bought fourteen of the locomotives in 1947–9, eight directly from a war surplus sale and six from the old Midland Terminal RR. They had

Plate 312   USA/TC 4015 first series Alco-built official photograph (Photo: R. Tourret Collection)

Plate 313   USA/TC 4063 second series Lima-built official photograph (Photo: H. L. Goldsmith Collection)

rebuilt three of them 4028/50/1 into 2–6–0s, but the N&PBL reconverted them back to 0–6–0s. Nos 50–7 were 1944 Lima-built nos 4065/1/0/50/1/64/70/68 and were known as Class S-6, and 60–5 were 1942 Alco-built 4016, three unknown and 4028/14 known as Class S-6a. Nos 53–6 and 64/5 came via the MTR. All but 51 were scrapped by about 1958. USA/TC 4056/45/73/2/4/57–9/48/04 went to the Alaska RR and became ARR 310–9 in order. USA/TC 4005/7/10 were sold to the Norwegian State Railways in July 1948 but, in the event, they were not used but broken up for parts.

Dimensions	**4000–42**	**4043–79**
Cylinders, two inside	21in x 28in	21in x 28in
Wheel diameter, coupled	4ft 2in	4ft 2in
Wheelbase, engine	11ft 0in	11ft 0in
Wheelbase, engine & tender	43ft 1½in	43ft 0½in
Heating surface, tubes	2273sq ft	2273sq ft
firebox	136sq ft	135sq ft
total	2409sq ft	2408sq ft
Grate area	33.2sq ft	33.1sq ft
Boiler pressure	190psi	190psi
Tractive effort at 85% BP	40,000lb	40,000lb
Weight, engine	69 ton 0cwt	71 ton 3cwt
tender	52 ton 0cwt	47 ton 10cwt
total	121 ton 0cwt	118 ton 13cwt
Tender, coal capacity	8 ton	9 ton
oil capacity	–	1800 US gl
water capacity	6000 US gl	6000 US gl
Length over couplings	56ft 10½in	56ft 8in

Plate 314   USA/TC 4026 at Lincoln in Nebraska in October 1945 (Photo: A. Holck)

Plate 315   USA/TC 4076 at Portland in Oregon in May 1948 (Photo: R. Tourret Collection)

Plate 316   Minnesota Transfer Railway 485 (ex USA/TC 4013) at St Paul in Minnesota in September 1949 (Photo: H. L. Goldsmith)

Plate 317 Duluth and North Eastern RR Co 29 (ex USA/TC 4047) at Cloquet in Minnesota in August 1957 (Photo: H. L. Goldsmith Collection)

Chapter 55

FINNISH STATE RAILWAYS 0–6–0STs, USA/TC 6740–63

In 1945, the Vulcan Ironworks of Wilkesbarre, Pa, commenced construction of an order for 0–6–0STs for Russia. Their weight was 70 US ton and the gauge 5ft 0in. Twenty four engines were built, USA/TC 6740–63, Vulcan 4630–53. Originally the order was up to 6781 but the rest were cancelled, either because of the end of the war or because the Russians rejected them because of "weak" frames. They were ordered through the USA/TC because of being built under "Lease-Lend" and accordingly the engines were delivered to USA/TC Depots for store, 6740–4 to Marietta TC Depot in April 1945, 6745–9 to Marietta in May 1945, 6750–62 to Elmira QMD Depot in 1945 and 6763 to Burlington in 1945.

Since the USA/TC had no use for them, they were turned over to the War Assets Administration and were offered for sale at the beginning of 1947. On 5 January 1948, the sale of all twenty-four locomotives to the Finnish Purchasing Commission was approved. They were sold at $7000 each plus $500 for one set of spare parts (probably 6763).

They were originally VR Class Vr4. All were rebuilt (including the spare parts) into 0–6–2T becoming VR Class Vr5 Nos 1400–23 during 1951–5.

Plate 318 USA/TC 6740 0–6–0ST official photograph. Later lettered "USA". Photographed at Vulcan plant in 1945 (Photo: H. L. Goldsmith Collection)

Plate 319   VR Class Vr5 No 1403 rebuilt into 0–6–2T at Pasila Helsinki in May 1962 (Photo: P. J. Kelley)

Plate 320   VR Class Vr5 No 1414 0–6–2T at Tampere shed in May 1962 (Photo: P. J. Kelley)

Chapter 56

THE LIMA 2–8–0s, USA/TC 6994–9

In 1942, Lima built six 2–8–0 locomotives, USA/TC 6994–9, Lima Works Nos 7875–80, for internal service in the United States at places such as Holabird TC Depot, Fort Eustis and Fort Belvoir. The design was a typical American steam 2–8–0 and the cylinders were 21in by 26in, driving wheel diameter 4ft 2in, tractive effort at 85% boiler pressure 57,100lb and weight of engine in working order 80ton 18cwt.

Some time after the war, five of the engines, USA/TC 6994–6/8/9, went to the Alaska Railroad and became ARR 505/6/4/1/2 in order (USA/TC 503 was ex-USA/TC 10). Later, the numbers were decreased by 100. In February 1958, the five engines were sold to Ferrocarril de Langreo en Asturias in Spain. By 1960, 404 had been through works and was painted green, 406 was in works and the rest were stored at either Abono or Pinzales. The new cut-off tunnel, for which these engines were required, had then not yet been finished.

USA/TC 6997 was renumbered 620 in the postwar series in 1952.

Plate 322 USA/TC 6994 at Fort Belvoir in Virginia in August 1947. The feedwater heater originally fitted has now been removed (Photo: C. W. Witbeck)

Plate 321 USA/TC 6998 official photograph. Note the feedwater heater in front of the smokebox door (Photo: H. L. Goldsmith Collection)

Plate 323 USA/TC 620 (in post-war renumbering, originally USA/TC 6997) at Fort Eustis in Virginia in 1954 (Photo: H. L. Goldsmith Collection)

Plate 324 Ferrocarril de Langreo en Asturias 404 (ex ARR 404 ex USA/TC 6996) Csijon shed in May 1960 (Photo: J. D. Blythe)

Chapter 57

GENERAL ELECTRIC 75 ton DIESEL LOCOMOTIVES
USA/TC 7228–37

These ten large 75 ton 500hp locomotives, USA/TC 7228–37, had two Cummins L1–600 diesel engines driving two GE Model GT–549 generators, which in turn powered four GE Model GHM–833 traction motors.

Dimensions were as follows:

Wheel arrangement	Bo-Bo
Minimum radius of curve	75ft
Tractive effort	
Starting, 30% adhesion	48,000lb
5 mph	24,000lb
10 mph	12,000lb
15 mph	9,000lb
Maximum permissible speed	40mph
Fuel capacity	400 US gl
Wheel diameter	3ft 6in
Wheelbase	30ft 1in
Length over buffers	42ft 3½in
Length over truck centres	23ft 1in
Truck wheelbase	7ft 0in
Height, rail to cab top	12ft 2⅛in
Width	9ft 3½in

USA/TC 7228–33/6/7 arrived at Newport Ebbw Junction GWR USA/TC workshops in June 1944, USA/TC 7234/5 arriving in July. USA/TC 7231 was the first to go on trial after assembly, going to Risca on 16 June. The others had their trial runs during July. USA/TC 7233 travelled 38 miles on its trial trip on 25 July, and it is interesting to speculate where it might have got to. This batch was despatched from Ebbw, probably made up into one train, on 12 August, and were quickly shipped to the Continent, arriving in France in August and September.

In Europe, they were used for shunting and operating long-distance military freight and ambulance trains. After the war, USA/TC 7228–37 became D4028–37 in order, on the Société General de Chemin de Fer et de Transportes Automobiles at St Symphorien, Gironde.

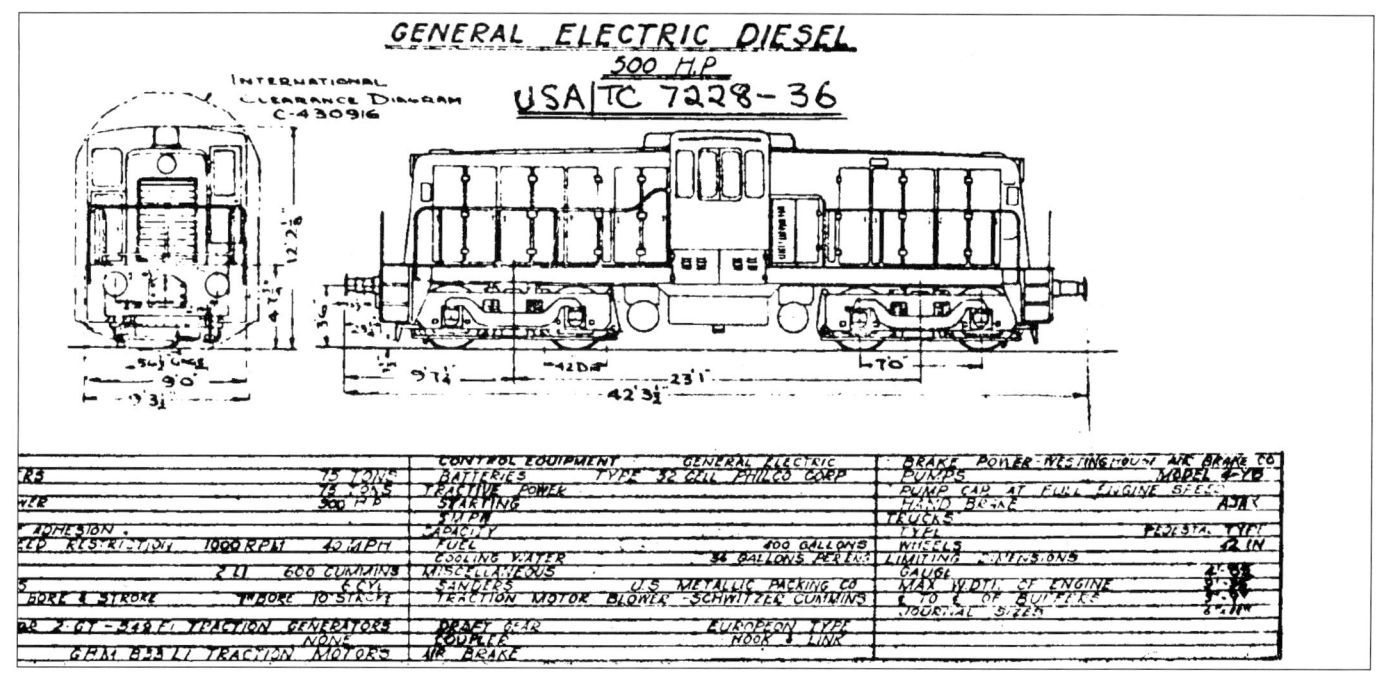

Fig. 38 General Electric 500hp diesel USA/TC 7228–36

Chapter 58

EVANS AUTORAILERS 235hp 0–6–0Ds, USA/TC 7731–8

Some small shunting diesel locomotives of rather unusual design, which could be used on the railway or on the road, were built for the USA/TC. Most, if not all, saw service in the Naples and Rome areas in Italy. They probably arrived at Naples around 1945 and some were still in Italy in 1947.

The cab was placed at one end with one pair of wheels underneath, while the engine was carried on the remaining two pairs of wheels. A headlamp, exhaust silencer, bell and hooter were carried on top of the bonnet. All six wheels were driven via a hydraulic transmission and were fitted with ordinary lorry tyres which rested on the rails and carried the entire weight of the locomotive. To keep the rubber tyres on the rails, four 16in diameter flanged guide wheels were provided, one pair between the wheels under the engine and the other pair behind the wheels under the cab so that the wheel arrangement appeared thus "OoO Oo". These guide wheels were retractable, enabling the locomotive to be used on the road, and the rear pair of wheels under the cab were then used for steering.

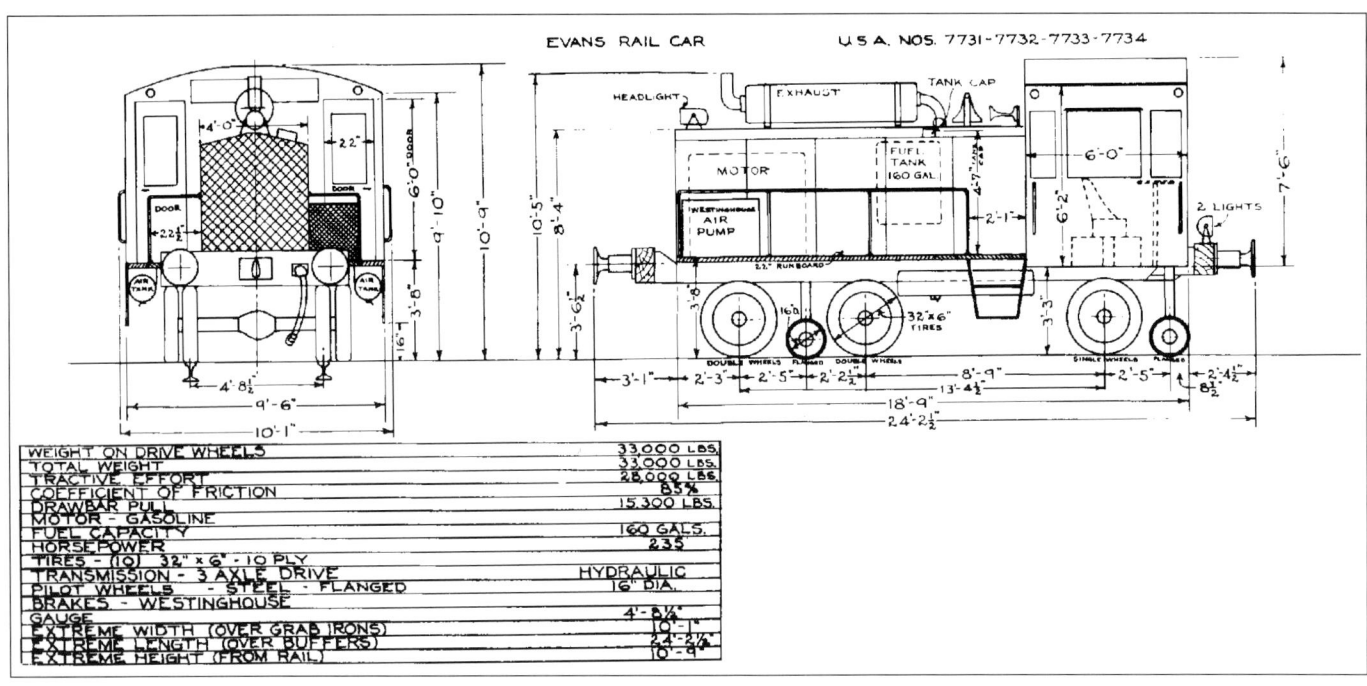

Fig. 39　Evans Autorailer 235hp diesel USA/TC 7731–4

Plate 325　Evans Autorailer USA/TC 7731, for use on either road or rail (Photo: R. Tourret Collection)

Chapter 59

GENERAL ELECTRIC 25ton DIESEL LOCOMOTIVES
USA/TC 7770–9

These small 25ton 150hp 0-4-0DE units were intended for use as small easily-handled motive-power units for the initial phases of invasion operations, being built to give long service with minimum maintenance. They were fitted with a Cummins type HB1-600 diesel engine rated at 150hp at 1800rpm driving a GE type GT-1503 shunt-wound DC generator. A single GE type GE-733 traction motor drove the axles through double-reduction gear. The axles were coupled together by a chain drive. The locomotives were fitted with a large cab at one end. The frames were outside the wheels and the roller-bearing axleboxes were connected by a compensating beam with coil springs to take the weight of the locomotive. The brakes were straight air.

USA/TC 7770–9 were shipped to Great Britain during April, May and June 1944. Most, if not all, appeared at Eastleigh Works, 7770–5 arriving on 12 June, followed by 7776 on 2 July. Presumably they were checked over and started up, and then prepared for further shipment. USA/TC 7774/5 were sent to Southampton Docks on 14 June for shipment to France and were probably the first to leave England, while 7778/9 were observed at Millbrook awaiting shipment on 17 July.

Two of these locomotives were unloaded from a tank landing craft at Utah Beach on 10 July 1944, the first Allied railway equipment to arrive in France. USA/TC 7774 arrived at Cherbourg on board the "Hampton Ferry" in August 1944, and all ten had been despatched by October 1944.

Little is known of their work on the Continent, but judging from photographs they were used for reconstruction work close behind the fighting forces. After the war, these units went back to the USA.

Dimensions were as follows:

Minimum radius of curve	40ft
Tractive, effort	
Starting, 30% adhesion	15,000lb
5 mph	7,000lb
10 mph	3,700lb
15 mph	2,300lb
Maximum permissible	
speed	20mph
Fuel capacity	75 US gl
Wheel diameter	2ft 9in
Wheelbase	6ft 0½in
Length over buffers	18ft 0in
Height, rail to cab top	10ft 4in
Width	8ft 0in

Plate 326 USA/TC 7775 and 7774 just arrived in France in June 1944, loaded up with drums of diesel fuel for immediate service (Photo: R. Tourret Collection)

268

Plate 327 USA/TC 7770 at Laon in France in August 1944 (Photo: US Army)

Plate 328 USA/TC 7777 at Arsenal Docks, Cherbourg in France in November 1944 (Photo: R. Tourret Collection)

Plate 329 USA/TC 7773 at Herzogenrath just over the border into Germany in December 1944 (Photo: US Army)

Chapter 60

GENERAL ELECTRIC 45ton DIESEL LOCOMOTIVES
7800–29, 7924–9, 8390, 8499–8528 & 8532–9/60–73

The General Electric Co Ltd of America built several hundred diesel-electric locomotives for various war purposes during the period 1940 to 1945. General Electric, in common with most American manufacturers of diesel locomotives, built locomotives on a production line basis in quantity lots. This practice differed from the customary British arrangement whereby locomotives were built only against specific orders and was possible only when designs were standardised and customers were willing to accept standard designs.

Because of this method of manufacture, individual locomotives were often assigned to the customers from the production line and individual locomotives in a particular order may have either consecutive or random works numbers, depending on the relative priority of the various orders outstanding at the time. Most of the locomotives ordered by the USA/TC were the subject of small orders, and for these reasons the works numbers were generally not consecutive. These engines were supplied to various supply, ordnance, Army Depots or US Air Force bases, and large industrial plants which were engaged on war work. Many of these locomotives carried road numbers for the defence plant or location where the locomotive was first operated and these often belonged to a special local series. Most of these locomotives were subsequently renumbered into the general USA/TC series. These locomotives are not dealt with here, but are listed in Chapter 45.

Some somewhat larger orders were placed for locomotives intended for service in Europe or India and, probably because of the high priority of these orders, the works numbers were largely consecutive. It is these locomotives which are dealt with in this Chapter. All these locomotives were standard General Electric types, although some were slightly modified to suit USA/TC requirements.

Later locomotives, including those intended for overseas, were numbered in the general USA/TC series when they were built. The locomotives that saw service in Europe and India came from three classes. USA/TC 7800–29, 7924–9, 8390, 8499–8528 and 8532–9/60–73 were 45ton locomotives (GE classified their types by nominal weight); USA/TC 7228–37 were 75ton locomotives (see Chapter 57) and USA/TC 7770–9 were small 25ton units (see Chapter 59).

The 45ton 380hp Bo-Bo DE locomotives were built to GE Specification No 4130 and US Army Specification No 4342. USA/TC 7800–29 were GE 27656–85 all built in 1944, USA/TC 7924–9 were GE 27631–96 built in 1944, USA/TC 8390 was GE 27792 built in 1945, USA/TC 8499–8528 were GE 27577–27606 all built in 1944, USA/TC

8532–9 were various built in 1944 and USA/TC 8560–73 were GE 27698–711 all built in 1944.

These locomotives had a central cab with a headlamp and a bonnet at each end housing the two power units. It was a light railroad design intended for lines with restricted axleweight and loading limits. The range of gauges for which the design could be adapted was extremely wide, ranging from metre to 5ft 6in and this was accomplished by merely changing the power trucks.

The power units were two Caterpillar diesel eight-cylinder V-form four-stroke engines. All electrical equipment was naturally provided by GE. The motors drove all axles on the bogies through 11.25:1 ratio reduction gears. Multiple-unit type controls and Westinghouse braking gear were fitted.

Most of the locomotives saw service in the European Theatre of Operations. USA/TC 7924–9 and 8499–8528 all visited Great Britain in 1944. USA/TC 7924–9 arrived at Ebbw Junction GWR USA/TC works in late April for assembly and trials, which took place in May with some second runs later. This batch remained at Ebbw until August, when they left for overseas. USA/TC 8499–8509 arrived in May and had their initial trials in June, usually working in tandem. This batch did not stay at Ebbw long, most being shipped from Southampton during July. The last batch, USA/TC 8521–8, did not arrive at Ebbw until August, and had their trial runs from 28 August to 1 September, after which they were quickly despatched for overseas duty. The missing series, USA/TC 8510–20, appear to have been assembled and used at military depots in the USA, before arriving in Great Britain in July 1944, thus allowing them to be shipped to the Continent straight away without going to Ebbw Junction.

On the Continent, these locomotives were joined by USA/TC 8560–73 sent direct from USA to France. They were used chiefly for shunting but occasionally for various other purposes. Some were allocated to Versailles Matelots for banking trains up the incline from the yard to St Cyr. They were also used occasionally for long-distance freight and ambulance train workings, especially in times of pressure when the supply of steam 2–8–0s was insufficient to meet traffic demands. The first was so noted in September 1944. The usual practice was to operate in pairs but on odd occasions they appeared singly or in threes. USA/TC 7924/6, 8499 and 8500/5/7–9/15–7/9/22–5 were amongst those noted on these duties. USA/TC 8510/60/3–7/71/2 were noted stored at Brussels Forest Midi shed in July 1945.

USA/TC 7800–29 went to India in July to September 1944, except 7808 which went to the Colombo Port Commission as No 4 in August. USA/TC 7800–7/9–29 became Indian Government Railways 6500–7/9–29. USA/TC 7800–2/4/6/12/7/8/21 went into service in 1944 initially on the Bombay Baroda and Central India Railway, 7803/5/10/1/3–6 on the North Western Railway, 7807/9/19/20/2/3/6–9 on the Great Indian Peninsula Railway and 7824/5 probably on the Bengal Assam Railway. There were some later changes, for instance 7807/9/19/20/2/3 went to the BBCIR in 1946.

USA/TC 7808 was replaced by USA/TC 8390 which arrived in India in March 1945 and became IGR 6590. It has often been assumed that this locomotive was USA/TC 7890, probably because of the manner of renumbering of the original batch, but this is incorrect. IGR 6590 entered service on the BBCIR in May 1945.

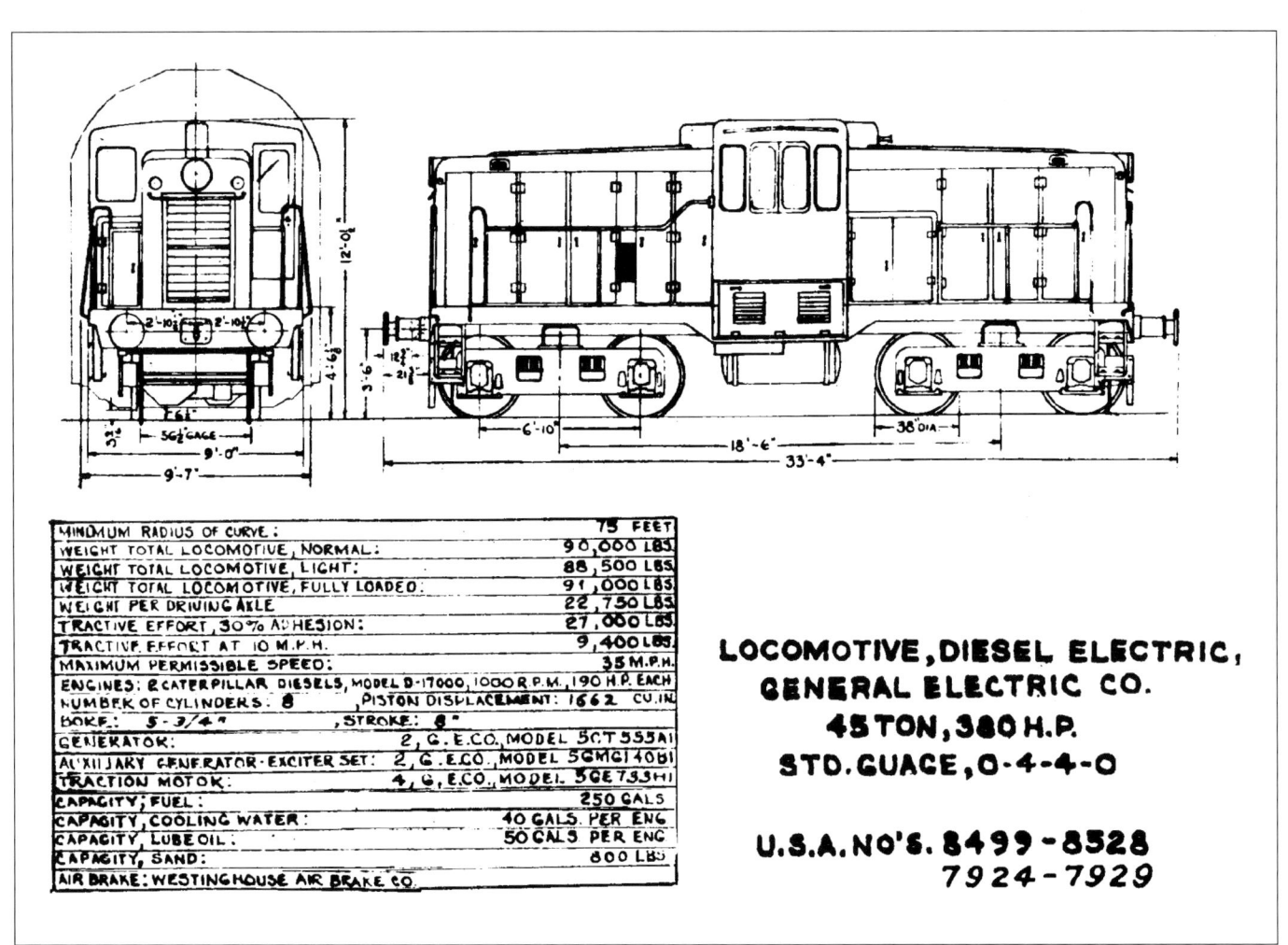

Fig. 40   General Electric 380hp diesel USA/TC 7924–9 and 8499–8528

Plate 330   USA/TC 7800 General Electric Bo–BoDE 45ton 380hp locomotive official photograph (Photo: R. Tourret Collection)

Fourteen locomotives, IGR 6500/1/3/5/10/1/3–6/24–7, remained on the NWR which went to Pakistan on Partition. They were all stationed at Karachi and were used for shunting duties and hauling local passenger trains of five to seven bogie coaches. One route was Karachi to Landhi, some 40 miles. Certain of the locomotives, at least, had no vacuum-brake equipment for operating train brakes, but all had headlamps, which was probably just as well! One or two of the engines were fitted with unusual towing links on the frames for dock shunting duties. All fourteen were still in service in 1960.

Unlike the USA/TC steam locomotives, once the war was over most of these GE diesel-electric locomotives were rapidly returned to the United States, apparently in 1945. Probably it was intended to use them in the Pacific war, but in the event, this was finished too rapidly for any to be transhipped to that area. Most of the locomotives remained under USA/TC control, although a few were sold to industry around 1946/7. The only exceptions were the Indian locomotives which were presumably sold to the IGR since they remained in India.

USA/TC 8532–9 were similar 45 ton Bo-Bo DE units, built GE 18040–2/5/39/46–8 in 1944, and sent immediately to Iran, arriving in February 1944. However, they were rated only at 300hp, presumably being down-rated somewhat for service in the hot, and often high-altitude, locations in Iran.

In May 1945, they were crated up and returned to the USA, being distributed to various US military depots as follows. USA/TC 8532 went to Montgomery Army Services Forces Depot in Alabama, 8533 to Carteret Ordnance Depot in NJ, 8534 to Camp Stewart Ga, 8535 to Brookley Field in Mobile Ala, 8536 to Gadsden Army Air Force Depot Ala, 8537/8 to the Army Air Force Depot in Topeka, Kansas and 8539 to the Transportation Corps Railroad Shops at Fort Benning Ga. Later, USA/TC 8532 went to Jackson AFB Miss and then to South Korea in 1953/4 but returned to the USA in 1955. Some, such as 8534/6/8, were sold for industrial use.

Plate 331   USA/TC 8505 General Electric Bo–BoDE 45ton 380hp locomotive official photograph (Photo: R. Tourret Collection)

Plate 332 USA/TC 8506 being loaded in an English port for the Channel crossing to France in September 1944 (Photo: R. Tourret Collection)

Plate 333 IGR 6500 (ex USA/TC 7800) on NWR in Pakistan hauling passenger train up to Karachi City from Landi, at Karachi Cantonment Station, in April 1948 (Photo: E. A. S. Cotton)

Plate 334 IGR 6516 (ex USA/TC 7816) at NWR Karachi shed in August 1948. This locomotive was adapted for shunting, mainly in the docks area. Note the low hooks on the side frames (Photo: E. A. S. Cotton)

273

Plate 335   USA/TC 8573 back in the United States in April 1951 (Photo: H. L. Goldsmith Collection)

Plate 336   USA/TC 8524 at Fort Eustis in Virginia in April 1957 (Photo: H. L. Goldsmith Collection)

Plate 337   USA/TC 8528 at Clover in Utah in April 1966 (Photo: H. L. Goldsmith Collection)

Chapter 61

WHITCOMB 65ton DIESEL LOCOMOTIVES, USA/TC 7961–90, 8120–47, 8400–98 & 8800–11 & MRS 1300–67

These 65 ton 650hp 0–4–4–0 diesel-electric locomotives, fitted for multiple-unit control, were built by Whitcomb to Specification No 65–DE–19A for general use on all European standard-gauge lines. The design was developed from the WD 12XX and 13XX series, 65–DE–14, 65–DE–14A and 65–DE–14B used in the Middle East (See Chapter 25). With a maximum speed of 45mph, they could be used for mainline service as well as for shunting. Several minor variants of this basic model, one of the USA/TC standard designs, were produced and armour plating could be fitted.

The design was quite conventional by American standards, the locomotives being fitted with headlamps and central cabs. The two diesel engines were supercharged Buda type 6–DCS–1879, each rated at 325hp at 1200rpm. All electrical equipment was by the Westinghouse Electrical & Manufacturing Corporation and consisted of generator type 197A, auxiliary generator type YG–41–B and four nose-suspended traction motors type 970A fitted with 14:72 ratio single-reduction gearing.

The works numbers were:

7961–90	60331–60	1943
8120–47	60361–88	1944
8400–98	60406–504	1944
8800–2	60515–7	1944
8803–11	60518–26	1945

Almost all of the first three series were sent overseas. The locomotives were shipped in three crates, one 40ft 4in by 12ft 8in by 10ft 4in weighing just under fifty tons which contained the chassis, odd parts and tools, and two 12ft 3in by 9ft 4in by 4ft 11in weighing 14$\frac{1}{2}$ tons, each containing a truck assembly. The final series, 8800–11, however, were used in the United States at various depots and Arsenals.

Some of these diesels which were used in the European Theatre of Operations, visited Great Britain in 1944 prior to shipment to the Continent. USA/TC 7961–90 all came to Great Britain, the first being 7964/5 in December 1943. Most of the series 7961–80 came in December 1943, being shipped into this country at Cardiff Docks although six, at least, arrived at Barry Docks. Newport Ebbw Junction GWR USA/TC workshops were used to assemble and prepare the diesels for service. USA/TC 7965 was the first to go on trial on 28 December and went to Rogerstone Yard, but from February 1944 onwards trial runs were always to Risca. There are unconfirmed reports of one or two diesels working goods trains as far as Gloucester. Some observations were USA/TC 7964/5/7/70 at Newport on 21 January 1944, 7963/74/5/8/80 on 23 February, 7971/2 on 28 April, while on 16 July 7967/8/74/5/7 were in the yards.

USA/TC 8120–9 were the next to arrive, also at Cardiff Docks, and were at Ebbw Junction by March 1944. Their initial trials took place from 23 March to 21 April, apart from 8123 on 8 May. Most of the diesels had two or three trials, so it would appear that the runs were also intended to keep the locomotives in trim.

Many of these diesels remained stored in the Ebbw Junction area during the summer of 1944. Six, USA/TC 7971/2/8 and 8120/2/7, were sent to the GWR engine shed at Llanelly for store. They probably went there in May and returned late July or early August.

The Whitcomb diesels in South Wales were sent to Southampton Docks in late July and early August, from where they were shipped to Cherbourg and Le Havre. For some unknown reason, USA/TC 8121 remained at Ebbw Junction for several weeks and was still there on 15 September.

USA/TC 7961/73/6/9/81–90 arrived at the Longmoor Military Railway in February 1944, painted a light sandy colour (similar to desert camouflage used in MEF). They were put into working order, painted black, and used on passenger trains before going into store. USA/TC 7976/87–9 were working passenger trains in May and June, for instance. USA/TC 7966, which went to the Melbourne Military Railway in February 1944, came to Longmoor in May. By August, however, nearly all of them had departed and their progress to the Continent via Southampton has been

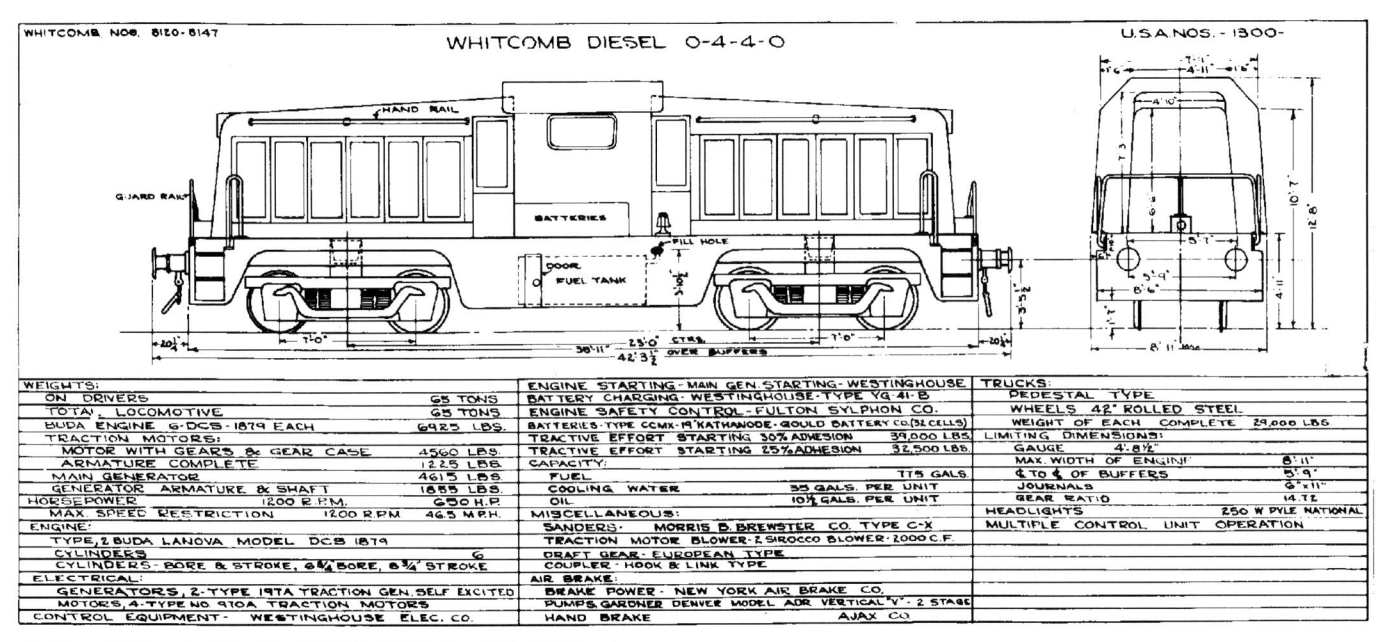

Fig. 41   Whitcomb 650hp diesel USA/TC 8120–47 and MRS 1300 series

Plate 338 USA/TC 7963 Whitcomb diesel locomotive official photograph (Photo: R. Tourret Collection)

fairly well recorded. USA/TC 7979 was the Eastleigh North Yard shunter on 30 June, while 7973/9/81/3/5 were at Southampton in July and 7976/84/5/90 on 31 July. USA/TC 7961, however, appeared at Cricklewood on 1 August and 7969 at Didcot on 29 July.

On the Continent, these locomotives arrived from June to August 1944, and were joined by others sent direct from USA to France, also in 1944. The complete series in France was USA/TC 7961–90, 8120–9 and 8422/40–7/57–64/6/9–76/8–82/91–4. They were used for shunting and various other purposes. USA/TC 8125 was the first Allied military locomotive to arrive in Paris. Some were allocated to Versailles Matelots for banking trains up the incline from the yard to St Cyr. They were occasionally used on long-distance freight and ambulance workings, especially in times of pressure when there were insufficient steam 2–8–0s. The first was so noted in September 1944. They were then usually used in pairs but on odd occasions they appeared singly or in threes.

The locomotives from the 8400–98 series almost all arrived directly from the United States, although 8457/8/63/4 briefly landed in the UK. These locomotives, which arrived new and painted brown, were prepared for service at a diesel repair shop established at Batignolles. They were then repainted green and despatched for service to other parts of France and to Belgium. USA/TC 7980 and 8445–7/57/8/60/6/80/91–4 were noted stored at Brussels Forest Midi shed in July 1945.

Sixty-eight of the 81XX and 84XX series were sent to Italy in 1944 directly from the United States. They were allotted numbers MRS 1300–67, probably in the order in which they arrived at Naples. Unfortunately, not all of the works numbers or USA/TC numbers are known and so the relationship of the two series cannot be determined completely, but details so far as are known are given on the following page.

Because of the end of the war in Europe, all the MRS 1300–67 series in Italy, together with the majority of the

Plate 339 Whitcomb diesel locomotives, USA/TC 7988 leading, lined up at Newport Ebbw Junction shed probably in January 1944. Note the light sand colour livery, presumably applied because desert service was in mind when the order was placed (Photo: R. Tourret Collection)

Plate 340 Whitcomb diesel locomotives, USA/TC 8122 leading, lined up at Newport in April 1944, alongside a line of USA/TC bogie petroleum tank wagons (Photo: R. Tourret Collection)

MRS	0	1	2	3	4	5	6	7	8	9
130X	?	?	?	8139	?	8143	8136	?	?	8145
131X	?	8401	?	?	?	?	?	8409	8406	8402
132X	8403	8408	8410	8411	8412	?	8132	?	?	8147
133X	8404	?	?	?	8418	8419	?	?	8424	8425
134X	8426	?	?	8432	8433	8434	8414	8421	8453?	?
135X	8427	?	?	8436	8438	?	?	?	8423	8454
136X	8455	8456	8452	?	8487	?	8489	8490	–	–

locomotives that had been shipped in to France, were sent back to the United States during the summer of 1945. Some 118 of these were stored at Hawkins Point, near Baltimore, including all the ex-MRS locomotives. A full list has never been found, but 7966/7/73/4/8/87, 8132/6/9/43/7 and 8401–6/8–12/4/5 8–21/3–7/32–4/6/8/42/52–6/66/86/7/9/90 are known to have been at Hawkins Point. It was intended to recondition these locomotives and send them west to aid the war against Japan, but this plan was abandoned because of the rapid conclusion of the war in the Far East. The existing order for further locomotives of this class, which would have been USA/TC 8812–8909 Whitcomb 60527–624 of 1945, was cancelled about the same time.

During the next two years or so, all these locomotives were sold out of USA/TC service, mostly to private firms in the United States. Some were exported to countries like Canada, Mexico and Cuba. A few were sold back to Whitcomb who rebuilt them to class 70–DE–26, and then resold them. The 88XX series locomotives were also sold.

Twenty of the locomotives which had been used in Europe were purchased by the Nederlandsche Spoorwegen, USA/TC 7962/79/84/5, 8129 and 8447/60/9–76/8/9/81/2 becoming NS class "600" Nos 601–19 in that order, and 7961 being used to provide spare parts. The Buda engines did not prove entirely satisfactory and they were first derated and then

Plate 342 MRS 1308 and a sister locomotive on war service in Italy, bringing the first train from Naples to Rome past the rubble of Cassino yard in July 1944. Note the bell on the running plate (Photo: US Army)

Plate 341 Whitcomb diesel USA/TC 7987 being loaded at Southampton for shipment to France in the summer of 1944. Note that the livery is now black (Photo: R. Tourret Collection)

replaced by Thomassen 6 Fe engines of 300hp by Thomassen Motoren-Fabriek, De Steeg. USA/TC 7962, 8129 and 8460/9/71/8/82 were never used in NS service before they were rebuilt. At the same time, new electric motors (Stork) and equipment were installed. The first one to be rebuilt was 604 which was rebuilt in 1951 presumably as a trial which proved successful, since the remainder were rebuilt in 1953/4 (except for 603 which was scrapped in 1953). The rebuilding was carried out at Tilburg Works, the engines being renumbered into the 20XX series in order in 1953, No 601 becoming No 2001, except that USA/TC 8482 NS 619 was renumbered to 2003 since NS 603 was scrapped because of the bad condition of its frames. They were used for shunting and freight trains on branch lines, until withdrawn 1958–60.

Plate 343 The first freight train to enter Rome on 20 July 1944, presumably the same train as shown in Plate 342 but now decorated up for the occasion, which was attended by US Secretary of War, Henry L. Stimson (Photo: US Army)

Plate 344   USA/TC 7981 crossing the newly-completed bridge across the Rhine at Wesel in April 1945 (Photo: US Army)

Plate 345   A more detailed photograph of USA/TC 7981 taken on the same occasion, crossing the Rhine in April 1945 (Photo: US Army)

Plate 346 Butler Brothers 8422 (ex USA/TC 8422) at Cooley in Minnesota in September 1949 (Photo: H. L. Goldsmith Collection)

Plate 347 USA/TC 8810 with the US Reclamation Service at Hoover Dam in Nevada in 1950 (Photo H. L. Goldsmith Collection)

Plate 348 Louisiana Southern 503 (ex USA/TC 8496) (Photo: H. K. Vollrath)

Chapter 62

ALCO–GE 127 ton DIESEL LOCOMOTIVES, USA/TC 8000–56 & 8600–99

This design of locomotive originated from a Bo-Bo shunting engine which went into service in 1938. This was developed into a mixed-traffic design which first went into service in 1942. Some of these engines were ordered for service in the United States (USA/TC 7122–5 and 8932–9, for instance) and these had four-wheeled bogies. For overseas service in areas where the axle-loading was considered likely to be limited, six-wheel bogies were fitted. It is these six-wheel bogie locomotives that this Chapter deals with.

The welded underframe was carried on two bogies, each carrying two nose-suspended traction motors. The six-wheeled bogies were similar to the four-wheeled ones except for the addition of an extra axle. In the front were situated the radiators and main fan, followed by the engine-generator set and then the driving cab which was sited to the rear of the locomotive followed only by the housing behind the cab for the heating boiler and accessories if fitted. A 1000hp Alco series 539 six-cylinder four-stroke supercharged diesel engine drove, besides auxiliaries, the main generator which supplied current to the electric traction motors.

The first series, USA/TC 8000–12, carried miscellaneous maker's numbers and were originally 0–4–4–0DE built for the following lines; New York, Susquehanna & Western Railroad 231/3 became 8000/1; Chicago, Milwaukee, St Paul & Pacific Railroad 1678/9 became 8002/3; Chicago, Rock Island & Pacific Railroad 747–9/6 became 8004–7; Tennessee Coal, Iron & Railroad Co Nos unknown became 8008/9 and Atlanta & St Andrews Bay Railroad 901–3 became 8010–2.

These locomotives were probably delivered in early 1942 and taken over by the USA/TC about October 1942. They were rebuilt from 0–4–4–0DE to 0–6–6–0DE with new bogies in the United States and renumbered into the USA/TC series. Further locomotives were built specially for the USA/TC, 8013–56 being Order No S–1898 of 1942, which also covered the early rebogied units. All were Alco class 606–DL–254. USA/TC 8600–99 were Order No S–1952 of 1944.

The Alco works numbers were as follows:

8000/1	69992/3	1942
8002/3	69567/8	1942
8004	69570	1942
8005/6	69424/5	1942
8007	69569	1942
8008	69428	1942
8009	69566	1942
8010/1	69426/7	1942
8012	69800	1942
8013–33	70634–54	1942
8034–56	70655–77	1943
8600–38	72073–111	1944
8639–49	72112–22	1945
8650–79	72143–72	1945
8680–99	72123–42	1945

In October 1942 it was decided that American personnel should take over the operation of the Trans-Iranian Railway in 1943 as far north as Teheran. At this time the American Mikados (WD/USA series 1000–1199) had just started working in Iran, although it was realised that the extreme temperatures in the southern plains and above all the scarcity of good water along the whole line made the operation of heavy trains by steam locomotives extremely difficult. Moreover, the 1000ton "Aid-to-Russia" trains required double-heading over the mountain sections, where gradients of 1 in 67 were frequent and the fact that there were 144 tunnels in 165 miles meant that locomotive crews suffered considerable hardship from smoke and oil fumes.

Accordingly, it was decided to send some of the 1000hp diesel-electric locomotives to work the worst sections of this line, and to suit the 67 to 75lb/yd rails in Iran six-wheeled bogies were used. USA/TC 8000–12 arrived about March 1943, and were normally used singly on the comparatively level lines in the southern plains, hauling goods and passenger trains between Ahwaz and Bandar Shalpur, Khorramshahr, Tanuma and Andhimishk. Later, when the second batch came, some were used further north.

The second batch, USA/TC 8013–56, were fitted for multiple-unit working so that two locomotives could be worked with only one engine crew. They arrived in April 1943. They were stationed at Andhimishk and Arak, and normally worked in pairs hauling all the heavy northbound freight trains over the mountainous sections between these two places. On the return journey, as many as five were coupled together to work back to Andhimishk. In May 1943, the situation was that USA/TC 8007/9–12/28/9/31/4–56 were not erected, 8000–5/13/5/8/30 were allocated to the southern Division and 8006/8/

Plate 349 USA/TC 8008 official photograph (Photo: R. Tourret Collection)

Plate 350 USA/TC 8048 at Durud in Iran in June 1945. In Iran, the heat was so intense that the Alco diesels operated with the engine access doors removed, despite the increased risk of damage due to the ingress of sand (Photo: H. C. Hughes)

14/6/7/9–27/32/3 were allocated to the Andhimishk-Arak pool. From September 1943, some of them worked as far north as Qum and by May 1944 some were working regularly through to Teheran. Between Arak and Teheran it became a common sight to see a diesel and a USA/TC steam 2–8–2 coupled together at the head of a train, and on at least one occasion two diesels and a 2–8–2 were used on a passenger train.

The Soviet government was impressed with the performance of these Alco 127 ton units in Iran and requested 70 for use in Russia. Accordingly, USA/TC 8600–49/80–99 were built with 5ft 0in gauge bogies for Russia, the last twenty being built before the ones destined for Europe. USA/TC 8621/6/30–49 were landed in Great Britain before transhipment to Russia via the Arctic convoys. USA/TC 8630–40/9 were lost en route. They became Russian SZD Class Da20–1 to 58, presumably standing for "Diesel, American". Russia wanted more of these locomotives in 1946, but this was now politically impossible so the Russians built a copy as their Class TE–1 (except for the cab). Several hundred were built between 1947 and 1950. TEM–1, TEM–2 and TEM–2A were similar types built during the 1960s, and these led to further developments as classes TEM–7 and TEM–12 over the years.

Some Da 20 class locomotives are still in service today (1991), and are even receiving new "computor" numbers.

Plate 351 USA/TC 8014 and a sister locomotive haul a freight train in Iran, coming straight out of a tunnel on to a bridge, showing the tough nature of the line (Photo: R. Tourret Collection)

Plate 352 USA/TC 8605, USSR Da 20.6, bound for Russia, official photograph (Photo: R. Tourret Collection)

Plate 353   USA/TC 8015 at Stockton in California in 1948 (Photo: H. L. Goldsmith)

diesels were sold to and went to Alaska in small batches, the first of these is believed to have been a group of nine which reached Alaska in mid-1946, while 8005/19/20/3 arrived in September 1950 and are believed to have been either the last or last but one batch. Certainly, all arrived before January 1951. Another eight were leased by the ARR and arrived between March and July 1951. While the USA/TC were releasing these locomotives, the Alaska Railroad obtained some new engines, and it appears that the two series of engines were numbered in order of delivery to the ARR.

Later diesels of this type, USA/TC 8650–79, were sent to Europe around May and June 1945. They were not used much. USA/TC 8650/3/60/2/4/5/70/1 were noted stored at Brussels Forest Midi shed in July 1945. They were all returned to the USA in 1946.

In Iran, the heavy "Aid-to-Russia" traffic had terminated by May 1945 and the 0–6–6–0DEs were crated at Ahwaz and shipped back to the United States in June and July 1945, where they were sent to Fort Holabird Military Railway Shop for a thorough overhaul. Most were then sent to New Cumberland Army Depot near Harrisburg, Pa, and placed in store. Three units, USA/TC 8014–6, were sent to the Tonopah and Goldfield to serve an Army Air Force Field in the desert.

In 1948/9, USA/TC 8021 (together with a similar unit) was tried on the Churchill (Hudson bay) line, operated by the Canadian National Railway, for cold weather testing, but was extensively damaged by a fire.

Plate 354   USA/TC 8669 at Cedar Hill Yard, New Haven, in September 1955 (Photo: H. L. Goldsmith)

Thirty-six of the Iranian 80XX series, as well as USA/TC 8650/64, went to the Alaska Railroad and were renumbered in their 10XX series. Twenty-eight of these

Details of the renumbering of the ex-USA/TC locomotives is given opposite:

The Alaska Railroad found that the open-type or tight-fitting hood over the

Plate 355   USA/TC 8033 in the service of the US Air Force at EAFB, Florida, in June 1955 (Photo: H. L. Goldsmith)

ARR	0	1	2	3	4	5	6	7	8	9
100X	–	–	8038	–	–	–	–	–	–	–
101X	8041	8051	8043	8044	8045	8035	8026	8664	8048	–
102X	–	8002	–	–	–	–	8042	8049	8019	8023
103X	8020	8005	8024	8039	8011	8013	8650	–	–	–
104X	–	8004	8006	8003	–	–	–	–	–	–
105X	8040	8054	8055	–	8056	8038*	–	8001	–	–
106X	–	–	–	–	–	8035*	–	8026*	–	8002*
107X	8047	–	8036	–	8052	8051*	8046	8043*	8053	–
108X	–	–	–	–	–	–	–	–	8021	

*subsequent renumbering

engine of the ex-military locomotives was not very good for maintenance in the sub-zero weather sometimes experienced, and a programme was started to rebuild their own locomotives into shrouded units. The leased locomotives, ARR 1032–6/41–3, were not so treated, however. The rebuilt locomotives either had a cab and were termed "A" units or were without a cab and were known as "B" or booster units. At the same time, units without multiple-unit control were so fitted and the six-wheel bogies were interchanged for roller-bearing four-wheel units (except ARR 1050/1). The increased axle loading was acceptable since the ARR was laid with 90 to 115 lb/yd rail.

The locomotives were rebuilt by the International Railway Car & Equipment Manufacturing Co, Kenton, Ohio; the Puget Sound Bridge & Dredging Co, Seattle, Washington; and the Anchorage Shops of the ARR itself. About half the programme was finished by January 1952, at which time the remaining locomotives were to be modified in the ARR shops at a rate of four or five a year. USA/TC 8001/43/51 were renumbered ARR 1021/12/1 respectively before being rebuilt into Nos 1069/77/5. Locomotives 8040/54 were rebuilt as streamline units for the ARR "Aurora" train. These locomotives retained their six-wheeled bogies for a while before being fitted with four-wheeled bogies. They were originally renumbered ARR 1050–A and 1051–A for a short period.

The remainder of the class were gradually put back into service of the USA/TC at various camps and depots in the United States. USA/TC 8037 was exhibited at the first annual Armed Forces Day Exhibition at Washington DC, in 1950.

Dimensions	6w bogies (8000–56)
Weight of engine in WO	127 tons (short)
Diesel engine, rating	1000hp
number of cylinders	6
cylinder bore and stroke	12½in x 13in
Traction motors, number	6
type	CE 731–B
gear ratio	4.69
Tractive effort, starting	
30% adhesion	76,200lb
5.5mph continuous	43,800lb
Maximum speed	60mph
Wheelbase, rigid	11ft 3in
total	50ft 3in
Driving wheel diameter	3ft 4in
Fuel oil capacity	1600 US gl

Plate 356 A long-lasting specimen in the USSR, USSR Da 20.47 at Tuxopeyk Tihoreckay in April 1991. USSR Da 20.49 was also on shed at this date. Note that 20.47 also carries its new "computor" number 15120471, which splits down as class 1512, locomotive number 047, and computor check number 1. Officially 50 still exist, although it is likely that many are stored out of service. USSR Da 20.031 is preserved in the Railway Museum at Shushary near St Petersburg (Photo: R. Tourret Collection)

Chapter 63

JAPANESE "MIKAI" CLASS 2–8–2s, USA/TC 9400–32

About the time of the fighting in Korea, the USA/TC ordered some steam 2–8–2 locomotives. It is not clear whether these were ordered to help put the Japanese locomotive manufacturers back on their feet or whether they were ordered specifically for the Korean conflict, but certainly they were shipped to Korea and used in that country. Not many details are known of these locomotives but it may be mentioned that "Mikai" means Mikado.

USA/TC Nos	Builder	Works Nos	Date
9400–3	Nippon Sharyo	1549–52	1950
9404–8	Kawasaki	3209–13	1950
9409–11	Kisha Seizo	2604–6	1950
9412–5	Hitachi	1938/9/41/2	1950
9416–8	Mitsubishi	709–11	1950
9419–28	Nippon Sharyo	1562/58/61/60/59/5/7/4/6/3	1951
9429–32	Kawasaki	3214–7	1951

Plate 357   USA/TC 9430 at Pusan in Korea in April 1952 (Photo: H. L. Goldsmith Collection)

Plate 358   USA/TC 9426 at Talga in Korea in October 1953 (Photo: H. K. Vollrath)

Chapter 64

BROAD-GAUGE 2–8–2s FOR THE INDIA RAILWAYS

These locomotives were built in Canada and the United States to the order of the Indian Railway Board, the co-ordinating authority between the Government-owned and the Company-owned railways of India. Lease-Lend is believed to have played a part in financing their purchase. The Railway Board had for many years drawn up designs and specifications for standard types of locomotives and the individual railways were encouraged to follow these designs as far as possible and to order jointly from builders in Britain or Europe through the Board. Among the standard designs were those for the XD and XE class 2–8–2 engines for the broad (5ft 6in) gauge, both having 5ft 1½in diameter coupled wheels and being suitable for heavy through-freight working. The 17ton axleload XD class had two cylinders 22½in by 28in, but the 22½ton axleload XE class was a very large locomotive with a tractive effort of over 48,000lb and had cylinders 23½in by 30in. As war-time traffic increased in 1942/3, the need for large numbers of such engines became apparent to the northern lines but British builders were unable to undertake urgent repeat orders for these designs.

Accordingly, it was arranged that trans-Atlantic builders should construct 2–8–2 engines to the general dimensions of the XD and XE classes but adopting manufacturing methods with which they were familiar. The result was the CWD (Canadian War Department) class which corresponded with the XD class and was at first known in India as the "X-Dominion". The American-built engines which followed the same design were known as the AWD class. In fact, this design was virtually identical to the US Army S200 class (WD & USA/TC 1000–1199) discussed in Chapter 48. Concurrently with the earlier CWD engines, there appeared the very large AWE or "X-Eagle" class, which corresponded with the large British XE class.

The CWD and AWD engines had bar frames and American-type trailing trucks, connected by equalising bars to the engine springing, also diamond-framed tender bogies. The leading pony truck and coupled axleboxes were grease lubricated, while the trailing truck and tender bogies had oil-fed axleboxes. In common with other locomotives for India, they had right-hand drive and screw reversing. The regulator handles were of the horizontal pull-out type, with ratchet. Two water gauges were fitted from the start, unlike the practice on some other wartime locomotives built in the United States. The grates were rocked by hand, "finger"-type firebars being used in accordance with Indian practice. There was a dump section to the grate, and a hopper ashpan. A permanent damper opening was provided by side apertures, which also permitted the hopper to be raked out.

The usual American features were also apparent in the AWE design. Notwithstanding a grate area of 63.2sq ft, this was hand-fired, two firemen being carried in India. The frames, suspension, wheels, axlebox lubrication and grate were generally similar to those of the CWD and AWD designs, likewise the reversing gear and regulator. Nathan injectors and British solid-jet vacuum ejectors were fitted, also a Detroit hydrostatic lubricator, and one water gauge column supplemented by test cocks. Another American feature, common also to the CWD and AWD classes, was the smokebox saddle cast in two halves, each integral with one cylinder, and the two halves bolted together on the centre line of the locomotive.

Dimensions

The main dimensions of the Canadian and American 2–8–2 engines for the 5ft 6in gauge are given below, together with those of the British-built 2–8–2s of classes XD and XE for comparison.

Class	XD	XE	AWD & CWD	AWE	XD
Date	1928	1929–31	1943–6	1943	1945/6
Cylinders, two, in	22½ x 28	23½ x 30	21 x 28	23½ x 30	22½ x 28
Wheel dia, coupled	5ft 1½in	5ft 1½in	5ft 0in	5ft 1½in	5ft 1½in
leading	3ft 0in	3ft 0in	2ft 6in	3ft 0in	3ft 0in
trailing	3ft 7in	3ft 7in	3ft 6in	3ft 6in	3ft 7in
Wheelbase, coupled	17ft 3in	17ft 3in	15ft 9in	17ft 3in	17ft 3in
total, engine	35ft 0in	36ft 5in	32ft 9in	36ft 5in	35ft 0in
Heating, tubes & flues	1962	2728	1985	2765	1930
surface, firebox	190	260	162	245(a)	190
sq ft, arch tubes	24	26	17	26	25
total evaporative	2176	3014	2164	3036	2145
superheater	540	763	623	765	540
combined total	2716	3777	2787	3801	2685
Grate area, sq ft	45	60	47	63.2	45
Boiler pressure, psi	180	210	200	210	180
TE at 85% BP, lb	35264	48086	35000	48100	35264
Adhesive weight	68t 0c	89t 16c	62t 19c	90t 12c	68t 0c
Weight of engine in WO	95t 15c	120t 7c	88t 8c	118t 16c	98t 7c
Tender, wheel diameter	3ft 7in	3ft 7in	3ft 0in	3ft 0in	3ft 7in
wheelbase	22ft 6in	22ft 6in	17ft 0in	21ft 3in	22ft 6in
water capacity, gl	4500	6000	4500	6000	4500
coal capacity, tons	10	14	12(b)	14	13
weight, full	63t 2c	78t 1c	55t 5c	64t 16c	66t 10c
Weight, engine & tender in WO	158t 17c	198t 8c	143t 13c	183t 12c	164t 17c

Notes
(a) Includes 55sq ft for combustion chamber
(b) Variously quoted as 12 tons and 13 tons

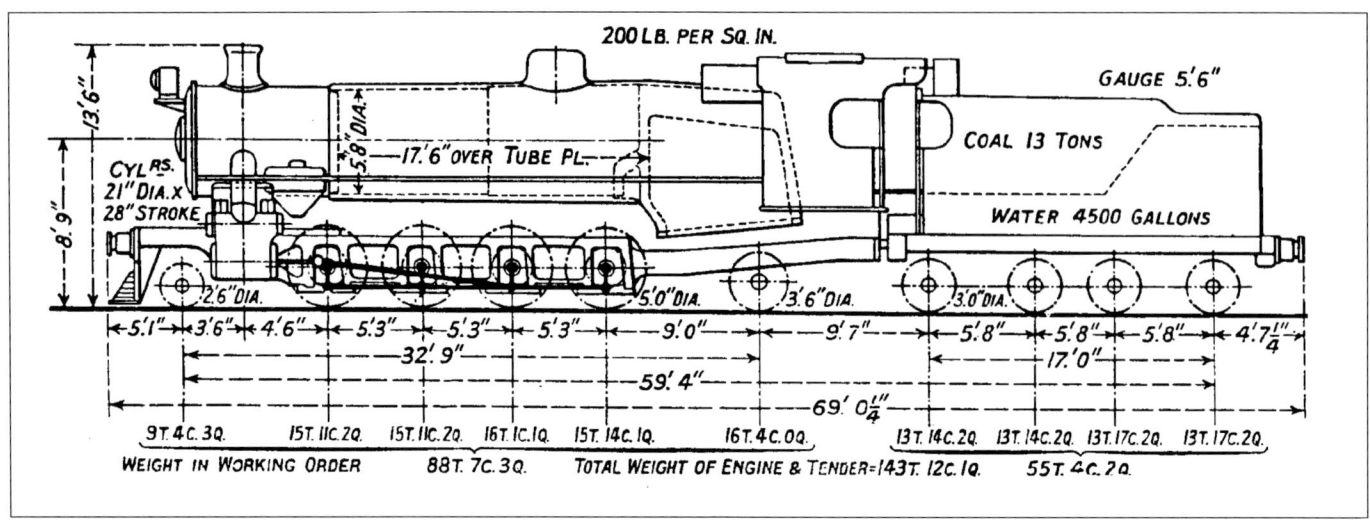

Fig 42 Canadian Locomotive Co CWD class 2–8–2 built for Indian railways (Courtesy Railway Gazette)

CWD Class, IGR 5001–5190 & 5501–5747

These appeared from the Canadian Locomotive Company of Kingston, Ontario, numbered serially from C1 upwards and from the Montreal Locomotive Works numbered from M1 upwards. These "C" & "M" numbers were stencilled on the cabsides. Nos C1–75 and M1–70 were ordered in 1943 and construction commenced the same year. M1–70 were US Army Class S 205. Further batches, C76–190 and M71–247, were ordered in 1945. Nos M71–247 were US Army Class S 198. The Montreal Locomotive Works numbers were, of course, in the same series as the Alco Works Nos.

The locomotives were delivered partially assembled, the boilers travelling separately from the chassis. No C1 was erected in India and put to work on 20 February 1944, C4 preceding it by one day. No M1 went into traffic on 6 April, preceded by M8 on 24 March and M14 on 3 April. The others followed quickly. M22–4 (IGR 5522–4) were lost en route to India.

Full details are as follows:

C/M Nos	IGR Nos	Contract Nos	Works	Works Nos	Delivered
C1–26	5001–26	C600	CLC	2045–70	Oct-Dec 1943
C27–75	5027–75	C600	CLC	2071–2119	Jan-May 1944
C76–150	5076–5150	C601	CLC	2171–2245	June-Nov 1945
C151–71	5151–71	C602	CLC	2246–66	Nov-Dec 1945
C172/3	5172/3	C602	CLC	2267/8	1946?
C174–90	5174–90	C602	CLC	2269–85	1946
M1–18	5501–18	Q399	MLW	71187–71204	Nov-Dec 1943
M19–70	5519–70	Q399	MLW	71205–56	Jan-April 1944
M71–90	5571–90	Q402	MLW	72173–92	
M91/2	5591/2	Q402	MLW	72948/9	
M93–186	5593–5686	Q402	MLW	72960–73055	Jan-May 1945
M187	5687	Q402	MLW	73081	
M188–247	5688–5747	Q403	MLW	73508–67	May-July 1945

Plate 359   USA/TC 5098 built by Baldwin in 1945. Became AWD Class IGR 7098. Official photograph (Photo: R. Tourret Collection)

The first engines went into traffic on the Bengal and Assam Railway main line from Calcutta (Sealdah) northwards and were at once painted black, generally with "B&A" painted on the tender. Initially, from February to April 1944, C1–25 and M1–11 were given BAR Nos 1–36, the first thirty of which were blanks in that Railway's own stock list at that time, but the last six of which conflicted with the 4–6–0 "Mail" engines then running regularly on the same main line. Details are as follows:

BAR	0	1	2	3	4	5	6	7	8	9
X	–	C1	C2	C3	C4	C5	C6	C7	M8	C9
1X	C10	C11	C12	C13	M11	C15	C16	C17	C18	C19
2X	C20	C21	C22	M1	M6	M10	C23	C24	M4	M7
3X	C8	M9	C25	M3	C14	M2	M5	–	–	–

About August 1944, however, an IGR system of numbering was started, series C1 upwards becoming 5001 upwards, and M1 upwards becoming 5501 upwards, in each case in order of the makers numbering. This took the place of the short-lived BAR scheme and was applied to all locomotives as they were erected. These 5XXX numbers were chosen so as to be higher than the highest numbers carried by the locomotives of any individual Indian railway and hence the CWD class could be operated, during and after the war, on any line in the sub-continent without confusion resulting.

The "C" and "M" prefixes were retained in some cases for a considerable time in conjunction with the new numbers. The tenders carried the initials of the Railway to which each engine was allocated, for example "B&A", "EIR", "GIP", etc but after a few months they began to appear with the letters "ISR" and by 1946 this in turn gave place to "IGR".

In one or two cases there was possible confusion as to the identity of the locomotives. Thus, by October 1944, only a few months after being first put into traffic, IGR 5025 carried maker's plates C 2058/43 and the engine to which they officially belonged, IGR 5014, carried C2069/43: the maker's plates were on the smokebox so this might merely denote a change of boilers but it was clear that the number "5014" was superimposed on the cabside since the figures "5025" were visible underneath. Again, IGR 5666–8 should be M 73033–5 and were recorded as such in the records of the shops which erected them, but they carried, certainly within a few months, the plates 73042/37/40 respectively. Other engines noted running within a short time of erection with maker's plates out of serial order or with no plates at all were IGR 5599, 5614/7/8/26/7/33/51–3/83/5/6/8/91 and 5730/1/9/40. Confusion of makers' plates is common in India but can usually be ascribed to carelessness with splashers, which become changed over in shops between engines of the same class.

However, in the case of the CWD locomotives it is probable that the confusion arose during erection in India, most of the engines concerned having been turned out at Karachi within the space of a few months. IGR 5685/6 have been recorded as M 73052/3 respectively, and this suggests that IGR 5684–7 may be M 73051–4, notwithstanding the information to the contrary from Canada quoted earlier. IGR 5688 has been recorded as M 73440, but this is difficult to accept. Engines M 22–4, which would have been IGR 5522–4, were lost at sea by enemy action and the IGR numbers were never filled, but the 1945 orders included three extra locomotives as replacements.

Erection of the 434 locomotives of class CWD was fairly equally divided between the Great Indian Peninsular Railway and the North Western Railway. The former erected some in their Parel Workshops at Bombay but the majority were dealt with in the Carriage and Wagon shops at Matunga, a few miles further out in the suburbs. The North Western's Workshops were at Moghalpura, Lahore, but these wartime locomotives were erected at a "Field Workshops" established at Karachi. These last-mentioned shops were unusual in being largely in the open air, a feature possible because of the infrequency of rain in Karachi. It is believed that three engines, IGR 5011–3, were assembled by the Bengal and Assam Railway at their Kanchrapara Shops, north of Calcutta. This would probably have been due to the diversion of the ship carrying these engines to Calcutta instead of the west coast docks of Bombay or Karachi.

Following assembly and delivery to the BAR, several of the first arrivals were stored for a month or two awaiting delivery of the ejectors from British makers. These ejectors were of the solid-jet type and overcame many of the delays which had been customary due to leaky train pipes, since in India all freight vehi-

Plate 360   IGR Class CWD 5174 (Photo: C. Smith)

cles were piped for vacuum brake and the majority were braked. Another helpful feature was the steam brake on the engine. In the event of difficulty in releasing the train brakes it was possible to avoid applying them again by running, most unofficially, on the engine brakes.

From the start, the CWD class met an urgent need. The Bengal and Assam Railway carried most of the traffic from Calcutta Docks, or from exchange points with other railways, to the Assam and North Burma fronts. Hence, it received the first allocation and more engines followed later. The BAR allocation was 5001–25/35/61/84 and 5501–11/25/36/8/41/7/51–3/9/62/71/89–98.

The East Indian, Bengal Nagpur, GIP and Nizam's State Railways were the other lines which received CWD locomotives in 1944, as they were carrying supplies and military personnel across the country to converge on the BAR system. The EIR eventually had 5037/43–7/52/4/5/8/62–72/6–8/82/3/6/91, 5115/21/3/5–8/32/6/7/42–56, 5520/1/6/7/9–35/40/6/54–6/67/8/70, 5611/31/2/4/7/56/60–2/9/70/3–7/84/9/92/4/5/7–9 and 5700–2/5/7/9–11/6/8–20/4/5/9/32/7/8/42–6/7. The BNR had 5026–32/4/6/8–42/51/3, 5512–9/28/48–50/72/83/8, 5601–4/7/8/15/6/8/35/48/9/81 and 5712–4/22. The GIP had 5048–50/9/73–5, 5101/30/1, 5537/9/42–5/58/60/1/3–6/9/76–80/6, 5609/10/36/8/9/41–5/50/7/9/63/4/71/2/8–80/2/6 and 5743/4. The NSR had only five locomotives, 5035/56/7/60 and 5557.

The work was chiefly in the category of express freight, but also included troop trains and the long trip to Poona with loaded ambulance trains over the BAR, BNR and GIP Railways. Their arrival considerably improved the speed and standard of running. Their "crack" jobs were the motor-vehicle trains. These were usually made up to sixty flat trucks and brake, loaded with motor vehicles and their crews, and were run to a booked path. These loads were around 800 tons but the petrol trains, which had to maintain almost the same average speed, often weighed double this figure and were a stiff proposition for an engine with 5ft 0in wheels.

As more engines of the class came into service in 1945/6, and peace-time conditions returned, they were allocated more widely. The EIR received more (some from the BAR) and so did the GIP, whilst the NWR, BBCI and MSM Railways received allocations.

The NWR received the most, having 5079–81/5/7–90/2/4/5/8/9, 5100/2–14/6–20/2/4/9/33–5/8–41/57–90,

Plate 361 IGR Class CWD C-5117 at NWR Rawalpindi shed in April 1948 (Photo: E. A. S. Cotton)

5581/7, 5612/7/26/7/33/54/83/7/90/1 and 5704/6/15/7/21/6–8/30/1/3–6/9–41/5. The BBCI received 5093/6/7, 5623/85/93/6 and 5703/8/23. The MSM was allocated 5573–5/82/4/5/99, 5600/5/6/13/4/9–22/4/5/8–30/40/6/7/51–3/5/8/65–8/88.

On 15 August 1947, India was partitioned into India and Pakistan. The NWR was split into two parts, the NWR of Pakistan and the Eastern Punjab Railway which was India's share. Some months earlier, on 31 March 1947, the NWR had 114 of these engines, all but five stationed in the Karachi, Lahore, Multan and Rawalpindi Divisions, so that most of the engines should have gone to the NWR(P). However, it appears that at the Partition the Indian Government retained as much stock as possible and in the 1948–9 returns the EPR was stated to have 61 CWD class locomotives, of which 42 were stated to have come from the NWR. The NWR(P) then had 72 class CWD, 5080/5/7–9/92/4/5/8/9, 5100/3–7/9–14/6–20/2/4/33/4/57/6/4/7/8/70/2–4/7–9/88/9, 5581/7/99, 5606/12/7/22/6/7/83/90/1, 5704/6/15/7/21/6–8/30/4–6/9/40/5. Presumably the EPR had the remainder of those which were on the NWR before the Partition. By December 1948, only one, 5026, remained on the BNR, and the MSM had lost many of theirs.

The Bengal Assam Railway was also partitioned in August 1947, the broad gauge portions being curtailed by cessions to the EIR. The remainder became the EBR of Pakistan. Twenty-four CWD's were retained by the EBR as follows, 5004/14/7/38/59, 5514/5/8/36–8/49/53/63/8/70/89–92/5–8, making a total of 96 of these engines going to Pakistan.

During 1948/9, ninety locomotives of the CWD class were built for the IGR by

Plate 362 IGR Class CWD 5730, specially painted for hauling VIP trains, at NWR Rawalpindi shed in May 1948 (Photo: E. A. S. Cotton)

Plate 363   IGR Class CWD 5704 at Karachi NWR shed in June 1948 (Photo E. A. S. Cotton)

the Montreal Locomotive Works M248–337 under Order No Q418; and 60 were built by Canadian Locomotive Co numbers C191–250 under Order No C611. They were renumbered IGR 8001–150, not in order, but according to the railway to which they were allocated, 8001–90 to EIR, 8091–110 to EPR and 8111–50 to GIP.

By 1978, nineteen CWD locomotives were in Bangladesh, allocated to the Paksey Division. At January 1984, Pakistan had 67 CWDs, allocated as follows; 23 to Khanewal, two to Multan, two to Rawalpindi, six at Rohri and 34 at Samasata.

AWD Class, IGR 5750–5914 and 7061–7120

As already explained, the AWD Class consisted of engines similar to the Canadian-built CWD class but built in America. They were ordered and built by Baldwin in two batches, both ordered in 1944. USA/TC 3750–3914 were Baldwin 71761–71925 all built in 1944 and USA/TC 5061–5120 were Baldwin 72113–72 all built in 1945. In all, there were 225 locomotives.

The engines came out to India partially erected, like the CWD class. They carried their USA/TC numbers on plates on the right-hand side of the smokebox, while the maker's plates were carried on the left-hand side. The first lot were given IGR Nos 5750–5914, two thousand higher to bring them above 5000, and the second lot, whose numbers clashed with the Canadian Locomotive Company series, likewise had two thousand added, to make them 7061–7120. Like the CWD locomotives, the erection was divided between the GIP (Matunga) and the NWR (Karachi).

The first arrived in December 1944 and by June 1945 all the first batch had arrived and been put into service. They helped during the peak traffic towards the close of the war in Asia. The final batch of sixty arrived from August 1945 to February 1946, and were at first somewhat redundant. In April 1946, twenty lay in the EIR shed at Asansol, painted grey and without siderods or motion, but these were later taken into traffic.

The GIP was allocated 5750/4–9/65–7/70–3/5–9/90–2/4/5,5803/8/10/1/4/6–8/23/4/7/31/5/40–6/50/2–5/7–64/6/7/9/71–3/8/84/93–7, 5914 and 7066/7. The EIR had 5751–3/60/2/74/82/5/98/9, 5800/1/4/26/9/30–2–4/6/8/9/47–9/70/9/88–92, 5901–7, 7061–5/8/70–2/9–89/93–9, 7100/3/5–15/7/9/20. The BBCI had 5761, 5802/5–7/9/12/3/9–22/37/68/98/9, 5900, 7092 and 7101/4/16. The BNR had 5763/4/8/9/80/1/3/4/6–9/93/6/7, 5815/25/8/51/6/65/74–7/80–3/5–7, 5908–13, 7069/73–8/90/1 and 7102/18.

By 1948/9, many were at work on the GIP and BBCI (some of the latter having previously been on the BNR) and it is believed that the rest were on the EIR. Those transferred to the BBCI by 1948 included 5764/8/9/78–81/3/4/6–9/93/7, 5825/8/48/9/51/6/65/74–7/80–3/5–7, 5908–13, 7069/73–5/90/1 and 7102/18.

AWD/CWD IGR 5001–5190, 5501–5747, 5750–5914, 7061–7120 and 8001–8150

From Independence Day, 15 August 1947, the IGR naturally began to treat the AWD and CWD classes as one big class. This comprised 225 AWD and 434 CWD engines, less the 96 engines that went to Pakistan, plus the post-Independence 150 1948/9 built CWD, making a total of 713 in all.

In the All-India renumbering, they became 12000 to 12716. The general scheme was to allot number blocks to different railways in turn, and the Central Railway was given 12000–174, Eastern Railway 12175–383, Northern Railway (ex EIR) 12384–419, Northern Railway (ex EPR) 12420–98, Northern Railway (ex EIR) 12499–617 and Western Railway 12618–716. The CR was the old GIP, the ER part of EIR and part of BAR, the NR the other part of EIR and the EPR, and the WR the old BBCI. However, there was some

Plate 364   Departure of the "Pakistan Mail" leaving Rawalpindi at 5pm in charge of IGR Class CWD 5587 in 1948 (Photo: E. A. S. Cotton)

All-India	0	1	2	3	4	5	6	7	8	9
1200X	5027	5028	5029	5030	5031	5033	5034	5036	5039	5042
1201X	5056	5057	5060	5101	5616	5131	5138	5512	5517	5670
1202X	5557	5575	5576	5695	5579	5580	5586	5588	5609	5610
1203X	5613	5619	5621	5624	5636	5637	5638	5639	5641	5643
1204X	5644	5645	5650	5651	5655	5657	5658	5659	5663	5664
1205X	5665	5667	5668	5671	5672	5678	5679	5680	5684	5686
1206X	5712	5713	5714	5733	5741	5699	5744	5750	5754	5755
1207X	5756	5757	5758	5759	5765	5766	5767	5770	5771	5772
1208X	5773	5775	5776	5777	5790	5791	5792	5794	5795	5796
1209X	5808	5810	5811	5815	5816	5817	5818	5823	5824	5827
1210X	5831	5835	5841	5842	5843	5844	5845	5846	5850	5852
1211X	5853	5854	5855	5857	5859	5860	5861	–	5863	5864
1212X	5866	5867	5869	5871	5872	5873	5878	5879	5884	5893
1213X	5894	5895	5897	7066	7067	8111	8112	8113	8114	8115
1214X	8116	8117	8118	8119	8120	8121	8122	8123	8124	8125
1215X	8126	8127	8128	8129	8130	8131	8132	8133	8134	8135
1216X	8136	8137	8138	8139	8140	8141	8142	8143	8144	8145
1217X	8146	8147	8148	8149	8150	5829	5892	5901	5906	7061
1218X	7062	7063	7064	7065	7068	7070	7071	7072	7076	7077
1219X	7078	7079	7080	7081	7082	7083	7084	7085	7086	7087
1220X	7088	7089	7093	7094	7095	7096	7097	7098	7099	7100
1221X	7103	7105	7106	7107	7108	7109	7110	7111	7112	7113
1222X	7114	7115	7120	5001	5002	5005	5006	5007	5009	5010
1223X	5011	5013	5015	5018	5019	5021	5024	5026	5032	5035
1224X	5037	5046	5050	5067	5073	5077	5078	5083	5084	5086
1225X	5115	5123	5125	5127	5128	5129	5136	5137	5143	5144
1226X	5145	5146	5147	5149	5150	5151	5152	5153	5154	5155
1227X	5156	5160	5506	5507	5508	5509	5510	5511	5525	5539
1228X	5540	5543	5546	5547	5551	5552	5555	5556	5559	5561
1299X	5562	5571	5593	5611	5614	5615	5682	5629	5632	5648
1230X	5649	–	–	–	5707	5718	5720	5729	5732	5737
1231X	5738	5742	5746	8001	8002	8003	8004	8005	8006	8007
1232X	8008	8009	8010	8011	8012	8013	8014	8015	8016	8017
1233X	8018	8019	8020	8021	8022	8023	8024	8025	8026	8027
1234X	8028	8029	8030	8031	8032	8033	8034	8035	8036	8037
1235X	8038	8039	8040	8041	8042	8043	8044	8045	8046	8047
1236X	8048	8049	8051	8052	8053	8070	8071	8072	8073	8074
1237X	8075	8077	8078	8079	8080	8081	8082	8083	8084	8085
1238X	8087	8088	8089	8090	5751	5752	5753	5760	5762	5763
1239X	5774	5782	5785	5798	5799	5800	5801	5804	5826	5830
1240X	5832	5833	5834	5836	5838	5839	5847	5870	5888	5889
1241X	5890	5891	5902	5903	5904	5905	5907	7117	7118	7119
1242X	5041	5053	5076	5079	5081	5090	5093	5096	5097	5102
1243X	5108	5121	5135	5139	5140	5141	5159	5161	5162	5163
1244X	5165	5166	5169	5171	5175	5176	5180	5181	5182	5183
1245X	5184	5185	5186	5187	5190	5513	5516	5528	5550	5574
1246X	5583	5600	5604	5605	5607	5608	5618	5620	5625	5634
1247X	5646	5647	5652	5653	5654	5687	5703	5722	5731	8091
1248X	8092	8093	8094	8095	8096	8097	8098	8099	8100	8101

confusion over the renumbering because a few engines on loan at the time were at first allotted two numbers, and others were under transfer. In the end, there were four blanks in the series. Full details of the renumbering follow, but the few cases where an original allotment was altered are ignored.

AWE Class, IGR 6103–42

Forty of these large locomotives, USA/TC 4103–42, were ordered and built by Baldwin in 1943, works numbers being 69674–69713 and dates of construction between June and about August 1943. The USA/TC 41XX numbers were carried at first but renumbering in the IGR 61XX series was carried out in 1944/5. The original classification on the Indian railways was "XE/1". The letters "USA" painted on the tenders subsequently gave way to the initials "EIR" and "GIP" and later to "IGR".

Twenty-nine were erected at the EIR's Jamalpur Shops and eleven by the GIP, in early 1944. The former were the engines which had been shipped into Calcutta, and the latter those which had arrived in Bombay Docks. From the start the AWE Class have been allocated between the EIR and the GIP, the EIR having 6103–10/5/7–27/9/32–7/9 and the GIP 6111–4/6/28/30/1/8/40–2. There was subsequently a certain amount of re-allocation between the EIR and GIP of individual locomotives, and by 1949 the GIP had fifteen and the EIR the balance.

Their work was the heaviest of the through freight category. On the EIR this was mainly between Asansol and Moghal Serai, over the banks of the Grand Chord "cut-off" on the Calcutta-Delhi route. On the GIP, they worked from Igatpuri (the end of the electrified Hill section from Bombay) to Bhusaval, focal point and site of the largest locomotive shed in India (then allocated over 180 engines).

The final 15 allocated to the GIP were 6107/11–4/6/28–32/8/40–2. In the 1951 zoning, they went to the Central Railway, and in the All-India renumbering became 22901–15. The EIR engines were 6103–6/8–10/5/7–27/33–7/9. In the

Plate 365 Canadian M271, the post-war version of the CWD Class, built directly for the Indian State Railways, official photograph (Photo: R. Tourret Collection)

All-India	0	1	2	3	4	5	6	7	8	9
1249X	8102	8103	8104	8105	8106	8107	8108	8109	8110	5003
1250X	5008	5012	5016	5020	5022	5023	5025	5040	5043	5044
1251X	5045	5047	5048	5049	5051	5052	5054	5055	5058	5061
1252X	5062	5063	5064	5065	5066	5068	5069	5070	5071	5072
1253X	5074	5075	5082	5091	5126	5132	5142	5148	5501	5502
1254X	5503	5504	5505	5520	5521	5526	5527	5529	5530	5531
1255X	5532	5533	5534	5535	5541	5542	5544	5545	5554	5558
1256X	5560	5564	5565	5566	5567	5569	5594	5628	5630	5631
1257X	5633	5635	5656	5660	5661	5662	5666	5669	5673	5674
1258X	5675	5676	5677	5681	5688	5689	5692	5694	5697	5716
1259X	5700	5701	5702	5705	5710	5711	5719	5724	5747	8050
1260X	8054	8055	8056	8057	8058	8059	8060	8061	8062	8063
1261X	8064	8065	8066	8067	8068	8069	8076	8086	5130	5519
1262X	5548	5572	5573	5577	5578	5582	5584	5585	5601	5602
1263X	5603	5623	5640	5642	5685	5693	5696	5698	5708	5709
1264X	5723	5725	5743	5761	5764	5768	5769	5778	5779	5780
1265X	5781	5783	5784	5786	5787	5788	5789	5793	5797	5802
1266X	5803	5805	5806	5807	5809	5812	5813	5814	5819	5820
1267X	5821	5822	5825	5828	5837	5840	5848	5849	5851	5856
1268X	5858	5862	5865	5868	5874	5875	5876	5877	5880	5881
1269X	5882	5883	5885	5886	5887	5896	5898	5899	5900	5908
1270X	5909	5910	5911	5912	5913	5914	7069	7073	7074	7075
1271X	7090	7091	7092	7101	7102	7104	7116	–	–	–

zoning, they went to the Western Railway, and in the All-India renumbering became 22916–40.

By 1978, three AWE class locomotives were reported as sold out of service to the Madhya Pradesh Electricity Board, Amrai Power Station between Bilaspur and Shahdol.

Plate 366   USA/TC 4117 built by Baldwin in 1943. Became IGR Class AWE 6117. Official photograph (Photo: R. Tourret Collection)

Plate 367   IGR Class AWE 6122 at Jamalpur in May 1945 (Photo: A. B. Crompton)

Plate 368   IGR Class AWE 6133 at Asansol in May 1945 (Photo: A. B. Crompton)

Chapter 65

THE MRS NUMBERING SCHEME USED IN ITALY

In Italy, the railways were initially operated by the Allied Armies, that is, by the British Royal Engineers and the American MRS (Military Railway Service). The Americans devised a numbering scheme for the captured Italian locomotives based on the stock at the beginning of 1943 or perhaps earlier, which was partially carried out although never very popular. It was in use for a year, from November 1943 to November 1944, for locomotives on the mainland but not for engines in Sicily or Sardinia. Several Sicilian locomotives were transferred to the mainland and were renumbered, however.

It should be noted that these numbers were MRS and not WD or USA/TC as commonly supposed. At the time, an MRS classification was prepared, but this was used even less than the numbering scheme. The numbers were painted in white above the FS numberplate and the class below; the South Eastern Railway in addition shading the numbers in red, which made them look quite smart.

The numbers were applied to all locomotives as the Allied Armies advanced up to Rome and even to Florence, whether in service or derelict, but thereafter the scheme fell into disuse and the numbers were not painted on locomotives in the north of Italy. Very soon afterwards, they were removed altogether.

Certain classes found only in the north never received MRS numbers at all, although allowance had been made for them. Railcars, narrow-gauge and electric locomotives were not included in the scheme.

Class A1 (FS 800) consisted of nine engines and was allocated numbers 1–9. In south Italy there was only one engine of the 800 class, but an engine of the 801 class was found at Naples which did not fit into the original scheme, being a departmental engine and not in the capital stock. This was classified A2 and allocated No 5.

The blank classes B1, B2, B6 and B7 are a bit of a mystery, since to fill them there were only the FS classes 822 (two engines), 885 (sixteen engines) and 899 (one engine). This suggests that the originators of the MRS scheme might have based their classification on an out-of-date list and included some classes that had been scrapped.

The B5 class originally had numbers 428–631 correctly giving a total of 204 engines. However, on the South Eastern Railway of Italy, 23 engines of the FS 870 class were found which had been sold out

Plate 369   MRS 100 (ex FS 835.088) "General Mark Clark Special" at Naples in November 1943 (Photo: US Army)

Outline of MRS Numbering Scheme			
MRS Nos	**MRS Class**	**Type**	**FS Class**
1–9	A1	0–4–0T	800
10–5	B2	0–6–0T	829
16–57	B3	0–6–0T	830
58–427	B4	0–6–0T	835
428–550	B5	0–6–0T	851
551–631	B5A	0–6–0T	870
649–60	B8	0–6–0T (Rack)	980
661–8	B9	0–6–0T (Rack)	981
669	B10	0–6–2T	900
700–99	C1	0–6–0	290
800–10	D1	0–8–0	420
?	E1 or E2	0–8–0T	893
912–1017	E3	0–8–0T	895
1018–46	E4	0–8–0T	896
2400–14	F1	0–10–0	470
2415–2542	F2	0–10–0	471
2543–51	F3	0–10–0	473
2552	F4	0–10–0	474
2553–81	F5	0–10–0	475
2582–2653	F6	0–10–0	476
2654–2731	F7	0–10–0	477
2732–2820	H2	2–6–0T	875
2826–2913	H3	2–6–0T	880
2914–80	H4	2–6–0T	905
3021–70	J1	2–8–2T	940
3100–3499	K1	2–6–0	625
3500–3699?	K2	2–6–0	640
3700–23	K3	2–6–0	645
3800–3	L1	2–6–2	680
3804–17	L2	2–6–2	681
3818–29	L3	2–6–2	682
3900–4242	L4	2–6–2	685
4243–86?	L5	2–6–2	S685(a)
4287–4314?	L6	2–6–2	688
4400–34	M1	2–8–0	728
4435–4550	M2	2–8–0	729
4551–4738	M3	2–8–0	730
4739–5131	M4	2–8–0	735
5132–5601	M5	2–8–0	740
5602–51	M6	2–8–0	744
5652–5724	M7	2–8–0	745
5800–59	N1	2–8–2	746
5900–4	P1	2–10–0	478
5905–13	P2	2–10–0	479
5914–31	P3	2–10–0	480
5932–?	P4	2–10–0	482

Note (a) The prefix "S" was used to denote 685 class engines with a boiler pressure of 200psi instead of the usual 170psi.

of service, the 870 class being extinct on the FS. The South Eastern Railways were created in 1932 by the amalgamation of three railways and since then they had purchased second-hand locomotives from two other systems but had not renumbered any of them! As these 870 class locomotives therefore still carried their old FS numberplates, the B5A class was specially created for them and they were allocated numbers from 551 upwards. Similarly, some H3 engines (FS 880) owned by the South Eastern Railway also received MRS numbers.

In addition to class D1, there was probably a class D2 and D3 to cover FS classes 422 (22 engines) and 460 (45 engines) which would carry the number series up to 877.

Class E1 or E2 was FS class 893 of twelve locomotives, so that they could be covered by the numbers 900–11. Class F7 (FS 477) originally consisted of 77 engines but probably quite a number had been scrapped or possibly those sent to Russia in 1942 for the war had been written off.

Class H1 must have been FS class 876, of which all locomotives had been withdrawn by 1944 and probably not more than one or two remained unscrapped. It is believed that class H2 consisted of 92 engines and the series probably started at 2745 or possibly 2750.

Blank MRS classes were G, I and O. FS classes not covered were 552 (13 4–4–0s), 691 (33 Pacifics), 819 (a second-hand 0–4–2WT acquired in 1938), 897 (two 0–10–0Ts) and 910 (54 2–6–2WTs of which some may have been scrapped). Possibly class 910 was I1 and carried Nos 2981–3020 and class 691 was O1, leaving G1 for the two class 897 0–10–Ts. In this case, class 552 might have been classified Q1.

Details of the FS locomotives are given in the book "Italian State Railways Steam Locomotives" by P. M. Kalla-Bishop, also published by Tourret Publishing.

Locomotives Actually Renumbered

The following list gives all the locomotives known to have been actually renumbered.

MRS No	FS No
1	800.007
5	801.004
16	830.012
58	835.088
59	835.275
60	835.362
61	835.274
62	835.120
63	835.180
64	835.201
65	835.257
66	835.319
69	835.129
70	835.321
72	835.068
73	835.193
76	835.138
77	835.296
78	835.182
79	835.015
80	835.025
81	835.035
82	835.064
83	835.099
84	835.104
85	835.123
86	835.125
87	835.150
88	835.171

Plate 370   MRS 101 (ex FS 835.275) "General Gray" at Naples in November 1943 (Photo: US Army)

MRS No	FS No	MRS No	FS No	MRS No	FS No
89	835.200	159	835.206	459	851.139
90	835.205	160	835.210	460	851.148
91	835.233	161	835.225	461	851.156
92	835.230	162	835.265	462	851.159
93	835.238	163	835.278	463	851.160
94	835.294	164	835.289	464	851.163
95	835.298	169	835.084	465	851.166
96	835.324	428	851.026	466	851.169
97	835.327	430	851.058?	467	851.172
98	835.361	431	851.104	468	851.173
99	835.364	432	851.107	469	851.180(i)
100	835.088	433	851.183	470	851.196
101	835.275	434	851.064	471	851.197
102	835.272	435	851.179	472	851.198
104	835.216	436	851.116	473	851.199
109	835.333	437	851.138	474	851.149
111	835.285	438	851.055	475	851.127
112	835.178	439	851.001	476	851.206
113	835.297	440	851.008	477	851.205
115	835.127	441	851.011	485	851.176
116	835.202	442	851.017	493	851.093
117	835.320	443	851.022	494	851.147
118	835.325	444	851.032	495	851.174
120	835.186	445	851.039	551	870.011
133	835.005	446	851.040(h)	552	870.012
134	835.024	447	851.043	553	870.023
135	835.034	448	851.045	554	870.043
136	835.039	449	851.059	555	870.072
141	835.155	450	851.060	556	870.075
145	835.224	451	851.061	557	870.082
146	835.228	452	851.062	558	870.092
147	835.229	453	851.070	559	870.096
150	835.284	454	851.074	560	870.099
151	835.303	455	851.105	561	870.100
152	835.318	456	851.123	562	870.105
157	835.090	457	851.128	563	870.110
158	835.143	458	851.134	564	870.116

MRS No	FS No	MRS No	FS No	MRS No	FS No
565	870.133	717	290.294	1031	896.026
566	870.135	718	290.313	2400	470.113
567	870.137	719	290.319	2401	471.116(c)
568	870.151	720	290.321	2402	470.127
569	870.166	726	290.256	2415	471.288
570	870.136	727	290.295	2416	471.104
571	870.015	800	420.230	2417	471.240
572	870.019	801	420.245	2418	471.115
649	980.009	802	420.253	2419	471.008
650	980.002	803	420.260	2420	471.112
651	980.004	804	420.285	2421	471.118
652	980.007	805	420.286	2423	471.080
653	980.010	806	420.290	2424	471.093
654	980.011	912	895.016	2553	475.029
655	980.012	913	895.031	2554	475.026
656	980.006	914	895.121	2555	475.012
661	981.004	915	895.152	2556	475.004
662	981.001	916	895.157	2557	475.007
663	981.002	917	895.008	2558	475.014
664	981.003	918	895.040	2559	475.022(j)
665	981.005	926	895.037	2582	476.020
666	981.006	927	895.154	2583	476.046
667	981.007	928	895.011	2584	476.056
668	981.008	929	895.012	2586	476.012
700	290.228	930	895.022	2587	476.002
701	290.229	931	895.149	2588	476.022
702	290.309	932	895.150	2589	476.024
703	290.281	935	895.021	2590	476.026
704	290.304	1018	896.011	2591	476.031
705	290.323	1019	896.019	2592	476.032
706	290.287	1020	896.003	2593	476.034
707	290.250	1021	896.001	2594	476.048
708	290.320	1022	896.008	2595	476.057
709	290.310	1023	896.009	2596	476.065
710	290.314	1024	896.013	2597	476.072
711	290.333	1025	896.028	2598	476.014
712	290.175	1026	896.030	2599	476.023
713	290.326	1027	896.012	2601	476.013(d)
714	290.187	1028	896.022	2602	476.055
715	290.262	1029	896.024	2603	476.062
716	290.293	1030	896.023	2604	476.004

Plate 371   MRS 4744 FS Class 735 shunting at Naples in December 1943 (Photo: US Army)

MRS No	FS No	MRS No	FS No	MRS No	FS No
2605	476.061	3104	625.477	3167	625.128
2606	476.027	3105	625.389	3168	625.045
2607	476.003(d)	3106	625.515	3169	625.055
2608	476.064	3107	625.026	3170	625.456
2609	476.007	3108	625.032	3171	625.487(b)
2610	476.052	3109	625.327	3172	625.115
2611	476.019	3110	625.329	3173	625.133
2612	476.051	3111	625.365	3174	625.001
2613	476.045(a)	3112	625.471	3175	625.002
2614	476.058(a)	3113	625.367	3176	625.004
2615	476.018(d, m)	3114	625.455	3177	625.005
2616	476.008(d)	3115	625.494	3178	625.010
2617	476.009(d)	3116	625.522	3179	625.011
2618	476.053	3117	625.351	3180	625.018
2622	476.071	3118	625.363	3181	625.019
2654	477.072	3119	625.410	3182	625.027
2826	880.006(b)	3120	625.436	3183	625.028
2827	880.021(b)	3121	625.534	3184	625.030
2828	880.022(b)	3122	625.411	3185	625.042
2829	880.032(b)	3123	625.003	3186	625.052
2830	880.035(b)	3124	625.064	3187	625.054
2831	880.037(b)	3125	625.079	3188	625.075
2832	880.041(b)	3126	625.080	3189	625.076
2833	880.042(b)	3127	625.301	3190	625.077
2834	880.046(b)	3128	625.311	3191	625.081
2835	880.216(b)	3129	625.316	3192	625.083
2836	880.001	3130	625.323	3193	625.084
2837	880.010	3131	625.326	3194	625.108
2838	880.012	3132	625.330	3195	625.122
2839	880.017	3133	625.341	3196	625.123
2840	880.028	3134	625.342	3197	625.129
2841	880.051	3135	625.343	3198	625.136
2842	880.159	3136	625.356	3199	625.161
2843	880.003	3137	625.368	3200	625.304
2844	880.008	3138	625.369	3201	625.305
2845	880.011	3139	625.370	3202	625.306
2846	880.015	3140	625.382	3203	625.307
2847	880.029	3141	625.384	3204	625.312
2848	880.036	3142	625.400	3205	625.314
2849	880.040	3143	625.407	3206	625.315
2850	880.043	3144	625.408	3207	625.317
2851	880.044	3145	625.422	3208	625.318
2852	880.053	3146	625.432	3209	625.319
2853	880.056	3147	625.440	3210	625.320
2854	880.136	3148	625.442	3211	625.321
2855	880.177	3149	625.443	3212	625.325
2856	880.213	3150	625.469	3213	625.328
2914	905.032	3151	625.473	3214	625.331
2915	905.038	3152	625.474	3215	625.337
2916	905.069	3153	625.478	3216	625.339
2917	905.036	3154	625.482	3217	625.346
2918	905.015	3155	625.501	3218	625.349
2924	905.018	3156	625.502	3219	625.354
2925	905.034	3157	625.504	3220	625.358
2926	905.054	3158	625.516	3221	625.371
2927	905.056	3159	625.520	3222	625.372
2928	905.077	3160	625.524	3223	625.374
2929	905.075	3161	625.531	3224	625.376
3021	940.009	3162	625.543	3225	625.386
3100	625.303	3163	625.544	3226	625.390
3101	625.507	3164	625.340	3227	625.394
3102	625.308	3165	625.160	3228	625.402
3103	625.383	3166	625.398	3229	625.404

MRS No	FS No	MRS No	FS No	MRS No	FS No
3230	625.406	3711	645.011	3963	685.132
3231	625.409	3720	645.019	3967	685.195
3232	625.412	3818	682.032	3968	685.393
3233	625.413	3900	685.136	3969	685.222
3234	625.416	3901	685.060	3970	685.352
3235	625.417	3902	685.099	3972	685.209
3236	625.426	3903	685.216	3973	685.070
3237	625.427	3904	685.152	4400	728.012
3238	625.428	3905	685.109	4551	730.110
3239	625.429	3906	685.126	4554	730.149
3240	625.435	3907	685.543	4557	730.075
3241	625.437	3908	685.145	4558	730.088
3242	625.438	3909	685.015	4561	730.096
3243	625.445	3910	685.026	4563	730.122
3244	625.446	3911	685.033	4565	730.023
3245	625.449	3912	685.036	4567	730.158
3246	625.453	3913	685.059	4568	730.151
3247	625.464	3914	685.076	4569	735.009(e)
3248	625.465	3915	685.078	4570	730.155
3249	625.475	3916	685.087	4739	735.102
3250	625.481	3917	685.114	4740	735.245
3251	625.483	3918	685.122	4741	735.330
3252	625.488	3919	685.140	4742	735.385
3253	625.492/6?	3920	685.141	4743	735.387
3254	625.497	3921	685.147	4744	735.?
3255	625.498	3922	685.151	4745	735.023
3256	625.503	3923	685.153	4746	735.265
3257	625.505	3924	685.154	4747	735.022
3258	625.506	3925	685.155	4748	735.168
3259	625.508	3926	685.157	4749	735.106
3260	625.509	3927	685.158	4750	735.321
3261	625.511	3928	685.159	4751	735.315
3262	625.514	3929	685.160	4752	735.351
3263	625.518	3930	685.173	4753	735.229
3264	625.525	3939	685.178	4754	735.341
3265	625.526	3932	685.185	4755	735.157
3266	625.527	3933	685.187	4756	735.371
3267	625.528	3934	685.189	4757	735.256
3268	625.532	3935	685.203	4758	735.243
3269	625.537	3936	685.507	4759	735.?
3270	625.538	3937	685.519	4760	735.338
3271	625.539	3938	685.524	4761	735.129
3272	625.541	3939	685.525	4762	735.189
3273	625.542	3940	685.530	4763	735.091
3274	625.548	3941	685.538	4764	735.278
3275	625.332	3942	685.544	4765	735.214
3276	625.495	3943	685.549	4766	735.335
3277	625.441	3944	685.553	4767	735.356
3278	625.378	3945	685.555	4768	735.089
3279	625.046	3946	685.559	4769	735.164
3280	625.059	3947	685.563	4770	735.305
3286	625.144	3948	685.567	4771	735.352
3500	640.127	3949	685.574	4772	735.079
3700	645.012	3950	685.576	4773	735.216
3701	645.020	3951	685.579	4774	735.005
3702	645.009	3952	685.581	4775	735.007
3703	645.006	3953	685.586	4776	735.019
3704	645.014	3954	685.605	4777	735.020
3705	645.022	3955	685.630	4778	735.027
3706	645.010	3956	685.632	4779	735.033
3707	645.021	3957	685.637	4780	735.035
3708	645.002	3961	685.027	4781	735.037
3709	645.007	3962	685.062	4782	735.042

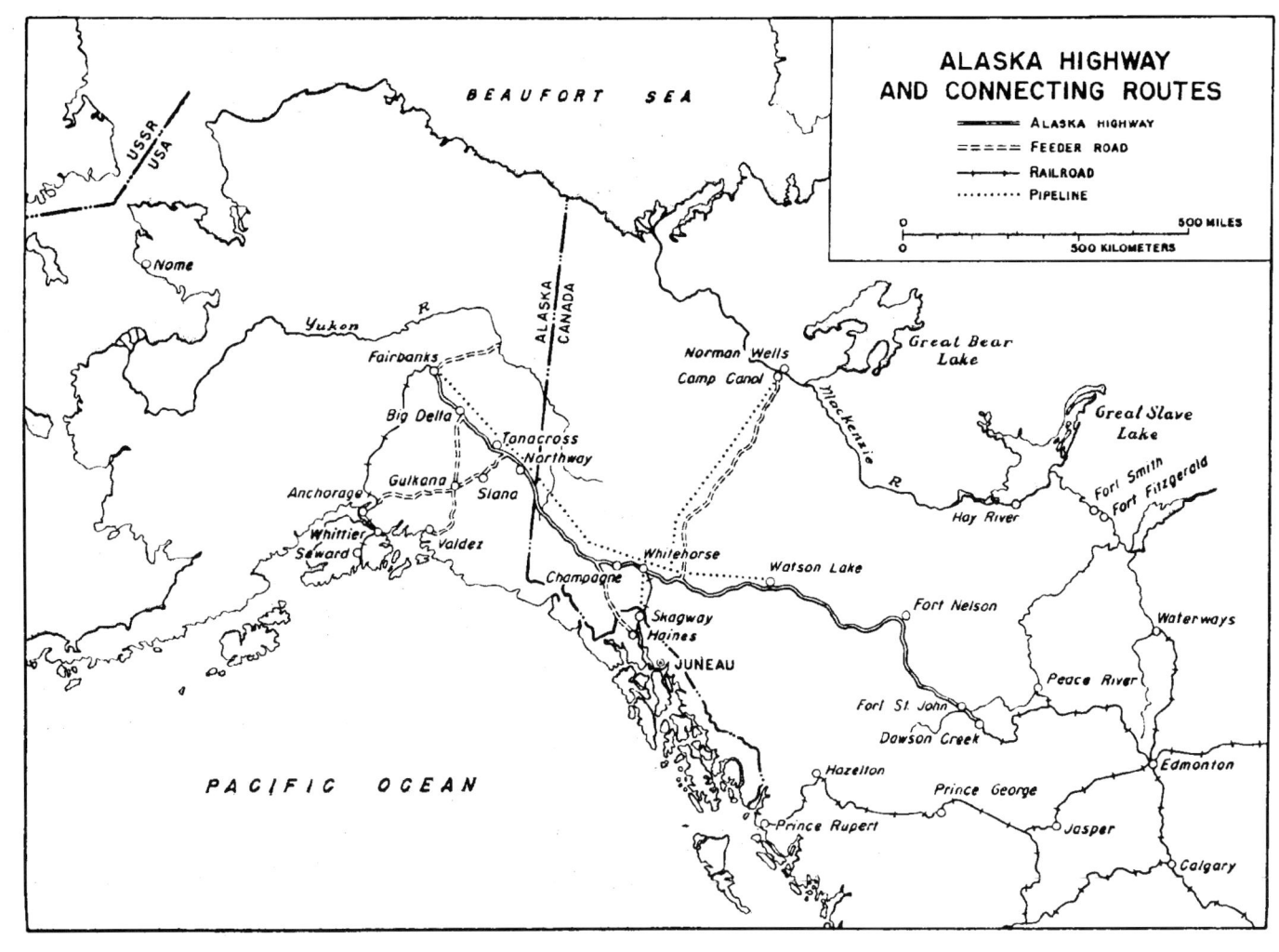

Map 27 Railways in Alaska and Yukon, showing the White Pass and Yukon Route running from Skagway to Whitehorse, and the Alaska Railroad running from Seward to Fairbanks, and their connections to the Alaska Highway (J. R. Crowley, Courtesy US Army)

originally Pacific Coast RR and then WP&YR No 1 in July 1898. It was subsequently renumbered 51 and was the museum engine at White Horse.

Now the WP&YR is a three-feet gauge line and there were not many serviceable locomotives of that gauge in the United States at that time. Seven Denver & Rio Grande Western Railroad Class 470 Engines Nos 470–2/4/5/7/9 built by Alco in 1923, stored at Alamosa and Salida, Colorado, were purchased by the American Government. They were then transported by rail to Seattle and then by barge to Skagway where they were put into service as USA/TC 250–6 in 1942. Two Eastern Tennessee and Western North Carolina engines, Baldwin 4–6–0s built in 1916 and 1919, were bought in 1942, rebuilt in Northern Pacific Railroad's Tacoma Workshops and sent to the WP&YR as 10 and 14, only to be destroyed by fire, probably in 1943.

Colorado & Southern 69 and 70, 2–8–0s built by Baldwin 11355/6 in 1890; and Silverton, Gladstone & Northern 3, 4 and 34, 2–8–0s built by Baldwin 24109/04, 27977/06 and 24130/04, were purchased in 1943 and sent to the WP&YR as 20–4. Baldwin 53296/20, a 4–6–0, was obtained from the Tanana Valley RR, renumbered 152 and sent to the WP&YR. Freight cars were also collected and, for instance, some steel boxcars intended for South America were diverted to the WP&YR.

In 1943, eleven new "MacArthur" 2–8–2 locomotives (see Chapter 47), USA/TC 190–200, Baldwin 69425–35 built in 1943, were rebuilt from metre gauge to three-feet gauge, and despatched to the WP&YR. By early 1943, there was stated to be on the WP&YR ten WP&YR and 26 USA/TC locomotives. The former would come from 4, 59–62, 66/7/9, 70/1, 80/1 and the latter would consist of 10/4, 20–4, 152 and 250–6 purchased secondhand and 190–200 new. Also by early 1943 there were 24 WP&YR and 2 USA/TC passenger cars, 83 WP&YR and 258 USA/TC freight wagons, and 22 WP&YR and 4 USA/TC work equipment trucks.

From 1938 to 1941, the WP&YR handled about 25,000 tons per year. For the first nine months of 1942, 67,500 tons were handled and for the last three months under USA/TC supervision 25,800 tons were handled. Subsequent figures were 282,000 tons 1943 and 133,500 tons in 1944, dropping to 38,500 tons in 1945. For the first four months in 1946, 10,600 tons were handled, after which the railway was passed back to civilian control and 25,600 tons handled during the remainder of the year. For the next year or two, traffic was fairly steady at about 65,000 tons per annum.

After the war, WP&YR 4 went to the Railroad Fan Club for Oak Creek Central RR in 1955. Nos 20–3 and 250–6 went back to the USA in 1945, were sold to M. Block & Co of Seattle and scrapped. No 24 was scrapped at Skagway in 1951, Nos 59–62/7 were probably scrapped in 1947 and No 66 was scrapped in 1953. No 69 was withdrawn in 1954 and sold to the Blackhills Central RR in 1956 where it was named "Klondike Casey". No 152 was returned to the USA in 1945 and scrapped or sold shortly afterwards.

In November 1951, the White Pass &

Yukon Railway Co sold all the capital issues of the three railway companies mentioned in the first paragraph and the capital issues of the British Yukon Navigation Co, to the White Pass & Yukon Corporation, a Canadian corporation with head office in Vancouver. Traffic had meanwhile been increasing and by 1955 the traffic was 103,000 tons by railway and 42,000 tons by pipeline. Two new GE diesel locomotives Nos 90/1 were brought into use in 1954 and three more in 1956, Nos 92–4.

In the autumn of 1955, a fifth wholly-owned subsidiary of the White Pass & Yukon Corporation was formed. This was the British Yukon Ocean Services Ltd, which began to operate a 4000 ton steamer on the Pacific Ocean between Vancouver, British Columbia and Skagway, Alaska, to make a complete service (with the railway) from Vancouver to Yukon.

Dimensions

WP&YR Number	Cylinders, in	DWD, in	Engine weight lb	Tractive effort lb	Boiler pressure, psi
4	15 x 20	37	120,000	15,000	160
Duchess	10 x 12	30	22,470	5,100	150
10/4	16 x 22	45	165,000	19,100	180
20/1	16 x 21	37	114,000	18,800	150
22–4	16 x 20	37	132,000	18,800	160
51	14½ x 18	42	95,900	12,975	160
59 & 60	17 x 20	42	161,000	18,900	180
61	17 x 20	38	167,000	22,100	180
62	17 x 22	44	160,000	18,500	180
66/7	17 x 20	42	161,000	18,900	180
69	21 x 22	42	213,000	28,260	160
70/1	17 x 22	44	230,500	25,200	215
80/1	19 x 20	44	213,000	23,700	170

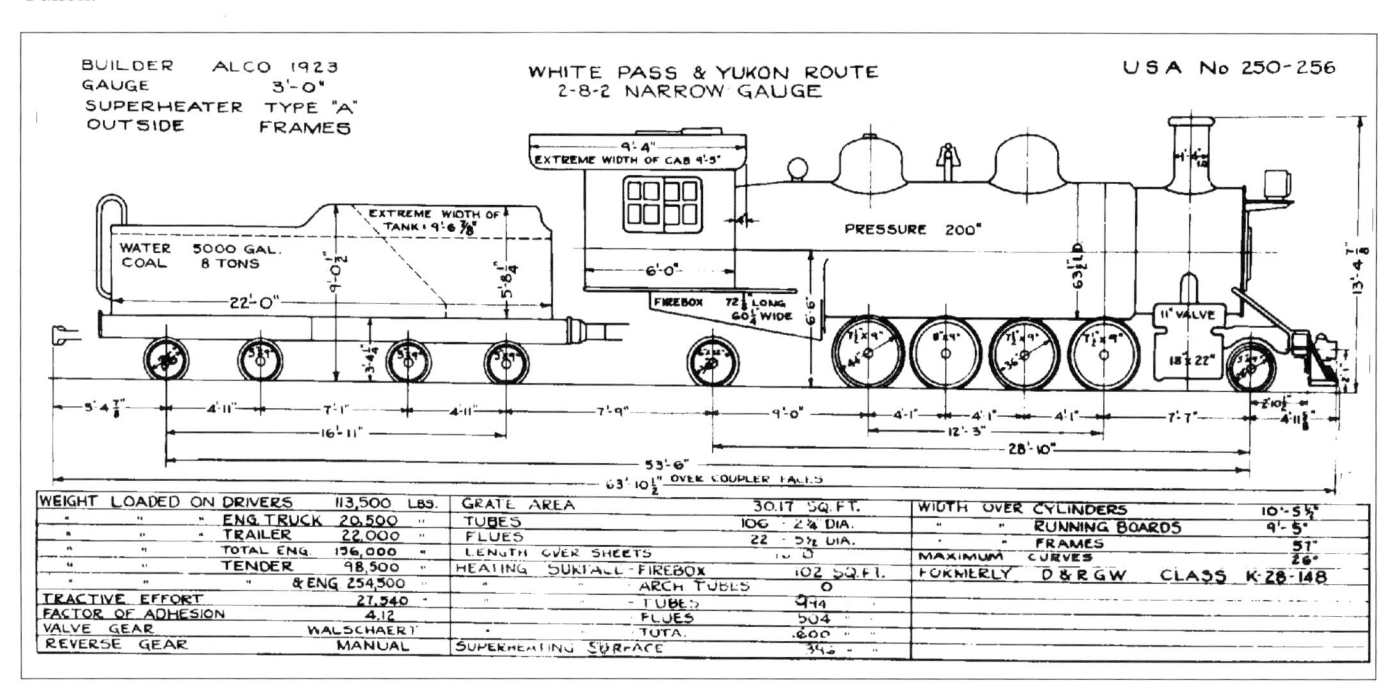

Fig 43   White Pass and Yukon Route narrow-gauge 2–8–2s USA/TC 250–6, ex Denver & Rio Grande Western Railroad Class 470 engine

Plate 372   Denver & Rio Grande Western RR 475 (later USA/TC 254) in July 1939 (Photo: B. H. Ward)

Chapter 67

ALASKA RAILROAD

The Alaska Railroad was built by the United States Government pursant to two Acts of Congress, one in August 1912 and the other in March 1914. These set up two Commissions, who surveyed the possible routes. Construction began in 1915 and was completed on 15 July 1923, the standard-gauge line then running from Seward on Resurrection Bay via Anchorage some 412 miles to a point on the Tanana River. Later, the line was extended to Fairbanks.

In 1941, a 12-mile cut-off was constructed by the US Corps of Engineers from Portage Bay to a new port terminal at Whittier. This cut-off, completed in 1943, by-passed the difficult southern section and shortened the distance to the northern railway stations by 52 miles. This new line included two tunnels, one 13,090 feet long and the other 4911 feet long. In 1943, the Alaska Railroad was about 470 miles long and had a maximum curvature of 15° and a gradient of 2 per cent.

The Alaska Railroad, although government owned, acted as a private carrier. Because of greatly increased wartime traffic, manpower leaving for better-paid jobs, and a severe winter in 1942/3, the railway was not performing as well as the military authorities wished. In February 1943, it was decided to send MRS troops in and the 714 ROB was selected, arriving in April 1943.

No 714 ROB rebuilt much of the track and rebuilt or repaired 50 bridges. Seven locomotives were brought in to help carry the military traffic. Traffic figures were 474,884 tons in 1941, 519,452 tons in 1942, 699,246 tons in 1943 and a peak of 764,775 tons in 1944. The average number of freight cars moved per month during 1942 was 3150, in 1943 5080 and a peak of 6600 cars in October 1943. No 714 ROB left the AR in May 1945.

INDEX

Alaska Railroad 188, 245, 261, 264, 282/3, 302
Algeria (CFA) 236
Ambulance trains 233, 243, 265, 275
Ardennes 19
Armour 60, 81, 83, 98, 138–40, 147
Assam Railway 134, 194
Ataka & Adibiya Military Railway 210
Auburn TC Depot 199
Austerity 79, 103, 120
Austria 214, 240

Battle of the Bulge 19
Belgium 15, 20, 210, 234/5
Bengal & Assam Railway 22, 132/3, 192/3, 238, 270, 287/8
Bengal Nagpur Railway 288
Benghazi, Barce and Soluch Railway 6, 69
Bombay, Baroda & Central India Railway 270, 288/9
Burma Railway 132, 133

Cadoxton 229
Camp Claiborne 187–9
Camp Polk 187
Central Mediterranean Force 204
Chemins de Fer Algeriens 11, 12
Chemins de Fer Damas, Hamah et Prolonguements 29, 76–8, 124
Chemis de Fer de Sfax à Gafsa 11, 12
Chemin de Fer de Tanger à Fez 11
Chemins de Fer du Maroc 11
Chemins de Fer du Mozambique 136, 137
Chemin de Fer Franco-Ethiopien 200
Chemins de Fer Tunisiens 11, 12, 107
Chemins de Fer Vicinaux du Congo 129
Cherbourg 230/2
China 142–4, 160/1, 239, 245
CMF – See Italy
Coal mining 107/8
Congo-Ocean Railway 136
Czechoslovakia (CSD) 243

Dean Goods 48–56
Demolition 14, 151
Deutsche Reichsbahn 123
Dreux 232
Dunkirk 39, 43

East African Railways & Harbours 134/5, 138, 196, 198
East Indian Railway 22, 238, 288–90
East Kent Railway 51

Egypt 5, 59, 60, 76, 142, 212
Elham Valley 38, 53
Explosions 246–8

Ferrocarril del Sor 200
Ferrocarril Nacional de Honduras 200
Finland 259, 262/3
Fort Eustis 188, 200, 239, 260/4
France (SNCF) 15–21, 214/5, 230, 232–5, 270, 275
Franch Cameroons 199

German numbering system 7
Germany 19–22
Gold Coast Railway 136, 198
Great Indian Peninsular Railway 238, 270, 287–90
Greece 124/5
Ground nut scheme 134

Haifa Beirut Tripoli Railway 7, 8, 62/3, 76/7, 100/1, 202–5
Hellenic State Railways 215, 240/1
Hungary (MAV) 242

India 22–4, 132/3, 192–5, 237/8, 270/1, 285–92
Iran 9, 10, 143/4
Iranian State Railway 205/6, 280/1
Iraq 63, 78, 112, 143
Iraqi State Railway 193, 197, 205, 210
Italian colonies 69–74
Italy (CMF) 13–15, 63, 101/2, 206/7, 213, 237, 247/8, 266, 275/6, 292–9

Jamaica Government Railway 213, 239/40
Japan 26
Jodhpur Railway 196
Jordan Railways 116

Kenya and Uganda Railway 134/7
Korea, South (KNR) 26/7, 245, 284
Kowloon Canton Railway 96/7, 142, 160/1, 206

Langreo, F.C., Spain 245, 264
Livery 2, 75, 82, 104, 121, 152/3, 192
Longmoor Military Railway 44, 58, 85, 102, 113, 128, 144–53, 208, 228, 236, 274
Louvain 235

Madras & Southern Mahratta Railway 193

Malayan Railway 196, 255
Manila Railroad 199
Martin Mill Military Railway 38, 158–60
Melbourne Military Railway 118, 154/5, 208, 274
Middle East (MEF) 5–9, 201–5, 210–3
Middle East Force Stock List 31
Military railways 1/2
Morocco 236
MRS 292–9
Mysore State Railway 194, 288

National Coal Board 107/9
Nederlandsche Spoorwegen 46, 87–9, 106, 122–4, 276
Newbury WD Depot 210
Newport, GWR 208, 228/9, 234, 270, 274
Nigerian Railway 197/8
Nizam's State Railways 288
Norfolk & Portsmouth Belt Line Railroad 260
North Africa 11/2, 191/2, 213, 236/7
North Western Railway 270, 287–9
Norwegian State Railway 261

Palestine Railway 8, 62–5, 76–8, 201–5, 210–3
Pelopennesus Railway 200
Penrhos 229, 236
Persia – see Iran
Peru Central Railway 240
Philippine Islands 25/6
Poland (PKP) 244/5

Qena-Sofaga Railway 7, 22, 115
Queensland Government Railways 198/9

Raritan River Railroad 260
Rhine 21
Riddles 56, 79, 120
Robinson 75
Royal Engineers 67
Russia 216, 223, 238, 256–9, 262, 281

Scarifier 14, 151
Shoeburyness Tramway 155/6
Shropshire & Montgomeryshire Railway 157/8
Siam, Royal State Railways 193, 196/7
Sicily 13
Sierra Leone Railway 131
South African Railway 29, 33
South East Asia Command 255
Southern Railway 213/4, 228
South Indian Railway 131, 193/4

303

Stanier 56
Sudan Government Railway 117
Sudbury WD Depot 228
Suez 8, 98, 100, 115, 118, 142
Swedish State Railway 89
Syria 7, 8

Tanganyika Railways 134
Tela Railroad 200
Trans-Zambesia Railway 118/9
Treforest 229, 235
Tripolitanian Railway 7, 70/1
Turkey (TCDD) 59, 205/6, 242
Tunisia (CFT) 236/7

United Fruit Company 200
UNRRA (United Nations Relief & Rehabilitation Association) 55, 206/7, 210, 236
USA/TC Grand Division 3
USA/TC MRS 3, 101
USA/TC organisation 3

Voorheesville TC Depot 259

War Department 28
War Department (India) 3, 140/1
WD Renumbering Scheme 33
Weaversdown Light Railway 150

Western Desert Extension Railway 5, 59, 60, 98
Western Australian Government Railway 118
West Yermo TC Depot 191, 197, 199, 200
Whitcomb 97–102, 274–9
White Pass & Yukon Route 199, 299–301
Woolmer Instructional Military Railway 145

Yugoslavia (JDZ) 210, 215, 240